the ULTIMATE Baby Names book

DIANE STAFFORD

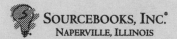

SOURCEBOOKS, INC.
NAPERVILLE, ILLINOIS

Copyright © 2005 by Diane Stafford
Cover and internal design © 2005 by Sourcebooks, Inc.
Cover photo © Canopy Pictures/Veer
Sourcebooks and the colophon are registered trademarks of
Sourcebooks, Inc.

All rights reserved. No part of this book may be reproduced in
any form or by any electronic or mechanical means including
information storage and retrieval systems—except in the case of
brief quotations embodied in critical articles or reviews—with-
out permission in writing from its publisher, Sourcebooks, Inc.

Published by Sourcebooks, Inc.
PO Box 4410, Naperville, Illinois 60567-4410
(630) 961-3900
Fax: (630) 961-2168
www.sourcebooks.com

Library of Congress Cataloging-in-Publication Data
Stafford, Diane.
  The ultimate baby names book / by Diane Stafford.
     p. cm.
  ISBN 1-4022-0413-2 (alk. paper)
  1. Names, Personal--Dictionaries. I. Title.

CS2377.S574 2005
929.4'4'03--dc22

                                        2004026866

Printed and bound in the United States of America
          QW 10 9 8 7 6 5 4 3 2

dedication

To my wonderful daughter, Jennifer, whose loving ways have brought me happiness every day of her life—and to my darling grandson, Ben, whose sweetness and charm are constant joys.

Acknowledgments

Sincere thanks to: Ed Knappman of New England Publishing Associates, for giving me the opportunity to write this book—and to Elizabeth Frost Knappman, literary agent and friend, who has made my dreams come true.

Hillel Black of Sourcebooks, for his patience, support, direction, and kindness. To Bethany Brown, Kelly Barrales-Saylor, Dan Bulla, Kristin Esch, Samantha Raue, and Morgan Hrejsa for their hard work.

Dana Chandler, Slavek Rotkiewicz, Camilla Pierce, Gabriela Baeza Ventura, and Jennifer Shoquist San Luis, for their help with this book.

And special thanks to my wonderful family and friends, whose names will always be tops on my list of favorites:

Jennifer, Benjamin, Robert, Clinton, Belle, Allen, Christina, Austin, Xanthe, Richard, Camilla, Britt, Gina, Curtis, Lindsay, Cameron, Josh, Jake, David, Amber, Dan, Fletcher, Russ, Martin, Dinah, Chris, Donna, Annie, Angela, Jami, Lucy, Tessie, Bob, Lily, Carolyn, Beth, Dot, Laurens, Cynthia, Laura, Jeffrey, Dana, Clarence, Eddi, Jay, Jim, Martha, Carrie, Natasha, Kathleen, Rachel, Renee, Wendy, Kristina, Jennifer, Liz, Elizabeth, Christy, Shannon, John, Shari, JoAnn, Alice, Gary, C.D., Bernice, Karla, Karen, Doug, Michael, Tom, Joanne, Mark, Fred, Spiker, Scott, Dominique, Russell, Evin, Dennis, Patrick, Cari.

Contents

INtro

Enjoy the Extreme Sport of Baby Naming

Ever consider Quincy or Harvest for your baby girl? Graydon or Wilbur for a boy? Eddie Murphy's faux-twins Monique and Unique *(Beverly Hills Cop II)* were just two of thousands of names-meant-to-titillate that have made us smile.

We're getting jiggy with it

You have to admit—today's parents are creating some unbelievable names. But, all of the names in my three baby-name books are strictly legitimate. They belong to someone out there somewhere—whether you agree that these are "real names" or not. So, before you decide to set yourself up as a name Nazi, remember that truth is always stranger than fiction.

Many people can't believe, for example, that a mom and dad actually sat down and put together "Dijon" (of Dijon mustard) and "aise" (of mayonnaise) and came up with a condiment name for their baby girl: "Hey, Dijonnaise works for us! *Cool*—that's what we'll call her!"

And while name inventing is by far the fastest-growing trend, it's certainly not the only one prevalent today. Check out these:

Invented names: While people do laugh about name "concoctions," the fact remains—parents have the right to enjoy choosing a name. If you're the one who's going to be getting up night after night for two a.m. feedings, you're entitled to choose the name you want to croon 50,000 times. Examples: Sharokina, Caneisha, Duron, Karlette, Shartese.

Recycled names with avant-garde spellings: Bring back an oldie but goodie and give it a fresh, foxy new spelling. Examples: Rozanna, Jenephur, Jayson, Markee.

Circa-'50s names revisited: Revisiting *Beach Blanket Bingo* days, we're seeing reincarnations of Darren, Tammy, Rita, Eddie, Sandy, Frankie, Deon.

Ethnic names unleashed: No longer does the first name have to fit the last name's ethnic slant. People put "Pedro" with Johnson and use "Marco" with Smith. Few people will throw stones (not big ones, anyway).

Goal names: These say something about the parents' priorities or goals for the child. Examples: Mercedes, Diamond, Alpha, Punk, Meadowlark, Prayer, Harley.

Names newly unisex: This is a growing category, with more and more names doing the crossover thing. Examples: Quincy, Brook, Gavin, Val, Devin, Rory, Ryan.

Glitzorama names: Grab a name from a pro athlete, actor, or another luminary (we'll undoubtedly see a bumper crop of little Parises, thanks to Paris Hilton). Other examples: Jemima, Melania, Catalina, Shar, Famke, Bree, Mischa, Taye, Warrick, Nigella, Keala, Stanford.

Tough-guy boy names: Nate, Slater, Viggo, Steele, Rocco, Mack, Gus, Dax.

Place names: Ireland, Savannah, Cayman, Venice, Asia, China, Macon, Yukon, Austin.

If your baby could speak, he might say, "Don't name me that!"

How do I know so much? *You* told me. When my fat little book *40,001 Best Baby Names* became a best-seller (luckily), talk-show listeners called in to chat about this very personal issue.

People had lots of reasons for disliking their names:

"I hated growing up with a grandmother-sound-ing name." (Dorothy)

"My name was too odd." (Khaki)

"No one could pronounce my name." (Camilla)

"No one who was popular had my name." (Wendy)

"Every other kid in school had my name." (Dylan)

"My name sounds too old-fashioned." (Gladys)

"People always asked if I was born at Christmas, and then I'd say, no, my mother was just a little nutty…" (Noelle)

"People made fun of me—they would say, 'oh, you're the tire.'" (Michelin)

And, about half said they had always been fond of their names.

"My name was a good fit." (Venus, Selena, Loibeth, Tony, Kyle)

"My name's easy to remember." (Jinx, Cameron, Derek)

"My name sounds good with my last name." (Karen Brinlee, Lindsay Liem)

"It felt comfortable to me." (Dana, Christina, Josh, David)

Eternal truths about baby naming

Most people hold their names near and dear—or they suspect that their names held them back. Some people think they have been adversely affected by names that are too weird, too scary, too hard to pronounce, or simply too different.

Here are things I've learned about names:

- Your name can give you a leg up socially. Where would The Donald be if he'd been named Buddy?
- Your name can be a liability. Do you think Zsa-Zsa Burgundy will have a chance at a run for the senate?

Is it just me or do some names seem superfreaky?

Today's name game is wilder and woollier than ever, which says something good about parents (they're creative and uninhibited) and something not-so-good (some focus so much on the cool quotient that they forget to consider how the name will work for the child carrying it around).

Roughly speaking, parents typically take one of three routes in choosing a baby name:

1. **Hot and trendy:** These come from mothers' maiden names, star athletes, and babies of movie stars (or the stars themselves). Examples: Roman, Ava, Monet, Tia, Myesha, Lola, Miranda, Parker, Fowler, Wylie, Logan, Karcher.

2. **Traditional:** These ebb and flow in popularity but usually land in the top 100 decade after decade. These are "safe" names. Examples: Emma, Emily, Jennifer, Michael, William, David, Scott.

3. **Family:** Many couples fall back on the comfort food of names—good old tried-and-true standards, ranging from venerable classics (Will, Robert, Rose, Elizabeth, Edward) to more dubious choices (Bertha, Elmer) to what's old is new again (Harry, Lana, Margaret).

You can settle matters by following the name rules

Sit down with your list of finalist names, and let these rules help you sort:

- Consider the name's baggage. Some names carry significant weight: Forbes sounds stuffy, Knievel daredevily, Bessy cowish. And, Drusella reminds us of an evil stepsister we wouldn't want to know. Teena makes us wonder why the parents couldn't spell Tina. And, well, Madonna or Arnold in this era of larger-than-life songbird

Madonna and governator Arnold? Count on seeing the taunting lasting until, well, maybe the kid's 40th birthday.

- Try the sound of the name with the surname. Say it out loud and watch for tongue-twisters or double-wides. Often, you'll find that a long last name works best with a short name, and vice versa. Avoid rhymes—Barley Farley or Carrie Derryberry.
- Watch the double vowels. A first name ending in a vowel paired with a last name that starts with a vowel can be a tough duo. Ava Amazon, for example, is simply hard to say.

- Go into baby naming with eyes wide open. You know what's going to happen if you give your child a crowd-pleaser name. Sarah, Britney, and Justin will be in a roomful of kids with the same names. But your daughter Courtney may not mind one bit being surrounded by Courtneys when she sees her friend Jemima get teased daily for being "Pancake Girl." You can be sure that your child named Pronzilda will someday ask you "why me?" But so will the child named Jennifer or Robert. ("Why couldn't you have been more original, Mom?")

- Don't even think about a pun. Yes, Ima Hogg was a rich Houston philanthropist, and she probably had a perfectly nice life—but I'll bet she would have swapped names with Mary or Susan in a heartbeat.

- Understand the fate of a child with a "different" name. You may love telling friends that you're naming your baby Bloom or Wilmer, but how will the child like it? When your son says "My name is Steele," the other person is going to say, "It's what?"

- Weigh the gene pool. One child may have the chutzpah to pull off the name King, while another may shrivel at the mention of it. It takes some swagger to be Dalia or Royston, Veronique or Malo…so ask yourself if your child has a bit of bravado in his genes. Personally, I'd bet big money that little Sam Sheen, baby daughter of actors Denise Richards and Charlie Sheen, has enough beauty potential to pull off her unisex name (did you see her baby pix—wow!). But not every family is packing the legacy of two gorgeous parents, so giving your girl baby a male name may just mean you end up with a boyish-looking girl slogging around with a boy name. Big problems out by the lockers.

- Think baby's comfort level, first and last. If in doubt, opt out of the idea of the zany name. Some research even suggests that kids with odd names are less well socialized because of the taunting they get from peers. Some become defensive; others turn into bullies; still others end up shy or aloof. On the other hand, a boy named Stone may get the life beat out of him in junior high, but when he's grown and the bruises are gone, he may decide he actually likes having a unique name.

- Rethink the importance of carrying on that family name that the originator didn't even like. Maybe Aunt Matilda did great with her name— she was Rodeo Queen, after all—but how will your tiny tot Matilda feel in 2005, stuck in a classroom full of Ambers and Samanthas? Some old-fashioned names do work their way back into fashion, but others won't resurface, thankfully. Do you think your child really wants to be Durwood or Ethel?

- Keep in mind the confusion that comes with being a namesake. And who is dying to be called "Little Al" or "Junior"? Also, he'll have to deal with confusion in regard to credit cards and credit reports and other personal I.D. info. Some psychiatrists caution that giving a child a name all his or her own makes for a much better jumpstart than creating a spinoff or mini-me. At the same time, we all know at least one Trey who loves having a name with strong tradition.

- Put the family/background name in the middle. Let your baby's name reflect his heritage or religion in a subtle way. This is a good backup plan for those who prefer mainstream names. You can fill both needs by using the ancestry name for a middle name and put that trendy one out front.

- Take a look at the name's meaning. For some people, name meanings count, big time. What if your child grows up to be a family-tree-snooper? She may hate finding out that her name Cresinelda means "whimpering guttersnipe trollop" and may ask why you stuck her with such an awful name.

- Check out the acronyms. Initials can cause considerable backlash. Don't think that your child's friends will fail to notice his initials spell out "W.I.M.P." Check out the shortened version of a first name, too. Your baby Catalina is destined to be "Cat." Your boy Roupen will end up "Roup."

- Give the name a test run. Say it out loud; see how it feels and sounds. Say, "Hannibal Higgins, please eat your fava beans." Or: "Avril Makena Sunhee Smith, do you want a karaoke set for Christmas?"

The name game

When you get ready to name a baby, you may experience one of these three feelings:

- You're madcap crazy with power.
- You're weak in the knees with the hefty responsibility.
- You're happy to come up with a pretty/viable/worthwhile name for that precious little doll. (Then again, who's to say what's pretty? Or what rolls off the tongue nicely? Or what name is truly worthwhile?)

Wait for your lightbulb moment

Take the quiz below to discover types of names most natural for you. That will point you toward the category that you and your child may be happiest with in the long run. Select your favorite of each list of three:

1. Choose:
   a. Julia
   b. Primalia
   c. Kayla

2. Choose:
   a. Emily
   b. Catalina
   c. Alexis

3. Choose:
   a. Samantha
   b. Dayanara
   c. Madison

4. Choose:

   a. Jacob

   b. Dixon

   c. Chad

5. Choose:

   a. Ethan

   b. Marco

   c. Brent

6. Choose:

   a. Joshua

   b. Linc

   c. Kevin

7. Choose:

   a. Michael

   b. Hudson

   c. Dirk

8. Choose:

   a. Charlie

   b. Maximillian

   c. Jack

9. Choose:

   a. Matt

   b. Dexter

   c. Grant

10. Choose:

   a. Brad
   b. Hewitt
   c. Hunter

What your choices say about your name preferences:

A's: If you chose mostly A's, you like dignified names. You're probably best served choosing from the top-10 lists, and your child will thank you. Top of the lists for 2004: Jacob and Emily.

B's: If you chose mostly B's, you like fun, off-the-wall names. You're a pistol, and maybe your spouse is, too. You'll probably have a quirky kid, so go crazy with baby naming. And what if you end up with a throwback to serious Grandma Myrtle—well, a wild-child name like Cinnamon or Massimo is sure to perk the kid up.

C's: You're a middle-of-the-road namer. You play it safe on the big issues. Chances are, you and your mate will be happy with Jenna or Hunter, Abby or Ashley, Christopher or Anthony, and your child will adore the name you choose.

Adding pluses and minuses...

To plow through 50,001 names, here are tips for paring down thousands to a manageable few:

- Sit down separately with the big, fat name book. Make a list of 10 names you like for each gender.

- Next, get with your mate and eliminate the ones you can't stand.

- So, now that you have only two of the twenty names left, try out these with your last name. Do you like the feel? The flow?

- Picture a fast-moving toddler with newly burgeoning language skills saying his name and smiling at the sound of it.

- Finally, when you've made the big decision, tuck away the secret name. Otherwise, relatives and friends will tell you all the reasons you shouldn't use that name and supply a string of "better" ones. Or they'll start calling your unborn baby by the name, which will be unfortunate if you end up going with something else.

And, what about little Apple? Looks like Gwyneth Paltrow really wasn't that far out in left field after all.

Bottom line, you should go with the name that *feels* right. Say it early. Say it often. Say it over and over. (Thanks, Jennifer, for making *me* the luckiest mom in the world.)

Lists

Powerful Names for Winners

Girls	Boys
Anna	Andrew
Blake	Barrett
Campbell	Burke
Celeste	Charles
Claire	Cole
Grace	Easton
Harper	Graham
Honor	Julian
Margaret	Justice
Merit	Liam
Pace	Mason
Quinn	Nash
Reeve	Nathaniel
Sydney	Nolan
Wylie	Quentin

Great Names to Grow Up With

Girls	Boys
Allison	Allen
Ashley	Ben
Becca	Brian
Carrie	Daniel
Danielle	Dave
Emily	Jake
Isabel	Jason
Jessica	Josh
Jordan	Justin
Kim	Logan
Lauren	Mike
Liz	Nicholas
Nicole	Rob
Rachel	Ryan
Samantha	Tyler

Exotic Names

Girls	Boys
Chiara	Desiderio
Kimone	Destin
Laurent	Diego
Pax	Enrique
Pepita	Enzo
Phaedra	Francesco
Philomena	Frederic
Phyllida	Gaston
Quanda	Genaro
Rania	Giancarlo
Rasheeda	Hansel
Santana	Hermes
Sequoia	Honorato
Shoshana	Janus
Solange	Johann

Overwhelming Names

Girls	Boys
Antigone	Axelrod
Chastity	Baldridge
Clotilde	Balthazar
Elspeth	Durwood
Henrietta	Ervin
Keturah	Gershom
Majidah	Hercules
Millicent	Ignatius
Panther	Lazarus
Prudence	Lothario
Purity	Marmaduke
Siphronia	Maverick
Vixen	Oswald
Zona	Montague
Zuwena	Thor

Playful Names

Girls	Boys
Bliss	Ballyhoo
Bunny	Boots
Cheer	Buffalo
Cookie	Bumble
Delight	Champ
Dreamy	Chum
Fantastica	Corky
Fluffy	Dusty
Pixie	Happy
Precious	Jinx
Punky	Pal
Queenie	Rabbit
Sundancer	Ritz
Trixie	Rodeo
Tweetie	Skip

High-Energy Names

Girls	Boys
Aviva	Bucky
Brandi	Dario
Fantasia	Flint
Frisky	Grasshopper
Frolic	Jagger
Gleam	Jazz
Infinity	Jovan
KayKay	Lynus
Lively	Rage
Mandy	Rockney
Poni	Ryder
Suzy	Sonic
Vivica	Sparky
Waverly	Spike
Yvette	Vito

Outdoorsy Names

Girls	Boys
Autumn	Camper
Breezy	Canyon
Eartha	Cliff
Flora	Dune
Galaxy	Dusk
Hillary	Ford
Holly	Frost
Misty	Montana
Oceana	Orbit
Rainbow	Rain
Ravine	River
Season	Sky
Sierra	Storm
Summer	Typhoon
Star	Winter

Girlie Girls and Macho Men

Girls	Boys
Annabelle	Bucko
Bay	Butch
Darcy	Cash
Dolce	Duke
Dove	Evander
Faith	Hud
Goldie	Hugo
Greta	Jock
Honey	Ram
Julianna	Rebel
Laurel	Rip
Marina	Rocco
Rosa	Spike
Sarah-Jessica	Stone
Tammy	Zoom

Future Artists

Girls	Boys
Ashantia	Ballard
Caramia	Blaze
Chantal	Ceron
Emelle	Eduardo
Eve	Francoise
Kavita	Hector
Lace	Laurent
Lavonne	Lionel
Margina	Octavio
Michaele	Oscar
Mona	Paulo
Neva	Pash
Prema	Pedro
Regine	Sancho
Sisteene	Sebastian

Future Authors

Girls	Boys
Alcott	Beckett
Anais	Bertolt
Djuna	Borges
Eudora	Cervantes
Flannery	Chekhov
Harper	Faulkner
Jamaica	Fenimore
Louisa May	Hemingway
Maeve	Italo
Maryse	Nabokov
Sandra	Steinbeck
Simone	T.S.
Virginia	Umberto
Willa	Upton
Zora	Vladimir

Future Chefs

Girls

Angelica
Candy
Caraway
Cassia
Genievre
Ginger
Honey
Julia
Marjolaine
Nigella
Poppy
Rosemary
Saffron
Sarriette
Verbena

Boys

Alton
Baker
Basil
Bayless
Coriander
Cook
Delmonico
Emeril
Herb
Hiroyuki
Jamie
Lawson
Tamarind
Tarragon
Wolfgang

Future Cowboys and Cowgirls

Girls	Boys
Abilene	Austin
Angeline	Beau
Arizona	Chaparro
Cassidy	Cody
Cheyenne	Dallas
Conroe	Doc
Dacey	Dustin
Dixie	Earp
Dobie	Gene
Jessie	Rusty
Johanna	Shane
Luella	Stetson
Montana	Vaquero
Oakley	Wadell
Rosita	Wyatt

Future Nobel Prize Winners

Girls	Boys
Alva	Archer
Christiane	Baruch
Corrigan	Cordell
Gabriela	Desmond
Gordimer	Hamilton
Grazia	Jacinto
Jody	Kenzaburo
Mairead	Linus
Nadine	Niels
Pearl	Peyton
Rigoberta	Renato
Rosalyn	Romain
Selma	Sinclair
Shirin	Susumu
Sigrid	Winston

Future Politicians

Girls	Boys
Albright	Ambrose
Barbara	Ari
Carter	Barack
Chelsea	Charlton
Cheney	Clinton
Condoleezza	Delano
Eleanor	Lyndon
Gloria	Newt
Hillary	Nixon
Jacqueline	Orrin
Joycelyn	Powell
Kerry	Spiro
Lady Bird	Theodore
Lilibet	Truman
Tipper	Zell

Future Drama Queens and Kings

Girls	**Boys**
Azalea	Alvie
Babette	Amadeo
Bella	Bonnard
Breanna	Chyrell
Carmen	Danton
Chanina	Deno
Dyana	Ellison
Estella	Fabrizio
Isra	Gabino
Janaye	Garrick
Janelle	Lonzo
Lisel	Mario
Liliana	Ransom
Marva	Zach
Roxanne	Zennie

Pop Superstars of Tomorrow

Girls	Boys
Adora	Angus
Blondelle	Arturo
Bonita	Carlos
Dantea	Diego
Elle	Francisco
Jandrea	Gabe
Jasmine	Giancarlo
Kiki	Heath
Liliana	Jair
Lourdes	Jude
Lysette	Reno
Natalia	Rory
Nicolette	Ruben
Shae	Sly
Shyla	Smith

Future Doctors

Girls	**Boys**
Ann	Bryant
Athena	Dimitri
Brenda	Frazier
Bryce	Lister
Catrice	Martin
Dana	Murray
Elizabeth	Newell
Freda	Niles
Greta	Peter
Lydia	Philip
Lynn	Randall
Maureen	Reagan
Miriam	Rell
Suzanne	Russell
Victoria	Sabin

Future Lawyers

Girls	Boys
Campbell	Atticus
Carlisle	Caleb
Joanna	Carlson
Justine	Gary
Kendra	Lawrence
Lane	Noble
Mariel	Preston
Mason	Price
Meg	Quinn
Parker	Reese
Rachel	Rourke
Serena	Ryder
Sloan	Samuel
Taylor	Sander
Terese	Sandford

Future Olympians

Girls	Boys
Carly	Aaron
Chris	Alexei
Fanny	Andre
Hamill	Apollo
Katarina	Crawford
Kerrigan	Derek
Kristi	Dwight
Mariel	Eldredge
Mia	Emmons
Nadia	Gatlin
Peggy	Greg
Sasha	Hamilton
Sonja	Phelps
Tristan	Rulon
Vonetta	Tyler

Future Sports Legends

Girls	Boys
Althea	A.J.
Annika	Babe
Billie Jean	Barry
Bonnie	DiMaggio
Cammi	Foreman
Chamique	Gordie
Florence	Hakeem
Gale	Hank
Glenna	Hogan
Hazel	Jackie
Mickey	Lemiuex
Senda	O.J.
Steffi	Rocky
Swoopes	Rogers
Tamara	Satchel

Soap Opera Names

Girls	Boys
Allura	Bo
Amber	Dax
Brisa	Deone
Charmaine	Destin
Desiree	Diego
Hope	Duke
Laura	Fabio
Madonna	Keller
Salome	Luke
Saskia	Rico
Tatiana	Rip
Tawny	Romeo
Tish	Sebastian
Treece	Shiloh
Yolie	Thor

Sitcom Names

Girls	Boys
Blossom	Balki
Dharma	Chachi
Jeannie	Conan
Laverne	Elvin
Lorelai	Gil
Lucy	Grady
Meadow	Gunther
Miranda	Kramer
Phoebe	Mork
Prue	Niles
Rhoda	Odafin
Scully	Raymond
Sidney	Ricky
Tabitha	Vinnie
Topanga	Wilson

Celebrity Names

Girls	Boys
Charlize	Antonio
Demi	Ashton
Drea	Casey
Drew	Casper
Halle	Crowe
Julia	Cruise
Hudson	Damon
Lara	Denzel
Liv	Goran
Natasha	Griffin
Oprah	Keenan
Portia	Kiefer
Reese	Liam
Renee	Mel
Uma	Russell

Literary Names

Girls	Boys
Austen	Boswell
Bronte	Cummings
Browning	Dryden
Charlotte	Emerson
Colette	Foster
Godiva	Grimm
Grisham	Keats
Kipling	Lowell
McMurtry	Milton
Millay	Norman
Sadie	Quixote
Scarlett	Rhett
Scout	Sherman
Stella	Wordsworth
Whittier	Yeats

Colorful Names

Girls	Boys
Blanche	Amarillo
Bionda	Auburn
Burgundy	Brinley
Carmine	Brown
Cerise	Laban
Crimson	Loden
Cyanetta	Red
Henna	Rudd
Indigo	Russet
Iona	Rusty
Jade	Sable
Jetta	Slate
Lavender	Stone
Melina	Tyrian
Peridot	Umber

Globetrotters

Girls	Boys
Asia	Aberdeen
Bali	Aleppo
Cairo	Beaumont
China	Bexley
Dallas	Billings
Dayton	Bradford
Egypt	Cuba
Flanders	Cyprus
Georgia	Dodge
Ireland	Elam
Kentucky	Gobi
Kenya	Macon
Persia	Orlando
Savannah	Rainier
Venice	Yukon

Mythological Names

Girls	Boys
Adonia	Acheron
Aegina	Ajax
Amalthea	Asariel
Berecyntia	Bacchus
Castalia	Cadmus
Chloris	Creon
Decembra	Janus
Devi	Kanaloa
Elektra	Leander
Evadne	Percival
Halcyon	Philemon
Inanna	Regin
Kalliope	Tiki
Niobe	Vidar
Polyxena	Zethus

Names for Heroes

Girls	Boys
Aphrodite	Army
Cordelia	Arthur
Liberty	Braveheart
Loyalty	Bravo
Navy	Captain
Pacifica	Gallant
Patience	Hercules
Pilot	Leander
Salute	Leon
Shera	Lincoln
Star	Manfred
True	Odysseus
Valerie	Patriot
Victory	Sailor
Xena	Savion

Last Names as First Names

Girls	Boys
Childers	Afton
Fields	Brandt
Gilmore	Chatwin
Garson	Corbitt
Harrison	Deagan
Keaton	Easton
Jennings	Greer
Lancaster	Halliwell
Mackenzie	Laskey
Maclaine	Mackeane
O'Brien	Orton
Pace	Prescott
Payton	Rollins
Pfeiffer	Tomlin
Rainey	Wingate

Inventive Names

Girls	Boys
Alexakai	Albanese
Amberkalay	Arnome
Bryelle	Damarcus
Dalondra	Derlin
Dasmine	Devonte
Davelyn	Donyell
Dawntelle	Jabari
Jaleesa	Jaquawn
Jameka	Jashon
Kaneesha	Javaris
Keoshawn	Kyan
Noemi	Preemoh
Quanisha	Raekwon
Shalonda	Shawnell
Tearah	Tevin

Out-of-Date and Overused Names

Girls	Boys
Betty	Al
Carla	Bob
Delores	Dennis
Edith	Donald
Frances	Ernie
Judy	Frank
Loretta	Harold
Myrna	Harvey
Nancy	Jason
Nina	Jerry
Priscilla	Marvin
Stacy	Oscar
Tiffany	Randy
Veronica	Rick
Wanda	Todd

Retro Cool Names

Girls	Boys
Alma	Barney
Annette	Chester
Arden	Clem
Arlene	Curtis
Ava	Dexter
Betsy	Duke
Corinna	Elmer
Hazel	Gill
Inez	Harvey
Isabel	Homer
Kay	Mort
Loretta	Myron
Mabel	Oscar
Polly	Otis
Trudy	Wilbur

Cutting-Edge Names

Girls	**Boys**
Addison	Brand
Aja	Cortland
Amelie	Dolen
Ashland	Ender
Campton	Mac
Emmaline	Moore
Gracia	Noble
Jaycey	Pratt
Jemma	Questyn
Lexia	Rogan
Lotte	Sage
Maitlyn	Sevarius
Riley	Trav
Tria	Trystyn
Vy	Zane

Tongue Twister Names

Girls	Boys
Aleithea	Dionysus
Carenleigh	Flody
Chesskwana	Gyth
Deighan	Hamif
Falesyia	Hieronymos
Gisbelle	Iago
Gresia	Ioannis
Madchen	Isidro
Maromisa	Larrmyne
Mayghaen	Mihow
Meyka	Mischa
Naeemah	Moey
Nunibelle	Revin
Rhonwen	Sladkey
Ruthemma	Slavek

Biblical and Saintly Names

Girls	Boys
Bathsheba	Abel
Deborah	Adam
Delilah	Ezekiel
Dinah	Isaiah
Esther	Jonah
Eve	Joseph
Leah	Joshua
Magdalene	Lazarus
Mary	Luke
Naamah	Moses
Naomi	Noah
Salome	Paul
Sarah	Peter
Tamar	Samuel
Zipporah	Solomon

African Names

Girls	Boys
Aamori	Addae
Abayomi	Adio
Femi	Dumisani
Habiba	Hamidi
Hasina	Harun
Jumoke	Hasani
Kibibi	Runako
Kissa	Saeed
Lateefa	Salehe
Oni	Salim
Rufaro	Sekani
Salama	Themba
Taliba	Umi
Tisa	Zikomo
Zahra	Zuberi

Arabic and Islamic Names

Girls	Boys
Almira	Ali
Bathsira	Amir
Fatima	Dawud
Hadil	Fariol
Hayfa	Hamid
Ihab	Hasan
Jamila	Ibrahim
Karima	Kareem
Laila	Khalid
Malak	Mahmud
Nada	Muhammad
Nima	Nuri
Rashidah	Rafi
Salima	Sharif
Zulema	Yasir

Asian Names

Girls	Boys
Bao	Hiro
Bay	Huang
Ha	Ibu
Lei	Ji
Li	Jin
Mai	Jing
Min	Ju-Long
Niu	Kang
Nu	Li
Pang	Liang
Tam	Pin
Thim	Quon
Veata	Shen
Zhong	Tan
Zi	Zhong

English Names

Girls	Boys
Alexandra	Arthur
Althea	Clinton
Andie	Clive
Connie	Colin
Cynthia	Earl
Elizabeth	Edward
Esther	Nicholas
Georgina	Nigel
Hayley	Norman
Ida	Peter
Margaret	Roland
Moira	Ronald
Pippa	Toby
Rhonda	William
Wendy	Winston

French Names

Girls	Boys
Aimee	Alain
Angelique	Claude
Antoinette	Gaston
Arianne	Gerard
Daniele	Germain
Desiree	Isidore
Dominique	Jacques
Emmanuelle	Jean
Esmee	Jean-Claude
Gabrielle	Laurent
Genevieve	Louis
Giselle	Luc
Monique	Marcel
Yvette	Maxime
Yvonne	Yves

German Names

Girls	Boys
Anneliese	Folker
Annemarie	Freiderich
Beata	Garrick
Clotilda	Gerhard
Constanze	Gunther
Cordula	Gustaf
Emma	Karl
Felicie	Konrad
Gudrun	Norbert
Heidi	Oswald
Hilda	Otto
Katharina	Ralph
Kristina	Stefan
Margarite	Wilhelm
Martina	Wolfgang

Greek Names

Girls	Boys
Athena	Demetrios
Calista	Demos
Calla	Flavian
Damalla	Hilarion
Delos	Markos
Diona	Nikos
Filia	Sander
Isadora	Socrates
Kali	Stephanos
Kalidas	Theo
Kori	Theodoros
Kynthia	Theophilos
Leandra	Tito
Nia	Verniamin
Xanthe	Zeno

Irish Names

Girls	Boys
Aileen	Brendan
Briana	Colin
Ciara	Curran
Deirdre	Devin
Dorren	Farris
Eavan	Fergus
Eliza	Finn
Emma	Ian
Ethnea	Kevin
Maggie	Kieran
Molly	Killian
Nessa	Liam
Polly	Lochlain
Riona	Owen
Sinead	Rowan

Italian Names

Girls	Boys
Carlotta	Aldo
Chiara	Alessandro
Donna	Angelo
Elda	Anthony
Elena	Arturo
Eliana	Carlo
Elisa	Carmine
Elletra	Emilio
Faustina	Enrico
Fidelia	Franco
Gina	Gianni
Isabella	Gino
Maria	Lorenzo
Melania	Luciano
Nicola	Vincenzo

Jewish and Hebrew Names

Girls	Boys
Esther	Barry
Golda	Benjamin
Hannah	Daniel
Ilana	David
Judith	Eli
Leah	Esau
Lena	Gabriel
Lillian	Ira
Miriam	Isaac
Naomi	Joshua
Rachel	Levi
Shara	Marvin
Sophie	Saul
Sylvia	Sheldon
Tovah	Solomon

Polish Names

Girls	Boys
Celestyna	Aniol
Gizela	Anzelm
Grazyna	Boleslaw
Hanna	Czeslaw
Honorata	Dobromir
Iwona	Karol
Jadwiga	Kazimierz
Karolina	Krzysztof
Krysta	Marek
Krystyna	Pawel
Lucja	Witold
Otylia	Wladymir
Roksana	Wladyslaw
Waleria	Wojtek
Wiktoria	Zbigniew

Russian Names

Girls	Boys
Anastasiya	Adya
Anninka	Alek
Dariya	Dmitri
Elena	Grigori
Evelina	Igor
Inessa	Ivan
Kira	Mikhail
Lara	Misha
Lia	Nikita
Masha	Pavel
Natasha	Sasha
Oksana	Sergei
Olga	Sidor
Polina	Vladimir
Tatiana	Vladja

Scandinavian Names

Girls	Boys
Astrid	Aksel
Birgit	Anders
Bonnevie	Anton
Dufvenius	Bjorn
Gudrun	Dirk
Gunilla	Erik
Inge	Gustav
Ingrid	Hendrik
Janna	Ingmar
Mini	Karl
Sabina	Knut
Sanna	Matts
Sigrid	Mikael
Ursula	Oskar
Wilhelmina	Stellan

Scottish Names

Girls	Boys
Annella	Ainsley
Dina	Angus
Fiona	Bean
Lexine	Bennett
Lindsay	Clement
Maidie	Conall
Maisie	Donald
Margaret	Fergus
Nan	Gregor
Netta	Iagan
Nora	Ian
Peigi	Jock
Robina	Kenneth
Rona	Peader
Rowena	Roddy

Spanish Names

Girls	Boys
Beilarosa	Benito
Bonita	Damaso
Caliopa	Felipe
Consuelo	Fiero
Delicia	Francisco
Delfina	Hector
Destina	Isidoro
Elena	Jaime
Guadalupe	Javier
Honoria	Julio
Mariposa	Miguel
Odelita	Mundo
Paloma	Raoul
Primalia	Roberto
Soledad	Tomas

Most Popular Names of the 1950s

Girls

1. Mary
2. Linda
3. Patricia
4. Susan
5. Deborah
6. Barbara
7. Debra
8. Karen
9. Nancy
10. Donna
11. Cynthia
12. Sandra
13. Pamela
14. Sharon
15. Kathleen

Boys

1. Michael
2. James
3. Robert
4. John
5. David
6. William
7. Richard
8. Thomas
9. Mark
10. Charles
11. Steven
12. Gary
13. Joseph
14. Donald
15. Ronald

Most Popular Names of the 1960s

Girls

1. Lisa
2. Mary
3. Karen
4. Susan
5. Kimberly
6. Patricia
7. Linda
8. Donna
9. Michelle
10. Cynthia
11. Sandra
12. Deborah
13. Pamela
14. Tammy
15. Laura

Boys

1. Michael
2. David
3. John
4. James
5. Robert
6. Mark
7. William
8. Richard
9. Thomas
10. Jeffrey
11. Steven
12. Joseph
13. Timothy
14. Kevin
15. Scott

Most Popular Names of the 1970s

Girls	Boys
1. Jennifer	1. Michael
2. Amy	2. Christopher
3. Melissa	3. Jason
4. Michelle	4. David
5. Kimberly	5. James
6. Lisa	6. John
7. Angela	7. Robert
8. Heather	8. Brian
9. Stephanie	9. William
10. Jessica	10. Matthew
11. Elizabeth	11. Daniel
12. Nicole	12. Joseph
13. Rebecca	13. Kevin
14. Kelly	14. Eric
15. Mary	15. Jeffrey

Most Popular Names of the 1980s

Girls

1. Jessica
2. Jennifer
3. Amanda
4. Ashley
5. Sarah
6. Stephanie
7. Melissa
8. Nicole
9. Elizabeth
10. Heather
11. Tiffany
12. Michelle
13. Amber
14. Megan
15. Rachel

Boys

1. Michael
2. Christopher
3. Matthew
4. Joshua
5. David
6. Daniel
7. James
8. Robert
9. John
10. Joseph
11. Jason
12. Justin
13. Andrew
14. Ryan
15. William

Most Popular Names of the 1990s

Girls	Boys
1. Ashley	1. Michael
2. Jessica	2. Christopher
3. Emily	3. Matthew
4. Sarah	4. Joshua
5. Samantha	5. Jacob
6. Brittany	6. Andrew
7. Amanda	7. Daniel
8. Elizabeth	8. Nicholas
9. Taylor	9. Tyler
10. Megan	10. Joseph
11. Stephanie	11. David
12. Kayla	12. Brandon
13. Lauren	13. James
14. Jennifer	14. John
15. Rachel	15. Ryan

Most Popular Names of 2003

Girls

1. Emily
2. Emma
3. Madison
4. Hannah
5. Olivia
6. Abigail
7. Alexis
8. Ashley
9. Elizabeth
10. Samantha
11. Isabella
12. Sarah
13. Grace
14. Alyssa
15. Lauren

Boys

1. Jacob
2. Michael
3. Joshua
4. Matthew
5. Andrew
6. Joseph
7. Ethan
8. Daniel
9. Christopher
10. Anthony
11. William
12. Ryan
13. Nicholas
14. David
15. Tyler

Girls

Aaliyah
(Hebrew) moving up
Aliya

Aamori
(African) good

Abay
(Native American) growing
Abai, Abbay, Abey, Abeye

Abayomi
(African) giving joy

Abby
(English) happy
*Abbee, Abbey, Abbi,
Abbie, Abbye*

Abella
(French) vulnerable;
capable
*Abela, Abele, Abell, Bela,
Bella*

Abery
(Last name as first name)
supportive
Abby, Aberee, Abrie, Abry

Abia
(Arabic) excellent
Ab, Aba, Abiah, Abbie

Abigail
(Hebrew, English, Irish)
joyful
*Abagail, Abbegayle,
Abbey, Abbie, Abby,
Abegail, Abey, Abigal,
Abigale, Abigayle,
Abygail, Abygale,
Abygayle, Gail, Gayle*

Abilene
(Place name) Texas town;
southern girl
Abalene, Abi, Abiline, Aby

Abiola
(Spanish) God-loving
Abby, Abi, Biola

Abira
(Hebrew) strong

Abra
(Hebrew) form of Abraham;
strong and exemplary
*Aba, Abbee, Abbey, Abbie,
Abby*

Abrianna
(American) insightful
*Abriana, Abryana,
Abryanna, Abryannah*

Abrielle
(American) form of
Abigail; rejoices
*Abby, Abree, Abrey, Abrie,
Abriella, Abryelle*

Acacia
(Greek) everlasting; tree
*Akaysha, Cacia, Cacie,
Case, Casey, Casha, Casia,
Caysha, Kassy, Kaykay*

Acantha
(Greek) thorny; difficult

Accalia
(Latin) stand-in
Accal, Accalya, Ace, Ackie

Achantay
(African American) reliable
Achantae, Achanté

Ada
(German) noble; joyful
Adah, Addah, Adeia, Aida

Adaani
(French) pretty; noble
*Adan, Adane, Adani,
Daani, Dani*

Adabelle
(American) combo of Ada
and Belle; noble beauty
*Ada, Adabel, Addabel,
Belle*

Adaeze
(African) prepared
Adaese

Adah
(Biblical) decorated
Ada, Adie, Adina, Dina

Adair
(Scottish) innovative
*Ada, Adare, Adayr, Adayre,
Adda*

Adalia
(Spanish) spunky
*Adahlia, Adailya, Adallyuh,
Adaylia*

Adalind
(American) from Adaline;
noble

Adalinda
(French) from Adele;
nobility

Adamina
(Hebrew) earth child

Adanna
(Spanish) beautiful baby
Adana

Adar
(Hebrew) respected

Adara
(Greek) lovely
Adarah, Adrah

Addison
(English) awesome
*Addeson, Addie, Addisen,
Addison, Addy, Addyson,
Adeson, Adisen, Adison*

Addy
(English) nickname for
Addison; distinctive;
smiling
*Addee, Addie, Addy,
Addye, Adie, Ady*

Adeen
(American) decorated
*Addy, Adeene, Aden,
Adene, Adin*

Adela
(Polish) peacemaker

Adelaide
(German) calming;
distinguished
*Ada, Adalaid, Adalaide,
Adelade, Adelaid, Laidey*

Adeline
(English) sweet
*Adaline, Adealline,
Adelenne, Adelina,
Adelind, Adlin, Adline*

Adelita
(Spanish) form of Adela;
noble
*Adalina, Adalita, Adelaina,
Adelaine, Adeleta, Adey,
Audilita, Lita, Lite*

Adelka
(German) form of
Adelaide; noble
*Addie, Addy, Adel,
Adelkah, Adie*

Adelle
(German) giving
Adel, Adell, Addy

Adelpha
(Greek) beloved sister
Adelfa, Adelphe

Adena
(Hebrew) precious
*Ada, Adenna, Adina,
Adynna, Deena, Dena*

Aderyn
(Hebrew) from Adira;
powerful

Adesina
(African) threshold child

Adia
(African) God's gift

Adiel
(African) goat; tough-
willed
Adie, Adiell, Adiella

Adina
(Hebrew) high hopes
*Addy, Adeen, Adeena,
Adine, Deena, Dena, Dina*

Adisa
(Hispanic) friendly
Adesa, Adissa

Aditi
(Hindi) free

Adiva
(Arabic) gracious

Adjanys
(Hispanic) lively
Adjanice, Adjanis

Adline
(German) reliable
*Addee, Addie, Addy,
Adleen, Adlene, Adlyne*

Adolpha
(German) noble wolf;
strong girl
Adolpham

Adonia
(Greek) beauty
*Adona, Adonea, Adoniah,
Adonis*

Adora
(Latin) adored child
*Adorae, Adoray, Dora,
Dore, Dorey, Dori, Dorree,
Dorrie, Dorry*

Adorna
(Latin) adorned

Adra
(Greek) beauty

Adria
(Latin) place name
Adrea

Adrian
(English) rich
Adrien, Adryan, Adryen

Adrianna
(Greek, Latin) rich; exotic
*Addy, Adree, Adriana,
Adrie, Adrin, Anna*

Adrienne
(Latin) wealthy
*Adreah, Adreanne,
Adrenne, Adriah, Adrian,
Adrien, Adrienn, Adrin,
Adrina*

Aereale
(Hebrew) form of Ariel;
light and sprite
Aereal, Aeriel, Areale

Aeronwenn
(Welsh) white; aggressor
Awynn

Affrica
(Irish) nice

Afra
(Arabic) deer; lithe
Aphra, Aphrah, Ayfara

Afton
(English) confident
Aft, Aftan, Aften, Aftie

Africa
(Place name) continent
Afrika

Afua
(African) baby born on
Friday
Afuah

Agafi
(Greek) form of Agnes;
pure
*Ag, Aga, Agafee, Agaffi,
Aggie*

Agapi
(Greek) love
Agapay, Agappe, Agape

Agasha
(Greek) form of Agatha;
long-suffering
Agashah, Agashe

Agata
(Italian) good girl

Agate
(English) gemstone;
precious girl
Agatte, Aget, Aggey, Aggie

Agatha
(Greek) kind-hearted
*Agath, Agathah, Agathe,
Aggey, Aggie, Aggy*

Agatta
(Greek) form of Agatha;
honorable and patient
*Ag, Agata, Agathi, Aggie,
Agi, Agoti, Agotti*

Agave
(Botanical) strong-spined;
genus of plants
Ag, Agavay, Aggie, Agovay

Agentina
(Spanish) form of
Argentina; colorful
Agen, Agente, Tina

Aggie
(Greek) kind-hearted
Aggee, Aggy

Aglaia
(Greek) goddess of
beauty; splendid

Agnes
(Greek) pure
*Ag, Aggie, Aggnes, Aggy,
Agnas, Agnes, Agness,
Agnie, Agnus, Nessie*

Aharona
(Hebrew) beloved
Arni, Arnina, Arona

Ahimsa
(Hindu) virtuous

Ahulani
(Hawaiian) heavenly place

Ahvanti
(African) focused
Avanti

Aida
(Arabic) gift
Aeeda, Ayda, Ayeeda, Ieeda

Aidan
(Irish) from the masculine
name Aidan; fiery
Aden, Aiden, Aidyn

Aileen
(Irish, Scottish) fair-haired
beauty
*Aleen, Alene, Alenee,
Aline, Allee, Alleen, Allene,
Allie, Ally*

Ailey
(Irish) form of Aileen; light
and friendly
Aila, Ailee, Ailie, Ailli, Allie

Ailsa
(Irish) noble

Aimee
(French) beloved
*Aime, Aimey, Aimi, Aimme,
Amee, Amy*

Aimee-Lynn
(American) combo of
Aimee and Lynn; lovable
*Aimee Lynn, Aimeelin,
Aimeelynn*

Aimer
(German) leader; loved
Aimery, Ame, Amie

Aine
(Irish) blissful
Ayne

Ainsley
(Scottish) meadow;
outdoorsy
*Ainslea, Ainslee,
Ainsleigh, Ainslie, Anes,
Anslie, Aynslee, Aynsley*

Aintre
(Irish) joyous estate
*Aintree, Aintrey, Antre,
Antry*

Aisha
(Arabic, African) life; lively
Aaisha, Aaysha, Aeesha, Aiesha, Aieshah, Ayeesha, Ayisha, Aysha, Ieashia, Ieeshah, Iesha

Aisling
(Irish) dreamy
Aislinn, Ashling, Isleen

Aislinn
(Irish) dreamy
Aisling, Aislyn, Aislynn

Aithne
(Irish) fiery
Aine, Eithne, Ena, Ethne

Akako
(Japanese) red; blushes

Akala
(Hawaiian) respected

Akasha
(American) combo of A and Kasha; happy; swimmer

Ala
(Arabic) excellent
Alla

Alabama
(Place name) western
Bama

Alaine
(Gaelic) lovely
Alaina, Alaiyne, Alenne, Aleyna, Aleyne, Allaine, Allayne

Alala
(Roman mythology) sister of Mars; protected
Alalah

Alameda
(Spanish) poplar tree; growth

Alana
(Scottish) pretty girl
Alahna, Alahnah, Alaina, Alainah, Alanah, Alanna, Alannah, Allana, Allie, Ally

Alanis
(French) shining star
Alaniss, Alannis, Alannys, Alanys

Alason
(German) form of Alison; noble; bright
Ala, Alas

Alathea
(English) heals and helps
Aleta, Letitia, Letty

Alaula
(English) heals and helps

Alaygrah
(Invented) form of Allegra; frisky
Alay, Allay

Alaytheea
(Invented) form of Aleithea; honest
Alay, Thea, Theea

Alba
(Italian) white

Alberta
(French) bright-eyed
Alb, Albertah, Albie, Albirta, Alburta, Bertie, Berty

Albertina
(Portuguese) bright

Albertine
(English) form of Albert; bright
Albertyne, Albie, Albyrtine, Teeny

Albie
(American) casual
Albee, Albey, Alby, Albye

Albina
(Italian) white
Albyna

Alcina
(Greek) magical; strong-willed
Alcee, Alcie, Als, Alsena, Alsie. Cina, Seena, Sina

Alda
   (German) the older child
Aldona
   (American) sweet
   Aldone
Alea
   (Arabic) excellent
   Alaya, Aleah, Aleeah, Alia,
   Ally
Aleah
   (American) combo of Allie
   and Leah
   Alayah, Alayja
Aleeza
   (Hebrew) joy
   Aliza
Alegria
   (Spanish) beautiful
   movement
   Allegria
Aleksandra
   (Polish, Russian) helpful
Aleshia
   (Greek) honest
   Aleeshia, Aleeshya,
   Aleshya, Alyshia, Alyshya
Alejandra
   (Spanish) defender
   Alijandra, Alyjandra
Alessa
   (Italian) helper
   Alesa
Alessandra
   (Italian) defender of
   mankind
   Aless, Alessa
Alessia
   (Italian) nice
   Alesha, Alyshia, Allyshia
Alethea
   (Greek) truthful
   Alathea, Aleethia, Aletha,
   Aletie, Altheia, Lathea,
   Lathey

Aletta
   (Greek) carefree
   Aleta, Aletta, Eletta, Letti,
   Lettie, Letty
Alex
   (English) protector
Alexa
   (Greek) short for
   Alexandra
   Alecksa, Aleksah, Alex,
   Alexia, Alixa, Alyxa
Alexakai
   (American) combo of
   Alexa and Kai; merry
   Alexikai, Lexi, Kai
Alexandra
   (Greek, English, Scottish,
   Spanish) regal protector
   Alejandra, Alejaundro,
   Alex, Alexandrah,
   Alexandria, Alexis,
   Alezandra, Allesandro,
   Ally, Lex, Lexi, Lexie
Alexandrine
   (French) helpful
   Alexandrie, Alex, Ally, Lexi,
   Lexie
Alexi
   (Greek) short for Alexis;
   defends; sweet
   Alexie, Alexy, Alixi, Alixie,
   Alixy, Alyxi, Alyxie
Alexia
   (Greek) helpful, bright
   Alexea, Alexiah, Alixea,
   Lex, Lexey, Lexie, Lexy
Alexis
   (Greek) short for
   Alexandra; helpful; pretty
   Aleksus, Alexius, Alexus,
   Alexys, Lex, Lexey, Lexi,
   Lexie, Lexis, Lexus

Alfonsith
(German) aggressive
*Alf, Alfee, Alfey, Alfey,
Alfie, Alfonsine, Allfrie,
Alphonsine, Alphonsith*

Alfre
(English) short for Alfreda;
seer
*Alfree, Alfrey, Alfri, Alfrie,
Alfry*

Alfreda
(English) wise advisor
*Alfi, Alfie, Alfred, Alfredah,
Alfrede, Alfredeh, Freda,
Freddy*

Ali
(Greek) short for
Alexandra; defending
Aley, Allee, Alley, Ally, Aly

Alianet
(Spanish) honest; noble
Alia, Aliane

Alice
(Greek) honest
*Alece, Alicea, Alise, Alliss,
Ally, Allys, Alyse, Alysse,
Lisie, Lisy, Lysse*

Aliceann
(American) combo of Alice
and Ann; well-born;
southern feel
*Alice Ann, Alicean, Alice-
Ann*

Alicia
(Greek) delicate; lovely
Alisha

Alida
(Greek) stylish
*Aleda, Aleta, Aletta,
Alidah, Alita, Lee, Lida,
Lita, Lyda*

Alima
(Hebrew) strong

Alina
(Scottish, Slavic) fair-
haired
*Aleena, Alene, Aline,
Allene, Allie, Ally, Allyne,
Alyna, Lena, Lina*

Aline
(Polish) variant of Alina;
noble family

Alisa
(Hebrew) happy
*Alissa, Allisa, Allissah,
Alyssa*

Alisha
(Greek) happy; truthful
*Aleesha, Alesha, Alicia,
Ally, Allyshah, Alysha,
Lesha, Lisha*

Alison
(Scottish) noble
Alisen

Alissa
(Greek) pretty
*Alesa, Alessa, Alise,
Alissah, Allee, Allie, Ally,
Allyssa, Alyssea*

Alita
(Native American)
sparkling

Aliya
(Hebrew) rises;
sweetheart
Aleeya, Alya

Alka
(Polish) distinctive
Alk, Alkae

Allegra
(Italian) snappy
*Aligra, All, Allagrah, Allie,
Alligra, Ally*

Allena
(Greek) outstanding
*Alena, Alenah, Allana,
Allie, Ally*

Allene
(Greek) wonderful
Alerie, Alyne

Allessandra
(Italian) kind-hearted
Allesandra

Allie
(Greek) smiling
Ali, Allee, Alli, Ally, Allye

Allison
(English) kind-hearted
*Alisen, Alison, Allie,
Allisan, Allisen, Allisun,
Ally, Allysen, Allyson,
Alysen, Alyson, Sonny*

Allura
(Hispanic) alluring
Alura

Ally
(Greek) pure heart
*Allee, Alleigh, Alley, Alli,
Allie*

Allyson
(English) another form of
Allison; sweet
*Alisaune, Allysen, Allysun,
Alyson*

Allysse
(Greek) smooth
Allice, Allyce, Allyss

Alma
(Latin) good; soulful
Almah, Almie, Almy

Almeria
(Arabic) princess
*Alma, Almara, Almaria,
Almer, Almurea, Als*

Almirah
(Spanish, Arabic) princess
*Allmeerah, Almira, Elmira,
Mira*

Alodie
(Origin unknown) thriving
Alodee

Aloha
(Hawaiian) love

Alona
(Jewish) sturdy oak
Allona

Alondra
(Spanish) bright
Alond, Alondre, Alonn

Alouette
(French) birdlike
*Allie, Allo, Allou, Allouetta,
Alou, Alowette*

Aloyse
(German) renowned
Aloice, Aloise, Aloyce

Alpha
(Greek) first; superior
*Alf, Alfa, Alfie, Alph,
Alphah, Alphie*

Alston
(English) a place for a
noble
*Allie, Ally, Alstan, Alsten,
Alstun*

Alta
(Latin) high place; fresh

Altea
(Polish) healer

Althaea
(Latin, Italian) healing

Althea
(Greek, English) demure;
healer
*Althe, Althey, Althia,
Althie, Althy, Thea, They*

Alva
(Spanish) fair; bright
Alvah

Alvada
(American) evasive
Alvadah, Alvayda

Alverna
(English) elf friend
Alver, Alverne, Alvernette

Alvernise
(English) form of Alverne;
honest, elf friend
Alvenice

Alvina
(English) beloved; friendly
*Alvee, Alveena, Alvie,
Alvine, Alvy*

Alvita
(Latin) charismatic

Alyda
(French) soaring
*Aleda, Alida, Alita, Lida,
Lyda*

Alys
(English) noble

Alysia
(Greek) compelling
*Aleecia, Alesha, Alicia,
Alish, Alycia*

Alyssa
(Greek) flourishing
*Alissa, Allissa, Allissae,
Ilyssah, Lissa, Lyssa, Lyssy*

Alyx
(English) variant of Alex;
protects

Amabe
(Latin) loved
Ama

Amabelle
(American) loved
Amabel, Amahbel

Amada
(Latin, Spanish) loved one
Ama, Amadah

Amal
(Arabic) optimistic
Amahl

Amalia
(Hungarian) industrious

Amalina
(German) worker
*Am, Ama, Amaleen,
Amaline, Amalyne*

Amalita
(Spanish) hopeful

Amanda
(Latin, English, Irish)
lovable
*Amand, Amandah,
Amandy, Manda, Mandee,
Mandi, Mandy*

Amandra
(American) variant of
Amanda; lovely
*Amand, Mandee, Mandi,
Mandra, Mandree,
Mandry, Mandy*

Amara
(Greek, Italian) unfading
beauty
*Am, Amarah, Amareh,
Amera, Amura, Mara*

Amarillo
(Place name) city in Texas;
(Spanish) yellow
*Ama, Amari, Amarilla,
Amy, Rillo*

Amaris
(Hebrew) beloved;
dedicated
Amares

Amaryllis
(Greek) fresh flower
Ama, Amarillis

Amber
(French) gorgeous and
golden; semiprecious
stone
*Ambar, Amberre, Ambur,
Amburr*

Amber-Dee
(American) combination of
Amber and Dee; golden
jewel; spontaneous
Amber D, Amber Dee

Amberkalay
(American) combo of
Amber and Kalay;
beautiful energy
Amber-Kalé, Amber-Kalet

Amberlee
(American) combo of
Amber and Lee
*Amberlea, Amberleigh,
Amberley, Amberli,
Amberly, Amburlee*

Amberlyn
(American) combo of
Amber and Lyn
*Amberl, Amberlin,
Amberlynn, Amlynn*

Amboree
(Last name as first name)
precocious
Ambor, Ambree

Ambrin
(Greek) long life

Ambrosette
(Greek) eternal
*Amber, Ambie, Ambro,
Ambrosa, Ambrose*

Ambrosia
(Greek) eternal
*Ambroze, Ambrozeah,
Ambrozia*

Ambrosina
(Greek) everlasting
Ambrosine

Amelia
(German) industrious
*Amalee, Amaylyuh, Amele,
Ameleah, Ameli, Amelie,
Amelya, Amilia*

Amera
(Arabic) of regal birth
Ameera, Amira

America
(American) patriotic
*Amer, Amerca, Americah,
Amerika, Amur*

Amethyst
(Greek) precious gem
Amathist, Ameth

Amica
(Latin) good friend
Ameca, Ami, Amika

Amici
(Italian) friend
Amicie, Amie, Amisie

Amie
(French) loved one

Amiga
(Spanish) friend
Amigah

Amina
(Arabic) trustworthy
Amena, Amine

Aminta
(Latin) protects

Amira
(Arabic) nurturer

Amity
(Latin) a good friend
Amitee, Amitey, Amiti

Amor
(Spanish) love
Amora, Amore

Amora
(Spanish) love

Amorelle
(French) lover
*Amoray, Amore, Amorel,
Amorell*

Amoretta
(French) little love
*Amoreta, Amorreta,
Amorretta*

Amorette
(French) tiny love
Amorrette

Amorita
(Spanish) loved

Amy
(Latin) loved one
*Aimee, Amee, Amey,
Ameyye, Ami, Amie, Amye,
Amye*

Amykay
(American) combo of Amy
and Kay
Amikae

Amylynn
(American) combo of Amy
and Lynn
Ameelyn, Amilynn, Amylyn

Amyrka
(Spanish) lively
*Amerka, Amurka, Amyrk,
Amyrrka*

Anabelle
(American) combo of Ana
and Belle; lovely
*Anabel, Anabell,
Annabelle, Anabella*

Anabril
(Spanish) merciful; pretty
Anabrelle, Anna, Annabril

Anais
(French) variant of Anne;
graceful

Anala
(Hindi) fiery

Analia
(Hebrew) gracious; hopeful
*Ana, Analea, Analeah,
Analiah, Analya*

Analeese
(Scandinavian) gracious
*Analece, Analeece,
Annaleese*

Analicia
(Spanish) combo of Ana
and Licia; gracious
sweetheart
*Analice, Analicea,
Analisha, Licia*

Analisa
(American) combo of Ana
and Lisa; lovely
*Analise, Annalisa, Anna-
Lisa*

Analy
(American) graceful;
gracious
Analee, Anali

Analynne
(American) combo of Ana
and Lynne
*Analinn, Analynn,
Annalinne, Annalynn*

Anand
(Hindi) joyful; profound
Anan, Ananda

Anastace
(Spanish) from Anastasia;
reborn
*Anastayce, Anestace,
Anestayce, Anystace,
Anystayce*

Anastasiya
(Greek, Russian) reborn;
royal
Anastasia, Anastasya

Anastay
(Greek) born again;
renewed
Ana, Anastae, Anastie

Anastice
(Latin) from Anatasia;
reborn
*Anasteece, Anesteece,
Anestice, Anysteece,
Anystice*

Anatola
(Greek, French) dawn
Anatol, Anatole

Anayancy
(Spanish) combo of Ana
and Yancy; buoyant
*Ana Yancy, Anayanci,
Anayancie, Ana-Yancy*

Anaysis
(Latin) from Anatasia;
reborn
Anaysys

Anchoret
(Welsh) beloved girl

Ancret
(Welsh) short for
Anchoret; beloved

Ander
(Greek) feminine

Anders
(Scandinavian) stunning
*Andars, Andie, Andurs,
Andy*

Andes
(Greek) feminine
Andee

Andi
(English) casual
*Andee, Andey, Andie,
Andy*

Andraa
(Greek, French) feminine
Andrah

Andrea
(Greek) feminine
*Andee, Andi, Andie,
Andra, Andrae, Andre,
Andreah, Andreena*

Andreana
(Greek) bold heart
*Andreanna, Andriana,
Andrianna, Andryana,
Andryanna*

Andreanne
(American) combo of
Andrea and Anne
Andreane, Andrie, Andry

Andree
(Greek) strong woman
Andrey, Andrie, Andry

Andrenna
(Scottish) pretty; gracious
Andreene, Adrena

Andrianna
(Greek) feminine
Andree, Andy

Andromeda
(Greek) beautiful star
Andromedah

Aneka
(Polish) forgiving

Anemone
(Greek) breath of fresh air

Anewk
(Invented) form of Anouk

Ange
(Greek) from Angela;
angelic

Angel
(Latin) sweet; angelic
*Angelle, Angie, Anjel,
Annjell*

Angela
(Greek) divine; angelic
*Angelena, Angelica,
Angelina, Angelle, Angie,
Gela, Nini*

Angelia
(American) angelic
messenger
Angelea, Angeliah

Angelica
(Latin) angelic messenger
*Angie, Anjeleka, Anjelica,
Anjelika, Anjie*

Angelika
(Greek) angel
*Angelyka, Anglīka,
Angilyka, Angylika*

Angelina
(Latin) angelic
*Ange, Angelyna, Angie,
Anje, Anjelina, Anjie*

Angeline
(American) angelic
Angelene, Angelline

Angelique
(Latin, French) angelic
*Angel, Angeleek, Angelik,
Angie, Anjee, Anjel,
Anjelique*

Angelle
(Latin) angelic
*Ange, Angell, Anje, Anjell,
Anjelle*

Angharad
(Welsh) graceful
Angahard

Angie
(Latin) angelic
Angey, Angi, Angye, Anjie

Aniece
(Hebrew) gracious
*Ana, Anesse, Ani, Anice,
Annis, Annissa*

Aniela
(Polish) sent by God
Ahneela

Anika
(Hebrew) hospitable
*Anec, Anecca, Aneek,
Aneeka, Anic, Anica, Anik,
Annika*

Anila
(Hindi) wind girl

Anisha
(English) purest one
Aneesha, Anysha

Anissa
(Greek) a completed spirit
*Anisa, Anise, Anysa,
Anyssa, Anysse*

Anita
(Spanish) gracious
*Aneda, Aneeta, Anitta,
Anyta*

Anitra
(Invented) combo of Anita
and Debra
Anetra, Anitrah, Annitra

Anjali
(Hindi) pretty; honored
Anjaly

Anjana
(Hindi) merciful; pretty
Anjann

Anjelica
(Latin) angelic
Anjelika

Anjeliett
(Spanish) little angel
*Anjel, Anjeli, Jelette,
Jeliett, Jeliette, Jell, Jelly*

Anjul
(French) jovial
*Angie, Anjewel, Anji, Anjie,
Anjool*

Ann
(Hebrew) loving;
hospitable
*Aine, An, Ana, Anna, Anne,
Annie, Ayn*

Ann-Dee
(American) variant of
Andy; graceful
*Andee, Andey, Andi, Andy,
Ann Dee, Anndi*

Anna
(English, Italian, German,
Russian, Polish) gracious
*Ana, Anae, Anah, Annah,
Anne, Anuh*

Annabella
(Italian) lovely girl
*Anabela, Anabella,
Annabela*

Annabelle
(English) lovely girl
*Anabell, Anabelle,
Annabell*

Annairis
(American) combo of Anna
and Iris; sweet
Anairis, Ana-Iris, Anna Iris

Annamaria
(Italian) combo of Anna and Maria; merciful and holy
Anamaria, Anna-Maria, Annamarie

Anna-Pearl
(American) combo of Anna and Pearl; classic
Anapearl, Anna Pearl, Annapearl

Anne
(English) generous

Anneka
(Scandinavian) from Ann; gracious girl
Anneke

Anneliese
(Scandinavian) gracious; (German) religious
Aneliece, Aneliese

Annella
(Scottish) graceful
Anell, Anella, Anelle

Annemarie
(German) combo of Anne and Marie
Anmarie, Ann Marie, Anne-Marie, Annmarie

Annes
(Hebrew) hospitable

Annette
(American) vivacious; giving
Anette, Ann, Anne, Annett, Annetta, Annie, Anny

Anne-Louise
(American) combo of Anne and Louise; sweet
Anlouise, Ann Louise, Annelouise, Annlouise, Ann-Loweez

Annice
(English) pure of heart

Annie
(Hebrew, Irish) gracious; hip
Ann, Annee, Anney, Anni, Anny

Annika
(Scandinavian) gracious
Anika

Anninka
(Russian) gracious; graceful

Annis
(English) pure

Annissa
(Greek) gracious; complete
Anissa, Anni, Annie, Annisa

Annunciata
(Italian) noticed

Anona
(Botanical) pineapple; fresh

Anora
(Latin) honored

Anouk
(French) form of Ann

Anshaunee
(African American) combo of Ann and Shaunee; happy
Annshaunee, Anshawnee

Ansley
(English) happy in the meadow
Annesleigh, Ans, Anslea, Anslee, Ansleigh, Ansli, Anslie

Anstass
(Greek) resurrected; eternal
Ans, Anstase, Stace, Stacey, Stass, Stassee

Anstice
(Greek) everlasting
Anst, Steece, Steese, Stice

Anthea
(Greek) flowering
Anthia

Antigone
(Greek) impulsive; defiant

Antique
(Word as name) old soul
Anteek, Antik

Antoinette
(Latin) quintessential;
(French) feminine form of
Antoine
*Antoine, Antoinet,
Antwanett, Antwonette,
Antwonette, Toinette,
Tonette*

Antonetta
(Greek) praised
Antoneta

Antonia
(Latin) perfect
Antone, Antonea, Antoneah

Antonian
(Latin) valuable
*Antoinette, Antonetta,
Toni, Tonia, Tonya*

Antonine
(Greek) praised
Antonyne

Antwanette
(African American) prized
Antwan, Antwanett

Anusha
(Armenian) sweet

Anya
(Russian) grace

Aoife
(Irish) beauty

Aphra
(Hebrew) earthy;
sentimental
*Af, Affee, Affey, Affy, Afra,
Aphree, Aphrie*

Aphrodite
(Greek) goddess of love
and beauty
Afrodite, Aphrodytee

Apolinaria
(Spanish) form of Greek
god Apollonia; martyr
Apolinara

Apollonia
(Greek) sun goddess
*Apolinia, Apolyne,
Appollonia*

Apple
(Botanical) fruit; quirky
Apel, Appell

April
(Latin) month; springlike
Aprel, Aprile, Aprille, Apryl

Aqua
(Spanish) colorful
Akwa

Arabella
(Latin) answer to a prayer;
beauty
*Arabel, Arabela, Arabelle,
Arbel, Arbella, Bella, Belle,
Orabele, Orabella*

Arabelle
(Latin) divine
Arabell

Araceli
(Latin) heavenly
Ara, Aracelli, Ari

Aracelle
(Spanish) flamboyant;
heavenly
*Ara, Aracel, Aracell,
Araseli, Celi*

Arachne
(Greek) weaver; spider

Araminta
(English) unique; precious
dawn
*Ara, Arama, Aramynta,
Minta*

Araylia
(Latin) golden
Araelea, Aray, Rae, Ray

Arbra
(American) form of Abra;
sensitive
Arbrae

Arcelia
(Spanish) treasured
*Arcey, Arci, Arcilia, Arla,
Arlia*

Arcelious
(African American)
treasured
*Arce, Arcel, Arcelus, Arcy,
Arselious*

Archon
(American) capable
*Arch, Archee, Archi,
Arshon*

Ardath
(Hebrew) ardent
*Ardee, Ardie, Ardith,
Ardon*

Ardele
(Latin) enthusiastic;
dedicated
*Ardell, Ardella, Ardelle,
Ardine*

Arden
(Latin) ardent; sincere
*Ardan, Ardena, Ardin,
Ardon, Ardyn*

Ardiana
(Spanish) ardent
Ardi, Ardie, Diana

Ardie
(American) enthusiastic;
special
Ardee, Ardi

Areika
(Spanish) pure
Areka, Areke, Arika, Arike

Arekah
(Greek) virtuous; loving

Arelie
(Latin) golden girl
Arelee, Arely, Arlea

Aretha
(Greek) virtuous; vocalist
Areetha

Aretta
(Greek) virtuous
Arette, Arie

Argenta
(Latin) silver

Argentina
(Place name) confident;
land of silver
*Arge, Argen, Argent,
Argenta, Argie, Tina, Tinee*

Argosy
(French) bright
Argosee, Argosie

Argus
(Greek) bright
Arguss

Argyle
(French, American)
complicated
Argie, Argile, Argy, Argylle

Ari
(Hebrew) short for Ariel;
lioness
Aree, Arey, Arie, Ary

Aria
(Hebrew) from Ariel;
lioness
Arya

Ariadne
(Greek) holiness
Aryadne

Ariana
(Greek) righteous

Arianda
(Greek) helper
Ariand

Ariane
(Greek) very gracious
Arianne, Aryahn

Arianne
(French) kind
Ana, Ari, Ariann

Arianwen
(Welsh) from Aeronwen;
blessed

Aridatha
(Hebrew) flourishing
Ar, Arid, Datha

Arisca
(Greek) form of Arista;
best; delight
Ariska, Ariske, Arista

Ariel
(French, Hebrew) heavenly
singer
Aeriel, Airey, Arielle

Ariella
(French) lioness
Ariela, Aryela, Aryella

Aries
(Latin) zodiac sign of the
ram; contentious
Arees

Arin
(Arabic) spreads truth
Aryn

Arista
(Greek) wonderful

Aristelle
(Greek) wonder
Aristela, Aristella

Aritha
(Greek) virtuous
Arete, Aretha

Arizona
(Place name) U.S. state;
grand
Zona

Arketta
(Invented) outspoken
Arkett, Arkette, Arky

Arlea
(Greek) heavenly
*Airlea, Arlee, Arleigh, Arlie,
Arly*

Arleana
(American) form of Arlene;
dedicated
Arlena, Arlina

Arlen
(Irish) devoted
Arlin, Arlyn

Arlena
(Irish) dedicated
*Arlana, Arlen, Arlenna,
Arlie, Arlina, Arlyna,
Arrlina, Lena, Lina, Linney*

Arlene
(Irish) dedicated
*Arlee, Arleen, Arlie, Arline,
Arlyne, Arlynn, Lena, Lina*

Arlette
(French) loyal
Arlet

Armanda
(French) disciplined

Armani
(Italian) fashionable
*Armanee, Armanie,
Armond, Armonee,
Armoni, Armonie*

Armida
(Latin) armed; prepared
Armi, Armid, Army

Arminell
(Latin) nobility
Arminel

Arnette
(English) little eagle;
observant
*Arn, Arnee, Arnet, Arnett,
Ornette*

Arosell
(Last name as first name)
loyal
Arosel

Arpine
(Romanian) dedicated
Arpyne

Artemisia
(Mythology) from Artemis,
goddess of moon/hunting
Arta, Arte, Artema

Arthlese
(Irish) rich
Arth, Arthlice, Artis

Artriece
(Irish) stable
Artee, Artreese, Arty

Aruna
(Hindi) baby of dawn

Arvis
(American) special
*Arvee, Arvess, Arvie,
Arviss, Arvy*

Asabi
(African) outstanding

Ash
(Hebrew) short for Asha;
lucky
Ashe

Asha
(Hebrew) lucky
Aasha, Ashah, Ashra

Ashandra
(African American)
dreamer
Ashan, Ashandre

Ashanti
(African) graceful
Ashantay, Anshante

Ashantia
(American) outgoing
Ashantea, Ashantiah

Asharaf
(Hindi) wishful
Asha, Ashara

Ashby
(English) farm of ash trees
Ashbee

Asher
(Hebrew) blessed
Ash

Ashla
(English) form of Ashley;
gentle

Ashland
(Irish) dreamlike
*Ashelyn, Ashlan, Ashleen,
Ashlin, Ashlind, Ashline,
Ashlinn*

Ashlei
(English) variant of Ashley;
pretty
Ashee, Ashie, Ashly, Ashy

Ashleigh
(English) from the ash tree
meadow
Ashlynn, Ashton

Ashley
(English) woodland sprite
*Ash, Ashie, Ashlay, Ashlea,
Ashlee, Ashleigh, Ashli,
Ashlie, Ashly*

Ashlyn
(English) natural
Ashlin, Ashlinn, Ashlynn

Ashonika
(African American) pretty
Ashon, Ashoneka, Shon

Ashton
(English) from an eastern
town; sassy
*Ashe, Ashten, Ashtun,
Ashtyn*

Asia
(Greek) reborn;
(Place name) continent
*Ashah, Asiah, Asya, Aysia,
Azhuh*

Asma
(Arabic) exalted; loyal

Asmay
(Origin unknown) special
Asmae, Asmaye

Asoka
(Japanese) from Asako;
morning baby

Asp
(Greek) short for Aspasia;
witty
Aspasia
(Greek) witty
Aspashia, Aspasya
Aspen
(Place name) city in
Colorado; earth mother
Aspin, Aspyn, Azpen
Asphodel
(Greek) lily beauty
Asra
(Hindi) pure
Azra
Asta
(Greek) star
Astera
(Greek) starlike
*Asteria, Astra, Astree,
Astrie*
Astra
(Greek) starlike
Astrah, Astrey
Astrid
(Scandinavian, German)
beautiful goddess
*Aster, Asti, Astred, Astri,
Astridd, Astryd, Astrydd,
Atty, Estrid*
Asysa
(Arabic) lively
Aesha, Asha, Aysah
Atalanta
(Greek) athletic; fleet-
footed
Addi, Atlante, Attie
Athalia
(Hebrew) ambitious
AthaSue
(American) combo of Atha
and Sue; sweet and
discriminating
Atha, Athasue, Atha-Sue

Athelean
(Greek) eternal;
precocious
Athey, Athi
Athene
(Chinese) wise
Athena
(Greek) wise woman;
goddess of wisdom in
mythology
*Athene, Athenea, Athina,
Xena, Zena*
Athie
(Hebrew) wise
Athee, Athey, Athy
Atifa
(Arabic) compassionate
Ateefah
Atropos
(Mythology) one of the
Greek Fates; cutter
Aube
(French) from Aubrey;
experiments
Aubrey
(German) noble being;
(French) blonde leader
*Aubery, Aubey, Aubrea,
Aubree, Aubreye, Aubri,
Aubrie, Aubry*
Auburne
(American) tough-minded
*Aubee, Aubern, Auberne,
Aubey, Aubi, Aubie,
Auburn, Auby*
Audie
(French) rich;
(American) daring
*Audee, Audey, Audi, Audy,
Audye*
Audra
(English) exciting
Audrah, Audray

Audrey
(Old English) strong and regal
Audi, Audie, Audra, Audree, Audreen, Audreye, Audri, Audrianna, Audrianne, Audrie, Audrina, Audry

Augustina
(Latin) great
Agustico, Agustin, Augusine, Augustine, Gusty, Tina, Tino

Augusta
(Latin) revered
Augustah, Auguste, Augustia, Augustyna, Austina

Augustine
(Latin) dignified; worthwhile
Augestinn, Augusta, Augustina, Augustyna, Augustyne, Austie, Austina, Austine, Tina

Aunjanue
(French) sparkling

Aunshaunte
(African American) believer
Anshauntay, Aunshauntay, Aunshawntay, Aunshawnte, Shauntae, Shauntay, Shaunte

Aura
(Greek) breeze
Arra

Aurease
(Latin) excellent, golden
Auree, Aureese, Aurey, Auriece, Aury

Aurelia
(Latin) dawn goddess
Arelia, Aura, Auralea, Aurel, Aurelie, Auria, Auriel, Aurielle

Auriel
(Latin) gold
Auriol

Aurora
(Latin) morning glow
Aurorah, Aurore, Rory

Aurysia
(Latin) gold
Arys, Arysia, Aurys

Austen
(Literature) for author Jane Austen; charming
Austyn

Austeena
(American) statuesque
Austeenah, Austie, Austina

Austine
(Latin) respected
Austen, Austene, Austine, Austin

Autra
(Latin) gold

Autumn
(Latin) joy of changing seasons
Autum, Autumm

Ava
(Latin) pretty; delicate bird
Avah, Eva

Avalon
(Celtic) paradise

Avalynne
(American) combo of Ava and Lynne
Avaline, Avalinn, Avalynn, Avelinn

Avena
(Latin) basic; oat field

Avengelica
(Spanish) avenging
Angelica, Avenga, Avengele, Gelica

Averil
(French) flighty
*Ava, Averile, Averill,
Averyl, Averyll, Aviril*

Avery
(French) flirtatious
Avary, Averee, Averi, Averie

Aves
(Greek) breath of fresh air

Avis
(Latin) little bird

Aviana
(Latin) fresh

Avianca
(Latin) fresh

Avisae
(American) springlike
Ava, Avas, Aves, Avi

Aviva
(Hebrew) springlike
Avivah

Avolonne
(African American) happy
*Avalonn, Ave, Avelon,
Avlon, Avo, Avolon,
Avolunne*

Avon
(English) graceful
*Avaughn, Avaugn, Avonn,
Avonne*

Avril
(French) April; springlike

Avrit
(Hebrew) fresh
Avie, Avree, Avret, Avrie

Axelle
(French) serene
Axel, Axell

Aya
(Hebrew) bird in flight

Ayan
(Hindi) pure
Ayun

Ayanna
(Hindi) innocent
Ayunna

Ayeisha
(Arabic) feminine
*Aeesha, Aieshah, Asha,
Ayeeshea, Ayisa, Iasha,
Yeisha, Yeishee, Yisha,
Yishie*

Ayla
(Hebrew) strong as an oak

Aylee
(Hebrew) light

Ayleen
(Hebrew) light-hearted
Aylene

Aylin
(Spanish) strong
Aylen

Aylwin
(Welsh) beloved
Ayle, Aylwie

Aynona
(Hebrew) form of Anne;
graceful
*Ayn, Aynon, Aynonna,
Aynonne*

Azalea
(Latin) earthy; flowering
Azalee, Azelea

Azenet
(Spanish) sun god's gift
Aza, Azey

Azriella
(Hebrew) variant of
Ariella; lioness
Azriela, Azryela, Azryella

Azimah
(Japanese) from Azami;
flower

Aziza
(African) beloved; vibrant
Asisa

Azucena
(Spanish) lily pure
Azu, Azuce, Azucina

Azura
   (French) blue-eyed
   *Azuhre, Azur, Azure,
   Azurre, Azzura*

Baako
   (Japanese) promising;
   happy
Baba
   (American) fun-loving
Bachiko
   (Japanese) happy
Babe
   (Latin) little darling; baby
Babette
   (French) little Barbara
Babianne
   (American) combo of Babi
   and Anne; fun-loving
   *Babi, Babiane, Babyann,
   Biann, Bianne*
Babs
   (American) short for
   Barbara; lively
Bachi
   (Japanese) happy
   *Bachee, Bachey, Bachie,
   Bochee*
Baden
   (German) friendly
   Boden, Bodey
Baderinwa
   (African) worthy
Badger
   (Irish) badger
   Badge

Badriyyah
   (Arabic) surprise
Baek
   (Origin unknown)
   mysterious
Bagent
   (Last name as first name)
   baggage
   Bage
Bagula
   (German) enthused
Bahaar
   (Hindi) spring
Bahama
   (Place name) islands; sun-
   loving
   Baham
Bahati
   (African) lucky girl
   Baha, Bahah
Bahija
   (Arabic) excelling
   Bahiga
Bahir
   (Arabic) striking
   Bah, Baheer, Bahi
Bahira
   (Arabic) bright mind
Bai
   (Chinese) outgoing
Baiben
   (Irish) sweet; exotic
   *Babe, Babe, Bai, Baib,
   Baibe, Baibie, Baibin*
Bailey
   (English) bailiff
   *Bailee, Baylee, Bayley,
   Baylie*
Bailon
   (American) variant of
   Bailey; dancing; happy
   Bai, Baye, Baylon
Bain
   (American) thorn; pale
   Baine, Bane, Bayne

Baird
(Irish) ballad singer
Bayrde

Bairn
(Scottish) child
Bairne

Baize
(Polish) from Bazyli;
royalty
Bayze, Baze

Baka
(Hindi) crane; long-legged
Baca

Bakara
(African) noble

Bakul
(Hindi) flowering
Bakula

Bakura
(Hebrew) ripe; prime
Bikura

Balala
(Hindi) hopes

Balaniki
(Hawaiian) angelic

Balbina
(Latin) stammers
Balbine

Baldree
(German) brave;
loquacious
Baldry

Bali
(Place name) island near
Indonesia; exotic

Ballou
(American) outspoken
Bailou, Balou

Balvino
(Spanish) powerful
Balvene, Balveno

Bambi
(Italian) childlike; baby girl
*Bambee, Bambie,
Bambina, Bamby*

Banan
(Punjabi) held close

Banessa
(American) combo of B
and Vanessa; hopeful
B'Nessa, Banesa, Benessa

Banht
(Hindi) fire

Banita
(Hindi) girl; thoughtful

Banjoko
(Asian) joy

Bano
(Persian) bride
*Bannie, Banny, Banoah,
Banoh*

Bao
(Chinese) adorable;
creative

Bao-Jin
(Chinese) precious gold

Bao-Yo
(Chinese) jade; pretty

Baptista
(Latin) one who baptizes
*Baptiste, Batista, Battista,
Bautista*

Bara
(Hebrew) chosen
Bari, Barra

Barb
(Latin) short for Barbara

Barbara
(Greek, Latin) unusual
stranger
*Babb, Babbett, Babbette,
Babe, Babett, Babette,
Babina, Babita, Babs,
Barb, Barbary, Barbe,
Barbette, Barbey, Barbi,
Barbie, Barbra, Barby,
Basha, Basia, Bobbie,
Bobi*

Barbro
(Swedish) extraordinary
Bar, Barb, Barbar

Barcelona
(Place name) city in Spain;
exotic
Barce, Lona

Barcie
(American) sassy
Barsey, Barsi

Bariah
(Arabic) does well

Barika
(Hebrew) chosen one

Barkait
(Arabic) shines
Barkat

Barran
(Arabic) song

Barrett
(Last name as first name)
happy girl
*Bari, Barret, Barrette,
Barry, Berrett*

Barrie
(Irish) markswoman;
from masculine name
Barry
Bari, Barri

Barron
(Last name as first name)
bright
*Bare, Baron, Barrie, Beren,
Beron*

Barrow
(Last name as first name)
sharp; sly
Barow

Basey
(Last name as first name)
beauty
Bacie, Basi

Baseylea
(American) combo of
Basey and Lee; pretty
*Basey, Basilea, Basilee,
Leelee*

Bashiyra
(Arabic) joyful

Basia
(Greek) regal
Basha, Basya

Basilia
(Greek) regal
Basila, Basilea, Basilie

Basimah
(Arabic) smiling
Basima, Basma

Bastienna
(French) from masculine
name Bastien; clever
Bastee, Bastienne

Bat
(German) female warrior
Bet

Bathia
(German) warrior woman
*Basha, Baspa, Batia,
Batya, Bitya*

Bathilda
(German) woman in war
*Bathild, Bathilde,
Berthilda, Berthilde*

Bathsheba
(Hebrew) beautiful;
daughter of Sheba
*Bathseva, Batsheba,
Batsheva, Batshua, Sheba*

Bathshira
(Arabic) happy; seventh

Batia
(Hebrew) daughter of God
Batea, Batya

Batice
(American) warrior;
attractive
*Bateese, Batese, Batiece,
Batty*

Batini
(African) ponders much
Batzra
(Hebrew) daughter of God
Bay
(Vietnamese) Saturday's child; patient; unique
Bae, Baye
Baylor
(French) of the bay; water-loving
Bayler
Bayo
(African) bringing joy
Baynes
(American) from masculine name Baines; confident
Bain, Baines, Bayne
Bayonne
(Greek) joyful victor
Bay, Baye, Bayonn, Bayonna, Bayunn
Bea
(American) short for Beatrice
Beata
(German) blessed
Bayahta, Beate
Beatha
(Latin) blessed
Betha
Beatrice
(Latin) blessed woman, joyful
Beat, Beatrisa, Beatrise, Beattie, Bebe, Bee, Beitris, Beitriss, Bibi, Treece, Trice
Beatrix
(Latin) happy
Beatriz
(Spanish) joyful
Bebe
(French) baby
Babee, Baby, Bebee

Bebhinn
(Irish) sweet girl
Becca
(Hebrew) short for Rebecca; lively
Bekka
Bechira
(Hebrew) chosen child
Becky
(English) short for Rebecca; spunky
Becki, Beki
Bedelia
(Irish) form of Bridget; powerful
Bedriska
(Irish) from Bedelia; active
Beegee
(American) laidback; calm
B.G., Begee, Be-Gee
Beeja
(Hindi) the beginning; happy
Beej
Bee-Sun
(Filipino) nature-loving; glad
Bee Sun
Bego
(Hispanic) spunky
Beago
Begonia
(Botanical) flower
Behira
(Hebrew) shines
Behorah
(Invented) friend
Be, Behi, Behie, Behora
Beige
(American) tawny; calm
Bayge
Beige-Dawn
(American) clear morning
Bayge-Dawn, Beige Dawn

Beila
(Spanish) beautiful
Beilarosa
(Spanish) combo of Beila
and Rosa; beautiful rose
*Beila, Beila-Rosa, Beila-
Rose, Beiliarose, Rose*
Bel
(Latin) beauty
Bela
(Czech) white
Belah
Belanie
(Invented) combo of B and
Melanie; lovely
*Bela, Belan, Belanee,
Belaney, Belani, Belle*
Belann
(Spanish) pretty
*Bela, Belan, Belana,
Belane, Belanna*
Belem
(Spanish) pretty
Bel, Beleme, Bella
Belen
(Latin) beauty
Belgica
(American) white
*Belgika, Belgike, Belgyke,
Bellgica*
Belia
(Spanish) beauty
*Belea, Beliano, Belica,
Belicia, Belya, Belyah*
Belicia
(Spanish) believer
Belia
Belinda
(Latin, Spanish) beautiful
serpent
Belynda
Belita
(Spanish) pretty little one;
(French) beauty
Bella
(Italian) beautiful

Bellace
(Invented) pretty
Bellase, Bellece, Bellice
Belle
(French) beautiful
Bela, Bele, Bell, Bella
Bellina
(French) beautiful
Belva
(Latin) beautiful view
Belvia
(Invented) practical
Bell, Belva, Belve, Belveah
Bemedikta
(Scandinavian) from
Benedicta; blessed
Benedikte
Bena
(Native American)
pheasant; highbrow
Bendite
(Latin) well blessed
*Ben, Bendee, Bendi,
Bennie, Benny, Binni*
Bene
(Latin) blessed
Benecia
(Latin) short for Benedicta
Benedetta
(Latin) blessed
*Benedicta, Benedicte,
Benedikta, Benetta,
Benita, Benni, Benoite*
Benedicta
(Latin) woman blessed
Benna, Benni
Beneva
(American) combo of Ben
and Eva; kind
*Benevah, Benna, Benni,
Bennie, Benny, Bineva*
Bening
(Filipino) blessing

Benita
(Latin, Spanish) lovely
*Bena, Benetta, Benitri,
Bennie, Binnie*

Benni
(Latin) short for
Benedicta; blessed
Bennie, Binny

Bente
(Latin) blessed

Bentley
(English) meadow; luxury
life
*Bentlea, Bentlee,
Bentleigh, Bently*

Bera
(German) bearish

Berachan
(Hebrew) blessing
*Beracha, Berucha,
Beruchiya, Beruchya*

Berdina
(German) bright; robust
*Berd, Berdie, Berdine,
Berdyne, Burdine,
Burdynne, Dina, Dine*

Berdine
(German) glows

Berecyntia
(Mythology) earth
goddess

Bergen
(American) pretty
Berg, Bergin

Berget
(Irish) form of Bridget
Bergette

Berit
(Scandinavian) glorious
Beret, Berette

Berkley
(American) smart
*Berkeley, Berkie, Berklie,
Berkly*

Berlynn
(English) combo of Bertha
and Lynn
Berla, Berlinda, Berlyn

Bermuda
(Place name) island;
personable
Bermudoh

Bernadette
(French) form of
Bernadine
*Berna, Bernadene,
Bernadett, Bernadina,
Bernadine, Bernarda,
Bernardina, Bernardine,
Berneta, Bernetta,
Bernette, Berni, Bernie,
Bernita, Berny*

Bernadine
(German) brave; (English)
feminine form of Bernard
Bernadene, Berni, Bernie

Berneen
(Irish) hearty

Bernice
(Greek) victorious
*Beranice, Berenice,
Bernelle, Berneta,
Bernetta, Bernette, Berni,
Bernicia, Bernie, Bernyce*

Bernie
(American) winning
*Bernee, Berney, Berni,
Berny*

Bernita
(Greek) from Bernice;
winning

Berry
(Botanical) tiny; succulent
Berree, Berri, Berrie

Bersaida
(American) sensitive
*Bersaid, Bersaide, Bersey,
Bersy, Sada, Saida*

Bertha
(German) bright
*Barta, Berta, Berte,
Berthe, Berti, Bertie,
Bertilda, Bertilde, Bertina,
Bertine, Bertita, Bertuska,
Berty, Bird, Birdie, Birdy,
Birtha*

Bertie
(German) bright
Bert, Bertee, Bertey, Berty

Bertille
(German) from Bertilde;
bright maiden

Bertina
(German) shining bright;
feminine form of Bert

Berule
(Greek) bright; pure
Berue, Berulle

Berura
(Hebrew) chaste
Beruria

Beryl
(Greek) bright and shining
gem
*Beril, Berlie, Berri, Berrill,
Berry, Beryla, Beryle,
Beryn*

Bess
(Hebrew) form of Elizabeth
Bessie

Bet
(Hebrew) daughter

Beta
(Greek) from Greek
alphabet; beginning
Betka, Betuska

Beth
(Hebrew) form of Elizabeth

Betha
(Welsh) devoted to God
Bethah, Bethanne

Bethann
(English); combo of Beth
and Ann; devout
*B-Anne, Bethan, Beth-ann,
Bethanne*

Bethany
(Hebrew) God's disciple
*Beth, Bethanee, Bethani,
Bethania, Bethanie,
Bethann, Bethanne,
Bethannie, Bethanny,
Betheny, Bethina*

Bethel
(Hebrew) in God's house;
holy child

Bethesda
(Hebrew) child of a merry
home

Bethia
(Hebrew) Jehovah's
daughter
Betia, Bithia

Beti
(English) small woman

Betriss
(Welsh) blessed
Betrys

Betsy
(Hebrew) form of Elizabeth
*Bet, Betsey, Betsi, Betsie,
Betts*

Bette
(French) lively; God-loving

Bettina
(Spanish) combo of Beth
and Tina
Betina, Betti, Bettine

Betty
(Hebrew) God-loving; form
of Elizabeth
Bett, Betti, Bettye

Betuel
(Hebrew) in God's house
Bethuel

Betula
(Hebrew) dedicated;
religious
*Bee, Bet, Bethula,
Bethulah, Bett, Betulah*

Beulah
(Hebrew) married
Bealah, Beula, Bew, Bewla

Bev
(English) short for Beverly;
friendly

Beverly
(English) beavers by the
stream; friendly
*Bev, Beverelle, Beverle,
Beverlee, Beverley,
Beverlie, Beverlye, Bevvy,
Verly*

Bevina
(Irish) vocalist
*Beavena, Bev, Beve,
Beven, Bevena, Bevin,
Bevy, Bovana*

Bevinn
(Irish) royal
Bevan

Bhamini
(Hindi) beautiful girl

Bhanumati
(Hindi) bright

Bharaati
(Hindi) careful

Bhavika
(Hindi) devoted girl

Bhuma
(Hindi) of the earth

Bian
(Vietnamese) hides from
life

Bianca
(Italian) white
*Beanka, Beonca, Beyonca,
Biancha, Biancia, Bionca,
Bionka, Blanca, Blancha*

Bibi
(Arabic, Latin, French) girl;
lively
*Bebe, Bibiana, Bibianna,
Bibianne, Bibyana*

Bibiane
(Latin) vibrant

Bidelia
(Irish) from Bridget; lively
Bedilia, Biddy, Bidina

Bienvenida
(Spanish) welcomed baby

Bijou
(French) jewel
*Bejeaux, Bejou, Bejue,
Bidge, Bija, Bijie, Bijy*

Bik
(Chinese) jade

Bikini
(Place name) island girl;
fun-loving
Bikinee

Billie
(German) form of
Wilhelmina;
(English) strong-willed
*Billa, Billee, Billey, Billi,
Billy, Billye*

Billie-Jean
(American) combo of Billie
and Jean
Billie Jean, Billijean

Billie-Jo
(American) combo of Billie
and Jo
Billie Jo, Billyjo

Billie-Sue
(American) combo of Billie
and Sue
Billie Sue, Billysue

Billina
(English) from masculine
name Bill; kind
*Belli, Bill, Billee, Billie,
Billy*

Billings
(American) bright
Billey, Billie, Billing, Billy,
Billye, Billyngs, Byllings

Bina
(Hebrew) perceptive
woman
Bena, Binah, Byna

Binali
(Hindi) music girl

Binase
(Hebrew) bright
Beanase, Benace, Bina,
Binah, Binahse

Binti
(African) dancer

Binyamina
(Hebrew) from Benjamin;
loyal

Bionda
(Italian) black
Beonda, Biondah

Bira
(Hebrew) fortified; strong
Biria, Biriya

Bircit
(Scandinavian) from
Bridget; best

Bird
(English) birdlike
Birdy

Birdie
(English) bird
Birdee, Birdey, Birdi,
Byrdie

Birgit
(Scandinavian) spectacular
Bergette, Berit, Birgetta,
Birgite, Britta, Byrget,
Byrgitt

Birgitta
(Scandinavian) strong;
(Swedish) excellent
splendor
Birgette, Brita, Byrgetta,
Byrgitta

Birgitte
(Scandinavian) strong

Birte
(Scandinavian) form of
Bridget; powerful
Berty, Birt, Birtey, Byrt,
Byrtee

Bishop
(Last name as first name)
loyal
Byshop

Bithia
(Hebrew) Jehovah's
daughter

Bithron
(Biblical) resounding

Bitki
(Spanish) variant of
Beatrix; happy

Bitsie
(American) small
Bitsee, Bitzee, Bitzi,
Bytsey

Bitta
(Scandinavian) variant of
Bridget; excellent
Bit, Bitt, Bittey

Bittan
(Origin unknown) gives joy

Bivona
(African American) feisty
BeBe, Biv, Bivon, Bivonne

Bjork
(Icelandic) unique
Byork

Blade
(English) glorified
Blaide, Blayde

Blaine
(Irish) thin
Blane, Blayne

Blair
(Scottish) plains-dweller
Blaire, Blayre

Blaise
(Latin, French) stammerer
Blaize, Blasé, Blaze

Blake
(English) dark

Blakely
(English) dark
Blakelee, Blakeley, Blakeli

Blanca
(Spanish) white
Blancah, Blonka, Blonkah

Blanche
(French) white
*Blanca, Blanch, Blancha,
Blanchette, Blanka,
Blanshe, Blenda*

Blanchefleur
(French) white flower;
pretty

Blanda
(Latin) seductive
Blandina, Blandine

Blasia
(Spanish) from Blaise;
stutters

Blath
(Irish) flower

Blaze
(Englush) fiery
Blaize, Blayze

Bless
(American) blessed
Blessie

Blessing
(English) dedicated

Bleu
(French) blue
Blue

Blima
(Hebrew) blossoming girl
Blimah, Blime

Bliss
(English) blissful girl

Blodwen
(Welsh) white flower
Blodwyn, Blodyn

Blom
(Hebrew) from Blum;
flower

Blondelle
(French) blonde girl
Blondell, Blondie, Blondy

Blondie
(American) blonde
Blondee

Blossom
(English) flower

Bluebell
(Botanical) pretty
*Belle, Blu, Blubel, Blubell,
Blue, Bluebelle*

Blum
(Hebrew) flower
Bluma

Blush
(American) pink-cheeked
Blushe

Bly
(American) soft; sensual
Blye

Blythe
(English) carefree
Blithe, Blyth

Bo
(Chinese) precious girl

Boanah
(American) good
*Boana, Bonaa, Bonah,
Bonita*

Bobbi
(American) form of
Roberta
*Bobbee, Bobbette,
Bobbie, Bobby, Bobbye,
Bobi, Bobina*

Bobbiechristine
(American) combo of
Bobbie and Christine
*BobbiChris,
Bobbichristine, Bobbie-
Christine*

Bobbi-Ann
(American) combo of
Bobbi and Ann
*Bobbiann, Bobbyann,
Bobbyanne*

Bobbi-Jo
(American) combo of
Bobbi and Jo
Bobbiejo, Bobbijo, Bobijo

Bobbi-Lee
(American) combo of
Bobbi and Lee
Bobbilee, Bobbylee

Bobby-Kay
(American) combo of
Bobby and Kay
Bobbikay

Bobby-Sue
(American) combo of
Bobby and Sue
Bobbisue, Boby-Sue

Bodil
(Polish) heroic
Bothild, Botilda

Bogdana
(Polish) gift from God
*Boana, Bocdana, Bogda,
Bogna, Bohdana,
Bohdana, Bohna*

Bogumila
(Polish) loved by God

Boguslawa
(Polish) in God's glory

Boinaiv
(Native American) girl in
the grass

Bola
(Origin unknown) clever
Bolo

Bolade
(African) honored girl

Bolanile
(African) rich in spirit

Boleslawa
(Polish) strong

Bona
(Latin, Italian, Polish,
Spanish) good
Bonah, Bonna

Bonda
(Spanish) good
Bona

Bonfilia
(Italian) good daughter

Bong-Cha
(Korean) excellent
daughter

Bonita
(Spanish) good; pretty
*Bo, Bona, Boni, Bonie,
Bonitah, Nita*

Bonn
(French) satisfied; good
Bon, Bonne

Bonnevie
(Scandinavian) good life

Bonnie
(English, Scottish) pretty
face
*Boni, Bonie, Bonne,
Bonnebell, Bonnee,
Bonni, Bonnibel,
Bonnibell, Bonnibelle,
Bonny*

Bonnie-Bell
(American) combo of
Bonnie and Belle; lovely
*Bonnebell, Bonnebelle,
Bonnibelle*

Booth
(German) from the
dwelling; home-loving
Boothe

Bootsey
(American) cowgirl
Boots, Bootsie

Borghild
(Scandinavian) prepared

Borgny
   (Scandinavian) fortified;
   strong
Bors
   (Latin) foreign
   Borse
Boske
   (Hungarian) strays
Boston
   (Place name) city in
   Massachussets; courteous
   Boste, Bosten, Bostin
Boswell
   (Last name as first name)
   intellectual
   Boz, Bozwell
Boupha
   (Vietnamese) flower girl
Bowdy
   (American) outgoing
   Bow, Bowdee, Bowdey,
   Bowdie
Boxidara
   (Slavic) divine
   Boza, Bozena, Bozka
Bracha
   (Hebrew) blessed; sways
   in wind
   Brocha
Bradley
   (English) girl of the broad
   meadow; carefree
   Bradlee, Bradleigh,
   Bradlie, Bradly
Brady
   (Irish) spirited child
   Bradee, Bradey, Bradi,
   Bradie
Braisly
   (American) cautious
   Braise, Braislee, Braize,
   Braze
Branca
   (American) from Blanca;
   white

Brandy
   (Dutch) sweet as wine;
   fun-loving
   Bran, Brandais, Brande,
   Brandea, Brandee,
   Brandeli, Brandi, Brandye,
   Brandyn, Brani, Branndea
Brandy-Lynn
   (American) combo of
   Brandy and Lynn
   Brandelyn, Brandilynn,
   Brandlin, Brandy-Lyn
Branka
   (Czech) glory
   Bran, Branca, Bronca,
   Bronka
Brayden
   (American) humorous
   Braden, Brae, Braeden,
   Bray, Brayd, Braydan,
   Braydon
Braxton
   (English) from town of
   Brock; safe
   Braxten
Breana
   (Irish) form of Briana
   Bre-Anna, Breanne,
   Breeana, Briana, Briane,
   Briann, Brianna, Brianne,
   Briona, Bryanna, Bryanne
Breann
   (Irish) form of Briana
   Bre-Ann, Bree, Breean,
   Breeann
Breck
   (Irish) freckled
Bree
   (Irish) upbeat
   Brea, Bria, Brie, Brielle
Breena
   (Irish) glowing
   Brena

Breeshonna
(African American) happy-go-lucky
Bree, Brie, Brieshona

Breezy
(American) easygoing
Breezee, Breezie

Brehea
(American) self-sufficient
Breahay, Brehae, Brehay

Bren
(American) short for Brenda
Breyn

Brena
(Irish) strong-willed
Brenna

Brenda
(Irish) royal; glowing
Bren, Brendalynn, Brenn, Brenna, Brennda, Brenndah, Brinda, Brindah, Brinna

Brenda-Lee
(American) combo of Brenda and Lee
Brandalee, Brindlee, Brinlee

Brendette
(French) small and royal

Brendie
(American) form of Brenda
Brendee, Brendi

Brendelle
(American) distinctive

Brendolyn
(Invented) combo of Brenda and Lyn; intelligent
Brend, Brendo, Brendolynn, Brendy

Brenna
(Irish) form of Brenda; dark-haired
Bren, Brenn, Brenie

Bretislava
(Polish) glorious
Breeka, Breticka

Brett
(Latin) jolly
Bret, Bretta, Brette

Breyawna
(African American) variant of Brianna
Bryawn, Bryawna, Bryawne

Bria
(Irish) short for Briana; pure; spirited

Briana
(Irish) virtuous; strong
Breana, Breann, Bria, Brianna, Briannah, Brie-Ann, Bryanna

Brianne
(Irish) strong
Briane, Brienne, Bryn

Briar
(French) heather
Brear, Brier

Briar-Rose
(Literature) from "Sleeping Beauty"; princess

Brice
(English) quick

Bryce
(Welsh) aware

Briceidy
(English) precocious
Brice, Bricedi, Briceidee, Briceidey

Bride
(Scottish) from Bridget; wise

Bridey
(Irish) wise
Bredee, Breedee, Bride, Bryde

Bridged
(Scottish) has the strength of fire
Bridgid, Briged, Brigid

Bridget
(Irish) powerful
Birgit, Birgitt, Birgitte, Breeda, Brid, Bride, Bridge, Bridgett, Bridgette, Bridgitte, Bridgey, Brigantia, Briget, Brigette, Brighid, Brigid, Brigida, Brigit, Brigitt, Brigitta, Brigitte, Brijette, Brygett, Brygida, Brygitka

Brie
(French) from the French town Rozay-en-Brie
Bree, Brielle

Brielle
(Invented) combo of Bri and Elle
Briell, Bryelle

Brier
(French) heather
Briar

Briesha
(African American) giving
Bri, Brieshe

Brigida
(Italian) strong
Brigeeda

Brigidine
(Invented) combo of Brigit and Dine (from Geraldine)
Brige, Brigid

Brigitta
(Romanian) strong
Brigeeta, Brigeetta, Brigita

Bril
(American) strong
Brill

Briley
(Last name as first name) popular
BeBe, Bri, Brile

Brina
(Latin) short for Sabrina
Breena, Brena, Brinna, Bryn, Bryna, Brynn, Brynna, Brynne

Brindle
(Irish) versatile
Bryndle

Brine
(Irish) strong
Bryne

Brinlee
(American) sweetheart
Brendlie, Brenlee, Brenly

Brionna
(Irish) happy
Breona, Briona

Brinkelle
(American) independent nature
Binkee, Binky, Brinkee, Brinkel, Brinkell, Brinkie

Brisa
(Spanish) beloved
Breezy, Breza, Brisha, Brisia, Brissa, Briza, Bryssa

Brisco
(American) high-energy woman
Briscoe, Briss, Brissie, Brissy

Briseis
(Mythology) prized; loved

Brissellies
(Spanish) happy
Briselle, Briss, Brisse, Brissel, Brissell, Brissey, Brissi, Brissies

Brit
(Latin) British

Britaney
(English) from Britain
Britanee, Britani, Briteny, Brittaney, Brittenie, Britnee, Britney, Britni

Brites
(Spanish) strong
Britt
(Latin) from Britain
Brit
Britta
(Swedish) strong woman
Brita
Brittany
(English) from Britain;
trendy
*Brinnee, Britany, Briteney,
Britney, Britni, Brittan,
Brittaney, Brittani,
Brittania, Brittanie,
Brittannia, Britteny,
Brittni, Brittnie, Brittny*
Britty
(Irish) short for Brittney;
girl from Britain
*Britee, Britey, Briti, Britie,
Brittee, Brittey, Britti,
Brittie, Brity*
Brody
(Irish) girl from the canal
*Brodee, Brodey, Brodi,
Brodie*
Brona
(Italian) brown-haired girl
Bronislava
(Polish) protective
*Brana, Branislava, Branka,
Brona, Bronicka, Bronka*
Bronislawa
(Polish) protective
Bronya
Bronte
(Literature) for authors
Charlotte and Emily
Bronte; romantic
Brontae, Brontay
Bronwyn
(Welsh) white-breasted
*Bron, Bronwen,
Bronwhen, Bronwynn*

Brook
(English) sophisticated
Brooke, Brooky
Brooklyn
(Place name)
neighborhood in New York
*Brookelyn, Brookelynn,
Brooklynn, Brooklynne*
Browning
(Literature) for poet
Elizabeth Barrett
Browning; pensive
Brucie
(French) from Bruce; royal
Brucina, Brucine
Bruenetta
(French) brown-haired
Bru, Brunetta
Bruna
(Italian) brown-haired girl
Bruneita
(German) brown-haired
*Broon, Brune, Bruneite,
Brunny*
Brunella
(German) intelligent
*Brun, Brunela, Brunella,
Brunelle, Brunetta,
Brunette, Brunilla, Brunne*
Brunhilda
(German) warrior
*Brunhild, Brunhilde,
Brunnhilda, Brunnhilde,
Brynhild, Brynhilda, Hilda*
Bryanna
(Gaelic) powerful female
Breanna, Brianna, Bryana
Bryanta
(American) form of
masculine name Bryan;
strong
Brianta, Bryan, Bryianta
Bryce
(American) happy
Brice

Bryleigh
    (English) spinoff of
    Brittany; jovial
    Brilee, Briley, Brily, Brilye,
    Brylee, Brylie
Bryn
    (Welsh) hopeful; climbing
    a hill
    Brenne, Brinn, Brynn,
    Brynne, Brynnie
Brynn
    (Welsh) hopeful
    Brenn, Brinn, Brynne
Brynna
    (Welsh) optimistic
    Brinn, Brinna
Bryonie
    (Latin) clinging vine
    Breeonee, Brioni, Bryony
Bryony
    (Latin) vine; clingy
    Briony, Bronie, Bryonie
Bua
    (Vietnamese) fortunate
    Boo, Bu
Bubbles
    (American) perky
    Bubb
Buena
    (Spanish) goodness
Buffy
    (American) plains-dweller
    Buffee, Buffey, Buffie
Bukola
    (African) wealthy
    Bucola
Bunard
    (American) good
    Bunerd, Bunn, Bunny
Bunmi
    (Hindi) earth
Bunny
    (English) little rabbit;
    bouncy
    Bunnee, Bunni, Bunnie

Burgundy
    (French) red wine; unique
    Burgandi, Burgandy
Burke
    (American) loud
    Berk, Burk, Burkie
Burkeley
    (English) birches;
    outdoorsy
    Burkelee, Burkeleigh,
    Burkeli, Burkelie, Berkeley,
    Burkely, Burklee,
    Burkleigh, Burkley, Burkli,
    Burklie, Burkly
Burns
    (Last name as first name)
    presumptuous
    Bernes, Berns, Burn,
    Burnee, Burnes, Burney,
    Burni, Burny
Buseje
    (African) interesting
Buthaayna
    (Arabic) lovely body
    Busayna, Buthaynah
Butte
    (Place name) landscape
Butter
    (American) smooth
Buzzie
    (American) spirited
    Buzz, Buzzi
Bwyana
    (African American) smart
    Bwya, Bwyanne
Byhalia
    (Native American) strong
    oak
Byronae
    (American) form of Byron;
    smart
    Byrona, Byronay

Cabot
(French) fresh-faced

Cabrina
(American) combo of C and Sabrina; innovator

Cabriole
(French) adorable
Cabb, Cabby, Cabriolle, Kabriole

Cacalia
(Botanical) accommodating

Cachay
(African American) distinctive

Cachet
(French) fetching
Cache, Cachee

Caddy
(American) elusive; alluring

Cade
(American) precocious
Kade, Kaid

Cadena
(Latin) rhythmic

Cadence
(American) musical
Kadence

Cady
(English) fun-loving
Cadee, Cadey, Cadye, Caidee, Caidy, Kadee, Kady

Caesaria
(Greek) from Caesar; leader

Cai
(Chinese) wealthy; girlish

Cailida
(Spanish) passionate

Cailidora
(Greek) gifted with a beautiful face

Cailin
(American) happy
Cailyn, Cailynn, Calyn, Cayleen, Caylin, Caylyn, Caylynne

Caimile
(Spanish) helps

Cainwen
(Welsh) lovely treasure
Ceinwen, Kayne, Keyne

Cairo
(Place name) Egypt's capital; confident
Kairo, Kayro

Cait
(Greek) purest
Cate, Kate

Caitlin
(Irish) virginal
Cailin, Caitleen, Caitlen, Caitlinn, Caitlyn, Catlin, Catlyn, Catlynne

Caitrin
(Irish) pure of heart

Cakusola
(African) lionhearted

Cala
(Arabic) strong
Calla, Callah

Calandra
(Greek) lark
Calendra, Calondra, Kalandra

Calantha
(Greek) gorgeous flower
Calanth, Calanthe, Callantha, Calli

Calatea
(Greek) flowering
Calatee

Cale
(Latin) respected
Kale

Caledonia
(Latin) from Scotland;
worthy
Kaledonia

Caleigh
(American) beauty
Calleigh

Caley
(American) warm
Caleigh, Kaylee

Calhoun
(Last name as first name)
surprising

Calia
(American) beauty

Calida
(Spanish) warmth

California
(Place name) U.S. state;
cool
Callie, Kalifornia, Kallie

Calinda
(American) combo of Cal
and Linda
*Cal, Calenda, Calli, Callie,
Cally, Kalenda, Kalinda*

Caliopa
(Greek, Spanish) singing
beautifully
Kaliopa

Calise
(Greek) gorgeous

Calista
(Greek) most beautiful
*Calysta, Kali, Kalista, Kalli,
Kallista, Callista*

Calla
(Greek) beautiful
Cala, Callie, Cally

Callidora
(Greek) gift of beauty

Callie
(Greek) beautiful
*Caleigh, Callee, Calley,
Calli, Cally, Kali, Kallee,
Kallie*

Calligenia
(Italian) beauty's child

Calliope
(Greek) poetry muse
Kalliope, Kallyope

Callison
(American) combo of Calli
and Allison; pretty
offspring
*Cal, Calli, Callice, Callis,
Callisen, Callisun*

Callista
(Greek) most beautiful
*Calesta, Calista, Callista,
Calysta, Kallista*

Callula
(Latin) beautiful

Caltha
(Latin) gold flower

Calumina
(Scottish) calm

Calvina
(Latin) has no hair
Calvine

Calypso
(Greek) sea nymph

Cam
(American) short for
Cameron
Cami, Camie, Cammie

Camaren
(American) from Cameron;
crooked nose

Camassia
(American) combo of
Camey and Massia; aloof

Cambay
(American) saucy
Cambaye, Kambay

Camber
(American) from Amber;
has potential
Cambie, Cambre, Cammy,
Kamber

Cambree
(Place name) from
Cambria, Wales; ingenious
Cambre, Cambrie, Cambry,
Cambry, Kambree,
Kambrie

Cambria
(English) the people

Camden
(American) glorious face
Cam, Camdon, Cammi,
Cammie, Cammy

Cameka
(African American) form of
Tameka/Tamika
Cammey, Cammi, Cammy,
Kameka, Kammy

Camellia
(Italian) flower
Camelia, Kamelia

Camelina
(American) from Camilla;
shy

Camelot
(English) elegant
Cam, Cami, Camie, Camy

Cameo
(French) piece of jewelry;
singular
Cameoh, Cammie, Kameo

Camera
(Word as name) stunning
Kamera

Camerino
(Spanish) unblemished
Cam, Cammy

Cameron
(Scottish) popular;
crooked nose
Cameran, Camren,
Camryn, Kameron, Kamryn

Cami
(French) short for Camille,
Camilla, or Cameron
Camey, Camie, Cammie,
Cammy

Camilla
(Latin, Italian) wonderful
Cam, Camelia, Camellia,
Camila, Camile, Camille,
Camillia

Camille
(French) swift runner;
great innocence
Camila, Cammille, Cammy,
Camylle, Kamille

Cammy
(American) short for
Camilla; helps

Camp
(American) outsider
Cam, Campy

Campbell
(Last name as first name)
amazing
Cam, Cambell, Camey,
Cami, Camie, Camy

Camrin
(American) variant of
Cameron
Camren, Camryn

Canace
(American) from Candace;
white brilliance

Canada
(Place name) country in
North American; decisive
Cann, Kanada

Candace
(Greek) glowing girl
Caddy, Candice, Candis,
Candys, Kandace

Candelara
(Spanish) spiritual
Cande, Candee,
Candelaria, Candi, Candy,
Lara

Candenza
(Italian) from Candace; white brilliance

Candida
(Latin) white

Candra
(Latin) she who glows
Candria, Kandra

Candy
(American) short for Candace; glowing
Candee, Candi, Candie

Caneadea
(Native American) the horizon; far-reaching goals

Canei
(Greek) pure

Cannes
(Place name) town in France; selective
Can, Kan

Cannon
(American) vital

Cantara
(Arabic) bridge
Canta, Kanta, Kantara

Capelta
(American) fanciful
Capeltah, Capp, Cappy

Caplice
(American) spontaneous
Capleece, Capleese, Kapleese

Capri
(Place name) island off coast of Italy
Caprie, Kapri

Caprice
(Italian) playful; capricious
Caprece, Capreese, Capricia, Caprise

Capote
(Spanish) cloak; protected

Capucine
(French) cloak
Cappy

Car
(American) driven
Carr, Kar, Karr

Cara
(Latin, Italian) dear one
Carah, Kara

Caramia
(Italian) my dear
Cara Mia, Cara-Mia

Cardia
(Spanish) giving
Cardi, Kardia

Caren
(American) dear
Carine, Caryn, Karen, Karyn

Carenleigh
(American) combo of Caren and Leigh
Caren-Leigh

Caresse
(Greek) well-loved

Carey
(Welsh) by a castle; fond
Caree, Cari, Carrie, Cary

Cari
(Latin) giving

Caridad
(Spanish) giving
Cari

Carie
(Latin) generous

Carina
(Greek, Italian) dearest
Careena, Carena, Carin, Carine, Kareena, Karina

Carinthia
(Place name) city in Austria; dear girl

Carissa
(Greek, Italian) beloved
Carisa, Caryssa, Karessa, Karissa

Carita
(Latin) giving; loved
Caritta, Carrita, Carritta, Karita

Caritina
(Spanish) combo of Cari and Tina; dearest
Cari, Cartine, Tina

Carla
(German) feminine of Charles
Carlah, Carlee, Carli, Carlia, Carlie, Carly, Karla, Karlah

Carleas
(American) from Carlissa; smooth moves

Carlee
(German) darling
Carleigh, Carley, Carli, Carly, Karlee, Karley

Carlene
(American) sweet
Carleen, Carlina, Carline, Carlyn

Carlanda
(American) darling
Carlan, Carland, Carlande, Carlee, Carlie, Carly, Karlanda

Carlessa
(American) combo of Carla and Lessa; restless

Carlett
(Spanish) affectionate
Carle, Carlet, Carletta, Carlette, Carley, Carli

Carlianne
(American) combo of Carli and Anne; affectionate

Carlin
(Latin, German) winner
Caline, Carlan, Carlen

Carlisle
(Place name) city on the border of England and Scotland; sharp
Carlile, Carrie, Karlisle

Carlisa
(Italian) combo of Carla and Lisa; fond of friends
Carlie, Carlissa, Carly, Carlysa, Karlese, Karlisa

Carlissa
(American) pleasant
Carleeza, Carlisse

Carlita
(Italian) outstanding

Carlotta
(Italian, Spanish) feminine form of Carlo and Carlos; sweetheart
Karlotta

Carly
(German) darling
Carlee, Carley, Carli, Carlie, Karlee

Carma
(Hebrew) short for Carmel; special garden
Car, Carmee, Carmi, Carmie, Karma

Carmel
(Hebrew) garden
Carmela, Carmella, Karmel

Carmela
(Hebrew, Italian) fruitful
Carmalla, Carmel, Carmella, Carmie, Carmilla

Carmelina
(Italian) combo of Carmelo and Lina; in the garden
Carmalina, Carmelena, Carmela, Carmelita

Carmen
(Hebrew) crimson
*Carma, Carman, Carmela,
Carmelinda, Carmita,
Carmynne, Chita, Mela,
Melita*

Carmensita
(Spanish) dear girl
*Carma, Carmens,
Carmense, Karmence*

Carmiela
(Hebrew) from Carmel;
garden girl

Carmiya
(Hebrew) from Carmel;
garden girl

Carmine
(Italian) attractive
Carmyne, Karmine

Carminia
(Italian) dearest
*Carma, Carmine,
Carmynea, Karm,
Karminia, Karmynea*

Carna
(Latin) horn; sound of joy

Carni
(Latin) horn; vocal
*Carna, Carney, Carnia,
Carnie, Carniela, Carniella,
Carniya, Carny, Karni,
Karnia, Karniela, Karniella,
Karniya*

Carnation
(Botanical) abundant
flower
*Carn, Carna, Carnee,
Carney, Carny*

Carnethia
(Invented) fragrant
*Carnee, Carney, Carnithia,
Karnethia*

Carnie
(American) happy
Carni, Karni, Karnie

Carody
(American) humorous
*Caridee, Caridey, Carodee,
Carodey, Carrie, Karodee,
Karody*

Carol
(English) feminine;
(French) joyful song;
(German) farming woman
*Carole, Carroll, Caryl,
Karol, Karrole*

Carolanne
(American) combo of Carol
and Anne
Carolane, Carolann

Carole
(French) joyous song
Karol, Karole

Carolina
(Italian) feminine
Carrolena, Karolina

Caroline
(German) petite woman
*Caraline, Carilene,
Cariline, Caroleen, Carolin,
Carrie, Karalyn, Karolina,
Karoline, Karolyn,
Karolynne*

Carolyn
(English) womanly
*Carilyn, Carilynn, Carolyne,
Carolynn, Karolyn*

Caron
(Welsh) giving heart
Carron, Karon

Caronsy
(American) form of Caron;
sweet
*Caronnsie, Caronsi,
Karonsy*

Carrelle
(American) lively
Carrele

Carrie
(French, English) joyful song
Carey, Cari, Carri, Carry, Kari

Carson
(Nordic) dramatic
Carse, Carsen, Carsun, Karrson, Karsen, Karson

Carsyn
(American) variant of Carson; confident

Carylan
(American) combo of Caryl and An; soft
Carolann, Caryland, Carylanna, Karylan

Caryn
(Danish) form of Karen; loving
Caren, Carrin, Caryne, Carynn

Carys
(Welsh) love

Casey
(Greek, Irish) attentive female
Casie, Cassee, Cassey, Casy, Caysee, Caysie, Caysy, Kasey

Cashonya
(African American) monied; lively
Kashonya

Casielee
(American) combo of Casie and Lee; popular
Caseylee, Casie Lee, Casielea, Casie-Lee, Casieleigh

Casilda
(Latin) from the dwelling

Casilde
(Spanish) combative
Casilda, Casill, Cass, Cassey, Cassie

Cason
(Greek) seer; spirited
Case, Casey, Kason

Cassandra
(Greek) insightful
Casandra, Casandria, Cass, Cassie, Cassondra, Kassandra

Cassia
(Greek) spicy; cinnamon

Cassidy
(Irish) clever girl
Casadee, Cass, Cassidee, Cassidi, Kassidy

Cassie
(Greek) short for Cassandra; tricky
Cassey, Cassi

Cassiopeia
(Greek) starry-eyed
Cass, Cassi, Kass, Kassiopia

Cassis
(American) variant of Carson; confident

Casta
(Spanish) short for Castalina; chaste

Castalia
(Mythology) ill-fated

Castalina
(Spanish) variant of Catalina; chaste

Castara
(Greek) from Catherine; pure
Castera, Castora

Catalina
(Spanish) pure
Catalena, Katalena, Katalina

Catarina
(Greek, Italian) pure
Caterina, Catrina, Katarina

Catava
(Greek) uncorrupted

Catharina
(Greek) from Catherine; pure

Cather
(Literature) for author Willa Cather; earthy
Kather

Catherine
(Greek, Irish, English) pure
Cartharine, Cathrine, Cathryn, Katherine

Cathleen
(Irish) pure; immaculate
Cathelin, Cathleyn, Cathlinne, Cathlyn, Cathy

Cathresha
(African American) pure; outspoken
Cathrisha, Cathy, Kathresha, Resha

Cathryn
(Greek) pure female; form of Catherine

Cathy
(Greek) pure; innocent
Cathee, Cathey, Cathie, Kathy

Catima
(Greek) pure
Cattima

Catline
(Irish) form of Caitlin; virtuous
Cataleen, Catalena, Catleen, Catlen, Katline

Catrice
(Greek) form of Catherine; wholesome
Catrece, Catreece, Catreese, Katreece, Katrice

Catrina
(Greek) pure
Catreena, Catreene, Catrene, Katrina

Catriona
(Greek) from Catherine; pure
Katriona

Cavender
(American) emotional
Cav, Cavey, Kav, Kavender

Cayenne
(Word as name) peppery; spice

Caykee
(American) combo of Cay and Kee; lively
Caycay, Caykie, Kaykee, Kee

Cayla
(Hebrew) unblemished
Cailie, Calee, Cayley, Caylie, Kayla

Cayley
(American) joyful
Caelee, Caeley, Cailey, Cailie, Caylea, Caylee, Cayleigh, Caylie

Caylisa
(American) combo of Cay and Lisa; lighthearted
Cayelesa, Cayl, Cay-Lisa, Caylise, Kayl, Kaylisa

Cayman
(Place name) the islands; free spirit
Caman, Caymanne, Kayman

Cayne
(American) generous
Cain, Kaine

Ceara
(Irish) variant of Ciara; clear-eyed

Ceaskarshenna
(African American) ostentatious
Ceaskar, Karshenna, Shenna

Cece
(Latin) from Cecilia; blind; hopeful

Ceci
(Latin) short for Cecilia; dignified

Cecile
(Latin) short for Cecilia; genteel
Cecily

Cecilia
(Latin, Polish) blind; short-sighted
Cacelia, Cece, Cecelia, Ceil, Celia, Cice, Cicilia, Cilley, Secilia, Sissy

Cedrica
(English) chief; leader

Cedrice
(American) form of masculine name Cedric; feisty
Ced, Cedrise

Ceil
(Latin) blythe
Ceel, Ciel

Ceinwen
(Welsh) blessed baby

Ceirra
(Irish) clear-eyed
CeAirra, Cierra

Ceiteag
(Scottish) purest

Celand
(Latin) heavenward
Cel, Cela, Celanda, Celle

Celandine
(Greek) wildflower; natural beauty

Celebration
(American) word as name; celebrant
Cela, Sela

Celena
(Greek) heavenly; form of Selena
Celeena, Celene

Celery
(Botanical) refreshing
Cel, Celeree, Celree, Celry, Sel, Selery, Selry

Celeste
(Latin) gentle and heavenly
Celest, Celestial, Celestine, Seleste

Celestia
(Latin) heavenly
Celeste, Celestea, Celestiah, Seleste, Selestia

Celestyna
(Polish) heavenly
Cela, Celeste, Celesteenah, Celestinah, Celestyne

Celina
(Greek) loving; form of Celena
Selina, Celena

Celine
(Greek) lovely
Celeen, Celene

Celisha
(Greek) flaming; passionate

Celka
(Latin) celestial
Celk, Celkee, Celkie, Selk, Selka

Celkee
(Latin) form of Celeste; sweet
Celkea, Celkie, Cell, Selkee

Celosia
(Greek) flaming

Cena
(English) special
Cenna, Sena

Cenobia
(Spanish) power of Zeus;
strong girl
Cenobie, Zenobia, Zenobie

Cerella
(Latin) springlike

Cerelia
(Latin) spring baby

Ceporah
(Hebrew) variant of
Zipporah; bird; dainty

Cera
(French) colorful

Cerea
(Greek) thriving
Serea

Cerelia
(Latin) spring
Cerallua, Cerellia, Cerelly

Ceres
(Latin) joyful

Ceridwen
(Welsh) poetic; blessed
Ceri, Ceridwyn

Cerina
(Latin) variant of Serena;
peaceful girl

Cerise
(French) cherry red
*Cerese, Cerice, Cerrice,
Ceryce*

Cerys
(Mythology) harvest
goddess
Ceri, Ceries, Cerri, Cerrie

Cesaria
(Latin) from Caesar; leader

Cesarina
(Latin) strong spirit
Cesarea, Cesarie, Cesarin

Cesary
(Polish) outspoken
Cesarie, Cezary, Ceze

Cesia
(Spanish) celestial
Cesea, Sesia

Chablis
(French) white wine
Chabli

Chacita
(Spanish) lively girl
*Chaca, Chacie, Chaseeta,
Chaseta*

Chadee
(French) goddess
Shadee

Chaemarique
(Invented) pretty
*Chae, Chaemareek,
Marique, Shaymarique*

Chafin
(Last name as first name)
sure-footed
Chaffin, Shafin

Chahna
(Hindi) she lights the world

Chai
(Hebrew) life-giving
Chae, Chaeli

Chaitali
(Hindi) light

Chaka-Khan
(Invented) singer

Chaille
(American) variant of
Chelle, short for Michelle
or Rochelle; feminine

Chakra
(Sanskrit) energy
*Chak, Chaka, Chakara,
Chakyra*

Chala
(African American)
exuberant
*Chalah, Chalee, Chaley,
Chalie*

Chalese
(French) goblet; toasts life

Chalette
(American) good taste
*Chalett, Challe, Challie,
Shalette*

Chalice
(French) a goblet; toasting
*Chalace, Chalece, Chalyse,
Chalyssie*

Chalina
(Spanish) rose; fragrant

Chaline
(American) smiling
Chacha, Chaleen, Chalene

Chalis
(African American) sunny
disposition
Chal, Chaleese, Chalise

Chalissa
(African American)
optimistic
Chalisa, Chalysa, Chalyssa

Challie
(American) charismatic
Challee, Challi, Chally

Chalondra
(African American) pretty
*Chacha, Chalon,
Chalondrah, Cheilonndra,
Chelondra*

Chalsey
(American) variation of
Chelsea
*Chalsea, Chalsee, Chalsi,
Chalsie, Chalsie*

Chamania
(Hebrew) sunflower;
bright
*Chamaniya, Hamania,
Hamaniya*

Chamaran
(Hebrew) from Chamania;
sunflower

Chambray
(French) fabric; hardy
Chambree

Chameli
(Hindi) jasmine; fragrant

Champagne
(French) sparkling;
luxurious

Chan
(Vietnamese) fragrant

Chana
(Hindi) moonlike

Chanah
(Hebrew) graceful
Chanach, Channah

Chanal
(American) moonlike

Chanda
(Hindi) moon goddess
Chandi, Chandie, Shanda

Chandani
(Hindi) moonbeams
*Chandni, Chandree,
Chandrika*

Chandelle
(French) candle-lighter
*Chandal, Shandalle,
Shandel*

Chandi
(Sanskrit) goddess

Chandler
(English) romantic;
candle-maker
Chandlee, Shandler

Chandra
(Hindi) of the moon
*Chandre, Shandra,
Shandre*

Chanel
(French) fashionable;
designer name
*Chan, Chanell, Chanelle,
Channel, Shanel, Shanell,
Shanelle*

Chanelle
(American) stylish
Shanell, Shanelle

Chaney
(English) short for
Chandler; cute
Chanie, Chaynee, Chayney

Chania
(Hebrew) blessed by
Lord's grace
Chaniya, Hania, Haniya

Chanicka
(African American) loved
*Chaneeka, Chani, Chanika,
Nicka, Nika, Shanicka*

Chanina
(Hebrew) knows a
gracious Lord

Chanise
(American) adored
Chanese, Shanise

Chanit
(Hebrew) spear; ready for
combat
Chanita, Hanit, Hanita

Channa
(Hindi) chickpea; little
thing

Channary
(Vietnamese) moon girl

Channing
(Last name as first name)
clever

Chanon
(American) shining
*Chanen, Chann, Channon,
Chanun*

Chansanique
(African American) girl
singing
*Chansan, Chansaneek,
Chansani, Chansanike,
Shansanique*

Chantal
(French) singer of songs
*Chandal, Chantale,
Chantalle, Chante,
Chantee, Chantel,
Chantell, Chantelle,
Chantile, Chantille,
Chawntelle, Shanta,
Shantel, Shawntel,
Shontelle*

Chantee
(American) singer
*Chante, Chantey, Chanti,
Chantie, Shantee, Shantey*

Chanterelle
(French) singer; prized

Chanti
(American) melodious
Chantee, Chantie

Chantilly
(French) beautiful lace
Chantille, Shantilly

Chantou
(French) singer

Chantrea
(Vietnamese) moonlight

Chantrice
(French) singer of songs
Shantreece, Treece

Chanya
(Hebrew) blessed by
Jehovah's love

Chanyce
(American) risk-taker
*Chance, Chancie,
Chaneese, Chaniece,
Chanycey*

Chapa
(Native American) beaver

Chapawee
(Native American) active

Chaquanne
(African American) sassy
Chaq, Chaquann, Shakwan

Chara
(Greek) from Charis;
graceful movements
Charo

Charanne
(American) combo of Char
and Anne; charitable
Charann, Cherann

Charbonnet
(French) loving and giving
Charbonay, Charbonet, Charbonnay, Sharbonet, Sharbonnet

Charde
(French) wine
Charday, Chardea, Shardae

Chardonnay
(French) white wine
Char, Chardonee, Chardonnae, Shardonnay

Charelle
(French) feminine

Charian
(French) womanly

Charie
(Greek) from Charis; feminine
Chari

Charille
(French) variant of Charlotte; feminine; delightful
Char, Chari, Charill, Shar, Sharille

Charis
(Greek) graceful
Charice, Charisse

Charish
(American) cherished
Chareesh

Charisma
(American) charming
Char, Karismah

Charissa
(Greek) giving
Char, Charesa, Charisse, Charissey

Charita
(Spanish) sweet
Cherita

Charity
(Latin) loving; affectionate
Carisa, Charis, Charita, Chariti, Charry, Cherry, Chirity, Sharity

Charla
(French) from Charlotte; feminine
Char

Charlaine
(English) small woman; form of Charlene
Charlane

Charlana
(American) form of Charlene; feminine
Chalanna

Charlene
(French) petite and beautiful
Charla, Charlaine, Charleen, Charline, Sharlene

Charlesetta
(German) form of Charles; royal
Charlesette, Charlsetta

Charlesia
(American) form of Charles; royal
Charlese, Charlisce, Charlise, Charlsie, Charlsy, Sharlesia

Charlesey
(American) expansive; generous
Charlesee, Charlie, Charlsie, Charlsy

Charli
(English) feminine

Charlianne
(American) combo of Charlie and Anne
Charlann, Charleyann

Charlie
(American) easygoing
Charl, Charlee, Charley,
Charli

Charlize
(American) pretty

Charlotta
(French) womanly

Charlotte
(French) little woman
Carly, Charla, Charle,
Charlott, Charolot

Charlottie
(French) small
Charlotty

Charlsheah
(American) happy

Charlsie
(French) womanly

Charluce
(American) form of
Charles; feminine; royal
Charl, Charla, Charluse

Charm
(Greek) short for
Charmian; charming
Charma, Charmay, Sharm

Charmaine
(Latin) womanly; (French)
singer
Charma, Charmagne,
Charmain, Charmane,
Charmayne, Charmian,
Charmine, Charmyn,
Sharmaine, Sharmane,
Sharmayne, Sharmyne

Charmian
(Greek) joy baby;
charming

Charmine
(French) charming
Charmen, Charmin

Charminique
(African American)
dashing
Charmineek

Charmonique
(African American)
charming
Charm, Charmi, Charmon,
Charmoneek, Charmoni,
Charmonik, Sharmonique

Charnee
(American) effervescent
Charney, Charnie, Charny

Charneeka
(African American)
obsessive
Charn, Charnika, Charny

Charnelle
(American) sparkling
Charn, Charnel, Charnell,
Charney, Sharnell,
Sharnelle

Charnesa
(African American) noticed
Charnessa, Charnessah

Charo
(Spanish) flower
Charro

Charra
(French) womanly

Charron
(African American) variant
of Sharon; pretty
Charryn, Cheiron

Charsetta
(American) form of
Charlene; emotional
Charsee, Charsette,
Charsey, Charsy

Chartra
(American) classy
Chartrah

Chartres
(French) planner
Chartrys

Charu
(Hindi) gorgeous

Charumat
(Hindi) lovely and smart

Charysse
(Greek) graceful girl
*Charece, Charese,
Charisse*

Chashmona
(Hebrew) princess

Chasia
(Hebrew) sheltered
Chasya, Hasia, Hasya

Chasida
(Hebrew) religious
Chasidah, Hasida

Chasina
(Aramaic) strength of
character

Chasity
(Latin) pure
Chassity

Chassie
(Latin) form of Chastity;
virtuous
Chass, Chassey, Chassi

Chastity
(Latin) pure woman
Chasta, Chastitie

Chateria
(Vietnamese) moonlight

Chau
(Aramaic) strength of
character

Chaucer
(English) demure
Chauser, Chawcer, Chawser

Chava
(Hebrew) life-giving
Chavah, Chave, Hava

Chavi
(Gypsy) girlish

Chaviva
(Hebrew) beloved

Chavon
(Hebrew) life
Chavonne

Chaya
(Jewish) living

Chayan
(Native American) variant
of Cheyenne; tribe
*Chay, Chayanne, Chi,
Shayan, Shy*

Chazmin
(American) from Jasmine;
exuberant
Jasmine

Chazona
(Hebrew) seer

Chea
(American) witty
Chea, Cheeah

Chedra
(Hebrew) happy

Cheer
(American) joyful

Cheifa
(Hebrew) enjoys a safe
harbor

Chekia
(Invented) cheeky
Chekie, Shekia

Chela
(Spanish) exuberant
Chelan, Chelena

Cheletha
(African American) smiling
Chelethe, Cheley

Chelle
(American) short for
Chelsea or Michelle;
secure
Shell

Chelsea
(Old English) safe harbor
*Chelcy, Cheli, Chellsie,
Chelse, Chelsee, Chelsei,
Chelsey, Chelsie, Kelsey,
Shelsee*

Chemarin
(French) fertile; dark

Chemash
(Hebrew) servant of God
*Chema, Chemesh,
Chemosh*

Chemda
(Hebrew) charismatic

Chemdiah
(Hebrew) loves God
*Chemdia, Chemdiya,
Hemdia, Hemdiah*

Chenia
(Hebrew) lives by the
grace of God
*Chen, Chenya, Hen, Henia,
Henya*

Chenille
(American) soft
Chenelle, Chenile, Chinille

Chenoa
(American) form of Genoa;
fun
Cheney, Cheno

Cher
(French) dear
Chere, Sher

Cherelle
(French) dear
Charell, Cherrelle, Sharelle

Cherie
(French) dear
*Cherey, Cheri, Cherice,
Cherree, Cherrie, Cherry,
Cherye*

Cherika
(French) form of Cherry;
kind; dear
Chereka, Cherikah

Cherilynn
(American) combo of
Cheryl and Lynn; kind-
hearted
*Cheryl-Lynn, Cherylynne,
Sherilyn, Sherilynn,
Sherralin*

Cherinne
(American) happy
Charinn, Cherin, Cherry

Cherise
(French) cherry
*Cherece, Cherice, Cherish,
Cherrise*

Cherish
(French) precious girl
*Charish, Cherishe,
Sherishe*

Cherisha
(American) endearing
Cherishah, Cherishuh

Cherita
(Spanish) dearest
Cheritt, Cheritta, Cherrita

Cheritte
(American) held dear
Cher, Cherette, Cheritta

Cherly
(American) form of
Shirley; natural; bright
meadow
Cherlee, Sherly

Cherlyn
(American) combo of Cher
and Lyn; dear one
*Cherlin, Cherlinn,
Cherlynn, Cherlynne*

Chermona
(Hebrew) goes to the
sacred mountain

Cherokee
(Native American) Indian
tribe member

Cherron
(American) graceful
dancer
Cher, Cheron, Cherronne

Cherry
(Latin, French) cherry red
*Cheree, Cherey, Cherrye,
Chery*

Cherrylee
(American) combo of
Cherry and Lee; lively
*Charalee, Charralee,
Cheralee, Cherilea,
Cherilee, Cherileese, Cher-
Lea, Cherry-Lee, Cherylee,
Sharilee, Sheralea,
Sherryleigh*

Cherry-Sue
(American) combo of
Cherry and Sue

Cheryl
(French) beloved
*Charyl, Cherel, Cherelle,
Cheryll*

Chesley
(English) pretty; meadow
*Ches, Cheslay, Cheslea,
Chesleigh*

Chesma
(Slavic) peace-loving

Chesna
(Slavic) peace
Ches, Chesnah

Chesney
(English) peacemaker
*Chesnee, Chesni, Chesnie,
Chessnea*

Chessa
(Slavic) peace

Chesskwana
(African American) evoker
*Chesskwan, Chessquana,
Chessy*

Chessteen
(American) needed
*Ches, Chessy, Chesteen,
Chestene*

Chestnut
(Botanical) unique

Chet
(American) vivacious
Chett

Chevona
(Irish) loves a gracious
God

Chevy
(American) funny
Chev, Chevee

Cheyann
(Native American) tribe;
optimist

Cheye
(American) from
Cheyenne; optimist

Cheyenne
(Native American) Indian
tribe
*Chayanne, Cheyan,
Cheyanna, Cheyene,
Chynne, Shayan, Shayann,
Sheyenne*

Chhaya
(Hebrew) life; vibrant

Chi
(African) Ibo god; light

Chiante
(Italian) wine
Chianti

Chiara
(Italian) bright and clear
*Cheara, Chiarra, Kiara,
Kiarra*

Chiba
(Hebrew) love

Chica
(Spanish) girl
Chika

Chick
(American) fun-loving
Chicki, Chickie

Chickadee
(American) cute little girl
*Chicka, Chickady, Chickee,
Chickey, Chicky*

Chidi
(Spanish) cheerful

Chidori
(Japanese) shorebird
Chika
(Japanese) dear girl; wise
Chikira
(Spanish) dancer
Shakira
Chiku
(African) loquacious
Chilali
(Native American)
snowbird
Childe
(American) offspring
Child
Childers
(Last name as first name)
dignified
*Chelders, Childie,
Chillders, Chylders*
Chimalis
(Native American)
snowbird
Chimene
(French) self-starter; eager
China
(Place name) unique
Chinnah, Chyna, Chynna
Chinadoll
(Word as name) delicate
*China Doll, China-Doll,
Chynadoll*
Chinasia
(Place name) China and
Asia; different
Chinenye
(Place name) from China
Chinue
(African) blessed by Chi
Chipo
(American) from Chip;
alike
Chiquida
(Spanish) form of
Chiquita; small
Chiquide

Chiquita
(Spanish) small girl
*Chica, Chick, Chickie,
Chikita, Chiquitia,
Chiquitta, Shiquita*
Chiriga
(African) triumphant;
capable
Chirline
(American) variant of
Charline; sweet
*Chirl, Chirlene, Shirl,
Shirline*
Chislaine
(French) loyal
Chita
(Spanish) girlish; from
Chica
Chitsa
(Spanish) from Carmen;
runs the orchard
Chivonne
(American) happy
*Chevonne, Chivaughan,
Chivaughn, Chivon,
Chivonn*
Chiyena
(Hebrew) in the Lord's
grace
Chiyoko
(Japanese) forever
Chizoba
(African) well-protected;
strong
Chizu
(Japanese) a thousand
storks; bountiful
Chizuko
(Japanese) abundant
Chloe
(Greek) flowering
*Chloee, Clo, Cloe, Cloee,
Cloey, Khloe, Kloe*
Chloris
(Greek) pale-skinned
Chloras, Cloris, Kloris

Cho
(Japanese) dawn of day
Choko, Choyo

Chofa
(Polish) able

Cholena
(Native American) birdlike;
sings

Chris
(Greek) form of Christina;
best
Chrissie, Chrissy, Kris

Chrisana
(American) boisterous
Chris, Chrisanah, Crisane

Chriselda
(German) from Griselda;
fights

Chrissa
(Greek) form of Christina
Crissa, Cryssa, Krissa

Chrissy
(English) short for Christina
Chrissie, Chrysie, Krissy

Christa
(German, Greek) loving
Crista, Krista

Christabelle
(American) combo of
Christa and Belle
Cristabel

Christal
(Latin) form of Crystal
*Christall, Christalle,
Christel*

Christalin
(American) combo of
Christa and Lin
Christalinn, Christalynn

Christanda
(American) smart
Christandah, Christawnda

Christauna
(American) spiritual
*Christaun, Christawna,
Christown, Christwan*

Christen
(Greek) form of Christina;
Christian
*Christan, Christin, Cristen,
Kristen*

Christian
(Greek) a Christian

Christiana
(Greek, German) Christ's
follower
*Christa, Christianna,
Christianne, Christie,
Chystyana, Crystianne,
Crysty-Ann, Kristiana*

Christie
(Greek) short for Christina
Christi, Kristi, Kristie

Christina
(Greek, Scottish, German,
Irish) the anointed one
*Chris, Chrissie, Christi,
Christiana, Chrystina,
Crista, Kristina*

Christine
(French, English, Latin)
faithful
*Christene, Christin,
Cristine, Kristine*

Christmas
(English) Christmas baby

Christopher
(Greek) devout Christian
*Kris, Krissie, Krissy, Krista,
Kristofer, Kristopher*

Christy
(Scottish) Christian
Christee, Christi, Christie

Chrysanthemum
(American) flower
*Chrys, Chrysanthe,
Chrysie, Mum*

Chrysanthum
(Invented) from flower
chrysanthemum; flowering
Chrys, Chrysan, Chrysanth

Chuki
(African) born in a sour time

Chula
(Native American) flower; colorful

Chulda
(Hebrew) fortune-teller
Hulda, Huldah

Chulisa
(Invented) clever
Chully, Ulisa

Chuma
(Hebrew) warm
Chumi, Huma, Humi

Chumana
(Native American) dew; morning fresh

Chumani
(Native American) dewdrop

Chumina
(Hebrew) warmth

Chun
(Chinese) springlike

Chyan
(American) variant of Cheyenne; able

Chynna
(Chinese) China; wise; musical
Chyna

Ciandra
(Italian) light

Ciannait
(Irish) an old soul

Ciannata
(Latin) old spirit

Ciara
(Irish) brunette
Cearra, Ciarah, Ciarra, Ciera, Keera, Keerah

Cicely
(Latin) form of Cecilia; clever
Cicelie, Cici, Sicely

Cid
(American) fun
Cyd, Syd

Cida
(American) from Cindy; light

Cidni
(American) jovial
Cidnee, Cidney, Cidnie

Cidrah
(American) unusual
Cid, Ciddie, Ciddy, Cidra

Cieara
(Spanish) dark
CiCi, Ciear, Sieara

Ciera
(Irish) dark
Ciera, Cia, Cieera, Cierra, Ciere

Cilla
(Greek) vivacious
Cika, Sica, Sika

Cille
(American) short for Lucille
Ceele

Cima
(Place name) short for Cimarron; western

Cimm
(Place name) short for Cimarron; western

Cinderella
(French) girl in the ashes
Cinda, Cindi, Cindie, Cindy

Cindy
(Greek, Latin) moon goddess
Cindee, Cindi, Cyndee, Cyndi, Cyndie, Sindee, Syndi, Syndie, Syndy

Cinnamon
(English) savory spice
Cenamon, Cinna, Cinnammon, Cinnamond, Cinamen, Cynamon

Cinta
(Spanish) mountain of good

Cinzia
(Italian) mountain; reasonable

Ciona
(American) steadfast
Cinonah, Cionna, Cyona

Ciprianna
(Italian) from Ciprus; cautious
Cipri, Cipriannah, Cypriana, Cyprianna, Cyprianne, Sipriana, Siprianna

Circe
(Greek) sorceress deity; mysterious
Circee, Cirsey, Cirsie

Ciri
(Latin) regal
Ceree, Ceri, Seree, Siri

Cirila
(Latin) heavenly
Ceri, Cerila, Cerilla, Cerille, Cerine, Ciria, Cirine

Cissy
(American) sweet
Ciss, Cissey, Cissi, Sissi

Cita
(American) from the musical instrument sitar

Citare
(Greek) musical; variant of the Indian lute sitar
Citara, Sitare

Claire
(Latin, French) smart
Clair, Clairee, Claireen, Claireta, Clairy, Clare, Clarette, Clarry, Klair

Clarieca
(Latin) bright
Claire, Clare, Clari, Clarieka, Clary, Klarieca, Klarieka

Clancey
(American) a devil-may-care attitude
Clance, Clancee, Clancie, Clancy

Clara
(Latin) bright one
Clarie, Clarine, Clareta, Clarette, Clare, Claire, Clary

Clarabelle
(Latin) combo of Clara and Belle; bright lovely woman
Claribel

Claresta
(Greek) from Clarissa; smart

Clareta
(Spanish) from Clarita; bright

Clarice
(Latin, Italian) insightful
Clairece, Claireece, Clairice, Clarece, Clareece, Clariece, Clarise

Clarimond
(Latin) shining defender; bright

Clarinda
(Latin) from Claire; bright

Clarissa
(Latin, Greek) smart and clear-minded
Claressa, Clarice, Clarisa, Clarise, Clerissa

Clarity
(Word as name) clear-minded
Clare, Claritee, Claritie

Clasina
(Latin) bright

Claudia
(Latin, German, Italian) persevering
Claudelle, Claudie, Claudina, Clodia, Klaudia

Claudia-Rose
(American) combo of
Claudia and Rose

Claudette
(French) persistant
*Claude, Claudee, Claudet,
Claudi, Claudie, Claudy*

Clava
(Spanish) earnest; sincere

Clea
(Invented) short for
Cleanthe and Cleopatra;
famed
Clia, Klea, Klee

Cleanthe
(English) famed
*Clea, Cleantha, Cliantha,
Klea, Kleanth*

Clelia
(Latin) glorious girl

Clematia
(Greek) winding vine

Clematis
(Greek) vine; clings

Clemence
(Latin) easygoing; merciful
*Clem, Clemense, Clements,
Clemmie, Clemmy*

Clementina
(Spanish) kind; forgiving
*Clementas, Clementi,
Clementis, Clementyna,
Clymentyna, Klementina*

Clementine
(Latin) gentle; (German)
merciful
*Clemencie, Klementine,
Klementynne*

Cleo
(Greek) short for
Cleopatra

Cleodal
(Latin) glory
Cleodel, Cleodell

Cleopatra
(Greek) Egyptian queen
Cleo, Clee, Kleeo, Kleo

Cleva
(English) from the hill

Cliantha
(Greek) flower of glory
*Cleantha, Cleanthe,
Clianthe*

Clio
(Greek) history muse
Kleeo, Klio

Cliodhna
(Irish) dark
Clidna, Cliona

Cliona
(Greek) from Clio (history
muse); remembers well

Cloe
(Greek) flourishing
Cloee, Cloey

Cloreen
(American) happy
*Clo, Cloreane, Cloree,
Cloreene, Corean, Klo,
Klorean, Kloreen*

Cloressa
(American) consoling
Cloresse, Kloressa

Clorinda
(Latin) happy
*Cloee, Cloey, Clorinde,
Clorynda, Klorinda*

Cloris
(Latin) pale
Chloris

Clotho
(Mythology) one of the
Greek Fates; spins web of
fate

Clory
(Spanish) smiling
Clori, Clorie, Kloree, Klory

Closetta
(Spanish) secretive
Close, Closette, Klosetta,
Klosette

Clotilda
(German) famed fighter
Clotilde, Clothilde, Tïlda,
Tillie, Tilly

Clotilde
(French) combative

Cloud
(Word as name) airy
Cloudee, Cloudie, Cloudy

Clove
(Botanical) distinctive
spice
Klove

Clover
(Botanical) lucky
Clovah, Clove, Kloverr

Clydette
(American) form of Clyde
Clidette, Clydett, Clydie,
Klyde, Klydette

Clymene
(Greek) famous

Clytie
(Greek) excellent; in love
with love
Cly, Clytee, Clytey, Clyty,
Klytee, Klytie

Co
(American) jovial
Coco, Ko, Koko

Coahoma
(Native American)
panther; stealthy

Coby
(American) glad
Cobe, Cobey, Cobie

Cochava
(Hebrew) star girl

Cocheta
(Italian) from Concetta;
pure

Coco
(Spanish) coconut
Koko

Cocoa
(Spanish) chocolate;
spunky girl

Cody
(English) soft-hearted;
pillow
Codi, Codie, Kodie

Coffey
(American) lovely
Cofee, Caufey

Coiya
(American) coquettish
Coyuh, Koya

Cokey
(American) intelligent
Cokie

Colanda
(African American) from
Yolanda; generous

Colberdee
(American) combo of
Colber (Colby) and Dee;
ostentatious

Colby
(English) enduring
Cobie, Colbi, Kolbee

Cole
(Last name as first name)
laughing
Coe, Colie, Kohl

Colemand
(American) adventurer
Colmyand

Colette
(French) spiritual; victorious
Coey, Collette, Kolette

Colina
(American) righteous
Colena, Colin, Colinn

Coline
(Irish) from Colin; girlish

Colinette
from Colleen; victorious
Colisa
(English) delightful
Colissa, Collisa, Collissa
Colleen
(Irish) young girl
Coleen, Colene, Coley,
Colleene, Collen, Colli,
Kolene, Kolleen
Colley
(English) fearful; worrier
Col, Collie, Kolley
Colmbyne
(Latin) from Columbine;
dove; serene
Colola
(African American)
combination of Co and
Lola; victor
Co, Cola, Colo
Coloma
(Spanish) calm
Colo, Colom, Colome
Columbia
(Latin) from Columbine;
dove; serene
Colombe, Columba,
Columbine
Columbine
(Latin) dove; flower
Comfort
(American) comforting;
easygoing
Komfort
Comfortyne
(French) comforting
Comfort, Comfortine,
Comfurtine, Comfy
Comsa
(Greek) variant of Cosma;
universal spirit
Concepcion
(Spanish) conceived;
begins
Conception

Concetta
(Italian) pure female
Conchetta
(Spanish) wholesome
Concheta, Conchette
Conchie
(Latin) conception
Conchee, Conchi, Konchie
Conchita
(Spanish) girl of the
conception
Chita, Concha, Conchi
Conchiteen
(Spanish) pure
Conchita, Conchitee,
Connie
Conchobarre
(Irish) willful
Concordia
(Latin) goddess of peace
Condoleezza
(American) smart; with
sweetness
Condeleesa, Condilesa,
Condolissa
Coneisha
(African American) giving
Coneisha, Conisha,
Conishah, Conniesha
Conesa
(American) free-flowing
nature
Conisa, Connesa, Konesa
Conlee
(American) form of
Connelly; radiant
Con, Conlee, Conley, Conlie,
Conly, Conly, Connie,
Konlee, Konlee, Konlie
Conner
(American) brave
Con, Coner, Coni, Connie,
Connor, Conny, Conor

Connie
(Latin, English) short for
Constance; constant
Con, Conni, Conny, Konnie

Connie-Kim
(Vietnamese) golden girl
Conni-Kim

Conradina
(German) form of Conrad;
brave
*Connie, Conradine,
Conradyna, Konnie,
Konradina*

Conroe
(Place name) small town
in Texas
Conn, Connie, Konroe

Conroy
(Last name as first name)
stately; literary
Conroi, Konroi, Konroy

Conseja
(Spanish) advises

Consolata
(Spanish) consoles others

Constance
(Latin) loyal
*Con, Connie, Conny,
Constantia, Constantina,
Constantine, Constanza*

Constantina
(Italian) loyal; constant
*Conn, Connee, Conni,
Connie, Conny, Constance,
Constanteena,
Constantinah*

Constanza
(Hebrew) constant
Constanz, Connstanzah

Constanze
(German) unchanging
Con, Connie, Stanzi

Consuelo
(Spanish) comfort-giver
*Chelo, Consolata,
Consuela*

Contessa
(Italian) pretty
*Contesa, Contessah,
Contesse*

Cookie
(American) cute
Cooki

Copeland
(Last name as first name)
adaptable
*Copelan, Copelyn,
Copelynn*

Copper
(American) redhead
Coppyr

Coppola
(Italian) theatrical
*Copla, Coppi, Coppo,
Coppy, Kopla, Kopola,
Koppola*

Cora
(Greek) maid; giving girl
*Corah, Corra, Correna,
Corene, Coretta, Corette,
Corrie, Corinna, Kora*

Coral
(Latin) natural; small
stone
*Corall, Coralle, Coraly,
Core, Corel, Koral, Koraly*

Coralee
(American) combo of Cora
and Lee
Cora-Lee, Coralie, Koralie

Coraline
(American) country girl

Coralynn
(American) combo of Cora
and Lynn
*Coralene, Coralyn,Cora-
Lyn, Cora-Lynn, Coralynne,
Corline, Corlynn*

Corazon
(Spanish) heart
Cora, Corrie, Zon, Zonn

Corby
(Latin) raven; dark

Corday
(English) prepared; heart
*Cord, Cordae, Cordie,
Cordy, Korday*

Cordelia
(Latin) warm-hearted
woman
*Cordeelia, Cordalia,
Cordelie, Cordi, Cordie,
Cordilia, Kordelia, Kordey,
Kordi*

Cordelita
(Latin, Spanish) heartfelt
*Cordelia, Cordelite,
Cordella*

Cordillera
(Latin) from Cordelia; kind
heart

Cordula
(Latin) heart; (German)
jewel
*Cord, Cordie, Cordoola,
Cordoolah, Cordy*

Corette
(Greek) from Cora; sweet
maiden

Corey
(Irish) perky
*Cori, Corree, Corrie, Korey,
Korri, Korrie*

Corgie
(American) funny
Corgi, Korgee, Korgie

Cori
(Greek, Irish) caring
person
Corey, Corri, Corrie, Cory

Coriander
(Botanical) seasoning;
simplistic

Corinna
(Greek) young girl
*Corina, Corrinna, Corryna,
Corynna*

Corinne
(Greek) maiden; (French)
protective
*Coreen, Corina, Corine,
Corinna, Corrina, Coryn,
Corynn, Koreene, Korinne*

Corinthian
(Place name) Corinth, a
town in Greece; religious

Coris
(Greek) singer
Corris, Koris, Korris

Corissa
(Greek) kind-hearted
Korissa

Corky
(American) energetic
*Corkee, Corkey, Corki,
Corkie, Korkee, Korky*

Corlinda
(American) combo of Cora
and Linda; pretty, yellow-
haired girl

Corliss
(English) open-hearted
*Corless, Corlise, Corly,
Korlis, Korliss*

Corly
(American) active
*Corlee, Corli, Corlie, Korli,
Korly*

Corlyn
(American) innovative
*Corlin, Corlinn, Corlynn,
Corlynne, Korlin, Korlyn*

Cormella
(Italian) fiery
*Cormee, Cormela,
Cormelah, Cormellia,
Cormey, Cormie*

Cornae
(Origin unknown) all
seeing
Coma, Korna, Kornae

Cornecia
(Latin) yellow hair; horn

Cornelia
(Latin) practical
Carnelia, Corney, Corni

Cornelius
(Latin) realistic
Corneal, Corneelyus, Corney, Corny

Cornesha
(African American) talkative
Cornee, Corneshah, Cornesia

Corona
(Spanish) crowned
Corone, Coronna, Korona

Correne
(American) musical
Coree, Coreen, Correen, Correna, Korrene, Korene

Corrianna
(American) joyful
Coreanne, Corey, Corianna, Corri, Corriana

Corrie
(English) variant of Coral; delight

Corrinda
(French) girlish
Corri, Corrin, Korin, Korinda

Cortanie
(American) variation on Courtney
Cortanny, Cortany

Cortland
(American) distinctive
Cortlan, Courte, Courtland, Courtlin

Cortlinn
(American) happy
Cortlenn, Cortlin, Cortlyn, Cortlynn

Corvette
(Word as name) speedy
Corv, Corva, Corve, Korvette

Corvina
(Latin) raven; brunette

Cosetta
(French) pretty thing

Cosette
(French) warm
Cossette

Cosima
(Greek, German, Italian) the universe in harmony
Coseema, Koseema, Kosima

Cosmee
(Greek) organized
Cos, Cosmi, Cosmie

Cossette
(French) winning
Coss, Cossie, Cossy, Kossee, Kossette

Costanza
(Last name as first name) strong-willed; funny

Costner
(American) embraced
Cosner, Cost, Costnar, Costnor, Costnur

Cota
(Spanish) lively

Cotcha
(African American) stylish
Kasha, Katcha, Katshay, Kotsha

Cotia
(Spanish) full of vitality

Cotrena
(American) form of Katrina; pure
Catreena, Catrina, Catrine, Cotrene, Katrine, Kotrene

Cotton
(American) comforting
Cottie

Countess
(English) blueblood
Contessa

Cournette
(American) form of coronet; regal
Courney, Kournette

Courney
(English) from Courtney; in the court; involved

Courtney
(English) regal; (French) patient
Cortney, Courtenay, Courteney, Courtnay, Courtnee, Courtny, Kortnee, Kortney

Covin
(American) unpredictable
Covan, Cove, Coven, Covyn

Coy
(American) sly
Coye, Koi, Koy

Coyah
(American) singular
Coya, Coyia

Coyote
(American) wild
Coyo, Kaiote, Kaiotee

Cozette
(French) darling

Cramer
(American) jolly
Cramar, Cramir, Kramer

Cramisa
(Invented) nice
Cramissa, Kramisa

Cree
(American) wild spirit
Crea, Creeah

Creed
(American) boisterous
Crede, Cree, Kreed

Creirwy
(Welsh) lucky amulet

Cresa
(English) fickle

Crescente
(American) impressive
Crescent, Cresent, Cress, Cressie

Crescentia
(Spanish) crescent-faced; smiling
Creseantia, Crescent, Cressentt

Cressa
(Greek) delicate; from the name Cressida
Cresa, Cressah, Cresse, Cress, Kressa

Cressida
(Greek) infidel
Cresida, Cresiduh, Cresside

Cressie
(American) growing; good
Cress, Cressy, Kress, Kressie

Creston
(American) worthy
Crest, Crestan, Creste, Cresten, Crestey, Cresti, Crestie

Cresusa
(English) fickle

Cricket
(American) energetic
Kricket

Crimson
(American) deep
Cremsen, Crims, Crimsen, Crimsonn, Crimsun

Criselda
(Spanish) wild
Crisselda

Crishonna
(American) beautiful
Crishona, Crisshone, Crissie, Crissy, Krishona, Krishonna

Crisiant
(Welsh) crystal; clear
Cris, Crissie
Crispa
(Latin) curly hair
Crispina
(Latin) curly-haired girl
Crispy
(Invented) fun-loving; zany
Crispee, Krispy
Crista
(Italian) form of Christina
Krista
Cristin
(Irish) dedicated
*Cristen, Crystyn, Kristin,
Krystyn*
Cristina
(Greek) form of Christina;
devout
Christina, Kristina
Cristos
(Greek) dedicated
Criss, Crissie, Christos
Cristy
(English) spiritual
Cristi, Crysti, Krystie, Kristi
Crystal
(Latin) clear; open-minded
*Christal, Chrystal, Cristal,
Cristalle, Crys, Crystelle,
Krystal*
Crystilis
(Spanish) focused
*Chrysilis, Crys, Cryssi,
Cryssie, Crystylis*
Csilla
(Hungarian) defensive
Cuba
(Place name) island; fun-
loving girl
Cullen
(Irish) attractive
Cullan, Cullie, Cullun, Cully

Cumale
(American) open-hearted
*Cue, Cuemalie, Cue-maly,
Cumahli*
Cumthia
(American) open-minded
*Cumthea, Cumthee,
Cumthi, Cumthie, Cumthy*
Cupid
(American) romantic
Cupide
Curine
(American) attractive
*Curina, Curinne, Curri,
Currin*
Curry
(American) languid
*Curree, Currey, Curri,
Currie*
Cursten
(American) form of Kirsten
*Curst, Curstee, Curstie,
Curstin*
Cushaun
(American) elegant
*Cooshaun, Cooshawn,
Cue, Cushawn, Cushonn,
Cushun*
Cyan
(American) colorful
Cyanne, Cyenna, Cyun
Cyanea
(Greek) blue-eyed baby
Cyanetta
(Greek) little blue
*Cyan, Cyanette, Syan,
Syanette*
Cybele
(Greek) conflicted
Cybill
(Latin) prophetess
*Cybell, Cybelle, Cybil,
Sibyl, Sibyle*

Cydell
(American) country girl
*Cydee, Cydel, Cydie,
Cydile, Cydy*

Cydney
(American) perky
Cyd, Cydni, Cydnie

Cylee
(American) darling
*Cye, Cyle, Cylea, Cyli, Cylie,
Cyly*

Cylene
(American) melodious
Cylena, Cyline

Cyllene
(American) sweet

Cyma
(Greek) does well

Cymbeline
(Greek) benevolent ruler
*Beline, Cymba, Cymbe,
Cymbie, Cyme, Cymmie,
Symbe*

Cyn
(Greek) short for Cynthia
Cynnae, Cynnie, Syn

Cynara
(Greek) prickly; particular
Cynarra

Cynder
(English) having
wanderlust
*Cindee, Cinder, Cindy, Cyn,
Cyndee, Cyndie, Cyndy*

Cyntanah
(American) singer
Cintanna, Cyntanna

Cynthia
(Greek, English) moon
goddess
*Cindy, Cyn, Cyndee, Cyndy,
Cynthea, Cynthee, Cynthie*

Cyntia
(Greek) variant of Cynthia;
smiling goddess
*Cyn, Cyntea, Cynthie,
Cyntie, Syntia*

Cyntrille
(African American) gossipy
*Cynn, Cyntrell, Cyntrelle,
Cyntrie*

Cypress
(Botanical) swaying
*Cypres, Cyprice, Cypris,
Cypriss, Cyprus*

Cyra
(American) willing
Cye, Cyrah, Syra

Cyreen
(American) sensual
Cyree, Cyrene, Cyrie

Cyrena
(American) variant of
Serena; siren

Cyrenian
(American) bewitching
*Cyree, Cyren, Cyrenean,
Cyrey, Siren, Syrenian*

Cyrenna
(American)
straightforward
*Cyrena, Cyrennah, Cyrinna,
Cyryna, Cyrynna*

Cyriece
(American) artistic
*Cyreece, Cyree, Cyreese,
Cyrie*

Cyrilla
(Latin) royal; little minx
Cirila

Cytherea
(Greek) from Cythera;
celestial

Czarina
(Russian) royal

Daba
(Hebrew) kindhearted
D'Anna
(Hebrew) special
Dacey
(Irish) a southerner
Dace, Dacee, Daci, Dacia,
Dacie, Dacy, Daicie, Daycee
Dacia
(Latin) old soul
Dacie, Dachia, Dachi
Dae
(English) day
Day, Daye
Daelan
(English) aware
Dael, Daelan, Daeleen,
Daelena, Daelin, Daely,
Daelyn, Daelynne, Dale,
Daley, Daylan, Daylin,
Daylind, Dee
Daeshawna
(American) combo of Dae
and Shawna; daylight
Daeshan, Daeshanda,
Daeshandra, Daeshandria,
Daeshaun, Daeshauna,
Daeshaundra,
Daeshaundria, Daeshavon,
Daeshawn, Daeshawnda,
Daeshawndra,
Daeshawndria,
Daeshawntia, Daeshon,
Daeshona, Daeshonda,
Daeshondra, Daeshondria

Daeshonda
(African American) combo
of Dae and Shonda
Daeshanda, Daeshawna,
Daeshondra
Daffodil
(Botanical) flower
Daffy
Dafnee
(Greek, American) form of
Daphne; pretty
Dafney, Dafnie
Dagmar
(German, Scandinavian)
glorious day
Dag, Dagmara, Dagmarr
Dagny
(Scandinavian) day
Dagna, Dagnanna, Dagne,
Dagney
Dahlia
(Scandinavian) flower
Dahl, Dollie
Dai
(Welsh, Japanese) beloved
one of great importance
Daira
(American) outgoing
D'Aira, Daire, Dairrah,
Darrah, Derrah
Daisha
(American) sparkling
D'Aisha, Daish, Daishe,
Dasha, Dashah
Daisy
(English) flower; day's eye
Daisee, Daisey, Daisi,
Daisia, Daisie, Daissy,
Daizee, Daizi, Daizy,
Dasey, Dasi, Dasie, Dasy,
Daysee, Daysie, Daysy

Daisyetta
(American) combo of
Daisy and Etta; spunky;
the day's eye
Daiseyetta, Daizie,
Daiziette, Dasie,
Dazeyetta, Daziette

Daiton
(American) wondrous
Day, Dayten, Dayton

Daja
(American) intuitive
Dajah

Dajanae
(African American)
persuasive
Daije, Daja, Dajainay,
Dayjanah

Dajon
(American) gifted
D'Jon, Dajo, Dajohn,
Dajonn, Dajonnay, Dajonne

Dakara
(American) firebrand
Dacara, Dakarah, Dakarea,
Dakarra

Daking
(Asian) friendly

Dakota
(Native American) tribal
name; solid friend
Dacota, Dakohta,
Dakotah, Dakotha,
Dakotta, Dekoda, Dekota,
Dekotah, Dekotha

Dalacie
(American) brilliant
Dalaci, Dalacy, Dalasie,
Dalce, Dalci, Dalse

Dalaina
(American) spirited
Dalana, Dalayna, Delaina,
Delaine, Delayna

Dalaney
(American) hopeful
Dalanee, Dalaynee,
Dalayni

Dale
(English) valley-life
Daile, Daleleana, Dalena,
Dalina, Dayle

Daleah
(American) pretty
Dalea

Daley
(Irish) leader
Dailey, Dalea, Daleigh,
Dali, Dalie, Daly

Dalia
(Spanish) flower
Daliah, Daliyah, Dayliah,
Doliah, Dolliah, Dolya

Dalian
(American) joy
Dalean

Daliana
(American) joyful spirit
Daliane, Dalianna, Dilial,
Dollianna

Dalice
(American) able
Daleese, Dalleece

Dalila
(African) gentle
Dahlila, Dahlila, Dalia,
Dalilah, Dalilia

Dalin
(American) calm
Dalen, Dalenn, Dalun

Dalita
(American) smooth
Daleta, Daletta, Dalite,
Dalitee, Dalitta

Dallas
(Place name) city in Texas;
confident
*Dalis, Dalisse, Daliz,
Dallice, Dallis, Dallsyon,
Dallus, Dallys, Dalyce,
Dalys*

Dallen
(American) outspoken
Dal, Dalin, Dallin, Dalen

Dallise
(American) gentle
*Dalise, Dallece, Dalleece,
Dalleese*

Dalondra
(Invented) generous
*Dalandra, Dalon,
Dalondrah, Delondra*

Dalonna
(Invented) generous
Dalohn, Dalona, Dalonne

Dalphine
(French) form of Delphine;
delicate and svelte
*Dal, Dalf, Dalfeen,
Dalfene, Dalphene*

Dalton
(American) smart
*Dallee, Dalli, Dallie,
Dallton, Dally, Daltawyn*

Daltrey
(American) quiet
Daltree, Daltri, Daltrie

Dalyn
(American) smart
*Dalin, Dalinne, Dalynn,
Dalynne*

Dama
(Hindi) temptress

Damalla
(Greek) fledgling; young
*Damala, Damalas,
Damalis, Damall*

Damara
(Greek) gentle
Damaris, Damarra

Damaris
(Greek) calm
*Damalis, Damar, Damara,
Damares, Damaret,
Damarius, Damary,
Damarys, Dameress,
Dameris, Damiris,
Dammaris, Dammeris,
Damrez, Damris, Demaras,
Demaris, Demarays*

Damecia
(Invented) sweet
*Dameisha, Damesha,
Demecia, Demisha,
Demeshe*

Dami
(Greek) short for Damia;
spirited
*Damee, Damey, Damie,
Damy*

Damia
(Greek) spirited
*Damiah, Damya, Damyah,
Damyen, Damyenne,
Damyuh*

Damianne
(Greek) one who soothes
Damiana

Damica
(French) open-spirited
*Dameeka, Dameka,
Damekah, Damicah,
Damie, Damika, Damikah,
Demeeka, Demeka,
Demekah, Demica,
Demicah*

Damita
(Spanish) small woman of
nobility
*Dama, Damah, Damee,
Damesha, Dameshia,
Damesia, Dametia,
Dametra, Dametrah*

Damon
(American) sprightly
Damoane, Damone

Damone
(American) mighty
Dame

Dana
(English) bright gift of God
Daina, Dainna, Danae,
Danah, Danai, Danaia,
Danalee, Danan, Danarra,
Danayla, Dane, Danean,
Danee, Daniah, Danie,
Danna, Dayna, Daynah

Danae
(Greek) bright and pure
Danay, Danayla, Danays,
Danea, Danee, Dannae,
Danays, Danee, Denae,
Denee

Danala
(English) happy; golden
Dan, Danalla, Danee,
Danela, Danney, Danny

Danasha
(African American) combo
of Dana and Tasha;
spirited
Anasha, Danas, Danash,
Danashah, Daneash,
Danesha

Danasia
(American) combo of Dana
and Asia; dances

Danay
(American) happy
D'Nay, Dánay, Danaye

Dancel
(French) energetic
Dance, Dancell, Dancelle,
Dancey, Dancie, Danse,
Dansel, Danselle

Dancie
(American) from the word
dancer
Dancy

Daneil
(Hebrew) judged by God;
spiritual
Daneal, Daneala, Daneale,
Daneel, Daneela, Daneila

Danelle
(Hebrew) kind-hearted
Danael, Danalle, Danel,
Danele, Danell, Danella,
Dani, Dannele, Danny

Danelly
(Spanish) form of Daniel;
judged by God
Daneli, Danellie,
Dannelley, Dannelly

Danessa
(American) dainty
Danesa, Danese, Danesha,
Danesse, Daniesa,
Daniesha, Danisa,
Danisha, Danissa

Danessia
(American) delicate child
Danesia, Danieshia,
Danisla, Danissia

Danette
(American) form of Danielle
Danetra, Danett, Danetta

Dangela
(Latin) form of Angela;
angelic
Angee, Angelle, Angie,
Dangelah, Dangelia,
Dangey, Dangi, Dangie

Dani
(Hebrew) short for
Danielle; judged by God
Danee, Danie, Danne,
Dannee, Danni, Dannie,
Danny, Dany

Dania
(Hebrew) short for
Danielle
Daniah, Danya, Danyah

Daniah
(Hebrew) judged
Dan, Dania, Danny, Danya

Danica
(Latin, Polish) star of the morning
Daneeka, Danika, Danneeka, Dannica, Dannika

Danice
(American) combo of Danelle and Janice; romantic

Danielle
(Hebrew, French) form of Daniel; judged by God alone
Danelle, Daniell, Daniele, Danniella, Danyel

Daniella
(Italian) form of Danielle
Danilla

Danir
(American) fresh
Daner

Danit
(Hebrew) judged by God
Danett, Danis, Danisha, Daniss, Danita, Danitra, Danitza, Daniz, Danni

Danita
(American) combo of Dan and Anita; gregarious
Danni, Danny, Denita, Denny

Danna
(American) cheerful
D'Ana, D'Anna, Dannae, Danni, Danny

Danube
(Place name) river; flowing spirit

Danuta
(Polish) God's gift

Daphiney
(Greek) form of Daphne; nymph
Daff, Daph

Daphne
(Greek) pretty nymph
Daphane, Daphaney, Daphanie, Daphany, Daphiney, Daphnee, Daphney, Daphnie, Daphny, Daphonie, Daphy

Daquisha
(African American) talkative

Dara
(Hebrew) compassionate
Dahra, Dahrah, Darah, Darra, Darrah

Daralice
(Greek) beloved
Dara, Daraleese, Daraliece

Daravia
(Hebrew) loving

Darby
(Irish) a free woman
Darb, Darbee, Darbi, Darbie, Darbye

Darceece
(Irish) from Darci; dark

Darcelle
(American) secretive
Darce, Darcel, Darcell, Darcey

Darci
(Irish) dark
Darce, Darcee, Darcie, Darcy, Dars, Darsey

Darda
(Hebrew) wise

Dari
(Czech) rich

Daria
(Greek, Italian) rich woman of luxury
Dare, Darea, Dareah, Dari, Darian, Darianne, Darria, Darya

Darian
(Anglo-Saxon) precious
Dare, Darien, Darry, Derian, Derian

Darice
(English) contemporary
Dareese, Darese, Dari, Dariece, Darri, Darrie, Darry

Darielle
(French) rich
Darell, Darelle, Dariel, Darriel, Darrielle

Darienne
(Greek) great

Darilyn
(American) darling
Darilin, Darilinn, Darilynn, Derilyn

Darina
(Greek) rich

Darionne
(American) adventuresome
Dareon, Darion, Darionn, Darionna

Dariya
(Russian) sweet
Dara, Darya

Darla
(English) short for Darlene
Darl, Darlee, Darley, Darli, Darlie, Darly

Darlee
(English) darling
Darl, Darley, Darli, Darlie

Darlene
(French) darling girl
Darlean, Darleen, Darlena, Darlenia, Darlin, Darling

Darlie-Lynn
(American) combo of Darlie and Lynn

Darling
(American) precious
Darline, Darly, Darlyng

Darlonna
(African American) darling
Darlona

Darlye
(French) darling

Darnelle
(Irish) seamstress
Darnel, Darnell, Darnella, Darnyell

Daroma
(American) treasured

Daron
(Irish) great woman
Daren, Darun, Daryn

Darrelle
(English) loved

Darrien
(Irish) great

Darrow
(Last name as first name) cautious
Darro, Darroh

Darryl
(French, English) beloved
Darel, Darelle, Daril, Darrell, Darrill, Daryl, Daryll, Derel, Derrell

Darshelle
(African American) confident
Darshel, Darshell

Dart
(English) tenacious
Darte, Dartee, Dartt

Daruce
(Hindi) from Daru; pine tree; sturdy

Darva
(Invented) sensible
Darv, Darvah, Darvee,
Darvey, Darvi, Darvie

Daryn
(Greek, Irish) gift-giver
Daryan, Darynn, Darynne

Dash
(American) fast-moving
Dashee, Dasher, Dashy

Dasha
(Russian) darling
Dashah

Dashanda
(African American) loving
Dashan, Dashande

Dashawn
(African American) brash
Dashawna, Dashay

Dashawntay
(African American) careful
Dash, Dashauntay

Dashea
(Hebrew) patient

Dasheena
(African American) flashy
Dashea, Dasheana

Dashelle
(African American) striking
Dachelle, Dashel, Dashell,
Dashy

Dashika
(African American) runner
Dash, Dasheka

Dashiki
(African) loose shirt;
casual
Dashi, Dashika, Dashka,
Desheka, Deshiki

Dashilan
(American) solemn
Dashelin, Dashelin,
Dashlinne, Dashlyn,
Dashlynn, Dasialyn

Dasmine
(Invented) sleek
Dasmeen, Dasmin,
Dazmeen, Dazmine

Dassia
(American) pretty
Dasie, Dassea, Dasseah,
Dassee, Dassi, Dassie,
Deassiah

Dati
(Hebrew) believer

Dativa
(Hebrew) believer

Daureen
(American) darling
Dareen, Daurean, Daurie,
Daury, Dawreen

Davalynn
(American) combo of Dava
and Lynn; sparkling eyes
Davalin, Davalinda,
Davalyn, Davalynda,
Davalynne, Davelin,
Davelyn, Davelynn,
Davelynne, Davilin,
Davilyn, Davilynn,
Davilynne

Daveena
(Scottish) form of David;
loved
Daveen, Davena, Davey,
Davina, Davinna

Davelyn
(Invented) combo of Dave
and Lynn; loved
Davalin, Davalynn,
Davalynne, Dave, Davey,
Davie, Davilynn

Davianna
(English) beloved

Davida
(Hebrew) beloved one
Daveeda, Daveisha,
Davesia, Daveta, Davetta,
Davette, Davika, Davisha,
Davita

Davina
(Hebrew) believer;
beloved
*Dava, Daveena, Davene,
Davida, Davita, Devina,
Devinia, Devinya*

Davincia
(Spanish) God-loving;
winner
Davince, Davinse, Vincia

Davinique
(African American)
believer; unique
Davin, Davineek, Vineek

Davis
(American) boyish
Daves

Davisnell
(Invented) vivacious
Daviesnell, DavisNell

Davonna
(Scottish) well-loved
Davon, Davona, Davonda

Davonne
(African American) splashy
*Davaughan, Davaughn,
Davion, Daviona, Davon,
Davone, Davonn*

Davrush
(Yiddish) loves others

Dawa
(Tibetan) girl born on
Monday

Dawanda
(African American)
righteous
*Dawana, Dawand,
Dawanna, Dawauna,
Dawonda, Dawonna,
Dwanda*

Dawn
(English) daybreak
Daun, Dawna, Dawne

Dawna
(English) eloquence of
dawn
*Dauna, Daunda, Dawn,
Dawnah, Dawnna, Dawny,
Dawnya*

Dawnika
(African American) dawn
*Dawneka, Dawneeka,
Dawnica, Donika*

Dawnisha
(African American) breath
of dawn
*Daunisha, Dawnish,
Dawny, Nisa, Nisha*

Dawntelle
(African American)
morning bright
*Dawntel, Dawntell,
Dontelle*

Dawona
(African American) smart
Dawonna, Dawonne

Day
(English) day; bright

Dayana
(American) variant of
Diana; darling
Dayannah, Dyana

Dayanara
(Spanish) form of
Deyanira; forceful;
destructive
*Day, Daya, Dayan,
Dianara, Diannare, Nara*

Daylee
(American) calm; reserved
Dailee, Day, Dayley, Dayly

Dayna
(English) variant of Dana;
bright gift of God
Daynah

Daysha
(Russian) serene
Dasha, Dayeisha

Dayshanay
(African American) saucy
Daysh, Dayshanae,
Dayshannay, Dayshie

Dayshawna
(American) laughing
Dayshauna, Dayshona,
Dashonah

Dayshay
(African American) lovable
Dashae, Dashay, Dashea

Dayton
(Place name) town in
Ohio; fast

Daytona
(American) speedy
Dayto, Daytonna

Dayvonne
(African American) careful
Dave, Davey, Davonne,
Dayvaughn

De
(Chinese) virtuous

Deacon
(Greek) joyful messenger
Deak, Deakon, Deecon,
Deke

Dean
(English) practical
Deanie, Deanni

Deana
(Latin) divine girl
Deane, Danielle, Deanna

Deandra
(English) combo of Deanna
and Sandra; pretty face
Andie, Andra, Dee

Deandralina
(American) combo of
Deandra and Lina; divine
seer
Deandra-Lina, Deandra
Lina. Deanalina, Lina,
Deandra, Dee, DeeDee

Deandria
(American) sweetheart
Deandreah, Deandriah

Deanie
(English) form of Dean;
from the valley
Deanee, Deaney, Deani

Deanna
(Latin, English) divine girl
Deana, Deanne, Dee

Deanne
(Latin) from Diana; moon
goddess
Deann, Dee, Deeann

Dearbhail
(Welsh) held close

Dearon
(American) dear one
Dear, Dearan, Dearen,
Deary

Dearoven
(American) form of Dearon
Derovan, Deroven

Deasa
(Spanish) delightful

Debarath
(Hebrew) bee; busy
Deborath, Daberath

Debbie
(Hebrew) short for Deborah
Deb, Debbee, Debbey,
Debbi, Debby, Debbye,
Debee, Debi, Debie

Debbie-Jean
(American) combo of
Debbie and Jean

Debbielou
(American) combo of
Debbie and Lou
Debilou

Debbie-Sue
(American) combo of
Debbi and Sue
Debbisue

Deborah
    (Hebrew) prophetess
    Debbie, Debbora,
    Debborah, Debor,
    Deboreh, Deborrah, Debra

Debra
    (Hebrew) prophetess
    Debbra, Debbrah, Debrah

Debran
    (American) form of
    Deborah

Debray
    (American) form of
    Deborah; prophetess
    Dabrae, Deb, Debrae,
    Debraye

Debra-Jean
    (American) combo of
    Debra and Jean

DeChell
    (Invented) combo of De
    and Chell; quiet
    Dechelle, Dee

Decima
    (Latin) tenth girl

Decuma
    (Mythology) one of the
    Roman Fates; measures

Dedra
    (American) spirited
    Dee, DeeDee, Deeddra,
    Deedra, Deedrea, Deedrie,
    Deidra, Deirdre

Dee
    (English, Irish) lucky one
    Dedee, Dea, Deah,
    DeeDee, Dee-Dee, Didee

Deedee
    (American) short for D
    names; vivacious
    D.D., Dee Dee, DeeDee,
    Dee-Dee

Deena
    (American) soothes

Deepa
    (Hindi) light

DeErica
    (African American)
    audacious
    Dee-Erica

Deesha
    (American) dancing
    Dedee, Dee, Deesh,
    Deeshah, Deisha

Deidra
    (Irish) sparkling
    Deedra, Deidre, Dierdra

Deighan
    (American) exciting
    Daygan, Deigan

Deiondra
    (Greek) partier; wine-
    loving
    Deandrah, Deann,
    Deanndra, Dee, Deean,
    Deeann, DeeDee, Deondra

Deirdre
    (Irish) passionate
    Dedra, Dee, Deedee,
    Deedrah, Deerdra,
    Deerdre, Didi

Deishauna
    (African American) combo
    of Dei and Shauna; pious;
    day of God
    Dayshauna, Deisha,
    Deishaun, Deishaune,
    Shauna

Deissy
    (Greek) form of Desma;
    sworn; loyal
    Deisi, Deissey, Deissie,
    Desma, Desmee, Desmer,
    Dessi

Deitra
    (Greek) goddess-like
    Deetra, Detria

Deja
    (French) already seen
    D'Ja, Dejah

Deja-Marie
(American) combo of Deja and Marie
Deja, Dejamarie

Dejon
(French) she came before
Daijon, Dajan, Dajona

Deka
(African) a pleasure
Dekah, Dekka

Dela
(English) dramatic

Delace
(American) combo of De and Lace; smart

Delaine
(American) combo of D and Elaine; smart
D'Laine, Delane

Delana
(German) protective
Dalana, Dalanna, Dalayna, Daleena, Dalena, Dalenna, Dalina, Dalinna, Deedee, Delaina, Delainah, Delena

Delanah
(American) wise
Delana, Dellana, Delano

Delandra
(American) outgoing
Delan, Delande

Delaney
(Irish) bouncy; enthusiastic
Dalanie, Delaine, Delainey, Delane, DeLayney, Dellie, Dulaney

Delcarmen
(Spanish) combo of Del and Carmen; worldly
Del, Del Carmen, Del-Carmen, Delcee, Delcy

Delcia
(Latin) delightful

Delcine
(Latin) a delight

Delcy
(American) friendly
Del, Delcee, Delci

Dele
(American) rash; noble
Del, Dell

Delfina
(Latin, Italian) flowering
Dellfina, Delphina

Delgadina
(Spanish) derivative of Delgado; slender
Delga, Delgado

Delia
(Greek) lovely; moon goddess
Dehlia, Deilyuh, Del, Delea, Deli, Dellia, Dellya, Delya, Delyah

Delicia
(English) delights
Delesha, Delice, Delisa, Delise, Delisha, Delisiah, Delya, Delys, Delyse, Delysia

Delight
(French) wonderful

Delilah
(Hebrew) beautiful temptress
Dalia, Dalila, Delila, Lilah

Delinda
(American) form of Melinda; pretty
Delin, Delinde, Delynda

Delise
(Latin) delicious
Del, Delice, Delicia, Delisa, Delissa

Delite
(American) a pleasure
Delight

Dell
(Greek) kind
Del

Della
(Greek) kind
Dee, Del, Dela, Dell, Delle, Delli, Dells

Dellana
(Irish) form of Delaney; vibrant; delight
Delaine, Delana, Dell, Dellaina, Dellane, Dellann

Delma
(American) combo of Dell and Velma; practical

Dell-Marie
(American) combo of Dell and Marie; helpful; gracious
Dell Marie, Delmaria, Delmarie

Delma-Lee
(American) combo of Delma and Lee; uncomplicated
Delmalea, Delmalee

Delmee
(American) star
Del, Delmey, Delmi, Delmy

Delmys
(American) incredible
Del, Delmas, Delmis

Delon
(American) musical
Delonn, Delonne

Delora
(Spanish) from Delores; pensive
Dellora, Delorita

Delores
(Spanish) woman of sorrowful leaning
Del, Delora, Delore, Dolores, Deloria, Delories, Deloris, Delorise

Delos
(Greek) beautiful brunette; a small Aegean isle; stunning
Delas

Delpha
(Greek) from Delphi, or the flower delphinium; flourishing
Delfa

Delphina
(Greek) dolphin; smart

Delphine
(Latin) swimmer
Delfina, Delfine, Delpha, Delphe, Delphene, Delphi, Delphia, Delphina, Delphinia, Delvina

Delta
(Greek) door; (American) land-loving
Del, Dell, Dellta, Delte, Deltra

Deltrese
(African American) jubilant
Del, Delltrese, Delt, Delta, Deltreese, Deltrice

Delwyn
(English, Welsh) beautiful friend
Delwen, Delwenne, Delwin

Demery
(American) combo of D and Emery; demure

Demetress
(Greek) form of Demetria, goddess of harvest
Deme, Demetra, Demetres, Demetri, Demetria, Dimi, Tress, Tressie, Tressy

Demetria
(Greek) harvest goddess
Deitra, Demeta,
Demeteria, Demetra,
Demetrice, Demetris,
Demetrish, Demetrius,
Demi, Demita, Demitra

Demi
(French) half
Demiah, Demie

Dena
(English) laid back; valley
Deane, Deena, Deeyn,
Denae, Denah, Dene,
Denea, Deney, Denna

Denae
(Hebrew) from Dena;
shows the truth
Danay, Denee

Deneane
(English) from Denise;
lively

Denedra
(American) lively; natural
Den, Dene, Denney

Denee
(French) robust

Deneen
(American) absolved
Denean, Denene

Denes
(English) nature-lover
Denis, Denne, Denny

Denesha
(American) rowdy

Denetria
(Greek) from God
Denitria, Denny, Dentria

Denetrice
(African American)
optimistic
Denetrise, Denitrise,
Denny

Denise
(French) wine-lover
Danice, Daniece, Danise,
Denese, Deni, Denica,
Deniece, Denni, Denny

Denisha
(American) jubilant
Danisha, Deneesha,
Deneesha, Denesha,
Deneshea, Deniesha,
Denishia

Denton
(Place name) town in
Texas; from a holy town
Dent, Dentun, Denty,
Dentyn

Denver
(English) born in a green
valley
Denv, Denvie

Denz
(Invented) lively
Dens

Deoniece
(African American)
feminine
Dee, DeeDee, Deo, Deone,
Deoneece, Deoneese

Deonsha
(American) from Deone;
charismatic

Dericka
(American) dancer
D'ericka, Derica, Dericca,
Derika, Derrica, Derricka,
Derrika

Derie
(Hebrew) form of Derora;
dear; bird
Derey, Drora, Drorah

Deronique
(African American) unique
girl
Deron, Deroneek

Derrona
(American) natural
Derona, Derone, Derry

Derry
(Irish) red-haired woman
Deri, Derrie

Deryn
(Welsh) birdlike; small
*Derren, Derrin, Derrine,
Deryne*

Desdemona
(Greek) tragic figure;
destined
Des, Desde, Dez

Deshawna
(African American)
vivacious
*Dashawna, Deshan,
Deshanda, Deshandra,
Deshane, Deshaun,
Deshauna, Deshaundra,
Deshaune, Deshawnna,
Deshawn, Deshawndra,
Desheania, Deshona,
Deshonda, Deshonna*

Deshaye
(American) combo of Dee
and Shaye; romantic

Deshette
(African American) dishy
Deshett

Deshondra
(African American)
vivacious
*Deshaundra, Deshondrah,
Deshondria*

Desi
(French) short for Desiree
Dezi, Dezzie

Desiah
(French) from Desiree;
desired

Desire
(English) desired
Dezire

Desiree
(French) desired
*Des'ree, Desairee,
Desarae, Desaray,
Desaraye, Desaree,
Desarhea, Desary, Deseri,
Desree, Des-Ree, Dezaray,
Deziree, Dezray*

Destin
(American) destiny
Destinn, Destyn

Destina
(Spanish) destiny
Desteena, Desteenah

Destiny
(French) fated
*Destanee, Destanie,
Desteney, Destinay,
Destinee, Destinei, Destini,
Destinyi, Destnay, Destney,
Destonie, Destony, Destyni*

Destry
(American) well-fated;
western feel
Destrey, Destri, Destrie

Deterrion
(Latin) form of Detra;
blessed
*Deterr, Deterreyon, Detra,
Detrae*

Detra
(Latin) form of Detta;
blessed
Detraye

Deva
(Hindi) moon goddess;
wielder of power
Devi

Devahuti
(Hindi) from Deva, moon
goddess

Devalca
(Spanish) generous
Deval

Devan
(Irish) poetic
Devana, Devn

Devashka
(Hebrew) variant of
Devasha; honey

Devi
(Hindi) beloved goddess
*Devia, Deviann, Devian,
Devie, Devri*

Devin
(Irish) poetic
*Devan, Devane, Devanie,
Devany, Deven, Devena,
Deveny, Deveyn, Devine,
Devinne, Devn, Devyn,
Devynne*

Devina
(Irish) divine; creative
*Davena, Devie, Devine,
Devy, Divine*

Devon
(English) poetic
*Dev, Devaughan,
Devaughn, Devie,
Devonne, Devy*

Devonna
(English) girl from
Devonshire; happy
*Davonna, Devon, Devona,
Devonda, Devondra*

Devorah
(American) combo of
Devon and Deborah
*Devora, Devore, Devra,
Devrah*

Dew
(Word as name) Misty;
fresh
Dewi, Dewie

Dewanna
(African American) clingy
*D'Wana, Dewana,
Dewanne*

Dexhiana
(Origin Unknown) nimble

Dexter
(English) spunky;
dexterous
*Dex, Dexee, Dexey, Dexie,
Dext, Dextar, Dextur, Dexy*

Dextra
(Latin) skilled

Deyanira
(Spanish) aggressor
*Deyan, Deyann, Dianira,
Nira*

Dharcia
(American) sparkler
Darch, Darsha, Dharsha

Dharika
(American) sad
Darica, Darika

Dharma
(Hindi) morality; beliefs
Darma, Darmah

Dhazalai
(African) sweet
Dhaze, Dhazie

Dhelal
(Arabic) coy

Dhessie
(American) glowing
*Dhessee, Dhessey, Dhessi,
Dhessy*

Dhumma
(Hebrew) from Dumia;
quiet

Di
(Latin) short for Diane or
Diana
Didi, Dy

Dia
(Greek) shining
Deah

Diaelza
(Spanish) divine; pretty
Diael, Dialza, Elza

Diah
(American) pretty
Dia

Diamantina
(Spanish) sparkling
Diama, Diamante, Mantina

Diamond
(Latin) precious gemstone
*Diamin, Diamon,
Diamonda, Diamonds,
Diamonte, Diamun,
Diamyn, Diamynd,
Dyamond*

Diamondah
(African American)
glowing
Diamonda, Diamonde

Diamondique
(African American)
sparkling
Diamondik

Diamony
(American) gem
*Diamonee, Diamoney,
Diamoni, Diamonie*

Diana
(Latin) divine woman;
goddess of the hunt and
fertility
*Dee, Di, Diahana, Diahna,
Dianah, Diannah, Didi,
Dihanna, Dyanna,
Dyannah, Dyhana*

Dianalynn
(American) combo of
Diana and Lynn
*Dianalin, Dianalinne,
Dianalyn*

Diandro
(American) special
*Diandra, Diandrea,
Diandroh*

Diane
(Latin) goddess-like;
divine
*Deane, Deanne, Deeann,
Deeanne, Deedee, Di,
Diahann, Dian, Diann,
Dianne, Didi*

Dianette
(American) combo of
Diane and Ette; high-
spirited
*Di, Diane, Dianett, Didi,
Diette, Diyannette, Dyan,
Dyanette, Dyanne,
Dyenette*

Diantha
(Greek) flower; heavenly
Dianth

Diarah
(American) pretty
*Dearah, Di, Diara, Diarra,
Dierra*

Diavonne
(African American) jovial
*Diavone, Diavonna,
Diavonni*

Dicey
(American) impulsive
*Di, Dice, Dicee, Dicy,
Dycee, Dycey*

Dicia
(American) wild
Desha, Dicy

Diedre
(Irish) variant of Deidre;
spunky
Diedra, Diedré

Diella
(Latin) worships
Dielle

Diesha
(African American) zany
*Diecia, Dieshah, Dieshie,
Dieshay*

Diethild
(German) believer

Diggs
(American) tomboyish
Digs, Dyggs

Dihana
(American) natural
Dihanna

Dijonnay
(American) fun-loving
*Dijon, Dijonae, Dijonay,
Dijonnae, Dijonnaie*

Dilan
(American) form of Dylan
Dillan, Dilon

Dillyana
(English) worshipful
*Diliann, Dilli, Dillianna,
Dilly*

Dilsey
(American) dependable;
one who endures

Dilynn
(American) variant of
Dylan; loving the sea
*Di, Dilenn, Dilinn, Dilyn,
Lynn*

Dima
(American) high-spirited
Deemah, Dema

Dimond
(American) from Diamond;
shines

Dina
(Hebrew, Scottish) right;
royal

Dinah
(Hebrew) fair judge
*Dina, Dinah, Dinna, Dyna,
Dynah*

Dinesha
(American) happy
*Dineisha, Dineshe,
Diniesha*

Dini
(American) joyful
Dinee, Diney, Dinie

Dinora
(Spanish) judged by God
Dina, Dino, Nora

Dioma
(Greek) from Diona; loves
God

Diona
(Greek) divine woman
*Dee, Di, Dion, Dionah,
Dionuh*

Dioneece
(American) daring
*Dee, DeeDee, Deon,
Deone, Deonece,
Deoneece, Dioniece,
Neece, Neecey*

Dionicia
(Spanish) vixen
*Di, Dione, Dionice,
Dionise, Nicia, Nise, Nisee*

Dionndra
(American) loving
*Diondra, Diondrah,
Diondruh*

Dionne
(Greek) love goddess
*Deona, Deondra, Deonia,
Deonna, Deonne, Dion,
Dione, Dionna*

Dionshay
(African American) combo
of Dion and Shay; loving
*Dionsha, Dionshae,
Dionshaye*

Dior
(French) stylish
*Diora, Diorah, Diore,
Diorra, Diorre*

Diotima
(Latin) in the time of God

Dira
(Arabic) soft-spoken

Direll
(American) svelte
Di, Direl, Direlle

Dirisha
(African American)
outgoing
Di, Diresha, Direshe
Disa
(Scandinavian) goddess
Disha
(American) fine
Dishae, Dishuh
Dishawna
(African American) special
*Dishana, Dishauna,
Dishawnah, Dishona,
Dishonna*
Divina
(American) divine being
Divine
(Italian) divine soul
Divin, Divina
Divinity
(American) sweet; devout
Divinitee, Diviniti, Divinitie
Dix
(French) live wire
Dixann
(American) combo of Dixie
and Ann
*Dixan, Dixanne, Dixiana,
Dixieanna*
Dixie
(English, French,
American) Southern girl
Dixee, Dixi, Dixy
D'Nicola
(American) combo of D
and Nicola
*D'nicole, Deenicola,
Dnicola*
Dnisha
(African American)
rejoicing
*D'Nisha, Dnisa, Dnish,
Dnishay, Dnishe*

Dobie
(American) cowgirl
Dobee, Dobey, Dobi
Docia
(Latin) from Docilla; docile
Docie
Docilla
(Latin) docile
Docila, Docile
Dodie
(Greek, Hebrew) short for
Dorothy; beloved woman
Doda, Dodee, Dodi, Dody
Dodona
(Greek) ancient city in
Greece
Doherty
(American) ambitious
*Dhoertey, Dohertee,
Dohertie*
Dolcy
(American) a vision
Dolcee, Dolcie, Dolsee
Dolly
(American) toylike
*Dol, Doll, Dollee, Dolli,
Dollie*
Dolores
(Spanish) woman of
sorrowful leaning
Delores
Domel
(American) steadfast;
faithful
Domela, Domella
Dometria
(American) form of Greek
Demetria; goddess;
fruitful
*Dome, Dometrea, Domi,
Domini, Domitra*
Domina
(Latin) ladylike

Domini
(Latin) form of Dominick
*Dom, Dominee,
Domineke, Dominey,
Dominie, Dominika,
Domino, Dominy*

Dominica
(Latin) follower of God
*Domenica, Domenika,
Domineca, Domineka,
Domini, Dominika,
Domenika, Domineca,
Dom, Domonica,
Domonika*

Dominique
(French) bright; masterful
*Dom, Domanique,
Domeneque, Domenique,
Domino, Domonik*

Dona
(Latin) always giving
*Donail, Donalea, Donalisa,
Donay, Donelle, Donetta,
Doni, Donia, Donice,
Donie, Donise, Donisha,
Donishia, Donita, Donitrae*

Donalda
(Scottish) loves all
*Donalda, Donaldina,
Donaleen, Donelda,
Donella, Donellia,
Donette, Doni, Donita,
Donnella, Donnelle*

Donata
(Italian) celebrating
*Donada, Donatah,
Donatha, Donatta, Donni,
Donnie, Donny*

Donatella
(Latin, Italian) gift
Don, Donnie, Donny

Donava
(African) jubilant
Donavah

Donela
(Italian) leader
Donella

Donia
(American) from Donna;
controls

Donika
(African American) from
Donna; home-loving
Donica

Donisha
(African American)
laughing; cozy
*Daneesha, Danisha,
Doneesha*

Donna
(Italian) ladylike and
genteel
*Dom, Don, Dona, Dondi,
Donnie, Donya*

Donnata
(Latin) giving
Dona, Donata, Donni

Donnelly
(Italian) lush
*Donally, Donelly, Donnell,
Donnelli, Donnellie,
Donni, Donnie, Donny*

Donnis
(American) pleasant;
giving
Donnice

Donserena
(American) dancer; giving
*Donce, Doncie, Dons,
Donse, Donsee, Donser,
Donsey*

Donyale
(African American) form of
Danielle; kind
Donyelle

Dora
(Greek) gift from God
*Dorah, Dori, Dorie, Dorra,
Dorrah*

Dorat
(French) a gift
Doratt, Dorey, Dorie

Dorcea
(Greek) sea girl
Dorcia

Dore
(Irish) from Dora;
comtemplative

Doreen
(Greek, Irish) capricious
Dorene, Dorine, Dory

Dori
(French) adorned
*Dore, Dorey, Dorie, Dory,
Dorree, Dorri, Dorrie,
Dorry*

Doria
(Greek) from Dorian;
secrets
*Dori, Doriana, Doriann,
Dorianna, Dorianne*

Dorian
(Greek) happy
*Dorean, Doreane, Doree,
Doriane, Dorri, Dorry*

Dorianne
(American) combo of Doris
and Ann; sparkly

Dorika
(Greek) God's gift
Doreek, Dorike, Dory

Dorin
(Greek) from Dorian; sea-
loving

Dorina
(Hawaiian) loved

Dorinda
(Spanish) loved

Doris
(Greek) sea-loving; sea
nymph
*Dor, Dori, Dorice, Dorise,
Doriss, Dorris, Dorrise,
Dorrys, Dory*

Dorit
(Greek) God's gift; shy
Dooritt

Dornay
(American) involved
*Dorn, Dornae, Dornee,
Dorny*

Dorothea
(Greek) gift from God
*Dorethea, Dorotha,
Dorothia, Dorotthea,
Dorthea, Dorthia*

Dorothy
(Greek) gift of God
Dorathy, Dorthy

Dorren
(Irish) sad-faced
Doren

Dorte
(Scandinavian) God's gift

Dortha
(Greek) God's gift; studious
*Dorth, Dorthee, Dorthey,
Dorthy*

Dory
(French) gilded; gold hair
Dora, Dore, Dorie

Dorthe
(Scandinavian) God's gift

Dosia
(Russian) happy

Dossey
(Last name as first name)
rambunctious
*Dosse, Dossi, Dossie,
Dossy, Dozze*

Dot
(Greek) spunky
Dottee, Dottie, Dotty

Dottie
(Greek) from Dorothy;
God's gift; spunky

Douce
(French) sweet
*Doucia, Dulce, Dulci,
Dulcie*

Dougiana
(American) combo of
Dougi and Ana
Dougi

Dove
(Greek) dreamy

Doxie
(Greek) fine
Doxy

Drahomira
(Czech) dearest

Draven
(American) loyal
Dravan, Dravin, Dravine

Draxy
(American) faithful
Drax, Draxee, Draxey, Draxi

Drea
(American) adorable

Dream
(American) dream girl;
misty
*Dreama, Dreamee,
Dreamey, Dreami,
Dreamie, Dreamy*

Dreda
(Anglo-Saxon) thoughtful
Drida

Dree
(American) soft-spoken

Dreena
(American) cautious
Dreenah, Drina

Drelan
(Origin Unknown) watches

Drew
(Greek) woman of valor
Dru, Drue

Drover
(American) surprising
Drovah, Drovar

Dru
(American) bright
Drew, Drue

Druanna
(American) bold
*Drewann, Drewanne,
Druanah, Druannah*

Drucelle
(American) smart
*Druce, Drucee, Drucel,
Drucell, Drucey, Druci,
Drucy*

Druella
(Latin) from Drusilla;
strong

Drusa
(Latin) from Drusilla;
forceful
Drusie, Drucie

Drusi
(Latin) strong girl
*Drucey, Drucie, Drucy,
Drusey, Drusie, Drusy*

Drusilla
(Latin) strong
Dru, Drucilla

Dryden
(Last name as first name)
special
Dydie

Duana
(Irish) dark
Dwana

Dubethza
(Invented) sad
Dubeth

Duchess
(American) fancy
*Duc, Duchesse, Ducy,
Dutch, Dutchey, Dutchie,
Dutchy*

Duena
(Spanish) chaperones;
guards

Duffy
(Irish) spunky

Dufvenius
(Swedish) lovely
Duf, Duff

Duhnell
(Hebrew) kind-hearted
Danee, Danny, Nell

Dulce-Maria
(Spanish) sweet Mary
Dulce, Dulcey

Dulce
(Latin, Spanish) sweet one
Dulce, Dulcey, Dulcy

Dulcinea
(Latin) sweet nature

Duma
(African) quiet help
Dumah

Duna
(Spanish) protects

Dune
(American) summery
Doone, Dunah, Dunie

Dumia
(Hebrew) quiet
Dumi

Dunesha
(African American) warm
Dunisha

Dupre
(American) soft-spoken
Dupray, Duprey

Durene
(American) combo of Dura and Renne; planner

Durrah
(Hindi) heroine

Dusanka
(Slavic) soulful
Dusan, Dusana, Dusank, Sanka

Duscha
(Russian) happy
Dusa, Duschah, Dusha, Dushenka

Dusky
(Invented) dreamy

Dusky-Dream
(Invented) dreamy
Duskee-Dream

Dustine
(German) go-getter
Dustee, Dusteen, Dustene, Dusti, Dustie, Dustina, Dusty

Dusty
(American) southern
Dustee, Dusti, Dustie, Dustey

Dwanda
(American) athletic
Dwana, Dwayna, Dwunda

Dyan
(Latin) form of Diane; divine
Dian, Dyana, Dyane, Dyani, Dyann, Dyanna, Dyanne

Dyandra
(Latin) sleek
Diandra, Dianndrah, Dyan, Dyandruh

Dylan
(Welsh) creative; from the sea
Dilann, Dyl, Dylane, Dylann, Dylanne, Dylen, Dylin, Dyllan, Dylynn

Dylana
(Welsh) sea-loving

Dymond
(American) variant of diamond
Dymahn, Dymon, Dymonn, Dymund

Dymphia
(Irish) poetic
Dimphia

Dynasty
(Word as name) substantial; rich

Dyney
(American) consoling others
Diney, DiNey, Dy

Dyonne
(American) marvelous
Dyonn, Dyonna, Dyonnae

Dyronisha
(African American) fine
Dyron

Dyshaunna
(African American)
dedicated
*Dyshaune, Dyshawn,
Dyshawna*

Dyshawna
(American) combo of Dy
and Shawna; outrageous;
smiles
*Dyshanta, Dyshawn,
Dyshonda, Dyshonna*

Dywon
(American) bubbly
*Diwon, Dywan, Dywann,
Dywaughn, Dywonne*

Dzidzo
(African) universal child

E

Eadrianne
(American) standout
*Eddey, Eddi, Eddy,
Edreiann, Edrian, Edrie*

Earla
(English) leader
*Earlah, Erla, Erlene,
Erletta, Erlette*

Earlean
(Irish) dedicated
*Earla, Earlecia, Earleen,
Earlena, Earlene, Earlina,
Earlinda, Earline, Erla,
Erlana, Erlene, Erlenne,
Erlina, Erlinda, Erline,
Erlisha*

Early
(American) bright
Earlee, Earlie, Earlye, Erly

Eartha
(English) earth mother

Easter
(American) born on
Easter; springlike

Easton
(American) wholesome
*Eastan, Easten, Eeston,
Eastun, Estynn*

Eavan
(Irish) beautiful
Evaughn, Eevonne

Ebba
(English, Scandinavian)
strong
Eb, Eba, Ebbah

Ebban
(American) pretty; affluent
Ebann, Ebbayn

Ebony
(Greek) hard and dark
*Eb, Ebanie, Ebbeny, Ebbie,
Ebonea, Ebonee, Eboney,
Eboni, Ebonie, Ebonni*

Ebrel
(Cornish) from the month
April
*Ebby, Ebrelle, Ebrie,
Ebrielle*

Echo
(Greek) smitten
Eko

Ecstasy
(American) joyful
Ecstasey, Ecstasie, Stase

Eda
  (Irish) from Edith;
  treasured
Edaena
  (Irish) fiery; energetic
  Ed, Eda, Edae, Edana,
  Edanah, Edaneah, Eddi
Edalene
  (German) refined
  Eda, Edalyne, Edeline,
  Ediline, Lena, Lene
Edana
  (Irish) flaming energy
  Eda, Edan, Edanna
Eddi
  (English) form of Edwina;
  spirited brunette
  Eddie, Eddy, Edy
Edel
  (German) clever; noble
  Edell, Eddi
Eden
  (Hebrew) paradise of
  delights
  Ede, Edena, Edene, Edin,
  Edyn
Edenathene
  (American) combo of Eden
  and Athene
Edie
  (English) short for Edith;
  blessed
  Eadie, Edee, Edi, Edy,
  Edye, Eydie
Edith
  (English) a blessed girl
  who is a gift to mankind
  Eadith, Ede, Edetta,
  Edette, Edie, Edithe,
  Editta, Ediva, Edy, Edyth,
  Edythe, Eydie
Edju
  (Origin unknown) giving
  Eddju

Edlin
  (German) noble;
  sophisticated
  Eddi, Eddy, Edlan, Edland,
  Edlen
Edmee
  (American) spontaneous
  Edmey, Edmi, Edmy,
  Edmye
Edmonda
  (English) form of Edmond;
  rich
  Edmon, Edmond, Edmund,
  Edmunda, Monda
Edna
  (Hebrew) youthful
  Eddie, Ednah, Edneisha,
  Ednita, Eydie
Edreanna
  (American) merry
  Edrean, Edreana,
  Edreanne, Edrianna
Edrina
  (American) old-fashioned
  Ed, Eddi, Eddrina, Edrena,
  Edrinah
Edsel
  (American) plain
  Eds, Edsell, Edzel
Edshone
  (American) wealthy
  Ed, Eds, Edshun
Edwina
  (English) prospering
  female
  Eddi, Eddy, Edina,
  Edweena, Edwena,
  Edwenna, Edwine,
  Edwyna, Edwynna
Effemy
  (Greek, German) good
  singer
  Efemie, Efemy, Effee,
  Effemie, Effey, Effie, Effy

Effie
(Greek) of high morals;
(German) good singer
Effi, Effia, Effy, Ephie

Efrat
(Hebrew) bountiful
Efrata

Egan
(American) wholesome
Egen, Egun

Egypt
(Place name) country;
exotic
Egyppt

Egzanth
(Invented) form of Xanthe;
beautiful blonde

Eileen
(Irish) bright and spirited
*Eilean, Eilee, Eileena,
Eileene, Eilena, Eilene,
Eiley, Eilleen, Eillen, Eilyn,
Elene, Ellie*

Eireen
(Scandinavian)
peacemaker
Eirena, Erene, Ireen, Irene

Eires
(Greek) peaceful
Eiress, Eres, Heris

Eirianne
(English) peaceful
Eirian, Eriann

Elaine
(French) dependable girl
*Elain, Elaina, Elainia,
Elainna, Elan, Elana,
Elane, Elania, Elanie,
Elanna, Elayn, Elayna,
Elayne, Ellaine*

Elana
(Greek) pretty
*Ela, Elan, Elani, Elanie,
Lainie*

Elata
(Latin) bright; well-
positioned
Ela, Elate, Elatt, Elle, Elota

Elda
(Italian) protective

Eldora
(Spanish) golden girl
*Eldoree, Eldorey, Eldori,
Eldoria, Eldorie, Eldory*

Eleacie
(American) forthright
Acey, Elea, Eleasie

Eleanora
(Greek) light

Eldee
(American) light
El, Eldah, Elde

Eldora
(Spanish) golden spirit

Eleanor
(Greek) light-hearted
*Elana, Elanor, Elanore,
Eleanora, Elenor,
Elenorah, Eleonor,
Eleonore, Elinor, Elinore,
Ellie, Ellinor, Ellinore,
Elynor, Elynore, Lenore*

Eleanora
(Greek) light
*Elenora, Eleonora, Eleora,
Ella nora, Ellora, Ellenora,
Ellenorah, Elnora, Elora,
Elynora*

Electra
(Greek) resilient and
bright
Elec, Elek, Elektra

Elegy
(American) lasting
*Elegee, Eleggee, Elegie,
Eligey*

Elek
(American) star-like
Elec, Ellie, Elly

Elena
(Greek, Russian, Italian, Spanish) light and bright; beautiful
Elana, Eleana, Eleen, Eleena, Elen, Elene, Eleni, Ilena, Ilene, Lena, Leni, Lennie, Lina, Nina

Eleni
(Greek) sweet
Elenee

Eleonore
(Greek, German) light and bright
Elenore, Elle, Elnore

Eleri
(Welsh) smooth
Elere, Eleree

Elettra
(Latin, Italian) shining

Elfin
(American) small girl
El, Elf, Elfan, Elfee, Elfey, Elfie, Elfun, Els

Elfrida
(German) peaceful spirit
Elfie, Elfrea, Elfredda, Elfreeda, Elfreyda, Elfryda

Eliana
(Latin, Greek, Italian) sunny
Eliane, Elianna, Elianne, Elliana, Ellianne, Ellie, Liana, Liane

Eliane
(French) cheerful; sunny

Elicia
(Hebrew) dedicated
Ellicia

Elisa
(English, Italian) God-loving; grace
Elecea, Eleesa, Elesa, Elesia, Elisia, Elissa, Elisse, Elisya, Ellisa, Ellisia, Ellissa, Ellissia, Ellissya, Ellisya, Elysa, Elysia, Elyssia, Elyssya, Elysya, Leese, Leesie, Lisa

Elisabet
(Hebrew, Scandinavian) God as her oath
Bet, Elsa, Else, Elisa

Elisabeth
(Hebrew, French, German) sworn to God
Bett, Bettina, Elisa, Elise, Els, Elsa, Elsie, Ilsa, Ilyse, Liesa, Liese, Lisbeth, Lise

Elise
(French, English) soft-mannered
Elice, Elisse, Elle, Ellyse, Lisie

Elisha
(Greek) God-loving
Eleacia, Eleasha, Elecia, Eleesha, Eleisha, Elesha, Eleshia, Elicia, Eliesha, Ellie, Lisha

Elissa
(Greek) God-loving
Ellissa, Ellyssa, Elyssa, Ilissa, Ilyssa

Elita
(French) selected one
Elida, Elitia, Elitie, Ellita, Ellitia, Ellitie, Ilida, Ilita, Litia

Elite
(Latin) best
Elita

Eliza
(Irish) sworn to God
Aliza, Elieza, Elize, Elyza

Elizabeth
(Hebrew) God-directed;
beauty
*Beth, Betsy, Elisabeth,
Elizebeth, Lissie, Liza*

Elke
(Dutch) distinguished
Elki, Ilki

Elkie
(Dutch) variant of Elke;
distinguished
Elk, Elka

Ella
(Greek) beautiful and
fanciful
*Ellamae, Elle, Ellia, Ellie,
Elly*

Ella Bleu
(Invented) combo of Ella
and Bleu; gorgeous
daughter of fame
Ella-Bleu

Ellaina
(American) sincere
Elaina, Ellana, Ellanuh

Ellan
(American) coy
Elan, Ellane, Ellyn

Elle
(Scandinavian) woman
Ele

Ellen
(English) open-minded
*El, Elen, Elenee, Eleny,
Elin, Ellene, Ellie, Ellyn,
Ellynn, Elyn*

Ellender
(American) decisive
*Elender, Ellander, Elle,
Ellie*

Elletra
(Greek, Italian) shining
Elletrah, Illetrah

Elli
(Scandinavian) aged
Ell, Elle, Ellie

Ellice
(English) loves God
Ellecia, Ellyce, Elyce

Ellie
(English) candid
Ele, Elie, Elly

Ellyanne
(American) combo of Elly
and Anne
*Elian, Elianne, Ellyann,
Elyann*

Elma
(Turkish) sweet
El

Elmas
(Armenian) diamondlike
Elmaz, Elmes, Elmis

Elnora
(American) sturdy
Ellie, Elnor, Elnorah

Elodia
(Spanish) flowering
Elodi

Eloise
(German) high-spirited
Eluise, Luise

Elora
(American) fresh-faced
Elorah, Flory, Floree

Elpidia
(Spanish) shining
El, Elpey, Elpi, Elpie

Elrica
(German) leader
*Elrick, Elrika, Elrike, Rica,
Rika*

Elsa
(Hebrew, Scandinavian,
German) patient; regal
*Ellsa, Ellse, Ellsey, Els,
Elsah, Elseh, Elsie, Ellsee*

Elsie
(German) hard-working
Elsee, Elsi, Elsy

Elsiy
(Spanish) God-loving
El, Els, Elsa, Elsee, Elsi, Elsy

Elspeth
(Scottish) loved by God
El, Elle, Els

Elton
(American) spontaneous
Elt, Elten, Eltone, Eltun

Elva
(English) tiny
Elvenea, Elvia, Elvie, Elvina, Elvinea, Elvineah, Elvah

Elvia
(Latin) sunny
Elvea, Elviah, Elvie

Elvira
(Latin, German) light-haired and quiet
Elva, Elvie, Elvina, Elwire, Vira

Elyanna
(American) good friend
Elyana, Elyannah, Elyunna

Elyse
(English) soft-mannered
Elice, Elle, Elysee, Elysia, Ilysha, Ilysia

Elyssa
(Greek) loving the ocean;
(English) lovely and happy
Elisa, Elissa, Elysa, Illysa, Lyssa

Elysia
(Latin) joyful
Elyse, Elysee, Elysha, Elyshia

Emalee
(German) thoughtful
Emalea, Emaleigh, Emaley, Emaline, Emally, Emaly, Emmalynn, Emmeline, Emmelyne

Emann
(American) soft-spoken
Eman

Ember
(American) temperamental
Embere, Embre

Emberatriz
(Spanish) respected
Emb, Ember, Embera, Emberatrice, Emberatryce, Embertrice, Embertrise

Emberli
(American) pretty
Em, Emb, Ember, Emberlee, Emberley, Emberly

Eme
(German) short for Emma;
strong
Emee, Emme, Emmee

Eme
(Hawaiian) loved
Em, Emee, Emm, Emmee, Emmie, Emmy

Emelle
(American) kind
Emell

Emely
(German) go-getter
Emel, Emelee, Emelie

Emena
(Latin) of fortunate birth
Em, Emen, Emene, Emina, Emine

Emerald
(French) bright as a
gemstone
Em, Emmie

Emestina
(American) form of
Ernestina; competitive
Emee, Emes, Emest, Tina

Emilee
(American) combo of
Emma and Lee

Emilie
(French) charmer

Emilia
(Italian) soft-spirited
Emalia, Emelia, Emila

Emily
(German) poised;
(English) competitor
*Em, Emalie, Emilee, Emili,
Emilie, Emmi, Emmie*

Emilyann
(American) combo of
Emily and Ann; traditional
girl

Emma
(German, Irish) strong
*Em, Emmah, Emme,
Emmie, Emmi, Emmot,
Emmy, Emmye, Emott*

Emmalee
(American) combo of
Emma and Lee
*Em, Emalea, Emalee,
Emilee, Emliee, Emma-Lee,
Emmali, Emmie*

Emmaline
(French, German) form of
Emily
*Em, Emaline, Emalyne,
Emiline, Emmie*

Emmalynn
(American) combo of Emma
and Lynn; today's child
*Emelyn, Emelyne,
Emelynne, Emilyn,
Emilynn, Emilynne, Emlyn,
Emlynn, Emlynne,
Emmalyn, Emmalynne*

Emmanuelle
(Hebrew, French) believer
Em, Emmi, Emmie, Emmy

Emmalise
(American) combo of
Emma and Lise; lovely
*Emalise, Emmalisa,
Emmelise*

Emmanuelle
(Hebrew) knows God
Emmanuela, Emmanuella

Emme
(German) feminine
Em

Emmi
(German) pretty
Emmee, Emmey, Emmy

Emmylou
(American) combo of
Emmy and Lou
*Emmilou, Emmi-Lou,
Emylou*

Emylinda
(American) combo of Emy
and Linda; happy and
pretty
*Emi, Emilind, Emilynd,
Emy, Emylin, Emylynda*

Ena
(Hawaiian) intense
Eana, En, Enna, Ina

Enchantay
(American) enchanting
Enchantee

Endah
(Irish) flighty
Ena, End, Enda

Endia
(American) variant of
India; magical
*Endee, Endey, Endie, Endy,
India, Ndia*

Enedina
(Spanish) praised, spirited
Dina, Ened

Enid
(Welsh) lively
Eneid

Enore
(English) careful
Enoor, Enora

Enslie
(American) emotional
Ens, Enslee, Ensley, Ensly, Enz

Enya
(Irish) fiery; musician
Enyah, Nya

Epifania
(Spanish) proof
Epi, Epifaina, Epifanea, Eppie, Pifanie, Piffy

Eppy
(Greek) lively
Ep, Eppee, Eppey, Eppi, Eps

Equoia
(African American) great equalizer
Ekowya

Eranth
(Greek) spring bloomer
Erantha, Eranthae, Eranthe

Erasema
(Spanish) happy
Eraseme

Ercilia
(American) frank
Erci, Ercilya

Eres
(Greek) goddess of chaos
Era, Ere, Eris

Erika
(Scandinavian) honorable; leading others
Erica, Ericah, Ericca, Ericha, Ericka, Erikka, Errica, Errika, Eryka, Erykka, Eryka

Erin
(Irish) peace-making
Eran, Eren, Erena, Erene, Ereni, Eri, Erian, Erine, Erinn, Erinne, Eryn, Erynn, Erynne

Erina
(American) peaceful
Era, Erinna, Erinne, Eryna, Erynne

Erla
(Irish) playful

Erlind
(Hebrew) from Erlinda; angelic
Erlinda, Erlinde

Erma
(Latin) wealthy
Erm, Irma

Ermelinda
(Spanish) fresh-faced
Ermalinda, Ermelind, Ermelynda

Ermine
(Latin) rich
Erma, Ermeen, Ermie, Ermin, Ermina, Erminda, Erminia, Erminie

Erna
(English) short for Ernestine; knowing; earnest
Emae, Ernea, Ernie

Ernestine
(English) sincere spirit
Erna, Ernaline, Ernesia, Ernesta, Ernestina, Ernestyne

Ertha
(English) variant of Eartha; also from Bertha; earth woman

Eryn
(Irish) calm

Es
(American) short for Estella
Esa, Essie

Esbelda
(Spanish) black-haired beauty
Es, Esbilda, Ezbelda

Esdey
(American) warm-hearted
Esdee, Esdy, Essdey

Eshah
(African) exuberant
Esha

Eshe
(African) life
Eshay

Eshey
(American) life
Es, Esh, Eshae, Eshay

Esmee
(French) much loved
Esma, Esme, Esmie

Esmeralda
(Spanish) emerald; shiny and bright
Emelda, Es, Esmerelda, Esmerilda, Esmie, Esmiralda, Esmirilda, Ezmerelda, Ezmirilda

Esne
(English) happy
Es, Esnee, Esney, Esny, Essie

Esperanza
(Spanish) hopeful
Es, Espe, Esperance, Esperans, Esperanta, Esperanz, Esperanza

Essence
(American) ingenious
Esence, Essens, Essense

Essie
(English) shining
Es, Essa, Essey, Essie, Essy

Esta
(Hebrew) bright star
Es, Estah

Estee
(English) brightest
Esti

Estella
(French) radiant star
Es, Estel, Estell, Estelle, Estie, Stell, Stella

Estelle
(French) glowing star
Es, Essie, Estee, Estel, Estele, Estell, Estie

Estevina
(Spanish) adorned; wreathed
Estafania, Este, Estebana, Estefania, Estevan, Estevana

Esthelia
(Spanish) shining
Esthe, Esthel, Esthele, Esthelya

Esther
(Persian, English) shining star
Es, Essie, Estee, Ester, Esthur

Estherita
(Spanish) bright
Estereta

Estime
(French) esteemed
Es

Estrella
(Latin) shining star
Estrell, Estrelle, Estrilla

Eta
(German) short for Henrietta
Etah

Etaney
(Hebrew) focused
Eta, Etana, Etanah, Etanee

Ethel
(English) class
*Ethelda, Ethelin, Etheline,
Ethelle, Ethelyn, Ethelynn,
Ethelynne, Ethyl*

Ethelene
(American) form of Ethel;
noble
Ethe, Etheline

Ethne
(Irish) blueblood
Eth, Ethnee, Ethnie, Ethny

Ethnea
(Irish) kernel; piece of the
puzzle
Ethna, Ethnia

Etta
(German, English) short
for Henrietta; energetic
Etti, Ettie, Etty

Eudlina
(Slavic) generous; affluent
*Eudie, Eudlyna, Udie,
Udlina*

Eudocia
(Greek) fine
Eude, Eudocea, Eudosia

Eudora
(Greek) cherished

Eudore
(Greek) treasured

Eugenia
(Greek) regal and polished
*Eugeneia, Eugenie,
Eugenina, Eugina, Gee,
Gina*

Eula
(Greek) specific
Eulia

Eulala
(Greek) spoken sweetly
Eulalah

Eulalia
(Greek, Italian) spoken
sweetly
Eula, Eulia, Eulie

Eulanda
(American) fair
Eudlande, Eulee, Eulie

Eunice
(Greek) joyful; winning
*Euna, Euniece, Eunique,
Eunise, Euniss*

Eupheme
(Greek) well-spoken
*Eu, Euphemee, Euphemi,
Euphemie*

Euphemia
(Greek) respected
*Effam, Eufemia, Euphan,
Euphie, Uphie*

Euphrosyne
(Greek) mirth, merriment

Eurydice
(Greek) adventurous
*Euridice, Euridyce,
Eurydyce*

Eustacia
(Greek) industrious
Eustace, Stacey, Stacy

Euvenia
(American) hardworking
Euvene, Euvenea

Eva
(Hebrew, Scandinavian)
life
Evah, Evalea, Evalee

Evadne
(Greek) pleasing; lucky
*Eva, Evad, Evadnee,
Evadny*

Evaline
(French) form of Evelyn;
matter-of-fact
Evalyn, Eveleen

Evalouise
(American) combo of Eva
and Louise; witty
Eva-Louise, Evaluise

Eva-Marie
(American) combo of Eva
and Marie; generous

Evan
(American) bright;
precocious
Evann, Evin

Evana
(Greek) lovely woman
Eve, Ivana, Ivanna, Evania

Evangelina
(Greek) bringing joy
*Eva, Evangelia,
Evangelica, Evangeline,
Evania, Eve, Lina*

Evania
(Irish) spirited
*Ev, Evana, Evanea, Evann,
Evanna, Evanne, Evany,
Eve, Eveania, Evvanne,
Evyan*

Evanthie
(Greek) flowering well
*Evanthe, Evanthee,
Evanthi*

Eve
(French, Hebrew) first
woman
Eva, Evie, Evvy

Evelina
(Russian) lively
Evalina, Evalinna

Evelyn
(English) optimistic
*Aveline, Ev, Evaleen,
Evalene, Evaline, Evalenne,
Evalyn, Evalynn, Evalynne,
Eveleen, Eveline, Evelyne,
Evelynn, Evelynne, Evline*

Ever
(Word as name) eternal
Ev

Everilde
(Origin unknown) hunter

Evette
(French) dainty
Evett, Ivette

Evline
(French) nature girl
*Evleen, Evlene, Evlin,
Evlina, Evlyn, Evlynn,
Evlynne*

Evonne
(French) form of Yvonne;
sensual
Evanne, Eve, Evie, Yvonne

Ewelina
(Polish) life
Eva, Lina

Eydie
(American) endearing
Eidey, Eydee

Eyote
(Native American) great
Eyotee

Ezra
(Hebrew) happy; helpful
Ezrah, Ezruh

Ezza
(American) healthy
Eza

Faba
(Latin) bean; thin
Fabah, Fava

Fabia
(Latin) fabulous; special
*Fabiann, Fabianna,
Fabianne*

Fabienne
(French) farming beans

Fabio
(Latin) fabulous
Fabeeo, Fabeo, Fabeoh

Fabiola
(Spanish) royalty

Fabrizia
(Italian) manual worker
*Fabrice, Fabricia,
Fabrienne, Fabriqua,
Fabritzia*

Fae
(English) variant of Faye;
fairy girl

Fahimah
(Arabic) from Fatima;
renowned

Faida
(Arabic) bountiful
Fayda

Faillace
(French) delicate beauty
*Faill, Faillaise, Faillase,
Falace*

Faine
(English) happy
Fai, Fainne, Fay, Fayne

Fairlee
(English) lovely
Fair, Fairlea, Fairley, Fairly

Faith
(English) loyal woman
Fay, Fayth

Falesyia
(Hispanic) exotic
Falesyiah, Falisyia

Faline
(Latin, French) lively
Faleen, Falene

Fall
(Word as name)
changeable
Falle

Fallon
(Irish) fetching; from the
ruling class
Falan, Fallen, Fallyn, Falyn

Falsette
(American) fanciful
Falcette

Fanchon
(French) from France
*Fan, Fanchee, Fanchie,
Fanny, Fran, Frannie,
Franny*

Fancy
(English) fanciful
Fanci, Fancie

Fane
(American) strict
Fain, Faine

Fanfara
(Last name as first name)
fanfare; excitement
Fann, Fanny

Fang
(Chinese) pleasantly
scented

Fanny
(Latin) from France; bold
Fan, Fani, Fannie

Fantasia
(American) inventive
*Fantasha, Fantasiah,
Fantasya, Fantazia*

Fanteen
(English) clever
*Fan, Fannee, Fanney,
Fanny, Fantene, Fantine*

Farah
(English) lovely
Farrah

Faredah
(Arabic) special
Farida

Farhanah
(Arabic) lovely

Farica
(German) leader
Faricka, Fericka, Flicka

Farida
(Arabic) wanders far

Farina
(Latin) flour
Fareena

Faris
(American) forgiving
Fair, Farris, Pharis, Pharris

Farrah
(Arabic) beautiful;
(English) joyful
Fara, Farah

Farren
(American) fair
Faren, Farin

Farrow
(American) narrow-minded
Farow, Farro

Faryl
(American) inspiring
Farel, Farelle

Fashion
(American) stylish
Fashon, Fashy, Fashyun

Fatima
(Arabic) wise woman;
(African) dedicated
Fatema, Fatimah, Fatime

Faulk
(American) respected
Falk

Fauna
(Roman mythology)
goddess of nature
Faunah, Fawna, Fawnah

Faunee
(Latin) nature-loving
*Fauney, Fauneye, Fawnae,
Fawni, Fawny*

Faustene
(French, American) envied
*Fausteen, Faustine, Fausty,
Fawsteen*

Faustiana
(Spanish) good fortune
*Faust, Fausti, Faustia,
Faustina*

Faustina
(Italian) lucky
*Fausta, Faustine,
Fawsteena, Fostina,
Fostynna*

Favianna
(Italian) confident
Faviana

Fawn
(French) gentle
Faun, Fawne

Fawna
(French) soft-spoken
Fawnna, Fawnah, Fawnuh

Faye
(English, French) light-
spirited
Fae, Fay, Fey

Fayette
(American) southern
*Fayet, Fayett, Fayetta,
Fayitte*

Fayleen
(American) quiet
*Faylene, Fayline, Falyn,
Falynn, Faye, Fayla*

Fayth
(American) form of Faith;
faithful
Faithe, Faythe

Feather
(Native American) svelte
Feathyr

Febe
(Polish, Greek) bright
Febee

February
(Latin) icy
Feb

Fedora
(Greek) God's gift

Felda
(German) field girl

Felder
(Last name as first name)
bright
Felde, Feldy

Felice
(Latin) happy
Felece, Felise

Felicia
(Latin) joyful
*Faleshia, Falesia, Felecia,
Felisha*

Felicie
(Latin) happy;
(German) fortunate
*Feliccie, Felicee, Felicy,
Felisie*

Felicita
(Spanish) gracious
*Felice, Felicitas, Felicitee,
Felisita*

Felicity
(Latin) happy girl
*Felice, Felicite, Felicitee,
Felisitee*

Felise
(German) joyful
Felis

Femay
(American) classy
Femae

Femi
(African) love-seeking
Femmi

Femise
(African American) asking
for love
Femeese, Femmis

Fenella
(Irish) white
Fionola, Fionnuala

Fenia
(Scandinavian) gold worker
Fenja, Fenya

Fenn
(American) bright
Fen, Fynn

Feo
(Greek) given by God
Fee, Feeo

Feodora
(Greek) God-given girl
Fedora

Fern
(German, English) natural
Ferne

Fernanda
(German) bold
Ferdie, Fernnande

Fernilia
(American) successful
*Fern, Fernelia, Ferny,
Fyrnilia*

Fernley
(English) from the fern
meadow; nature girl

Feven
(American) shy
Fevan, Fevun

Ffion
(Irish) pale face
Fi

Fia
(Scandinavian) perky

Fiamma
(Italian) fiery spirit
*Feamma, Fee, Fia, Fiama,
Fiammette, Fifi*

Fiby
(Spanish) bright

Fidela
(Spanish) loyal
Fidele, Fidella, Fidelle

Fidelia
(Italian) faithful
Fidele

Fidelity
(Latin) loyal
Fidele, Fidelia

Fidelma
(Irish) loyal

Fife
(American) dancing eyes;
musical
Fifer, Fifey, Fyfe

Fifi
(French) jazzy
Fifee

Fifia
(African) Friday's child
FeeFee, Fifeea

Filia
(Greek) devoted
Filea, Feleah, Filiah

Filipa
(Italian) loves horses

Fillis
(Greek) form of Phyllis;
devoted
*Filis, Fill, Fillees, Filly,
Fillys, Fylis*

Filma
(Greek) loved

Filomena
(Polish) beloved

Fina
(Spanish) blessed by God

Finch
(English) bird; sings

Finelle
(Irish) fair-faced
*Fee, Finell, Finn, Finny,
Fynelle*

Finesse
(American) smooth
Fin, Finese, Finess

Finn
(Irish) cool

Finola
(Italian) white

Fion
(Irish) blonde

Fiona
(Irish) fair-haired
Fi, Fionna

Fionnuala
(Irish) white
Nuala

Fiorella
(Irish) spirited
Fee, Feorella, Rella

Fire
(American) feisty
Firey, Fyre

Flair
(English) stylish
Flaire, Flairey, Flare

Flame
(Word as name) fiery

Flaminia
(Latin) flaming spirit

Flana
(Irish) red-haired
*Flanagh, Flanna,
Flannerey, Flannery*

Flanders
(Place name) region of
Belgium; creative
Fland, Flann

Flannery
(Irish) warm; red-haired
Flann

Flavia
(Latin) light-haired
Flavie

Flax
(Botanical) plant with blue
flowers
Flacks, Flaxx

Fleming
(Last name as first name)
adorable
*Flemma, Flemmie,
Flemming, Flyming*

Flemmi
(Italian) pretty
Flemmy

Fleur
(French) flower
*Fleura, Fleuretta,
Fleurette, Fleuronne*

Flicky
(American) vivacious

Flirt
(Word as name) flirtatious
Flyrtt

Flis
(Polish) from Felicyta;
good girl

Flo
(American) short for
Florence

Flor
(Spanish) blooming
*Flo, Flora, Floralia,
Florencia, Florencita,
Florens, Florensia, Flores,
Floria, Floriole, Florita,
Florite*

Flora
(Latin, Spanish) flowering
Floria, Florie

Floramaria
(American) combo of Flora
and Maria; Mary's flower
Flora Maria, Flora-Maria

Flordeperla
(Spanish) pearly blooms

Florella
(Latin) girl from Florence;
blooming

Florence
(Latin, Italian) place name;
flourishing and giving
*Flo, Flora, Florencia,
Florense, Florenze, Florie,
Florina, Florrie, Flos,
Flossie, Floy*

Florens
(Polish) blooming
Floren

Florent
(French) flowering
*Flor, Floren, Florentine,
Florin*

Florida
(Place name) U.S. state;
flowered
Flora, Flory

Florine
(American) blooming
*Flo, Flora, Floren, Floryne,
Florynne*

Florizel
(Literature)
Shakespearean name; in
bloom
Flora, Flori, Florisel

Florrie
(English) blooms

Flossie
(English) grows beautifully

Flower
(American) blossoming
beauty
Flo

Floy
(English) blooms

Fluffy
(American) fun-loving
Fluff, Fluffi, Fluffie

Flynn
(Irish) red-haired
Flenn, Flinn, Flyn

Fog
(American) dreamy
Fogg, Foggee, Foggy

Fola
   (African) honored
   Folah
Fonda
   (American) risk-taker
   Fond
Fondice
   (American) fond of friends
   Fondeese, Fondie
Fontaine
   (French) fountaining
   bounty
   Fontane, Fontanna,
   Fontanne
Fontenot
   (French) special girl;
   fountain of beauty
   Fonny, Fontay, Fonte,
   Fonteno
Ford
   (Last name as first name)
   confident
   Forde
Fortney
   (Latin) strength
   Fortnea, Fortnee,
   Fortneigh, Fortnie, Fortny
Fortuna
   (Latin) good fortune
   Fortunata
Forsythia
   (Botanical) flower girl
Fortune
   (Latin) excellent fate;
   prized
Fotine
   (Greek) light-hearted
   Foty, Fotyne
Fowler
   (Last name as first name)
   stylish
   Fowla, Fowlar, Fowlir
Fran
   (Latin) from France;
   freewheeling
   Frann, Franni, Frannie

Franca
   (Italian) free spirit
France
   (Place name) country;
   French girl
   Frans, Franse
Francene
   (French) free
   Francine
Frances
   (Latin) free; of French
   origin
   Fanny, Fran, Francey,
   Franci, Francie, Franse
Francesca
   (Italian) form of Frances;
   open-hearted
   Fran, Francessca,
   Franchesca, Francie,
   Frankie, Frannie
Franchelle
   (French) from France
   Franshell, Franchelle,
   Franchey
Franchesca
   (Italian) smiling
   Cheka, Chekkie,
   Francheska, Francheska,
   Franchessca
Francine
   (French) form of Frances;
   beautiful
   Fran, Franceen, Francene,
   Francie
Françoise
   (French) free
Franisbel
   (Spanish) beautiful French
   girl
   Franisbella, Franisbelle
Frankie
   (American) a form of
   Frances; tomboyish
   Franki, Franky

Frannie
(English) friendly
Franni, Franny

Fransabelle
(Latin) beauty from France
Fransabella, Franzabelle

Frayda
(Scandinavian) fertile
woman
*Frayde, Fraydel, Freyda,
Freyde, Freydel*

Frea
(Scandinavian) noble;
hearty
Fray, Freas, Freya

Freda
(German) serene

Freddie
(English) short for
Frederica; spunky
Fredi, Freddy

Fredella
(American) combo of
Freda and Della; striking
Fredelle

Frederica
(German) peacemaking
*Federica, Fred, Freda,
Freddie, Freida, Frida,
Fritze, Rica*

Frederique
(German) serene

Free
(Word as name) liberated
spirit

Freesia
(Botanical) fragrant flower

Freida
(German) short for
Frederica and Alfreda;
graceful
Freda, Frida, Frieda

Frenchie
(French, American) saucy
*French, Frenchee, Frenchi,
Frenchy*

Freya
(Scandinavian) goddess;
beautiful
Freja, Freyja

Frida
(Scandinavian) lovely

Frieda
(German) happy
Freda

Friedelinde
(German) gentle girl
Friedalinda

Frigg
(Scandinavian) loved one

Frigga
(Scandinavian) beloved
Fri, Friga, Frigg

Fritzi
(German) leads in peace

Frond
(Botanical) growing

Frosty
(Word as name) crisp and
cool
Frostie

Frula
(German) hardworking

Fuchsia
(Botanical) blossoming
pink
Fuesha

Fructuose
(Latin) bountiful
Fru, Fructuosa, Fruta

Fruma
(Hebrew) devout

Frythe
(English) calm
Frith, Fryth

Fudge
(American) stubborn
Fudgey

Fuensanta
(Spanish) holy fountain
Fuenta

Fulgencia
(Latin) glowing
Fulvia
(Latin) blonde
Fulvy
(Latin) blonde
Full, Fulvee, Fulvie
Fury
(Latin) raging anger
Furee, Furey, Furie
Fushy
(American) animated;
vivid
Fooshy, Fueshy, Fushee

Gable
(German) farming woman
*Gabbie, Gabby, Gabe,
Gabel, Gabell, Gabl*
Gabor
(French) conflicted
Gaber, Gabi
Gabriela
(Italian, Spanish) God is
her strength
*Caby, Gabela, Gabi,
Gabrela, Gabriela,
Gabriella, Gabryela,
Gabryella*

Gabrielle
(French, Hebrew) strong,
by faith in God
*Gabi, Gabraelle, Gabreelle,
Gabreille, Gabríelle,
Gabriele, Gabriella,
Gabrilla, Gabrille,
Gabryele, Gabryelle, Gaby,
Gaebriell, Gaebrielle,
Garbreal*
Gaby
(French) from Gabrielle;
devoted
Gabey, Gabi, Gabie
Gadar
(Armenian) perfect girl
*Gad, Gadahr, Gaddie,
Gaddy*
Gae
(Greek) short for Gaea;
earth goddess
Gay, Gaye
Gaea
(Greek) earth goddess
Gaia
Gaegae
(Greek) from Gaea;
earthy; happy
Gae, Gaege, Gaegie
Gaenor
(Welsh) beautiful
Gaia
(Greek) goddess of earth
Gaea, Gaya
Gail
(Hebrew) short for Abigail;
energetic
Gaelle, Gale, Gayle
Gaily
(American) fun-loving
Gailai, Galhy
Gaitlynn
(American) hopeful
*Gaitlin, Gaitline, Gaitlinn,
Gaitlyn, Gaytlyn*

Gala
(French, Scandinavian)
joyful celebrant
*Gaila, Gailah, Galaa,
Galuh, Gayla*

Galatea
(Greek) sea nymph in
mythology
Gal, Gala

Galaxy
(American) universal
Gal, Galaxee, Galaxi

Galen
(American) decisive
*Galin, Galine, Galyn, Gaye,
Gaylen, Gaylin, Gaylyn*

Galena
(Latin) metal; tough
Galyna, Galynna

Galiana
(German) vaulted
Galiyana, Galli, Galliana

Galienna
(Russian) steady
*Galiena, Galyena,
Galyenna*

Galina
(Russian) deserving
*Gailina, Gailinna, Galyna,
Galynna*

Galise
(American) joyful
*Galeece, Galeese, Galice,
Galyce*

Galya
(Hebrew) redeemed;
merry
Galia

Garcelle
(French) flowered
Garcel, Garsell, Garselle

Gardenia
(Botanical) sweet flower
baby

Garland
(American) fancy
*Garlan, Garlande, Garlinn,
Garlynn*

Garlanda
(French) flowered wreath;
pretty girl
*Gar, Garl, Garlynd,
Garlynda*

Garlin
(French) variant of
Garland; decorative;
pretty
Garlinn, Garlyn, Garlynn

Garner
(American) style-setter
Garnar, Garnir

Garnet
(English) pretty; semi-
precious stone

Garnett
(English) red gemstone;
valued

Garnetta
(French) gemstone;
precious
*Garna, Garnet, Garnie,
Garny*

Garrett
(Last name as first name)
bashful
Garret, Gerrett

Garri
(American) energetic
*Garree, Garrey, Garry,
Garrye*

Garrielle
(American) competent
Gariele, Garielle, Garriella

Garrison
(American) sturdy
*Garisen, Garisun, Garrisen,
Garrisun*

Garrity
(American) smiling
Garety, Garrety, Garity, Garritee, Garritie

Gartha
(American) form of masculine name Garth; nature-loving

Garyn
(American) svelte
Garen, Garin, Garinne, Garun, Garynn, Garynne

Gates
(Last name as first name) careful
Gate

Gauri
(Hindi) golden goddess

Gavin
(American) smart
Gave, Gaven, Gavey, Gavun

Gavion
(American) daring
Gaveon, Gavionne

Gaviotte
(French) graceful
Gaveott, Gaviot, Gaviott

Gavit
(French) from Gabrielle; devoted
Gavitt, Gavyt, Gavytt

Gavotte
(French) dancer
Gav, Gavott

Gavrielle
(French) from Gabrielle; heroine
Gavriele, Gavryele, Gavryelle

Gay
(French) jolly
Gae, Gaye

Gayla
(American) planner
Gaila, Gailah, Gala, Gaye, Gaylah, Gayluh

Gayle
(Hebrew) rejoicing

Gaylynn
(American) combo of Gay and Lynn
Gaelen, Gaylene, Gaylyn, Gay-Lynn

Gaynelle
(American) combo of Gay and Nelle
Gaye, Gaynel, Gaynell, Gaynie

Gaynor
(American) precocious
Ganor, Gayner, Gaynorre

Geanna
(American) ostentatious
Geannah, Gianna

Geary
(Hebrew) variant of Jerry; able
Gearee, Gearey, Geari, Gearie, Geeree, Geerey, Geeri, Geery

Geena
(Italian) form of Gina; statuesque
Gina, Ginah

Geeta
(Italian) pearl

Gelacia
(Spanish) treasure
Gela, Gelasha, Gelasia

Gelda
(American) gloomy
Geilda, Geldah, Gelduh

Gelsey
(American) combo of G and Kelsey; vivacious
Gelsee, Gelsey, Gelsl, Gelsie, Gelsy

Gem
(American) shining
Gemmy, Gim, Jim

Gemesha
(African American)
dramatic
*Gemeisha, Gemiesha,
Gemme, Gemmy, Gimesha*

Gemini
(Greek) twin
Gem, Gemelle, Gemmy

Gemma
(Latin, Italian, French)
jewel-like
*Gem, Gema, Gemmie,
Gemmy*

Gemmy
(Italian) gem
Gemmee, Gemmi, Gimmy

Gems
(American) shining gem
Gem, Gemmie, Gemmy

Gena
(French) form of Gina;
short for Genevieve
*Geena, Gen, Genah, Geni,
Genia*

Genell
(American) form of Janelle
Genill

Genera
(Greek) highborn
Gen, Genere

Generosa
(Spanish) generous
Generosah, Generossa

Genesis
(Latin) fast starter;
beginning
*Gen, Gena, Genesys,
Geney, Genisis, Genisys,
Genysis, Genysys, Jenesis*

Geneva
(French) city in Switzerland;
flourishing; like juniper
*Gena, Geneeva, Genyva,
Janeva, Jeneva*

Genevieve
(German, French) high-
minded
*Gen, Gena, Genna,
Genavieve, Geneveeve,
Geniveeve, Genivieve,
Genovieve, Genyveeve,
Genyvieve*

Genica
(American) intelligent
*Gen, Genicah, Genicuh,
Genika, Gennica, Jen,
Jenika, Jennika*

Genie
(Greek) of high birth;
tricky
*Geenee, Geeney, Geeni,
Geenie, Geeny, Genee,
Geney, Geni, Geny*

Genna
(English) womanly
Gen, Genny, Jenna

Gennelle
(American) combo of Genn
and Elle; graceful
*Genel, Genelle, Ginelle,
Jenele, Jenelle*

Gennese
(American) helpful
*Gen, Geneece, Geniece,
Genny, Ginece, Gineese*

Gennifer
(American) form of
Jennifer
*Genefer, Genephur,
Genifer*

Genny
(Greek) of high birth;
loving
Genney, Genni, Gennie

Genoa
(Italian) playful
Geenoa, Genoah, Jenoa

Genoveva
(American) form of
Genevieve; white; light
Genny, Geno

Gentle
(American) kind
*Gen, Gentil, Gentille,
Gentlle*

Gentry
(American) sweet
*Gen, Gentree, Gentrie,
Jentrie, Jentry*

Geoma
(American) outstanding
*Gee, GeeGee, Geo,
Geomah, Geome, Gigi,
Jeoma, Oma, Omah*

Geonna
(American) sparkling
*Gee, Geionna, Geone,
Geonne, Geonnuh*

Georgann
(English) bright-eyed
*Georganne, Jorgann,
Joryann*

Georganna
(English) from Georgia;
gracious
*Georgana, Georgeana,
Georgeanna*

Georgene
(English) wandering
*Georgeene, Georgena,
Georgene, Georgyne,
Jorgeen, Jorjene*

Georgette
(French) lively and little
*Georgett, Georgitt,
Georgitte, Jorgette*

Georgia
(Greek, English) cordial
*Georgi, Georgie, Georgina,
Georgya, Giorgi, Jorga,
Jorgia, Jorja*

Georgianna
(English) combo of
Georgia and Anna; bright-
eyed
*Georganna, Georgeanna,
Jorjeana, Jorgianna*

Georgie
(English) short for
Georgia; sassy
*Georgee, Georgey, Georgi,
Georgy*

Georgina
(Greek, English) earthy

Geraldine
(German) strong
*Geraldyne, Geri, Gerri,
Gerry*

Geralena
(French) leader
*Gera, Geraleen, Geralen,
Geralene, Gerre, Gerrilyn,
Gerry, Jerrileena, Lena*

Germaine
(French) of German origin;
important
*Germain, Germane,
Germayne, Jermaine*

Gerry
(German) short for
Geraldine; leader

Gertrude
(German) beloved
Gerdie, Gerti, Gertie

Gervaise
(French) strong
Gerva, Gervaisa

Gessalin
(American) loving
*Gessilin, Gessalyn,
Gessalynn, Jessalin,
Jessalyn*

Gessica
(American) form of Jessica
Gesica, Gesika, Gessika

Gethsemane
(Biblical) peaceful
*Geth, Gethse,
Gethsemanee,
Gethsemaney,
Gethsemanie, Gethy*

Geynille
(American) womanly
Geynel

Gezelle
(American) lithe
Gezzelle, Gizele, Gizelle

Ghada
(Arabic) graceful
Ghad, Ghadah

Ghadeah
(Arabic) graceful
Gadea, Gadeah

Ghandia
(African) able
*Gandia, Ghanda,
Ghandee, Ghandy, Gondia,
Gondiah*

Ghea
(American) confident
Ghia, Jeah, Jeeah

Gherlan
(American) forgiving;
joyful
Gerlan, Gherli

Ghislaine
(French) loyal

Ghita
(Italian) pearl
Gita, Gite

Gia
(Italian) lovely

Giacinte
(Italian) hyacinth; flowering
Gia, Giacin, Giacinta

Gianina
(Italian) believer
*Gia, Giane, Giannina,
Gianyna, Janeena, Janina,
Jeanina*

Gianna
(Italian) forgiving
*Geonna, Giana, Gianne,
Gianne, Gianni, Giannie,
Gianny, Ginny, Gyana,
Gyanna*

Gianne
(Italian) combo of Gi and
Anne; divine
Gia, Gian, Giann, Gigi

Giannelle
(American) hearty
*Geanelle, Gianella,
Gianelle, Gianne*

Giannesha
(African American) friendly
*Geannesha, Gianesha,
Giannesh, Gianneshah,
Gianneshuh*

Giara
(Italian) sensual
Gee, Geara, Gia, Giarah

Gidget
(American) cute
*Gidge, Gidgett, Gidgette,
Gydget*

Gift
(American) blessed
Gifte, Gyft

Gigi
(French) small, spunky
Geegee, Giggi

Gila
(Hebrew) joyful
Gilla, Gyla, Gylla

Gilberta
(German) smart
Bertie, Gill

Gilberte
(German) shining

Gilda
(English) gold-encrusted
Gildi, Gildie, Gill

Gillaine
(Latin) young

Gilleese
(American) funny
Gill, Gillee, Gilleece, Gillie, Gilly

Gillen
(American) humorous
Gill, Gilly, Gillyn, Gyllen

Gilli
(American) joyful
Gill, Gillee, Gilly

Gillian
(Latin) youthful
Gila, Gili, Gilian, Giliana, Gilien, Gilliana, Gilliane, Gillie, Gillien, Gilly, Gillyan, Gillyen, Gilyan, Gilyen, Jillian

Gillis
(Last name as first name)
conservative
Gillice, Gillis, Gilise, Gylis, Gyllis

Gilma
(American) form of Wilma;
fortified
Gee, Gilly

Gilmore
(Last name as first name)
striking
Gilmoor, Gill, Gillmore, Gylmore

Gina
(Italian) well-born
Geena, Gena, Gin, Ginah, Ginny, Gyna, Gynah, Jenah

Ginacarol
(American) combo of Gina
and Carol
Gina-Carol, Gina-Carroll, Gyna-Carole

Ginamarie
(Italian) combo of Gina
and Marie
Gina-Marie, Ginamaria

Ginane
(French) well-born
Gigi, Gina, Gine, Jeanan, Jeanine

Ginerva
(American) combo of G
and Minerva; strong spirit
Gynerva

Ginette
(Italian) flower

Ginevieve
(Irish) from Genevieva;
womanly
Gineveeve, Giniveeve, Ginivieve, Ginyveeve, Ginyvieve

Ginger
(Botanical) pale orange;
spicy
Gin, Ginny, Jinger

Ginnifer
(American) form of
Jennifer
Gini, Ginifer, Giniferr, Ginifir, Ginn

Ginny
(English) from Virginia;
virginal; purest girl
Ginnee, Ginney, Ginni, Ginnie

Gioconda
(Italian) pleasing
Gio, Giocona

Giono
(Last name as first name)
delight; friendly
Gio, Gionna, Gionno

Giorgio
(Italian) form of George;
earthy; vivacious
Giorgi, Giorgie, Jorgio

Giovanna
(Italian) gracious believer; great entertainer
Geo, Geovanna, Gio, Giovahna, Giovana

Giritha
(Sri Lankan) melodic
Giri, Girith

Gisbelle
(American) lovely girl
Gisbel

Gisella
(German) pledged for service
Gisela

Giselle
(German) naïve; (French) devoted friend
Gis, Gisel, Gisela, Gisele, Gisell, Gissel, Gissell, Gissella, Gisselle, Gissie, Jizele

Gita
(Sanskrit) song
Geta, Gete, Git, Gitah

Gitana
(Spanish) gypsy

Gitele
(Hebrew) good
Gitel

Githa
(Slavic) good girl; from Gita
Gytha

Gitika
(Sanskrit) little singer
Getika, Gita, Giti, Gitikah

Giulia
(Italian) little girl

Giuletta
(Italian) tiny girl

Giva
(Sanskrit) from Gita; song
Givah, Gyva, Gyvah

Givonnah
(Italian) loyal; believer
Gevonna, Gevonnuh, Givonn, Givonna, Givonne, Jevonah, Jevonna, Jivonnah, Juvona

Gizela
(Polish) dedicated
Giz, Gizele, Gizella, Gizzy

Gizelle
(German) pledged to serve
Giselle, Gizel, Gizele, Gizell

Gizmo
(American) tricky
Gis, Gismo, Giz

Glad
(Welsh) from Gladys; lame; light

Gladiola
(Botanical) blooming; flower
Glad, Gladdee, Gladdy

Gladys
(Welsh) flower; princess
Glad, Gladice, Gladis, Gladise, Gladiss, Gladdie

Glafira
(Spanish) giving
Glafee, Glafera, Glafi

Gleam
(American) bright girl
Glee, Gleem

Glenda
(Welsh) bright; good
Glinda, Glynda, Glynn, Glynnie

Glenys
(Welsh) holy
Glenice, Glenis

Glenn
(Irish) glen; from a sylvan setting
Glen

Glenna
(Irish) valley-living
*Glena, Glenah, Glenuh,
Glyn, Glynna*

Glennesha
(African American) special
*Glenesha, Gleneshuh,
Gleniesha, Glenn,
Glenneshah, Glenny,
Glinnesha*

Glennice
(American) top notch
*Glenis, Glennis, Glenys,
Glenysse, Glynnece,
Glynnice*

Glenys
(Welsh) holy
Glenis, Gleniss, Glenyss

Gloria
(Latin) glorious
*Glorea, Glorey, Glori,
Gloriah, Glorrie, Glory*

Glorianne
(American) combo of
Gloria and Anne
*Gloriann, Glori-Ann,
Glorianna, Gloryann,
Glory-Anne*

Glorielle
(American) generous
*Gloriel, Gloriele, Glory,
Gloree, Glori*

Gloris
(American) glorious
*Gloeeca, Glores, Gloresa,
Glorisa, Glorus, Gloryssa*

Glory
(Latin) shining
Gloree, Glorey, Glori, Glorie

Gloss
(American) showy
*Glosse, Glossee, Glossie,
Glossy*

Glynis
(Welsh) from the glen
Glyniss, Glynys, Glynyss

Glynisha
(African American) vibrant
*Glynesh, Glynn, Glynnecia,
Glynnesha, Glynnie,
Glynnisha*

Glynn
(Welsh) from the glen
Glin, Glinn, Glyn

Glynnis
(Welsh) vivacious; glen
*Glenice, Glenis, Glennis,
Glinice, Glinnis, Glynn,
Glynnie, Glynny*

Goala
(American) goal-oriented
Go, GoGo, Gola

Gobnat
(Irish) cuddly

Goddess
(American) gorgeous
Godess, Goddesse

Godiva
(English) God's gift; brazen
Godeva, Godivah

Golda
(English) golden
Goldi, Goldie

Golden
(American) shining
*Goldene, Goldon, Goldun,
Goldy*

Goldie
(English) bright and
golden girl
*Goldee, Goldey, Goldi,
Goldy*

Goliad
(Spanish) goal-oriented
Goleade, Goliade

Goneril
(Literature) Shakespearean
name; ruthless
*Gonarell, Gonarille,
Gonereal*

Govindi
(Sanskrit) devout; faithful

Grable
(American) handsome
woman
Gray, Graybell

Grace
(Latin) graceful
*Graci, Gracie, Gracy,
Graice, Gray, Grayce*

Graceann
(American) girl of grace
*Gracean, Grace-Ann,
Graceanna, Graceanne,
Gracee, Gracy*

Gracie
(Latin) graceful
*Gracee, Gracey, Graci,
Gracy, Graecie, Gray*

Graciela
(Spanish) pleasant; full of
grace
*Chita, Gracee, Gracella,
Gracey, Gracie, Graciella,
Gracilla, Grasiela, Graziela*

Gracilia
(Latin) graceful girl
*Gracillia, Gracillya,
Gracilya*

Grady
(Irish) hardworking;
diligent

Graham
(American) sweet
Graehm, Grayhm

Grainne
(Irish) loving girl
Graine, Grayne, Graynne

Grania
(Irish) love
Grainee, Graini

Granya
(Russian) breech baby

Gratia
(Scandinavian) graceful;
gracious
*Gart, Gert, Gertie, Grasha,
Gratea, Grateah, Gratie*

Gray
(Last name as first name)
quiet
Graye, Grey

Grayson
(Last name as first) child
of quiet one
Graison, Grasen, Greyson

Grazie
(Italian) graceful; pleasant
Grasie, Grazee, Grazy

Grazyna
(Polish) graceful; pleasant

Greer
(Scottish) aware
Greere, Grear, Greare, Grier

Gregory
(American) scholarly
*Gregoree, Gregge, Greggy,
Gregoria, Gregorie*

Greshawn
(African American) lively
*Greeshawn, Greshaun,
Greshawna, Greshonn,
Greshun*

Gresia
(American) compelling
*Grecia, Grasea, Graysea,
Grayshea*

Greta
(German) pearl
*Gretah, Grete, Gretie,
Grette, Grytta*

Gretchen
(German) pearl
*Grechen, Grechin, Grechyn,
Gretch, Gretchin, Gretchun,
Gretchyn, Grethyn*

Gretel
(German) pearl; fanciful
*Gretal, Grettel, Gretell,
Gretelle*

Greyland
(American) focused
*Grey, Greylin, Greylyn,
Greylynne*

Griffie
(Welsh) royal
*Griff, Griffee, Griffey, Griffi,
Gryffie*

Griffin
(Welsh) royal
Griff

Grindelle
(American) live wire
*Dell, Delle, Grenn, Grin,
Grindee, Grindell, Grindy,
Renny*

Griselda
(German) patient
*Grezelda, Grisel, Grissy,
Grizel, Grizelda, Grizzie*

Grisham
(Last name as first name)
ambitious
Grish

Griselia
(Spanish) gray; patient
*Grise, Grisele, Grissy,
Seley, Selia*

Grizel
(Spanish) long-suffering
*Griz, Grizelda, Grizelle,
Grizzy*

Grushenka
(Russian) desirable

Guadalupe
(Spanish) patron saint;
easygoing
*Guadelupe, Guadrylupe,
Lupe, Lupeta, Lupita*

Gubby
(Irish) cuddly
Gub, Gubee, Gubbie

Gudrun
(Scandinavian) close friend;
(German) contentious
*Gudren, Gudrenne,
Gudrin, Gudrinne*

Guendolen
(Welsh) fair born

Guenevere
(Welsh) soft; white

Guenna
(Welsh) soft
Guena

Guinevere
(Welsh) queen; white
*Guenevere, Guenyveere,
Guin, Gwen*

Gulab
(Hindi) darken

Gunilla
(Scandinavian) warlike
Gun, Gunn

Gunun
(German) lively
Gunan, Gunen

Gurlene
(American) smart
*Gurl, Gurleen, Gurleene,
Gurline*

Gurshawn
(American) talkative
*Gurdie, Gurshauna,
Gurshaune, Gurshawna,
Gurty*

Gussie
(Latin) short for Augusta;
industrious
Gus, Gussy, Gustie

Gusta
(German) from Gustava;
watchful
*Gussy, Gusta, Gustana,
Gusty*

Gustava
(Scandinavian) royal

Guy
(French) guiding; assertive
Guye

Guylaine
(American) combo of Guy
and Laine; haughty
Guylane, Gylane

Guylynn
(American) combo of Guy
and Lynn; tough-minded
Guylinne, Guylyn, Guylyne

Gwen
(Welsh) short for
Gwendolyn; happy
*Gwyn, Gweni, Gwenn,
Gwenna*

Gwenda
(Welsh) beautiful
Guenda

Gwendolyn
(Welsh) mystery goddess;
bright
*Gwenda, Gwendalinne,
Gwendalyn, Gwendelynn,
Gwendolen, Gwendolin,
Gwendoline, Gwendolynn,
Gwennie, Gywnne*

Gwenless
(Invented) fair
Gwen, Gwenles, Gwenny

Gwenllian
(Welsh) lovely

Gwenna
(Welsh) beautiful
Gwena

Gwenora
(American) combo of
Gwen and Nora; playful;
fair-skinned
*Guinn, Guinna, Guinnora,
Guinnoray, Guinore, Gwen,
Gwena, Gwenda,
Gwendah, Gwenee,
Gwenna, Gwennie,
Gwennora, Gwenny,
Gwenorah, Gwenore,
Nora, Nore, Norra*

Gwladys
(Welsh) from Gladys;
happy

Gwyn
(Welsh) short for
Gwyneth; happy
*Gwenn, Gwinn, Gwynn,
Gwynne*

Gwynedd
(Welsh) blessed

Gwyneth
(Welsh) blessed
*Gwennie, Gwinith,
Gwynethe, Gwynith,
Gwynithe, Gwynne,
Gwynneth, Win, Winnie*

Gylla
(Spanish) from Guillermo;
determined
Guilla, Gye, Gyla, Jilla

Gynette
(American) form of
Jeannette; believer
*Gyn, Gynett, Gynnee,
Gynnie*

Gypsy
(English) adventurer
Gippie, Gipsie, Gypsie

Gyselle
(German) variant of
Giselle; naïve
Gysel, Gysele

Gythae
(English) feisty
Gith, Gyth, Gythay

Ha
(Vietnamese) happy

Haafizah
(Arabic) librarian
Hafeezah

Haalah
(Arabic) librarian

Haarisah
(Hindi) sun girl

Haarithah
(Arabic) angel

Habbai
(Arabic) well-loved

Habiba
(Arabic) well-loved
Habeebah, Habibah

Habika
(Arabic) loved and
cherished

Hadassah
(Hebrew) form of Esther;
myrtle; love
*Hadasa, Hadasah,
Hadaseh, Hadassa,
Haddasah, Haddee,
Haddi, Haddy*

Hadil
(Arabic) cooing

Hadlee
(English) girl in heather
*Hadlea, Hadley, Hadli,
Hadly*

Hady
(Greek) soulful
*Haddie, Hadee, Hadie,
Haidee, Haidie*

Hadyn
(American) smart
Haden

Haelee
(English) form of Hailey

Hagai
(Hebrew) abandoned;
alone
Haggai, Haggi, Hagi

Hagar
(Hebrew) stranger
Haggar, Hager, Hagur

Hagir
(Arabic) wanderer
Hajar

Haidee
(Greek) humble
Haydee

Hailey
(English) natural; hay
meadow
*Haile, Hailea, Hailee,
Hailie, Haily, Halee, Haley,
Halie, Hallie*

Halcyone
(Greek) calm
Halceonne, Halcyon

Halda
(Scandinavian) half-
Danish
*Haldaine, Haldana,
Haldane, Haldayne*

Halden
(Scandinavian) half-
Danish girl
Haldin, Haldyn

Haldi
(Scandinavian) variant of
Halda; half-Danish
Haldie, Haldis

Halena
(Russian) from Helen;
staunch supporter
Haleena, Halyna

Halene
(Russian) staunch
Haleen, Haleen, Halyne

Haletta
(Greek) little country girl
from the meadow
*Hale, Halette, Hallee,
Halletta, Halley, Hallie,
Hally, Letta, Lettie, Letty*

Haleyanne
(American) combo of
Haley and Anne
*Haleyana, Haleyanna,
Haley-Ann*

Halfrida
(German) peaceful

Hali
(English) heroic

Halia
(Hawaiian) remembering

Halima
(Arabic) gentle

Haleemah
(Arabic) speaks quietly

Halimeda
(Greek) sea-loving
Hallie, Hally, Meda

Halina
(Russian) faithful
Haleena, Halyna

Hall
(Last name as first name)
distinguished
Haul

Halle
(German) home ruler

Hallela
(Hebrew) from Halleli;
praiseworthy

Hallie
(German) high-spirited
*Halle, Hallee, Haleigh,
Hali, Halie, Hally, Hallye*

Halona
(Native American) lucky
baby
Halonna

Halsey
(American) playful
*Halcie, Halsea, Halsee,
Halsie*

Halston
(American) stylish
Hall, Halls, Halsten

Halzey
(American) leader
*Hals, Halsee, Halsi, Halsy,
Halze, Halzee*

Hameedah
(Arabic) grateful

Hamilton
(American) wishful
*Hamil, Hamilten,
Hamiltun, Hamma,
Hamme*

Hamony
(Latin) from Harmony;
together; in synch

Haneefah
(Arabic) true believer

Hanh
(Vietnamese) moral

Hanna
(Polish) grace

Hannabelle
(German) happy beauty;
from Hannibal
*Hannabell, Hannahbell,
Hannahbelle*

Hannah
(Hebrew) merciful; God-
blessed
*Hanae, Hanah, Hanan,
Hannaa, Hanne, Hanni*

Hannelore
(American) from Hannah;
gracious

Hannette
(American) form of
Jannette; graceful
Hann, Hanett, Hannett

Hansa
(Indian) swanlike
Hans, Hansah, Hansey,
Hanz

Happy
(English) joyful
Hap, Happee, Happi

Haralda
(Scandinavian) rules the
army
Harelda, Hallie, Hally,
Harilda

Harla
(English) country girl from
the fields
Harlah, Harlea, Harlee,
Harlen, Harlie, Harlun

Harlan
(English) athletic
Harlen, Harlon, Harlun

Harlequine
(Invented) romantic
Harlequinne, Harley

Harley
(English) wild thing
Harlea, Harlee, Harleey,
Harli, Harlie, Harly

Harlie
(English) in the field;
dreamy

Harlinne
(American) vivacious
Harleen, Harleene,
Harline, Harly

Harlow
(American) brash
Harlo, Harly

Harmon
(Last name as first name)
attuned
Harmen, Harmone,
Harmun, Harmyn

Harmony
(Latin) in synchrony
Harmonee, Harmoni,
Harmonia, Harmonie

Harper
(English) musician; writer
Harp

Harrah
(English) rejoicing;
merriment
Hara, Harah, Harra

Harrell
(American) leader
Harell, Harill, Haryl, Harryl

Harriet
(French) homebody
Harri, Harrie, Harriett,
Harriette, Harrott, Hat,
Hattie, Hatty, Hatti, Hattie

Harshita
(English) from Harrett;
home leader

Hart
(American) romantic
Harte, Hartee, Hartie,
Harty, Heart

Hartley
(Last name as first name)
having heart
Hartlee, Hartleigh, Hartli,
Hartlie, Hartly

Hasina
(African) beauty

Hassaanah
(African) first girl born

Hattie
(English) home-loving
Hatti, Hatty, Hettie, Hetty

Haute
(French, American) stylish
Hautie

Hava
(Hebrew) life; lively
Chaba, Chaya, Haya

Havana
(Cuban) loyal
Havanah, Havane,
Havanna, Havvanah,
Havanuh

Haven
(American) safe place; open
Havin, Havun

Haviland
(American) lively; talented
Havilan, Havilynd

Hawkins
(American) wily
Hawk, Hawkens, Hawkey, Hawkuns

Hawlee
(American) negotiator
Hawlea, Hawleigh, Hawlie, Hawley, Hawly

Haydee
(American) capable
Hady, Hadye, Haydie

Haydon
(American) knowing
Hayden, Hadyn

Hayfa
(Arabic) slim

Hayley
(English) natural; hay meadow
Hailey, Haley, Haylee, Hayleigh, Hayli, Haylie

Hayleyann
(American) combo of Hayley and Ann
Haleyan, Haylee-Ann, Hayley-Ann, Hayli-Ann

Haze
(American) word as a name; spontaneous
Haise, Hay, Hays, Hazee, Hazey, Hazy

Hazel
(English) powerful
Hazell, Hazelle, Hazie, Hazyl, Hazzell

Heart
(American) romantic
Hart, Hearte

Heath
(English) open; healthy
Heathe

Heather
(Scottish) flowering
Heath, Heathar, Heathor, Heathur

Heaven
(English) happy and beautiful
Heavyn, Hevin

Heavenly
(American) spiritual
Heaven, Heavenlee, Heavenley, Heavynlie, Hevin

Heba
(Greek) child; goddess of youth
Hebe

Hecate
(Greek) goddess of withcraft

Hedda
(German) capricious; warring
Heda, Heddi, Heddie, Hedi, Hedy, Hetta

Hedley
(Greek) sweet
Hedlee, Hedleigh, Hedli, Hedlie, Hedly

Hedy
(German) mercurial
Hedi

Hedy-Marie
(German) capricious

Heidi
(German) noble; watchful; perky
Heide, Heidee, Heidie, Heidy, Hidi

Heidirae
(American) combo of Heidi and Rae
Heidi-Rae, Heidiray

Heidrun
(German) from Heidi;
noble
Heija
(Korean) bright
Hia, Hya
Heirnine
(Greek) from Helen; light
Heirrierte
(English) from Harriet;
home leader
Helaine
(French) ray of light;
gorgeous
*Helainne, Helle, Helyna,
Hellyn*
Helanna
(Greek) lovely
*Helahna, Helana, Helani,
Heley, Hella*
Helbon
(Greek) from Helen; light
*Helbona, Helbonia,
Helbonna, Helbonnah*
Held
(Welsh) light
Helen
(Greek) beautiful and light
*Hela, Hele, Helena, Helyn,
Lena, Lenore*
Helena
(Greek) beautiful;
ingenious
*Helana, Helayna, Heleana,
Helene, Hellena, Helyena,
Lena*
Helene
(French) form of Helen;
pretty but contentious
Helaine, Heleen, Heline

Helenore
(American) combo of
Helen and Lenore; light;
darling
*Hele, Helen, Helenoor,
Helenor, Helia, Helie,
Hellena, Lena, Lennore,
Lenora, Lenore, Lenory,
Lina, Nora, Norey, Norie*
Helga
(Anglo-Saxon) pious
Helg
Helia
(Greek) sun
Heleah, Helya, Helyah
Helice
(Greek) from Helen; light
Helie
(Greek) sunny
Heley, Heli
Helina
(Greek) delightful
Helinah, Helinna, Helinnuh
Helki
(Native American) tender
Helkie, Helky
Hella
(Greek) from Helen; light
Helle
Helma
(German) helmet; well
protected
Heloise
(German) hearty
*Hale, Haley, Heley,
Heloese, Heloyse*
Helsa
(Scandinavian) God-loving
Helse, Helsie
Henda
(English) from Henna;
loves color
Hende, Hendel, Heneh
Hender
(American) embraced
Hendere

Henia
(English) from Henrietta; home leader
Henna, Henie, Henye

Henley
(American) sociable
Hendlee, Hendly, Henli, Henlie, Hinlie, Hynlie

Henna
(Hindi, Arabic) plant that releases colorful dye
Hena, Hennah, Hennuh, Henny

Henrietta
(English, German) home-ruler
Harriet, Hattie, Henny, Hetta, Hettie

Hensley
(American) ambitious
Henslee, Henslie, Hensly

Hera
(Greek) wife of Zeus; radiant

Herdis
(Scandinavian) army woman

Herendira
(Invented) tender and dear
Heren

Herise
(Invented) warm
Heree, Hereese, Herice

Herleen
(American) quiet
Herlee, Herlene, Hurleen, Herley, Herline, Herly

Hermelinda
(Spanish) earthy

Hermilla
(Spanish) fighter
Herm, Hermila, Hermille

Hermina
(Greek) of the earth
Hermine

Hermione
(Greek) sensual
Hermina, Hermine

Hermosa
(Spanish) beautiful
Ermosa

Hernanda
(Spanish) feminine for Hernando; daring

Herra
(Greek) earth girl
Herrah, Hera

Hersala
(Spanish) lithe and lovely
Hers, Hersila, Hersilia, Hersy

Hersilia
(Spanish) delicate

Hertha
(English) earth
Erta, Ertha, Eartha, Erda, Herta

Hertnia
(English) earth
Herrntia

Hesper
(Greek) night star
Hespera, Hespira

Hest
(Greek) starlike; variant of Hester
Hessie, Hesta, Hetty

Hesta
(Greek) starlike
Hestia

Hester
(American) literary
Esther, Hestar, Hesther, Hett, Hettie, Hetty

Hester-Mae
(American) combo of Hester and Mae; star
Hester May, Hestermae

Hestia
(Greek) hearth, fireside

Heti
(English) short for
Henrietta; rules
Hetta
(German) ruler
Hedda, Heta, Hettie, Hetty
Hetty
(English) short for
Henrietta; rules
Heven
(American) pretty
*Hevan, Hevin, Hevon,
Hevun, Hevven*
Heyzell
(American) form of Hazel;
tree; homebody
Hayzale, Heyzel, Heyzelle
Hiah
(Korean) form of Heija;
bright
Hia, Hy, Hya, Hye
Hiatt
(English) form of Hyatt;
splendid
Hi, Hye
Hibernia
(Place name) Latin word
for Ireland
Hibiscus
(Botanical) pretty
Hicks
(Last name as first name)
saucy
Hicksee, Hicksie
Hidee
(American) form of Heidi;
wry-humored
*Hidey, Hidie, Hidy, Hydee,
Hydeey*
Hideko
(Japanese) excellence
Hidie
(German) lively
Hilan
(Greek) happy

Hilaria
(Latin, Polish) merrymaker
Hilarea, Hilareeah, Hilariah
Hilary
(Latin) cheerful and
outgoing
*Hilaire, Hilaree, Hilari,
Hilaria, Hillarree, Hillary,
Hillerie, Hillery*
Hilda
(German) practical;
(Scandinavian) fighter
*Hild, Hilde, Hildi, Hildie,
Hildy*
Hildar
(Scandinavian) feisty
Hildebrand
(German) strong
Hildegard
(German, Scandinavian)
steadfast protector
*Hilda, Hildagarde,
Hildegarde, Hildred, Hillie*
Hildegunde
(Last name as first name)
princess
Hildemar
(German) strong
Hildreth
(German) struggles
Hilina
(Hawaiian) celestial
Hilma
(German) helmet; protects
herself
Helma
Hilton
(American) wealthy
*Hillie, Hilltawn, Hillton,
Hilly*
Himalaya
(Place name) mountain
range; upwardly mobile
Hima

Hindal
(Hebrew) from Hinda; doe; slight

Hinton
(American) affluent
Hintan, Hinten, Hintun, Hynton

Hiroko
(Japanese) giving; wise

Hisa
(Japanese) forever
Hissa, Hysa, Hyssa

Hisaye
(Japanese) longlasting

Hodel
(German) stern
Hodi

Hodge
(Last name as first name) confident
Hodj

Holda
(German) secretive

Holden
(English) willing
Holdan, Holdun

Holder
(English) beautiful voice
Holdar, Holdur

Holiday
(American) jazzy
Holidae, Holidaye, Holladay, Holliday, Holly

Holine
(American) special
Hauline, Holinn, Holli, Holyne

Hollah
(German) hides much

Holland
(Place name) expressive
Hollan, Hollyn, Holyn

Hollander
(Dutch) from Holland; benevolent
Holander, Holender, Holynder, Hollender, Hollynder

Hollis
(English) smart; girl by the holly
Hollice, Hollyce

Hollisha
(English) ingenious; Christmas-born; holly
Holicha, Hollice, Hollichia, Hollise

Holly
(Anglo-Saxon) Christmas-born; holly tree
Hollee, Holleigh, Holley, Holli, Hollie, Hollye

Holsey
(American) laidback
Holsee, Holsie

Holton
(American) whimsical
Holt, Holten, Holtun

Holyn
(American) fresh-faced
Holan, Holen, Holland, Hollee, Hollen, Holley, Hollie, Holly, Hollyn, Hollyn

Homer
(American) tomboyish
Homar, Home, Homera, Homie, Homir, Homma

Honesty
(American) truthful
Honeste, Honestee, Honesti, Honestie, Honestye

Honey
(Latin) sweet-hearted
Honie, Hunnie

Honor
(Latin) ethical
Honer, Honora, Honour

Honora
(Latin) honorable
Honorah, Honoree,
Honoria, Honoura

Honorata
(Polish) respected woman

Honoria
(Spanish) of high integrity;
a saint
Honoreah

Honorina
(Spanish) honored
Honor, Honora, Honoryna

Hope
(Anglo-Saxon) optimistic

Hopkins
(American) perky
Hopkin

Horatia
(Latin) keeps time; careful
Horacia

Horiya
(Japanese) gardens

Hortencia
(Spanish) green thumb
Hartencia, Hartense,
Hartensia, Hortence,
Hortense, Hortensia

Hortense
(Latin) caretaking the
garden
Hortence, Hortensia,
Hortinse

Hosanna
(Greek) time to pray;
worshipping
Hosana, Hosanah,
Hosannah

Hoshi
(Japanese) shines

Houston
(Place name) leader
Houst, Houstie, Huston

Hoyden
(Last name as first name)
having high spirits
Hoydin, Hoydyn

Huberta
(German) brilliant

Hud
(American) tomboyish
Hudd

Huda
(Arabic) the right way
Hoda

Hudel
(Scandinavian) lovable

Hudi
(Arabic) the right way

Hudson
(English) explorer;
adventuresome
Hud, Huds

Hueline
(German) smart
Hue, Huee, Huel, Huela,
Huelene, Huelette,
Huelyne, Huey, Hughee,
Hughie

Huella
(American) joyous
Huela, Huelle

Huette
(German) intellectual
Hughette, Huetta, Hugette

Hulda
(Scandinavian) sweetheart
Huldy, Huldie, Huldah

Humairaa
(Asian) generous

Hun
(American) short for Hunny
Hon

Hunter
(English) searching; jubilant
Hun, Huner, Hunner, Hunt,
Huntar, Huntter

Hurley
(English) fit
Hurlee, Hurlie, Hurly

Hutton
(English) right
Hutten, Huttun

Huxlee
(American) creative
Hux, Huxleigh, Huxley, Huxly

Hyacinth
(Greek) flower
Hy, Hycinth, Hyacinthe

Hyatt
(English) high gate; worthwhile
Hyat

Hyde
(American) tough-willed
Hide, Hydie

Hydie
(American) spirited
Hidi, Hydee, Hydey, Hydi

Hypatia
(Greek) tops

Iana
(Greek) flowering; from the flower name Iantha
Iann

Ianeke
(Hawaiian) believer in a gracious God
Ianete, Iani

Ianthe
(Greek) flowering
Ianthina, Ian, Iantha, Ianthiria

Ida
(German) kind; (English) industrious
Idah, Iduh

Idaa
(Hindi) earth woman

Idahlia
(Greek) sweet
Idali, Idalia, Idalina, Idaline, Idalis

Idalia
(Italian) sweet

Idarah
(American) social
Idara, Idare, Idareah

Idasia
(English) joyful

Ide
(Irish) thirsty

Ideh
(German) variant of Ida; thrives
Idit

Idelle
(Celtic) generous
Idele

Idetta
(German) serious worker
Ideta, Idettah, Idette

Idil
(Latin) pleasant
Idee, Idey, Idi, Idie, Idyll

Idola
(German) worker
Idolah, Idolia

Idolina
(American) idolizes
Idol, Idolena

Idona
(Scandinavian) fresh
Idonea, Idonia, Iduna, Idonah, Idonia, Idonna

Idony
(Scandinavian) reborn
Idowu
(African) baby after twins
Idra
(Aramaic) rich; fig tree;
flourishes
Idriya
(Hebrew) duck; rich
Idria
Iduna
(Scandinavian) fresh
Idun
Iduvina
(Spanish) dedicated
Iduvine, Iduvynna,Vina
Ieesh
(Arabic) feminine
*Ieasha, Ieesha, Iesha,
Yesha*
Ierne
(Irish) from Ireland
Iesha
(Arabic) feminine
Ifama
(African) well being
Ife
(African) loving
Ifigenia
(Spanish) from Effie; good
speaker
Ignacia
(Latin) passionate
Ignatia, Ignatzia, Ignacy
Ihab
(Arabic) gift
Iheoma
(Hawaiian) lifted by the
Lord
Ihsan
(Arabic) good will
Ihsana, Ihsanah
Ijada
(Spanish) jade; beauty

Ikabela
(Hawaiian) from Isabella;
dedicated to God
Ikapela
Ikea
(Scandinavian) smooth
Ikee, Ikeah, Ikie
Ikeida
(Invented) spontaneous
Ikae, Ikay
Iku
(Japanese) nurturing
Ila
(Hindi) of the earth; lovely
Ilamay
(French) sweet; from an
island
*Ila May, Ilamae, Ila-May,
Ilamaye*
Ilana
(Hebrew) tree; gorgeous
*Elana, Ilaina, Ilane, Ilani,
Illana, Lainie, Lanie*
Ilaria
(Greek) girl with a good
attitude
Ilda
(German) warring; feisty
Ildiko
(Hungarian) contentious;
warrior
Ileannah
(American) soaring
*Ileana, Ileanna, Ilene,
Iliana, Ilianna, Illeana,
Illiana*
Ilene
(American) svelte
Ileen, Ilenia
Ilena
(Greek) regal
Ileena, Ilina
Ilesha
(Hindi) loves the Lord of
the earth

Ilia
(Greek) from ancient city Ilion; traditional

Iliana
(Greek) woman of Troy
Ileanai, Illeana

Ilima
(Hawaiian) Oahu flower

Ilka
(Hungarian) beauty

Illana
(Greek) from Troy; Iliana; sweet beauty

Ilma
(American) stubborn

Ilona
(Hungarian) from Helen; beauty

Ilsa
(Scottish) glowing
Elyssa, Illisa, Illysa, Ilsah, Ilse, Lissie

Ilse
(German) from Elizabeth; loves God

Ilyssa
(English) variant of Alyssa; charming

Ima
(German) affluent;
(Japanese) current
Imah

Imaine
(Arabic) form of Iman; exotic; believer
Imain, Iman, Imane

Imala
(Native American) strongwilled

Iman
(Arabic, African) living in the present
Imen

Imana
(Arabic) faithful; true

Imani
(Arabic) faithful

Imanuela
(Spanish) faithful

Imara
(Hungarian) ruler

Imari
(Japanese) today's girl

Imelda
(German) contentious
Imalda

Imena
(African) dreamy

Imin
(Arabic) loyal

Immaculada
(Spanish) spotless

Imogen
(Celtic, Latin) girl who resembles her mother
Emogen, Imogene

Imperia
(Latin) imperial; stately

In
(Arabic) short for Inaya; generous

Ina
(Latin) small
Inah

Inaki
(Asian) generous spirit

Inam
(Arabic) generous

Inanna
(Mythology) goddess

Inas
(Arabic) friendly

Inca
(Indian) adventurer
Incah

India
(Place name) woman of India
Indeah, Indee, Indie, Indy, Indya

Indiana
(Place name) salt-of-the-earth; U.S. state
Inda, India, Indiana

Indiece
(American) capable
Indeece, Indeese

Indigo
(Latin) eyes of deep blue
Indego, Indigoh

Indira
(Hindi) ethereal; god of heaven and thunderstorms
Indra

Indra
(Hindi) goddess of thunder and rain; powerful
Indee, Indi, Indira, Indre

Indranee
(Hindi) sky god's wife

Indray
(American) outspoken
Indrae, Indee, Indree

Indre
(Hindi) splendor

Ineesha
(African American) sparkling
Inesha, Ineshah, Inisha

Ineke
(Japanese) nurtures

Ines
(Spanish) chaste
Inez, Innez, Ynez

Inessa
(Russian) pure
Inesa, Nessa

Inez
(Spanish) lovely
Ines

Infinity
(American) lasting
Infinitee, Infinitey, Infiniti, Infinitie

Inga
(Scandinavian) protected by Ing, god of peace and fertility

Ingalill
(Scandinavian) fertile

Ingalls
(American) peaceful

Inge
(Scandinavian) fertile
Inga

Ingeborg
(Scandinavian) fertile

Ingegerd
(Scandinavian) from Ingrid; fertile

Ingrad
(American) variant of Ingrid; beauty
Inger, Ingr

Ingrid
(Scandinavian) beautiful
Inga, Inge, Inger, Ingred

Ingrida
(Scandinavian) from Ingrid; beauty

Iniguez
(Spanish) good
Ina, Ini, Niqui

Innocence
(American) pure
Innoce, Innocents, Inocence, Inocencia, Inocents

Inoa
(Hawaiian) named

Inocencia
(Spanish) innocent
Inocenta, Inocentia

Inola
(Greek) from Iola; dawn in clouds

Integrity
(American) truthful
Integritee, Integritie

Iola
(Greek) dawn
Iole

Iolana
(Hawaiian) violet; pretty

Iolanthe
(English) violet; delicate
Iole, Iola

Iona
(Place name) for the Isle
of Iona in Scotland
Ione, Ionia

Iosepine
(Hawaiian) from
Josephine; blessed

Ira
(Hebrew) contented;
watchful
Irah

Ireland
(Place name) vibrant
*Irelan, Irelande, Irelyn,
Irelynn*

Irina
(Greek, Russian)
comforting
*Ireena, Irena, Irenah,
Irene, Irenia, Irenya*

Irene
(Greek) peace-loving;
goddess of peace
Irine

Ireta
(Greek) serene
Iretta, Irette

Iris
(Greek) bright; goddess of
the rainbow

Irma
(Latin) realistic
Irmah

Irmgard
(Latin) from Irma; noble

Irodell
(Invented) peaceful
Irodel, Irodelle

Irra
(Greek) serene

Irvette
(English) friend of the sea

Isa
(Spanish) dark-eyed
Isah

Isabel
(Spanish) God-loving
*Isabela, Isabella, Isabelle,
Issie, Iza*

Isabella
(Spanish, Italian)
dedicated to God
Isabela, Izabella

Isadora
(Greek) beautiful; gift of
Isis; fertile
Dora, Dori, Dory, Isidora

Isairis
(Spanish) lively
Isa, Isaire

Isamu
(Japanese) high-energy

Isatas
(Native American) snow
Istas

Isaura
(Greek) Asian country

Isela
(American) giving
Iselah

Iseult
(Irish) lovely

Isha
(Hindi) protected

Ishana
(Hindi) sheltered

Ishi
(Japanese) rock; safe
Ishie

Ishiko
(Japanese) rock;
dependable

Isis
(Egyptian) goddess supreme of moon and fertility

Isla
(Place name) river in Scotland; flows

Isleana
(Latin) sun girl; jolly
Islean, Isleen, Isaeileen

Ismaela
(Hebrew) from Ishmael; God hears
Isma, Mael, Maella

Ismat
(Arabic) protective

Ismene
(French) from the name Esme; respected
Isme, Ismyne

Ismenia
(Place name) region of Mars; loyal

Ismey
(French) variant of Esme; respected

Isoka
(African) given by God
Isoke, Soka

Isoke
(African) God's gift

Isolde
(Welsh) beautiful
Iseult, Isolda, Isolt, Izette, Yseult

Isotta
(Irish) princess

Isra
(Arabic) night mover

Istvan
(Hungarian) crowned

Ita
(Irish) thirsts for knowledge

Italia
(Italian) girl from Italy

Iti
(Irish) variant of Ita; thirsts for knowledge

Itiah
(Hebrew) God comforts her
Itia, Itiya

Itica
(Spanish) eloquent
Itaca, Iticah

Itidal
(Arabic) cautious

Itinsa
(Hawaiian) waterfall

Itka
(Irish) variant of Ita; thirsts for knowledge

Ito
(Japanese) thread; delicate

Ituha
(Native American) sturdy oak; white stone

Itzel
(Spanish) from Isabella; God-loving
Itz

Itzy
(American) lively
Itsee, Itzee, Itzie

Iuana
(Welsh) believes in gracious God

Iudita
(Hawaiian) praises; affectionate

Iuginia
(Hawaiian) highborn
Iugina

Iulaua
(Hawaiian) eloquent

Iulia
(Irish) from Julia; young girl

Iunia
(Hawaiian) from Iune, for June; goddess of marriage

Iusitina
(Hawaiian) justice

Iva
(Slavic) dedicated
Ivah

Ivanna
(Russian) gracious gift from God
Iva, Ivana, Ivanka, Ivie, Ivy

Ivelisa
(American) combo of Ivy and Lisa
Ivalisa, Ivelise, Ivelisee, Ivelissa, Ivelyse

Iverem
(African) lucky girl

Iveta
(French) athletic

Ivette
(French) clever and athletic
Ivet, Ivett

Ivey
(English, American) easygoing
Ivee, Ivie, Ivy

Iviannah
(American) adorned
Iviana, Ivianna, Ivie, Ivy

Ivisse
(American) graceful
Ivice, Iviece, Ivis, Ivise

Ivon
(Spanish) light
Ivonie, Ivonne

Ivona
(Slavic) gift
Ivana, Ivanna, Ivannah, Ivonah, Ivone, Ivonne

Ivonne
(French) athlete
Ivonn

Ivory
(Latin) white
Ivoree, Ivori, Ivorie

Ivria
(Hebrew) from Abraham's country
Ivriah, Ivrit

Ivy
(English) growing
Iv, Ivee, Ivey, Ivie

Iwa
(Japanese) strong character

Iwalani
(Hebrew) heavenly girl

Iwilla
(African American) I will rise

Iwona
(Polish) archer; athletic; gift
Iwonna

Iyabo
(African) her mother is home

Iyana
(Hebrew) sincere

Izabella
(American) variant of Isabella
Iza, Izabela, Izabelle, Izabell

Izanne
(American) calming
Iza, Izan, Izann, Izanna, Ize

Izdihar
(Arabic) blossoming

Izebe
(African) staunch supporter

Izegbe
(African) baby who was wanted

Izolde
(Greek) philosophical
Izo, Izolade, Izold

Izusa
(Native American) white rock; unique

Izzy
(American) zany
Izzee, Izzie

Jaala
(Arabic) seeks clarity

Jacalyn
(American) form of Jacqueline; discriminating
Jacelyn, Jacelyne, Jacelynn, Jacilyn, Jacilyne, Jacilynn, Jacolyn, Jacolyne, Jacolynn, Jacylyn, Jacylyne, Jacylynn

Jacey
(Greek) sparkling
J.C., Jace, Jacee, Jaci, Jacie, Jacy

Jacinda
(Greek) attractive girl
Jacenda, Jacey, Jaci, Jacinta

Jacinta
(Spanish) hyacinth; sweet
Jace, Jacee, Jacey, Jacinda, Jacinna, Jacintae, Jacinth, Jacinthia, Jacy, Jacynth

Jackalyn
(American) form of Jacqueline; cares
Jackalene, Jackalin, Jackaline, Jackalynn, Jackalynne, Jackelin, Jackeline, Jackelyn, Jackelynn, Jackelynne, Jackilin, Jackilyn, Jackilynn, Jackilynne, Jackolin, Jackoline, Jackolyn, Jackolynn, Jackolynne

Jackie
(French) short for Jacqueline
Jackee, Jacki, Jacky, Jaki, Jaky

Jacklyn
(American) careful
Jacklin, Jackline, Jackline, Jacklyne, Jacklynn, Jacklynne

Jackquel
(French) watchful
Jackquelin, Jackqueline, Jackquelyn, Jackquelynn, Jackquilin, Jackquiline, Jackquilyn, Jackquilynn, Jackquilynne

Jackson
(Last name as first name) swaggering
Jacksen, Jaksin, Jakson

Jaclyn
(French) form of Jacqueline
Jacalyn, Jackalene, Jackalin, Jackalyn, Jackeline, Jackolynne, Jacleen, Jaclin, Jacline, Jaclyne, Jaclynn

Jacoba
(Hebrew) replaces

Jacobi
(Hebrew) stand-in
Cobie, Coby

Jacomine
(Dutch) best girl, seductive
Jacoy
(French) from Jackie;
stand-in
Jacqueline
(French) little Jacquie;
small replacement
Jacki, Jackie, Jacklin,
Jacklyn, Jaclyn, Jacqualin,
Jacqualine, Jacqualyn,
Jacqualyne, Jacquel,
Jacquelyn, Jacquelynn,
Jacqui, Jacquie, Jakie,
Jakline, Jaklinn, Jaklynn,
Jaqueline, Jaquie
Jacquelyn
(French) highbrow
Jacquelyne, Jacquelynn
Jacquet
(Invented) form of
Jacquelyn
Jackett, Jackwet, Jacquee,
Jacquie, Jakkett
Jacqui
(French) short for
Jacquline
Jacquay, Jacque, Jacquee,
Jacquie, Jakki, Jaki, Jaquay,
Jaqui, Jaquie
Jacynth
(Spanish) hyacinth; flower
Jada
(Spanish) personable;
precious
Jadah
Jade
(Spanish) green gemstone;
courageous; adoring
Jada, Jadah, Jadda, Jadea,
Jadeann, Jadee, Jaden,
Jadera, Jadi, Jadie,
Jadielyn, Jadienne, Jady,
Jadzia, Jadziah, Jaeda,
Jaedra, Jaida, Jaide, Jaiyde,
Jaiden

Jaden
(African American) exotic
Jadi, Jadie, Jadin, Jadyn,
Jaeden, Jaiden
Jadwiga
(Polish) religious
Jad, Jadwig, Wiga
Jae
(Latin) small; jaybird
Jaea, Jay, Jayjay
Jael
(Hebrew) high-climbing
Jaela, Jaelee, Jaeli, Jaelie,
Jaelle
Jaela
(Hebrew) bright
Jael, Jaell, Jayla
Jaelyn
(African American)
ambitious
Jaela, Jaelynne, Jala, Jalyn,
Jaylyn
Jaenesha
(African American) spirited
Jacey, Jae, Jaeneisha,
Jaeniesha, Janesha,
Jaynesha, Nesha
Jaffa
(Hebrew) lovely
Jagan
(American) form of Jadan;
wholesome
Jag, Jagann, Jagen, Jagun
Jagger
(English) cutter
Jaeger, Jag, Jager
Jaguar
(American) runner
Jag, Jaggy, Jagwar, Jagwor
Jahnea
(Scandinavian) from John;
loves God
Jahnika
(Scandinavian) believes in
God

Jahnny
(American) form of Johnny
*Jahnae, Jahnay, Jahnie,
Jahnnee, Jahnney, Jahnnie,
Jahny*

Jaidan
(American) golden child
*Jaedan, Jai, Jaide, Jaidee,
Jaidi, Jaidon, Jaidun, Jaidy,
Jaidyn, Jaydan, Jaydyn*

Jaime
(French) girl who loves
*Jaeme, Jaemee, Jaima,
Jaimee, Jaimey, Jaimi,
Jaimie, Jaimy, Jamie,
Jaymee*

Jaime-Day
(American) loving

Jairia
(Spanish) taught by God's
lessons

Jakira
(Arabic) warmth

Jakisha
(African American) favored
Jakishe

Jakki
(American) form of Jackie;
carefree
Jakea, Jakia, Jakkia

Jaleesa
(African American) combo
of Ja and Leesa
Gilleesa, Jalesa, Jilleesa

Jalena
(American) combo of Jay
and Lena; outgoing
*Jalayna, Jalean, Jaleen,
Jalene, Jalina, Jaline,
Jalyna, Jelayna, Jelena,
Jelina, Jelyna*

Jalene
(American) combo of Jane
and Lene; pretty
*Jaleen, Jaline, Jalinn, Jalyn,
Jalyne, Jalynn, Jlayna*

Jaleshia
(American) combo of Jale
and Leshia; chatterer
Jalicia

Jalila
(Arabic) excellent
Jalile

Jalisa
(American) combo of Jay
and Lisa
Gillisa, Jalise, Jaylisa, Jelisa

Jalit
(American) sparkling
Jal, Jalitt, Jalitte, Jallit

Jamaica
(Place name) Caribbean
island
*Jama, Jamaika, Jamaka,
Jamake, Jamana, Jamea,
Jameca, Jameka, Jamica,
Jamika, Jamiqua, Jamoka,
Jemaica, Jemika, Jemyka*

Jamais
(French) ever
Jamay, Jamaye

Jamalita
(Invented) form of James;
little Jama
Jama

Jamar
(African American) strong
*Jam, Jamara, Jamareah,
Jamaree, Jamarr, Jamarra,
Jammy*

Jamashia
(African American) soulful
Jamash, Jamashea

Jameah
(African American) bold
Jamea, Jameea, Jamiah

Jamecka
(African American)
studious
*Jamecca, Jameeka,
Jameka, Jameke, Jamekka,
Jamie, Jamiea, Jamieka*

Jamesetta
(American) form of James
Jamesette

Jamesha
(African American)
outgoing
*Jamece, Jamecia,
Jameciah, Jameisha,
James, Jamese, Jameshia,
Jameshyia, Jamesia,
Jamesica, Jamesika,
Jamesina, Jamessa, Jamie,
Jamisha, Jay*

Jami
(Hebrew) replacement
Jamay, Jamia, Jamie, Jamy

Jamiann
(American) combo of Jami
and Ann
*Jami, Jamia, Jami-Ann,
Jamian, Jamiane*

Jamie
(Hebrew) supplants; fun-
loving
*Jami, Jamee, James,
Jaymee*

Jamielyn
(American) combo of
Jamie and Lyn; pretty
*Jameelyn, Jamelinn,
James, Jamie, Jamie-Lynn,
Jamilin, Jami-Lyn*

Jamika
(African American)
buoyant
*Jameeka, Jamey, Jamica,
Jamicka, Jamie*

Jamila
(Arabic) beautiful female
*Jahmela, Jahmilla, Jam,
Jameela, Jami, Jamie,
Jamil, Jamilah, Jamile,
Jamilla, Jamille, Jamilya,
Jammell, Jammie*

Jamisha
(American) combo of Jami
and Misha; organized

Jan
(English) short for Janet or
Janice; cute
*Jani, Jania, Jandy, Jannie,
Janny*

Jana
(Slavic, Scandinavian)
gracious
Janna, Janne

Janae
(American) giving
*Janea, Jannay, Jennae,
Jannah, Jennay*

Janaleigh
(American) combo of Jana
and Leigh; friendly
*Jana, Janalea, Janalee,
Janalee, Jana-Lee, Jana-
Leigh, Janlee, Jannalee,
LeeLee, Leigh*

Janalyn
(American) giving
*Jan, Janalynn, Janelyn,
Janilyn, Jannalyn, Jannnie,
Janny*

Janan
(Arabic) soulful
*Jananee, Janani, Jananie,
Janann, Jannani*

Janara
(American) generous
*Janarah, Janerah, Janira,
Janirah*

Janay
(American) forgiving
Janae, Janah, Janai

Janaya
(American) combo of Jana
and Anaya; comical

Jancy
(American) risk-taker
*Jan, Jance, Jancee, Jancey,
Janci, Jancie, Janny*

Jandy
(American) fun
Jandee, Jandey, Jandi

Jane
(Hebrew) believer in a
gracious God
*Jaine, Jan, Janelle, Janene,
Janeth, Janett, Janetta,
Janey, Janica, Janie, Jannie,
Jayne, Jaynie*

Janeana
(American) sweet
*Janea, Janean, Janeanah,
Janine*

Janel
(French) variant of Janelle;
dark eyes
*Janell, Jannel, Jaynel,
Jaynell*

Janene
(American) form of Jane
*Janeen, Jenean, Janine,
Jenine*

Janella
(American) combo of Jan
and Ella; sporty
Jan, Janela, Janelle, Janny

Janelle
(French) exuberant
*J'Nel, J'nell, Janel, Janell,
Jannel, Jenelle, Nell*

Janessa
(American) forgiving
*Janesha, Janeska,
Janessah, Janie, Janiesa,
Janiesha, Janisha, Janissa,
Jannesa, Jannesha,
Jannessa, Jannisa,
Jannisha, Jannissa,
Janyssa*

Janet
(English) small; forgiving
*Jan, Janett, Janetta,
Janette, Jannet, Jannett,
Janot, Jessie, Jinett,
Johnette, Jonetta, Jonette*

Janeth
(American) fascinating
Janith

Janice
(Hebrew) knowing God's
grace
*Genese, Jan, Janece,
Janecia, Janeese, Janeice,
Janiece, Jannice, Janyce,
Jynice*

Janie
(English) form of Jane
Janey, Jani, Jany

Janiece
(American) devout;
enthusiastic
*Janece, Janecia, Janeese,
Janese, Janesea, Janesse,
Janneece, Jeneece,
Jeneese*

Janiecia
(African American) sporty
*Janesha, Janeisha,
Janeshah, Janisha, Jan,
Jannes, Jannesa*

Janika
(Scandinavian) believer in
a gracious God
*Janica, Janicah, Janik,
Jannike, Janikka*

Janine
(American) kind
*Janean, Janeen, Janene,
Janey, Janie, Jannine,
Jannyne, Janyne, Jenine*

Janiqua
(American) combo of Jani
and Niqua; has a fortune

Janira
(American) combo of Jan
and Nira; entertaining

Janis
(English) form of Jane
*Janees, Janeesa, Janes,
Jenice, Jenis, Janise*

Janitza
(American) from Juanita; bright

Janjan
(Last name as first) sweet; believer
Jan Jan, Jange, Janja, Jan-Jan, Janje, Janni, Jannie, Janny

Janke
(Scandinavian) believer in God
Jankee, Jankey, Jankie

Jan-Marie
(American) combo of Jan and Marie; believer
Jan Marie, Janmarie, Jannemarie

Janna
(Hebrew) short for Johana; forgiving

Janneke
(Scandinavian) smart; believer

Jannette
(American) lovely
Jan, Janette, Jannett, Jannie, Janny

Jannie
(English) form of Jane and Jan
Janney, Janny, Jannye

Jansen
(Scandinavian) smooth
Jan, Jannsen, Jans, Jansie, Janson, Jansun, Jansy

Jaqualia
(American) combo of Jaquie and Alia; reserved

Jaquita
(Spanish) combo of Jaqui and Quita; temperamental

Jaqueline
(French) form of Jacquelyn
Jaqlinn, Jaqlyn, Jaqlynn, Jaqua, Jaquaeline, Jaqualine, Jaqualyn, Jaquelina, Jaquelyn, Jaquelynne, Jaquie, Jaqulene

Jaquonna
(African American) spoiled
Jakwona, Jakwonda, Jakwonna, Jaqui, Jaquie, Jaquon, Jaquona, Jaquonne

Jardana
(American) gardener
Jardana, Jarde, Jardee, Jardy

Jardena
(French) gardens
Jardan, Jardane, Jarden, Jardenia, Jardine, Jardyne

Jarene
(American) bright
Jare, Jaree, Jareen, Jaren, Jareni, Jarine, Jarry, Jaryne, Jerry

Jarita
(Arabic) carries water; befriends
Jara, Jari, Jaria, Jarica, Jarida, Jarietta, Jarika, Jarina, Jaritta, Jaritza

Jariya
(Arabic) from Jarita; totes water; hardworking

Jarmila
(Czech) beautiful spring

Jaranescia
(Scandinavian) magnificent

Jarone
(American) optimistic
Jaron, Jaroyne, Jerone, Jurone

Jaroslava
(Czech) glorious spring

Jarren
(American) lovable
Jaren, Jarran, Jarre

Jas
(American) from Jasmine;
saucy
Jass, Jaz, Jazz, Jazze, Jazzi

Jasalin
(American) devoted
*Jasalinne, Jasalyn,
Jasalynn, Jaselyn, Jasleen,
Jaslene, Jass, Jassalyn,
Jassy, Jazz, Jazzy*

Jasira
(Polish) from Jane; religious

Jasmarie
(American) combo of
Jasmine and Marie;
attractive

Jasmine
(Persian, Spanish)
fragrant; sweet
*Jas'mine, Jasamine,
Jasime, Jasimen, Jasimin,
Jasimine, Jasmaine,
Jasman, Jasme, Jasmie,
Jasmina, Jasminah,
Jasminen, Jasminne,
Jasmon, Jasmond,
Jasmone, Jasmyn,
Jasmynn, Jasmynne, Jazie,
Jazmaine, Jazman,
Jazmeen, Jazmein, Jazmen,
Jazmin, Jazmine, Jazmon,
Jazmond, Jazmyn,
Jazmyne, Jazs, Jazsmen,
Jazz, Jazza, Jazzamine,
Jazzee, Jazzi, Jazzmeen,
Jazzmin, Jazz-Mine,
Jazzmun, Jazzy*

Jasna
(American) talented
Jas, Jazna, Jazz

Jaspreet
(Punjabi) pure
*Jas, Jaspar, Jasparit,
Jasparita, Jasper, Jasprit,
Jasprita, Jasprite*

Jatara
(American) combo of Jay
and Tara; popular
*Jataria, Jatarra, Jatori,
Jatoria*

Ja-Tawn
(African American) tawny
J'Tawn, Ja Tawn, Jatawn

Jatsue
(Spanish) lively
Jat, Jatsey

Javana
(Asian) girl from Java;
dancer
*Javanna, Javanne, Javon,
Javonda, Javonna,
Javonne, Javonya, Jawana,
Jawanna, Jawn*

Javiera
(Spanish) owns a home
Javeera, Viera

Jawara
(Arabic) true gem

Jaya
(Hindi) winning
Jaea, Jaia, Jay, Jayah

Jayare
(African) winner

Jayci
(American) vivacious
*Jacee, Jacey, Jaci, Jacie,
Jacy, Jaycee, Jaycey, Jayci,
Jaycie*

Jaydee
(American) combo of Jay
and Dee; perky
*Jadee, Jadey, Jadi, Jadie,
Jady, Jayde, Jadey, Jayda,
Jayd, Jaydia, Jaydn, Jayia*

Jayden
(American) enthusiastic
*Jaden, Jay, Jaydeen,
Jaydon, Jaydyn, Jaye*

Jaydie
(American) lively
*Jadie, Jady, Jay-Dee,
Jaydeye, Jaydie*

Jaydra
(Spanish) treasured jewel;
jade
Jadra, Jay, Jaydrah

Jaye
(Latin) small as a jaybird
Jae, Jay

Jayla
(American) smiling
Jaila, Jaylah, Jayle, Jaylee

Jaylene
(American) combo of Jay
and Lene; conflicted
*Jayelene, Jayla, Jaylah,
Jaylan, Jayleana, Jaylee,
Jayleen*

Jaylo
(American) combo of
Jennifer and Lopez;
charismatic
*J. Lo, Jalo, Jayjay, Jaylla,
Jaylon, J-Lo*

Jaylynn
(American) combo of Jay
and Lynn; conflicted
*Jaelin, Jaeline, Jaelyn,
Jaelyne, Jaelynn, Jaelynne,
Jalin, Jaline, Jalyn, Jalyne,
Jalynn, Jalynne, Jaylin,
Jayline, Jaylyn, Jaylyne,
Jaylynne*

Jayme
(English) gracious;
feminine form of James
*Jami, Jamie, Jaymee, Jaymi,
Jaymia, Jaymie*

Jayna
(Hindi) winner
Jaynae

Jayne
(Hindi, American) winning
*Jane, Janey, Jani, Jayn,
Jaynee, Jayni, Jaynie,
Jaynita, Jaynne*

Jaynell
(American) combo of Jay
and Nell; southern belle
*Janell, Janelle, Jaynel,
Jaynelle, Jeanel, Jeanell,
Jeanelle, Jeanelly*

Jazlyn
(American) combo of Jazz
and Lynn; zany
*Jazleen, Jazlene, Jazlin,
Jazline, Jazlynn, Jazlynne,
Jazzleen, Jazzlene, Jazzlin,
Jazzline, Jazzlyn, Jazzlynn,
Jazzlynne*

Jazz
(American) rhythmic
*Jas, Jassie, Jaz, Jazzi,
Jazzie, Jazzle, Jazzy*

Jazzell
(American) spontaneous
*Jazel, Jazell, Jazz, Jazzee,
Jazzie*

Jazzlyn
(American) combo of Jazz
and Lyn
*Jaz, Jazilyn, Jazlin, Jazlinn,
Jazlinne, Jazlyn, Jazlynn,
Jazlynne*

Jean
(Scottish) God-loving and
gracious
*Jeana, Jeanie, Jeanne,
Jeannie, Jeanny, Jena,
Jenay, Jenna*

Jeana
(American) variant of Gina;
audacious
Jeanna

Jeanetta
(American) impish
Janetta, Jeannet, Jeannette, Jeanney, Jen, Jenett, Jennita

Jeanette
(French) lively
Janette, Jeannete, Jeanett, Jeanetta, Jeanita, Jeannete, Jeannett, Jeannetta, Jeannette, Jeannita, Jenet, Jenett, Jenette, Jennett, Jennetta, Jennette, Jennita, Jinetta, Jinette

Jeanie
(Scottish) devout; outspoken
Jeani, Jeannie, Jeanny, Jeany

Jeanine
(Scottish) peace-loving
Jeanene, Jeanina, Jeannina, Jeannine, Jenine, Jennine

Jeanisha
(African American) pretty
Jean, Jeaneesh, Jeanise, Jeanna, Jeannie, Jenisha

Jearlean
(American) vibrant
Jearlee, Jearlene, Jearley, Jearli, Jearline, Jearly, Jerline

Jebel
(Origin unknown) from Jezebel; treacherous

Jecelyn
(Invented) form of Jocelyn; innovative
Jece, Jecee, Jeselyn, Jess

Jeffrey
(German) peaceful; sparkling personality
Jef, Jeff, Jeffa, Jefferi, Jeffery, Jeffie, Jeffre, Jeffrie, Jeffy, Jefry

Jelana
(Russian) from Helen; upright

Jelane
(Russian) light heart
Jelaina, Jelaine, Jelanne, Jilane, Julane

Jelani
(American) pretty sky
Jelaney, Jelani, Jelanie, Jelainy, Jelanni

Jemima
(Hebrew) dove-like
Jamima, Jem, Jemi, Jemimah, Jemm, Jemma, Jemmi, Jemmia, Jemmiah, Jemmy, Jemora

Jemine
(American) treasured
Jem, Jemmy, Jemyne

Jemma
(Hebrew, English) nickname for Jemima; peaceful
Jem

Jems
(American) treasured
Gemas, Jemma, Jemmey, Jemmi, Jemmy

Jena
(Arabic); small
Jenaa, Janae, Jenaeh, Jenah, Jenai, Jenal, Jenay, Jenna

Jenavieve
(American) from Genevieve; generous

Jenaya
(African) hospitable

Jenci
(American) combo of Jen and Nanci; friend of all

Jencynn
(American) combo of Jen and Cynn; sweetheart
Jencin, Jen-Cynn, Jensynn

Jenell
(American) combo of
Jenny and Nell
*Janele, Jen, Jenaile,
Jenalle, Jenel, Jenella,
Jennelle, Jenny*

Jenesia
(American) combo of Jen
and Nesia; popular

Jeniece
(American) combo of Jen
and Niece; well-liked

Jenifer
(Welsh) beautiful; fair
*Gennefer, Gennifer,
Ginnifur, Ginnipher, Jay,
Jenefer, Jenifer, Jenjen,
Jenna, Jenni, Jennifer,
Jenny*

Jenilee
(American) combo of Jen
and Lee; fair and light
*Jenalea, Jenalee,
Jenaleigh, Jenaly, Jenelea,
Jenelee, Jeneleigh, Jenely,
Jenelly, Jenileigh, Jenily,
Jennely, Jennielee,
Jennilea, Jennilee, Jennilie*

Jenilynn
(American) combo of
Jenny and Lynn; precious
*Jennalyn, Jennilin,
Jennilinn, Jennilyn, Jenny-
Lynn, Jennylynn*

Jenisa
(American) combo of Jen
and Nisa; smart
*Jenisha, Jenissa, Jennisa,
Jennise, Jennisha,
Jennissa, Jennisse,
Jennysa, Jennyssa, Jenysa,
Jenyse, Jenyssa, Jenysse*

Jenna
(Scottish, English) sweet
*Jena, Jennah, Jennat,
Jennay, Jhenna, Jynna*

Jenni
(Welsh) from Jennifer;
beauty
*Jeni, Jenica, Jenie, Jenisa,
Jenka, Jenne, Jennee,
Jenney, Jennia, Jennier,
Jennita, Jennora, Jensine*

Jennifer
(Welsh, English) fair-
haired; beautiful
perfection
*Gennefur, Ginnifer, Jen,
Jenefer, Jenife, Jenifer,
Jeniferr, Jeniffer, Jenipher,
Jenn, Jenna, Jennae,
Jennafer, Jennefer, Jenni,
Jenniffe, Jenniffer,
Jenniffier, Jennifier,
Jenniphe, Jennipher,
Jenniphur, Jenny, Jennyfer,
Jennypher*

Jennilee
(American) combo of Jeni
and Lee; dependable
*Jennalea, Jennalee,
Jennielee, Jennilea,
Jennilie*

Jennilynn
(American) combo of Jenni
and Lynn; pretty
*Jennalin, Jennaline,
Jennalyn, Jennalyne,
Jennalynn, Jennalynne,
Jennilin, Jenniline,
Jennilyn, Jennilyne,
Jennilynne*

Jennings
(Last name as first name)
pretty
Jen, Jenny

Jennis
(American) white; patient
*J, Jay, Jen, Jenace, Jenice,
Jenis, Jenn, Jennice*

Jennison
(American) variant of
Jennifer; darling
*Gennison, Jenison,
Jennisyn, Jenson*

Jenny
(Scottish, English) short
for Jennifer; blessed;
sweetheart
*Jen, Jenae, Jeni, Jenjen,
Jenney, Jenni, Jennie,
Jennye, Jeny, Jinny*

Jeno
(Greek) heavenly

Jensen
(Scandinavian) athletic

Jenteale
(American) combo of Jen
and Teale; blue-eyed and
pretty
*Jen, Jenny, Jenteal, Jentelle,
Jyn, Jynteale, Teal, Teale*

Jenvie
(American) lovely
Jennvey, Jenvee, Jenvy

Jenz
(Scandinavian) form of
masculine name
Johannes; believer in God
Jen, Jens

Jeri
(American) hopeful
*Geri, Jere, Jerhie, Jerree,
Jerri, Jerry, Jerrye*

Jerica
(American) combo of Jeri
and Erica; conniving
*Jerice, Jericka, Jerika,
Jerreka, Jerricca, Jerrice,
Jerricka, Jerrika*

Jeridean
(American) combo of Jeri
and Dean; leader; musical
*Geridean, Jerdean, Jeri
Dean, Jeri-Dean, Jerridean,
Jerrydean*

Jerilee
(American) combo of Jeri
and Lee; political

Jerilyn
(American) combo of Jeri
and Lyn; plots
*Jeralin, Jeraline, Jeralyn,
Jeralyne, Jeralynn,
Jeralynne, Jerelin, Jereline,
Jerelyn, Jerelyne, Jerelynn,
Jerelynne, Jerilin, Jeriline,
Jerilyne, Jerilynn, Jerilynne,
Jerrilin, Jerriline, Jerrilyn,
Jerrilyne, Jerrilynn,
Jerrilynne*

Jerikah
(American) sparkling
*Jereca, Jerecka, Jeree, Jeri,
Jerica, Jerik, Jeriko, Jerrica,
Jerry*

Jerilyn
(American) combo of Jeri
and Lynn
*Jeralyn, Jeralynn, Jerrilin,
Jerrilyn*

Jerin
(American) daring
*Jere, Jeren, Jeron, Jerinn,
Jerun*

Jeritah
(American) combo of Jeri
and Rita; presides
Jerita

Jermaine
(French) form of Germaine
*Germaine, Jermain, Jerman,
Jermane, Jermanee,
Jermani, Jermany, Jermayne*

Jerrett
(American) spirited
*Jerett, Jeriette, Jerre, Jerret,
Jerrette, Jerrie, Jerry*

Jerrica
(American) free spirit
Jerrika

Jerusha
(Hebrew) wealthy

Jesenia
(Spanish) witty
*Jesene, Jess, Jessenia,
Jessie, Jessie, Jisenia,
Yesenia*

Jessa
(American) spontaneous
Jessah

Jessalyn
(American) combo of
Jessica and Lynn; exciting
*Jesalin, Jesaline, Jesalyn,
Jesalyne, Jesalynn,
Jesalynne, Jesilin, Jesline,
Jesilyn, Jesilyne, Jesilynn,
Jeslin, Jeslyn, Jessaline,
Jessie, Jesslin*

Jessamine
(French) form of Jasmine;
sassy
*Jesamyn, Jess, Jessamin,
Jessamon, Jessamy,
Jessamyn, Jessemin,
Jessemine, Jessie,
Jessmine, Jessmon,
Jessmy, Jessmyn*

Jesse
(Hebrew) friendly
Jesie, Jessey, Jessi, Jessy

Jessenia
(Arabic) flowering
Jescenia, Jesenia

Jessica
(Hebrew) rich
*Jesica, Jess, Jessa, Jessie,
Jessika, Jessy, Jezika*

Jessie
(Scottish) casual
*Jescie, Jesey, Jess, Jesse,
Jessee, Jessi, Jessye*

Jessie-Mae
(American) combo of
Jessie and Mae; country
girl
*Jessee-May, Jessemay,
Jessie Mae, Jessie May,
Jessiemae, Jessmae*

Jessika
(Hebrew) rich
*Jesika, Jessieka, Jessika,
Jessyka, Jezika*

Jesusa
(Spanish) form of Jesus;
worships

Jesusita
(Spanish) little Jesus

Jett
(American) high-flying
Jettie, Jetty

Jetta
(English) black gem;
knowing
Jette, Jettie

Jette
(German, Scandinavian)
lovely gem
*Jet, Jeta, Jetia, Jetta, Jette,
Jettee, Jettie*

Jeudi
(French) born on Thursday

Jeune-Fille
(French) young girl

Jevae
(Spanish) desired
Jevaie, Jevay

Jevette
(American) combo of Jen
and Yvette; compromises
Jetta, Jeva, Jeveta, Jevetta

Jevonne
(African American) kind
*Jev, Jevaughan, Jevaughn,
Jevie, Jevon, Jevona,
Jevonn, Jevvy*

Jewel
(French) pretty
Jeul, Jewelia, Jewelie, Jewell, Jewelle, Jewels, Juel, Jule

Jewellene
(American) combo of Jewel and Lene; treasured
Jewelene, Jeweline, Jewels, Julene

Jezebel
(Hebrew) wanton woman
Jessabel, Jessebel, Jessebelle, Jez, Jezabel, Jezabella, Jezabelle, Jeze, Jezebell, Jezel, Jezell, Jezybel, Jezzie

Jezenya
(American) flowering
Jesenya, Jeze, Jezey

Jhamesha
(African American) lovely; soft
Jamesha, Jmesha

Jianna
(Italian) trusts in God
Jiana, Jianina, Jianine

Jilan
(American) mover
Jilyn, Jillan, Jillyn, Jylan, Jylann

Jill
(English) short for Jillian; high-energy and youthful
Jil, Jilee, Jilli, Jillie, Jilly

Jillaine
(Latin) young-hearted
Jilaine, Jilane, Jilayne, Jillana, Jillane, Jillann, Jillanne, Jillayne

Jilleen
(American) energetic
Jil, Jileen, Jilene, Jiline, Jill, Jillain, Jilline, Jlynn

Jillian
(Latin) youthful
Giliana, Jill, Jillaine, Jillana, Jillena, Jilliane, Jilliann, Jillie, Jillion, Jillione, Jilly, Jilyan

Jimi
(Hebrew) replaces; reliable
Jimae

Jimmi
(American) assured
Jim, Jimi, Jimice, Jayjay

Jin
(Chinese) golden; gem
Jinn, Jinny

Jina
(Italian) variant of Gina; winning
Jena, Jinae, Jinan, Jinda, Jinna, Jinnae

Jinger
(American) form of Ginger; go-getter
Jin, Jinge

Jinkie
(American) bouncy
Jinkee, Jynki, Jinky

Jinny
(Scottish) form of Jenny
Jin, Jina, Jinae, Jinelle, Jinessa, Jinna, Jinnae, Jinnalee, Jinnee, Jinney, Jinni, Jinnie

Jinte
(Hindi) patient

Jinx
(Latin) a spell
Jin, Jinks, Jinxie, Jinxy, Jynx

Jinxia
(Latin) form of Jinx; spellbinder
Jinx, Jynx, Jynxia

Jirina
(Czech) works the earth

Jnae
(American) darling
J'Nay, Jenae, Jnay, Jnaye

J'Netta
(American) form of
Jeanetta; sweetness
*J'netta, J'Nette, Janetta,
Janny*

J-Nyl
(American) flirtatious

Jo
(American) short for
Josephine; spunky
Joey, Jojo

Jo-Allene
(American) combo of Jo
and Allene; effervescent
*Jo Allene, Joallene, Joallie,
Joeallene, Joealli, Jolene*

Joan
(Hebrew) heroine; God-
loving
*Joane, Joane, Joani,
Joanie, Joanni, Joannie,
Jonie*

Joana
(Hebrew) kind
*Joanah, Joanna, Joannah,
Jonah*

Joanie
(Hebrew) kind
*Joanney, Joanni, Joannie,
Joanny, Joany, Joni*

Jo-Ann
(French) believer;
gregarious
*Joahnn, JoAn, JoAnn,
Joann, Joanna, Joanne, Jo-
Anne, Joannie*

Joanna
(English) kind
*Jo, Joana, Joandra,
Joananna, Joananne,
Joannah, Joeanna,
Johannah, Josie*

Joanne
(English) form of Joan;
excellent friend
*JoAnn, Joann, Jo-Ann,
JoAnne, Joeanne*

Joannie
(Hebrew) forgiving
*Joani, Joany, Joanney,
Joanni*

Joappa
(Origin unknown) noisy

Jobelle
(American) combo of Jo
and Belle; beautiful
*Jobel, Jobell, Jobi, Jobie,
Joebel*

Jobeth
(American) combo of Jo
and Beth; vivacious
*Beth, Bethie, Jo, Jobee,
Jobie, Joby*

Jobi
(Hebrew) misunderstood;
inventive
Jobee, Jobey, Jobie, Joby

Jobina
(Hebrew) hurting
*Jobey, Jobie, Joby, Jobye,
Jobyna*

Jo-Carol
(American) combo of Jo
and Carol; lively
Jo Carol, Jocarol, Jocarole

Jocasta
(Italian) light

Jocelyn
(Latin) joyful
*Jocelie, Jocelin, Jocelle,
Jocelyne, Jocelynn, Joci,
Joclyn, Joclynn, Jocylan,
Jocylen, Joycelyn*

Joci
(Latin) happy
*Jocee, Jocey, Jocie, Jocy,
Josi*

Jocklyn
(American) combo of Jock and Lyn; athletic
Jock, Joklyn

Jocosa
(Latin) laughs; jokes

Jodase
(American) brilliant
Jo, Jodace, Jodasse, Jodie, Jody

Jode
(American) from Jody; happy

Jo-Dee
(American) combo of Jo and Dee
Jo Dee, Jodee, Joedee

Jodee-Marie
(American) combo of Jodee and Marie
Jodeemarie, Jodymarie

Jodelle
(American) combo of Jo and Delle
Jodel, Jodell, Jodie, Jody

Jodie
(American) happy girl
Jo, Jodee, Jodey, Jodi, Jody

Jodiann
(American) combo of Jodi and Ann; wanted
Jodianna, Jodianne, Jodyann, Jodyanna, Jodyanne

Joedy
(American) jolly
Joedey, Joedi, Joedie

Joe-Leigh
(American) combo of Joe and Leigh; happy
Joe Leigh, Joel, Joelea, Joesey, Jolee, Joleigh, Jolie, Jollee, Jose, Joze

Joelle
(Hebrew) willing
Jo, Joel, Joela, Joele, Joelee, Joeleen, Joelene, Joeli, Joeline, Joell, Joella, Joelle, Joellen, Joelly

Joellen
(American) combo of Jo and Ellen; popular

Joely
(Hebrew) believer; lively
Jo, Joe, Joey

Joelly
(American) kindhearted
Joelee, Joeli, Joely

Joetta
(American) combo of Jo and Etta; creative
Jo, Joe, Joettah, Joette

Joey
(American) easygoing
Joe, Joeye

Joezee
(American) form of Josey; attractive
Jo, Joe, Joes, Joezey, Joezy

Johanna
(German) believer in a gracious God
Johana, Johanah, Johanna, Jonna

Johnay
(American) steadfast
Johnae, Jonay, Jonaye, Jonnay

Johnnessa
(American) combo of Johna and Nessa; restless
Jahnessa, Johnecia, Johnesha, Johnetra, Johnisha, Johnishi, Johnnise, Jonyssa

Johnette
(Hebrew) from John; believer

Johnica
(American) form of John; believer in a gracious God
Jonica

Johnna
(American) upright
Jahna, John, Johna, Johnae, Jonna, Jonnie

Johnnell
(American) happy
Johnelle, Jonell, Jonnel

Johnnetta
(American) joyful
Johneta, Johnete, Johnetta, Johnette, Jonetta, Jonette, Jonietta

Johnnisha
(African American) steady
Johnisha, Johnnita, Johnny, Jonnisha

Johnson
(Last name as first name) confident
Johns

Johntell
(African American) sweet
Johna, Johntal, Johntel, Johntelle, Jontell

Johntria
(Hebrew) believer

Johppa
(Origin unknown) different
Johppah

Joi
(Latin) joyful
Joicy, Joie, Jojo, Joy

Jo-Kiesha
(African American) vibrant
Joekiesha

Jola
(Greek) violet flower

Jolanda
(Latin, Italian) violet; pretty flower
Jola, Jolan, Jolana, Jolande, Jolander, Jolane, Jolanka, Jolantha, Jolanthe, Joli

Jolanta
(Greek) lovely girl

Jolene
(American) jolly
Jo, Joeleane, Joeleen, Joelene, Joelynn, Joleen, Joleene, Jolen, Jolena, Joley, Jolie, Joline, Jolyn, Jolynn

Joletta
(American) happy-go-lucky
Jaletta, Jolette, Joley, Joli, Jolie, Jolitta

Jolie
(French) pretty
Jo, Jole, Jolea, Jolee, Joleigh, Joley, Joli, Jollee, Jollie, Jolly, Joly

Jolienne
(American) pretty
Joliane, Jolianne, Jolien, Jolina, Joline

Joline
(English) blessed

Jolisa
(American) combo of Jo and Lisa; cheerful
Joelisa, Joleesa, Joli, Jo-Lisa, Jolise, Jolissa, Jolysa, Jolyssa, Lisa

Jolyane
(American) sweetheart
Joliane, Jollyane, Jolyan, Jolyann, Jolyanne

Jolynn
(American) combo of Jo and Lynn
Jo, Jolene, Joline, Jolinn, Jolyn, Jolynda, Jolyne

Jomaralee
(American) combo of Jo and Mara and Lee; country girl

Jonelle
(American) combo of Joan and Elle
Jahnel, Jahnell, Jahnelle, Jo, Johnel, Johnell, Johnelle, Jonel, Jonell, Jonnell, Jynel

Jones
(American) saucy

Joni
(American) short for Joan
Joanie, Jonie, Jony

Jonica
(American) sweet soul

Jonice
(American) casual
Joneece, Joneese, Jonni, Jonise

Jonina
(Hebrew) sweetheart
Jona, Jonika, Joniqua, Jonita, Jonnina

Jonita
(Hebrew) pretty little one
Janita, Jonati, Jonit, Jonite, Jonta, Jontae

Jonquill
(American) flower
Jonn, Jonque, Jonquie, Jonquil, Jonquille

Jontelle
(American) musical
Jahntelle, Jontaya, Jontel, Jontell, Jontelle, Jontia, Jontlyl

Joplin
(Last name as first name) wild girl

Jorah
(Hebrew) fresh as rain
Jora

Jo-Rain
(American) combo of Jo and Rain; zany
Jo Rain, Jorain, JoRaine

Jordan
(Hebrew) excellent descendant
Johrdon, Jordaine, Jordane, Jorden, Jordenne, Jordeyn, Jordi, Jordie, Jordin, Jordon, Jordyn, Jordynne, Joudane, Jourdan

Jordana
(Hebrew) smart; departs; lonely
Giordanna, Jordain, Jordana, Jordane, Jordann, Jordanna, Jordanne, Jordannuh, Jorden, Jordenne, Jordi, Jordin, Jordine, Jordon, Jordona, Jordonna, Jordyn, Jordyne, Jori, Jorie, Jourdana, Jourdann, Jourdanna, Jourdanne

Jordy
(American) quick
Jordee, Jordey, Jordi, Jordie, Jorey

Jorgina
(Spanish) nurturing
Jorge, Jorgine, Jorgy, Jorgie, Jorgi, Georgina, Georgeena

Jorie
(Hebrew) short for Jordan
Joree, Jorey, Jorhee, Jorhie, Jori, Jorre, Jorrey, Jorri, Jory

Joriann
(American) combo of Jori and Ann; desirable
Joriaana, Jorianne, Jorriann, Jorryann, Jorryanna, Jorryanne, Joryann, Joryanna, Joryanne

Jorja
(American) smart
*Georgia, Jorge, Jorgia,
Jorgie, Jorgy*

Jorunn
(American) loved by God

Joscelin
(Latin) happy girl
*Josceline, Joscelyn,
Joscelyne, Joscelynn,
Joscelynne, Joselin,
Joseline, Joselyn, Joselyne,
Joselynn, Joselynne,
Joshlyn*

Josee
(American) delights
*Joesee, Joesell, Joesette,
Joselle, Josette, Josey, Josi,
Josiane, Josiann, Josianne,
Josielina, Josina, Josy,
Jozee, Jozelle, Jozette,
Jozie*

Josefat
(Spanish) form of Joseph;
gracious
*Fata, Fina, Josef, Josefa,
Josefana, Josefenna,
Josefita, Joseva, Josey,
Josie*

Josefina
(Hebrew) fertile
Jose, Josephina, Josey, Josie

Joselyn
(German) pretty
*Josalene, Joselene,
Joseline, Josey, Josiline,
Josilyn, Joslyn, Josselen,
Josseline, Josselyne,
Josslyn, Josslynn, Josylynn*

Josephine
(French) blessed
*Fena, Fifi, Fina, Jo, Joes,
Josefina, Josephene, Josie,
Jozaphine*

Josette
(French) little Josephine

Josetta
(French) she trusts in God

Josey
(Hebrew, American) saucy
Josee, Josi, Josie, Jozie

Joshana
(American) combo of Jo
and Shana; striking
beauty
Joshanna

Joshlyn
(Latin) saved by God
*Joshalin, Joshalyn,
Joshalynn, Joshalynne,
Joshann, Joshanna,
Joshanne, Joshleen,
Joshlene, Joshlin, Joshline,
Joshlyne, Joshlynn,
Joshlynne*

Joshi
(Hebrew) God loves

Josiann
(American) combo of Josey
and Ann; prettiest one
*Josann, Josiane, Josianne,
Joseyann*

Josie
(American) thrills
*Josee, Josey, Josi, Josy,
Josye*

Josie-Mae
(American) combo of Josie
and Mae
Josee-Mae, Josiemae

Josilin
(Latin) form of Jocelyn;
God saved
*Josielina, Josiline, Josilyn,
Josilyne, Josilynn,
Josilynne, Joslin, Josline,
Joslyn, Joslyne, Joslynn,
Joslynne*

Joslyn
(Latin) jocular
*Joclyn, Joslene, Joslinn,
Josslin, Josslyn, Josslynn*

Josnelle
(American) combo of Josne and Nelle; admired

Jossalin
(Latin) form of Jocelyn; God saved
Jossaline, Jossalyn, Jossalynn, Jossalynne, Josseline, Jossellen, Jossellin, Jossellyn, Josselyn, Josselyne, Josselynn, Josselynne, Jossie, Josslin, Jossline, Josslyn, Josslyne, Josslynn, Josslynne

Jostin
(American) adorable
Josten, Jostun, Josty, Jostyn

Jour
(French) day

Jovannah
(Latin) regal
Jeovana, Jeovanna, Jouvan, Jouvanna, Jovan, Jovana, Jovanee, Jovani, Jovanie, Jovann, Jovanna, Jovanne, Jovannie, Jovena, Jovon, Jovonna, Jovonne, Jowanna

Jovi
(Latin) jovial

Jovita
(Latin) glad
Joveeda, Joveeta, Jovena, Joveta, Jovetta, Jovi, Jovida, Jovie, Jovina, Jo-Vita, Jovitta, Jovy

Jovonne
(American) combo of Jo and Yvonne; queenly
Javonne, Jovaughn, Jovon, Jovonnie

Jowannah
(American) happy
Jowanna, Jowanne, Jowonna

Joy
(Latin) joyful
Joi, Joie, Joya, Joye

Joyce
(Latin) joyous
Joice, Joy, Joycey, Joyci, Joycie, Joysel

Joyleen
(American) combo of Joy and Eileen; happy lady
Joyleena, Joylene, Joyline

Joylyn
(American) combo of Joy and Lyn; joyful girl
Joyleen, Joylene, Joylin, Joyline, Joylyne, Joylynn, Joylynne

Joyous
(American) joyful
Joy, Joyus

Joyslyn
(American) form of Jocelyn; cheery
Joycelyn, Joyslin, Joyslinn

Juanisha
(African American) delightful
Juanesha, Juaneshia, Juannisha

Juanita
(Spanish) believer in a gracious God; forgiving
Juan, Juana, Juaneta, Juanika, Juanna, Juanne, Juannie, Juanny, Wanita

Juba
(Hebrew) ram; strongwilled

Jubelka
(African American) jubilant
Jube, Jubi, Jubie

Jubilee
(Hebrew) jubilant
Jubalie

Jubini
(American) grateful; jubilant
Jubi, Jubine

Jucinda
(American) relishing life
Jucin, Jucindah, Jucinde

Judalon
(Hebrew) merry
*Judalonn, Juddalone,
Judelon*

Jude
(French) confident
Judea, Judee, Judde

Judit
(Hebrew) Jewish
Jude, Judi, Juditt

Judith
(Hebrew) woman worthy
of praise
*Judana, Jude, Judi, Judie,
Judine, Juditha, Judy,
Judyth, Judythe*

Judy
(Hebrew) short for Judith
*Judi, Judie, Joodie, Judye,
Jude*

Judyann
(American) combo of Judy
and Ann; old-fashioned
*Judiann, Judianna,
Judianne, Judyanna,
Judyanne*

Juel
(American) dependable
Jewel, Juelle, Juels, Jule, Juile

Jueta
(Scandinavian) from
Judith; praises God
Juetta, Juta

Juirl
(American) careful
Ju, Juirll

Juleen
(American) sensual
Jule, Julene, Jules

Jules
(American) brooding
Jewels, Juels

Julia
(Latin) forever young
*Jula, Juliann, Julica, Julina,
Juline, Julisa, Julissa, Julya,
Julyssa*

Julian
(Latin) effervescent
*Jewelian, Julean, Juliann,
Julien, Juliene, Julienn,
Julyun*

Juliana
(Italian, German, Spanish)
youthful
*Juleanna, Julianna,
Juliannah, Julie-Anna,
Jullyana*

Julianne
(American) combo of Julie
and Anne
Juleann, Jules, Julieann

Julie
(English) young and vocal
*Juel, Jule, Julee, Juli,
Juliene, Jullie, July, Julye*

Juliet
(Italian) loving

Juliette
(French) romantic
Julie, Jules, Juliet, Julietta

Julimarie
(American) combo of Juli
and Marie; young; alluring
*Joolimarie, Julie Marie,
Juliemarie, Julie-Marie*

Julissa
(Latin) universally loved
Jula, Julessa, Julisa, Julisha

Julita
(Spanish) adorable; young
Juli, Julitte

Juliza
(Latin) from Julia; pretty
Juluette
(American) adorable;
young
Jule, Jules, Julett, Julette,
Julie, Julu, Julue, Juluett,
Julu-Ette, LuLu
July
(Latin) month; warm
Jumoke
(African) most popular
Jun
(Chinese) honest
June
(Latin) born in June
Juneth, Junie, Junieth,
Juney, Juny
Junieth
(Latin) from the month
June; heavenly
Juney, Juni, Junie, Juniethe
Junko
(American) from June;
warmth
Juno
(Latin) queenly
Juna, June
Juqwanza
(African American) bouncy
Jukwanza, Juqwann,
Qwanza
Justice
(Latin) fair-minded
Just, Justise, Justy
Justika
(American) dancing-girl
Justeeka, Justica, Justie,
Justy
Justina
(Latin) honest
Jestena, Jestina, Justeena,
Justena, Justinna, Justyna

Justine
(Italian, Latin) fair-minded
Jestine, Justa, Juste,
Justean, Justeen, Justena,
Justene, Justi, Justie,
Justina, Justinn, Justinna,
Justy, Justyne, Justynn,
Justynne, Juzteen
Jutta
(American) ebullient
Juta
Juvelia
(Spanish) young
Juvee, Juvelle, Juvelya,
Juvie, Juvilia, Velia, Velya
Juwanne
(African American) lively
Juwan, Juwann, Juwanna,
Juwon, Jwanna, Jwanne
Jynx
(American) variant of Jinx;
bewitching

Kacey
(Irish) daring
Casey, Casie, K.C., K.Cee,
Kace, Kacee, Kaci, Kacy,
Kasey, Kasie, Kaycee,
Kaycie, Kaysie
Kachina
(Native American) sacred
dancer; doll-like
Kacia Cachina, Kachena,
Kachine

Kacia
(Greek) variant of Acacia; has thorns; moody
Kaycia, Kaysia

Kacondra
(African American) bold
Condra, Connie, Conny, Kacon, Kacond, Kaecondra, Kakondra, Kaycondra

Kaden
(American) charismatic
Caden, Kadenn

Kadenza
(Latin) cadence; dances
Cadenza, Kadena, Kadence

Kadie
(American) virtuous
Kadee

Kady
(English) sassy
Cady, K.D., Kadee, Kadie, Kaydie, Kaydy

Kaela
(Arabic) sweet
Kaelah, Kayla, Kaylah, Keyla, Keylah

Kaelin
(Irish) pure; impetuous
Kaelan, Kaelen, Kaelinn, Kaelyn, Kaelynn, Kaelynne, Kaylin

Kaelynn
(American) combo of Kae and Lynn; beloved
Kaelin, Kailyn, Kay-Lynn

Kai
(Hawaiian, African) attractive
Kaia

Kailah
(Greek) virtuous
Kail, Kala, Kalae, Kalah

Kailey
(American) spunky
Kalee, Kaili, Kailie, Kaylee, Kaylei

Kaitlin
(Irish) pure-hearted
Caitlin, Caitlyn, Kaitlan, Kaitland, Kaitlinn, Kaitlyn, Kaitlynn, Kalyn, Katelyn, Katelynn, Katelynne, Kathlin, Kathlinne, Kathlyn

Kala
(Hindi) black; royal

Kalani
(Hawaiian) leader
Kalauni, Kaloni, Kaylanie

Kalea
(Arabic) sweet
Kahlea, Kahleah, Kailea, Kaileah, Kallea, Kalleah, Kaylea, Kayleah, Khalea, Khaleah

Kalei
(American) sweetheart
Kahlei, Kailei, Kallei, Kaylei, Khalei

Kaleigh
(Sanskrit) energetic; dark
Kalea

Kalena
(Hawaiian) chaste
Kaleena

Kalet
(French) beautiful energy
Kalay, Kalaye

Kaley
(Sanskrit) energetic
Kalee, Kaleigh, Kalleigh

Kali
(Greek) beauty
Kala, Kalli

Kalidas
(Greek) most beautiful
Kaleedus, Kali

Kalila
(Arabic) sweet; lovable
*Cailey, Cailie, Caylie,
Kailey, Kaililah, Kaleah,
Kalela, Kalie, Kalilah, Kaly,
Kay, Kaykay, Kaylee,
Kayllie, Kyle, Kylila, Kylilah*

Kalina
(Hawaiian) unblemished
Kalinna, Kalynna

Kalinda
(Hindi) mythical
mountains; goal-oriented
*Kaleenda, Kalindi,
Kalynda, Kalyndi*

Kalisa
(American) combo of Kay
and Lisa; pretty and loving
*Caylisa, Kaleesa, Kalisha,
Kalyssa, Kaylisa, Kaykay*

Kallan
(American) loving
Kall, Kallen, Kallun

Kallie
(Greek) beautiful
*Callie, Kalley, Kali, Kalie,
Kally*

Kalliope
(Greek) beautiful voice
*Calli, Calliope, Kalli,
Kallyope*

Kallista
(Greek) pretty; bright-eyed
*Cala, Calesta, Calista,
Callie, Callista, Cally, Kala,
Kalesta, Kalista, Kalli,
Kallie, Kally, Kallysta,
Kalysta*

Kalyn
(Arabic) loved
*Calynn, Calynne, Kaelyn,
Kaelynn, Kalen, Kalin,
Kalinn, Kallyn*

Kama
(Sanskrit) beloved

Kamala
(Arabic) perfection
Kamalah

Kamaria
(African) moonlike
Kamara, Kamaarie

Kambria
(Latin) girl from Wales
*Kambra, Kambrie,
Kambriea, Kambry*

Kamea
(Hawaiian) adored
Kameo

Kameko
(Japanese) turtle girl;
hides

Kameron
(American) variant of
Cameron; crooked nose;
kind
Kamren, Kamrin, Kamron

Kami
(Japanese) perfect aura
Cami

Kamilah
(Hindi) desires
Kamila, Kamilla, Kamillah

Kamilia
(Polish) pure

Kama
(Sanskrit) beloved; Hindu
god of love
Kam, Kamie

Kamala
(American) interesting
*Camala, Kam, Kamali,
Kamilla, Kammy*

Kamea
(Hawaiian) precious darling
Cammi, Kam, Kammie

Kamela
(Italian) form of Camilla;
wonderful
Kam, Kamila, Kammy

Kameron
(American) spiritual
*Cam, Cameron, Cami,
Cammie, Kamreen, Kamrin*

Kami
(Italian) spiritual little one
*Cami, Cammie, Cammy,
Kammie, Kammy*

Kamilah
(North African) perfect

Kamilia
(Polish) perfect character
*Kam, Kamila, Kammy,
Milla*

Kamyra
(American) light
Kamera

Kanara
(Hebrew) tiny bird; lithe
Kanarit, Kanarra

Kanda
(Native American) magical

Kandace
(Greek) charming; glowing
*Candace, Candie, Candy,
Dacie, Kandace, Kandi,
Kandice, Kandiss, Kandy*

Kandi
(American) short for
Kandace
Candi, Kandie, Kandy

Kandra
(American) light
Candra

Kaneesha
(American) dark-skinned
*Caneesha, Kaneesh,
Kaneice, Kaneisha,
Kanesha, Kaneshia, Kaney,
Kanish, Nesha*

Kanesha
(African American)
spontaneous
*Kaneesha, Kaneeshia,
Kaneisha, Kanisha,
Kannesha*

Kanga
(Australian) short for
kangaroo; jumpy

Kanisha
(American) pretty
*Kaneesha, Kanicia,
Kenisha, Kinicia, Kinisha,
Koneesha*

Kannitha
(Vietnamese) angelic

Kansas
(Place name) U.S. state
Kanny

Kanya
(Hindi) virginal
Kania

Kaprece
(American) capricious
*Caprice, Kapp, Kappy,
Kapreece, Kapri, Kaprise,
Kapryce, Karpreese*

Kapuki
(African) first girl in the
family

Kara
(Danish, Greek) dearest
*Cara, Carina, Carita, Kar,
Karah, Kari, Karie, Karina,
Karine, Karita, Karrah,
Karrie, Kera*

Karalee
(Invented) combo of Kara
and Lee

Karalenae
(American) combo of Kara
and Lenae
Kara-Lenae, Karalenay

Karalynn
(American) combo of Kara
and Lynn; smiling
sweetness

Karbie
(American) energetic
Karbi, Karby

Karelle
(French) joyful singer
Carel, Carelle, Karel

Karen
(Greek, Irish) pure-hearted
*Caren, Carin, Caron,
Caronn, Carren, Carrin,
Carron, Carryn, Caryn,
Carynn, Carynne, Kare,
Kareen, Karenna, Kari,
Karin, Karina, Karna,
Karon, Karron, Karryn,
Karyn, Keren, Kerran,
Kerrin, Kerron, Kerrynn,
Keryn, Kerynne, Taran,
Taren, Taryn*

Karenz
(English) from Kerenza;
sweet girl
Karence, Karens, Karense

Kari
(Scandinavian) pure
Cari, Karri, Karrie, Karry

Karian
(American) daring
Kerian

Karianne
(American) combo of Kari
and Anne
*Kariane, Kariann, Kari-
Ann, Karianna, Kerianne*

Karida
(Arabic) pure
Kareeda, Karita

Karilynne
(American) combo of Kari
and Lynne
Cariliynn, Kariline, Karylynn

Karima
(Arabic) giving
*Kareema, Kareemah,
Kareima, Kareimah,
Karimah*

Karin
(Scandinavian) kind-
hearted
Karen, Karine, Karinne

Karina
(Russian) best of heart;
(Latin) even
*Kare, Karinda, Karine,
Karinna, Karrie, Karrina,
Karyna*

Karine
(Russian) pure
Kaarrine, Karryne, Karyne

Karise
(Greek) graceful woman
Karis, Karisse, Karyce

Karissa
(Greek) longsuffering
Carissa, Karessa, Karisa

Karizma
(African) hopeful
Karisma

Karla
(German) bright-eyed;
feminine form of Carl/Karl
*Carla, Karlah, Karlie,
Karlla, Karrla*

Karla-Faye
(American) combo of Karla
and Faye

Karleen
(American) combo of Karla
and Arleen; witty
Karlene, Karline, Karly

Karlotta
(German) from Charlotte;
pretty
*Karlota, Karlotte, Lotta,
Lottee, Lottey, Lottie*

Karly
(Latin, American) strong-
voiced
Carly, Karlee, Karlie, Karlye

Karma
    (Hindi) destined for good
    things
    Karm, Karmie, Karmy
Karmel
    (Hebrew) garden
    Carmel, Karmela, Karmelle
Karmen
    (Hebrew) loving songs
    Carmen, Karmin, Karmine
Karnesha
    (American) spicy
    Carnesha, Karnisha, Karny
Karolanne
    (American) combo of Karol
    and Anne
    *Karol, Karolan, Karolane,
    Karolann, Karolen*
Karolina
    (Polish) form of Charles
    *Karaline, Karalyn,
    Karalynna, Karalynne,
    Karla, Karleen, Karlen,
    Karlena, Karlene, Karli,
    Karlie, Karlina, Karlinka,
    Karo, Karolina, Karolline,
    Karolinka, Karolyn,
    Karolyna, Karolyne,
    Karolynn, Karolynne,
    Leena, Lina, Lyna*
Karoline
    (German) form of Karl
    *Kare, Karola, Karolah,
    Karolina, Lina*
Karolyn
    (American) friendly
    *Carolyn, Kara, Karal,
    Karalyn, Karilynne,
    Karolynn*
Karri
    (American) from Karen;
    pure
    Kari, Karie, Karrie, Karry

Karrington
    (Last name as first name)
    admired
    Carrington, Kare, Karring
Karyn
    (American) sweet
    Caren, Karen
Kasey
    (American) spirited
    *Casey, Kacey, Kasie,
    Kaysie*
Kasha
    (Greek) variant of
    Katherine; pure
Kashawna
    (American) combo of
    Kasha and Shawna;
    debater
    *Kashana, Kashawn,
    Kashonda, Kashonna*
Kashmir
    (Place name) a region
    near India and Pakistan;
    fertile
    *Cahmere, Cashmir, Kash,
    Kashmere*
Kashonda
    (African American)
    dramatic
    *Kashanda, Kashawnda
    Koshonda*
Kashondra
    (African American) bright
    *Kachanne, Kachaundra,
    Kachee, Kashandra,
    Kashawndra, Kashee,
    Kashon, Kashondrah,
    Kashondre, Kashun*
Kasi
    (American) form of Cassie;
    seer
    Kass, Kassi, Kassie
Kasia
    (Polish) pet form of
    Katarzyna

Kasmira
(Slavic) peacemaker
Kassandra
(Greek) capricious
*Cassandra, Kass,
Kasandra, Kassandrah,
Kassie*
Kassidy
(Irish) clever
*Cassidy, Cassir, Kasadee,
Kass, Kassie, Kassy,
Kassydi*
Kassie
(American) clever
Kassee, Kassi, Kassy
Kat
(American) outrageous
Cat
Kataniya
(Hebrew) little girl
Katarina
(Greek) pure
*Katareena, Katarena,
Katarinna, Kataryna,
Katerina, Katryna*
Katarzyna
(Origin unknown) creative
Katarzina
Katchen
(Greek) virtuous
Kat, Katshen
Katchi
(American) sassy
*Catshy, Cotchy, Kat, Kata,
Katchie, Kati, Katshi,
Katshie, Katshy, Katty,
Kotchee, Kotchi, Kotchie*
Kate
(Greek, Irish) pure-hearted
*Cait, Caitie, Cate, Catee,
Catey, Catie, Kait, Kaite,
Kaitlin, Katee, Katey,
Kathe, Kati, Katie, Katy,
Kay-Kay*

Katelyn
(Irish) pure-hearted
*Caitlin, Kaitlin, Kaitlynne,
Kat, Katelin, Katelynn,
Kate-Lynn, Katline, Katy*
Katera
(Origin unknown)
celebrant
Katara, Katura
Katharine
(Greek) powerful; pure
*Kat, Katharin, Katherin,
Katwin, Katherine, Kathy,
Kathyrn, Kaykay*
Kathlaya
(American) fashionable
Kathleen
(Irish) brilliant; unflawed
*Cathaleen, Cathaline,
Cathleen, Kathaleen,
Kathaleya, Kathaleyna,
Kathaline, Kathelina,
Katheline, Kathlene,
Kathlin, Kathline,
Kathlynn, Kathlyn, Kathie,
Kathy*
Kathryn
(English) powerful and pure
*Kathreena, Kathren,
Kathrene, Kathrin,
Kathrine, Kathryne*
Kathy
(English) pure;
(Irish) spunky
*Cathie, Cathy, Kath, Kathe,
Kathee, Kathey, Kathi,
Kathie*
Katia
(French) stylish
Kateeya, Kati, Katya
Katie
(English) lively
*Kat, Katy, Kay, Kaykay,
Kate, Kaytie*

Katina
(American) form of
Katrina; virtuous
Kat, Kateen, Kateena

Katlynn
(Greek) pure
Kat, Katlinn, Katlyn

Katrice
(American) graceful
*Katreese, Katrese, Katrie,
Katrisse, Katry*

Katrina
(German) melodious
*Catreena, Catreina,
Catrina, Kaitrina, Katreena,
Katreina, Katryna, Kay,
Ketreina, Ketrina, Ketryna*

Katrine
(German, Polish) pure
*Catrene, Kati, Katrene,
Katrinna, Kati*

Katy
(English) lively
*Cady, Katie, Kattee, Kattie,
Kaytee*

Kaulana
(Hawaiian) well-known girl
Kaula, Kauna, Kahuna

Kavinli
(American) form of Kevin;
eager
*Cavin, Kaven, Kavin,
Kavinlee, Kavinley, Kavinly*

Kavita
(Hindi) poem
Kaveta, Kavitah

Kay
(Greek, Latin) fun-loving
Cay, Caye, Kaye, Kaykay

Kaya
(Native American)
intelligent
Kaja, Kayia

Kaycie
(American) merrymaker
*CayCee, K.C., Kaycee,
Kayci, Kaysie*

Kayla
(Hebrew, Arabic) sweet
*Cala, Cayla, Caylie, Kala,
Kaela, Kaila, Kaylah,
Kaylyn, Keyla*

Kaylee
(American) open
*Cayley, Kaelie, Kaylea,
Kaylie, Kayleigh*

Kayleen
(Hebrew) sweet;
(American) combo of Kay
and Eileen
*Kaileen, Kalene, Kay,
Kaylean, Kayleene, Kaykay*

Kayley
(Irish) combo of Kay and
Lee; effervescent
*Caleigh, Cayleigh, Cayley,
Kaeleigh, Kailee, Kaileigh,
Kailey, Kaili, Kaleigh,
Kaley, Kaylea, Kaylee,
Kaylie, Kaylleigh, Kaylley*

Kaylin
(American) combo of Kay
and Lynn
*Kailyn, Kaylan, Kaylanne,
Kaylen, Kaylinn, Kaylyn,
Kaylynn, Kaylynne*

Kaylinda
(American) combo of Kae
and Linda
*Kaelinda, Kaelynda, Kay-
Linda*

Kaylon
(American) form of Caylin;
outgoing
Kay, Kaylen, Kaylun

Kaylon
(Hebrew) crowned
*Kaylan, Kayln, Kaylond,
Kaylon, Kalonn*

Keane
(American) keen
*Kanee, Keanie, Keany,
Keen*

Keanna
(American) curious
Keana, Keannah

Keara
(Irish) darkness
*Kearia, Kearra, Keera,
Keerra, Keira, Keirra, Kera,
Kiara, Kiarra, Kiera, Kierra*

Kearney
(Irish) winning
*Kearne, Kearni, KeKe,
Kerney*

Keekee
(American) dancing
Keakea, Kee-Kee

Keeley
(Irish) noisy
*Kealey, Kealy, Keeley,
Keeli, Keelia, Keelie, Keely,
Keighley, Keighly, Keili,
Keilie, Keylee, Keyley,
Keylie, Keylley, Keyllie*

Keena
(Irish) courageous
Keenya, Kina

Keenan
(Irish) small
Keanan, Keen, Keeny

Kefira
(Hebrew) lioness
*Kefeera, Kefeira, Kefirah,
Kefirra*

Kehohtee
(Invented) alternate
spelling for Quixote

Kei
(Japanese) respectful

Keidra
(American) form of
Kendra; aware
Kedra, Keydra

Keiki
(Hawaiian) child

Keiko
(Hawaiian) child of joy
Kei

Keila
(Hebrew) crowned
Keilah

Keilani
(Hawaiian) graceful leader
Kei, Lani, Lanie

Keira
(Irish) dark-skinned
Keera, Kera

Keisha
(American) dark-eyed
*Keasha, Keesha, Keeshah,
Keicia, Keishah, Keshia,
Keysha, Kicia*

Keishla
(American) dark

Keita
(Scottish) lives in the
forest
Keiti

Keitha
(Scottish) from the forest
Keithana

Kelby
(English) lives in a
farmhouse
*Kelbea, Kelbeigh, Kelbey,
Kellbie*

Kelda
(Scandinavian) spring of
youth
Kellda

Kelila
(Hebrew) regal woman
*Kayla, Kayle, Kaylee,
Kelula, Kelulah, Kelulla,
Kelylah, Kyla, Kyle*

Keller
(Irish) daring
Kellers

Kelley
(Irish) brave
Keli, Kellie, Kelly, Kellye

Kellyn
(Irish) brave heart
Kelleen, Kellen, Kellene, Kellina, Kelline, Kellynn, Kellynne

Kelsey
(Scottish) opinionated
Kelcey, Kelcie, Kelcy, Kellsey, Kellsie, Kelsea, Kelsee, Kelseigh, Kelsi, Kelsie, Kelsy

Kember
(American) zany
Kem, Kemmie, Kimber

Kemella
(American) self-assured
Kemele, Kemellah, Kemelle

Kempley
(English) from a meadowland; rascal
Kemplea, Kempleigh, Kemplie, Kemply

Kenda
(English) aware
Kendi, Kendie, Kendy, Kennda, Kenndi, Kenndie, Kenndy

Kendall
(English) quiet
Kendahl, Kendal, Kendell, Kendelle, Kendie, Kendylle

Kendra
(American) ingenious
Ken, Kendrah, Kenna, Kennie, Kindra, Kinna, Kyndra

Keneisha
(American) combo of Ken and Aisha
Kaneesha, Kenesha, Kenisha, Kennie, Kaykay

Kenia
(African) giving; from the place name Kenya
Ken, Keneah

Kenna
(English) brilliant
Kenina, Kennah, Kennina, Kennette, Kynna

Kennae
(Irish) form of Ken; attractive
Kenae, Kenah

Kennedy
(Irish) formidable
Kennedie, Kenny

Kennice
(English) beauty
Kanice, Keneese, Kenese, Kennise

Kensington
(English) brash
Kensingtyn

Kentucky
(Place name) U.S. state
Kentuckie

Kenya
(Place name) country in Africa
Kenia, Kennya

Kenyatta
(African) from Kenya

Kenzie
(Scottish) pretty
Kensey, Kinsey

Keoshawn
(African American) clever
Keosh, Keoshaun

Kerdonna
(African American) loquacious
Donna, Kerdy, Kirdonna, Kyrdonna

Kerensa
(English) lovable
Karensa, Karenza, Kerenza

Kerra
(American) bright
Cara, Carrah, Kara, Kerrah

Kerry
(Irish) dark-haired
*Carrie, Kari, Kera, Keree,
Keri, Kerrey, Kerri, Kerria,
Kerridana, Kerrie*

Kerstin
(Scandinavian) a Christian
Kersten, Kerston, Kerstyn

Kerthia
(American) giving
*Kerth, Kerthea, Kerthi,
Kerthy*

Kesha
(American) laughing
Kecia, Kesa, Keshah

Keshia
(American) bouncy
*Kecia, Keishia, Keschia,
Kesia, Kesiah, Kessiah*

Keshon
(African American) happy
*Keshann, Keshaun,
Keshonn, Keshun,
Keshawn*

Keshondra
(African American) joy-
filled
*Keshaundra, Keshondrah,
Keshundra, Keshundrea,
Keshundria, Keshy*

Keshonna
(African American) happy
*Keshanna, Keshauna,
Keshaunna, Keshawna,
Keshona, Keshonna*

Kesi
(African) baby born in
hard times

Kessie
(African) fat baby cheeks
*Kess, Kessa, Kesse,
Kessey, Kessi, Kessia,
Kessiah*

Keturah
(African) long-suffering
Katura, Ketura

Kevine
(Irish) lively
*Kevina, Kevinne, Kevyn,
Kevynn, Kevynne*

Kevyn
(Irish) variant of Kevin;
lovely face
*Keva, Kevan, Kevina,
Kevone, Kevonna, Kevynn*

Keydy
(American) knowing
Keydee, Keydi, Keydie

Keyonna
(African American)
energetic

Keyshawn
(American) lively
*Keyshan, Keyshann,
Keyshaun, Keyshaunna,
Keyshon, Keyshona,
Keshonna, Keykey, Kiki*

Kezia
(Hebrew) from Cassis;
cinnamon; spicy
*Kazia, Kessie, Kessy,
Ketzia, Ketziah, Keziah,
Kezzie, Kissie, Kizzie, Kizzy*

Khadijah
(Arabic) sweetheart
*Kadija, Kadiya, Khadiya,
Khadyja*

Khai
(American) unusual
Ki, Kie

Khaki
(American) personality-
plus
*Kakee, Kaki, Kakie,
Khakee, Khakie*

Khali
(Origin unknown) lively
Khalee, Khalie, Koli, Kollie

Khalida
(Hindi) eternal
Khali, Khalia, Khalita

Khiana
(American) different
*Kheana, Khianah,
Khianna, Ki, Kianah,
Kianna, Kiannah*

Ki
(Korean) born again

Kia
(American) short for Kiana
Keeah, Kiah

Kiana
(American) graceful
*Kia, Kiah, Kianna,
Kiannah, Quiana, Quianna*

Kiara
(Irish) dark-skinned
*Chiara, Chiarra, Keearah,
Keearra, Kiarra*

Kibibi
(African) small girl

Kidre
(American) loyal
Kidrea, Kidrey, Kidri

Kiele
(Hawaiian) aromatic
flower; gardenia
*Kiela, Kieley, Kieli, Kielli,
Kielly*

Kienalle
(American) light
Kieana, Kienall, Kieny

Kienna
(Origin unknown) brash
Kiennah, Kienne

Kiera
(Irish) dark-skinned
Keara, Keera, Kierra

Kiersten
(Greek) blessed
*Kerston, Kierstin, Kierstn,
Kierstynn, Kirst, Kirsten,
Kirstie, Kirstin, Kirsty*

Kiki
(Spanish, American)
vivacious
Keiki, Ki, Kiekie, Kikee

Kiko
(Japanese) lively
Kiki, Kikoh

Kiku
(Japanese) flower (mum)
Kiko

Kiley
(Irish) pretty
*Kilea, Kilee, Kili, Kylee,
Kyley, Kylie*

Kim
(Vietnamese) sharp
Kimey, Kimmi, Kimmy, Kym

Kimana
(American) from Kim;
meadow girl; outdoors-
loving

Kimberlin
(American) combo of
Kimberly and Lin
*Kimberlinn, Kimberlyn,
Kimberlynn*

Kimberly
(English) leader
*Kim, Kimber-Lea,
Kimberlee, Kimberleigh,
Kimberley, Kimberli,
Kimberlie, Kimmy,
Kymberly, Kimmie*

Kimbrell
(African American) smiling
*Kim, Kimbree, Kimbrel,
Kimbrele, Kimby, Kimmy*

Kimeo
(American) form of Kim;
happy
Kim, Kime, Kimi

Kimetha
(American) form of Kim;
happy
Kimeth

Kimi
(Japanese) spiritual
Kimone
(Origin unknown) darling
Kimonne, Kymone
Kina
(Hawaiian) girl from China
Kineisha
(American) form of
Keneisha
*Keneesha, Keneisha,
Kineasha, Kinesha,
Kineshia, Kiness, Kinisha,
Kinnisha, Kinny*
Kineta
(Greek) energetic
Kinetta
Kinsey
(English) child
*Kensey, Kinnsee, Kinnsey,
Kinnsie, Kinsee, Kinsey,
Kinsie, Kinzee*
Kinsley
(Origin unknown) familiar
*Kingslea, Kingslee,
Kingslie, Kinslea, Kinslee,
Kinslie, Kinsly, Kinzlea,
Kinzlee, Kinzley, Kinzly*
Kintra
(American) joyous
Kentra, Kint, Kintrey
Kinza
(American) relative
Kioko
(Japanese) happy baby
Kiyo, Kiyoko
Kiona
(Native American) girl
from the hill
Kipling
(Last name as first name)
energetic
Kiplin

Kira
(Russian) sunny; light-
hearted
*Keera, Kera, Kiera, Kierra,
Kiria, Kiriah, Kirya, Kirra*
Kiran
(Irish) pretty
Kiara, Kiaran, Kira, Kiri
Kirby
(Anglo-Saxon) right
Kirbee, Kirbey, Kirbie
Kirima
(Eskimo) hill child; high
aspirations
Kirsta
(Scandinavian) Christian
Kirsten
(Scandinavian, Greek)
spiritual
*Karsten, Keerstin, Keirstin,
Kersten, Kerstin, Kiersten,
Kierstin, Kiersynn, Kirsteen,
Kirstene, Kirsti, Kirstie,
Kirstin, Kirston, Kirsty,
Kirstynn, Kristen, Kristin,
Kristyn, Krystene, Krystin*
Kirstie
(Scandinavian)
irrepressable
Kerstie, Kirstee, Kirsty
Kisha
(Russian) ingenious
Keshah
Kishi
(Japanese) eternal
Kismet
(Hindi) destiny; fate
Kismat, Kismete, Kismett
Kissa
(African) a baby born after
twins
Kit
(American) strong
Kitt
Kita
(Japanese) northerner

Kithos
(Greek) worthy

Kitty
(Greek, American) flirty
Kit, Kittee, Kittey, Kitti, Kittie

Kiva
(Origin unknown) bright
Keva

Kiwa
(Origin unknown) lively
Kiewah, Kiwah

Kiya
(Australian) from the name Kylie; always returning; pretty girl
Kya

Kizzie
(African) energetic
Kissee, Kissie, Kiz, Kizzee, Kizzi, Kizzie, Kizzy

Klara
(Hungarian) bright
Klari, Klarice, Klarika, Klarissa, Klarisza, Klaryssa

Klarissa
(German) bright-minded
Clarissa, Klarisa, Klarise

Klarybel
(Polish) beauty
Klaribel, Klaribelle

Klaudia
(Polish) lame

Klea
(American) bold
Clea, Kleah, Kleea, Kleeah

Klementina
(Polish) forgiving
Clemence, Clementine, Klementine, Klementyna

Kleta
(Greek) form of Cleopatra; noble-born; temptress
Cleta

Klotild
(Hungarian) famous
Klothild, Klothilda, Klothilde, Klotilda, Klotilde

Kobi
(American) California girl
Cobi, Kobe

Koffi
(African) Friday-born
Kaffe, Kaffi, Koffe, Koffie

Kogan
(Last name as first name) self-assured
Kogann, Kogen, Kogey, Kogi

Koko
(Japanese) the stork comes

Kona
(Hawaiian) feminine
Koni, Konia

Konstance
(Latin) loyal
Constance, Kon, Konnie, Konstanze, Stanze

Kora
(Greek) practical
Cora, Koko, Korey, Kori

Kori
(Greek) little girl; popular
Cori, Corrie, Koree, Korey, Kory

Korina
(Greek) strong-willed; (German) small girl
Corinna, Koreena, Korena, Korinna, Koryna

Kornelia
(Latin) straight-laced
Cornelia, Kornelya, Korney, Korni, Kornie

Kortney
(American, French) dignified
Courtney, Kortnee, Kortni, Kourtney, Kourtnie

Koshatta
(Native American) form of
Coushatta; diligent
*Coushatta, Kosha, Koshat,
Koshatte, Koshee, Koshi,
Koshie, Koushatta*

Kosta
(Latin) from Constance;
steady
Kostia, Kostusha, Kostya

Koto
(Japanese) harp; musical

Krenie
(American) capable
*Kren, Kreni, Krenn,
Krennie, Kreny*

Kris
(American) short for
Kristina
Kaykay, Krissie, Krissy

Krishen
(American) talkative
*Crishen, Kris, Krish,
Krishon*

Krissy
(American) friendly
Kris, Krisie, Krissey, Krissi

Krista
(German) short for
Christina
Khrista, Krysta

Kristalee
(American) combo of
Krista and Lee
*Kristalea, Krista-Lee,
Kristaleigh*

Kristen
(Greek) Christ's follower;
(German) bright-eyed
*Christen, Cristen, Kristin,
Kristyn*

Kristian
(Greek) Christian woman
*Kristiana, Kristianne,
Kristyanna*

Kristie
(American) saucy
Christi, Christy, Kristi

Kristin
(Scandinavian) high-energy
Kristen, Kristyne

Kristina
(Greek) anointed;
(Scandinavian) Christ's
follower
*Christina, Krista, Kristie,
Krysteena, Tina*

Kristine
(Swedish) Christ's follower
*Christine, Kristee,
Kristene, Kristi, Kristy*

Kristy
(American) short for
Kristine
Kristi, Kristie

Krysta
(Polish) clear
Chrsta, Krista

Krystal
(American) clear and
brilliant
*Cristalle, Cristel, Crysta,
Crystal, Crystalle,
Khristalle, Khristel,
Khrystle, Khrystalle,
Kristel, Kristle, Krys,
Krystalle, Krystalline,
Krystelle, Krystie, Krystle,
Krystylle*

Krystalee
(American) combo of
Krystal and Lee; seeks
clarity
*Kristalea, Kristaleah,
Kristalee, Krystalea,
Krystaleah, Krystlea,
Krystleah, Krystlee,
Krystlea, Krystleleah,
Krystlelee*

Krystalynn
(American) combo of
Krystal and Lynn; clear-
eyed
*Krystaleen, Krystalina,
Kristaline, Kristalyn,
Kristalynn, Kristilyn,
Kristilynn, Kristlyn,
Krystalin, Krystalyn*

Krystyna
(Polish) Christian

Kumiko
(Japanese) long hair in
braids
Kumi

Kurrsten
(Scandinavian, Greek)
form of Kirsten; spiritual
Kurrst, Kurst, Kurstie

Kyla
(Irish) pretty
Kiela, Kila, Ky

Kyle
(Irish) pretty
*Kyall, Kyel, Kylee, Kylie,
Kyll*

Kylee
(Australian, Irish) pretty
*Kielie, Kiely, Kiley, Kye,
Kyky, Kyleigh, Kylie*

Kylene
(American) cute
Kyline

Kylie
(Irish) graceful
*Keyely, Kilea, Kiley, Kylee,
Kyley*

Kylynne
(American) fashionable
Kilenne, Kilynn, Kyly

Kym
(American) favorite
*Kim, Kymm, Kymmi,
Kymmie, Kymy*

Kynthia
(Greek) goddess of the
moon
Cinthia, Cynthia

Kyoko
(Japanese) sees herself in
a mirror

Kyra
(Greek) feminine
*Kaira, Keera, Keira, Kira,
Kyrah, Kyreena, Kyrene,
Kyrha, Kyria, Kyrie, Kyrina,
Kyrra, Kyry*

Kyria
(Greek) form of Kyra;
ladylike
Kyrea, Kyree, Kyrie, Kyry

L

Labe
(American) slow-moving
Labie

Lace
(American) delicate
*Lacee, Lacey, Laci, Lacie,
Lase*

Lacey
(Greek) cheery
Lacee, Laci, Lacie, Lacy

Lachelle
(African American)
sweetheart
*Lachel, Lachell, Laschell,
Lashelle*

Lachesis
(Mythological) one of the Greek Fates; the measurer

Lachina
(African American) fragile

Lacole
(American) sly
Lucole

Lacreta
(Spanish) form of Lacretia; efficient
Lacrete, LaLa

Lacretia
(Latin) efficient
Lacracia, Lacrecia, Lacrisha, Lacy

LaDaune
(African American) the dawn
Ladaune, LaDawn

Ladda
(American) open
Lada

Ladonna
(American) combo of La and Donna; beautiful
Ladona, LaDonna

Lady
(American) feminine
Ladee, Ladie

Ladrenda
(African American) cagy
Ladee, Ladey, Ladren, Ladrende, Lady

Laela
(Hebrew) variation of Leila; dark

Laetitia
(Latin) joy
Leticia, Lateaciah, Lateacya, Latycia, Letisia, Letyziah

Lafonde
(American) combo of La and Fonde; fond

Laguna
(Place name) Laguna Beach, California; water-loving
Lagunah

Laila
(Scandinavian) dark beauty
Laili, Laleh, Layla, Laylah, Leila

Lainil
(American) soft-hearted
Lainie, Lanel, Lanelle

Lajean
(French) soothing; steadfast
L'Jean, LaJean, Lajeanne

Lajuana
(American) combo of La and Juana
Lajuana, Lala, Lawanna

Lake
(Astrology) graceful dancer

Lakeisha
(African American) the favorite; combo of La and Keisha

Lakela
(Hawaiian) feminine
Lakla

Lakesha
(African American) favored
Keishia, Lakaisha, Lakeesha, Lakeishah, Lakezia, Lakisha

Lakya
(Hindi) born on Thursday

Lala
(Slavic) pretty flower girl; tulip

Lalage
(Greek) talkative
Lal, Lallie, Lally

Lalaney
(American) form of Hawaiian name Leilani; celestial
Lala, Lalanee, Lalani

Laleema
(Spanish) devoted
Lalema, Lalima

Lalita
(Sanskrit) charmer
Lai, Lala, Lali, Lalitah, Lalite, Lalitte

Lally
(English) babbling
Lalli

Lalya
(Latin) eloquent
Lalia, Lall, Lalyah

Lamarian
(American) conflicted
Lamare, Lamarean

Lamia
(Egyptian) calm
Lami

Lamika
(African American) variant of Tamika; calm

L'Amour
(French) love
Amor, Amour, Lamore, Lamour, Lamoura

Lana
(Latin) pretty; peacemaker
Lan, Lanna, Lanny

Lanai
(Hawaiian) heavenly
Lenai

Land
(American) word as name; confident
Landd

Landa
(American) blonde beauty
Landah

Landry
(American) leader
Landa, Landree

Landy
(American) confident
Land, Landee, Landey, Landi

Lane
(Last name as first name) precocious
Laine, Lainey, Laney, Lanie, Layne, Laynie

Lanee
(Asian) graceful

LaNiece
(Invented) form of Lenice

Lanette
(American) healthy
La-Net, LaNett, LaNette

Langley
(American) special
Langlee, Langli, Langlie, Langly

Lani
(Hawaiian) short for Leilani
Lannie

Lansing
(Place name) hopeful
Lanseng

Lantana
(Botanical) flowering
Lantanna

Laquanna
(African American) outspoken
Kwanna, LaQuanna, LaQwana, Quanna

Laquisha
(American) combo of La and Quisha; a happy life

Laquita
(American) combo of La and Queta; fifth
Laqueta, Laquetta

Lara
(Russian) lovely

Laraine
(Latin) pretty
Lareine, Larene, Loraine

Larby
(American) form of Darby;
pretty
*Larbee, Larbey, Larbi,
Larbie*

Larch
(American) full of life

Lareina
(Greek) seagull; flies over
water
*Larayna, Larayne, Lareine,
Larena, Larrayna, Larreina*

Larhonda
(African American) combo
of La and Rhonda; flashy
LaRhonda, Laronda

Larinda
(American) smart
Lare, Larin, Larine, Lorinda

Larissa
(Latin) giving cheer
Laressa, Larisse, Laryssa

Lark
(American) pretty
Larke

Larkin
(American) pretty
Larken, Larkun

Larkspur
(Botanical) tall and stately

Larrie
(American) tomboyish
Larry

LaRue
(American) combo of La
and Rue
Laroo, Larue

Larsen
(Scandinavian) laurel-
crowned
Larson, Larssen, Larsson

Lasha
(Spanish) forlorn
Lash, Lass

Lashanda
(American) brassy
*Lala, Lasha, LaShanda,
LaShounda*

Lashauna
(American) happy
*Lashona, Leshauna,
Lashawna*

LaShea
(American) sparkling
Lashay, La-Shea, Lashea

Lashonda
(American) combo of La
and Shonda; the grace of
God

Lashoun
(African American) content
*Lashaun, Lashawn,
Lashown*

Lassie
(American) lass
Lass

Lata
(Hindi) lovely vine;
entwines

Latanya
(African American) combo
of La and Tanya; the queen

Latasha
(American) combo of La
and Tasha; born on
Christmas Day
*Latacha, LaTasha,
Latayshah, Latisha*

LaTeasa
(Spanish) tease
*Latea, Lateasa, LaTease,
LaTeese*

Lateefah
(Arabic, African, Hebrew)
kind queen
*Lateefa, Latifa, Latifah,
Lotifah, Tifa, Tifah*

Latesha
(Latin, American) joyful
Lateesha, Lateisha, Lateshah, Laticia, Latisha

Latifah
(Muslim) gentle
Lateefa, Latifa, Latiffe, Latifuh

Lathenia
(American) verbose
Lathene, Lathey

Latisehsha
(African American) happy; talkative
Lati, Latise, Latiseh, Latisha

Latona
(Latin) goddess

Latonia
(African American) rich
Latone, Latonea

Latosha
(African American) happy

Latoya
(American) combo of La and Toya
LaToya, Lata, Toy, Toya, Toyah

Latreece
(American) go-getter
Latreese, Latrice, Letrice, Lettie, Letty

Latrelle
(American) laughing
Lettie, Letrel, Letrelle, Litrelle

Latrice
(Latin) noble
Latreece, Latreese

Latricia
(American) happy
Latrecia, Latreesha, Latrisha, Latrishah

Latrisha
(African American) prissy
Latrishe

Lauda
(Latin) praised

Laudomia
(Italian) praiseworthy

Laufeia
(Scandinavian) thriving

Laura
(Latin) laurel-crowned; joyous
Lara, Lora

Laurain
(English) graceful

Laurann
(American) combo of Laura and Ann
Lauran, Laurana, Lauranna, Lauranne

Lauralee
(American) combo of Laura and Lee
Laura-Lee, Loralea, Loralee, Lorilee

Laureen
(American) old-fashioned
Laurie, Laurine, Loreen

Laurel
(American) flourishing; (Latin) graceful
Laurell, Lorel, Lorell, Laural, Laurell, Laurella, Laurelle, Lorel, Lorella, Lourelle

Lauren
(English, American) flowing
Laren, Laurene, Lauryn, Laryn, Loren

Laurencia
(Latin) crowned in laurels
Laurenciah, Laurens, Laurentana

Laurent
(French) graceful
Lorent, Laurente

Lauretta
(American) graceful
Laureta, Laurettah, Lauritta, Lauritte, Loretta

Laurette
(American) from Laura; graceful
Etta, Ette, Laure, Laurett, Lorette

Laurie
(English) careful
Lari, Lauri, Lori

Lauriann
(American) combo of Laurie and Ann
Laurian, Laurianne

Laurissaa
(Greek) pleased

Laveda
(Latin) pure
Lavella, Lavelle, Laveta, Lavetta, Lavette

Lavena
(French, Latin) purest woman
Lavi, Lavie, Lavina

Lavender
(Latin) pale purple flowers; peaceful

Laverne
(Latin) breath of spring
Lavern, Lavirne, Verna, Verne

Lavette
(Latin) pure; natural
Laveda, Lavede, Lavete, Lavett

Lavinia
(Latin) cleansed
Vin, Vina, Vinnie, Vinny

Lavina
(Latin) woman of Rome

Lavita
(American) charmer
Laveta, Lavitta, Lavitte

Lavinia
(Greek) ladylike
Lavenia

Lavonne
(American) combo of La and Yvonne
Lavaughan, Lavaughn, Lavon, Lavone, Lavonn, Lavonna, Lavonnah

Lawanda
(American) sassy
LaWanda, Lawonda

Layce
(American) spunky

Layla
(Arabic) dark
Laela, Laila, Lala, Laya, Laylah, Laylie, Leila

Layne
(French) from the meadow
Laine, Lainee, Lainey

Lea
(Hawaiian) goddess-like

Leaf
(Botanical) hip

Leah
(Hebrew) tired and burdened
Lea, Lee, Leeah, Leia, Lia

Leala
(French) steadfast

Leandra
(Greek) commanding as a lioness
Leandrea, Leanndra, Leeandra, Leedie

Leanna
(English) leaning
Leana, Leelee, Liana

Leanne
(English) sweet
Lean, Leann, Lee, Leelee, Lianne

Leanora
(Greek) light
Lenora, Lanora, Lanoriah

Leanore
(English, Greek) stately
Lanore

Leatrice
(American) charming
Leatrise

Lecia
(Latin) short for Leticia;
jubliation
*Leecia, Leesha, Lesha,
Lesia*

Leda
(Greek) feminine
Ledah, Lida, Lita

Lee
(English, American,
Chinese) light-footed
Lea, Leelee, Leigh

Leeanne
(English) combo of Lee
and Anne
*Lean, Leann, Lee Ann, Lee-
Ann, Leianne*

Leeannette
(Greek) form of Leandra;
lionine
*Leann, Lee Annette,
Leeanett, Lee-Annette,
Leiandra*

Leelee
(American, Slavic) short
for Leanne, Lena, Lisa,
Leona
Lee-Lee, Lele, Lelee

Leeline
(American) combo of Lee
and Line; pastural; loyal
*Lee, Leela, LeeLee,
Leelene*

Leena
(Latin) temptress
Lina, Lena

Leeo
(American) sunny
Leo

Leeza
(American) gorgeous
Leesa, Leeze, Liza, Lize

Legend
(American) memorable
Legen, Legende, Legund

Legia
(Spanish) bright
Legea

Lehava
(Hebrew) flaming

Lei
(Hawaiian) short for
Leilani
Leilei

Léi
(Chinese) open; truthful

Leigh
(English) light-footed
Lee, Leelee

Leila
(Arabic) beauty of the night
*Layla, Leela, Leilah, Lelah,
Leyla, Lila*

Leilani
(Hawaiian) heavenly girl
Lanie

Leith
(Scottish) from the river;
nature-loving
Leithe, Lethe

Lejoi
(French) joy
Joy, Lejoy

Leland
(American) special
Lelan, Lelande

Lelia
(Greek) articulate
Lee, Leelee

Lemuela
(Hebrew) loyal
*Lemuelah, Lemuella,
Lemuellah*

Lena
(Latin) siren
Leena, Lenette, Lina
Lenesha
(African American) smiling
Leneisha, Lenisha, Lenni,
Lennie, Neshie
Lenice
(American) delightful
Lenisa, Lenise
Lenita
(Latin) gentle spirit
Leneeta, Leneta, Lineta
Lenna
(Hebrew) shy
Lenoa
(Greek) form of Lenore;
light
Len, Lenor, Lenora
Lenore
(Greek) a form of Eleanor;
radiant
Leoda
(German) popular
Leota
Leola
(Latin) fierce; lionine
Lee, Leo, Leole
Leona
(Greek, American) brave-
hearted
Liona
Leonarda
(German) lionhearted
Lenarda, Lenda, Lennarda,
Leonarde
Leondrea
(Greek) strong
Leondreah, Leondria
Leonie
(Latin) lionlike; fierce
Leola, Leonee, Leoni,
Leoney, Leontine, Leony

Leonora
(English) bright light
Leanor, Leanora, Leanore,
Lenora, Lenore, Leonore
Leonore
(Greek) glowing light
Lenore, Leonor, Leonora
Leonsio
(Spanish) form of
masculine name Leon;
fierce
Leo, Leonsee, Leonsi
Leopoldina
(Invented) form of
Leopold; brave
Dina, Leo, Leopolde,
Leopoldyna
Leora
(Greek) light-hearted
Liora, Leorah
Lera
(Russian) strong
Lerae, Lerie, Lira
Leretta
(American) form of Loretta
Lere, Lerie, Loretta
Lesley
(Scottish) strong-willed
Les, Lesle, Lesli, Leslie,
Lesly, Leslye, Lezlie
Leslie
(Scottish) fiesty; beautiful
and smart
Les, Lesli
Leta
(Latin) happy
Leeta, Lita
Letha
(Greek) ladylike
Litha
Leticia
(Latin, Spanish) joyful
woman
Letecia, Leticia, Letisha,
Letitia, Lettice, Lettie,
Letty, Tiesha

Letichel
(American) happy;
important
*Chel, Chelle, Leti, Letichell,
Letishell, Lettichelle,
Lettychel*

Leto
(Greek) mother of Apollo

Letsey
(American) form of Letty;
glad
Letsee, Letsy

Lettice
(American) sweet
Letty

Lettie
(Latin, Spanish) happy
Lettee, Letti, Letty, Lettye

Levana
(Hebrew) fair
Lev, Liv, Livana

Leverne
(French) grove of trees

Levina
(Latin) lightning

Levitt
(American) straightforward
Levit

Levity
(American) humorous

Levora
(American) home-loving
*Levorah, Levore, Livee,
Livie, Livora, Livore*

Lewana
(Hebrew) moon bright

Lexa
(American) cheerful
Lex, Lexah

Lexi
(Greek) helpful; sparkling
*Lex, Lexie, Lexsey, Lexsie,
Lexy*

Lexine
(Scottish) helper

Lexus
(American) rich
*Lexi, Lexorus, Lexsis,
Lexuss, Lexxus*

Lexy
(Scottish) helper

Leya
(Spanish) true blue

Lezena
(American) smiling
Lezene, Lezina, Lyzena

Li
(Chinese) plum

Lia
(Greek, Russian, Italian)
singular
Li, Liah

Lian
(Latin, Chinese) graceful
Leane, Leanne, Liane

Liana
(Greek) flowering;
complicated
Leanna, Lee, Liane

Lianne
(English) light
Leann, Leanne, Leeann

Libby
(Hebrew) short for
Elizabeth; bubbly
Lib, Libbi, Libbie

Liber
(American) from the word
liberty; free
Lib, Libby, Lyber

Liberty
(Latin) free and open
Lib, Libbie

Librada
(Spanish) free
Libra, Libradah

Lichelle
(American) combo of Li
and Chelle
Leshel, Leshelle, Licha, Lili

Licia
(Greek) outdoorsy
Lisha

Lida
(Greek) beloved girl
Leedah, Lyda

Lidia
(Greek) pleasant spirit
Lydia

Liese
(German) given to God

Liesel
(German) pretty
Leesel, Leezel

Lieselotte
(Hebrew, French)
charming woman; combo
of Elizabeth and Charlotte

Light
(American) light-hearted
Li, Lite

Ligia
(Greek) talented musician
Ligea, Lygia, Lygy

Liguria
(Greek) music lover

Likiana
(Invented) likeable
Like, Likia

Lila
(American) short for
Delilah, form of Leila;
(Arabic) playful
Lilah, Lyla, Lylah

Lila-Lynn
(American) combo of Lila
and Lynn; night-loving;
delight
*Lilalinn, Lilalyn, Lilalynn,
Lilalynne*

Lilac
(Botanical) tiny blossom
Lila

Lilakay
(American) combo of Lila
and Kay
*Lilaka, Lilakae, Lila-Kay,
Lilakaye, Lylakay*

Lileah
(Latin) lily-like
Lili, Liliah, Lill, Lily, Lilya

Lilette
(Latin) little lily; delicate
Lill, Lillette, Lillith, Lilly, Lilly

Lilia
(American) flowing
Lileah, Lyleah, Lylia

Lilian
(Latin) pure beauty

Liliana
(Italian) pretty
Lilianah, Lylianah

Lilias
(Hebrew) night
Lilas, Lillas, Lillias

Liliash
(Spanish) lily; innocent
*Lil, Lileah, Liliosa, Lilya,
Lyliase, Lylish*

Lilibert
(English) combo of Lili and
Bert; bubbly
Lilibeth, Lillibet, Lilybet

Lilith
(Arabic) nocturnal
*Lilis, Lilita, Lill, Lilli, Lillie,
Lillith, Lilly, Lilyth, Lilythe*

Lillian
(Latin) pretty as a lily
*Lila, Lileane, Lilian,
Liliane, Lill, Lilla, Lillah,
Lillie, Lillyan, Lillyann,
Lilyanne, Liyan*

Lillias
(Hebrew) night

Lillibeth
(American) combo of Lilli
and Beth; flower; lovely
girl
Lilibeth, Lillibethe, Lilybeth

Lily
(Latin, Chinese) elegant
Lil, Lili, Lilie

Limor
(Hebrew) myrrh; treasured
Leemor

Lin
(English, Chinese)
beautiful
Linn, Lynn

Lina
(Greek, Latin, Scottish)
light of spirit; lake calm
Lena, Lin, Linah, Lynn

Linda
(Spanish) pretty girl
Lind, Lindy, Lynda

Linden
(American) harmonious
*Lindan, Lindun, Lynden,
Lynnden*

Lindsay
(English, Scottish)
calming; bright and
shining
*Lindsee, Lindsey, Lindsi,
Lindz, Lyndsie, Lyndzee,
Lynz*

Lindse
(Spanish) form of Lindsey;
enthusiastic
Linds, Lindz, Lindze, Lyndzy

Lindy
(American) music-lover
*Lind, Lindee, Lindi, Lindie,
Linney, Linnie, Linse, Linz,
Linze*

Linette
(French, English, American)
graceful and airy
*Lanette, Linet, Linnet,
Lynette*

Lin-Lin
(Chinese) beauty of a
tinkling bell
Lin, Lin Lin

Ling
(Chinese) delicate

Linnea
(Swedish) statuesque
*Lin, Linayah, Linea,
Linnay, Linny, Lynnea*

Linsey
(English) bright spirit
Linsie, Linsy, Linzi, Linzie

Linzetta
(American) form of Linzey;
pretty
Linze, Linzette, Linzey

Liora
(Hebrew) light
Leeor, Leeora, Lior, Liorit

Lisa
(Hebrew, American)
dedicated and spiritual
*Lee, Leelee, Leesa, Leesah,
Leeza, Leisa, Lesa, Lysa*

Lisamarie
(American) combo of Lisa
and Marie
*Lisamaree, Lisa-Marie,
Lise-Marie, Lis-Maree*

Lisarae
(American) combo of Lisa
and Rae
Lisa-Rae, Lisa-Ray, Lisaray

Lisbeth
(Hebrew) short for
Elizabeth

Lise
(German) form of Lisa;
solemn
Lesa

Lisette
(French) little Elizabeth
Lise, Lisete, Lissette, Liz

Lisha
(Hebrew) short for Elisha;
dark
Lish, Lishie

Lissa
(Greek) sweet
Lyssa

Lissandra
(Greek) defends others

Lisseth
(Hebrew) form of
Elizabeth; devout
*Liseta, Liseth, Lisette,
Lisith, Liss, Lisse, Lissi*

Lissie
(American) short for Elise;
flowery
Lis, Lissi, Lissey, Lissy

Lita
(Latin) short for Carmelita;
life-giving
Leta

Liv
(Latin, Scandinavian)
lively
Leev

Livia
(Hebrew) lively
Levia, Livya

Livona
(Hebrew) vibrant
Levona, Liv, Livvie, Livvy

Liya
(Russian) lily; lovely
Leeya

Liz
(English) short for
Elizabeth; excitable
Lis, Lissy, Lizy, Lizzi, Lizzie

Liza
(American) smiling
*Leeza, Liz, Lizah, Lizzie,
Lizzy, Lyza*

Lizbeth
(American) combo of Liz
and Beth; devout
Liz Beth, Liz-Beth, Lizeth

Lizeth
(Hebrew) ebullient
Liseth, Lizethe

Lizette
(Hebrew) lively
Lizet, Lizett

Lizibeth
(American) combo of Lizi
and Beth
*Lizabeth, Liza-Beth, Lizzie,
Lizziebeth*

Lizzie
(American) devout
*Liz, Liza, Lizae, Lizette,
Lizzee, Lizzey, Lizzi, Lizzy*

Lo
(American) spunky
Loe

Loanna
(American) combo of Lo
and Anna; loving
Lo, Loann, Loanne, LoLo

Loelia
(Arabic) nocturnal
Leila

Logan
(English) climbing
Lo, Logun

Loibeth
(American) combo of Loy
and Beth; popular
*Beth, Loi, Loy Beth, Loy,
Loybeth, Loy-Beth*

Loicy
(American) delightful
*Loice, Loisee, Loisey, Loisi,
Loy, Loyce, Loycy, Loyse,
Loysie*

Loire
(Place name) river in
France; lovely wonder
Loir, Loirane

Lois
(Greek) good
Lo, Loes

Lojean
(American) combo of Lo
and Jean; bravehearted
Lojeanne

Lola
(Spanish) pensive
Lo, Lolah, Lolita

Loleen
(American) jubilant
Lolene

Lolita
(Spanish) sad
Lo, Lola, Loleta, Lita

Lolly
(English) candy; sweet

Lomita
(Spanish) good

Lona
(Latin) lionlike
*Lonee, Lonie, Lonna,
Lonnie*

Londa
(American) shy
Londah, Londe, Londy

London
(Place name) calming
*Londen, Londun, Londy,
Loney, Lony*

Loni
(American) beauty
Loney, Lonie, Lonnie, Loney

Lonnette
(American) pretty
*Lonett, Lonette, Lonnie,
Lonn*

Lora
(Latin) regal
Laura, Lorah, Lorea, Loria

Loranden
(American) ingenious
*Lorandyn, Lorannden,
Luranden*

Loreen
(American) variation on
Lauren
Lorene

Lorel
(German) tempting
Loreal

Lorelei
(German) siren
*Loralee, Lorilie, LoraLee,
Lurleen, Lurlene*

Lorelle
(American) lovely
*Lore, Loreee, Lorel, Lorey,
Lori, Lorie, Lorille, Lorel,
Lorille*

Loren
(American) form of
Lauren; picture-perfect
*Lorren, Lorri, Lorrie,
Lorron, Lorryn, Lory, Loryn,
Lourie*

Lorena
(English) photogenic
*Loreen, Lorene, Lorrie,
Lorrine*

Lorenza
(Latin) variant of Laura;
wears laurel wreath
Laurenza

Loretta
(English) large-eyed beauty
Lauretta

Lori
(Latin) laurel-crowned and
nature-loving
Laurie, Loree, Lorie, Lory

Lorinda
(American) combo of Lori
and Linda; gregarious
*Larinda, Lorenda, Lori,
Lorie*

Loris
(Greek, Latin) fun-loving
Lorice, Lauris

Lorna
(Latin) laurel-crowned;
natural
Lorenah

Lorola
(Origin unknown) family

Lorraine
(Latin, French) sad-eyed
*Laraine, Lauraine, Lorain,
Loraine, Lorrie, Lors*

Lotta
(Swedish) sweet

Lottie
(American) old-fashioned
Lottee, Lotti, Lotty

Lotus
(Greek) flowery
Lolo, Lotie

Lou
(American) short for
Louise
Loulou, Lu

Louella
(English) elf
*Loella, Loellah, Loelle,
Luella, Luela*

Louie
(American) strong

Louisa
(English) patient
*Lou, Loulou, Luisa, Luizza,
Lu*

Louise
(German) hardworking
and brave
Lolah, Lou, Loulou, Luise

Lourdes
(French) girl from Lourdes,
France; hallowed
Lourd, Lordes, Lordez

Lordyn
(American) enchanting
*Lorden, Lordin, Lordine,
Lordun, Lordynn*

Love
(English, American) loving
Lovey, Lovi, Luv

Loveada
(Spanish) loving
Lova, Lovada

Loveanna
(American) combo of Love
and Anna; loving
*Lovanna, Love-Anna,
Loveanne, Luvana,
Luvanna*

Lovejoy
(Invented) combo of Love
and Joy; jubliant

Lovella
(Native American) soft
spirit
Lovela

Lovely
(American) loving
*Lovelee, Loveley, Loveli,
Lovey*

Lovie
(American) warm
Lovee, Lovey, Lovi, Lovy

Lovina
(American) warm
*Lovena, Lovey, Lovinah,
Lovinnah*

Lowell
(American) lovely
Lowel

Lowena
(American) from Louise;
warrior
Lowenek, Lowenna

Loyalty
(American) loyal
Loyaltie

Luann
(Hebrew) combo of Lou
and Ann; happy girl
*Lou, Louann, Louanne,
Loulou, Luan, Luanne*

Luba
(Yiddish) dear
Liba, Lubah, Lyuba

Luberda
(Spanish) light; dear
Luberdia

Luca
(Italian) light
Luka

Lucasta
(Spanish) bringer of light

Luceil
(French) light; lucky
Luce, Lucee, Lucy

Lucerne
(Latin) born into the light
Lucerna

Lucero
(Italian) light-hearted
Lucee, Lucey, Lucy

Lucetta
(English) radiating joy

Lucette
(French) pale light

Lucia
(Italian, Greek, Spanish)
light; lucky in love
Chia, Luceah, Lucey, Lucey, Luci

Luciana
(Italian) fortunate
Louciana, Luceana, Lucianah

Lucie
(French, American) lucky
girl
Lucy

Lucienne
(French) lucky
Lucien, Lucianne, Lucienn, Lucy-Ann

Lucilla
(English) from Lucille;
bright
Loucilla, Loucilah, Loucilla, Lucilah, Lucylla, Lusyla, Luzela

Lucille
(English) bright-eyed
Loucil, Loucile, Loucille, Lucyl, Lucie, Lucile, Lucy

Lucina
(American) happy
Lucena, Lucie, Lucinah, Lucy, Lucyna

Lucinda
(Latin) prissy
Cinda, Cindie, Lu, Luceenda, Lucynda, Lulu

Lucita
(Spanish) light
Lusita, Luzita

Lucja
(Polish) light
Luscia

Luckette
(Invented) lucky
Luckett

Lucretia
(Latin) wealthy woman
Lu, Lucrecia, Lucreesha, Lucritia

Lucy
(Latin, Scottish, Spanish)
light-hearted
Lu, Luca, Luce, Luci, Lucie

Lucyann
(American) combo of Lucy
and Ann; gracious light
Luce, Luciana, Luciann, Lucianne, Lucy, Lucyan, Lucy-Ann, Lucyanne

Lucylynn
(American) combo of Lucy
and Lynn; light-hearted
Lucilyn, Lucylin, Lucy-Lynn

Ludivina
(Slavic) loved

Ludmilla
(Slavic) beloved one
Lu, Ludie, Ludmila, Ludmylla, Lule, Lulu

Lue-Ella
(English) combo of Lue and Ella; tough; assertive
Louel, Luella, Luelle

Luella
(German) conniving
Loella, Louella, Lu, Lula, Lulah, Lulu

Luenetter
(American) egotistical
Lou, Lu, Luene, Luenette

Luisa
(Spanish) smiling
Louisa

Luisana
(Place name) form of Louisiana; combative
Luisanna, Luisanne, Luisiana

Luke
(American) bouncy
Luc, Luka, Lukey, Lukie

Lula
(German) all-encompassing
Lulu

Lulani
(Polynesian) heaven-sent
Lula, Lani, Lanie

Lulu
(German, English) kind
Lou, Loulou, Lu, Lulie

Lulubell
(American) combo of Lulu and Bell; well-known
Bell, Bella, Belle, Lulu, Lulubel, Lulu-Bell, Lulubelle

Luminosa
(Spanish) luminous

Luna
(Latin) moonstruck
Loona

Lund
(German) genius
Lun, Lunde

Lundy
(Scottish) grove by an island
Lundea, Lundee, Lundi

Lundyn
(American) different
Lundan, Lunden, Lundon

Lupe
(Spanish) enthusiastic
Loopy, Loopey, Lupeta, Lupey, Lupie, Lupita

Luquitha
(African American) fond
Luquetha, Luquith

Lura
(American) loquacious
Loora, Lur, Lurah, Lurie

Lurajane
(American) combo of Lura and Jane; cuddly little one
Janie, Loorajane, Lura-Jane, Luri, Lurijane

Lurissa
(American) beguiling
Luresa, Luressa, Luris, Lurisa, Lurissah, Lurly

Lurlene
(German) tempting; (Scandinavian) bold
Lura, Lurleen, Lurlie, Lurline

Luvelle
(American) light
Luvee, Luvell, Luvey, Luvy

Luvy
(American) spontaneous
Lovey, Luv

Lux
(Latin) light
Luxe, Luxee, Luxi, Luxy

Luz
(Spanish) light-hearted
Lusa, Luzana, Luzi

Luzille
(Spanish) light
Luz, Luzell

Lyanne
(Greek) melodious
*Liann, Lianne, Lyan,
Lyana, Lyaneth, Lyann*

Lyawonda
(African American) friend
*Lyawunda, Lywanda,
Lywonda*

Lycoris
(Greek) twilight

Lydia
(Greek) musical; unusual
*Lidia, Lidya, Lyddie, Lydie,
Lydy*

Lyla
(French) island girl
Lila, Lilah, Lile

Lyle
(English) strident
Lile

Lymekia
(Greek) form of Lydia; royal
Lymekea

Lynda
(Spanish) beautiful
*Linda, Lindi, Lynde,
Lyndie, Lynn*

Lyndsay
(Scottish) bright and
shining
Lindsay, Lindsey

Lynelle
(English) pretty girl; bright
as sunshine
Linelle, Lynel, Lynie, Lynn

Lynette
(French) small and fresh
*Lyn, Lynet, Lynnet,
Lynette, Lynnie*

Lynn
(English) fresh as spring
water
*Lin, Linn, Linnie, Lyn,
Lynne*

Lynsey
(American) form of
Lindsay
*Linzie, Lyndsey, Lynze,
Lynzy*

Lyra
(Greek) musical
Lyre

Lyric
(Greek) musical
Lyrec

Lyris
(Greek) plays the lyre
Liris, Lirisa, Lirise

Lysa
(Hebrew) God-loving
Leesa, Lisa

Lysandra
(Greek) liberator; she
frees others
Lyse, Lysie

Lysanne
(Greek) helpful
Lysann

Lysett
(American) pretty little
one
Lyse, Lysette

Lyssan
(Greek) form of Alexandra;
supportive
*Liss, Lissan, Lissana,
Lissandra, Lyss*

Lytanisha
(African American)
scintillating
*Litanisha, Lyta, Lytanis,
Lytanish, Lytanishia, Nisa,
Nisha*

Mab
(Literature)
Shakespearean queen of
fairies

Mabel
(Latin) well-loved
*Mabbel, Mabil, Mable,
Mabyl, Maybel, Maybie*

Macallister
(Irish) confident

Macarena
(Spanish) name of a
dance; blessed
*Macarene, Macaria,
Macarria, Rena*

Macaria
(Spanish) blessed
*Maca, Macarea, Macarie,
Maka*

Macey
(American) upbeat; happy
Mace, Macie, Macy

Mackenzie
(Irish) leader
*Mac, Mackenzee,
Mackenzey, Mackenzi,
Mackenzie, Mackenzy,
Mackie, Mackinsey,
Mckenzie, McKinsey,
McKinzie*

Mada
(American) helpful
Madah, Maida

Madalena
(Greek) from Madeline;
jaunty
*Madalayna, Madaleyna,
Madelyna, Madelayna,
Madelena, Madeleyna*

Madalyn
(Greek) high goals
Madelyn

Madchen
(German) girl
*Madchan, Madchin,
Maddchen*

Maddie
(English) form of Madeline
*Mad, Maddee, Maddey,
Maddi, Maddy, Mady*

Maddox
(English) giving
*Maddax, Maddee, Maddey,
Maddie, Maddux, Maddy*

Madelcarmen
(American) combo of
Madel and Carmen; old-
fashioned
*Madel-Carmen,
Madlecarmen*

Madeleine
(French) high-minded
Madelon

Madeline
(Greek) strength-giving
*Madaleine, Maddie,
Maddy, Madelene, Madi*

Madelyn
(Greek) strong woman
*Madalyn, Madlynne,
Madolyn*

Madge
(Greek, American) spunky
Madgie, Madg

Madhur
(Hindi) sweet girl

Madina
(Greek) form of Madeline;
happy
*Mada, Maddelina, Maddi,
Maddy, Madele, Madena,
Madlin*

Madison
(English) good-hearted
*Maddie, Maddison,
Maddy, Madisen, Madysin*

Madonna
(Latin) my lady; spirited

Madora
(Place name) from
Madeira, Spain; volcanic
Madorra

Madrina
(Spanish) godmother
*Madra, Madreena,
Madrine*

Madrona
(Spanish) mother;
maternal
Madrena

Mae
(English) bright flower
May

Maegan
(Irish) a gem of a woman
Megan

MaElena
(Spanish) light
Elena, Lena

Maeli
(English) great; from Mae
*Maelee, Maeley, Maelie,
Maely, Maylee, Mayley,
Mayli, Maylie, Mayly*

Maeve
(Irish) queen
Maive, Mave, Mayve

Maezelma
(American) combo of Mae
and Zelma; practical
*Mae Zelma, Maez, Mae-
Zelma, Maezie, Mayzelma*

Magan
(Greek) heavy-hearted
Mag, Magen, Maggie

Magda
(Scandinavian) believer
Mag, Maggie

Magdala
(Greek) girl in the tower
Magdalla

Magdalene
(Greek, Scandinavian)
spiritual
*Mag, Magda, Magdalena,
Magdaline, Magdalyn,
Magdelin, Magdylena
Maggie*

Maggie
(Greek, English, Irish)
priceless pearl
Mag, Maggee, Maggi

Magina
(Russian) hard-working
Mageena, Maginah

Magnolia
(Botanical) flower;
(Latin) flowering and
flourishing
*Mag, Maggi, Maggie,
Maggy, Magnole, Nolie*

Magryta
(Slavic) desired

Mahal
(Filipino) loving woman
Mah, Maha

Mahala
(Hebrew, Native American)
tender female
*Mah, Mahalah, Mahalia,
Mahla, Mahlie*

Mahelia
(Arabic) from Mahala;
tenderness
*Maheelia, Maheelya,
Mahelya*

Mahina
(Hawaiian) moonbeam

Mahira
(Hebrew) vibrant
Mahogany
(Spanish) rich as wood
Mahagonie, Mahogony
Mahoney
(American) high energy
Mahhony, Mahonay,
Mahonie, Mahony
Mai
(Scandinavian, Japanese)
treasure; flower; singular
Mae, May
Maia
(Greek) fertile; earth
goddess
Maya, Mya
Maida
(Greek) shy girl
Mady, Maidie, May, Mayda
Maidie
(Scottish) maiden; virgin
Maidee, Maydee, Maydie
Mair
(Irish) from Mary; religious
Maire
Maira
(Hebrew) bitter; saved
Mara, Marah
Maired
(Irish) pearl; treasured
Mairead, Mared
Mairin
(Irish) from Mary; reverent
Maisie
(Scottish) treasure
Maesee, Maesey, Maesi,
Maesie, Maesy, Maisee,
Maisey, Maisi, Maisy,
Maizie, Mazee
Maitland
(American) variant of
Maitlyn; generous
Maitlande, Mateland,
Matelande, Maytland,
Maytlande

Maitlin
(American) variant of
Maitlyn; kind
Maitlyn, Matelin, Matelyn,
Maytlin, Maytlyn
Maja
(Scandinavian) fertile
Majidah
(Arabic) slendid
Makala
(Hawaiian) natural
outdoors
Makal, Makie
Makayla
(American) magical
Makaila, Makala, Michaela,
Mikaela, Mikayla, Mikaylah
Makyll
(American) innovative
Makell
Makynna
(American) friendly
Makenna, Makinna
Malak
(Arabic) angelic
Malay
(Place name) from
Malaysia; softspoken
Malae
Malaya
(Filipino) free and open
Malea
Malene
(Scandinavian) in the tower
Maleen, Maleene, Malyne
Malha
(Hebrew) queenlike and
regal
Mali
(Thai) flowering beauty
Malee, Maley, Mali, Malie,
Malley, Mallie, Maly
Malia
(Hawaiian) thoughtful
Maylia

Maliaval
(Hawaiian) peaceful
Malika
(Hungarian) hardworking
and punctual
Maleeka
Malin
(Native American)
comfort-giver
Malen, Maline, Mallie
Malina
(Scandinavian) in the tower
*Maleena, Maleenah,
Malinah, Malyna, Malynah*
Malinda
(Greek, American) honey
Melinda
Malissa
(American, Greek) combo
of May and Melissa; sweet
Melissa
Mallika
(Indian) watchful; tending
the garden
Malika
Mallory
(French, German,
American) tough-minded;
spunky
*Mal, Malery, Mallari,
Mallery, Mallie, Mallorey,
Mallori, Mallorie, Maloree,
Malorey, Malori, Malorie,
Malory*
Malu
(Hawaiian) peaceful
Maloo
Malvina
(Scottish) romantic
*Malv, Malva, Malvie,
Melvina*
Mame
(American) from Margaret;
pearl; treasured
Maime, Mayme

Mamie
(American) from Margaret;
little pearl; treasured
*Mamee, Mamey, Mami,
Mamy*
Mancie
(American) hopeful
Manci, Mansey, Mansie
Manda
(American) short for
Amanda; beloved
*Amand, Mandee, Mandi,
Mandy*
Mandy
(Latin) lovable
*Manda, Mandee, Mandey,
Mandi, Mandie*
Mandymay
(American) combo of
Mandy and May
*Mandeemae, Mandimae,
Mandimay, Mandymae*
Mane
(American) top
Main, Manie
Manee
(Korean) peace giving
Mani, Manie
Manilow
(Last name as first name)
musical
Manisha
(African) kind; (Hindi)
intelligent
Manju
(Hindi) sweetheart
Manna
(Hawaiian) perceptive
Mana, Manah, Mannah
Manon
(French) exciting
Mantill
(American) guarded
Mant, Mantell, Mantie

Manuela
(Spanish) sophisticated
girl
Manuella
Manzie
(Native American) flower
Mansi
Mara
(Greek) thoughtful believer
Marah, Marra
Marajayne
(American) combo of Mara
and Jayne; lively
*Mara Jayne, Marajane,
Mara-Jayne, Maryjayne*
Maranda
(Latin) wonderful
Marandah, Miranda
Marbella
(Spanish) pretty
Marb, Marbela, Marbelle
Marbury
(American) substantial
Mar, Marbary
Marcelina
(Latin) contentious
*Marceleena, Marcelyna,
Marcileena, Marcilina,
Marcilyna, Marcyleena*
Marceline
(Latin) argumentative
*Marceleene, Marcelyne,
Marcileene, Marcilyne,
Marcyleene*
Marcella
(Latin) combative
*Marce, Marcela, Marci,
Marcie, Marse, Marsella*
Marcelline
(French) pretty
*Marceline, Marcelyne,
Marcie, Marcy, Marcyline*

Marcellita
(Spanish) desired, feisty
*Marcel, Marcelita,
Marcelite, Marcelle,
Marcelli, Marcey, Marci*
Marcena
(Latin, American) spirited
*Marce, Marceen, Marcene,
Marcie*
Marcia
(Latin, American)
combative
Marcie, Marsha
Marcie
(English) chummy
*Marcee, Marcey, Marci,
Marcy, Marsi, Marsie*
Marcilyn
(American) combo of
Marci and Lyn; physical
*Marce, Marcie-Lyn, Marci-
Lyn, Marclinne, Marclyn,
Marcy, Mars, Marse,
Marslin, Marslyn*
Marcine
(American) bright
Marceen, Marceene
Marcy
(English, American)
opinionated
Marci, Marsie, Marsy
Mardonia
(American) approving
*Mardee, Mardi, Mardone,
Mardonne, Mardy*
Mare
(American) living by the
ocean
Maren
(American) ocean-lover
Marin, Marren, Marrin
Maret
(English) from Mary;
bittersweet
*Marett, Marit, Maritt,
Maryt, Marytt*

Marg
(American) tenacious
Mar

Margaret
(Greek, Scottish, English)
treasured pearl; pure-
spirited
*Mag, Maggie, Marg,
Margerite, Margie, Margo,
Margret, Meg, Meggie*

Margaretta
(Spanish) pearl

Margarita
(Italian, Spanish) winning
*Marg, Margarit, Margarite,
Margie, Margrita,
Marguerita*

Margarite
(Greek, German) pearl
*Gretal, Marga,
Margareeta, Margaryta,
Margereeta, Margerita,
Margeryta, Margit, Margot*

Margaux
(French) variant of
Margaret; treasure

Marge
(English, American) short
for Marjorie; easygoing
Marg, Margie

Margery
(English) pearl
Marge, Margie

Marghanita
(Spanish) pearl

Margherita
(Italian, Greek) treasured
pearl
Marg

Margia
(American) form of
Margie; friendly
Marge, Margea, Margy

Margie
(English) friendly
Margey, Margy, Marjie

Margina
(American) centered

Margoletta
(French) little Margo;
spunky

Margot
(French) lively
Margaux, Margo

Margrita
(Spanish) treasure
Margreeta, Margrytaa

Marguerite
(French) stuffy
*Maggie, Marg, Margerite,
Margie, Margina, Margurite*

Mari
(Japanese) ball; round

Maria
(Latin, French, German,
Italian, Polish, Spanish)
desired child
*Maja, Malita, Mareea,
Marica, Marike, Marucha,
Mezi, Mitzi*

Mariah
(Hebrew) sorrowful singer
*Marayah, Mariahe,
Marriah, Meriah, Moriah*

Marializa
(Spanish) combo of Maria
and Liza; desired
*Liza, Maria Liza, Maria,
Maria-Liza, Mariliza*

Marialourdes
(Spanish) combo of Maria
and Lourdes; sweet
*Maria Lourdes, Maria-
Lourdes*

Mariamne
(French) form of Miriam;
sea of sadness
Mariam, Marianne

Marian
(English) thoughtful
*Mariane, Marianne,
Maryann, Maryanne*

Mariana
(Spanish) quiet girl
Maryanna

Marianella
(French) combo of Marian
and Ella; girl of the sea
Ella, Marian, Mariane

Mariangela
(American) combo of Mary
and Angela; angelic
Mary Angela, Mary-
Angela, Mariangelle

Maria-Teresa
(Spanish) combo of Maria
and Teresa; desired
Maria Teresa, Mariateresa,
Maria-Terese, Maria-
Theresa

Maribel
(French, English,
American) combo of Mary
and Belle
EmBee, Marabel,
Maribela, Merrybelle

Maribeth
(American) combo of Mari
and Beth
Mary Beth, Mary-Beth,
Marybeth

Marie
(French) form of Mary;
dignified and spiritual
Maree, Marye

Mariel
(German) spiritual
Mari, Mariele, Marielle

Marielena
(Spanish) combo of Marie
and Lena; desired
Mari, Mari-Elena, Marie-
Lena, Maryelenna

Mariella
(Italian) from Maria;
blessed

Mariellen
(American) combo of Mari
and Ellen; dancer
Mare, Marelle, Mariella,
Maryellen, MaryEllen

Mariene
(Spanish) devout
Mari, Marienne

Mariet
(French) variant of Marie;
bittersweet
Mariett, Mariette, Maryet,
Maryett, Maryette

Marietta
(French) combo of Mary
and Etta; spright spirit
Marieta, Maryeta,
Maryetta

Marigold
(Botanical) sunny
Maragold, Marigolde,
Marigole, Marrigold,
Marygold, Marygolde

Marihelen
(American) combo of Mary
and Helen; steadfast friend
Marihelene, MaryHelen

Marika
(Slavic, American)
thoughtful and brooding
Mareeca, Mareecka,
Mareeka, Marica, Maricka,
Maryca, Marycka, Maryka,
Merica, Merika, Merk,
Merkie

Marikaitlynn
(American) combo of Mari
and Kaitlynn; desired
Kait, Kaiti, Mari,
Marreekaitlyn, Mary
Kaitlynn, Mary-Kaitlynn

Marilee
(American) combo of Mary
and Lee; dancing
Marylee, Merilee, Merrilee

Marilene
(American) combo of Mari
and Ilene; talented
Marilou
(American) combo of Mary
and Lou; jubilant
*Marilu, Marrilou, Marylou,
Marylu*
Marilyn
(Hebrew) fond-spirited
*Maralynne, Mare, Marilin,
Mariline, Marilinn,
Marilynn, Marrie, Marrilyn,
Marylyn, Marylynn,
Merilyn, Merrilyn*
Marin
(Latin) sea-loving
Mare, Maren
Marina
(Latin) lover of the ocean
*Mareena, Marena, Marina,
Maryna*
Marinella
(French) combo of Marin
and Ella; soft
*Ella, Marin, Mari-Nella,
Marin-Ella, Nella*
Marion
(French) form of Mary;
delicate spirit
*Mare, Marien, Marrion,
Mary, Maryen, Maryian,
Maryon*
Mariposa
(Spanish) butterfly
*Mari, Mariposah,
Maryposa*
Mariquita
(Spanish) form of
Margaret; party-loving
*Marikita, Marrikita,
Marriquita*
Maris
(Latin) sea-loving
*Mere, Marice, Meris,
Marys*

Marisa
(Latin) sea-loving;
(Spanish) combo of Maria
and Luisa
*Marce, Maressa, Marissa,
Marisse, Mariza Marsie,
Marysa, Maryssa, Merisa*
Marisela
(Spanish) hearty
Marisella, Marysela
Mariska
(American) endearing
*Mareska, Marisca,
Mariskah*
Marisol
(Spanish) stunning
*Mare, Mari, Marizol,
Marrisol, Marzol, Merizol*
Maritza
(Place name) for St.
Moritz, Switzerland
Marixbel
(Spanish) pretty
Marix
Marjie
(Scottish) short for
Marjorie
Marji, Marjy
Marjorie
(Greek, English, Scottish)
bittersweet; pert
*Marg, Marge, Margerie,
Margery, Margorie, Marjie,
Marjori*
Marky
(American) mischievous
Marki, Markie
Marla
(German) believer;
easygoing
Marlah, Marlla
Marlaina
(American) form of
Marlene; dramatic
Marlaine, Marlane

Marlana
(Hebrew, Greek) vamp
Marlanna

Marleal
(American) form of Mary;
desired
Marle, Marleel, Marly

Marlee
(Greek) guarded
*Marleigh, Marley, Marli,
Marlie, Marly*

Marlen
(American) desired
Marl, Marla, Marlin

Marlena
(German) pretty;
bittersweet
*Marla, Marlaina,
Marleena, Marlina,
Marlyna, Marlynne,
Marnie*

Marlene
(Greek) high-minded;
attractive;
(English) adorned
*Marlean, Marlee, Marleen,
Marleene, Marley, Marline,
Marly, Marlyne*

Marley
(English) form of Marlene
Mar, Marlee, Marlie, Marly

Marlis
(German) combo of Maria
and Elisabeth; religious
Marl, Marlice

Marlise
(English) considerate
Marlice, Marlis, Marlys

Marlo
(American) vivacious
*Marloe, Marloh, Marlow,
Marlowe*

Marlycia
(Spanish) desired
Lycia, Marly, Marlysia

Marna
(French) from Marlene;
rejoices

Marnie
(Hebrew) storyteller
*Marn, Marnee, Marney,
Marni, Marny*

Marnina
(French) from Marlene;
joyful
Marneena, Marnyna

Marnita
(American) worrier
*Marneta, Marni, Marnite,
Marnitta, Marny*

Marolyn
(Invented) form of
Marilyn; desired; precious
Maro, Marolin, Marolinne

Maromisa
(Japanese) combo of Maro
and Misa; warm
Maromissa

Marquise
(French) noble-spirited
*Markeese, Marquees,
Marquisa, Mars*

Marquisha
(African American) form of
Marquise
Marquish

Marquita
(Spanish) happy girl
*Marqueda, Marquitta,
Marrie*

Marrie
(American) variant of
Mary; desired
Marry

Marsala
(Italian) of Marseille, Italy;
rambunctious
Marse, Marsela, Marsie

Marsha
(Latin) light-haired;
combative
Marcia, Mars, Marsie

Marshay
(American) exuberant
Marshae, Marshaya

Marta
(Danish) treasure
Mart, Marte, Marty, Merta

Marterrell
(American) changeable
Marte, Marterill, Martrell

Martha
(Aramaic) lady
*Marta, Marth, Marti,
Marty, Mattie*

Marthe
(Aramaic) ladylike

Marti
(English) short for Martha;
dreamy
*Martee, Martey, Martie,
Marty*

Martina
(Latin, German) combative
*Marteena, Martene, Marti,
Martinna, Martyna, Tina*

Martine
(French) combative

Martivanio
(Italian) form of Martina;
feisty; fighter
Mart, Marti, Tivanio

Martonette
(American) form of
masculine name Martin;
feisty little girl
*Martanette, Martinette,
Martonett*

Marty
(English) from Martha;
hopes
Marti

Marusya
(Slavic) soft-hearted

Marvel
(French) astounding;
marvelous

Marvella
(French) marvelous
woman
*Marva, Marvelle, Marvie,
Mavela*

Mary
(Hebrew) bitter; in the
Bible, the mother of Jesus
*Maire, Mara, Mare, Maree,
Mari, Marie, Mariel, Marlo,
Marye, Merree, Merry,
Mitzie*

Marya
(Arabic) white and bright
Marja

Maryalice
(American) combo of Mary
and Alice; friendly
Marialice, Maryalyce

Maryann
(English, American) combo
of Mary and Ann; special
*Mariann, Marianne,
Maryan, Maryann,
Maryanne*

Mary-Catherine
(American) combo of Mary
and Catherine; outgoing
*Maricatherine,
Marycatherine, Mary-
Kathryn*

Maryellen
(American) combo of Mary
and Ellen; satisfied
Maryellin, Maryellyn

Mary-Elizabeth
(American) combo of Mary
and Elizabeth; kind
*Marielizabeth, Mary
Elizabeth, Maryelizabeth*

Maryjo
(American) combo of Mary
and Jo; likable
Marijo

Marykate
(American) combo of Mary
and Kate; splendid
Marikate, Mary-Kate

Marykay
(American) combo of Mary
and Kay; adorned
Marikay, Marrikae

Maryke
(Dutch) kind; desired
*Mairek, Marika, Maryk,
Maryky*

Mary-Lou
(American) combo of Mary
and Lou; athletic
Mary Lou, Marylou

Mary-Marg
(American) dramatic
Marimarg

Mary-Margaret
(American) combo of Mary
and Margaret; dramatic,
kind
*Marimargaret, Mary
Margaret, Marymarg,
Marymargret*

Marypat
(American) combo of Mary
and Pat; easygoing
Mary-Pat, Mary Pat

Marysue
(American) combo of Mary
and Sue; country girl
MariSue, Merrysue, Mersue

Masha
(Russian) child who was
desired

Mashonda
(African American)
believer
Masho, Mashonde

Masina
(Last name as first)
charming; delightful

Mason
(French) diligent; reliable

Massey
(German) confident
Massi, Massie

Massiel
(American) giving
*Masie, Masiel, Massey,
Massielle*

Massim
(Latin) great
Massima, Maxim, Maxima

Matia
(Hebrew) a God-given gift
Matea, Mattea, Mattie

Matilda
(German) powerful fighter
*Mat, Mathilda, Mattie,
Tilda, Tillie, Tilly*

Mattie
(English) most honored
*Matt, Matte, Mattey, Matti,
Matty*

Matylda
(Polish) strong fighter
Matyld

Maude
(English) old-fashioned
Maud, Maudie

Maudeen
(American) countrified
*Maudie, Mawdeen,
Mawdine*

Maudisa
(African) sweet
Maudesa, Maudesah

Mauna
(American) attractive
Maune, Mawna, Mon

Maura
(Latin, Irish) dark
Moira, Maurie

Maureen
(Irish, French) night-loving
*Maura, Maurene, Maurine,
Moreen, Morene*

Maurelle
(French) petite
Maure, Maurie, Maurielle

Maurise
(French) dark
Morise, Maurice

Mauve
(French) gentle
Mauvey, Mauvie

Mave
(French) bird; melodic

Mavis
(French) singing bird
Mauvis, Mav, Mave

Maxeeme
(Latin) form of Maxime;
maximum

Maxie
(Latin) fine
Maxee, Maxey, Maxy

Maxime
(Latin) maximum
Maxey, Maxi, Maxim

Maxine
(Latin) greatest of all
*Max, Maxeen, Maxene,
Maxie, Maxy*

May
(Old English) bright flower
Mae, Maye

Maya
(Latin, Hindi, Mayan)
creative; mystical
*Maia, Maiya, Mayah, Mya,
Myah, Mye*

Maybelle
(American) combo of May
and Belle; lovely May
*Mabelle, Maebelle,
Maybell, May-Belle*

Maybelline
(Latin) variation of Mabel;
lovable
*Mabie, May, Maybeline,
Maybie, Maybleene*

Mayella
(American) combo of May
and Ella; jolly
*Ella, Maella, May, Mayela,
Mayell, Mella*

Mayghaen
(American) fortunate

Mayim
(Origin unknown) special
Mayum

Maykaylee
(American) ingenious
*Maykayli, Maykaylie,
Maykayly*

Mayo
(Place name) a county in
Ireland; vibrant
Mayoh

Mayra
(Spanish) flourishing;
creative
Mayrah

Mayrant
(Spanish) industrious
Maya, Mayrynt

Mazel
(American) form of Hazel;
shining; (Hebrew) lucky
girl
Masel, Mazil, Mazal

Mazie
(Scottish) form of Maisie

Mazu
(Chinese) goddess of the
sea

McCanna
(American) ebullient
Maccanna, McCannah

McCauley
(Irish) feisty
Mac, McCauly, McCawlie

McCay
(Irish) creative
Mackaylee, McCaylee

McCormick
(Irish) last name as first name
MacCormack, Mackey

McGown
(Irish) sensible
Mac, MacGowen, Mackie, McGowen

McKenna
(American) able
Mackenna, Makenna

McKenzie
(Scottish) form of Mackenzie
Mackie, McKinzie, Mickey

McMurtry
(Irish) last name as first name
Mac, McMurt

Mead
(Greek) honey-wine-loving
Meade, Meed, Meede

Meadhoh
(Irish) joyful

Meadow
(English) open land; calm
Meadoh

Meagan
(Irish) joyous; precious
Maegan, Meaghan, Meegan, Meg, Meganne, Meggie, Meggye, Meghan

Meara
(Irish) happy girl

Meashley
(American) charmer
Meash, Meashlee

Meatah
(American) athletic
Mea, Mia, Miata, Miatah

Meave
(Irish) sings

Medalle
(American) pretty
Medahl, Medoll

Medardo
(Spanish) pretty

Medea
(Greek) ruling; cruel
Medeia

Medusa
(Greek) contriver; temptress

Meena
(Hindi) fish

Meera
(Hindi) rich

Meg
(Greek) able; lovable
Megs

Megan
(Irish) precious, joyful
Meagan, Meaghen, Meggi, Meghan, Meghann

Meggie
(Greek) best
Meggey, Meggi, Meggy

Megha
(Welsh) pearl

Meghan
(Welsh) pearl
Meghen, Meghyn

Mehetabel
(Hebrew) won by faith
Mehitabel

Mehul
(Hindi) rain girl

Meirion
(Hebrew) light

Meissa
(Hindi) from Mesha; moonlike
Meisa, Meysa, Meyssa

Mel
(Greek) sporty
Mell

Melada
(Greek) from Melanie;
dark
Mel, Melli

Melana
(Greek) giving; dark

Melanna
(Greek) dark

Melancon
(French) dark beauty;
sweet
*Mel, Melance, Melaney,
Melanie, Melanse,
Melanson, Melonce,
Melonceson*

Melania
(Italian) giving;
philanthropic
Mel, Melly

Melanie
(Greek) dark; sweet
*Melanee, Melaney, Melani,
Melany, Meleni, Melenie,
Meleny*

Melantha
(Greek) dark-skinned;
sweet
Melanthah

Melba
(Australian) talented;
light-hearted
Melbah

Meleda
(Spanish) sweet
Meleeda, Melida, Melyda

Melia
(German) dedicated
*Meelia, Meleea, Melya,
Melyah*

Melicent
(English) variant of
Millicent; strong
Melisent

Melina
(Greek) honey; sweet
*Meleena, Melena,
Melinah, Melyna*

Melinda
(Latin) honey; sweetheart
*Linda, Linnie, Linny,
Lynda, Mellie, Melynda,
Milinda, Mindy, Mylinde*

Melisande
(French) strong
Melisenda

Melissa
(Greek) honey
*Melisa, Melysa, Melyssa,
Melyssuh*

Mellicent
(German) from Millicent;
royal born
*Melicent, Mellycent,
Melycent*

Mellie
(Greek) bee; busy

Melody
(Greek) song; musical
*Mel, Mellie, Melodee,
Melodey, Melodie*

Meloney
(American) form of
Melanie; dark and sweet
Mel, Melone, Meloni

Melora
(Latin) good
*Meliora, Melorah,
Melourah*

Melosa
(Greek) variant of Melissa;
bee; never rests
Melossa

Melrose
(English) honey of roses;
sweet girl
Mellrose, Melrosie

Melvia
(American) leader; dark
Mel, Mell, Melvea

Melvina
(Irish) prepared to lead
Malvina

Mena
(Egyptian) pretty
Meenah, Menah

Meosha
(African American)
talented
*Meeosha, Meoshe,
Miosha*

Merary
(American) merry
Marary, Meraree, Merarie

Mercedes
(Spanish) merciful;
rewarded
*Mercedez, Mercides,
Mersadez, Mersaydes*

Mercia
(English) variant of
Marcia; combative

Mercy
(English) forgiving
*Merce, Mercee, Mercey,
Merci, Mercie*

Meredith
(Welsh) protector
*Mer, Meredithe, Meredyth,
Merridith, Merry, Merydith,
Merydithe*

Meri
(Irish) by the sea
Merrie

Meridian
(American) perfect posture
Meredian, Meridiane

Merie
(French) secretive;
blackbird
Mer, Meri, Myrie

Meriel
(Irish) girl who shines like
the sea
*Meri, Merial, Merri,
Merriyl, Merry*

Merilyn
(English, American) combo
of Merry and Lynn
*Marilyn, Mer, Meralyn,
Merelyn, Meri, Merill,
Merilynn, Merilynne,
Merri, Merrill, Merrylyn*

Meris
(Latin) variant of Merissa;
the sea girl
*Meriss, Merris, Merrys,
Merys*

Merissa
(Latin) ocean-loving
Merisa, Meryssa

Merit
(American) deserving
*Merite, Meritt, Meritte,
Meryt, Merytt, Mirit*

Merle
(Irish) shining girl
Merl, Murl, Murle

Merribeth
(English) cheerful
Merri-Beth, Merrybeth

Merrilee
(American) combo of Merri
and Lee; happy
*Marilee, Merilee, Merrylee,
Merry-Lee*

Merrill
(Irish) shines
Merril

Merry
(English) cheerful
*Mer, Meri, Merie, Merree,
Merrey, Merri, Merrie,
Mery*

Merryjane
(English) combo of Merry
and Jane; happy
*Merijane, Merrijane,
Merrijayne, Merryjaine,
Merryjayne*

Mersaydes
(Invented) variant of
Mercedes
Mercy, Mersa, Mersy

Mersey
(English) River Mersey;
rich
Merce, Merse

Mersia
(Hebrew) variant of
Mersera; princess
*Mercy, Mers, Mersea,
Mersy*

Meryl
(German) well-known;
(Irish) shining sea
*Mer, Merel, Merri, Merrill,
Merryl, Meryll*

Mesa
(Place name) earthy
Mase, Maysa, Mesah

Mesha
(Hindi) born in lunar
month; moon-loving
Meshah

Meta
(Scandinavian) short for
Margaret; devoted

Mhari
(Scottish) from Mary;
religious
Mhairi

Mi
(Chinese) obsessive
My, Mye

Mia
(Scandinavian, Italian)
blessed; girl of mine
*Me, Mea, Meah, Meea,
Meya, Mya*

Miaka
(Japanese) influential

Miana
(American) combo of Mi
and Ana
Mianna

Micah
(Hebrew) religious
Mica, Mika, My, Myca

Micala
(Hebrew) from Michaela;
wonders
*Micalah, Michala,
Michalah, Mikala, Mikalah,
Mycala, Mycalah, Mychala,
Mychalah, Mykala, Mykalah*

Michaela
(Hebrew) God-loving
*Meeca, Micaela, Micela,
Michael, Michal, Michala,
Michalla, Michela, Mikaela,
Mikala, Mikela, Mycaela,
Mycaela, Mycela, Mychaela,
Mychela, Mykaela, Mykela*

Michaelannette
(American) combo of
Michael and Annette;
spirited
Annette, Michelannet

Michaele
(Hebrew) loving God

Michele
(Italian, French, American)
God-loving
*Machele, Machelle,
Mechele, Mia, Michell,
Michelle, Mischel,
Mischell, Mischelle, Mish,
Mishell, Mishelle*

Michelin
(American) lovable
Michalynn, Mish, Mishelin

Micheline
(French) form of Michele;
delightful
Mishelinne

Micki
(American) quirky
*Mick, Mickee, Mickey,
Micky, Miki, Mikie, Mycki*

Mickley
(American) form of
Mickey; fun-loving
*Mick, Mickaella, Micklee,
Mickley, Mickli, Miklea,
Miklee, Mikleigh, Mikley,
Myk, Mykkie*

Micole
(American) combo of
Micha and Nicole; happy-
go-lucky girl
Macole, Micolle

Mid
(American) middle child
Middi, Middy

Migon
(American) precious
*Mignonne, Migonette,
Migonn, Migonne*

Mignon
(French) cute
*Migonette, Mim, Mimi,
Minyon, Minyonne*

Miguelinda
(Spanish) combo of
Miguel and Linda; strong-
willed beauty
Miguel-Linda, Miguelynda

Mika
(Hebrew) wise and pious
Micah, Mikah, Mikie

Mikaela
(Hebrew) God-loving
*Mik, Mikayla, Mike,
Mikhaila, Miki*

Mila
(Russian, Italian) short for
Camilla; dearest
Milah, Milla, Millah, Mimi

Milagros
(Spanish) miracle
Mila, Milagro

Milantia
(Panamanian) calm
Mila

Mildred
(English) gentle
*Mil, Mildread, Mildrid,
Millie, Milly*

Milena
(Greek) loving girl
Mela, Mili, Milina

Miliani
(Hawaiian) one who
caresses
Mil, Mila

Milissa
(Greek) softspoken
Melissa, Missy

Milla
(Polish) gentle; pure
Mila, Millah

Millay
(Literature) for poet Edna
St. Vincent Millay; soft

Millicent
(Greek, German) soft-
hearted
*Melicent, Melly, Milicent,
Millie, Millisent, Milly,
Millycent, Milycent, Missy*

Millie
(English) short for Mildred
and Millicent
*Mil, Mili, Millee, Milley,
Milli, Milly*

Mim
(American) short for
Miriam; cute
Mimm, Mym, Mymm

Mima
(Burmese) feminine

Mimi
(French) short for Camilla;
willful
*Meemee, Mim, Mims,
Mimsie*

Mimosa
(Botanical) sensitive; tree

Min
(Chinese) sensitive; soft-hearted

Mina
(German, Polish) resolute protector; willful
Meena, Mena, Min, Minah, Myna, Mynah

Mindy
(Greek) short for Melinda; breezy
Mindee, Mindey, Mindi, Mindie, Myndee, Myndi

Minerva
(Latin, Greek) bright; strong
Menerva, Min, Minnie, Myn

Minette
(French) loyal woman
Min, Minnette, Minnie

Ming
(Chinese) shiny; hope of tomorrow

Minhtu
(Asian) light and clear

Mini
(Scandinavian) mine

Miniver
(English) assertive
Meniver, Minever, Miniverr

Minna
(German) sturdy
Mina, Minnie, Mynna

Minnie
(German) short for Minerva
Mini, Minni, Minny

Minta
(English) memorable
Minty

Mira
(Latin, Spanish) wonderful girl
Meara, Mirror

Mirabel
(Latin) marvelous; beautiful reflection
Marabelle, Mira, Mirabell, Mirabelle

Mirabella
(Italian) marvelous
Mira, Mirabellah, Mirabelle, Mirabell, Myrabell, Myrabelle

Miraclair
(Latin) combo of Mira and Clair; wonderful; gentle
Mira-Clair, Miraclaire, Miraclare

Miracle
(American) miracle baby
Merry, Mira, Mirakle, Mirry

Miranda
(Latin) unique and amazing
Maranda, Meranda, Mira, Mirrie, Myranda

Mirella
(Spanish) wonderful
Mira, Mirel, Mirela, Mirell, Mirelle, Myrela, Myrella

Mirelle
(Latin) wonder
Mirell, Myrell, Myrelle

Mireya
(Hebrew) form of Miriam; melancholy

Mireyli
(Spanish) wondrous; admirable
Mire, Mirey

Miri
(Gypsy) bittersweet
Meeri, Miree, Mirey, Mirie, Miry

Moirin
(Irish) exce...

Mokysha
(African Am...
dramatic
Kisha, Kysh...
Mokey

Moll
(Literature)
Defoe's Mo...
outgoing
Mol, Molly

Molly
(Irish) jovia...
Moli, Moll,
Mollie

Momo
(Japanese)

Mona
(Greek) sho...
shining-che...
Monah, Mo...

Monday
(American)
Monday; h...
Mondae

Moneek
(Invented) f...
Monique; s...
Moneeke

Monet
(French) art...
Mon, Mona...

Monica
(Greek) see...
of others
Mon, Mona...
Monika, Mo...

Monical
(American)
Monica an...
Monecal, M...
Monikal

Monika
(Polish) ad...

More
(American) bonus
Moore, Morie

Moreen
(English) good friend

Morgan
(Welsh) girl on the
seashore
*Mor, Morey, Morgane,
Morgannna, Morgen,
Morgyn*

Morgander
(American) soft-spoken;
divine

Moriah
(French) dark girl;
(Hebrew) God-taught
*Mareyeh, Mariah, Moorea,
More, Moria, Morie,
Morria, Morya*

Morine
(American) form of
Maureen; fond of night
Morri

Moritza
(Place name) St. Moritz,
Switzerland; playful

Morla
(American) form of Marla;
easygoing
Morley, Morly

Morna
(French) dark

Morta
(Mythological) one of the
Roman Fates; the cutter

Morven
(American) magical
Morvee, Morvey, Morvi

Morwenna
(Welsh) seamaiden
Mo, Morwen

Morwyn
(Welsh) maiden
*Morwen, Morwenn,
Morwynn, Morwynna*

Moselle
(Hebrew) uplifted
Mose, Mozelle, Mozie

Moya
(Scandinavian) mother
Moiya, Moy

Moyra
(Irish) excellent

Muadhnait
(Irish) little noble girl

Mudiwa
(African) beloved
Mudewa

Muirne
(Irish) affectionate

Muna
(Arabic) hopes
Moona

Munira
(Irish) wishful

Murali
(Irish) seagoing

Murdina
(Slavic) dark spirit
Murdi, Murdine

Muriel
(Celtic) shining
*Meriel, Mur, Murial,
Muriele, Muriell, Murielle,
Muryel, Muryell, Muryelle*

Murphy
(Irish) spirited
*Murphee, Murphey,
Murphi, Murphie*

Murray
(Last name as first name)
brisk
Muray, Murraye

Musa
(African) child; muse

Musetta
(French) instrument;
musical
Museta

Musette
(French) instrument;
musical
Musett

Musique
(French) musical
Museek, Museke, Musik

Mussie
(American) musical
Muss, Mussi, Mussy

Mwazi
(Israeli) type of fig

Myeshia
(African American) giving
Meyeshia, Mye, Myesha

Myfanwy
(Welsh) water baby

Mykala
(Scandinavian) giving
Mykaela, Mykela, Mykie

Mykelle
(American) generous
Mykell

Myla
(English) forgiving
Miela, Mylah

Mylene
(Greek) dark-skinned girl
Myleen

Mylie
(German) forgiving
Miley, Mylee, Myli

Myna
(English) talkative
Mina, Minah

Mynola
(Invented) smart
*Minola, Monoa, Mynolla,
Mynolle*

Myra
(Latin) fragrant
Mira, Myrah

Myriam
(French) bittersweet life

Myrischa
(African American)
fragrant doll
*Myresha, Myri, Myrish,
Myrisha, Rischa*

Myrna
(Irish) loved
Merna, Mirna, Murna

Myrtle
(Greek) loving
*Mertle, Mirtle, Myrt,
Myrtie*

Mysha
(Russian) form of Misha;
protective
*Mischa, Mish, Misha,
Mysh*

Mysta
(Invented) mysterious
Mista, Mystah

Mystique
(French) intriguing woman
*Mistie, Mistik, Mistique,
Misty, Mystica*

Naama
(Hebrew) sweet
Naamah, Naamit

Naamah
(Biblical) sweet
Nanay, Nayamah, Naynay

Naarah
(Aramaic) bright light
Naara

Naava
(Hebrew) delightful girl
Naavah, N'Ava

Nabiha
(Arabic) noble
Naihah

Nabila
(Arabic) noble
Nabeela, Nabilah, Nabilia

Nabulungi
(African) of nobility

Nada
(Arabic) morning dew;
giving

Nadelie
(American) form of Natalie;
Christmas-born; beauty
Nadey

Nadeline
(Invented) born on
Christmas
Nad, Nadelyne

Nadette
(French) darling girl

Nadezda
(Russian) hopeful
Nadeia

Nadia
(Slavic) hopeful
*Nada, Nadea, Nadeen,
Nadene, Nadi, Nadie,
Nadina, Nadine, Nady*

Natka
(Russian) wonders; hopes

Nadidaa
(Slavic) hopes
Nadidah

Nadine
(Russian, French) dancer
*Nadeen, Nadene, Nadie,
Nadyne, Naidyne*

Nadira
(Arabic) precious gem
Nadirah, Nadra

Nadya
(Russian) optimistic; life's
beginnings

Nadyan
(Hebrew) pond; reflective
Nadian

Nadzieja
(Greek) water nymph
Nadzia, Nata, Natia, Natka

Naeemah
(African) breathtaking

Nafshiya
(Persian) precious girl

Nagida
(Hebrew) thrives
*Nagia, Nagiah, Nagiya,
Najiah, Najiya, Najiyah,
Negida*

Nagisa
(Japanese) from the shore

Nahara
(Aramaic) light
Nehara, Nehora

Nahida
(Hebrew) rich
Nahid

Nahla
(Arabic) succeeds

Nahtanha
(African) warm

Nai
(Japanese) intelligent
Nayah

Naia
(Hawaiian) water nymph

Naida
(Greek) nymph-like
Naiad, Naya, Nayad, Nyad

Nailah
(African) successful
Naila

Naimah
(Arabic) happy
Naeemah, Naima

Naja
(Greek) form of Nadia
Najat
(Arabic) safe
Nagat
Najiba
(Arabic) safe
Nagiba, Nagibah, Najibah
Najla
(Arabic) large-eyed
Najwa
(Arabic) confidante
Nagwa
Nakesha
(African American) combo
of Na and Kesha
*Naka, Nakeisha, Nakie,
Nakisha*
Nakia
(Arabic) purest girl
Nakea
Nakita
(Russian) precocious
*Nakeeta, Nakeita, Nakya,
Naquita, Nikita*
Nala
(African) loved
Nalah, Nalo
Nalani
(Hawaiian) calming
Nalanie, Nalany
Nalin
(Native American) serene
maiden
Nallely
(Spanish) friend
Nalelee, Naleley, Nallel
Nalukea
(Hawaiian) sky girl
Nami
(Japanese) rides a wave
Namiko
Namisha
(African) content with life
Namono
(African) twin

Nampeyo
(Native American) female
snake; sly
Nampayo, Nampayu
Nan
(German, Scottish,
English) bold; graceful
Na, Nana, Nannie, Nanny
Nana
(Hebrew) from Ann;
graceful
Nanabah
(Hebrew) from Ann; full of
grace
Nanala
(Hebrew) from Ann; grace
Nanalie
(American) form of
Natalie; graceful;
Christmas-born
Nan, Nana, Nanalee
Nance
(American) giving
Nans
Nancy
(English, Irish) generous
woman
*Nan, Nancee, Nanci,
Nancie, Nansee, Nonie*
Nandana
(Hindi) delightful;
challenges
Nandini, Nandita
Nanek
(Hebrew) from Nancy;
moves with grace
Naneka, Naneki, Naneta
Nanette
(French) giving and
gracious
Nanet
Nani
(Greek) charming beauty
Nan, Nannie

Nanice
(American) open-hearted
*Nan, Naneece, Naneese,
Naniece*

Nanise
(American) variant of Nan;
mercurial

Nanna
(Scandinavian) brave
Nana

Nanon
(French) slow to anger
Nan, Nanen

Nanvah
(African) God's gift, an
infant

Nao
(Japanese) truthful;
pleasing

Naola
(American) from Naomi;
truthful

Naoma
(Hebrew) lovely

Naomi
(Hebrew) beautiful woman
*Naoma, Naomia, Naomie,
Naomy, Naynay, Nene,
Neoma, Noami, Noemi,
Noemie, Noma, Nomah,
Nomi*

Nara
(Greek, Japanese) happy;
dreamy
Narah, Nera

Narcissa
(Greek) narcissistic
*Narcisa, Narcisse,
Narkissa, Nars*

Narcissie
(Greek) conceited; daffodil
*Narci, Narcis, Narcissa,
Narcisse, Narcissey,
Narsee, Narsey, Narsis*

Narda
(Latin) fragrant

Narelle
(Australian) of the sea

Naresha
(Hindi) ruler; wise

Nari
(Japanese) thunders
loudly

Narilla
(Gypsy) boisterous
Narrila, Narrilla

Nascha
(Native American) owl;
watchful

Naseem
(Hindi) breezy

Nashota
(Native American) second
twin

Nashan
(Origin unknown) miracle
child

Nasia
(Hebrew) miraculous child
*Naseea, Naseeah, Nasiah,
Nasya, Nsayah*

Nasnan
(Native American) miracle
child; mystical

Naspa
(Hebrew) form of Nasia;
wondrous
Nasia, Nasya

Nasrin
(Hindi) wild rose
Nasreen

Nastasia
(Greek, Russian) gorgeous
girl
Nas, Nastasha, Natasie

Nasya
(Hebrew) God's miracle
Nasia

Nat
(American) short for
Natalie; Christmas baby
Natt

Nata
(Latin) saving

Natalia
(Russian, Latin) born on Christmas; beauty
Nat, Nata, Natala, Natalea, Natalee, Natalie, Natalya, Nati, Nattie, Nattlee, Natty

Natalie
(Latin) born on Christmas
Natala, Natalee, Natalene, Natalia, Natalina, Nataline, Natalka, Natalya, Natelie, Nathalia, Nathalie

Natane
(Native American) daughter; giving

Nataniah
(Hebrew) God's gift
Natania, Nataniela, Nataniella, Natanielle, Natanya, Nathania, Nathaniella, Nathanielle, Netana, Netanela, Netania, Netaniah, Netaniela, Netaniella, Netanya, Nethania, Nethanisah, Netina

Natarsha
(American) splendid
Natarsh, Natarshah

Natasha
(Latin, Russian) glorious; born on Christmas
Nastasia, Nastassia, Nastassja, Nastassya, Nastasya, Natacha, Natashah, Natashia, Natassia, Nitasha, Tashi, Tashia, Tasis, Tassa, Tassie

Natesa
(Hindi) goddess

Nathadria
(Hebrew) form of Nathan; gift of God
Natania, Nath, Nathe, Nathed, Nathedrea, Natty, Thedria

Nathalie
(French) born on Christmas
Natalie

Nathitfa
(Arabic) unflawed
Nathifa, Nathifah, Natifa, Natifah

Nation
(American) spirited; patriotic
Nashon, Nayshun

Natividad
(Spanish) Christmas baby

Natka
(Polish) hope for tomorrow

Natosha
(African American) form of Natasha; born on Christmas
Nat, Natosh, Natoshe, Natty

Natsu
(Japanese) summer's child
Natsuko, Natsuyo

Nauasia
(Latin) variant of Nausicaa, kind princess in *The Odyssey*

Naveen
(Spanish) snowing

Navita
(Hebrew) pleasure; (Hispanic) original
Nava, Navite

Navy
(American) daughter of a member of the Navy; dark blue

Nawal
(Arabic) gifted
Nayana
(Irish) form of Neala;
winner
Nayeli
(African) of beginnings
Nayo
(African) joy baby
Nazihah
(Arabic) truthful
Nazira
(Arabic) equality
Nazirah
Nazly
(American) idealistic
Nazlee, Nazli, Nazlie
Neal
(Irish) spirited
Neale, Neel, Neil
Neala
(Irish) spirited
*Neal, Nealie, Nealy, Neeli,
Neelie, Neely, Neila, Neile,
Neilla, Neille*
Nealy
(Irish) winner
*Nealee, Nealey, Neali,
Nealie*
Neary
(English) variant of
Nerissa; snail; slow
*Nearee, Nearey, Neari,
Nearie, Neeree, Neerey,
Neeri, Neerie, Neery*
Neata
(Russian) from Nataliya;
born on Christmas
Neeta
Neba
(Latin) misty
Neeba, Niba, Nyba
Necedah
(Native American) yellow
hair

Nechama
(Hebrew) comforts others
*Nachmi, Necha, Neche,
Nehama*
Neche
(Spanish) pure
Nechona
(Spanish) pure
Neci
(Hungarian) intense
Necie
(Hungarian) intense
Neci
Neda
(Slavic) Sunday baby
Nedda, Neddie, Nedi
Nedaviah
(Hebrew) generous girl
Nedavia, Nedavya, Nediva
Nedda
(English) born to money
Ned, Neddy
Nedra
(English) secretive
Ned, Nedre
Neely
(Irish) sparkling smile
Nealy, Neelee, Neilie, Nelie
Neema
(Hebrew) melodious
Neenah
(Native American) flowing
water
Nefris
(Spanish) glamorous
*Nef, Neff, Neffy, Nefras,
Nefres*
Neh
(Hebrew) from Nehara;
light
Neha
(Hindi) loves
Nehali, Nehi
Nehanda
(Hebrew) comforter

Neia
(African) promising
Neiley
(Irish) winner
*Neelee, Neeley, Neeli,
Neelie, Neely, Neilee, Neili,
Neilie, Neily*
Neima
(Hindi) growing; tree
Neith
(Egyptian) feminine
Neit, Neithe
Neka
(Native American) wild
Nekeisha
(African American) bold
spirit
*Nek, Nekeishah, Nekesha,
Nekisha, Nekkie*
Nekoma
(Native American)
uninhibited; new moon
Nelda
(American) friend
Neldah, Nell, Nellda, Nellie
Nelia
(Spanish) short for
Cornelia; yellow-haired
*Neelia, Neely, Nela, Nelie,
Nene*
Nelka
(Spanish) yellow hair
Nela
Nell
(English) sweet charmer
Nelle, Nellie
Nellie
(English) short for
Cornelia and Eleanor
*Nel, Nela, Nell, Nelle,
Nelli, Nelly*
Nelliene
(American) form of Nellie;
charming
Nell, Nelli, Nellienne

Nelvia
(Greek) brash
Nell, Nelvea
Nemera
(Hebrew) leopard; exotic
Nemesis
(Mythological) goddess of
justice and retribution
Nemoria
(American) crafty
Nemorea
Nenet
(Egyptian) sea goddess
Neola
(Greek) new baby
Neolah
Nepa
(Arabic) talented
Nera
(Hebrew) candlelight
Neria, Neriah, Neriya
Nereida
(Spanish) sea nymph
*Nere, Nereide, Nereyda,
Neri, Nireida*
Neressa
(Greek) coming from the
sea
*Narissa, Nene, Nerissa,
Nerisse*
Nerida
(Greek) sea nymph
*Nerice, Nerina, Nerine,
Nerisse, Neryssa, Rissa*
Nerissa
(English) snail; moves
slowly
Nerisa, Nerise
Nerthus
(Scandinavian) masterful
Nerys
(Welsh) ladylike
Neris, Neriss, Nerisse

Nesiah
(Greek) lamb; meek
*Nesia, Nessia, Nesya,
Nisia, Nisiah, Nisva*

Nessa
(Irish) devout
Nessah

Nessie
(Greek) short for Vanessa
Nese, Nesi, Ness

Nest
(Welsh) pure
Nesta

Nestora
(Spanish) she is leaving
Nesto, Nestor

Neta
(Hebrew) growing and
flourishing

Netia
(Hebrew) from Neta;
plant; growing

Netira
(Spanish) flourishing

Netis
(Native American)
worthwhile

Netra
(American) maturing well
Net, Netrah, Netrya, Nettie

Netta
(Scottish) champion
Nett, Nettie

Nettie
(French) gentle
*Net, Neta, Netta, Netti,
Nettia, Netty*

Nettiemae
(American) combo of
Nettie and Mae; small-
town girl
*Mae, Netimay, Nettemae,
Nettie, Nettiemay*

Neva
(Russian, English) the
newest; snow
Neeva, Neve, Niv

Nevada
(Place name) U.S. state;
(Spanish) girl who loves
snow
Nev, Nevadah

Neve
(Irish) promising princess

Neviah
(Irish) from Nevina;
worshipful
Nevia

Nevina
(Irish) she worships God
Nev, Niv, Nivena, Nivina

Newlin
(Last name as first name)
healing
*Newlinn, Newlinne,
Newlyn, Newlynn*

Neyda
(Spanish) pure
Ney

Neza
(Slavic) from Agnes;
prayerful
Neysa

Ngabile
(African) aware; knowing

Ngozi
(African) fortunate

Ngu
(African) peaceful

Nguyet
(Vietnamese) moon child

Nia
(Greek) priceless
Niah

Niabi
(Native American) fawn;
docile

Niamh
(Irish) promising

Niandrea
(Invented) form of
Diandrea; pretty
*Andrea, Nia, Niand,
Niandre*

Nibal
(Arabic) completed

Nicelda
(American) industrious
Niceld, Nicelde, Nicey

Nichele
(American) combo of
Nicole and Michele; dark-
skinned
Nichel, Nichelle, Nishele

Nichole
(French) light and lively
Nichol

Nichols
(Last name as first name)
smart
*Nick, Nickee, Nickels,
Nickey, Nicki, Nickie,
Nicky, Nikels*

Nick
(American) short for Nicole
Nik

Nicki
(French) short for Nicole
Nick, Nickey, Nicky, Niki

Nicks
(American) fashionable
*Nickee, Nickie, Nicksie,
Nicky, Nix*

Nico
(Italian) victorious
Nicco, Nicko, Nikko, Niko

Nicola
(Italian) lovely singer
*Nekola, Nick, Nikkie,
Nikola*

Nicolasa
(Spanish) spontaneous;
winning
Nico, Nicole

Nicole
(French) winning
*Nacole, Nichole, Nick,
Nickie, Nikki, Nikol, Nikole*

Nicolette
(French) a tiny Nicole;
little beauty
*Nettie, Nick, Nickie,
Nicoline, Nikkolette,
Nikolet*

Nicolie
(French) sweet
Nichollie, Nikolie

Nida
(Greek) sweet girl

Nidia
(Latin) home-loving
Nidie, Nidya

Niemi
(Origin unknown) beauty
Nyemi

Niesha
(African American) virginal
*Neisha, Nesha, Nesia,
Nessie*

Nieves
(Spanish) snows
Neaves, Ni, Nievez, Nievis

Nihal
(Greek) from Nicole; victor

Nike
(Greek) goddess of
victory; fleet of foot; a
winner

Nikeesha
(American) from Nikita;
joyful
*Niceesha, Nickeesha,
Nickisha, Nicquisha,
Nykesha*

Niki
(American) short for
Nicole and Nikita
*Nick, Nicki, Nicky, Nik,
Nikki, Nikky*

Niki-Lynn
(American) combo of Niki
and Lynn
*Nicki-Lynn, Nicky-Lynn,
Nikilinn, Nikilyn*
Nikita
(Russian) daring
*Nakeeta, Niki, Nikki,
Niquitta*
Nikithia
(African American)
winning; frank
Kithi, Kithia, Nikethia, Niki
Niko
(Greek) from Nikola;
winning
Neeko, Nyko
Nikole
(Greek) winning
Nik, Niki
Nili
(Hebrew) plant; flourishes
Nilsine
(Scandinavian) wine; ages
well
Nima
(Arabic) blessed
*Neema, Neemah, Nema,
Nimah*
Nimesha
(American) combo of Nima
and Mesha; skeptical
Nina
(Russian, Hebrew,
Spanish) bold girl
Neena, Nena, Ninah
Nina-Lina
(Spanish) combo of Nina
and Lina; lovely
*Nina Lina, Ninalena,
Ninalina*
Ninetta
(American) from Nanette;
cloud
Nineta

Ninette
(American) from Nanette;
cloud
Nini
(Hungarian) forgiving
*Ninee, Niney, Ninie,
Ninnee, Ninney, Ninni,
Ninnie, Niny*
Ninon
(French) feminine
Ninen
Ninovan
(American) combo of Nina
and Van; fast runner
Niobe
(Greek) vain
Nipa
(Hindi) stream
Nira
(Hindi) night
Neera, Nyra
Niranjana
(Hindi) full moon
Nirel
(Hebrew) light of
knowledge
Nirvana
(Hindi) completion;
oneness with God
Nirvahna, Nirvanah
Nirveli
(Hindi) water babe
Nisha
(Hindi) nighttime
Nishi
Nishi
(Japanese) from the west;
sincere
Nishie, Nishiko, Nishiyo
Nissa
(Hebrew) symbolic
Nisa, Niss, Nissah, Nissie
Nissie
(Scandinavian) pretty; elf
Nisse, Nissee

Nita
(Hebrew) short for Juanita
Neeta, Nitali, Nite, Nittie

Nitara
(Hindi) well grounded

Nitsa
(Greek) from Helen; lovely face

Nituna
(Native American) sweet daughter

Niu
(Chinese) girlish; confident

Niva
(Spanish) variant of Neva; snowy
Neva

Nixi
(German) mystical
Nixee, Nixie

Niy
(American) lively
Nye

Nizana
(Hebrew) from Nitzana; budding beauty
Nitza, Nitzana, Zana

Noa
(Hebrew) chosen
Noah

Noami
(Hebrew) variant of Naomi; attractive
Noamee, Noamey, Noamie, Noamy

Nobantu
(African) able

Noel
(Latin) born on Christmas
Noela, Noelle, Noellie, Noli

Noelan
(Hawaiian) Christmas girl

Noelle
(French) Christmas baby
Noel, Noell

Noga
(Hebrew) light of day

Nohelia
(Hispanic) kind
Nohelya

Noicha
(African) light heart
Nolcha

Noirin
(Irish) from Norin; honored

Nokomis
(Native American) moon child

Noksu
(African) princess

Nola
(Latin) sensual
Nolah, Nolana, Nole, Nolie

Nolan
(Latin) bell; from Nola; laughing
Nolen, Nolyn

Noleta
(Latin) reluctant
Nolita

Nomalanga
(Hawaiian) lingers

Nombeko
(African) honored child

Nombese
(African) wonder girl

Nomble
(African) beautiful
Nombi

Nomusa
(African) goodhearted

Nona
(Latin) ninth; knowing
Nonah, Noni, Nonie, Nonn, Nonna, Nonnah

Noni
(Latin) ninth child

Noor
(Hindi) lights the world
Noora

Nora
(Greek, Scandinavian, Scottish) light; bright; from the north
Norah, Noreh

Noranna
(Irish) combo of Nora and Anna; honorable
Anna, Nora, Norana, Norannah, Noranne, Noreena

Norazah
(Malaysian) light

Norberta
(German) famous girl from the north

Noreen
(Latin) acknowledging others
Noreena, Norene, Noire, Norin, Norine, Norinne, Nureen

Norell
(Scandinavian) northern girl
Narelle, Norelle

Nori
(Japanese) normal

Noriko
(Japanese) follows tradition

Norika
(Japanese) athletic
Nori, Norike

Norlaili
(Asian) northern

Norma
(Latin) gold standard
Noey, Nomah, Norm, Normah, Normie

Norna
(Scandinavian) time goddess

Norris
(English) serious
Nore, Norrus

Nota
(American) negative
Na, Nada, Not

Notaku
(Asian) dealing with grief

Noula
(Irish) from Nuala; white
Noulah

Noura
(Arabic) light girl
Nourah

Nourbese
(African) wonderful

Nova
(Latin) energetic; new
Noova, Novah, Novella, Novie

Novak
(Last name as first name) emphatic
Novac

Novella
(Latin) new

Novena
(Latin) blessing; prayerful
Noveena, Novina, Novyna

Novia
(Spanish) sweetheart
Nov, Novie, Nuvia

Nowell
(American) variant of Noelle; gives
Nowel, Nowele, Nowelle

Nu
(Vietnamese) confident
Niu

Nudar
(Arabic) golden girl

Nueva
(Spanish) new; fresh
Nue, Nuey

Nuha
(Arabic) great mind

Numa
(Spanish) delightful
Num

Numa-Noe
(Spanish) combo of Numa
and Noe; delight
Numanoe
Nuna
(Native American) girl of
the land
Nunia
(Native American) girl of
the land
Nunibelle
(American) combo of Nuni
and Belle; pretty
Nunibell, Nunnibelle
Nunu
(Vietnamese) friendly
Nur
(Arabic) bright light
Nura, Nuri, Nurya
Nura
(Aramaic) light-footed
Noora, Noura, Nurrie
Nuria
(Arabic) light
*Noor, Noura, Nur, Nuriah,
Nuriel*
Nurit
(Hebrew) from Nurita;
flower
Nurice, Nurita
Nurlene
(American) boisterous
Nerlene, Nurleen
Nuru
(African) light of day
Nusi
(Hungarian) from Hannah;
blessed girl
Nutan
(Native American) variant
of Nutah; heart
Nuvia
(American) new
Nuvea

Nydia
(Latin) nest-loving; home
and hearth woman
*Nidia, Nidiah, Ny, Nydiah,
Nydie, Nydya*
Nyla
(Arabic) successful;
astounding
Nila
Nylene
(American) shy
*Nyle, Nylean, Nyleen,
Nyles, Nyline*
Nyree
(Asian) seagoing
Nysa
(Greek) life-starting
*Nisa, Nissa, Nissie, Nysa,
Nyssa*
Nyura
(African) light
Nyx
(Greek) lively
Nix

Oba
(Mythology) river goddess
Obala
(African) from Oba; river
goddess
Oballa, Obla, Obola
Obede
(English) obedient
Obead

Obedience
(American) obedient
Obey

Obelia
(Greek) needle; cautious
Obellia, Obel, Obiel

Obey
(American) obedient

Obioma
(African) kind

Oceana
(Greek) ocean-loving;
name given to those with
astrological signs that
have to do with water
Oceonne, Ocie, Oh

Ocin
(Origin unknown) comes
into life

Octavia
(Latin) eighth child; born
on eighth day of the
month; musical
*Octave, Octavie, Octivia,
Octtavia, Ottavia, Tave,
Tavi, Tavia, Tavie*

Oda
(Hebrew) praises the Lord

Odalis
(Spanish) humorous
*Odales, Odallis, Odalous,
Odalus*

Oddrun
(Scandinavian) secret love
Oda, Odd, Oddr

Oddveig
(Scandinavian) woman
with spears

Ode
(African) born on a road

Odeda
(Hebrew) strength of
character

Odeen
(Hebrew) praises

Odele
(Hebrew, Greek)
melodious
Odela, Odelle, Odie

Odelette
(Greek) melodic; rich
Odelet, Odette

Odelia
(Hebrew, Greek) singer of
spiritual songs
*Odele, Odelle, Odie, Odila,
Odile, Othelia*

Odelinda
(Hebrew) praises

Odelita
(Spanish) vocalist
Odelite

Odera
(Hebrew) works the soil

Odessa
(English) traveler on an
odyssey
Odessah, Odie, Odissa

Odette
(French) good girl
Oddette, Odet, Odetta

Odhairnait
(Irish) little and green;
elfin-like

Odile
(French) sensuous
Odyll

Odilia
(Spanish) wealthy
*Eudalia, Odalia, Odella,
Odylia, Othilia*

Odina
(Native American)
mountain girl

Odine
(Scandinavian) rules

Odiya
(Hebrew) God's song

Ofa
(Polynesian) loving

Ofira
(Hebrew) golden girl

Ogin
(Native American) rose

Ohara
(Japanese) meditative
Oh

Ohela
(Hebrew) tent; nature-loving

Oheo
(Native American) beauty

Oira
(Latin) from Ora; prays

Okalani
(Hawaiian) heavenly child

Okei
(Japanese) from Oki;
ocean girl

Oki
(Japanese) born mid-ocean; loves the water

Oksana
(Russian) praise to God
Oksanah, Oksie

Ola
(Scandinavian) bold
Olah

Olabisi
(African) joy

Olaide
(American) lovely;
thoughtful
Olai, Olay, Olayde

Olaug
(Scandinavian) loves her
ancestors; loyal

Oldriska
(Czech) ruling noble
*Olda, Oldra, Oldrina,
Olina, Oluse*

Oleda
(Spanish) audacious

Oleia
(Greek) smooth

Olena
(Russian) generous
Olenya

Olenka
(Russian) from Helen;
lovely

Olenta
(Origin unknown) sweet

Olesia
(Greek) regal

Oleta
(Greek) true
Oletta

Olga
(Russian) holy woman
Ola, Olgah, Ollie

Oliana
(Polynesian) oleander;
beautiful

Olida
(Spanish) lighthearted
Oleda

Olidie
(Spanish) light
Oli, Olidee, Olydie

Olina
(Hawaiian) joy
Oleen, Oline

Olinda
(Latin) fragrant

Oline
(Hawaiian) happy
Olina

Olino
(Spanish) scented
Olina, Oline

Olisa
(African) loves God

Olive
(Latin) subtle
Olyve

Olivia
(English) flourishing
*Olive, Olivea, Oliveah,
Oliviah, Ollie*

Olubayo
(African) resplendent

Olufemi
(African) God loves her

Olva
(Latin) from Olivia; olive tree; natural girl

Olvyen
(Welsh) footprint in white; lasting impression

Olwen
(Welsh) magical; white
Olwynn

Olya
(Latin) perfect
Olyah

Olympia
(Greek) heavenly woman
Olimpia, Ollie, Olympe, Olympie

Olynda
(Invented) form of Lynda; fragrant; pretty
Lyn, Lynda, Olin, Olinda, Olynde

Oma
(German) grandmother; (Hebrew) pious
Omah

Omana
(Hindi) womanly

Omanie
(Origin unknown) exuberant
Omanee

Omayra
(Latin) fragrant; (Spanish) beloved
Oma, Omyra

Omega
(Greek) last is best

Omemee
(Native American) dove; peaceful

Omesha
(African American) splendid
Omesh, Omie, Omisha

Omie
(Italian) homebody
Omee

Ominotago
(Native American) sweet sound

Omolara
(African) birth timed well; welcome baby

Omora
(Arabic) red-haired

Omorose
(African) lovely

Omri
(Arabic) red-haired

Omusa
(African) adored

Omusupe
(African) precious baby

Ona
(Latin) the one
Oona

Onatah
(Native American) earth child

Onawa
(Native American) alert

Ondina
(Latin) water spirit
Ondi, Ondine, Onyda

Ondrea
(Czech) from Andrea; svelte
Ondra

Ondreja
(Czech) from Andrea; pretty girl

Oneida
(Native American) anticipated
Ona, Oneeda, Onida, Onie, Onyda

Oneshia
(American) combo of Oney and Neshia; one who waits

Oni
(African) desired child

Onia
(Latin) one and only

Onie
(Latin) flamboyant
Oh, Oona, Oonie, Una

Onora
(Latin) honorable
Onoria, Onorine

Ontina
(Origin unknown) an open mind
Ontine

Onyx
(Latin) pretty shine

Oona
(Latin) one alone
Oonagh, Oonah

Opa
(Native American) owl; stares

Opal
(Hindi) the opal; precious
Opale, Opalle, Opie

Opalina
(Sanskrit) gem
Opaline

Ophelia
(Greek) helpful woman; character from Shakespeare's *Hamlet*
Ofelia, Ofilia, Ophela, Ophelie, Ophlie, Phelia, Phelie

Ophira
(Hebrew) fawn; lovable
Ofira

Opportina
(Italian) sees opportunity; successful
Opportuna

Oprah
(Hebrew) one who soars; excellent
Ophie, Ophrie, Opra, Oprie, Orpah

Ora
(Greek) glowing
Orah, Orie

Orabel
(Latin) believes in prayer
Orabelle, Oribel, Oribella, Oribelle

Oraleyda
(Spanish) light of dawn
Ora, Oraleydea, Oralida

Oralie
(Hebrew) light of dawn
Oralee, Orali, Orla

Orange
(English) warm

Orbelina
(American) excited, dawn
Lina, Orbe, Orbee, Orbeline, Orbey, Orbi, Orby

Ordella
(Latin) from Ora; prays

Orea
(Latin) from Ora; prays

Oreille
(Latin) from Oriel; gold

Orela
(Latin) from Oriel; golden girl

Orella
(Latin) golden girl
Oralla

Orenda
(Place name) Orinda, California; lovely gold

Orene
(French) nurturing
Orane, Orynne

Orfelinda
(Spanish) pretty dawn
Orfelinde, Orfelynda

Orianna
(Latin) sunny; dawn
Oria, Orian, Oriana,
Oriane, Orianna,
Oriannah, Orie

Orin
(Irish) dark-haired
Oren, Orinn

Oringa
(Invented) variant of
Orinda; golden

Orino
(Japanese) works outside
Ori

Oriole
(Latin) golden light
Oreilda, Oreole, Oriel,
Oriella, Oriol, Oriola

Oritha
(Greek) motherly

Orithna
(Greek) natural

Orla
(Irish) gold

Orlain
(French) famed

Orlanda
(German) celebrity

Orlaith
(Irish) golden lady

Orlena
(Russian) sharp-eyed

Orlenda
(Russian) eagle-eyed
Orlinda

Orly
(French) busy
Orlee

Ormanda
(Latin) noble
Ormie

Orna
(Irish) dark-haired
Ornah, Ornas, Ornie

Ornice
(Irish) pale face

Orpah
(Hebrew) escapes; fawn
Ophra, Ophrah, Orpa,
Orpha, Orphy

Orsa
(Greek) from Ursula;
stubborn

Orseline
(Latin) bearlike

Ortensia
(Italian) from Hortense;
joiner

Orthia
(Greek) straightforward

Ortrud
(Scandinavian) variant of
Gertrude; fresh
Ortrude

Orva
(French) golden girl
Or, Orvan, Orvah

Orya
(Origin unknown)
forthcoming

Osana
(Latin) praises the Lord

Osarma
(Origin unknown) sleek

Osen
(Japanese) one in a
thousand

Oseye
(African) happy

Osithe
(Place name) variant of
Ostia, Italy; together
Osyth

Osyka
(Native American) eagle-
eyed

Otha
(German) excels

Otilie
(Czech) fortunate girl

Otina
(Origin unknown)
fortunate

Ottavia
(English) from Octavia;
eighth

Otthild
(German) prospers
*Ottila, Ottilia, Ottilie,
Otylia*

Ottilie
(Czech) lucky omen

Ottolee
(English) combo of Otto
and Lee; appealing
Ottalie, Ottilie

Otylia
(Polish) rich
Oteelya

Ouida
(Literature) for the
Victorian author Ouida;
romantic

Ourania
(Greek) heavenly

Ovalia
(Spanish) helpful
Ova, Ove, Ovelia

Ovida
(Hebrew) worships

Ovyena
(Spanish) helps

Owena
(Welsh) feisty
Oweina, Owina, Owinne

Oya
(Africa) invited to earth

Oyama
(African) called out

Oza
(African) strong

Ozara
(Hebrew) treasured
Ozarah

Ozera
(Hebrew) of merit

Ozioma
(Origin unknown) strength
of character

Ozora
(Hebrew) rich

P

Paavna
(Hindi) pure

Paavani
(Hindi) purity of the river

Pabiola
(Spanish) small girl
Pabby, Pabi, Pabiole

Paca
(Spanish) free girl

Pace
(Last name as first name)
charismatic
Pase

Pacifica
(Spanish) peaceful
Pacifika

Padgett
(French) growing and
learning; lovely-haired
*Padge, Padget, Paget,
Pagett, Pagette*

Padma
(Hindi) lotus blossom

Page
(French) sharp; eager
Pagie, Paige, Paje, Payge

Pageant
(American) theatrical
*Padg, Padge, Padgeant,
Padgent, Pagent*

Paili
(Irish) wished-for child
Paisley
(Scottish) patterned
Paislee, Pazley
Paiton
(English) from a warring
town; sad
Paka
(African) kitty cat
Pal
(American) friend; buddy
Pala
(Native American) water
Palakika
(Hawaiian) much loved
Palemon
(Spanish) kind
Palem, Palemond
Paley
(Last name as first name)
wise
Palee, Palie
Palila
(Polynesian) bird; free
flight
Palla
(Greek) from Pallas; wise
Pallas
(Greek) wise woman
Palace, Palas
Palma
(Latin) successful
*Palmah, Palmeda,
Palmedah*
Palmer
(Latin) palm tree; balmy
Palmira
(Spanish) palm-tree girl
Palmyra
Paloma
(Spanish) dove
*Palloma, Palometa,
Palomita, Peloma*

Pamela
(Greek) sweet as honey
*Pam, Pamala, Pamalia,
Pamalla, Pamee, Pamelia,
Pamelina, Pamelinn,
Pamella, Pamelyn, Pamilla,
Pammee, Pammela,
Pammi, Pammie, Pammy,
Pamyla, Pamylla*
Pana
(Native American)
partridge; small
Pandita
(Hindi) learned
Pandora
(Greek) a gift; curious
*Pan, Pand, Panda, Pandie,
Pandorah, Pandorra,
Panndora*
Pang
(Chinese) innovative
Pangiota
(Greek) all is holy
Panna
(Hindi) emerald; knowing
Panola
(Greek) all
Panphila
(Greek) all loving
Panfila, Panfyla, Panphyla
Pansy
(Greek) fragrant
*Pan, Pansey, Pansie,
Panze, Panzee, Panzie*
Panthea
(Greek) loves all gods
Panther
(Greek) wild; all gods
*Panthar, Panthea,
Panthur, Panth*
Panya
(Greek) she is crowned
Panyin
(African) the older twin
Paola
(Italian) firebrand

Paolabella
(Italian) lovely firebrand
Papina
(African) vine; clings
Paradise
(Word as name) dream girl
Paris
(French) capital of France;
graceful woman
*Pareece, Parie, Parice,
Parisa, Parris, Parrish*
Parker
(English) noticed; in the
park
Park, Parke, Parkie
Parminder
(Hindi) attractive
Parnelle
(French) small stone
*Parn, Parnel, Parnell,
Parney*
Parslee
(Botanical)
complementary
Pars, Parse, Parsley, Parsli
Parthenia
(Greek) from the
Parthenon; virtuous
*Parthania, Parthe,
Parthee, Parthena,
Parthene, Parthenie,
Parthina, Parthine,
Pathania, Pathena,
Pathenia, Pathina, Thenia*
Parthenope
(Greek) siren
Parvani
(Hindi) full moon
Parvina
Parvati
(Hindi) mountain child
Parvin
(Hindi) star
Parveen

Pascale
(French) born on a
religious holiday
*Pascal, Pascalette,
Pascaline, Pascalle,
Paschale, Paskel, Paskil*
Pascasia
(French) born on Easter
Paschasia
Paschel
(African) spiritual
Paschell
Pash
(French) clever
Pasch
Pasha
(Greek) lady by the sea
Passha
Passion
(American) sensual
*Pashun, Pasyun, Pass,
Passyun*
Pasua
(French) Easter child
Pat
(Latin) short for Patricia;
tough
Patt, Patty
Paterekia
(Hawaiian) patrician
Pakelekia
Pati
(African) gathers fish
Patia
(Latin) short for Patricia;
hard-minded
Patience
(English) woman of
patience
*Pacience, Paciencia, Pat,
Pattie*
Patrice
(French) form of Patricia;
svelte
*Pat, Patreas, Patreece,
Pattie, Pattrice, Trece, Treecc*

Patricia
(Latin) woman of nobility;
unbending
*Pat, Patreece, Patreice,
Patria, Patric, Patrica,
Patrice, Patricka, Patrizia,
Patrisha, Patsie, Patsy,
Patti, Pattie, Patty, Tricia,
Trish, Trisha*

Patrina
(American) noble;
patrician
*Patryna, Patrynna, Tryna,
Trynnie*

Patsy
(Latin) short for Patricia;
brassy
*Pat, Patsey, Patsi, Patsie,
Patti, Patty*

Patty
(English) short for Patricia
and Patrice; sweet
Pat, Pati, Patti, Pattie

Paula
(Latin) small and feminine
*Paola, Paolina, Paulah,
Paule, Pauleen, Paulene,
Pauletta, Paulette, Paulie,
Paulina, Pauline, Paulita,
Pauly, Paulyn, Pavla,
Pavlina, Pavlinka, Pawlah,
Pawlina, Pola*

Paulette
(French) form of Paula;
little Paula
*Paula, Paulett, Paulie,
Paullette*

Paulina
(Latin) small; (Italian)
lovely
Paula, Paulena, Paulie

Pauline
(Latin) short for Paula;
precocious
Pauleen, Paulene

Pausha
(Hindi) lunar month;
moonlike

Pavana
(Origin unknown) from
Paulina; ravishing
Pavani

Pax
(Latin) peace goddess

Paxton
(Latin) peaceful
Pax, Paxten, Paxtun

Payton
(Last name as first name)
aggressive
*Pay, Paye, Payten, Paytun,
Peyton*

Paz
(Hebrew, Spanish)
sparkling; peaceful
*Paza, Pazia, Paziah,
Pazice, Pazit, Paziya,
Pazya*

Paza
(Hebrew) golden child
Paz

Pazzy
(Latin) peaceful
Paz, Pazet

Peace
(English) peaceful woman
Pea, Peece

Peaches
(American) outrageously
sweet
Peach, Peachy

Peakalika
(Hawaiian) happiness

Pearl
(Latin) jewel from the sea
*Pearla, Pearle, Pearaleen,
Pearlena, Pearlette,
Pearley, Pearlie, Pearline,
Pearly, Perl, Perla, Perle,
Perlette, Perley, Perlie,
Perly*

Pecola
(American) brash
Pekola

Pedzi
(Origin unknown) gold

Pefilia
(Spanish) profile

Pega
(Greek) from Peggy; happy

Peggy
(Greek) pearl; priceless
Peg, Peggi, Peggie

Pegma
(Greek) happy

Pei
(Place name) village; from
Tang Pei, China

Peigi
(Scottish) pearl; priceless

Peke
(Hawaiian) from Bertha;
gives

Pela
(Polish) loves the sea;
special

Pelagia
(Polish) sea girl
*Pelage, Pelageia, Pelagie,
Pelegia, Pelgia, Pellagia*

Pelagla
(Greek) girl of the sea
*Pelagie, Pelagi, Pelagia,
Pelagias, Pelaga*

Pele
(Hawaiian) volcano;
conflicted

Peleka
(Hawaiian) strong; marvel

Pelham
(English) thoughtful
*Pelhim, Pellam, Pellham,
Pellie*

Pelia
(Hebrew) marvelous
Peliah, Pelya, Pelyia

Pelika
(Hawaiian) strong

Pelipa
(African) loves horses
Phillipa

Pelulio
(Hawaiian) sea treasure

Pemba
(African) powerful

Penda
(African) beloved

Pendant
(French) necklace;
adorned
Pendan, Pendanyt

Penelope
(Greek) patient; weaver of
dreams
*Pela, Pelcia, Pen,
Penalope, Penelopa,
Penina, Penine, Penna,
Pennelope, Penni, Pennie,
Penny, Pinelopi, Popi*

Peni
(Greek) thinker

Peninah
(Hebrew) pearl; lovely
*Peni, Penie, Penina,
Penini, Peninit, Penny*

Penny
(Greek) short for
Penelope; spunky
Pen, Penee, Penni, Pennie

Penthea
(Spanish) orchid; lovely
*Fentheam, Fentheas,
Pentha, Pentheam,
Pentheas*

Peony
(Greek) flowering; giving
praise
Pea, Peoni, Peonie

Peoria
(Place name) city in
Illinois; poised

Pepita
(Spanish) high-energy
Pepa, Peppita, Peta

Pepper
(Latin) spicy
Pep, Peppie, Peppyr

Peppy
(American) cheerful
Pep, Peppey, Peppi, Peps

Perach
(Hebrew) flowering
*Perah, Pericha, Pircha,
Pirchia, Pirchit, Pirchiya,
Pirha*

Perdita
(Latin) wanders away

Perel
(Latin) tested
Perele

Perfecta
(Spanish) perfection
Perfekta

Peril
(Latin) victor

Periwinkle
(Botanical) blue-eyed;
flower girl

Perla
(Latin) substantial
Perlah

Peridot
(Arabic) green gem;
treasured
Peri

Perlace
(Spanish) small pearl
*Perl, Perlahse, Perlase,
Perly*

Perlette
(French) pearl; treasured
*Pearl, Pearline, Peraline,
Perl, Perle, Perlett*

Perlie
(Latin) form of Pearl
Perli, Purlie, Perly

Perlina
(American) small pearl
*Pearl, Perl, Perlinna,
Perlyna*

Pernella
(Scandinavian) rock;
dependable
Pernelle, Parnella, Pernilla

Pernille
(Scandinavian) rock; safe

Peron
(Latin) travels

Perouze
(Armenian) turquoise
gemstone
*Perou, Perous, Perouz,
Perry*

Perpetua
(Spanish) lasting

Perri
(Greek, Latin) outdoorsy
Peri, Perr, Perrie, Perry

Persephone
(Greek) breath of spring
*Pers, Perse, Persefone,
Persey*

Persis
(Latin) from Persia; exotic
Perssis

Pesha
(Hebrew) flourishing
Peshah, Peshia

Peshe
(Hebrew) saved

Pershella
(American) philanthropic
*Pershe, Pershel, Pershelle,
Pershey, Persie, Persy*

Persia
(Place name) colorful
Persha, Perzha

Peta
(English) saucy
*Pet, Petra, Petrice,
Petrina, Petrona, Petty*

Petra
(Slavic) glamorous;
capable
*Pet, Peti, Petrah, Pett,
Petti, Pietra*

Petrine
(Scandinavian) rock

Petronilla
(Greek) form of Peter;
rock; dependable
*Petria, Petrina, Petrine,
Petro, Petrone, Petronela,
Petronella, Pett*

Petula
(Latin) petulant song
Pet, Petulah, Petulia

Petunia
(American) flower; perky
Pet, Petune

Pfeiffer
(Last name as first) lovely
blonde; talented

Phaedra
(Greek) bright
*Faydra, Faydrah, Padra,
Phae, Phedra*

Phan
(Asian) shares

Phashestha
(American) decorative
Phashey, Shesta

Pheakkley
(Vietnamese) faithful

Pheba
(Greek) smiling
Phibba

Phedra
(Greek) bright child
*Faydra, Fedra, Phadra,
Phaedra, Phedre*

Phemia
(Greek) language

Phenice
(Origin unknown) enjoys
life
*Phenicia, Pheni, Phenica,
Venice*

Pheodora
(Greek) God's gift to
mankind

Phernita
(American) articulate
Ferney, Phern

Phia
(Irish) saint

Phila
(Greek) loving
Phil, Philly

Philadelphia
(Greek) loving one's fellow
man
Fill, Phil, Philly

Philana
(Greek) loving
Filana, Filly, Philly

Philantha
(Greek) loves flowers

Philberta
(English) intellectual

Philene
(Greek) loving others

Philida
(Greek) loving others
Philina, Phillada, Phillida

Philippa
(Greek) horse lover
*Feefee, Felipa, Phil,
Philipa, Philippe, Phillie,
Phillipina, Phillippah,
Pippa, Pippy*

Philise
(Greek) loving
Felece, Felice, Philese

Philly
(Place name) from
Philadelphia, Pennsylvania
Filly, Philee, Phillie

Philomena
(Greek) beloved
Filomena, Filomina, Mena,
Phil, Phillomenah,
Philomen, Philomene,
Philomina

Phiona
(Scottish) variant of Fiona;
special
Phionna

Phira
(Greek) loves music

Phoebe
(Greek) bringing light
Febe, Fee, Feebe, Feebs,
Pheabe, Phebe, Phebee,
Pheby, Phobe, Phoeb,
Phoebey, Phoebie, Phoebs

Phoenix
(Place name) U.S. city;
(Greek) rebirth
Fee, Fenix, Fenny, Phenix,
Phoe

Phonsa
(Origin unknown) jubilant

Photina
(Origin unknown)
fashionable

Phylicia
(Greek) fortunate girl
Felicia, Phillie, Phyl,
Phylecia

Phyllida
(Greek) lovely; leafy
bough
Filida, Phyll, Phyllyda

Phyllis
(Greek) beautiful; leafy
bough; articulate; smitten
Fillice, Fillis, Phil, Philis,
Phillis, Philliss, Phillisse,
Phyl, Phylis, Phyllys

Pia
(Latin) devout
Peah, Piah

Picabo
(Place name) city in Idaho;
swift
Peekaboo

Piedad
(Spanish) devout

Pier
(Greek) form of Peter;
rock; reliable
Peer

Pierette
(Greek) reliable
Perett, Perette, Piere

Pierina
(Greek) dependable
Peir, Per, Perina, Perine,
Pieryna

Pilar
(Spanish) worthwhile;
pillar of strength

Pili
(Spanish) pillar; strength

Pililani
(Hawaiian) strong one

Pilisi
(Hawaiian) simple life

Piluki
(Hawaiian) little leaf;
small

Pilvi
(Italian) cheerful
Pilvee

Pineki
(Hawaiian) peanut; tiny
girl

Pinga
(Hindi) dark

Pingjarje
(Native American) shy;
little doe

Pink
(American) blushing
Pinkee, Pinkie, Pinky,
Pinkye, Pynk

Pinquana
(Native American) fragrant girl

Piper
(English) player of a pipe; musical

Pippa
(English) ebullient; horse-lover
Pip, Pipa

Pippi
(English) blushing;
(French) loving horses
Pip, Pippie, Pippy

Pirene
(French) rock; dependable

Pirouette
(French) ballet term
Piro, Pirouet, Pirouetta

Pita
(English) comforting

Pitana
(Origin unknown) accented

Pitarra
(American) interesting
Pitarr Peta, Petah

Pity
(American) sad
Pitee, Pitey, Pitie

Pixie
(American) small; perky
Pixee, Pixey, Pixi

Placida
(Latin) serenity
Plasida

Platinum
(English) from the Spanish *platinal*; fine metal
Plati, Platnum

Platona
(Spanish) good friend
Pleasance, Pleasant, Pleasants, Pleasence

Pleshette
(American) plush
Plesh

Pleun
(Origin unknown) wordsmith

Plum
(Botanical) fruit; healthy

Po
(Italian) effervescent
Poe

Pocahontas
(Native American) joyful
Poca, Poka

Poe
(Last name as first name) mysterious

Poetry
(Word as name) romantic
Poe, Poesy, Poet

Polete
(Hawaiian) small; kind
Poleke, Polina

Polina
(Russian) small
Po, Pola, Polya

Polly
(Irish) devout; joyous
Pauleigh, Paulie, Pol, Pollee, Polley, Polli, Pollie

Pollyanna
(American, English) combo of Polly and Anna; happy-go-lucky
Polianna, Polliana, Pollie-anna, Polly

Polyxena
(Mythology) very hospitable

Pomona
(Latin) apple of my eye
Pomonah

Pompa
(Last name as first name) pompous
Pompy

Pompey
(Place name) lavish
*Pomp, Pompee, Pompei,
Pompy*

Poni
(African) second daughter

Pony
(American) wild west girl
Poney, Ponie

Poodle
(American) sweet; curly-haired
Poo, Pood, Poodly

Poonam
(Hindi) kind soul

Poppy
(Latin) flower; bouncy girl
Pop, Poppi, Poppie

Pora
(Hebrew) fertile

Porsche
(Latin) giving; high-minded
*Porsh, Porsha, Porshe,
Porshie, Portia*

Porsha
(German) giving
Porshea

Portia
(Latin) a giving woman
*Porcha, Porscha, Porsh,
Porsha, Porshuh*

Posala
(Native American) good-bye to spring

Posh
(American) fancy girl
Posha

Posy
(American) sweet
Posee, Posey, Posie

Poupée
(French) doll
Pou

Powder
(American) gentle; light
*Pow, Powd, Powdy,
Powdyr, PowPow*

Pragyata
(Hindi) knowledgeable

Prarthana
(Hindi) prays

Pratibha
(Hindi) understanding

Precia
(Latin) important
*Preciah, Presha, Presheah,
Preshuh*

Precious
(English) beloved
*Precia, Preciosa, Preshie,
Preshuce, Preshus*

Prema
(Hindi) love

Premlata
(Hindi) loving

Prescilian
(Hispanic) fashionable
Pres, Priss

Presencia
(Spanish) presents well

Presley
(English) talented
*Preslee, Preslie, Presly,
Prezlee, Prezley, Prezly*

Pribislava
(Polish) glorifed; helpful
Pribena, Pribka, Pribuska

Price
(Welsh) loving
Pri, Prise, Pry, Pryce, Pryse

Prima
(Latin) first; fresh
*Primalia, Primetta, Primia,
Primie, Primina, Priminia,
Primma, Primula*

Primalia
(Spanish) prime; first

Primavera
(Italian) spring child

Primola
(Botanical) flower; from
primrose; first
Prim, Prym, Prymola

Primrose
(English) rosy; fragrant
Prim, Primie, Rosie, Rosy

Princess
(English) precious
*Prin, Prince, Princesa,
Princessa, Princie, Prinsess*

Prinscella
(American) combo of
Princess and Priscilla;
princess
*Princella, Prins, Prinsce,
Prinscilla, Prinsee, Prinsey*

Prisca
(Latin) old spirit

Prisciliana
(Spanish) wise; old
Cissy, Priscili, Priss, Prissy

Priscilla
(Latin) wisdom of the ages
*Cilla, Precilla, Prescilla,
Pricilla, Pris, Priscella,
Priscila, Prisilla, Priss,
Prissie, Prissilla, Prissy,
Prysilla*

Prisisima
(Spanish) wise and
feminine
Priss, Prissy, Sima

Prisma
(Hindi) cherished baby

Prissy
(Latin) short for Priscilla;
wise; feminine
Prisi, Priss, Prissie

Priti
(Hindi) lovely

Pristina
(Latin) pristine

Priya
(Hindi) sweetheart
Preeya, Preya, Priyah

Prochora
(Latin) leads

Promise
(American) sincere
Promis

Proserpine
(Mythology) queen of the
underworld; secretive

Prospera
(Latin) does well

Protima
(Hindi) dancing girl

Prova
(Place name) Provence,
France
Pro, Proa, Provah

Pru
(Latin) short for Prudence
Prudie, Prue

Prudence
(Latin) wise; careful
*Perd, Pru, Prudencia,
Prudie, Prudince, Pruds,
Prudu, Prudy, Prue*

Prunella
(Latin) shy
Pru, Prue, Prune, Prunie

Pryor
(Last name as first name)
wealthy
Prieyer, Pryar, Prye, Pryer

Psyche
(Greek) soulful
Sye, Sykie

Pua
(Hawaiian) flower

Pulcheria
(Italian) chubby; curvy
Pulchia

Puma
(American) cougar; wild
spirit
*Poom, Pooma, Poomah,
Pumah, Pume*

Purity
(English) virginal
Puretee, Puritie

Purnima
(Hindi) full moon baby

Pyera
(Italian) sturdy;
formidable; rock
Pyer, Pyerah

Pyllyon
(English) enthusiastic
Pillion, Pillyon, Pillyun

Pyrena
(Greek) fiery temper

Pyria
(Origin unknown)
cherished
Pyra, Pyrea

Pyrrha
(Latin) fire

Pythia
(Greek) prophet

Qadira
(Arabic) wields power
Kadira

Qamra
(Arabic) moon girl
Kamra

Qing
(Origin unknown) quick

Qitarah
(Arabic) aromatic

Qiturah
(Arabic) aromatic
*Qeturah, Quetura,
Queturah*

Q-Malee
(American) form of
Cumale; open-hearted
*Cue, Q, Quemalee,
Quemali, Quemalie*

Quan
(Chinese) goddess of
compassion

Quanda
(English) queenly
*Kwanda, Kwandah,
Quandah, Qwanda*

Quanella
(African American)
sparkling
Kwannie, Quanela

Quanesha
(African American) singing
*Kwaeesha, Kwannie,
Quaneisha, Quanisha*

Quanika
(American) combo of Quan
and Nika; joyful
*Quanikka, Quanikki,
Quanique, Quawanica*

Quantina
(American) brave queen
*Kwantina, Kwantynna,
Quantinna, Quantyna,
Tina*

Qubilah
(Arabic) easygoing

QueAnna
(American) combo of Que
and Anna; genuine
*Keana, KeAnna, KeeAnna,
Queana*

Queen
(English) regal; special
*Quanda, Queena,
Queenette, Queenie*

Queenie
(English) royal and dignified
Kweenie, Quee, Queen, Queeny

Queenverlyn
(Invented) combo of Queen and Verlyn; lady
Queenee, Queenie

Queisha
(American) contented child
Queysha, Queshia

Quenby
(Swedish) feminine
Quenbee, Quenbey, Quenbi, Quenbie, Quinbee, Quinbie, Quinby

Quenna
(English) feminine
Kwenna

Querida
(Spanish) dear one

Questa
(French) looking for love
Kesta

Queta
(Spanish) head of the house
Keta

Quiana
(Origin unknown) from Hannah; practical
Qiana, Qianna, Quianna, Quiyanna

Quilla
(English) writer
Kwila, Kwilla, Quila, Quillah, Quyla, Quylla

Quinby
(Scandinavian) living like royalty
Quenby, Quin, Quinbie, Quinnie

Quinceanos
(Spanish) fifteenth child
Quin, Quince, Quincy

Quincy
(French) fifth
Quince, Quincey, Quinci, Quincie, Quincy, Quinsy

Quincylla
(American) popular; fifth child
Cylla, Quince, Quincy

Quinella
(Latin) a girl who is as pretty as two
Quinn

Quinn
(English, Irish) smart
Quin, Quinnie

Quinta
(Latin) fifth day of the month

Quintana
(Latin) fifth; lovely girl
Quentana, Quinn

Quintessa
(Latin) essential goodness

Quintina
(Latin) fifth child
Quentina, Quintana, Quintessa, Quintona, Quintonette, Quintonice

Quintilla
(Latin) fifth girl
Quintina

Quintona
(Latin) fifth

Quintwana
(American) fifth girl in the family
Quintuana

Quinyette
(American) likeable; fifth child
Kwenyette, Quiny

Quirina
(Latin) contentious

Quisha
(African American)
beautiful mind
Keisha, Kesha, Key

Quita
(Latin) peaceful
Keeta, Keetah

R

Rabab
(Origin unknown) different

Rabiah
(Arabic) breezy

Rabbit
(American) lively; energetic
Rabit

Rabia
(Arabic) wind

Rachael
(Hebrew) peaceful as a
lamb
*Rach, Rachaele, Rachal,
Rachel, Rachie, Rae,
Raechal, Rasch, Ray, Raye*

Racheline
(American) combo of
Rachel and Line
Rachelene

Rachelle
(French) calm
*Rach, Rachell, Rashell,
Rashelle, Rochelle*

Racquel
(French) friendly
Racquelle, Raquel

Rada
(Polish) glad

Radha
(Hindi) successful
Radhika

Radmilla
(Slavic) glad; hardworking

Rae
(English) raving beauty
Raedie, Raena, Ray, Raye

Raegan
(French) delicate
Reagan, Regan, Regun

Raelene
(American) combo of Rae
and Lene; smart

Rafa
(Arabic) joyful girl
Rafah

Rafaela
(Hebrew) spiritual
Rafayela

Rafferty
(Irish) prospering
*Raferty, Raff, Raffarty,
Rafty*

Ragnild
(Scandinavian) goddess of
war
*Ragnhild, Ragnhilda,
Ragnhilde, Ragnilda,
Ranillda, Reinheld,
Renilda, Renilde, Reynilda,
Reynilde*

Raheel
(Hebrew) from Rachel;
sheep; meek
Raheela

Rahela
(Hawaiian) lamb

Rahil
(Hebrew) from Rachel;
sheep; meek

Rahima
(Pakistani) loving
Raheema, Raheema

Rain
(English) falling water
Rainie, Reign

Raina
(German) dramatic
Raine, Rainna, Rayna

Rainbow
(American) bright
*Rain, Rainbeau, Rainbo,
Rainie*

Raine
(Latin) helpful friend
*Raina, Rainie, Rana, Rane,
Rayne*

Rainey
(Last name as first name)
giving
Rainee, Rainie, Raney

Rainey-Anne
(American) combo of
Rainey and Anne; languid
*Rainee, Raineeann,
Rainee-Anne, Rainey,
Raneyann, Raneyanne*

Raisa
(Russian) embraced
Rasa

Raissa
(Russian) from Rose; rosy
cheeks

Raja
(Arabic) optimist

Rajani
(Hindi) dark; hopeful

Raji
(Hindi) royal

Rajni
(Hindi) dark night

Raka
(Hindi) royal

Raleigh
(Irish) admirable
*Raileigh, Railey, Raley,
Rawleigh, Rawley*

Ralphina
(American) from Ralph;
simplistic
Ralphine

Rama
(Hindi) godlike; good

Ramona
(Teutonic) beautiful
protector
*Rae, Ramonah, Ramonna,
Raymona*

Ramsay
(English) from the isle of
rams; country girl
Ramsey

Rana
(Hebrew) fresh;
(Hindi) beauty

Randa
(Latin) admired
Ran, Randah

Randall
(English) protective of her
own
Rand, Randal, Randi, Randy

Randelle
(American) wary
Randee, Randele

Randi
(English) audacious
Randee, Randie, Randy

Rane
(Scandinavian) queen-like
Rain, Raine, Ranie

Rani
(Hebrew) joyous; (Hindi)
queen
Rainie, Ranie

Rania
(Sanskrit) regal
*Ranea, Raneah, Raney,
Ranie*

Ranielle
(French) royal; frank

Ranita
(Hebrew) musical
*Ranit, Ranite, Ranitra,
Ranitta*

Raoule
(Spanish) from Raoul; wild
heart
Raoula, Raula

Rapa
(Hawaiian) lovely by
moonlight

Raphaela
(Hebrew) helping to heal
Rafaela, Rafe

Raquel
(Spanish) sensual
Racuell, Raquelle, Raqwel

Rasheeda
(Hindi) pious
*Rashee, Rashida, Rashie,
Rashy*

Rashidah
(Arabic) on the right path
Rashida

Rashinique
(African American) rash
Rash, Rashy

Raven
(English) blackbird
Ravan, Rave, Ravin

Ravenna
(English) blackbird

Rawnie
(Slavic) ladylike
Rawani, Rawn, Rawnee

Ray
(American) simplistic
approach
Rae, Raymonde

Rayleen
(American) popular
Raylene, Raylie, Rayly

Rayna
(Scandinavian) strong girl

Raynelle
(American) giving hope;
combo of Ray and Nelle
*Nellie, Rae, Raenel,
Raenelle*

Raynette
(American) ray of hope;
dancer
Raenette, Raynet

Razia
(Hebrew) secretive
Razeah, Raziah

Razina
(African) nice

Rea
(Polish) flowing
Raya

Reagan
(Last name as first name)
strong
Regan, Reganne, Reggie

Reannah
(English) combo of Rae
and Annah; divine
Reana, Reanna, Rennie

Reanne
(American) happy
*Reann, Rennie, Rere,
Rianne*

Reba
(Hebrew) fourth-born
Rebah, Ree, Reeba

Rebecca
(Hebrew) loyal
*Becca, Becki, Beckie,
Becky, Rebeca, Rebeka,
Rebekah*

Rebi
(Hebrew) friend who is
steadfast
Reby, Ree, Ribi

Rebop
(American) zany
Reebop

Reed
(English) red-haired
Read, Reade, Reid, Reida

Reenie
(Greek) peace-loving
Reena, Reeni, Reeny, Ren, Rena

Reese
(American) style-setting
Ree, Reece, Rees, Rere

Reeve
(Last name as first name)
strong

Regan
(Irish) queenly
Reagan

Regeana
(American) form of
Regina; queen
Rege, Regeanah, Regeane

Regina
(English, Latin) thoughtful
Gina, Rege, Regena, Reggie, Regine

Regine
(Latin) royal
Regene, Rejean

Rehema
(African) well-grounded
Rehemah, Rehemma, Rehima

Reiko
(Japanese) appreciative

Reine
(Spanish) from Reina;
queen

Rela
(German) everything
Reila, Rella

Reina
(Spanish) a thinker
Rein, Reinie, Rina

Reith
(American) shy
Ree, Reeth

Rella
(Origin unknown) rogue

Remah
(Hebrew) pale beauty
Rema, Remme, Remmie, Rima, Ryma

Remedios
(Spanish) helpful

Remember
(American) memorable
Remi, Remmi, Remmie, Remmy

Remi
(French) woman of
Rheims; jaded
Remee, Remie, Remy

Rena
(Hebrew) joyful singer
Reena, Rinah, Rinne

Renae
(French) form of Renee;
born again
Renay, Rennie, Rere

Renard
(French) fox; sly
Ren, Renarde, Rynard, Rynn

Renata
(French) reaching out
Renie, Renita, Rennie, Rinata

Rene
(Greek) hopeful
Reen, Reenie, Reney

Renea
(French) form of Renee;
renewal
Renny

Renee
(French) born again
Rene, Rennie, Rere

Renetta
(French) reborn
Ranetta, Renette

Renie
(Latin) renewal

Renita
(Latin) poised
Ren, Renetta, Rennie

Renite
(Latin) stubborn
Reneta, Renita

Renzia
(Greek) form of Renee;
peaceful
Renze

Resa
(Greek) productive;
laughing
Reesa, Reese, Risa

Reseda
(Spanish) helpful;
(Latin) fragrant flower
Res, Reseta

Reshauna
(African American) combo
of Re and Shauna
*Reshana, Reshawna,
Reshie*

Reshma
(African) compassionate

Reta
(African) shakes up
*Reda, Reeda, Reeta,
Rheta, Rhetta*

Reva
(Hebrew) rainmaker
Ree, Reeva, Rere

Reveca
(Spanish) form of
Rebecca; charming
Reba, Rebeca, Reva

Rexanne
(English) combo of Rex
and Anne; gracious
Rexan, Rexann, Rexanna

Rexella
(English) combo of Rex
and Ella; lighthearted
*Rexalla, Rexel, Rexela,
Rexell, Rexey, Rexi, Rexy*

Rexie
(American) confident
Rex, Rexi, Rexy

Reyna
(English) elegant; (Greek)
peaceful woman
Raina, Rayna, Rey

Reynalda
(German) wise
Raynalda, Rey, Reyrey

Reynolds
(Scottish) wispy
*Rey, Reye, Reynells,
Reynold*

Reza
(Czech) from Theresa;
playful
Rezi, Rezka, Riza

Rhea
(Greek) earthy; mother of
gods; strong
Ria

Rheta
(American) form of Rita;
intelligent

Rhianna
(Welsh) pure
Rheanna

Rhiannon
(Welsh) goddess; intuitive
*Rhian, Rhiane, Rhianen,
Rhiann, Rhianon, Rhyan,
Rhye, Riannon*

Rhoda
(Greek) rosy
*Rhodie, Roda, Rodi,
Rodie, Rody, Roe*

Rhodanthe
(Greek) from Rhodes;
thinker
Rhodante

Rhona
(Scottish) power-wielding
Rona, Ronne

Rhonda
(Welsh) vocal;
quintessential
Rhon, Ron, Ronda, Ronnie

Rhondie
(American) perfect
Rond, Rondie, Rondy

Rhonwen
(Welsh) lovely
*Rhonwenne, Rhonwin,
Ronwen*

Ria
(Spanish) water-loving;
river
Reah, Riah

Riana
(Irish) frisky
Reana, Rere, Rianna, Rinnie

Riane
(American) attractive
Reann, Reanne

Riannon
(Irish) free spirit
Rianna

Rica
(Spanish) celestial
*Ric, Ricca, Rickie, Rieka,
Rika, Ryka*

Ricarda
(German) has power

Richelle
(French) strong and
artistic
*Chelle, Chellie, Rich,
Richel, Richele, Richie*

Richenda
(German) rules

Richesse
(French) wealthy
Richess

Ricki
(American) sporty
*Rici, Rick, Rickie, Ricky,
Rik, Riki, Rikki*

Rickma
(Hindi) from Rukmi;
golden

Rico
(Italian) sexy
Reko, Ricco

Rida
(Arabic) satisfied
Ridah

Rihana
(Irish) pretty

Riley
(Irish) courageous; lively
*Reilly, Rylee, Ryleigh,
Ryley, Rylie*

Rilla
(German) lives by the
brook

Rima
(Arabic) graceful; antelope
*Rema, Remmee, Remmy,
Rimmy, Ryma*

Rimona
(Hebrew) pomegranate;
small

Rina
(Hebrew) joy
Renah

Rinda
(Scandinavian) loyal
Rindah

Ring
(American) magical
Ringe, Ryng

Riona
(Irish) regal
*Rina, Rine, Rionn, Rionna,
Rionne*

Ripley
(American) unique
Riplee, Ripli, Riplie

Riquette
(French) feminine form of Richard

Rissa
(Latin) laughing
Resa, Risa, Riss, Rissah, Rissie

Rita
(Greek) precious pearl
Reda, Reita, Rida

Ritalinda
(Spanish) combo of Rita and Linda; treasured
Linda, Retalinda, Retalynde, Rita, Ritalynd, Ritalynda

Ritsa
(Greek) short for Alexandra; noteworthy

Ritz
(American) rich
Rits

Riva
(Hebrew) joining; sparkling
Reva, Revi, Revvy

Rivalee
(Hebrew) combo of Riva and Lee; joined
Rivalea, Riva-Lee

River
(Latin) woman by the stream
Riv

Rivers
(American) trendy

Riza
(Greek) dignified
Reza, Rize

Roanna
(Spanish) brown skin
Ranna, Roanne, Ronni, Ronnie, Ronny

Roberta
(English) brilliant mind
Robbie, Robby, Robertah, Robi

Robin
(English) taken by the wind; bird
Robbie, Robby, Robinn, Robinne, Robyn

Robina
(Scottish) birdlike; robin
Robena

Robinetta
(American) combo of Robin and Etta; graceful dancer
Robbie, Robineta, Robinette

Rochelle
(French) small and strong-willed; (Hebrew) dream-like beauty
Roch, Roche, Rochel, Rochi, Rochie, Rochy, Roshelle

Rockella
(Invented) rocker
Rockell, Rockelle

Rocky
(American) tomboy
Rock, Rockee, Rockey, Rockie

Roda
(Polish) intelligent

Roddy
(German) well-known
Rod, Roddee, Roddey, Roddi, Roddie

Roderica
(German) princess
Rica, Roda, Roddie, Rodericka, Rodrika

Rogertha
(American) form of Roger; substantial
Rodge

Rohan
(Hindi) sandalwood; pretty

Rohana
(Hindi) sandalwood;
textured
Rohanna

Roisin
(Irish) rose

Roksana
(Polish) dawn
Roksanna, Roksona

Rolanda
(German) rich woman
Rolane, Rollande, Rollie

Rolandan
(German) form of Roland;
from a famous land
*Roland, Rolanden, Rollie,
Rolly*

Roline
(German) destined for
fame
*Roelene, Roeline, Rolene,
Rollene, Rolleen, Rollina,
Rolline, Rolyne*

Roma
(Italian) girl from Rome;
adventurous
Romy

Romaine
(French) daredevil
*Romain, Romane,
Romayne, Romi*

Roman
(Italian) adventurous
*Romi, Romie, Rommie,
Rommye, Romyn*

Romey
(Latin) sea-loving
Romy

Romilda
(Latin) striking
*Romelda, Romey, Romie,
Romy*

Romilla
(Latin) from Rome; she
who wanders
*Romella, Romi, Romie,
Romila*

Romilly
(Latin) wanderer
Romillee, Romillie, Romily

Romney
(Welsh) winding river

Romola
(Latin) from Rome; dark-
haired

Romona
(Spanish) form of Ramona
*Mona, Rome, Romie,
Romy*

Romy
(French) short for
Romaine; roaming
Roe. Romi, Romie

Rona
(Scandinavian, Scottish)
powerful
Rhona, Ronne, Ronni

Ronat
(Scandinavian) from
Rhona; smiles

Ronda
(Welsh) form of Rhonda; a
standout
Ronni

Ronelle
(English) winner
Ronnie

Roney
(Scandinavian) form of
Rona; lively
Roneye, Roni

Ronneta
(English) go-getter
*Roneda, Ronnete,
Ronnette, Ronnie*

Ronni
   (American) energetic
   Ron, Ronee, Roni, Ronnie,
   Ronny
Rori
   (Irish) spirited; brilliant
   Rory
Ros
   (English) from Rosalind;
   rosy and pretty
   Roz
Rosa
   (Italian) rose; (German)
   blushing beauty
   Rose, Rossah, Roza
Rosabella
   (Italian) combo of Rosa
   and Bella; beautiful rose
Rosabelle
   (French) combo of Rosa
   and Belle; beautiful rose
   Belle, Rosa, Rosabel,
   Rosa-Belle
Rosalba
   (Latin) glorious as a rose
   Rosalbah, Rosey, Rosi,
   Rosie, Rosy
Rosalia
   (Italian) hanging roses
   Rosa, Rosalea, Rosaleah,
   Rosaliah, Roselia, Rosey,
   Rosi, Rosie, Rossalia, Rosy
Rosalie
   (English) striking dark
   beauty
   Leelee, Rosa, Rosalee,
   RosaLee, Rosa-Lee, Rosie,
   Rossalie, Roz, Rozalee,
   Rozalie
Rosalind
   (Spanish) lovely rose
   Lind, Ros, Rosa, Rosalyn,
   Rosalynde, Rosie, Roslyn,
   Roslynn, Roz

Rosalinda
   (Spanish) lovely rose
   Rosa-Linda, Rosalynda
Rosaline
   (Spanish) a rose
   Rosalyn, Rosalynne,
   Roslyn
Rosalvo
   (Spanish) rosy-faced
   Rosa, Rosey
Rosamaria
   (Italian) combo of Rosa
   and Maria; rose; devout
   Rosa-Maria
Rosamond
   (English) beauty
   Rosa, Rosamun,
   Rosamund, Rose,
   Rosemond, Rosie, Roz
Rosanna
   (English) lovely
   Rosannah
Rosaoralia
   (Spanish) combo of Rosa
   and Oralia; rosy
   Rosa Oralia, Rosa-Oralia,
   RoseyO
Rose
   (Latin) rose; blushing
   beauty
   Rosa, Rosey, Rosi, Rosie,
   Rosy, Roze, Rozee
Roseandrea
   (Invented) combo of Rose
   and Andrea
Roseanna
   (English) combo of Rose
   and Anna
   Rosana, Rosannah, Rose,
   Roseana, Rosie
Roseanne
   (English) combo of Rose
   and Anne
   Rosann, Rosanne, Rose
   Ann, Rosie

Rosebud
(Latin) flowering
Roselle
(Latin) rose
Rosellen
(English) pretty
Roselinn, Roselyn
Rosemarie
(Latin, Scandinavian)
combo of Rose and Marie
Rose-Marie, Rosemary
Rosemary
(English) combo of Rose
and Mary; sweetheart
*Ro, Rose Mary, Rose,
Rosie*
Rosenda
(Spanish) rosy
*Rose, Rosend, Rosende,
Rosey, Rosie, Senda*
Rosetta
(Italian) longlasting
beauty
Rose, Rosy, Rozetta
Rosette
(Latin) flowering; rosy
Rosett, Rosetta
Roshall
(African American) form of
Rochelle; dreamy
Rochalle, Roshalle
Roshawna
(African American) combo
of Rose and Shawna
*Rosh, Roshanna, Roshie,
Roshona, Shawn*
Rosheen
(Latin) rose
Roshell
(French) form of Rochelle;
small and strong-willed
Rochelle, Roshelle
Roshni
(Sanskrit) light

Roshumba
(African American)
gorgeous
Rosh, Roshumbah
Roshunda
(African American)
flamboyant
*Rosey, Roshun, Roshund,
Rosie, Roz*
Rosie
(English) bright-cheeked
Rose, Rosi, Rosy
Rosina
(English) rose
Rosita
(Spanish) pretty
*Roseta, Rosey, Rosie,
Rositta*
Roslyn
(Scottish) combo of Rose
and Lyn; lovely girl
Ross
(Scottish) peninsula is
home
Rosse
Rotella
(American) smart
Rotel, Rotela
Roth
(American) studious
Rothe
Rotnei
(American) bright
Rotnay
Rowan
(Welsh) blonde
Rowanne
Rowena
(Scottish) blissful; beloved
friend
Roe, Roenna, Rowina
Roxanna
(Persian) bright
Roxana, Roxie

Roxanne
(Persian) lovely as the sun
*Roxane, Roxann, Roxie,
Roxy*

Roxy
(American) sunny
Rox, Roxi, Roxie

Royale
(English) of royal family
*Royalla, Royalene,
Roayalina, Royall, Royalle,
Royalyn, Royalynne*

Royce
(English) king's child
Roice

Royetta
(American) combo of Roy
and Etta; cowgirl
*Etta, Roy, Roye, Royett,
Royette*

Roynale
(American) motivated
Roy, Royna, Roynal

Roz
(French) short for Rosalind
Ros, Rozz, Rozzie

Rozena
(American) form of
Rosena; pretty
Roze, Rozenna

Rozonda
(American) pretty
Rosonde, Rozon, Rozond

Rube
(Hawaiian) ruby; gem

Rubena
(Hebrew) sassy
Rubyn, Rubyna, Rueben

Rubianney
(American) combo of Rubi
and Anney; shining
*Rubi, Rubianey, Rubianne,
Rubi-Anney, Rubyann*

Rubilee
(American) combo of Ruby
and Lee; shining
Ruby Lee, Rubylee

Rubina
(Pakistani) gem
Rubi

Rubra
(French) from Ruby; jewel
Rube, Rue

Ruby
(French) precious jewel
Rubi, Rubie, Rue

Ruby-Jewel
(American) combo of Ruby
and Jewel; sassy
*Rubijewel, Rubyjewel,
Ruby-Jule*

Ruchi
(German) brash

Rudelle
(English) ruddy skin
Rudella

Rudy
(German) sly
Rudee, Rudell, Rudie

Rue
(English, German) looking
back
Ru

Rufina
(Italian) red-haired
*Rufeena, Rufeine, Ruffina,
Ruphyna*

Ruelynn
(American) combo of Rue
and Lynn; smart and
famous
*Rue Lynn, Ruelin, Ruelinn,
Rue-Lynn, Rulynn*

Rufaro
(African) happy

Rula
(American) wild-spirited
Rue, Rulah, Rewela

Rumer
(English) unique
Ru, Rumor

Runa
(Scandinavian) secret

Rupli
(Hindi) beautiful

Ruri
(Japanese) emerald
Rure, Rurrie, RuRu

Rusbel
(Spanish) beautiful girl
with reddish hair
Rusbell, Rusbella

Russo
(American) happy
Russoh

Rusty
(English) red-haired girl
Rustee, Rusti

Ruta
(Lithuanian) practical
Rue, Rudah, Rutah

Ruth
(Hebrew) loyal friend
Rue, Ruthie, Ruthy

Ruthanne
(American) combo of Ruth
and Anne
Ruthann

Ruthemma
(American) combo of Ruth
and Emma
Routhemma, Ruthema

Ruthie
(Hebrew) friendly and
young
Ruth, Ruthey, Ruthi, Ruthy

Ryan
(Irish) royal; assertive
Ryann, Ryen, Ryunn, Rian

Ryanna
(Irish) leader
*Rianna, Rianne, Ryana,
Ryanne, Rynn*

Ryba
(Hebrew) traditional
Reba, Ree, Riba, Ribah

Rylee
(Irish) brave
*Rilee, Rili, Ryelee, Ryley,
Ryli, Ryly*

Ryn
(American) form of Wren
Ren, Rynn

Ryne
(Irish) form of Ryan;
divine; special
Rynea, Ryni, Rynie

Rynie
(American) loves the
woods
Rinnie, Ryn

Rynn
(American) outdoorsy
woman
Rin, Rynna, Rynnie, Wren

Rynnea
(American) sun-lover
Rynnee, Rynni, Rynnia

S

Saba
(Arabic) morning star
Sabah

Sabella
(English) spiritual
*Bella, Belle, Sabela,
Sabell, Sabelle, Sebelle*

Sabina
(Latin) desirable
Sabeena, Sabine,
Sabinna, Sabyna, Say

Sabine
(Latin) tribe in ancient
Italy
Sabeen, Sabienne, Sabin,
Sabyne

Sable
(English) chic
Sabelle, Sabie

Sablette
(American) luxurious
Sable, Sablet

Sabra
(Hebrew) substantial
Sabe, Sabera, Sabrah

Sabrina
(Latin) passionate
Breena, Brina, Brinna,
Sabe, Sabreena, Sabrinna

Sacha
(Greek) helpful girl
Sachie, Sachy

Sachi
(Japanese) girl
Sachee, Sachey, Sachie,
Sachy, Sashi, Shashie

Sadie
(Hebrew) charmer;
princess
Sade, Sadee, Sady, Sadye,
Shaday

Saffron
(Indian) spice
Saffrone, Safron

Saga
(Scandinavian) sensual
Sagah

Sagal
(American) action-oriented
Sagall, Segalle

Sage
(Latin) wise
Saige

Sahara
(Place name) desert;
wilderness
Saharra

Sahare
(American) loner

Sahila
(Hindi) guides others

Sahri
(Arabic) giving

Saida
(Hebrew) happy girl
Sada, Sadie

Sailor
(American) outdoorsy
Sail, Saile, Sailer, Saylor

Sajah
(Hindi) meritorious
Sajie, Sayah

Sakura
(Japanese) wealthy

Sal
(Italian) short for
Salvador; (American)
short for Sally

Salama
(African) safe

Salena
(Latin) needed; basic
Salene, Sally

Salima
(Arabic) healthy
Salma

Salina
(French) quiet and deep
Sale, Salena

Sally
(Hebrew) princess
Sal, Salli, Sallie

Salma
(Hebrew) peaceful;
(Spanish) ingenious;
(Hindi) safe
Sal, Sali, Sallee, Salley,
Salli, Sally, Salmah,
Salwah

Salome
(Hebrew) sensual; peaceful
Sal, Salohme, Salomey, Salomi

Salowmee
(Invented) form of Salome; peaceful
Sal, Salomee, Salomie, Salomy, Slowmee

Salvadora
(Spanish) saved
Sal, Salvadorah

Salvia
(Spanish) healthy

Sam
(Hebrew) God leads

Samantha
(Hebrew) good listener
Sam, Samath, Sammi, Sammie

Samara
(Hebrew) God-led; watchful
Sam, Samora

Samarantha
(Invented) combo of Samara and Samantha

Sami
(Hebrew) insightful
Sam, Sammie, Sammy

Samia
(Hindi) joyful
Sameah, Samee, Sameea, Samina, Sammy

Samimah
(Hebrew) praised

Samuela
(Hebrew) selected
Samm, Sammi, Sammy, Samula

Samyrah
(African American) music-loving
Samirah, Samyra

Sana
(Arabic) quintessential beauty

Sancha
(Spanish) sacred child
Sanchia

Sandi
(Greek) defends others
Sand, Sanda, Sandee, Sandie, Sandy

Sandip
(Hindi) knowing

Sandra
(Greek) helpful; protective
Sandrah, Sandy

Sandrea
(Greek) selfless
Sandreea, Sandie, Sanndria

Sandreen
(American) great
Sandrene, Sandrin, Sandrine

Sandy
(American) playful
Sandee, Sandey, Sandi, Sandie

Sanila
(Indian) full of praise
Sanilla

Saniyya
(Hindi) a special moment in time

Sanjuana
(Spanish) from San Juan; God-loving
Sanwanna

Sanjuanita
(Spanish) from San Juan; combo of San Juan and Juanita; believer
Juanita, Sanjuan

Sanna
(Scandinavian) truthful
Sana

Santa
(Latin) saint
Santana
(Spanish) saintly
*San, Santanne, Santie,
Santina*
Santeene
(Spanish) passionate
*Santeena, Santene,
Santie, Santina, Santine,
Satana*
Santia
(African) lovable
Santea
Santonina
(Spanish) ardent
Sapphire
(Greek) precious gem
*Safire, Saphire, Sapphie,
Sapphyre*
Sappho
(Greek) blue
Sara
(Hebrew) God's princess
Sae, Sarah, Saree, Sarrie
Sarafina
(Hebrew) angelic
Seraphina
Sarah-Jessica
(American) combo of
Sarah and Jessica;
charismatic
*Sarah Jessica, Sara-Jess,
Sarajessee, Sarajessica*
Sarai
(Hebrew) contentious
Sari
Saraid
(Irish) best
Sarajane
(American) combo of Sara
and Jane
Sarahjane
Saralee
(American) combo of Sara
and Lee

Saramay
(American) combo of Sara
and May
Sarah-May, Saramae
Saree
(Hebrew) woman of value
Sarie, Sary
Sari
(Hebrew, Arabic) noble
*Saree, Sarey, Sarie,
Sarree, Sarrey, Sarri*
Sarika
(Hindi) thrush; sings
Sarilla
(Spanish) princess
Sarella, Sarill, Sarille
Sarina
(Hebrew) strong
Sareena, Sarena, Sarrie
Sarit
(Hebrew) form of Sarah;
majestic
Saritt, Saryt, Sarytt
Sarita
(Spanish) regal
Sareeta, Sarie, Saritah
Sasha
(Russian) beautiful
courtesan; helpful
*Sacha, Sachie, Sascha,
Sasheen, Sashy*
Saskia
(Dutch) dramatic
Saskiah
Sassy
(Irish) Saxon girl; flirtatious
Sass, Sassi, Sassie
Satchel
(American) unusual
Satchal
Satin
(French) shiny
Saten

Saturine
(American) form of Saturn
Saturenne, Saturinne,
Saturn, Saturyne

Saundra
(Greek) defender
Sandi, Sandra, Sandrah

Savannah
(Spanish) open heart
Sava, Savana, Savanah,
Savanna, Seven

Savina
(Latin) form of Sabina
Saveena, Savyna

Sawyer
(Last name as first name)
industrious
Sawya, Sawyar, Sawyhr,
Sawyie, Sawyur

Sayde
(American) form of Sadie;
charming
Saydey, Saydie

Sayo
(Japanese) born at night
Saio, Sao

Scally
(Last name as first)
introspective
Scalley, Scalli

Scarlett
(English) red
Scarlet, Scarletta,
Scarlette

Schae
(Irish) variation of Shea;
fairy place
Schay

Schemika
(African American) form of
Shameka
Schemi, Schemike

Scherry
(American) form of Sherry
Scherri, Scherrie

Schmoopie
(American) baby; sweetie
Schmoopee, Schmoopey,
Schmoopy, Shmoopi

Schulyer
(Dutch) form of Skyler;
protective
Schulyar, Sky, Skye

Schylar
(Dutch) sheltering
Schylarr, Schyler, Schylerr,
Schylur, Schylurr

Scooter
(American) wild-spirit
Scooder, Scoot

Scotty
(Scottish) girl from
Scotland
Scota, Scotti, Scottie

Scout
(French) precocious
Scouts

Scully
(Irish) strong
Scullee, Sculleigh, Sculley,
Sculli, Scullie

Scyllaea
(Greek) mythological
monster; menace
Cilla, Scylla, Silla

Sea
(American) sea-loving;
flowing
Cee, See

Sealy
(Last name as first name)
fun-loving
Celie, Seal, Sealie

Sean
(Hebrew, Irish) God is
giving

Seana
(Irish) giving
Seane, Seanna, Suannea

Seandra
(American) form of
Deandra; intuitive
*Seandre, Seandreah,
Seanne*

Season
(Latin) special; change
*Seas, Seasee, Seasen,
Seasie, Seasun, Seazun,
Seezun*

Seaton
(English) from the coast
*Seaten, Seeten, Seeton,
Seten, Seton*

Sebastiane
(Latin) respected female
Sebastian, Sebbie

Seely
(English) bright
*Sealee, Sealey, Seali,
Sealie, Sealy, Seelee,
Seeley, Seeli, Seelie*

Seema
(Hebrew) treasured; soft-
hearted
Seem

Seine
(French) river; flowing
Sane

Sejal
(Origin unknown) together

Sela
(Hebrew) short for Cecilia;
substantial
Cela, Celia, Selah, Selia

Selda
(German) sure-footed
*Seda, Seldah, Selde,
Seldee, Seldey, Seldi,
Seldie*

Selena
(Greek) like the moon;
shapely
*Celina, Sela, Seleene,
Selene, Selina, Sylena*

Selene
(Greek) goddess of the
moon
Seleene, Seline, Selyne

Selima
(Hebrew) peacemaker
Selema, Selemmah

Selin
(Turkish) calm

Selina
(Greek) moon
Celina

Sella
(English) from Selena;
glowing
Sela

Selma
(German) fair-minded
female
*Selle, Sellma, Selmah,
Zele, Zelma*

Selona
(Greek) form of Selena;
goddess
*Celona, Sela, Seli, Selo,
Selone*

Selsa
(Hispanic) enthusiastic
Sel, Sels

Sema
(Greek) earthy
Semah, Semale, Semele

Semele
(Mythology) needs proof

Semilla
(Spanish) earth mother
*Samilla, Sem, Semila,
Semillah, Semmie,
Semmy, Sumilla*

Semiramis
(African) meets goals

Semone
(American) sentimental
Semonne

Sendy
(American) form of Cindy
Sendee, Sendie

Seneca
(Italian, Native American) leader
Seneka

September
(Latin) serious; month
Seppie, Sept

Septima
(Latin) seventh child
Septimma, Septyma

Sequoia
(Cherokee) giant redwood; formidable
Sekwoya

Serafina
(Hebrew) ardent
Serafeena, Serafeenah, Serafinah, Serafyna, Serafynah, Serifina, Seraphina, Seraphine

Seraphina
(Latin) angel
Serapheena, Serapheenah, Seraphinah, Seraphyna, Serphynah

Seren
(Latin) serene
Ceren, Seran

Serena
(Latin) calm
Sarina, Sereena, Serenah, Serina

Serendipity
(Invented) mercurial; lucky
Sere, Seren, Serendipitee, Serin

Serenity
(American) serene
Sera, Serenitee, Serenitie

Sesame
(American) inventive
Sesamee, Sezamee

Seth
(Hebrew) set; appointed; gentle
Sethe

Seville
(Place name) from Seville, Spain
Sevill, Sevyll, Sevylle

Seymoura
(Invented) form of masculine name Seymour; calm
Seymora

Shade
(English) cool
Shadee, Shadi, Shady

Shadow
(English) mysterious
Shado, Shadoh

Shae
(Hebrew) shy
Shay

Shaela
(Irish) pretty
Shae, Shaelie, Shala

Shaelin
(Irish) pretty
Shae, Shaelyn, Shaelynn, Shalyn

Shaeterral
(African American) well-shaped
Shatey, Shatrell, Shayterral

Shail
(American) pretty
Shale

Shaina
(Hebrew) beauty

Shaine
(Hebrew) pretty girl
Shanie, Shay, Shayne

Shainel
(African American) animated
Shainell, Shainelle, Shaynel

Shakira
(Arabic, Spanish) pretty movement
Shak, Shakeera, Shakeerah, Shakeira, Shakie, Shakyra, Skakarah

Shakonda
(African American) lovely

Shalanda
(African American) vivid
Shalande, Shally, Shalunda

Shaleah
(Hebrew) combo of Sha and Leah; funny
Shalea, Shalee, Shaleeah

Shaleina
(Turkish) humorist
Shalina, Shalyna, Shalyne

Shalene
(Hindi) giving

Shalonda
(African American) enthusiastic
Shalie, Shalondah, Shalonna, Shelonda

Shamara
(Arabic) assertive
Shamarah, Shemera

Shameena
(Arabic) beautiful
Shamee, Shameenah, Shamina, Shaminna

Shamika
(African American) loving
Shameika, Shameka, Shamekah, Shamika, Shemeca

Shamsa
(Pakistani) adorable

Shan
(Chinese) coral

Shana
(Hebrew) pretty girl
Shaina, Shan, Shanah, Shane, Shannah, Shanni, Shannie, Shanny, Shayna, Shayne

Shanae
(Irish) generous
Shan, Shanea, Shanee

Shandee
(English) hopeful
Shandi, Shandie, Shandy

Shandilyn
(American) not forsaken
Shandi, Shandy

Shandra
(American) fun-loving
Chandra, Shan, Shandrie

Shane
(Irish) soft-spoken
Shain, Shaine, Shanee, Shanie, Shayne

Shaneka
(African American) perky; pretty
Chaneka, Shan, Shanekah, Shanie, Shanika

Shanelle
(African American) variant of Chanel; stylish
Shanel, Shannel, Shannell, Shanny

Shani
(African) great

Shania
(African) ambitious; bright-eyed
Shane, Shaniah, Shanie, Shaniya, Shanya

Shanice
(African American) bright-eyed
Chaniece, Shaneese, Shani, Shaniece

Shanika
(African American) pretty;
optimistic
*Shan, Shane, Shanee,
Shaneeka, Shaneika,
Shaneikah, Shanequa,
Shaney, Shaneyka*

Shaniqua
(African American)
outgoing
*Shane, Shaneekwa,
Shaneequa, Shanequa,
Shanie, Shanikwa,
Shaniquah, Shanneequa*

Shanique
(African American)
outgoing

Shanisha
(African American) bright
*Chaneisha, Chanisha,
Shan, Shanecia,
Shaneisha, Shanie*

Shanna
(Irish) lovely
Shanah, Shanea, Shannah

Shannon
(Irish) smart
*Shann, Shanna, Shannen,
Shannyn, Shanon*

Shanny
(Irish) bubbly
Shannee, Shanni, Shannie

Shanta
(French) singing
Shantah, Shante, Shantie

Shantara
(French) bright-eyed
Shantay, Shantera, Shantie

Shante
(French) from Chantal;
song
Shantae, Shantay

Shantell
(American) bright singer
Chantel, Shantal, Shantel

Shanti
(Hindi) calm

Shaquan
(American) fine
*Shak, Shaq, Shaquanda,
Shaquanna, Shaquie,
Shaquonda*

Shaquita
(African American) delight
*Shaq, Shaqueita,
Shaqueta, Shaquie*

Shara
(Hebrew) form of Sharon;
open
Sharah, Sharra, Sherah

Shardae
(Arabic) wanderer
*Chardae, Sade, Shaday,
Sharday, SharDay*

Sharee
(American) dear
Sharie

Shari
(French) beloved girl
*Shar, Sharee, Sharree,
Sher, Sherri*

Sharice
(French) graceful
*Cherise, Shar, Shareese,
Shares*

Sharif
(Russian) mysterious
*Shar, Shareef, Sharey,
Shari, Sharrey, Shary*

Sharine
(Hebrew) from Sharon;
open heart
*Shareen, Shareene,
Sharyne*

Sharissa
(Hebrew) flat plain; quiet

Sharita
(French) charitable
Shar, Shareetah, Shareta

Sharla
(American) friendly
Sharlah

Sharlene
(German) form of Charlene
*Charleen, Charlene, Shar,
Sharl, Sharleen, Sharline,
Sharlyne*

Sharlott
(American) variant on
Charlotte; feminine
Charlotte

Sharmaine
(American) from
Charmaine; song

Sharmeal
(African American)
exhilarating
*Sharm, Sharma, Sharme,
Sharmele*

Sharna
(Hebrew) broad-minded
Sharn, Sharnah

Sharnea
(American) quiet
*Sharnay, Sharnee,
Sharney*

Sharnelle
(African American) spiritual
Sharnel, Sharnie, Sharny

Sharnette
(American) fighter
*Chanet, Charnette,
Shanet, Sharn, Sharnett,
Sharney*

Sharon
(Hebrew) open heart;
desert plain
*Shar, Sharen, Shari,
Sharin, Sharren, Sharron,
Sharry, Sharyn, Sheron,
Sherron*

Sharona
(Hebrew) from Sharon;
desert plain
*Sharonah, Sharonna,
Sharonnah*

Sharonda
(African American) open
Sharondah, Sheronda

Sharrona
(Hebrew) open
*Sharona, Sharonne,
Sherona, Shironah*

Sharterica
(African American)
beloved
*Sharter, Sharterika,
Shartrica, Sharty*

Shasta
(American) majestic mind
Shastah

Shatoya
(African American) spirited
*Shatoye, Shay, Shaytoya,
Toya*

Shauna
(Hebrew, Irish) giving heart
*Shauhna, Shaunie,
Shaunna, Shawna*

Shaune
(American) wide smile
Shaun, Shaunie, Shawn

Shauntee
(Irish) dancing eyes
*Shaun, Shawntey,
Shawntie, Shawnty*

Shavon
(Irish) devout; energetic
*Chavon, Chavonne,
Shavaun, Shavon,
Shavonne*

Shawana
(African American)
dramatic
*Shavaun, Shawahna,
Shawanna, Shawnie*

Shawandreka
(African American) gutsy
Shawan, Shawand,
Shawandrika, Shawann,
Shawuan

Shawn
(American) smiling
Shawne, Shawnee,
Shawnie, Shawny

Shawna
(Hebrew, Irish) form of
Sean; God is gracious
Shawnna

Shawnda
(Irish) helpful friend
Shaunda, Shaundah,
Shona

Shawneequa
(African American)
loquacious
Shauneequa,
Shawneekwa

Shawnel
(African American)
audacious
Shaune, Shaunel,
Shaunelle, Shawn,
Shawnee, Shawnelle,
Shawney, Shawni

Shawnie
(American) playful
Shaunie, Shawni

Shay
(Irish) fairy place
Shaye

Shayjuana
(African American) combo
of Shay and Juana;
cheerful
Shajuana, Shajuanna,
Shay

Shayla
(Irish) fairy palace

Shaylie
(Latin) playful
Shaleigh, Shaylea,
Shaylee, Shealee

Shayne
(Hebrew) form of Shane;
pretty
Shaine, Shane, Shay,
Sheyne

Shayonda
(African American) regal
Shay, Shaya, Shayon,
Shayonde, Sheyonda,
Yona, Yonda

Shea
(Irish) soft beauty
Shae, Shay

Sheba
(Hebrew) short for
Bathsheba; queenly
Chebah, Sheeba, Sheebah

Sheddreka
(African American)
dynamo
Shedd, Sheddrik,
Shedreke

Sheela
(Hindi) gentle spirit
Sheelah, Sheeli, Sheila

Sheelyah
(Irish) form of Shelia;
woman
Sheel, Sheil

Sheena
(Hebrew) shining
Sheen, Sheenah, Shena

Sheeneva
(American) combo of
Sheena and Eva; shiny
Shee, Sheen, Sheena,
Sheeny

Sheila
(Irish) vivacious; divine
woman
Shaylah, Sheela, Sheilia,
Sheilya, Shel

Shelagh
(Irish) fairy princess
Shelby
(English) dignified
*Chelby, Shel, Shelbee,
Shelbi, Shelbie*
Sheldon
(English) farm on the
ledge
Shelden
Shelia
(Irish) woman; gorgeous
Shelya, Shelyah, Shillya
Shelita
(Spanish) little girl
Chelita, Shelite, Shelitta
Shell
(English) meadow;
(French) from Michelle
Shel
Shelley
(English) outdoorsy;
meadow
Shelee, Shelli, Shelly
Shelton
(English) farm on a ledge
Shelten
Shena
(Irish) shining
Shenae, Shenea, Shenna
Sheneeka
(African American)
easygoing
*Shaneeka, Shaneka,
Sheneecah, Sheneka*
Shepard
(English) vigilant
*Shep, Sheperd, Shepherd,
Sheppie*
Shera
(Hebrew) light-hearted
Sheera, Sheerah, Sherah
Sheray
(French) saucy
Cheray, Sherayah

Sherael
(American) form of Sherry;
distinctive
*Sheraelle, Sherelle,
Sherryelle*
Sheree
(French) dearest girl
Sheeree, Sher, Shere
Sherele
(French) bouncy
Sher, Sherell, Sherrie
Sheresa
(American) dancer
*Sher, Sherisa, Sherissa,
Sherri*
Sheretta
(American) sparkling
Shere, Sherette
Sheri
(French) sparkling eyes
Sher, Sherri, Sherrie
Sherice
(French) artistic
*Cherise, Sher, Shereece,
Sherisse*
Sheridan
(Irish) free spirit;
outstanding
*Cheridan, Cheridyn,
Sheridyn, Sherridan*
Sherilyn
(American) combo of Sheri
and Lyn
*Sharilyn, Sheralyn, Sheri-
Lyn, Sheri-Lynn, Sherry-
Lynn*
Sherita
(French) stylish
Cherita, Sheretta
Sherleen
(American) easygoing
*Sherl, Sherlene, Sherline,
Sherlyn, Shirline*
Sherlitha
(Spanish) feminine
Sherl, Sherli

Sherolynna
(American) lovely
Cherolina, Sher, Sheralina, Sherrilina

Sherrill
(English) bright
Cheril, Cherrill, Sherelle, Sheril, Sherrell, Sheryl

Sherrunda
(African American) free spirit
Sharun, Sharunda, Sherr, Sherrunde, Sherunda

Sherry
(French) outgoing
Sher, Sheri, Sherreye, Sherri, Sherrie, Sherye

Sherrylynn
(American) combo of Sherry and Lynn
Sharolyn, Sher, Sherilyn, Sherry, Sherylyn

Sheryl
(French) beloved woman
Cheryl, Sharal, Sher, Sheral, Sheril, Sherill

Sherylin
(American) combo of Sheryl and Lynn
Sherylinn, Sherylyn, Sherylynn

Shevonne
(Gaelic) ambitious
Shavon, Shevaune, Shevon

Sheyenne
(Native American) form of Cheyenne; audacious
Shey, Shianne, Shyann, Shyanne, Shyenne

Sheyn
(Hebrew) beauty

Shibhan
(Irish) variation of Siobhan; God is gracious
Shiban, Shibann, Shibhann

Shiela
(Irish) blind

Shifra
(Hebrew) beautiful woman
Sheefra, Shifrah

Shikendra
(African American) spirited
Shiki, Shikie, Skikend

Shiloh
(Hebrew) gifted by God
Shilo, Shy

Shine
(American) shining example
Shena, Shina

Shiney
(American) glowing
Shine, Shiny

Shinikee
(African American) glorious
Shinakee, Shinikey, Shynikee

Shira
(Hebrew) song; singer
Shirah, Shiree

Shireen
(English) charmer
Shareen, Shiree, Shireene, Shirene, Shiri, Shiry, Shoreen, Shureen, Shurene

Shirleen
(American) nature-loving
Shirlene, Shirline

Shirley
(English) bright meadow; cheerful girl
Sherlee, Sherley, Sherly, Shir, Shirl, Shirly

Shlonda
(African American) bright
Londa, Schlonda, Shodie

Shola
(Hebrew) spirited
Sholah

Shon
(Irish) from Shona;
gracious; loving
Shonn

Shona
(Irish) open-hearted
Shonah, Shonie

Shonda
(Irish) runner
*Shondah, Shonday,
Shondie, Shounda,
Shoundah*

Shonta
(Irish) fearless
*Shauntah, Shawnta, Shon,
Shontie*

Shony
(Irish) shining
*Shona, Shonee, Shoni,
Shonie*

Shoshana
(Hebrew) beautiful; lily
*Shoshanna, Shoshannah,
Shoshauna*

Shula
(Arabic) flaming

Shulamit
(Hebrew) serene

Shulondia
(African American)
dynamic
*Shulee, Shuley, Shuli,
Shulonde, Shulondea,
Shulondiah*

Shuntay
(African American; Irish) a
form of Shonta; goodness
Shuntae

Shura
(Greek) protective

Shyama
(Native American) variant
of Cheyenne; thinker

Shyanne
(Native American) form of
Cheyanne
Shy

Shyla
(English) creative
Shila, Shy, Shylah

Shyne
(American) standout
Shine

Sia
(Welsh) calm; believer
Cia, Seea

Sian
(Welsh) believer

Siana
(Welsh) ebullient
Sian, Siane

Sib
(Anglo-Saxon) from
Sibley; friendly
Sibb

Sibley
(Anglo-Saxon) related
Siblee, Sibly

Sibyl
(Greek) intuitive
*Cibyl, Cyb, Cybil, Cybill,
Cybyl, Sib, Sibbi, Sibbie,
Sibby, Sibella, Sibil, Sibill,
Sibyll, Sibylla, Sybela,
Sybil, Sybyl*

Sid
(Place name) from Saint-
Denis, France; from Sidney
Sidd

Sidney
(Place name) from Saint-
Denis
Sidnee, Sidni, Sidny

Sidonia
(French) spiritual
Sid, Sidoneah, Sydonya

Sidonie
(French) appealing
Sidonee, Sidony, Sydoni

Sidra
(Latin) star
Cidra, Siddey, Siddie, Siddy, Sidi, Sidrie, Sydra

Sienna
(English) delicate; reddish-brown
Siena, Siene

Sierra
(Place name) peaks; outdoorsy
Cierra, Searah, Searrah, Siera, Sierrah, Sierre

Sigfrid
(German) peacemaker
Sig, Sigfred, Sigfreid, Siggy

Signe
(Latin) symbol
Sig, Signie, Signy

Sigourney
(English) leader who conquers
Sig, Siggie, Signe, Signy, Sigournay, Sygourny

Sigrid
(Scandinavian) lovely
Segred, Sig, Siggy, Sigrede

Sigrun
(Scandinavian) winning
Cigrun, Segrun

Sikita
(American) active
Sikite

Sile
(Turkish) misses home

Siline
(Greek) from Selene; moon
Sileen, Sileene, Silyne

Silvanna
(Spanish) nature-lover
Sil, Silva, Silvana, Silvane, Silvanne, Silver

Silver
(Anglo-Saxon) light-haired
Silva, Silvar, Sylver

Silvia
(Latin) deep; woods-loving
Sill, Silvy, Siviah, Sylvia

Simcha
(Hebrew) joyful
Simchah

Simi
(Lebanese) soft
Sim

Simica
(American) tender
Sim, Simika, Simmy

Simona
(American) form of Simon; wise
Sim, Simon, Sims

Simona
(Hebrew) svelte
Simonah, Symmie, Symona, Syms

Simone
(French) wise and thoughtful
Sim, Simonie, Symone

Sinai
(Place name) Mt. Sinai

Sinclair
(French) person from St. Clair; admired
Cinclair, Sinclare, Synclair, Synclare

Sindy
(American) left behind
Cindy

Sine
(Irish) God's gift

Sinead
(Irish) singer; believer in a gracious God
Shanade

Siobhan
(Irish) believer; lovely
Chevon, Chevonne, Chivon, Shavonne, Shevon

Siphronia
(Greek) sensible
Ciphronia, Sifronea, Sifronia, Syfronia

Siren
(Greek) enchantress
Syren

Sirena
(Greek) temptress
Sireena, Sirenah, Sirine, Sisi, Sissy, Syrena

Sirene
(Greek) enchantress
Sireen, Sireene, Siryne

Sisley
(Last name as first name) able

Sissy
(Latin) short for Cecilia or little sister; immature; ingenue
Cissee, Cissey, Cissy, Sis, Sissi, Sissie

Sistene
(Italian) spiritual
Sisteen, Sisteene

Sita
(Hindi) divine
Seeta, Seetha

Sivana
(Irish) from Sivney; easygoing
Sivanah

Sive
(Scandinavian) Siv, wife of Thor; she matters

Skye
(Scottish) high-minded; head in the clouds

Skyler
(Dutch) protective; sheltering
Schuyler, Skieler, Skilar, Skiler, Skye, Skyla, Skylar, Skylie, Skylor

Slane
(Irish) form of Sloane; striking
Slaine

Slaney
(Last name as first name) selective

Slava
(Russian) glory

Sloane
(Irish) strong
Sloan, Slone

Sly
(American) from Slyvestra

Slyvestra
(American) feminine form of Slyvester

Smiley
(American) radiant
Smile, Smilee, Smiles, Smili, Smily

Snooks
(American) sweetie
Snookee, Snookie

Snow
(American) quiet
Sno, Snowy

Snowdrop
(Botanical) white flower

Socorro
(Spanish) helpful
Socoro

Sofie
(Greek) wise

Sofya
(Russian) wise
Sofi, Sofie, Sofiya

Solana
(Spanish) sunny
Solanah, Soley, Solie

Solange
(French) sophisticated
Solie

Soledad
(Spanish) solitary woman
*Saleda, Solada, Solay,
Sole, Solee, Solie, Solita*

Soleil
(French) sun

Soline
(French) solemn
Solen, Solenne, Souline

Solita
(Latin) alone
Soleeta, Solyta

Soloma
(Hindi) from Soma; lunar

Sommer
(English) warm
Sommie, Summer, Summi

Sona
(Hindi) from Sonal;
sunshine

Sonal
(Hindi) golden girl of the
sun

Sonay
(Asian) bright-eyed
Sonnae

Sondra
(Greek) defender of
mankind

Sonel
(Hindi) from Sonal
Sonell

Song
(Chinese) independent

Sonia
(Slavic) effervescent
*Soni, Sonnie, Sonny,
Sonya*

Sonja
(Scandinavian) bright
woman

Sonnet
(American) poetic
Sonnett, Sonni, Sonny

Sonoma
(Place name) city in
California; wine-loving
Sonomah

Sonora
(English) easygoing
Sonorah

Sonseria
(American) giving
Seria, Sonsere, Sonsey

Sonya
(Greek) wise
Sonia, Sonje

Soo
(Korean) gentle spirit

Soon-Yi
(Chinese) delightful;
assertive

Soozi
(American) form of Suzy;
friendly
*Soos, Sooz, Souz, Souze,
Souzi*

Sophia
(Greek) wise one
*Sofeea, Sofi, Sofia, Sofie,
Sophea, Sopheea, Sophie,
Sophy*

Sophie
(Greek) from Sophia;
intelligent
*Sophee, Sophey, Sophi,
Sophy*

Sora
(Native American) chirping
bird
Sorra

Sorangel
(Spanish) heavenly
Sorange

Soraya
(Persian) royal
Sorcha
(Irish) bright
Shorshi, Sorsha, Sorshie
Sorele
(French) reddish-brown
hair
Sorrel
(English) delicate
Sorel, Sorell, Sorie, Sorree,
Sorrell, Sorri, Sorrie
Sosannah
(Hebrew) from Susannah;
rose
Sosana, Sosanah,
Sosanna
Soshana
(Hebrew) from
Shoshanah; lily
Soshanah
Sozos
(Hindi) clingy
Sosos
Spaulding
(English) divided field
Spalding
Spencer
(English) sophisticate
Spence, Spenser
Spirit
(American) lively; spirited
Spirite, Spyrit
Sprague
(American) respected
Sprage
Spring
(English) springtime; fresh
Spryng
Sri
(Hindi) glorious
Shree, Shri, Sree

Stacey
(Greek) hopeful and
spiritual
Stace, Staci, Stacie, Stacy,
Staycee
Stacia
(English) short for
Anastasia; devout
Stace, Stacie, Stasia,
Stayshah
Stanise
(American) darling
Stanee, Staneese, Stani,
Stanice, Staniece
Star
(English) a star
Starr
Starla
(American) shining
Starlah, Starlie
Starling
(English) glossy bird
Starlite
(American) extraordinary
Starlight, Starr
Stasia
(Greek, Russian)
resurrection
Stacie, Stasie, Stasya
Stefanie
(Greek) regal;
(German) crowned
Stafanie, Stefannye,
Stefany, Steff, Steffany,
Steffie, Stephanie
Steff
(Greek) short for
Stephanie; crowned
Steffi
(Greek) short for
Stephanie; crowned;
athletic
Steffie, Steffy, Stefi

Stefnee
(American) form of
Stephanie/Stefanie; regal
Stef, Steffy

Stella
(Latin) bright star
Stele, Stelie

Stephanie
(Greek) regal
*Stefanie, Steff, Steffie,
Stephenie, Stephney*

Stephene
(French, Greek) dignified
Steph, Stephie, Stephine

Stephney
(Greek) crowned
*Stef, Steph, Stephie,
Stephnie*

Sterla
(American) quality
Sterl, Sterlie, Stirla

Stevie
(Greek, American) jovial
*Steve, Stevee, Stevey,
Stevi*

Stockard
(English) stockyard; sturdy
Stockerd, Stockyrd

Storelle
(Invented) legend
*Storee, Storell, Storey,
Stori*

Storm
(English) powerful

Stormy
(American) impulsive
Storm, Stormi, Stormie

Story
(American) creative
Stori, Storie, Storee, Storey

Suanne
(American) combo of Sue
and Anne
Suann, Sueann, Sueanne

Sue
(Hebrew) flower-like; lily
Susy, Suze, Suzy

Suellen
(American) combo of Sue
and Ellen
SueEllen, Sue-Ellen

Sugar
(American) sweet
Shug

Sugy
(Spanish) short for the
name Sugar; sweet
Sug, Sugey, Sugie

Suki
(Japanese) beloved
Suke, Sukie, Suky

Sula
(Greek) sea-going
Soola, Sue, Suze

Sullivan
(Last name as first name)
brave-hearted
Sulli, Sullie, Sullivin, Sully

Summer
(English) summery; fresh
*Somer, Sommer, Sum,
Summie*

Sun
(Korean) obedient girl
Suna, Suni, Sunnie

Sundancer
(American) easygoing
Sunndance

Sunday
(Latin) day of the week;
sunny
*Sun, Sundae, Sundaye,
Sundee, Sunney, Sunni,
Sunnie, Sunny, Sunnye*

Sunila
(Hindi) blue sky

Sunita
(Hindi) Dharma's child
Suniti

Sunna
(American) sunny
Sun, Suna
Sunny
(English) bright attitude
*Sonny, Sun, Sunni,
Sunnye*
Sunshine
(American) sunny
Suprina
(American) supreme
Suprinna
Surbhi
(Indian) sweet smelling
Surrender
(Word as name) dramatic
Surren
Susan
(Hebrew) lily; pretty flower
*Soozan, Sue, Susahn,
Susanne, Susehn, Susie,
Suzan*
Susannah
(Hebrew) gentle
*Sue, Susah, Susanna,
Susie, Suzannah*
Susette
(French) from Susan;
flowering
Susett
Susie
(American) short for Susan
*Susey, Susi, Susy, Suze,
Suzi, Suzie, Suzy*
Sutton
(Last name as first name)
southern town
Suten, Sutten, Suton
Suz
(American) short for
Susan; lily; pretty flower
Suze
Suzan
(American) from Susan;
flower
Suzen

Suzanne
(English) fragrant
*Susanne, Suzan, Suzane,
Suzann, Suze*
Suzette
(French) pretty little one
Sue, Susette, Suze
Svea
(Swedish) patriotic
Svay
Svetlana
(Russian) star bright
Sveta, Svete
Swan
(Scandinavian) swan-like
Swanhildda
(Teutonic) swan-like;
graceful
*Swan, Swanhild, Swann,
Swanney, Swanni,
Swannie, Swanny*
Sweeney
(Irish) young and
rambunctious
Sweenee, Sweeny
Sweetpea
(American) sweet
Sweet-Pea, Sweetie
Swell
(Invented) good
Swelle
Swift
(word as name) bold
Swiftie, Swifty
Swoosie
(American) unique
Swoose, Swoozie
Syb
(Greek) from Sybil
Sybb
Sybil
(Greek) future-gazing
*Sibel, Sibyl, Syb, Sybill,
Sybille, Sybyl*

Syd
(French) from Sydney
Sydd
Sydel
(Hebrew) princess
Sydlyn
(American) quiet
Sidlyn, Sydlin, Sydlinne
Sydney
(French) enthusiastic
*Sidney, Syd, Sydnee,
Sydnie*
Syl
(Latin) loves the woods
Sill
Sylvan
(Latin) from the forest
*Silvan, Silven, Silvyn,
Sylven, Sylvyn*
Sylvana
(Latin) forest; natural
woman
Silvanna, Syl, Sylvie
Sylvestra
(English) lives in the woods
Sylvia
(Latin) sylvan; girl of the
forest
Syl, Sylvea
Sylvie
(Latin) sylvan;
peacefulness
*Sil, Silvie, Silvy, Syl,
Sylvey, Sylvi, Sylvy*
Sylwia
(Polish) serene; in the
woods
Silwia
Symira
(American) enthusiastic
Sym, Symra, Syms, Symyra
Symone
(Hebrew) good listener
Sym

Symphony
(American) musical
*Simphony, Symfonie,
Symfony, Symphonee,
Symphonie*
Syna
(Invented) sweet
Sina
Synora
(American) languid
*Cinora, Sinora, Synee,
Syni, Synor, Synore*
Synpha
(American) capable
Sinfa, Sinpha, Synfa
Syreta
(American) assertive
Sireta

T

Tabia
(African) talented girl
Tabina
(Arabic) follower of
Muhammed
Tabitha
(Greek) graceful; gazelle
*Tabatha, Tabbatha, Tabbi,
Tabytha*
Tabla
(Native American) wears a
tiara; regal
Tacey
(American) precious
Tace, Tacita

Tacha
(American) form of Tasha (from Natalie); born on Christmas
Tach

Tacho
(American) form of Tasha (from Natalie); born on Christmas

Taci
(American) strong

Tacie
(American) healthy
Tace, Taci, Tacy

Tadewi
(Native American) wind

Tadi
(Native American) variation of Tadewi

Tadita
(Native American) runner
Tadeta

Taesha
(American) sterling character
Tahisha, Taisha, Taisha, Tisha

Taeshawna
(American) combo of Tae and Shawna; glamorous
Taeseana, Taeshauna, Taeshona, Tayseana, Tayshauna, Tayshawna, Tayshona

Taffeta
(American) shiny
Tafeta, Taffetah, Taffi, Taffy

Taffy
(Welsh) sweet and beloved
Taffee, Taffey, Taffi

Taft
(English) loved
Tafte

Taghrid
(Arabic) singing bird

Tahcawin
(Native American) doe

Tahira
(Arabic) pure
Tahirah

Tahiyya
(Arabic) welcome
Tahiyyah

Tahnee
(English) little one

Tai
(American) fond
Tie, Tye

Taima
(Native American) thunder
Taimah, Taiomah

Tain
(Native American) new moon

Tainee
(Native American) variation of Tain

Taipa
(Native American) quail

Taiwo
(African) firstborn of twins

Tajudeen
(Spanish) clingy
Taj, Tajjy, Taju

Taka
(Japanese) honorable

Takala
(Native American) cornstalk
Takalah

Takara
(Japanese) beloved gem
Taka, Taki

Takayren
(Native American) commotion

Takeko
(Japanese) child of the bamboo

Takenya
(Native American) falcon in flight

Takeya
(African American) knowing
Takeyah

Taki
(Japanese) waterfall

Takia
(Arabic) spiritual
Taki, Tikia, Tykia

Takira
(American) combo of Ta and Kira; prayerful
Kira, Takera, Tikiri

Takisha
(African American) combo of Ta and Kisha; joyful
Takeisha, Takish, Tekisha, Tykisha

Takuhi
(Armenian) queen

Tala
(Native American) wolf

Talal
(Hebrew) dew

Talila
(Hebrew) dew

Talasi
(Native American) cornflower

Tale
(African) green

Talent
(American) self-assured
Talynt

Talesha
(African American) friendly
Tal, Taleesh, Taleisha, Talisha, Tallie, Telesha

Tali
(Hebrew) confident

Talia
(Greek) golden; dew from heaven
Tahlia, Tali, Tallie, Tally, Talya, Talyah

Talibah
(African) intellectual
Tali, Talib, Taliba

Talisa
(African American) variation of Lisa
Telisa

Talise
(Native American) beautiful creek

Talitha
(African American) inventive
Taleetha, Taleta, Taletha, Talith, Tally

Tallis
(English) forest

Tallulah
(Native American) leaping water; sparkling girl
Talie, Talley, Tallula, Talula, Talulah

Talluse
(American) bold
Talloose, Tallu, Taluce

Tally
(Native American) heroine
Tallee, Talley, Talli, Tally, Taly

Talma
(Hebrew) hill

Talou
(American) saucy
Talli, Tallou, Tally

Talutah
(Native American) red

Talya
(Hebrew) lamb
Talia

Tam
(Japanese) decorative
Tama

Tamah
(Hebrew) marvel
Tama

Tamaka
(Japanese) bracelet;
adorned female

Tamaki
(Japanese) bracelet

Tamala
(American) kind
*Tam, Tama, Tamela,
Tammie, Tammy*

Tamanna
(Hindu) desire

Tamar
(Hebrew) palm; breezy
Tama, Tamarr

Tamara
(Hebrew) royal female
*Tamera, Tammy, Tamora,
Tamra*

Tamas
(Hindu) palm tree
Tamasa, Tamasi, Tamasvini

Tamasine
(English) twin; feminine of
Thomas
*Tamasin, Tamsin, Tamsyn,
Tamzen, Tamzin*

Tamay
(American) form of
Tammy; soft
Tamae, Tamaye

Tambara
(American) high-energy
*Tam, Tamb, Tambra,
Tamby, Tammy*

Tamber
(American) combo of T
and Amber; energetic
*Amber, Tam, Tambey,
Tambur*

Tambusi
(African) frank
Tam, Tambussey, Tammy

Tame
(American) calm

Tamefa
(African American) form of
Tameka
Tamefah, Tamifa

Tamesha
(African American) open
face
*Tamesh, Tamisha, Tammie,
Tammy*

Tamesis
(Spanish) name for the
Thames River
Tam, Tamey

Tami
(Japanese) people
Tamie, Tamiko

Tamia
(Japanese) little gem
Tameea, Tamya

Tamika
(African American) lively
*Tameca, Tameeka,
Tameka, Tamieka,
Tamikah, Tammi, Tammie,
Tammy, Temeka*

Tamiko
(Japanese) the people's
child
Tami, Tamico, Tamika

Tamirisa
(Indian) night; dark
*Risa, Tami, Tamirysa,
Tamrisa, Tamyrisa*

Tammi
(American) sweetheart
*Tam, Tammie, Tammy,
Tammye*

Tamohara
(Hindu) the sun

Tamony
(Hebrew) from Tamara;
palm tree; warm
*Tamanee, Tamaney,
Tamani, Tamanie, Tamany,
Tamonee, Tamoney,
Tamoni, Tamonie*

Tamra
(Hebrew) sweet girl
Tammie, Tamora, Tamrah

Tamrika
(African) newly created
Tamreeka

Tamsin
(English) benevolent
*Tam, Tami, Tammee,
Tammey, Tammy, Tammye,
Tamsa, Tamsan, Tamsen*

Tamyrah
(African American) vocalist
Tamirah

Tana
(Slavic) petite princess
Taina, Tan, Tanah, Tanie

Tanaka
(Japanese) swamp dweller

Tanay
(African American) new
Tanee

Tanaya
(Hindu) daughter

Tandy
(English) team player
Tanda, Tandi, Tandie

Tane
(Polynesian) fertile

Tanesha
(African) strong
*Tanish, Tanisha, Tannesha,
Tannie*

Tangela
(American) combo of Tan
and Angela
T'Angela

Tangelia
(Greek) angel
Gelia, Tange, Tangey

Tangenika
(American) form of former
country Tanganyika
Tange, Tangi, Tangy

Tangi
(American) tangerine
Tangee

Tango
(Spanish) dance
Tangoh

Tangyla
(Invented) form of
Tangela; special
Tange, Tangy

Tani
(Slavic) glorious
Tahnie, Tanee, Tanie

Tania
(Russian, Slavic) queenly
Tannie, Tanny, Tanya

Tanina
(American) bold
*Tan, Tana, Tanena,
Taninah, Tanney, Tanni,
Tannie, Tanny, Tanye,
Tanyna*

Tanis
(Slavic) from Tania; fairy
queen
Taniss, Tanys, Tanyss

Tanise
(American) unique
Tanes, Tanis

Tanish
(Greek) eternal
Tan, Tanesh, Tanny

Tanisha
(African American) talkative
*Taniesha, Tannie, Tenisha,
Tinishah*

Tanith
(Irish) estate
Tanita, Tanitha
Tansy
(Latin) pretty
Tan, Tancy, Tansee, Tanzi
Tanuneka
(African American) gracious
Nuneka, Tanueka, Tanun
Tanvi
(Hindu) young woman
Tanya
(Russian) queenly bearing
Tahnya, Tan, Tanyie, Tawnyah, Tonya
Tanyanika
(African American) combo of Tayna and Nika; wild spirit
Nike, Tanya, Tanyani, Yanika
Tanyav
(Slavic) regal
Tanyev
Tanyette
(Italian) talkative
Tanye, Tanyee, Tanyett
Tanze
(Greek) form of Tansy; eternal
Tans, Tansee, Tanz, Tanzee, Tanzey, Tanzi
Tao
(Vietnamese) apple
Tapa
(Spanish) little snack
Tapas
Tapasya
(Hindu) bitter
Tapice
(Spanish) covered
Tapeece, Tapeese, Tapese, Tapiece, Tapp, Tappy

Taquanna
(African American) noisy
Takki, Takwana, Taquana, Taque, Taquie
Taquesha
(African American) joyful
Takie, Takwesha
Taquilla
(American) from the Spanish word tequila; lively
Takela, Takelah, Taque, Taquella, Taqui, Taquile, Taquille
Tara
(Gaelic) towering
Tarah, Tari, Tarra
Taral
(Hindu) rippling
Taran
(American) earthy
Taren, Tarran, Tarren, Tarryn, Taryn
Tarani
(Hindu) light
Taree
(Japanese) tree branch
Tarika
(Hindu) star
Tarlam
(Hindu) flowering
Taro
(Invented) card name; farsighted
Taroh **Tarsha**
(American) combo of Tasha and Tara
Tarsh, Tay
Tarub
(Arabic) cheerful

Taryn
(American) combo of Tara and Karyn; exuberant; (Irish) bright; combo of Tara and Erin
Taran, Taren, Tarran, Tarrin, Tarron

Tasha
(Russian) Christmas-born baby
Tacha, Tahshah, Tash, Tashie, Tasia, Tasie, Tasy, Tasya

Tashanah
(African American) spunky
Tash, Tashana

Tashanee
(African American) lively
Tashaunie

Tashawndra
(African American) bright smiling
Tasha, Tashaundra, Tashie

Tashel
(African American) studious
Tasha, Tashelle, Tashelle, Tochelle

Tashina
(African American) sparkles
Tasheena, Tasheenah, Tashinah

Tashka
(Russian) together
Tashca, Tashcka

Tashza
(African American) form of Tasha; bright
Tashi, Tashy, Tashzah

Tasida
(Native American) rides a horse

Tasma
(American) twin
Tasmah

Tasmind
(American) twin

Tasmine
(English) twin
Tasmin

Tassi
(Slavic) bold
Tassee, Tassey, Tassy

Tate
(English) short

Tateeahna
(Invented) form of Tatiana; snow queen

Tatiana
(Russian) snow queen
Tanya, Tatania, Tatia, Tatianna, Tatiannia, Tatie, Tattianna, Tatyana, Tatyanna

Tatsu
(Japanese) dragon

Tatum
(English) cheery; high-spirited
Tata, Tate, Tatie, Tayte

Taura
(Latin) bull-like; stubborn

Tavia
(Latin) short for Octavia; light
Tava, Taveah, Tavi

Tawannah
(African American) talkative
Tawana, Tawanda, Tawanna, Tawona

Tawanner
(American) loquacious
Tawanne, Twanner

Tawanta
(African American) smart
Tawan, Tawante

Tawia
(African) born after twins

Tawny
(American) tan-skinned
Tawn, Tawnee, Tawni,
Tawnie

Tawnya
(American) form of Tonya;
tan
Tawnie, Tawnyah, Tonya,
Tonyah

Tawyn
(American) reliable; tan
Tawenne, Tawin, Tawynne

Tayanita
(Native American) beaver

Tayla
(American) doll-like
Taila, Taylah

Taylor
(English) tailor by trade;
style-setter
Tailor, Talor, Tay, Taye,
Taylar, Tayler

Tazmin
(American) from Jasmine;
zany
Tazminn, Tazmyn,
Tazmynn

Tazmind
(American) from Jasmine;
outgoing

Tazu
(Japanese) stork

Teagan
(Irish) worldly; creative
Teague, Teegan, Tegan

Teague
(Irish) creative
Tee, Teegue, Tegue

Teah
(Greek) goddess
Tea

Teale
(English) blue-green; bird
Teal, Teala

Teamhair
(Irish) hill

Teamikka
(African American) form of
Tamika; lively
Teamika

Teana
(American) form of Tina;
high-energy
Teanah, Teane

Tecoa
(American) precocious
Tekoa

Teddi
(Greek) cuddly
Ted, Teddie, Teddy

Tedra
(Greek) outgoing
Teddra, Tedrah

Tegvyen
(Welsh) lovely

Tehara
(Native American) darling
Tihara, Tyhara

Tejuana
(Place name) Tijuana,
Mexico
T'Juana, Tijuana

Tekira
(American) legendary
Tekera, Teki

Tekla
(Greek) legend; divine
glory
Tekk, Teklah, Thekla, Tikla,
Tiklah

Tela
(Greek) wise
Tella

Teleri
(Welsh) variation of Eleri

Teleza
(African) slippery

Telina
(American) storyteller
Teline, Telyna, Telyne,
Tilina

Telma
(Greek) ambitious

Telsa
(American) form of Tessa; successful
Telly

Temetris
(African American) respected
Teme, Temi, Temitris, Temmy

Temira
(Hebrew) tall
Temora, Timora

Temperance
(Latin) moderation

Tempest
(French) tempestuous; stormy
Tempeste, Tempie, Tempyst

Templa
(Latin) spiritual; moderate
Temp, Templah

Tenesha
(African American) clever
Tenesia, Tenicha, Tenisha, Tennie

Tennille
(American) innovative
Tanielle, Tanile, Ten, Teneal, Tenile, Tenneal, Tennelle, Tennie

Tenuvah
(Hebrew) fruit and vegetables

Tenuva
(Hebrew) variation of Tenuvah

Teo
(Spanish) from masculine name Teodoro; God's gift
Teeo, Teoh

Teodora
(Scandinavian) God's gift
Teo, Teodore

Tequila
(Spanish) intoxicating
Tequela, Tequilla, Tiki, Tiquilia

Terena
(English) feminine version of Terence
Tereena, Terenia, Terina, Terrena, Terrina, Teryna

Teresa
(Greek) gardener
Taresa, Terese, Terhesa, Teri, Terre, Tess, Tessie, Treece, Tressa, Tressae

Terese
(Greek) nurturing
Tarese, Therese, Treece

Tereso
(Spanish) reaper
Tere, Terese

Teri
(Greek) reaper
Terre, Terri, Terrie

Terilyn
(American) combo of Teri and Lynn
Terelyn, Terrelynn, Terrilynn, Terri-Lynn

Terlah
(Arabic) of the earth

Terolyn
(American) combo of Tere and Carolyn; harvesting; flirtatious
Tarolyn, Tero, Terolinn, Terolinne

Terra
(Latin) earthy; name for someone born under an astrological earth sign
Tera, Terrie

Terrell
(Greek) hardy
Ter, Teral, Terell, Terrelle, Terrie, Teryl

Terrena
(Latin) smooth-talking
Terina, Terrina, Terry

Terry
(Greek) short for Theresa
Teri, Terre, Terrey, Terri, Tery

Tertia
(Latin) third
Ters, Tersh, Tersha, Tersia

Teshuah
(Hebrew) reprieve
Teshua, Teshura

Tess
(Greek) harvesting life
Tesse

Tessa
(Greek) reaping a harvest
Tesa, Tessie, Teza

Tessella
(Italian) countess
Tesela, Tesella, Tessela

Tessica
(American) form of
Jessica; friendly
*Tesica, Tess, Tessa, Tessie,
Tessika*

Tessie
(Greek) form of Theresa;
wonderful
Tessey, Tessi, Tezi

Tetsu
(Japanese) iron

Tevy
(Cambodian) angel

Thada
(Greek) appreciative
Thadda, Thaddeah

Thadyne
(Hebrew) worthy of praise
Thadee, Thadine, Thady

Thalassa
(Greek) sensitive
*Talassa, Thalassah,
Thalasse*

Thalia
(Greek) joyful; fun
Thalya

Thana
(Arabic) thanksgiving

Thandiwe
(African) affectionate

Thanh
(Vietnamese) brilliant

Thao
(Vietnamese) respect

Tharamel
(Invented) form of the
word caramel; dedicated
Thara

The
(Vietnamese) pledged

Thea
(Greek) goddess
*Teah, Teeah, Theah,
Theeah, Theo, Tiah*

Theda
(American) confident
Thada, Thedah

Theia
(Greek) divine one

Thia
(Greek) goddess

Thekia
(Greek) famous

Thekla
(Greek) famous; divine
Tecla, Tekla, Thecla

Thelma
(Greek) giver
Thel

Thema
(African) queen

Themba
(African) trusted

Theodora
(Greek) sweetheart; God's
gift
*Dora, Teddi, Teddie, Teddy,
Tedi, Tedra, Tedrah, Theda,
Theo, Theodorah,
Theodrah*

Theola
(Greek) excellent
Theo, Theolah, Thie

Theone
(Greek) serene
Theona, Theonne

Theophania
(Greek) god's features
Theophanie

Theophila
(Greek) loved by God
Theofila

Theora
(Greek) God's gift
*Theorah, Theorra,
Theorrah*

Theresa
(Greek) reaping a harvest
*Reza, Teresa, Terri, Terrie,
Terry*

Therese
(Greek) bountiful harvest
*Tereece, Terese, Terise,
Terry*

Therna
(Greek) wild
Thera

Theta
(Greek) letter in Greek
alphabet; substantial
Thayta, Thetah

Thetis
(Greek) mother of Achilles

Thi
(Vietnamese) poem

Thim
(Thai) ice cream; sweet

Thirzah
(Hebrew) pleasant
Thirza, Thursa, Thurza

Thocmetony
(Native American) flower
Tocmetone

Thomasina
(Hebrew) twin
*Tom, Toma, Tomasa,
Tomasina, Tomina,
Tommie, Toto*

Thora
(Scandinavian) like
thunder
Thorah

Thu
(Vietnamese) autumn

Thuy
(Vietnamese) gentle

Thyra
(Scandinavian) loud
Thira

Tia
(Greek) princess;
(Spanish) aunt
Teah, Tee, Teia, Tiah

Tian
(Greek) lovely
*Ti, Tiane, Tiann, Tianne,
Tyan, Tyann, Tyanne, Tye*

Tiana
(Greek) highest beauty
Tana, Teeana, Tiane, Tiona

Tianth
(American) pretty and
impetuous
Teanth, Tia, Tian, Tianeth

Tiara
(Latin) crowned goddess
*Teara, Tearra, Tee,
Teearah, Tierah, Tira*

Tibby
(American) frisky
Tib, Tibb, Tybbee

Tiberia
(Latin) majestic;
(Place name) Tiber River
Tibbie, Tibby

Tibisay
(American) uniter
Tibi, Tibisae

Tichanda
(African American) stylish
Tichaunda, Tishanda

Tiena
(Spanish) earthy
Teena

Tierah
(Latin) jeweled; ornament
Tia, Tiarra, Tiera

Tiernan
(English) lord

Tierney
(Irish) wealthy
*Teern, Teerney, Teerny,
Tiern*

Tifara
(Hebrew) festive
Tiferet, Tifhara

Tifaya
(Greek) form of Tiffany
Tifaya, Tifayane, Tiff, Tiffy

Tiffany
(Greek) lasting love
*Tifanie, Tiff, Tiffanie,
Tiffenie, Tiffi, Tiffie, Tiffy,
Tiphanie, Tyfannie*

Tigress
(Latin) wild
Tigris, Tye, Tygris

Tigris
(Irish) tiger

Tiki
(Polynesian) ancestor;
image
Tekee

Tilda
(German) short for
Matilda; powerful
Telda, Tildie, Till, Tylda

Tilla
(German) industrious
Tila

Tilly
(German) cute; strong
Till, Tillee, Tillie

Timmie
(Greek) short for Timothie;
honorable
Tim, Timi, Timmy

Timothea
(Greek) honoring God
*Timaula, Timi, Timie,
Timmi, Timmie*

Timothie
(Greek) honorable
*Tim, Timmie, Timothea,
Timothy*

Tina
(Latin, Spanish) little and
lively
Teena, Teenie, Tena, Tiny

Tionne
(American) hopeful
Tionn

Tiponya
(Native American) owl;
watchful

Tippah
(Hindi) from *tipo* (tiger);
ferocious

Tipper
(Irish) pourer of water;
nurturing
Tip, Tippy, Typper

Tippett
(American) giving

Tippie
(American) generous
Tippi, Tippy

Tira
(Hebrew) camp

Tirion
(Welsh) gentle

Tirrza
(Hebrew) sweet; precious
Thirza, Thirzah, Tirza, Tirzah

Tirtha
(Hindu) ford

Tirza
(Hebrew) kindness
Thirza, Tirza, Tirzah

Tisa
(African) ninth child
Tesa, Tesah, Tisah

Tish
(Latin) happy
Tysh

Tisha
(Latin) joyful
Tesha, Ticia, Tishah, Tishie

Tishra
(African American) original
Tishrah

Tishunette
(African American) happy
girl
Tish, Tisunette

Tita
(Greek) giant; large

Titania
(Greek) giant

Tivona
(Hebrew) lover of nature

Tiwa
(Native American) onion

Tobago
(Place name) West Indies
island; islander
Bago, ToTo

Tobi
(Hebrew) good
Tobie, Toby

Toffey
(American) spirited
*Toff, Toffee, Toffi, Toffie,
Toffy*

Tohuia
(Polynesian) flower

Toinette
(Latin) wonderful
*Toin, Toinett, Toney, Tony,
Toynet*

Toireasa
(Irish) strong
Treise

Toki
(Japanese) chance

Tokiwa
(Japanese) steady

Tolikna
(Native American) coyote
ears

Tollie
(Hebrew) confident
*Toll, Tollee, Tolli, Tolly,
Tollye*

Toloisi
(French) from Toulouse;
ingenious

Toma
(Latin) short for Tomasina
*Tomas, Tomgirl, Tommi,
Tommie, Tommy*

Tomazja
(Polish) twin

Tomeka
(African American) form of
Tamika
Tomeke

Tomiko
(Japanese) wealthy
Miko, Tamiko, Tomi

Tomitria
(African American) form of
Tommy
Tomi

Tommie
(Hebrew) sassy
Tom, Tomi, Tommy

Tomo
(Japanese) intelligence

Tonaya
(American) valuable
Tona, Tone

Tonia
(Latin) a wonder
Toneah, Tonya, Tonyah, Toyiah

Tonietta
(American) combo of Toni and Etta; valuable
Toni, Toniett, Toniette

Tonisha
(African American) lively
Nisha, Tona, Toneisha, Tonesha, Tonie, Tonish

Toni
(Latin) meritorious
Tone, Tonee, Tonie, Tony

Tonia
(Latin) daring
Tonni, Tonnie, Tony, Tonya

Tooka
(Japanese) ten days

Topaz
(Latin) gemstone; sparkling
Tophaz

Topekia
(American) form of Topeka
Topeka, Topeke, Topekea

Topsy
(English) topnotch
Toppie, Toppsy, Topsey, Topsi, Topsie

Tora
(Scandinavian) thunder

Torborg
(Scandinavian) thunder
Thorborg, Torbjorg

Tordis
(Scandinavian) Thor's goddess

Tori
(Scottish) rich and winning
Toree, Torri, Torrie, Torry, Tory

Torill
(Scandinavian) loud
Toril, Torille

Torrance
(Place name) town in California; confident
Torr, Torri

Torunn
(Scandinavian) loved by Thor

Tosha
(Slavic) priceless
Tosh, Toshia

Toshala
(Hindu) satisfied

Toshio
(Japanese) year-old child
Toshi, Toshie, Toshiko, Toshikyo

Toski
(Native American) bug

Totsi
(Native American) moccasins

Tova
(Hebrew) good woman
Tovah

Toy
(American) playful
Toia, Toya, Toye

Trace
(French) takes the right path
Traice, Trayce

Tracey
(Gaelic) aggressive
Trace, Tracee, Traci, Tracie, Tracy

Tracilyn
(American) combo of Tracy and Lynn; combative
Trace, Tracelynn, Tracilynne, Tracy-Lynn

Tracy
(English) summer
Trace, Tracee, Tracey, Traci, Tracie, Trasey, Treacy, Treesy

Tranell
(American) confident
Tranel, Tranelle, Traney, Trani

Trang
(Vietnamese) smart

Traniqua
(African American) hopeful
Tranaqua, Tranekwa, Tranequa, Trani, Tranikwa, Tranney, Tranniqua, Tranny

Trava
(Czech) grass

Traviata
(Italian) woman who wanders

Trazanna
(African American) talented
Traz, Trazannah, Traze

Tree
(American) sturdy

Treece
(American) short for Terese
Treese, Trice

Treena
(American) form of Trina
Treen

Trella
(Spanish) star; sparkles
Trela

Tremira
(African American) anxious
Tremera, Tremmi

Treneth
(American) smiling
Trenith, Trenny

Trenica
(African American) smiling
Trenika, Trinika

Trenise
(African American) songbird
Tranese, Tranise, Trannise, Treenie, Treneese, Treni, Trenniece, Trenny

Trenyce
(American) smiling
Trienyse, Trinyce

Tressa
(Greek) reaping life's harvest
Tresa, Tresah, Tress, Trisa

Tressie
(American) successful
Tress, Tressa, Tressee, Tressey, Tressi, Tressy

Treva
(English) homestead by the sea

Trevina
(English) variation of Treva; feminine Trevor

Tricia
(Latin) humorous
Treasha, Tresha, Trich, Tricha, Trish, Trisha

Trilby
(English) literary
Trilbie, Trilby

Trina
(Greek) perfect; scintillating
Tina, Treena, Trine, Trinie

Trinh
(Vietnamese) virgin

Trinidad
(Place name) island off of Venezuela; spiritual person
Trini, Trinny

Trinity
(Latin) triad
Trini, Trinita

Trinlee
(American) genuine
Trinley, Trinli, Trinly

Trish
(American) short for Patricia; funny
Trysh

Trisha
(American) short for Patricia: funny
Tricia

Trishelle
(African American) humorous girl
Trichelle, Trichillem, Trish, Trishel, Trishie

Trissy
(American) tall
Triss, Trissi, Trissie

Trista
(Latin) pensive; sparkling love
Tresta, Trist, Tristie, Trysta

Tristen
(Latin) bold
Tristan, Tristie, Tristin, Trysten

Tristica
(Spanish) form of Trista; pretty
Trist, Tristi, Tristika

Trixie
(Latin) personable
Trix, Trixi, Trixy

Trixiebelle
(American) combo of Trixie and Belle; sweet personality
Belle, Trix, Trixeebel, Trixiebell, Trixybell

Tru
(English) from Truly; true
True

Truc
(Vietnamese) desire

Trudy
(German) hopeful
Trude, Trudi, Trudie

True
(American) truthful
Truee, Truie, Truth

Truette
(American) truthful
Tru, True, Truett

Truffle
(French) delicacy
Truff, Truffy

Trulencia
(Spanish) honest
Lencia, Tru, Trulence, Trulens, Trulense

Truly
(American) honest
True, Trulee, Truley

Trusteen
(American) trusting
Trustean, Trustee, Trustine, Trusty, Trusyne

Truth
(American) honest
Truthe

Try
(American) earnest
Tri, Trie

Tryna
(Greek) form of Trina
Trine, Tryne, Trynna

Tsifira
(Hebrew) crown

Tsomah
(Native American) rose

Tsonka
(American) capricious
Sonky, Tesonka, Tisonka, Tsonk

Tsuhgi
(Japanese) second daughter

Tsula
(Native American) fox

Tua
(Polynesian) outdoors

Tualau
(Polynesian) outdoors

Tucker
(English) tailor
Tukker

Tuenchit
(Thai) mysterious

Tuesday
(English) weekday

Tuhina
(Hindu) snow

Tuki
(Japanese) moon

Tula
(Native American) moon

Tulia
(Spanish) glorious
Tuli, Tuliana, Tulie, Tuliea, Tuly

Tully
(Irish) powerful; dark spirit
Tull, Tulle, Tulli, Tullie

Tulsi
(Hindu) basil

Turin
(American) creative
Turan, Turen, Turrin, Turun

Turney
(Latin) wood worker
Turnee, Turni, Turnie, Turny

Turquoise
(French) blue-green
Turkoise, Turquie, Turrkoise

Tursha
(Slavic) warm
Tersha

Tusa
(Native American) prarie dog

Tuwa
(Native American) earth

Tuyen
(Vietnamese) angel
Tuyet

Twaina
(English) divided
Twayna

Tweetie
(American) vivacious
Tweetee, Tweetey, Tweeti

Twiggy
(English) slim
Twiggie, Twiggee, Twiggey

Twyla
(English) creative
Twila, Twilia

Twynceola
(African American) bold
Twin, Twyn, Twynce

Tyana
(African American) new

Tye
(American) talented

Tyeoka
(African American) rhythmic
Tioka, Tyeo, Tyeoke

Tyesha
(African American) duplicitous
Tesha, Tisha, Tyeisha, Tyiesha, Tyisha

Tyisha
(African American) sweet
Isha, Tisha, Ty, Tyeisha, Tyish

Tyler
(American) stylish; tailor
Tielyr, Tye

Tymitha
(African American) kind
Timitha, Tymi, Tymie, Tymith, Tymy, Tymytha

Tyndall
(Irish) dark
Tyndal, Tyndel, Tyndell, Tyndyl, Tyndyll

Tyne
(American) dramatic; (Old English) sylvan
Tie, Tine, Tye

Tyneil
(African American) combo of Ty and Neil; helpful
Tyne, Tyneal, Tyniel

Tynisha
(African American) fertile
Tinisha, Tynesha, Tynie

Tyra
(Scandinavian) assertive woman
Tye, Tyrah, Tyre, Tyrie

Tyrea
(African American) form of Thora; thunder
Tyree, Tyria

Tyrina
(American) ball of fire
Tierinna, Tye, Tyreena, Tyrinah

Tyronna
(African American) combo of Tyronne and Anna; special
Tierona, Tye, Tyrona, Tyronnah

Tyson
(French) son of Ty
Ty, Tysen

Tyzna
(American) ingenious, assertive
Tyze, Tyzie

Tzadika
(Hebrew) loyal
Zadika

Tzafra
(Hebrew) morning
Tzefira, Zafra, Zefira

Tzahala
(Hebrew) happy
Zahala

Tzeira
(Hebrew) young

Tzemicha
(Hebrew) in bloom
Zemicha

Tzeviya
(Hebrew) gazelle
Civia, Tzevia, Tzivia, Tzivya, Zibiah, Zivia

Tzigane
(Hungarian) gypsy
Tsigana, Tsigane

Tzila
(Hebrew) darkness
Tzili, Zila, Zili

Tzina
(Hebrew) shelter
Zina

Tzipiya
(Hebrew) hope
Tzipia, Zipia

Tziyona
(Hebrew) hill
Zeona, Ziona

Tzofi
(Hebrew) scout
Tzofia, Tzofit, Tzofiya, Zofi, Zofia, Zofit

Tzuriya
(Hebrew) God is powerful
Tzuria, Zuria

Uberta
(Italian) bright

Uchechi
(African) God's will

Udavine
(American) thriving
Uda

Udele
(English) prospering
woman
*Uda, Udela, Udell, Udella,
Udelle*

Uela
(Unknown) dedicated to
God
Uella

Uganda
(Place name) African
nation

Ula
(Celtic) jewel-like beauty
Eula, Ulah, Ule, Ulla, Ylla

Ulanda
(American) confident
Uland, Ulandah, Ulande

Ulani
(Hawaiian) happy;
(Polynesian) happy
Ulanee

Ulda
(Unknown origin)
prophetess

Ule
(Unknown origin) burdens

Ulielmi
(Unknown origin)
intelligent

Ulima
(Unknown origin) smart

Ulla
(German) powerful and
rich

Ulphi
(Unknown origin) lovely
Ulphia, Ulphiah

Ulrika
(Teutonic) leader
*Rica, Ulree, Ulric, Ulrica,
Ulrie, Ulry, Urik*

Ultima
(Latin) aloof

Ulva
(German) wolf; courage

Ulyssia
(Invented) from Ulysses;
wanderer
*Lyss, Lyssia, Uls, Ulsy,
Ulsyia*

Uma
(Hebrew) nation;
worldview
Umah

Umberlina
(Unknown origin) feminine
form of Umberto

Umeko
(Unknown origin) blossom

Umnia
(Arabic) desirable
Umniah, Umniya, Umniyah

Una
(Latin) unique
Ona, Oona, Unah

Undine
(Latin) from the ocean
Ondine, Undene, Undyne

Undra
(American) one;
longsuffering

Unice
(English) sensible
Eunice, Uniss

Unique
(Latin) singular
Uneek

Unity
(English) unity of spirit
Unitee

Unn
(Scandinavian) loving
Un

Ural
(Place name) Ural
Mountains
Ura, Uralle, Urine, Uris

Urania
(Greek) universal beauty
*Ranie, Uraine, Urana,
Uraneah, Uranie*

Urbai
(Unknown origin) gentle

Urbana
(Latin) born in the city
Urbani, Urbanna, Urbannai

Urbi
(Egyptian) princess

Uria
(Hebrew) God is my flame
*Ria, Uri, Uriah, Urial,
Urissa*

Uriela
(Hebrew) God's light
Uriella, Uriyella

Urith
(Hebrew) bright
Urit

Ursa
(Greek, Latin) star; bear-
like
Urs, Ursah, Ursie

Ursula
(Latin) little female bear
Ursa, Urse, Ursela, Ursila

Urta
(Latin) spiny plant

Usha
(Indian) dawn; awakening

Usher
(Word as name) helpful
Ush, Ushar, Ushur

Uta
(Teutonic) battle heroine

Utas
(Unknown origin) glorious

Ute
(German) rich and
powerful

Utica
(Native American)
Uticas, Uttica

Utopia
(American) idealistic
Uta, Utopiah

Uttasta
(Unknown origin) from the
homeland

Uzbek
(Place name) for
Uzbekistan
Usbek

Uzetta
(American) serious
Uzette

Uzia
(Hebrew) God is my
strength
Uzial, Uzzia, Uzzial

Uzma
(Spanish) capable
Usma, Uz, Uzmah

Uzoma
(African) the right way

Vacla
(Origin unknown) vain

Vaclava
(Origin unknown)
conceited

Vada
(German) form of Valda;
winner
Vaida, Vay

Vadnee
(Origin unknown) gives

Val
(Latin) short for Valerie; strong

Vala
(German) chosen one

Valarie
(Latin) strong
Val, Valaria, Valerie

Valborg
(Scandinavian) from power mountain
Valborga

Valda
(German) high spirits
Val, Valdah, Valida, Velda

Vale
(English) valley; natural
Vail, Vaylie

Valeda
(Latin) strong woman
Val, Valayda, Valedah

Valencia
(Place name) city in Spain; strong-willed
Val, Valecia, Valence, Valenica, Valensha, Valentia, Valenzia, Valincia

Valene
(Latin) strong girl
Valaine, Valean, Valeda, Valeen, Valen, Valena, Valeney, Vallen, Valina, Valine, Vallan, Vallen

Valentina
(Latin) romantic
Val, Vala, Valantina, Vale Valentin, Valentine, Valiaka, Valtina, Valyn, Valynn

Valeny
(American) hard
Val, Valenie

Valeria
(Spanish) having valor
Valeri, Valerie, Valery

Valerie
(Latin) robust
Vairy, Val, Valarae, Valaree, Valarey, Valari, Valarie, Vale, Valeree, Valeri, Valeriane, Valery, Vallarie, Valleree, Valleri, Vallerie, Vallery, Valli, Vallie, Vallirie, Valora, Valry, Veleria, Velerie

Valerta
(Invented) form of Valerie; courageous
Valer, Valert

Valeska
(Polish) joyous leader
Valese, Valeshia, Valeske, Valezka, Valisha

Valetta
(Italian) feminine
Valettah, Valita, Valitta

Valkie
(Scandinavian) from Valkyrie; fantastic
Val, Valkee, Valki, Valkry, Valky

Vallie
(Latin) natural
Val, Valli, Vally

Vallie-Mae
(Latin) from Valentina and Mae; romantic
Valliemae, Vallimae, Vallimay

Valma
(Scandinavian) loyal

Valonia
(Scandinavian) loyal
Vallon, Valona

Valora
(Latin) intimidating
Val, Valorah, Valori, Valoria, Valorie, Valory, Valorya

Valore
(Latin) courageous
Val, Valour

Valoria
(Spanish) brave
Vallee, Valora, Valore

Value
(Word as name) valued
Valu, Valyou

Valyn
(American) perky
Valind, Valinn, Valynn

Vamia
(Hispanic) energetic
Vamee, Vamie

Vanda
(German) smiling beauty
*Vandah, Vandana,
Vandelia, Vandetta, Vandi,
Vannda*

Vanessa
(Greek) flighty
*Nessa, Van, Vanassa,
Vanesa, Vanesah, Vanesha,
Vaneshia, Vanesia,
Vanessah, Vanesse,
Vanessia, Vanessica,
Veneza, Vaniece, Vaniessa,
Vanisa, Vanissa, Vanita,
Vanna, Vannessa, Vanneza,
Vanni, Vannie, Vanny,
Varnessa, Venesa, Venessa*

Vani
(Russian) from Vania;
hospitable

Vania
(Hebrew) gifted
Vaneah, Vanya

Vanille
(American) from vanilla;
simplistic
*Vana, Vani, Vanila, Vanile,
Vanna*

Vanity
(English) vain girl
Vanita, Vaniti

Vanna
(Greek) golden girl
*Van, Vana, Vanae, Vannah,
Vannalee, Vannaleigh*

Vanora
(Welsh) wave; mercurial
Vannora

Vanthe
(Greek) variant of Xanthe;
yellow-haired

Vantrice
(American) combo of Van
and Trice; retreats
*Vantrece, Vantricia,
Vantrisa*

Vanya
(American) form of Vanna;
self-assured
Vani, Vanja, Vanni, Vanyuh

Vara
(Greek) strange
Varah, Vare

Varda
(Hebrew) rosy
*Vadit, Vardah, Vardia,
Vardice, Vardina, Vardis,
Vardit*

Varaina
(Invented) form of Loraine

Varina
(Czech) from Barbara;
strange

Varna
(Origin unknown) no trace
of vanity

Vashti
(Persian) beauty
Vashtee, Vashtie

Vasta
(Persian) pretty
Vastah

Vasteen
(American) capable
Vas, Vastene, Vastine, Vasty

Vaughan
(Last name as first name)
smooth talker
Vaughn, Vawn, Vawne

Vaydell
(American) combo of Vay
and Dell; jokester

Veata
(Cambodian) smart;
organized
Veatah

Veda
(Sanskrit) wise woman
*Vedad, Vedah, Vedis,
Veeda, Veida, Vida, Vita*

Vedette
(French) watchful
Veda, Vedett, Vedetta

Vedi
(Sanskrit) wisdom

Vega
(Scandinavian) star
Vay, Vayga, Vegah, Veguh

Velacy
(Origin unknown) delicate

Velda
(German) famous leader
Veleda, Valeda

Veleda
(German) intelligent
Vel, Veladah, Velayda

Velika
(Slavic) wonder

Velinda
(American) form of
Melinda; practical
*Vel, Velin, Velind, Vell,
Velly, Velynda*

Vell
(American) short for
Velma; practical
Vel, Velly, Vels

Velma
(German) hardworking
*Valma, Vel, Vellma,
Velmah, Vilma, Vilna*

Velonie
(American) combo of V
and Melonie; smooth
*Val, Vallonia, Valoniah,
Valonia*

Velore
(Origin unknown) poised

Velvet
(French) luxurious
Vel, Vell, Velvete, Velvett

Venecia
(Italian) girl from Venice;
sparkles
*Vanecia, Vanetia, Veneise,
Venesa, Venesha,
Venesher, Venesse,
Venessia, Venetia,
Venette, Venezia, Venice,
Venicia, Veniece, Veniesa,
Venise, Venisha, Venishia,
Venita, Venitia, Venize,
Vennesa, Vennice,
Vennisa, Vennise, Vonitia,
Vonizia*

Veneradah
(Spanish) honored;
venerable
Ven, Venera, Venerada

Veneranda
(Spanish) venerated;
respected

Venetia
(Latin) girl from Venice

Venice
(Place name) city in Italy;
coming of age
*Vanice, Vaniece, Veneece,
Veneese*

Venitia
(Italian) forgiving
*Esha, Venesha, Venn,
Venney, Venni, Vennie,
Venny*

Venke
(Polish) from Venice

Vennita
 (Italian) from Venice, Italy; having arrived
 Nita, Vanecia, Ven, Venesha, Venetia, Venita, Vennie, Vinetia

Ventura
 (Spanish) fortunate

Venus
 (Latin) loving; goddess of love
 Venis, Venise, Vennie, Venusa, Vinny

Vera
 (Russian) faithful friend
 Vara, Veera, Veira, Veradis, Verah, Vere, Verie, Vira

Verbena
 (Latin) natural beauty

Verda
 (Latin) breath of spring
 Ver, Vera, Verdah, Verde, Verdi, Verdie, Viridiana, Viridis

Verdad
 (Spanish) verdant; honest
 Verda, Verdade, Verdie, Verdine, Verdite

Verdie
 (Latin) fresh as springtime
 Verd, Verda, Verdee, Verdi, Verdy

Verena
 (English) honest
 Veren, Verenah, Verene, Verenis, Vereniz, Verina, Verina, Verine, Virena, Virna

Verenase
 (Swiss) flourishing; truthful
 Ver, Verenese, Verennase, Vy, Vyrenase, Vyrennace

Verity
 (French) truthful
 Verety, Verita, Veritee, Veriti, Veritie

Verla
 (Latin) truthful

Verlene
 (Latin) vivacious
 Verleen, Verlena, Verlie, Verlin, Verlina, Verlinda, Verline, Verlyn, Verlynne

Verlita
 (Spanish) growing

Vermekia
 (African American) natural
 Meki, Mekia, Verme, Vermekea, Vermy, Vermye

Verna
 (Latin) springlike
 Vernah, Verne, Vernese, Vernesha, Verneshia, Vernessa, Vernetia, Vernetta, Vernette, Vernia, Vernice, Vernis, Vernisha, Vernishela, Vernita, Verusya, Viera, Virida, Virna, Virnell

Verneta
 (Latin) verdant
 Vernita, Verna, Virena, Virna

Vernice
 (American) natural
 Verna, Vernica, Vernicca, Vernie, Verniece, Vernique

Vernicia
 (Spanish) form of Vernice; springtime
 Vern, Verni, Vernisia

Vernita
 (Latin) of the spring

Verona
 (Place name) city in Italy; flourishes; honest

Veronica
(Latin) girl's image; real
*Nica, Ronica, Varonica,
Veron, Verhonica, Verinica,
Verohnica, Veron, Verone,
Veronic, Veronice,
Veronika, Veronne,
Veronnica, Vironica, Vonni,
Von, Vonni, Vonnie, Vonny,
Vron, Vronica*

Veronique
(French) realistic woman;
form of Veronica
*Veroneek, Veroneese,
Veroniece*

Versperah
(Latin) evening star
Vesp, Vespa, Vespera

Vertrelle
(African American)
organized
*Vertey, Verti, Vertrel,
Vetrell*

Vesela
(Origin unknown) open
Vess

Vespera
(Latin) evening star

Vesta
(Latin) home-loving;
goddess of the home
*Vess, Vessie, Vessy, Vest,
Vestah, Vesteria*

Veste
(Latin) keeps home fires
burning
Esta, Vesta

Vetaria
(Slavic) regal woman

Vevay
(Latin) form of Vivian;
lively
*Vevah, Vi, Viv, Vivay, Vivi,
Vivie*

Vevila
(Irish) vivacious

Vevina
(Latin) sweetheart

Vi
(Latin) short for Viola; kind
Vy, Vye

Vianca
(American) from Bianca;
white

Vianey
(Spanish) form of Vivian;
alive
*Via, Viana, Viane, Viani,
Vianne, Vianney, Viany*

Vianna
(American) combo of Vi
and Dianna; special
Viana, Viann, Vianne

Vianne
(French) striking
Vi, Viane, Viann

Vibeke
(Hindi) vibrant

Vicky
(Latin) short for Victoria
*Vic, Viccy, Vick, Vickee,
Vickey, Vicki, Vickie,
Vikkey, Vikki, Viky*

Victoria
(Latin) winner
*Vic, Vicki, Vicky, Victoriah,
Victoriana, Victorie,
Victorina, Victorine,
Victory, Vikki, Viktoria,
Vyctoria*

Victory
(Latin) a winning woman
Vic, Viktorie

Vida
(Hebrew) short for Davida
Veeda

Vidella
(Spanish) life
Veda, Vida, Videline, Vydell

Vidette
(Hebrew) loved
*Viddey, Viddi, Viddie,
Vidett, Videy*

Vidonia
(Portuguese) vine; winding

Vienna
(Place name) a city in
Austria
*Veena, Vena, Venna,
Viena, Viennah, Vienne,
Vienette, Vina*

Viennese
(Place name) from Vienna
Vee, Viena, Vienne

Viera
(Spanish) smart; alive

Viet
(Place name) form of
Vietnam
Vee, Viette

Vigdis
(Scandinavian) war
goddess

Vigilia
(Latin) vigilant

Vignette
(American) special scene

Vilhelmina
(Scandinavian) from
Wilhelmina; perseveres
Velma, Vilhelmine, Vilma

Villette
(French) little village girl
Vietta

Vilma
(Spanish) form of Velma;
industrious
Vi, Vil

Vimala
(Hindi) attractive

Vina
(Hindi) musical instrument
*Veena, Vena, Vin, Vinah,
Vinesha, Vinessa, Vinia,
Viniece, Vinique, Vinisha,
Vinita, Vinna, Vinni,
Vinnie, Vinny, Vinora, Vyna*

Vinah
(American) up-and-coming
Vi, Vyna

Vincentia
(Latin) winner
*Vicenta, Vin, Vincenta,
Vincentena, Vincentina,
Vincentine, Vincenza,
Vincy, Vinnie*

Vincia
(Spanish) forthright;
winning
Vincenta, Vincey, Vinci

Vinefrida
(Scandinavian) from
Winnifred; bold

Vinia
(Spanish) vineyard woman

Vinita
(Hindi) she comes home

Vinne
(American) from the
vineyard

Viola
(Latin) violet; lovely lady
*Vi, Violah, Violaine,
Violanta, Viole, Violeine*

Violanth
(Latin) from the purple
flower violet
*Vi, Viol, Viola, Violanta,
Violante*

Violet
(English, French) purple
flower
*Vi, Viole, Violette, Vylolet,
Vyoletta, Vyolette*

Violyne
(Latin) from the purple
flower violet
*Vi, Vio, Viola, Violene,
Violine*

Virgilee
(American) combo of Virgi
and Lee; pure girl
*Virge, Virgee, Virgi,
Virgilea, Virgileigh, Virgy,
Virgylee*

Virgilia
(Latin) bears all; stoic
Virgillia

Virginia
(Latin) pure female
*Giniah, Verginia, Verginya,
Virge, Virgen, Virgenia,
Virgenya, Virgie, Virgine,
Virginio, Virginnia,
Virginya, Virgy, Virjeana*

Viridas
(Latin) green; growing
Viridis

Viridiana
(Spanish) combo of Viri
and Diana; ostentatious
*Di, Diana, Diane, Viri,
Viridi, Viridiane*

Viridis
(Latin) green and verdant
*Virdis, Virida, Viridia,
Viridiana*

Virtue
(Latin) strong; pure

Vision
(Word as name) visionary

Vita
(Latin) animated; lively;
life
*Veda, Veeta, Veta, Vete,
Vitaliana, Vitalina, Vitel,
Vitella, Vitia, Vitka, Vitke*

Viv
(Latin) short for Vivian;
vital

Viva
(Latin) alive; lively
Veeva, Vivan, Vivva

Vivecca
(Scandinavian) lively;
energetic
*Viv, Viveca, Vivecka,
Viveka, Vivica, Vivie,
Vyveca*

Vivi
(Hindi) vital
Viv

Vivian
(Latin) bubbling with life
*Viv, Viva, Vive, Vivee, Vivi,
Vivia, Viviana, Viviane,
Vivie, Vivien, Vivienne,
Vivina, Vivion, Vivyan,
Vyvyan*

Vivianna
(American) inventive
Viviannah, Vivianne

Vivilyn
(American) vital
Viv, Vivi

Vix
(American) short for Vixen
Vixa, Vixie, Vyx

Vixen
(American) flirt
Vix, Vixee, Vixie

Vlasta
(Slavic) likeable

Voila
(French) attention; seen
Vwala

Volante
(Italian) veiled

Voletta
(French) mysterious
Volette, Volettie

Vona
(French) pretty woman

Vonda
(Czech) loving; talented
Vondah, Vondi

Vondrah
(Czech) loving
Vona
(French) pretty woman
Vonda
(Czech) loving; talented
Vondah, Vondi
Vondrah
(Czech) loving
Vond, Vonda, Vondie,
Vondra, Vondrea
Voneisha
(American) combo of Von
and Neisha; precocious
Voneishia, Vonesha,
Voneshia
Vonese
(American) form of
Vanessa; pretty
Vonesa, Vonise, Vonne,
Vonnesa, Vonny
Voni
(Slavic) affectionate
Vonee, Vonie
Vonna
(French) graceful
Vona, Vonah, Vonne,
Vonni, Vonnie, Vonny
Vonnala
(American) sweet
Von, Vonala, Vonnalah,
Vonnie
Vonshae
(American) combo of Von
and Shae; confident
Von, Vonshay
Vontricia
(American) combo of Von
and Tricia; thinks
Vontrece, Vontrese,
Vontrice, Vontriece
Voyage
(Word as name) trip;
wanderer
Voy

Vyera
(Spanish) variant of Viera;
lively; smart

Wade
(American) campy
Wafa
(Arabic) loyal
Wakana
(Japanese) plant; thriving
Wakanda
(Native American) magical
Wakenda
Wakeen
(American) spunky
Wakeene, Wakey, Wakine
Wakeishah
(African American) happy
Wake, Wakeisha, Wakesha
Walburga
(German) protective
Walberga, Wallburga,
Walpurgis
Walda
(German) powerful woman
Waldah, Waldena,
Waldette, Waldina,
Wallda, Wally, Welda,
Wellda
Waleria
(Polish) sweet
Waleska
(Last name as first name)
effervescent
Wal, Walesk, Wally

Walker
(English) active; mover
Wallker

Walkiria
(Mythology) from Valkyrie;
woodland nymph

Wallis
(English) from Wales;
open-minded
*Walis, Wallace, Walless,
Wallie, Walliss, Wally,
Wallys*

Wanda
(Polish) wild; wandering
*Vanda, Wahnda, Wandah,
Wandie, Wandis, Wandy,
Wannda, Wenda,
Wendaline, Wendall,
Wendeline, Wendy,
Wohnda, Wonda, Wonnda*

Wanetta
(English) fair
Waneta, Wanette, Wanita

Warda
(German) guards her own
Wardia, Wardine

Warma
(American) warmth-filled
Warm

Warna
(German) defends her own

Warner
(German) outgoing; fighter
Warna, Warnar, Warnir

Waverly
(English) wavers in the
meadow of swaying
aspens
Waverley

Waynette
(English) makes wagons;
crafts wood
*Waynel, Waynelle,
Waynlyn*

Weeko
(Native American) pretty

Wehilani
(Hawaiian) heaven

Wenda
(German) adventurer
Wend, Wendah, Wendy

Wendell
(English) has wanderlust
*Wendaline, Wendall,
Wendelle*

Wendy
(English) friendly; childlike
*Wenda, Wendaline,
Wende, Wendee,
Wendeline, Wendey,
Wendi, Wendie, Wendye*

Weslee
(English) girl from
meadows of the west
*Weslea, Weslene, Wesley,
Weslia, Weslie, Weslyn*

Weslia
(English) meadow in the
west
Wesleya, Weslie

Weslie
(English) woman in the
meadow
Wes, Weslee, Wesli

Wheeler
(English) inventive
Wheelah, Wheelar

Whitley
(English) outdoorsy
*Whitelea, Whitlea, Whitlee,
Whitly, Whittley, Witlee*

Whitman
(English) white-haired
Whit, Wittman

Whitney
(English) white; fresh
*Whit, Whiteney, Whitne,
Whitnea, Whitnee,
Whitneigh, Whitni,
Whitnie, Whitny,
Whittaney, Whittany,
Whittney, Whytnie*

Whitson
(Last name as first) white
Whits, Whitty, Witte, Witty

Whittier
(Literature) for the poet
John Greenleaf Whittier;
distinguished
Whitt

Whoopi
(English) excitable
*Whoopee, Whoopie,
Whoopy*

Whynesha
(African American) kind-
hearted
*Whynesa, Wynes, Wynesa,
Wynesha*

Wibeke
(Scandinavian) vibrant
Wiebke, Wiweca

Wiktoria
(Polish) victor
Wikta

Wilda
(English) wild-haired girl
Willda, Willie, Wylda, Wyle

Wile
(American) coy; wily
Wiles, Wyle

Wilfreda
(English) goal-oriented
Wilfridda, Wilfrieda

Wilhelmina
(German) able protector
*Willa, Willhelmena, Willie,
Wilma*

Willa
(English) desirable
Will, Willah

Willette
(American) open
Wilet, Wilett, Will, Willett

Willine
(American) form of Will;
willowy
Will, Willene, Willy, Willyne

Willis
(American) sparkling
Wilice, Will, Willice

Willow
(American) free spirit;
willow tree
Willo

Wilona
(English) desirable
*Wilo, Wiloh, Wilonah,
Wylona*

Wilma
(German) sturdy
*Willma, Wilmah, Wilmina,
Wylm, Wylma*

Wilmot
(English) from William;
prissy; God-fearing

Wilona
(English) desired child
Willonoa, Willone, Wilone

Win
(German) flirty
Winnie, Wyn, Wynne

Wind
(American) breezy
*Winde, Windee, Windey,
Windi, Windy, Wynd*

Winda
(African) hunts for prey

Windy
(English) likes the wind
*Windee, Windey, Windi,
Windie, Wyndee, Wyndy*

Winema
(Native American) leader

Winetta
(American) peaceful;
country girl
*Winette, Winietta, Wyna,
Wynette*

Winifred
(German) peaceful woman
*Win, Wina, Winafred,
Windy, Winefred,
Winefride, Winefried,
Winfreda, Winfrieda,
Winifryd, Winne, Winnie,
Winniefred, Winnifreed,
Wynafred, Wynifred,
Wynn, Wynne, Wynnifred*

Winkie
(American) vital
Winkee, Winky

Winna
(African) friendly
Winnah

Winner
(American) outstanding

Winnie
(English) winning
Wini, Winny, Wynnie

Winnielle
(African) victorious female
*Winielle, Winniele,
Wynnielle*

Winola
(German) vivacious

Winona
(Native American)
firstborn girl
*Wenona, Wenonah,
Winnie, Winnona,
Winoena, Winonah, Wye,
Wynnona, Wynona,
Wynonah, Wynonna*

Winsome
(English) nice; beauty
Wynsome

Winter
(English) child born in
winter
Wynter

Wisdom
(English) discerning

Wistar
(German) respected
Wistarr, Wister

Wisteria
(Botanical) vine;
entangles
Wistaria

Wonder
(American) filled with
wonder
*Wander, Wonda, Wondee,
Wondy, Wunder*

Wonila
(African American)
swaying
Waunila, Wonilla, Wonny

Wood
(American) smooth talker
*Woode, Woodee, Woodie,
Woody, Woodye*

Wova
(American) brassy
Whova, Wovah

Wren
(English) flighty girl; bird
Renn, Wrin, Wryn, Wrynne

Wyanda
(American) form of
Wanda; gregarious
Wyan

Wyanet
(Native American) lovely
*Wyanetta, Wyonet,
Wyonetta*

Wyetta
(French) feisty
Wyette

Wylie
(American) wily
Wylee, Wyley, Wyli

Wymette
(American) vocalist
*Wimet, Wimette, Wymet,
Wynette*

Wynne
(Welsh) fair-haired
*Win, Winne, Winnie,
Winny, Winwin, Wyn,
Wynee, Wynn, Wynnie*

Wynstelle
(Latin) chaste; star
*Winstella, Winstelle,
Wynnestella, Wynnestelle*

Wyomie
(Native American) horse-
rider on the plains
*Why, Wyome, Wyomee,
Wyomeh, Wyomia*

Wyoming
(Native American) U.S.
state; cowgirl
Wy, Wye, Wyoh, Wyomia

Wysandra
(Greek) fair; protects

Wyss
(Welsh) spontaneous; fair
Whyse

Xanadu
(Place name) an idyllic,
exotic, fictional place
Zanadu

Xandra
(Greek) protective
*Xandrae, Zan, Zandie,
Zandra*

Xanthe
(Greek) beautiful blonde;
yellow
*X, Xanth, X-Anth, Xantha,
Xanthie, Xes, Zane,
Zanthie*

Xanthippe
(Greek) form of Xanthe;
wife of Socrates

Xaverine
(Invented) combo of
Katherine and Xanthe

Xavia
(Origin unknown) feminine
form of Xavier; familiar

Xaviera
(French) smart
*Zavey, Zavie, Zaviera,
Zavierah, Zavy*

Xara
(Hebrew) form of Sara

Xena
(Greek) girl from afar
Xenia, Zen, Zena, Zennie

Xeniah
(Greek) gracious
entertainer
Xen, Xenia, Zenia, Zeniah

Ximena
(Greek) greets

Ximenia
(Spanish) form of Serena;
peaceful

Xiomara
(Spanish) congenial

Xylene
(Greek) outdoorsy
*Leen, Lene, Xyleen, Xyline,
Zylee, Zyleen, Zylie*

Xylia
(Greek) woods-loving
Zylea, Zylia

Xylophila
(Greek) lover of nature

Y

Yadira
(Hindi) dearest

Yael
(Hebrew) strength of God
Yaele, Yayl, Yayle

Yaeshona
(American) combo of Yae
and Shona; worries
*Yaeseana, Yaeshauna,
Yaeshawna, Yayseana,
Yayshauna, Yayshawna,
Yayshona*

Yaffa
(Hebrew) beautiful girl
Yafa, Yafah, Yaffah, Yapha

Yahaira
(Hebrew) precious
Yajaira

Yahnnie
(Greek) giving
Yahn, Yanni, Yannie, Yannis

Yaki
(Japanese) tenacious
Yakee

Yakira
(Hebrew) adored baby

Yale
(English) fertile moor
Yaile, Yayle

Yamileth
(Spanish) girl of grace
Yami

Yamilla
(Arabic) form of
Jamila/Camilla; beautiful
Yamila, Yamyla, Yamylla

Yamille
(Arabic) beautiful
*Yamill, Yamyl, Yamyle,
Yamylle*

Yana
(Slavic) lovely
*Yanah, Yanna, Yanni,
Yannie, Yanny*

Yancy
(Native American) Yankee;
sassy
*Yancee, Yancey, Yanci,
Yancie*

Yanessa
(American) form of
Vanessa; smooth
*Yanesa, Yanisa, Yanissa,
Yanysa, Yanyssa*

Yanisha
(American) combo of Yanis
and Nisha; high hopes
Yaneesha, Yanysha

Yannette
(American) combo of Y
and Annette; melodic
Yanett, Yannett, Yanny

Yaquelin
(Spanish) form of
Jaqueline
*Yackie, Yacque, Yacquelyn,
Yaki, Yakie, Yaque,
Yaquelinn, Yaquelinne*

Yara
(Spanish) expansive;
princess
Yarah, Yare, Yarey

Yardena
(Hebrew) flows naturally

Yardley
(English) open-minded
*Yardlee, Yardleigh, Yardli,
Yardlie, Yardly*

Yarine
(Russian) peaceful
Yari, Yarina

Yarita
(Spanish) flashy

Yarkona
(Hebrew) growing

Yashona
(Hindi) rich
*Yaseana, Yashauna,
Yashawna, Yeseana,
Yeshauna, Yeshawna,
Yeshona*

Yasmine
(Arabic) pretty
*Yasmeen, Yasmen,
Yasmin, Yasminn, Yasmyn,
Yasmynn*

Yasmina
(Hindi) from Jasmine;
blossoms
Yasmeena, Yasmyna

Yaura
(American) desirous
Yara, Yaur, YaYa

Yazmin
(Persian) pretty flower
*Yazmen, Yazminn, Yazmyn,
Yazmynn*

Yeardley
(English) home enclosed
in meadow
*Yeardlee, Yeardleigh,
Yeardli, Yeardlie, Yeardly*

Yebenette
(American) little
Yebe, Yebey, Yebi

Yelena
(Russian) friendly

Yelisabeta
(Russian) form of Elizabeth
Yelizabet

Yemaya
(African) smart; quirky
Yemye

Yenny
(American) combo of Y
and Jenny; happy
Yen, Yeni, Yenney, Yenni

Yessenia
(Spanish) devout
Jesenia, Yesenia

Yetta
(English) head of home

Yeva
(Russian) lively; loving
Yevka

Yina
(Spanish) winning
Yena

Ynez
(Spanish) from Inez; pure

Yoanna
(Hebrew) form of John;
believer
Yoana, Yoanah, Yoannah

Yodelle
(American) old-fashioned
*Yode, Yodell, Yodelly,
Yodette, Yodey*

Yoella
(Hebrew) loves Jehovah
Yoela, Yoelah, Yoellah

Yohanna
(Greek) violet; textured
*Yohana, Yohanah,
Yohannah*

Yoko
(Japanese) good; striving
Yokoh

Yola
(Spanish) form of Yolanda;
violet
Yolanda, Yoli

Yolanda
(Greek) pretty as a violet
flower
*Yola, Yolana, Yolandah,
Yolie, Yoyly*

Yolie
(Greek) violet; flower
Yolee, Yoley, Yoli, Yoly

Yon
(Korean) lotus; lovely
Yonn

Yona
(Hebrew) dove; calm
Yonah, Yonna, Yonnah

Yonaide
(American)
Yonade, Yonaid

Yonina
(Hebrew) dove; calm
Yonyna

Yonit
(Hebrew) passive
Yonitt, Yonyt, Yonytt

Yordaine
(French) from Jorden;
descends
Yordane, Yordayne

Yordan
(Hebrew) from Jordan;
descends
Yorden, Yordyn

Yordana
(Hebrew) humble
*Yordanah, Yordanna,
Yordannah*

Yori
(Japanese) dependable
Yoree, Yorey, Yorie, Yory

York
(English) forthright
Yorkie, Yorkke

Yosepha
(Hebrew) from Josephine;
pleasure

Yoshe
(Japanese) from Yoshi;
good girl
*Yoshee, Yoshey, Yoshi,
Yoshie, Yoshy*

Young
(Korean) forever

Yovona
(African American) from
Yvonne; joy
*Yovaana, Yovanna,
Yovhana, Yovhanna,
Yoviana, Yovianna*

Ysabel
(Spanish) from Isabel;
clever
*Ysabell, Ysabelle, Ysebel,
Ysebell, Ysebelle, Ysybel,
Ysybell, Ysybelle*

Ysabella
(Spanish) smart and witty
*Ysabela, Ysebela, Ysebella,
Ysybela, Ysybella*

Ysanne
(English) graceful
*Esan, Esanne, Essan,
Ysan, Ysann*

Yseult
(Irish) prettiness
Yseulte

Yu
(Asian) jade; a gem

Yue
(Asian) happy

Yuette
(American) capable
Yue, Yuete, Yuetta

Yuki
(Japanese) snow child

Yulan
(Spanish) splendid

Yule
(Spanish) from Yulene;
competitive

Yuliana
(Invented) combo of Y and
Juliana
Ana, Yuli, Yuliann, Yulianne

Yuna
(African) gorgeous
Yunah

Yurianna
   (Invented) combo of Yuri
   and Anna; royal
   Yuri, Yuriann, Yurianne

Yuta
   (American) dramatic
   Uta

Yves
   (French) clever

Yvette
   (French) lively archer
   *Yavet, Yevette, Yvete,
   Yvett*

Yvonne
   (French) athletic
   *Vonne, Vonnie, Yavonne,
   Yvone, Yvonna*

Yzabel
   (Hebrew) variant of Isabel;
   clever
   *Yzabell, Yzabelle, Yzebel,
   Yzebell, Yzebelle, Yzybel,
   Yzybell, Yzybelle*

Z

Zabrina
   (American) from Sabrina;
   clever; fruitful
   Zabreena, Zabryna

Zachah
   (Hebrew) Lord
   remembered; brave-
   hearted
   *Zach, Zacha, Zachie,
   Zachrie*

Zada
   (Arabic) fortunate
   Zaida, Zayda

Zafira
   (Arabic) successful
   Zafirah

Zahara
   (African) flower
   Zahari, Zaharit

Zahavah
   (Hebrew) golden girl
   Zahava, Zeheva, Zev

Zahira
   (African) flower
   *Zahara, Zahirah, Zahrah,
   Zara, Zuhra*

Zahra
   (African) blossoming
   Zara, Zarah

Zaida
   (Spanish) peacemaker
   *Zada, Zai_*

Zainab
   (Arabic) brave

Zaira
   (Arabic) flower
   Zara, Zarah, Zaria, Zayeera

Zaire
   (Place name) country in
   Africa
   Zai, Zay, Zayaire

Zakah
   (African) smart
   Zaka, Zakia, Zakiah

Zakiya
   (Arabic) chaste
   Zakiyah

Zale
   (Greek) strong force of the
   sea
   Zaile, Zayle

Zalika
   (African) born to royalty

Zaltana
   (Native American) high
   mountain

Zambee
(Place name) from Zambia
*Zambi, Zambie, Zamby,
Zamby*

Zamilla
(Greek) strong force of the
sea
Zamila, Zamyla, Zamylla

Zamir
(Hebrew) intelligent leader
Zameer, Zamyr

Zan
(Greek) supportive;
(Chinese) praiseworthy
Zander, Zann

Zana
(Greek) defender;
energetic
Zanah

Zandra
(Greek) shy; helpful
Zan, Zondra

Zane
(Scandinavian) bold girl
Zain

Zaneta
(Spanish) God is good

Zanita
(American) gifted
*Zaneta, Zanetta, Zanette,
Zanitt, Zeneta*

Zanna
(Hebrew) lily
Zana, Zanah, Zannah

Zanth
(Greek) leader
*Zanthe, Zanthi, Zanthie,
Zanthy*

Zara
(Hebrew) dawn; glorious
Zahra, Zarah, Zaree

Zarena
(Hebrew) dawn
Zareena, Zarina, Zaryna

Zarifa
(Arabic) successful

Zarina
(Hebrew) form of Sarika

Zarita
(Hebrew) form of Sarah;
princess

Zarmina
(Origin unknown) bright
Zar, Zarmynna

Zashawna
(American) combo of
Zasha and Shawna;
spontaneous
*Zaseana, Zashauna,
Zashona, Zeseana,
Zeshauna, Zeshawna,
Zeshona*

Zawadi
(African) gift

Zayit
(Hebrew) olive

Zaylee
(English) heavenly
*Zay, Zayle, Zayley, Zayli,
Zaylie*

Zayna
(Arabic) wonderful
Zayne

Zaynab
(Iranian) child of Ali
Zainab

Zaza
(Hebrew) golden

Zazalesha
(African American) zany
*Lesha, Zaza, Zazalese,
Zazalesh*

Zazula
(Polish) outstanding

Zdenka
(Czech) one from Sidon;
winding sheet
*Zdena, Zdenicka, Zdenina,
Zdeninka, Zdenuska*

Zdeslava
(Czech) present glory
Zdevsa, Zdisa, Zdiska,
Zdislava

Zea
(Latin) grain
Zia

Zeandrea
(American) from
Deandrea; noticed
Zeandraea, Zeandraya,
Zeandria, Zeandrya

Zeb
(Hebrew) Jehovah's gift

Zeborah
(Invented) combo of
Deborah and Zea

Zef
(Polish) moves with the
wind
Zeff

Zeffa
(Origin unknown) breezy

Zefiryn
(Polish) a form of Zephyr;
windlike

Zehara
(Hebrew) light

Zehava
(Hebrew) gold
Zahava, Zehovit, Zehuva,
Zehuvit

Zehira
(Hebrew) careful

Zel
(Persian) cymbal

Zela
(Greek) blessed; smiling

Zelda
(German) practical
Zell, Zellie

Zelenka
(Czech) fresh

Zelfa
(African American) in
control

Zelia
(Spanish) sunshine
Zeleah

Zella
(German) resistant

Zelma
(German) divine

Zemira
(Hebrew) song

Zemorah
(Hebrew) tree branch
Zemora

Zenae
(Greek) helpful
Zen, Zenah, Zennie

Zenaida
(Greek) daughter of Zeus

Zenana
(Hebrew) woman
Zena, Zenia

Zenda
(Hebrew) holy

Zenia
(Greek) open
Zeniah, Zenney, Zenni,
Zennie, Zenny, Zenya

Zenobia
(Greek) strength of Zeus

Zephyr
(Greek) the west wind;
wandering girl
Zefir, Zeph, Zephie, Zephir,
Zephira, Zephyra

Zeppelina
(English) beautiful storm

Zera
(Hebrew) seeds

Zeraldina
(Polish) spear ruler

Zerafina
(Greek) the west wind;
zephyr
Zerafeena, Zerafyna

Zerdali
(Turkish) wild apricot

Zerena
(Turkish) golden woman
Zereena, Zerina, Zeryna

Zerlinda
(Hebrew) dawn
Zerlina

Zerren
(English) flower

Zesiro
(African) first of twins

Zesta
(American) zestful
Zestah, Zestie, Zesty

Zeta
(English) rose; (Greek)
letter of alphabet
Zetah, Zetta

Zett
(Hebrew) olive; flourishing
Zeta, Zetta

Zevida
(Hebrew) current
Zevuda

Zhane
(African American)
feminine of Shane

Zhen
(Chinese) pure

Zhenia
(Latin) bright
Zennia, Zhen, Zhenie

Zhi
(Chinese) of high
character; ethical

Zho
(Chinese) character

Zhong
(Chinese) honorable

Zhuo
(Chinese) smart; wonderful
Zuo

Zi
(Chinese) flourishing;
giving

Zia
(Latin) textured
Zea, Ziah

Zigana
(Hungarian) gypsy

Zihna
(Native American) spinning

Zila
(Hebrew) shadowy
Zilah, Zilla, Zillah, Zylla

Zilias
(Hebrew) shadow
Zillia, Zillya, Zilya

Zilpah
(Hebrew) dignity
*Zillpha, Zilpha, Zulpha,
Zylpha*

Zimbab
(Place name) from
Zimbabwe, country in
Africa
Zimbob

Zimriah
(Hebrew) songs
Zimria, Zimriya

Zina
(Greek) hospitable woman
Zena, Zinah, Zine, Zinnie

Zinnia
(Botanical) flower
*Zenia, Zinia, Zinny, Zinnya,
Zinya*

Ziona
(Hebrew) symbol of good
Zionah, Zyona, Zyonah

Zipporah
(Hebrew) bird in flight
*Ziporah, Zippi, Zippie,
Zippora, Zippy*

Ziracuny
(Native American) water

Zirah
(Hebrew) coliseum
Zira

Zita
(Spanish) rose;
(Arabic) mistress
Zeeta, Zitah

Ziva
(Hebrew) brilliant
Zeeva, Ziv

Ziz
(Hungarian) dedicated
Zizz, Zyz, Zyzz

Zlata
(Czech) golden

Zoa
(Greek) life; vibrant

Zoann
(American) combo of Zo
and Ann; alive
Zoan, Zoanne, Zoayn

Zocha
(Polish) wisdom

Zoe
(Greek) lively; vibrant
Zoee, Zoey, Zoie, Zooey

Zofia
(Polish) skilled

Zofie
(Czech) wise

Zoheret
(Hebrew) shining

Zola
(French) earthy
Zolah

Zolema
(American) confessor
Zolem

Zona
(Latin) funny; brash
Zonah, Zonia, Zonna

Zonia
(English) flower

Zonta
(Native American) honest

Zooey
(Greek) life

Zoom
(American) energetic
Zoomi, Zoomy, Zoom-Zoom

Zora
(Slavic) beauty of dawn
Zara, Zorah, Zorrah, Zorre, Zorrie

Zoralle
(Slavic) ethereal
Zoral, Zoralye, Zorre, Zorrie

Zore
(Slavic) dawn of day

Zorianna
(American) combo of Zori
and Ann; practical
Zoree, Zori, Zoriannah, Zory

Zorina
(Slavic) golden
Zorana

Zorka
(Slavic) dawn
Zorke, Zorky

Zorna
(Slavic) golden

Zosa
(Greek) lively
Zosah

Zowie
(Irish) vibrant
Zowee, Zowey, Zowi, Zowy

ZsaZsa
(Hungarian) wild-spirited
Zsa, Zsaey

Zuba
(English) musical

Zubaida
(Arabic) laborer
Zubaidah, Zubeda

Zudora
(Sanskrit) laborer

Zulah
(African) country-loving
Zoola, Zoolah, Zula

Zuleyka
(Arabic) brilliant,
sparkling
*Zelekha, Zue, Zuleika,
Zuley*

Zulema
(Arabic) lovely
Zulima

Zulma
(Arabic) vibrant
Zul, Zule, Zulmah

Zuma
(Arabic) vital**Zuni**
(Native American) creative
Zu

Zuri
(African) beautiful

Zuriel
(American) from Ariel;
special

Zuwena
(African) good

Zuzanna
(Polish) misunderstood
Zu, Zue, Zuzan, Zuzana

BoyS

Aabid
(Arabic) loyal

Aalam
(Arabic) universal spirit

Aarcuus
(Greek) rambunctious

Aaron
(Hebrew) revered; sharer
*Aahron, Aaran, Aaren,
Aareon, Aarin, Aarone,
Aaronn, Aarron, Aaryn,
Aeron, Aharon, Ahran,
Ahren, Ahron, Aranne,
Aren, Arin, Aron, Arron*

Aashiq
(Arabic) fights evil

Aasif
(Hindi) brash

Aasim
(Hindi) in God's grace;
from Aamin

Aatiq
(Arabic) caring

Abacus
(Word as name) device for
doing calcalutions; clever
Abacas, Abakus, Abba

Abaddon
(Hebrew) knows God

Abahu
(Hindi) hopeful

Abanobi
(Mythology) water lover

Abasi
(African) strict

Abbas
(Arabic) harsh
Ab, Abba

Abbey
(Hebrew) spiritual
Abbie, Abie, Abby

Abbo
(Italian) short for
Abbondio; abundance

Abbott
(Hebrew) father; leader
Abbitt, Abott, Abotte

Abdiel
(Arabic) serving Allah

Abdon
(Greek) God's worker

Abdul
(Arabic) servant of Allah
*Ab, Abdal, Abdeel, Abdel,
Abdoul, Abdu, Abdual,
Abul*

Abdul-Jabbar
(Arabic) comforting

Abdulaziz
(Hindi) servant of a friend
*Abdelazim, Abdelaziz,
Abdulazaz, Abdulazeez*

Abdullah
(Arabic) Allah's servant
*Abdalah, Abdalla,
Abdallah, Abdualla,
Abdulah, Abdulla, Abdulahi*

Abe
(Hebrew) short for
Abraham; father of many
Abey, Abie

Abednego
(Aramaic) faithful

Abeeku
(African) Wednesday-born

Abel
(Hebrew) vital
*Abe, Abele, Abell, Abey,
Abie, Able, Adal, Avel*

Abelard
(German) firm
*Ab, Abalard, Abbey, Abby,
Abe, Abel, Abelerd,
Abelhard, Abilard,
Adalard, Adelard*

Abelino
(Spanish) from Biblical
Abel, son of Adam and
Eve; naïve
Abel, Able

Abercius
(Latin) open mind

Aberdeen
(Place name) serene
Aber, Dean, Deen

Aberlin
(German) ambitious

Abi
(Turkish) family's oldest
brother

Abiah
(Hebrew) child of Jehovah
*Abia, Abiel, Abija, Abijah,
Abisha, Abishai, Aviya,
Aviyah*

Abidla
(Arabic) worshipping

Abiezer
(Hebrew) father's light

Abijah
(Hebrew) God's gift
Abish

Abilene
(Place name) town in
Texas; good-old-boy
Abalene, Abileen

Abimbola
(African) destined for
riches

Abimelech
(Hebrew) believer

Abinadab
(African) Tuesday-born

Abioye
(African) he loves God

Abir
(Hebrew) strong
Abeer

Abisia
(Hebrew) God's gift; gifted
child
Abixah, Absa

Abner
(Hebrew) cheerful leader
*Ab, Abnir, Abnor, Avner,
Ebner*

Aboo
(African) father; wise

Abosi
(African) remembered

Abraham
(Hebrew) fathering
multitudes
*Abarran, Abe, Aberham,
Abey, Abhiram, Abie,
Abrahim, Abrahm, Abram,
Bram, Ibrahim*

Abram
(Hebrew) short for
Abraham
Abe, Abrams, Avram, Bram

Abraar
(Hebrew) fathers many

Abraxas
(Spanish) bright
Aba

Abrasha
(Hebrew) father

Abs
(Hebrew) short for
Absalom; muscular
Abe

Absalom
(Hebrew) peaceful;
handsome
*Abe, Abs, Absalon,
Avshalom*

Abundio
(Spanish) living in
abundance
Abun, Abund

Acacius
(Latin) blameless

Ace
(Latin) one; unity
Acer, Acey, Acie

Achard
(Last name as first name)
dark mind

Achilles
(Greek) hero of *The Iliad*
*Achill, Achille, Achillea,
Achillios, Ackill, Akil, Akili,
Akilles*

Acisclo
(Spanish) frantic

Acisclus
(Greek) from Achelous;
river god

Acker
(American) oak tree
Aker

Ackerley
(English) born of the
meadow; nature-loving
*Accerley, Ackerlea,
Ackerleigh, Ackersley,
Acklea, Ackleigh, Ackley,
Acklie*

Acton
(English) sturdy; oaks
*Acten, Actin, Actohn,
Actone*

Adael
(Hebrew) decorated by
God

Adair
(Scottish) negotiator
Adaire, Adare, Ade

Adal
(German) noble man
Adall, Adel

Adalberto
(Spanish) bright; dignified
Adal, Berto

Adalai
(Hebrew) my witness

Adalard
(German) brave

Adam
(Hebrew) first man; original
*Ad, Adahm, Adama,
Adamo, Adas, Addam,
Addams, Addie, Addy,
Adem, Adham*

Adomas
(African) blessed

Adamson
(Hebrew) Adam's son
*Adams, Adamsen,
Adamsson, Addamson*

Adan
(Irish) bold spirit
*Aden, Adin, Adyn, Aidan,
Aiden*

Adar
(Hebrew) fire; spirited
Addar

Adaucus
(Latin) from Daucus;
audacious

Addae
(African) the sun

Addis
(English) short for
Addison; masculine
*Addace, Addice, Addy,
Adis*

Addison
(English) Adam's son
*Ad, Addis, Adison,
Adisson*

Addy
(German) awesome;
outgoing
Addey, Addi, Addie, Adi

Ade
(German) short form of
Adel; noble man

Adebayo
(African) joyfully born

Adeeb
(African) twelfth son

Adel
(German) royal
Adal, Addey, Addie, Addy

Adelaido
(Latin) adorned

Adelard
(German) brave
*Adalar, Adalard, Addy,
Adel, Adelar, Adelarde*

Adelmo
(German) protects others

Adelpho
(Greek) breathes
Adelfo

Adeone
(Welsh) royal
Addy, Adeon

Adeoye
(Latin) God-given

Adewale
(Welsh) in flight; soars

Adigun
(American) distinctive

Adin
(Hebrew) good-looking
Adan

Adio
(African) devout

Adir
(Hindi) lightning

Adlai
(Hebrew) ornamented
*Ad, Addy, Adlay, Adley,
Adlie*

Adler
(German) eagle-eyed
Ad, Addler, Adlar

Adlay
(Hebrew) God's haven
Adlei, Adley

Adna
(Hebrew) physical

Adnee
(English) loner
Adni, Adny

Ado
(American) respected
Ad, Addy

Adolf
(German) sly wolf
Ad, Adolfe, Adolph

Adolfus
(German) form of
Adolphus
Adulphus

Adom
(African) blessed

Adonaldo
(Spanish) baby of hope

Adonijah
(Hebrew) believer

Adonis
(Greek) gorgeous
(Aphrodite's love in
mythology)
*Addonis, Adon Adones,
Adonnis, Adonys,
Andonice*

Adrian
(Latin) wealthy; dark-
skinned
*Adarian, Ade, Addie,
Adorjan, Adrain, Adreeyan,
Adreian, Adreyan, Adriaan,
Adriane, Adriann, Adrien,
Adrion, Adron, Adryan,
Adryon, Aydrien,
Aydrienne*

Adriano
(Italian) wealthy
Adriannho, Adrianno

Adriel
(Hebrew) God's follower
Adrial, Adryel

Adrien
(French) form of Adrian
Ade, Adriene, Adrienn

Adya
(Russian) man from Adria

Adyn
(Irish) manly
Adann, Ade, Aden, Aidan,
Ayden

Aedan
(Welsh) fire; fiery
temperament

Aeneas
(Greek) worthy of praise
Aineas, Aineias, Eneas,
Eneis

Aeolus
(Greek) ruler of the winds

Afan
(Russian) short for Afansi;
forever

Afanasy
(Russian) forever
Afanasi

Afdhaal
(Arabic) quiet

Afililio
(Hispanic) commentator

Afton
(English) dignified
Affton, Aftawn, Aften

Agamemnon
(Greek) slow but sure
Agamem

Agapito
(Spanish) loving

Agapius
(Greek) love

Agnar
(Irish) purity

Agricola
(Irish) farms

Agripino
(Hispanic) grieves

Agueleo
(Greek) wise one

Agustin
(Latin) dignified
Aguste, Auggie, Augustin

Ahab
(Hebrew) father's brother;
sea captain in *Moby Dick*

Ahaziah
(Hebrew) beloved

Ahearn
(Irish) horsetender
Ahearne, Aherin, Ahern,
Aherne, Hearn

Aherin
(Hebrew) held on high
Aharon, Ahern, Aherne

Ahimelech
(Biblical) religious support

Ahmad
(Arabic) praised man
Achmad, Achmed,
Ahamad, Ahamada,
Ahamed, Ahmaad,
Ahmaud, Amad, Amahd,
Amed

Ahmoz
(African) praised

Ahsan
(Hindi) gracious

Aidan
(Irish) fiery spirit
Adan, Aden, Adin, Aiden,
Aydan, Ayden, Aydin

Aided
(Irish) spirited, fiery

Aigars
(Russian) content

Aignan
(Greek) pure

Aiken
(English) hardy; oak-hewn
Aicken, Aikin, Ayken, Aykin

Ailbhe
(Irish) saint, noble

Ailred
(Last name as first name)
spiritual

Aimery
(German) leader
*Aime, Aimerey, Aimeric,
Amerey, Aymeric, Aymery*

Ainsley
(Scottish) in a meadow
*Ainsleigh, Ainslie, Ansley,
Ainslee, Ainsli, Aynslee,
Aynsley, Aynslie*

Ainsworth
(Last name as first name)
joyful

Aiwar
(Arabic) from Anwar;
bright

Aiyetoro
(African) destined for a
peaceful life

Ajani
(African) victorious

Ajax
(Greek) daring
Ajacks

Ajay
(American) spontaneous
A.J., Aj, Ajah, Ajai

Ajmal
(African) depressed

Akar
(Hindi) lightning
Akara

Akbar
(Hindi) Muslim king;
giving

Akeem
(Arab) form of Hakeem;
skilled; introspective
*Ackeem, Ackim, Akieme,
Akim, Hakeem, Hakim*

Akevy
(Hebrew) from Akiva;
replacing

Aki
(Scandinavian) blameless

Akil
(Arabic) intelligent
*Ahkeel, Akeel, Akeyla,
Akhil, Akiel, Akili*

Akilles
(Greek) form of Achilles;
heroic

Akim
(Russian) loved by God
*Achim, Ackeem, Ackim,
Ahkieme, Akeam, Akee,
Akeem, Akiem, Akima,
Arkeem*

Akinori
(Japanese) from Aki; born
in the fall

Akins
(African) brave

Akira
(Japanese) intellectual

Akiva
(Hebrew) cunning,
replacement
Akiba, Kiva

Akram
(Arabic) kind

Aksel
(Scandinavian) calm

Akwasi
(African) hopes

Akwete
(African) second-born twin

Al
(Irish) short for Alexander
and Alan; attractive

Aladdin
(Arabic) believer
*Al, Ala, Alaa, Alaaddin,
Aladdein, Aladean, Aladen*

Alain
(French) form of Alan and
Allen
*Alaen, Alainn, Alayn,
Allain, Alun*

Alair
(Gaelic) happy
Alaire

Alan
(Irish) handsome boy
*Ailin, Al, Aland, Alen,
Allan, Allen, Alley, Allie,
Allin, Allyn, Alon, Alun*

Alander
(American) argumentative;
cogitative

Alando
(Spanish) form of Alan;
attractive
*Al, Alaindo, Alan, Aland,
Alano, Allen, Allie, Alun,
Alundo, Alyn*

Alanson
(Last name as first name)
son of Alan; handsome
*Alansen, Alenson,
Allanson*

Alaric
(German) ruler
*Alarick, Alarik, Aleric,
Allaric, Allarick, Alric,
Alrick*

Alasdair
(Scottish) form of Alistair;
highbrow
*Al, Alaisdair, Alasdaire,
Alasdare, Alisdair,
Allysdair*

Alastair
(Scottish) strong leader
*Alaistair, Alasteir, Alastere,
Alastaire, Alastor,
Aleistere, Alester, Alistair,
Allaistar, Allastair, Allastir,
Alystair*

Alaster
(American) form of
Alastair; staunch advocate
Alaste, Alester, Allaster

Alban
(Latin) white man; from
Alba's white hill
*Abion, Albain, Albany,
Albean, Albee, Albein,
Alben, Albi, Albie, Albin,
Alby, Auban*

Albanse
(Invented) from the place
name Albany, New York;
white
*Alban, Albance, Albanee,
Albany, Albie, Alby*

Albany
(Place name) town in New
York; restless
Albanee, Albanie

Albe
(Latin) from Alba; white
hill

Alberic
(German) ruler; tough
Albric

Albert
(German) distinguished
*Al, Alberto, Alberts, Albie,
Albrecht, Alby, Ally, Aubert*

Alberto
(Italian) distinguished
Al, Albert, Bertie, Berto

Albie
(German) short for Albert;
smart
Albee, Albi, Alby

Albion
(Greek) old-fashioned
Albionne, Albyon

Alcordia
(American) in accord with
others
Alcord, Alkie, Alky

Alcott
(English) cottage-dweller
*Alcot, Alkokt, Alkott, Allcot,
Allcott, Allkot, Allkott*

Alden
(English) wise
Al, Aldan, Aldin, Aldon, Elden

Alder
(English) revered; kind

Aldo
(Italian) older one; jovial
Aldoh

Aldorse
(American) form of Aldo; old
Al, Aldo, Aldorce, Aldors

Aldous
(German) wealthy
Aldis, Aldus, Aldas

Aldred
(English) advisor; judgmental
Al, Aldrid, Aldy, Alldred, Eldred

Aldren
(English) old friend
Al, Aldran, Aldie, Aldrun, Aldy, Aldryn

Aldrich
(English) wise advisor
Aldie, Aldric, Aldrick, Aldridge, Aldrige, Aldrish, Aldritch, Alldric, Alldrich, Alldrick, Alldridge, Eldridge

Alec
(Greek) high-minded
Al, Aleck, Alek, Alic

Alejandro
(Spanish) defender; bold and brave
Alejandra, Alejo, Alex, Alexjandro

Alek
(Russian) short for Aleksei; brilliant
Aleks

Aleksander
(Greek and Polish) defender
Alek, Sander

Aleksei
(Russian) defender; brilliant
Alek, Alik, Alexi

Aleksey
(Russian) smart

Alemet
(African) world leader

Aleppo
(Place name) easygoing
Alepo

Aleric
(Scandinavian) rules all
Alarik, Alerick, Alleric, Allerick

Aleron
(French) the knight's armor; protected

Alessandro
(Italian) helpful; defender
Allessandro, Alessand

Alessio
(Italian) defensive

Alex
(Greek) short for Alexander; leader
Alax, Alecs, Alix, Allax, Allex

Alexander
(Greek) great leader; helpful
Al, Alec, Alecsander, Aleksandar, Aleksander, Aleksandur, Alex, Alexandar, Alexandor, Alexandr, Alexis, Alexsander, Alexxander, Alexzander, Alisander, Alixander, Alixandre

Alexandros
(Greek) form of Alexander;
helpful
Alesandros, Alexandras

Alexis
(Greek) short for
Alexander
*Alexace, Alexei, Alexes,
Alexey, Alexi, Alexie,
Alexius, Alexiz, Alexy, Lex*

Alf
(Italian) short for Alfonso;
noble

Alfalfa
(Botanical) sprite

Alfeus
(Hebrew) follower
Alpheus

Alfie
(English) short for Alfred;
friendly
Alf, Alfi, Alfy

Alfonso
(Spanish) bright; prepared
*Alf, Alfie, Alfons, Alfonsin,
Alfonso, Alfonsus, Alfonz,
Alfonza, Alfonzo, Alfonzus,
Alphonsus, Fons, Fonzie,
Fonzy*

Alford
(English) wise

Alfred
(English) counselor
*Al, Alf, Alfeo, Alfie, Alfrede,
Alfryd*

Alfredo
(Italian, Spanish) advisor
Alf, Alfie, Alfreedo, Alfrido

Alfredrick
(American) combo of
Alfred and Fredrick;
pretentious
*Al, Alf, Alfred, Freddy,
Fredrik*

Alger
(German) hardworking
Algar, Allgar

Algernon
(English) man with facial
hair
*Al, Algenon, Alger, Algie,
Algin, Algon, Algy*

Algia
(German) prepared; kind
Alge, Algie

Ali
(Arabic) greatest
Alee, Aly

Ali-Baba
(Literature) from *A
Thousand and One
Nights*; cunning

Alicio
(Spanish) noble; dignified

Alim
(Arabic) musical

Alipi
(Spanish) calm

Alireza
(Hebrew) joyful

Alisander
(Greek) form of Alexander
*Alisander, Alissander,
Allisandre, Alsandair,
Alsandare, Alsander*

Alisen
(Irish) honest

Allan
(Irish) form of Alan
Allane, Allayne

Allard
(English) brave man
Alard, Ellard

Allegheny
(Place name) mountains
of the Appalachian
system; grand
*Al, Alleg, Alleganie,
Alleghenie*

Allen
(Irish) handsome
Al, Alen, Alley, Alleyn, Alleyne, Allie, Allin, Allon, Allyn, Alon

Allward
(Polish) brave

Almagor
(Hebrew) courageous

Almar
(German) form of Almarine; strong
Al, Almarr, Almer

Almere
(American) director
Almer

Almo
(American) form of Elmo; easygoing

Almund
(Botanical) form of almond; wise

Alois
(Czech) famous warrior
Aloysius, Aloisio

Alonzo
(Spanish) enthusiastic
Alano, Alanzo, Alon, Alonso, Alonza, Alonze, Elonzo, Lon, Lonnie

Aloysius
(German) famed
Alaois, Alois, Aloisius, Aloisio

Alpar
(Hindi) champions downtrodden

Alpheus
(Hebrew) form of Alfeus; follower
Alphaeus

Alphonse
(German) distinguished
Alf, Alfonse, Alphons, Alphonsa, Alphonso, Alphonzus, Fonsi, Fonsie, Fonz, Fonzie

Alpin
(Scottish) man from alpine area

Alps
(Place name) climber
Alp

Alquince
(American) old; fifth
Al, Alquense, Alquin, Alquins, Alquinse, Alqwence

Alrick
(German) leader
Alrec, Alric

Alroy
(American) combo of Al and Roy; sedate
Al, Alroi

Alston
(English) serious; nobleman
Allston, Alsten, Alstin

Alsworth
(English) from a manor; rich

Altair
(Scottish) defender

Altarius
(African American) from Altair; shining star
Altare, Altair, Altareus, Alterius, Alltair, Al

Alter
(Hebrew) old; will live to be old

Altman
(German) wise
Altmann, Atman

Alto
(Place name) town in
Texas; alto voice;
easygoing
Al

Alton
(English) excellent; kind
Allton, Altawn, Alten, Altyn

Altus
(Latin) form of Alta; high
Al, Alta

Alula
(Latin) winged

Alva
(Hebrew) intelligent;
beloved friend
Alvah

Alvado
(Spanish) fair

Alvar
(Spanish) careful
Alvaro, Alver

Alvarado
(Spanish) peacemaker
*Alvaradoh, Alvaro, Alvie,
Alvy*

Alvaro
(Spanish) just
*Alvaroh, Alvarro, Alvey,
Alvie, Alvy*

Alvern
(English) old friend
Al, Alverne, Alvurn

Alvin
(Latin) light-haired; loved
*Alv, Alvan, Alven, Alvie,
Alvy, Alvyn*

Alvincent
(American) combo of Alvin
and Vincent; giving friend
*Alvin, Alvince, Vin, Vince,
Vincent, Vinse*

Alvis
(American) form of Elvis;
old friend
Al, Alviss, Alvy

Alvord
(Greek) cautious

Alwin
(German) variant of Alvin;
loved
*Allwyn, Alwyn, Alwynn,
Aylwin*

Alzado
(Arabic) forlorn

Amaan
(African) loyal
Aman, Amman

Amadayus
(Invented) form of
Amadeus
Amadayes

Amadeo
(Italian) blessed by God;
artistic

Amadeus
(Latin) God-loving
*Amad, Amadayus,
Amadeaus, Amadei,
Amadio, Amadis, Amado,
Amador, Amadou,
Amedeo, Amodaos*

Amado
(Spanish) loved
*Amadee, Amadeo, Amadi,
Amadis, Amadus, Amando*

Amadour
(French) loved
Amador, Amadore

Amadus
(Latin) adores God
Amandus

Amal
(Hebrew) hardworking;
optimistic
Amahl, Amhall

Amancio
(Spanish) faithful

Amandeep
(Hindi) light of peace
*Amandip, Amanjit,
Amanjot, Amanpreet*

Amar
(Arabic) making a home
Amari, Amario, Amaris,
Ammar, Ammer

Amaramto
(Latin) beauty does not
fade

Amarillo
(Place name) town in
Texas; in Spanish, it
means yellow; renegade
Amarille, Amarilo

Amasa
(Hebrew) carries a heavy
load

Amato
(Italian) loving
Amahto, Amatoh

Amazu
(Hebrew) burdened

Ambert
(Arabic) golden boy

Ambrose
(German) everlasting
Amba, Ambie, Ambroce,
Ambrus, Amby

Ameer
(Arabic) rules

America
(Place name) patriotic

Americo
(Spanish) patriotic
Ame, America, Americus,
Ameriko

Amerigo
(Italian) ruler; name of
Italian explorer
Amer, Americo, Ameriko

Amery
(Arabic) regal birth
Amory

Ames
(French) friendly
Aims

Amias
(Latin) devoted to God
Amyas

Amichai
(Hebrew) my nation lives

Amiel
(Hebrew) my people's God
Ameal, Amheel, Ammiel

Amin
(Arabic) honorable;
dependable
Aman, Ameen

Amir
(Arabic) royal; ruler
Ameer, Amire

Amit
(Hindi) forever;
(Hebrew) truth
Amitan, Amreet, Amrit

Amiti
(Japanese) endless friend

Ammon
(Irish) hidden
Amnon

Amor
(Latin) love
Amerie, Amoree, Amori,
Amorie

Amory
(German) home ruler
Amery, Amor

Amos
(Hebrew) strong
Amus

Ampah
(African) certainty

Ampy
(American) fast
Amp, Ampee, Ampey,
Amps

Amund
(Scandinavian) fearless

Amyas
(Latin) lovable
Aimeus, Ameus, Amias,
Amyes

An
 (Chinese) peaceful; safe
 Ana

Anan
 (Irish) outdoorsy
 An, Annan

Anand
 (Hindi) delightful
 Ananda, Anant, Ananth

Ananias
 (Biblical) pious

Anarolio
 (Spanish) called forth

Anas
 (Czech) born again

Anastasius
 (Greek) reborn
 *Anas, Anastagio, Anastas,
 Anastase, Anastasi,
 Anastasio, Anastastios,
 Anastice, Anasticius,
 Anastisis, Athanasius*

Anatole
 (French) exotic
 *Anatol, Anatoli, Anatolijus,
 Anatolio, Anatoly, Anitolle*

Ancel
 (French) creative
 *Ance, Ancell, Anse, Ansel,
 Ansell*

Andel
 (Scandinavian) honored

Ander
 (English) form of Andrew;
 masculine

Anders
 (Swedish) masculine
 *Ander, Andersen,
 Anderson, Andirs, Andries,
 Andy*

Andras
 (French) form of Andrew;
 masculine
 *Andrae, Andres, Andrus,
 Ondrae, Ondras*

André
 (French) masculine
 *Andra, Andrae, Andre,
 Anrecito, Andree, Aundré,
 Andrei*

Andreas
 (Greek) masculine
 *Andrieas, Andries Adryus,
 Andy*

Andrere
 (Greek) from Andreios;
 manly

Andres
 (Spanish) macho
 *Andras, Andrés, Andrez,
 Andy*

Andretti
 (Italian) speedy
 Andrette, Andy

Andrew
 (Greek) manly and brave
 *Aindrew, Anders, Andery,
 Andi, Andie, Andreas,
 Andres, Andrews, Andru,
 Andrue, Andy, Audrew*

Andronicus
 (Greek) clever

Andros
 (Polish) masculine
 Andris, Andrus

Andru
 (Greek) form of Andrew;
 masculine
 Andrue

Andrzej
 (Polish) manly

Andy
 (Greek) short for Andrew;
 masculine
 Andee, Andie

Aneurin
 (Welsh) golden child
 Aneirin

Anfanio
 (Spanish) secretive

Anferny
(American) variation of
Anthony
*Andee, Anfernee,
Anferney, Anferni,
Anfernie, Anfurny*

Angel
(Greek) angelic messenger
*Ange, Angele, Angell,
Angie, Angy*

Angelberto
(Spanish) shining angel
*Angel, Angelbert, Bert,
Berto*

Angelo
(Italian) angelic
*Ange, Angelito, Angeloh,
Angelos, Anglo, Anjelo*

Angits
(Celtic) divine, exceptional

Angle
(Word as name) spin
doctor
Ange, Angul

Anglin
(Greek) angelic
Anglen, Anglinn, Anglun

Angus
(Scottish) standout;
important
Ange, Angos, Aonghas

Anh
(Vietnamese) smart

Anibal
(Spanish) brave noble

Aniello
(Italian) risk-taker

Anil
(Hindi) air
Aneel, Anel, Aniel, Aniello

Aniol
(Polish) angel
Ahnjol, Ahnyolle

Anka
(Polish) gracious; stems
from Anna

Ankoma
(African) last-born child

Annan
(African) second; from
Annar

Annatto
(Botanical) tree; tough
Annatta

Annibale
(Phoenician) from
Hannibal; bold

Anniel
(Biblical) angel

Anolus
(Greek) masculine
Ano, Anol

Anrue
(American) masculine
Anrae, Anroo

Anscom
(English) awesome man
Anscomb

Ansel
(French) creative
Ancell, Ansa, Anse, Ansell

Anselm
(German) protective
Anse, Ansehlm, Ansellm

Anselmo
(Spanish) protected by God
*Ancel, Ancelmo, Anse,
Ansel, Anselm, Anzelmo,
Selmo*

Anshel
(Hindi) blessed
Anshel, Anshl

Anskar
(German) brusque

Ansley
(English) loner
*Anslea, Anslee, Ansleigh,
Anslie, Ansly, Ansy*

Anson
(German) divine male
Anse, Ansonn, Ansun

Antal
(Latin) princely

Antero
(Greek) moves with grace

Anthony
(Latin) outstanding
*Anathony, Anothony, Anth,
Anthawn, Anthey,
Anthoney, Anthoni,
Anthonie, Anthonio,
Anthyonny, Anton, Antony,
Tony*

Antipas
(Greek) father

Antoan
(Latin) variant of Anthony;
priceless

Antoine
(French) worthy of praise
*Antone, Antons, Antos,
Antwan, Antwon, Antwone*

Anton
(Latin) outstanding
Antan, Antawn

Antonce
(African American) form of
Anthony; valued
Antawnce

Antonio
(Spanish) superb
*Antinio, Antonello,
Antoino, Antone,
Antonino, Antonioh,
Antonnio, Antonyio,
Antonyo, Antonyia, Tony*

Antony
(Latin) good
*Antawny, Antini, Antonah,
Antone, Antoney, Antoni,
Antonie, Anty, Tone, Tony*

Antrinell
(African American) valued
Antrie, Antrinel, Antry

Antroy
(African American) form of
Anthony; prized
Antroe, Antroye

Antwan
(American) form of
Antoine; achiever
*Antawan, Antawn,
Anthawn, Antowine,
Antowne, Antown,
Antwain, Antwaine,
Antwaion, Antwane,
Antwann, Antwanne,
Antwaun, Antwen,
Antwian, Antwine,
Antwion, Antwoan,
Antwoin, Antwoine,
Antwon, Antwonn,
Antwonne, Antwuan,
Antyon, Antywon*

Antwone
(American) variant of
Antoine; achiever
Antwonn

Anwar
(Arabic) shining
Anour, Anouar, Anwhour

Anwyl
(Welsh) beloved
Anwyll, Anwell

Anyon
(Latin) from Anthony;
priceless

Anzelm
(Polish) protective
Ahnzselm

Apolinar
(Spanish) manly and wise
Apollo

Apollo
(Greek) masculine; a god
in mythology
*Apolloh, Apolo,
Apoloniah, Applonian,
Appollo*

Apolonio
(Greek) from Apollo, god
of music, poetry, prophesy

Apostle
(Greek) follower; disciple
Apos

Apostolos
(Greek) disciple
Apos

Apple
(American) favorite;
wholesome
Apel

Aquan
(Native American) tranquil

Aquila
(Spanish) eagle-eyed
*Acquilla, Aquil, Aquilas,
Aquile, Aquilla, Aquillino*

Aquileo
(Spanish) warrior
Akweleo, Aquilo

Aram
(Syrian) noble; honorable
Ara, Aramia, Arra

Aramis
(French) clever
*Airamis, Arames, Aramith,
Aramys, Aramyse,
Arhames*

Aracin
(Latin) ready; heaven's
gate

Araldo
(German) army leader

Aralt
(Irish) army leader

Arber
(American) from arbor;
adorned

Arbet
(Last name as first name)
high
Arb, Arby

Arbogast
(German) covered

Arceneaux
(French) friendly; heavenly
Arce, Arcen, Arceno

Arch
(English) short for Archie
and Archibald; athletic
Arche

Archard
(English) bold

Archer
(English) athletic; bowman
Arch, Archie

Archibald
(German) bold leader
Arch, Archibold, Archie

Archie
(English) short for
Archibald; bold
Arch, Archi, Archy

Ardan
(Latin) passion; eagle

Ardee
(American) ardent
Ard, Ardie, Ardy

Ardell
(Latin) go-getter
Ardel

Arden
(Latin) ball of fire
*Ard, Arda, Ardie, Ardin,
Ardon, Arrden*

Ardley
(English) with dedication

Ardmohr
(Latin) more ardent than
others
Ard, Ardmoor, Ardmore

Ardolph
(German) ardent

Areeb
(Arabic) passionate

Arelus
(Latin) form of Aurelius;
golden son

Aren
(Dutch) from Arnold; form
of Aaron

Arenda
(Spanish) eager

Aristeo
(Spanish) best
Aris, Aristio, Aristo, Ary

Argan
(American) leader
*Argee, Argen, Argey, Argi,
Argie, Argun*

Argento
(Spanish) silver
Arge, Argey, Argi, Argy

Argus
(Greek) careful; bright
Agos, Arjus

Argyle
(English) diamond
pattern; planning
Argile

Ari
(Greek) best
*Ahree, Aria, Arias, Arie,
Arih, Arij, Arri*

Aribert
(German) holy

Aribold
(German) holy

Aric
(English) leader
*Aaric, Arec, Areck, Arick,
Arik, Arric, Arrick, Arrik*

Ariel
(Hebrew) God's spirited
lion
*Airel, Arel, Arell, Ari, Arie,
Ariele, Arielle, Ariya,
Ariyel, Arrial, Arriel*

Aries
(Greek) god of war;
mythology
Arees, Arie, Ariez

Arik
(German) leads

Arild
(Hebrew) God's lion

Ario
(Spanish) warring
Ari, Arrio

Arion
(Greek) enchanted man
*Ari, Arian, Ariane, Arien,
Arrian, Arie, Ariohn*

Aristides
(Greek) son of the
outstanding
Ari, Aris, Aristidis

Aristophanes
(Greek) playwright

Aristotle
(Greek) best man
*Ari, Aris, Aristie, Aristito,
Aristo, Aristokles,
Aristotelis, Aristottle*

Arjan
(Hindi) one Pandavas
Arjun

Arkady
(Russian) revered

Arki
(Greek) ruler

Arkyn
(Scandinavian) royal
offspring
*Aricin, Ark, Arkeen, Arken,
Arkin*

Arle
(Irish) sworn
Arlee, Arley, Arly

Arledge
(English) lives by a lake
*Arleedj, Arles, Arlidge,
Arlledge*

Arleigh
(Irish) sworn
Arly

Arlen
(Irish) dedicated
*Arl, Arlan, Arland, Arle,
Arlend, Arlin, Arlyn, Arlynn*

Arley
(English) meadow-loving;
outdoorsy
Arleigh, Arlie, Arly

Arlis
(Hebrew) dedicated; in
charge
Arlas, Arles, Arless, Arly

Arlo
(German) strong
Arloh

Arlonn
(Irish) sworn; cheerful
Arlan, Arlann, Arlen, Arlon

Arlys
(Hebrew) pledged
Arlis

Arm
(English) arm
Arma, Arman, Arme

Arman
(German) army man;
defender
Armaan

Armand
(German) strong soldier
*Armad, Armanda,
Armando, Armands,
Armanno, Armaude, Arme,
Armenta, Armond,
Ormand*

Armando
(Spanish) entertainer
Armand, Arme, Armondo

Armani
(Italian) army; disciplined
talent
*Amani, Arman, Armanie,
Armon, Armoni*

Armen
(Spanish) from the name
Armenta; soldier
Arme, Arment, Armenta

Armitage
(Last name as first name)
safe haven
Armi, Armita, Army

Armon
(Hebrew) strong as a
fortress
*Arman, Arme, Armen,
Armin, Armino, Armoni,
Armons*

Armro
(Italian) from Armino;
warrior

Armstrong
(English) strong-armed
Arme, Army

Arnaud
(French) strong
Arnaldo, Arnauld

Arnborn
(Scandinavian) eagle-
bear; animal instincts
*Arn, Arne, Arnborne,
Arnbourne*

Arndt
(German) strong
*Arne, Arnee, Arney, Arni,
Arnie*

Arne
(German) short for Arnold;
ruler
Arn, Arna, Arnel, Arnell

Arnette
(Dutch) little eagle
Arnat, Arnet, Arnot, Arnott

Arnie
(German) short for Arnold;
ruler
*Arne, Arney, Arni, Arnny,
Arny*

Arnithan
(African American) form of
Arnie and Jonathan; eagle-
eyed
Arnee, Arnie, Nithan

Arno
(German) far-sighted
*Arn, Arne, Arnoh, Arnou,
Arnoux*

Arnold
(German) ruler; strong
*Arnald, Arne, Arndt, Arnie,
Arnoll, Arny*

Arnome
(Invented) powerful
Arnom

Arnon
(German) eagle

Arnot
(French) from Arnold;
eagle-eyed
Arnott, Arnart, Arnett

Arnst
(Scandinavian) eagle-eyed
(arn means eagle)
Arn

Arnulfo
(Spanish) strong
Arne, Arnie, Arny

Aroldo
(German) eagle; strong

Aron
(Hebrew) generous
Aaron, Arron, Erinn

Arpad
(Hungarian) prince; sunny

Arrigo
(Italian) ruler

Arsenio
(Greek) macho; virile
*Arne, Arsen, Arsenius,
Arseny, Arsinio, Arsonio*

Arshad
(Iranian) revered

Arshaq
(Arabic) supports

Art
(English) bear-like;
wealthy
Arte, Artie

Artemus
(Greek) gifted
*Art, Artemas, Artemio,
Artemis, Artie, Artimas,
Artimis, Artimus*

Arthisus
(Origin unknown) stuffy
Arth, Arthi, Arthy

Arthur
(English) distinguished
*Art, Arth, Arther, Arthor,
Artie, Artor, Artur, Arty,
Aurther, Aurthur*

Artie
(English) short for Arthur;
wealthy
Art, Artee, Arty

Arturo
(Italian) talented
*Art, Arthuro, Artur, Arture,
Arturro*

Arun
(Hindi) the color of the sky
before dawn
Aruns

Arundel
(English) lives with eagles;
soars

Arvai
(Hebrew) roams
Arve

Arvel
(German) friendly

Arvid
(Hebrew) full of
wanderlust
*Arv, Arvad, Arve, Arvie,
Arvind, Arvinder, Arvydas*

Arvin
(German) friendly
*Arv, Arven, Arvie, Arvind,
Arvinder, Arvon, Arvy*

Arwen
(German) friend
*Arwee, Arwene, Arwhen,
Arwy*

Ary
(Hebrew) lion; fierce
Ari, Arye

Asa
(Hebrew) healer
Ase, Aza

Asád
(Arabic) happy
Asaad, Asad, Asid, Assad, Azad

Ascot
(English) cottage-dweller

Asgar
(Scandinavian) God's home

Ash
(Botanical) tree; bold
Ashbey, Ashby, Ashe

Asharious
(Mythology) Ashur, god of war; combative boy

Ashbel
(Hebrew) fiery god

Ashby
(Scandinavian) brash
Ashbee, Ashbey, Ashie, Ashy

Asher
(Hebrew) joyful
Ash, Ashar, Ashor, Ashur

Ashfaaq
(Arabic) honorable

Ashford
(English) spunky
Ash, Ashferd, Ashtin

Ashley
(English) smooth
Ash, Asheley, Ashelie, Ashely, Ashie, Ashlan, Ashlee, Ashleigh, Ashlen, Ashlie, Ashlin, Ashling, Ashlinn, Ashlone, Ashly, Ashlyn, Ashlynn, Aslan

Ashlin
(English) from Ashley; lives in a forest

Ashraf
(Arabic) honors others

Ashton
(English) handsome
Ashteen, Ashtin

Ashur
(Hebrew) happy

Asifa
(Hebrew) gathers

Aslan
(Literature) from Lewis' Narnia series; lion-like

Asmus
(German) well-known

Asner
(Hebrew) giving

Aspah
(Greek) from Aspar; leader; welcomed

Asriel
(Hebrew) praised

Aston
(English) eastern
Asten, Astin

Aswin
(English) from the land of ash trees

Atam
(American) form of Adam; tough
Atame, Atom, Atym

Atanacio
(Spanish) everlasting
Atan, Atanasio

Ateeq
(Arabic) affectionate

Athanasius
(Greek) from Athanasios; immortal
Atanasio, Atanas

Athar
(English) lives on a farm

Atherton
(English) coming from a farm

Atilano
(Greek) strong

Atinuwa
(African) aware

Atkins
(Last name as first name) linked; known
Atkin

Atlas
(Greek) courier of greatness
Atlass

Atley
(English) from the meadow
Atlea, Atlee, Atleigh, Atli, Attley

Atsu
(African) second-born twin

Atticus
(Greek) ethical
Aticus, Attikus

Attila
(Gothic) powerful
Atalik, Atila, Atilio, Atiya, Atlya, Att

Atwater
(English) living by the water

Atwell
(English) the well; full of gusto

Atwood
(English) the woods; outdoorsy

Atworth
(English) farmer

Atyab
(Arabic) cultivated

Auberon
(German) like a bear; highborn
Aube, Auberron, Aubrey

Aubert
(German) leader
Auber, Aubey

Aubin
(French) ruler; elfin
Auben

Aubrey
(English) ruler
Aubary, Aube, Aubery, Aubree, Aubry, Aubury, Bree

Auburn
(Latin) brown with red cast; tenacious
Aubern, Aubie, Auburne

Auden
(English) old friend
Aude, Audie

Audencio
(Spanish) companion
Auden

Audie
(German) strong man
Aude, Audee, Audi, Audiel, Audley

Audley
(English) rich
Audlea, Audlee, Audleigh, Audly

Audon
(Scandinavian) alone

Audelon
(French) wealthy

Audras
(Scandinavian) having wealth
Audres

Audric
(French) wise ruler

Audun
(Scandinavian) form of Audon; alone

Audwin
(English) rich

Augie
(Latin) short for Augustus
Aug, Auggie, Augy

August
(Latin) determined
Auge, Augie

Augustine
(Latin) serious and revered
Agostino, Agoston, Agustin, Aug, Augie, August, Augustene, Augustin

Augusto
(Spanish) respected; serious
Agusto, Augey, Auggie, Austeo

Augustus
(Latin) highly esteemed
Aug, Auge, Augie, August

Aulie
(English) form of Audley
Awlie

Aurek
(Latin) golden

Aurelius
(Latin) golden son
Arelian, Areliano, Aurel, Aurey, Aurie, Auriel, Aury

Aust
(American) from Austin; kind

Austin
(Latin) capital of Texas; ingenious; southwestern
Astin, Aust, Austen, Austine, Auston, Austyn

Auther
(American) form of Arthur; brave and smart
Authar, Authur

Autry
(Latin) golden

Avan
(Hindi) short for Avanidra; lord of earth

Avenall
(English) from the woods; calm
Avenel, Avenell

Avent
(French) up-and-coming
Aventin, Aventino

Averill
(French) April-born child
Ave, Averel, Averell, Averiel, Averil, Averyl, Averyll, Avrel, Avrell, Avrill, Avryl

Avrylle
(French) hunter
Avryll

Avery
(English) soft-spoken
Avary, Ave, Aveary, Averey, Averie, Avry

Avi
(Hebrew) springlike
Avian, Avidan, Avidor, Aviel, Avion

Aviaz
(Hebrew) believer

Avinoam
(Biblical) pleasant brother

Avion
(French) flyer
Aveonn, Avyon, Avyun

Aviv
(Hebrew) spring

Avner
(Hebrew) father of light
Avneet, Avniel

Avniel
(Hebrew) God is my rock

Avram
(Hebrew) almighty father
Arram, Avraham, Avrom, Avrum

Axel
(German) peaceful;
contemporary
Aksel, Ax, Axe, Axil, Axill, Axl

Awet
(Welsh) from Awst; great

Axton
(German) town of peace;
peacemaker

Aydin
(Irish) masculine

Ayers
(Last name as first)
industrious

Aylmer
(English) of noble birth

Aylward
(English) guards best

Aylwin
(Welsh) elf friend

Ayo
(African) happy

Ayson
(Origin unknown) lucky
Aison

Azad
(Arabic) lucky

Azael
(Spanish) God-loved

Azariah
(Biblical) aided by Jehovah

Azeem
(Arabic) cherished
Aseem, Asim

Azeez
(Arabic) strong

Azhar
(Arabic) flourishes

Azi
(African) a child

Azim
(Arabic) grandiose

Aziz
(Arabic) powerful

Azizi
(African) beloved

Azrae
(Mythology) Azrael, angel
of God

Azriel
(Hebrew) the Lord's angel

Azuriah
(Hebrew) aided by God
Azaria, Azariah, Azuria

B

Babar
(Turkish) lion
Baber

Babe
(American) athlete

Babu
(Hindi) fierce

Bacchus
(Greek) reveler; jaded
Baakus, Bakkus, Bakus

Bach
(Last name as first name)
talented
Bok

Bachir
(Hebrew) oldest son;
reliable
Bachur

Bacon
(English) literary;
outspoken
Baco, Bake, Bakon

Badar
(Hindi) full moon

Baden
(German) bathes;
cleansed

Badger
(Last name as first name)
difficult
*Badge, Badgeant, Bage,
Bagent*

Badr
(African) full moon; lucky

Badru
(African) full moon; lucky

Baha
(Arabic) splendid

Bahir
(Arabic) magnificent

Bailey
(French) attentive
Baile, Baily, Baley, Baylie

Bainbridge
(Irish) bridge; negotiator
Bain, Banebridge, Beebee

Baines
(Last name as first name)
pale
Baine, Baynes

Bainlon
(American) form of Bailey;
pale
Bailey, Baily

Baird
(Irish) singer/poet;
creative
Bard, Bayrde

Bakari
(African) promising

Baker
(English) cook
Baiker, Baykar

Bal
(Hindi) strong

Bala
(Hindi) young

Baldemar
(Spanish) form of
Balthasar; brave and wise
Baldy

Balder
(Scandinavian) good
prince
Baldur, Baudier

Baldev
(Hindi) strong God

Baldie
(German) nickname for
Baldwin; brave friend

Baldric
(German) leader
*Baldrick, Baledric,
Bauldric*

Baldridge
(English) persuasive

Baldwin
(German) steadfast friend
Baldwinn, Baldwynn, Bally

Balendin
(Place name) Balen,
Belgium; sylvan

Baley
(American) form of Bailey
Baleye

Balfour
(Scottish) landowner
Balf, Balfore

Balfre
(Spanish) brave

Balin
(Hungarian) from Balint;
healthy

Ballance
(American) courageous
Balance, Ballans

Ballard
(German) brave
Ballerd

Balraj
(Hindi) strong king

Balthasar
(Greek) God save the king
Bath, Bathazar

Balu
(Hindi) young

Balwin
(Last name as first name)
friendly; brave
Ball, Winn

Banan
(Irish) white

Bancroft
(English) bean field;
gardener
Banc, Bankie, Bankroft

Bandy
(Origin unknown)
gregarious
Bandee, Bandi

Banks
(Last name as first name)
focused
Bank

Banning
(Irish) fair-haired
Bannie, Banny, Bannyng

Bao
(Chinese) prized boy

Baptist
(Latin) one who has been
baptized

Barak
(Hebrew) lightning;
success
Barrak, Barack

Baram
(Hebrew) son of the
people

Barclay
(Scottish) audacious man;
birch tree meadow
*Bar, Barclaye, Bark,
Barklay, Barky*

Bard
(Irish) singer
Bar, Barr

Barden
(English) peaceful; valley-
dweller
Bardon

Bardolf
(German) wily hero

Bardrick
(English) sings ballads
Bardric

Barend
(Scandinavian) bearlike

Bargo
(Last name as first name)
outspoken
Barg

Bark
(English) short for Barker;
outgoing
Birk

Barker
(English) handles bark;
lumberjack
Bark, Barkker

Barlow
(English) hardy
Barloe, Barlowe

Barman
(Last name as first name)
bright; blessed
Barr

Barn
(American) word as name;
works in barns
Barnee, Barney, Barny

Barnabas
(Hebrew) seer; comforter
*Barn, Barnaby, Barnebus,
Barney, Barnie, Barny*

Barnaby
(Hebrew) companionable
*Barn, Barnabee, Barnabie,
Barnie, Barny*

Barner
(English) mercurial
*Barn, Barnerr, Barney,
Barny*

Barnes
(English) powerful; bear

Barnett
(English) leader of men
Barn, Barnet, Barney

Barney
(English) short for Barnett
Barn, Barni, Barnie, Barny

Barnum
(German) safe; barn
Barnham, Barnhem, Barnie

Baron
(English) noble leader
Bare, Baren, Barren, Baryne

Barra
(Irish) fair-haired

Barrett
(German) strong and bearlike
Bar, Baret, Barett, Barette, Barry

Barrington
(English) dignified
Bare, Baring, Berrington

Barry
(Irish) candid
Barre, Barrie, Bary

Bart
(Hebrew) persistent
Bartee, Bartie, Barty

Bartley
(Last name as first name) rural man
Bart, Bartle, Bartlee, Bartli, Bartly

Barth
(Hebrew) protective
Bart, Barthe, Barts

Bartholomew
(Hebrew) friendly; earthy
Bart, Barthlolmewe, Bartie

Bartlett
(Last name as first name) motivated

Barto
(Spanish) form of Bartholomew; upward
Bartelo, Bartol, Bartoli, Bartolo, Bartolomeo

Barton
(English) persistent man; Bart's town
Bart, Barty

Bartram
(English) intelligent
Bart, Barty

Baruch
(Hebrew) most blessed
Barry

Baruti
(African) teaches

Basant
(Arabic) smiling

Basford
(American) charming; low-profile
Bas, Basferd, Basfor

Bash
(American) party-loving
Bashi, Bashey, Bashy

Basil
(Greek) regal
Basel, Basey, Basile, Bazil

Basim
(Arabic) smiles
Bassam

Basir
(Turkish) smart

Bass
(Last name as first name) fish; charmer
Bassee, Bassey, Bassi, Bassy

Bassett
(English) small man
Baset, Basett, Basey, Basse

Bastian
(Greek) respected
Bastien, Bastyun

Basye
(American) home-based; centered
Base, Basey

Batch
(French) short for bachelor; unmarried man
Bat, Bats, Batsh

Bates
(English) romantic
Bate

Baudoin
(Latin) winning

Baul
(Gypsy) slow-moving

Baurice
(African American) from Maurice; dark man

Bavol
(Gypsy) windblown

Baxley
(English) from the meadow; outdoorsy
Bax, Baxlee, Baxli

Baxter
(English) tenacious
Bax, Baxey, Baxie, Baxther

Bay
(English) hair of russet; vocal
Baye, Bayie

Bayard
(English) russet-haired
Bay, Baye, Bayerd

Baylon
(English) from the bay; outdoorsman

Bazzy
(American) loud
Bazzee, Bazzi, Bazzie

Bazooka
(American) fun-loving; unusual
Bazookah

Beacan
(Irish) small boy
Beag, Bec, Becan

Beach
(English) fun-loving
Bee, Beech

Beacher
(English) pale-skinned; beech tree
Beach, Beachie, Beachy, Beecher

Beagan
(Irish) small
Beagen, Beagin

Beale
(French) attractive
Beal, Beally

Beaman
(English) tends bees
Beamann, Beamen, Beeman

Beamer
(English) musician
Beam, Beamy, Beemer

Bean
(Scottish) lively
Beann

Beanon
(Irish) good boy
Beinean, Beineon, Binean

Bearach
(Irish) spearing
Bearchan, Bercnan, Bergin

Beasley
(English) nurturing; pea field
Beas, Beasie, Beesly

Beate
(German) serious
Bay, Baye, Bayahtah, Beahta, Beahtae

Beattie
(Irish) happy

Beau
(French) handsome man
Beaubeau, Bo, Boo, Bow

Beauford
(French) attractive
Beau, Beauf, Beaufort

Beaumont
(French) attractive and
strong
*Bo, Bomont, Bowmont,
Beau*

Beauregard
(French) a face much
admired
*Beau, Beauregarde,
Beaurigard, Bobo*

Beaver
(French) tenacious
Beav, Beever, Bevoh, Beave

Bebe
(Spanish) baby
Be-Be

Becher
(Hebrew) firstborn
Bee

Beck
(English) stream; laid-back
*Bec, Becc, Becke, Becker,
Bek*

Becker
(English) calm
Bekker

Beckett
(English) methodical
Beck, Beket, Bekette

Bede
(English) prayerful
Bea, Bead, Beda, Bedah

Bedford
(Last name as first name)
laid-back

Bedrich
(Czech) rules peacefully

Bedro
(Spanish) form of Pedro;
surprising
Bed

Beebe
(English) tending bees;
tenacious
B.B., Bee-be, Beebee

Beeson
(Last name as first name)
son of beekeeper; wary
Bees

Beggs
(Last name as first name)
admired
Begg, Begs

Beige
(American) calm
Bayge

Beinish
(Latin) from Benedict;
blessed

Beircheart
(Welsh) spears

Bela
(Hawaiian) beauty

Belden
(English) plain-spoken
*Beld, Beldene, Beldon,
Bell, Bellden, Belldon*

Belen
(Greek) following the
arrow's straight path

Bell
(French) handsome man

Bellamy
(French) beautiful friend
*Belamie, Bell, Bellamie,
Bellmee, Belmy*

Bellindo
(German) ferocious;
attractive
Balindo, Belindo, Belyndo

Bello
(African) advocates Islam

Belmount
(French) gracious
*Belmon, Belmond,
Belmonde, Belmont,
Belmonta*

Belton
(English) from a lovely
town of bells
Beltan, Belten

Belvin
(American) form of Melvin;
attractive
Belven

Bem
(African) peaceful

Ben
(Hebrew) short for
Benjamin; wonderful
*Benjy, Bennie, Benno,
Benny*

Benaiah
(Hebrew) God-built; wars
Benaya, Benayahu

Bence
(American) short for
Benson; good
Bens, Bense, Binse

Bend
(American) word as name;
lithe

Bendell
(Last name used as first
name) loving
Ben

Benedict
(Latin) blessed man
*Ben, Benedik, Benne,
Bennie, Benny*

Bender
(American) tweaker;
diplomatic
Ben, Bend

Bendo
(American) soothing
Ben, Bend

Benes
(Czech) blessed

Beniah
(Hebrew) articulate
Benia, Benyah

Benicio
(Spanish) adventurous
Benecio, Benito

Benito
(Italian) blessed
Benedo, Beni, Beno

Benjamin
(Hebrew) son of right
hand; wonderful boy
*Behnjamin, Ben,
Benjamen, Benjamine,
Benjie, Benjy, Benni,
Bennie, Benny, Benyamin*

Benjiro
(Japanese) promotes
peace

Bennett
(French) blessed
*Ben, Benet, Benett,
Bennet, Bennette, Benny*

Benno
(Italian) form of Ben;
wonderful; best
Beno

Benny
(Hebrew) short for
Benjamin
*Benge, Benjy, Benni,
Bennie*

Benoit
(French) growing and
flourishing
Ben, Benoyt

Benoni
(Hebrew) sorrow

Bensey
(American) easygoing; fine
Bence, Bens, Bensee

Benson
(Hebrew) son of Ben;
brave heart
Bensahn, Bensen

Bent
(English) short for Benton
Bynt

Bentley
(English) clever
Bent, Bentlee, Leye

Benton
(English) formidable
*Bentan, Bentawn,
Bentone*

Benvenuto
(Italian) welcomed child
Ben

Benz
(German) from carmaker
Mercedes-Benz; upscale
Bens

Benzi
(Hebrew) blessed

Beowulf
(Literature) warrior

Ber
(Hebrew) bear

Berdy
(German) bright

Beresford
(English) place of spears
Berresford

Berfit
(Origin unknown) farming;
outdoorsman
Berf

Berg
(German) tall; mountain
Bergh, Berj, Burg, Burgh

Bergen
(Irish) little spear man
Bergin, Birgin

Berger
(French) watchful;
shepherd
Bergher, Bergie

Bergin
(Swedish) loquacious;
lives on the hill
*Bergan, Berge, Bergen,
Berger, Bergin, Birgin*

Berk
(Turkish) rough-hewn

Berkeley
(English) idolized; (Place
name) town in California
*Berk, Berkeley, Berki,
Berkie, Berklee, Berkley,
Berklie, Berkly, Berky*

Berko
(Hebrew) bear
Ber

Berks
(American) adored
*Berk, Berke, Berkelee,
Berkey, Berkli, Berksie,
Berkslee, Berky, Birklee,
Birksey, Burks, Burksey*

Berman
(German) steady
Bermahn, Bermen, Bermin

Bernabe
(German) bold
*Bernabee, Bernabey,
Bernaby, Bernby, Bernebe,
Berns, Bernus, Burnby*

Bernal
(German) bearlike
Bern

Bernard
(German) brave and
dependable
*Bern, Bernarde, Bernee,
Bernerd, Bernie, Berny,
Burnard*

Bernardo
(Spanish) brave; bear
*Berna, Bernardo,
Barnardoh, Berny*

Bernave
(American) form of
Bernard; smart
*Bernav, Bernee, Berneve,
Berni*

Bernd
(German) bearlike
*Bern, Berne, Bernee,
Berney, Berny*

Berne
(German) courageous
Bern, Berni, Bernie,
Bernne, Berny

Bernie
(German) brave boy
Bern, Berni, Berny, Birnie,
Burney

Berry
(English) botanical;
flourishing

Bert
(English) shining example
Berti, Bertie, Berty, Birt,
Burt

Berthold
(German) bold ruler
Bert, Berthol, Berthuld,
Berty, Bertolt

Berthrand
(German) form of Bertram;
strong; raven
Bert, Berthran, Bertie,
Bertrand, Berty

Bertil
(Scandinavian) bright
Bertel

Bertin
(English) form of Burton;
dramatic
Berton, Burtun

Bertoldo
(Spanish) ruler
Bert

Berton
(American) form of
Burton; brave; dramatic
Bert, Bertan, Berty

Bertram
(German) outstanding
Bert, Bertie, Bertrem,
Bertrom, Berty

Bertrand
(German) bright
Bert, Bertie, Bertran,
Bertrund, Birtryn

Berty
(English) form of Bert;
shining
Bert, Bertie, Burty

Bervick
(American) upwardly
mobile; brave
Bervey

Berwyn
(English) loyal friend
Berrie, Berwin, Berwynd,
Berwynne

Besley
(Last name as first name)
calm
Bes, Bez

Best
(American) word as name;
quintessential man
Beste

Bethel
(Hebrew) loves the house
of God
Bethell

Bettis
(American) vocal
Bettes, Bettus, Betus

Beuford
(Last name as first name)
form of Buford; country
boy
Beuf, Bu, Bueford

Beval
(Welsh) vivacious

Bevan
(Welsh) beguiling
Bev, Bevahn, Beven, Bevin

Bever
(English) form of Bevis;
sophisticated

Beverly
(English) from a stream of
beavers; natural

Bevil
(English) form of Bevis;
dignified

Bevis
(French) strong-willed
Bev, Bevas, Beves, Bevvis,
Bevys, Bevyss

Bexal
(American) studious
Bex, Bexlee, Bexly, Bexy

Bexley
(Place name)
distinguished

Bhakati
(Hindi) devoted man

Bhanu
(Hindi) sun-loving

Bharat
(Hindi) fire

Bhaskar
(Hindi) shining

Biaggio
(Italian) stutters; unsure
Biage, Biagio

Bialas
(Polish) white-haired
Bialy

Bickford
(English) wields an ax;
chops

Biffy
(American) popular
Bibbee, Biff

Bigram
(Origin unknown)
handsome
Bigraham, Bygram

Bijou
(French) jewel

Bilal
(Arabic) selected one

Bill
(German) short for
William; strong; resolute
Billi, Billie, Billy

Billings
(Place name)
sophisticated

Billy
(German) short for
William; strong
Bilie, Bill, Billee, Billi,
Billie, Bily

Billybob
(American) combo of Billy
and Bob
B.B., Billibob, Billiebob,
BillyBob, Billy Bob

Billy-Dale
(American) from William
and Dale; countrified
Billidell, Billydale

Billyjoe
(American) combo of Billy
and Joe
Billiejoe, Billijo, Billjo,
BillyJoe

Billymack
(American) combo of Billy
and Mack
Billiemac, Billimac, Billy,
BillyMack, Mackie

Billyray
(American) combo of Billy
and Ray
Billirae, Billy Ray

Bing
(German) outgoing
Beng

Bingo
(American) spunky
Bengo, Bingoh

Binh
(Vietnamese) a part of the
whole

Binkie
(English) energetic
Bink, Binki, Binky

Birch
(English) white and
shining; birch tree
Berch, Bir, Burch

Bird
(American) soaring
Byrd

Biren
(American) form of Byron
Biran

Birger
(Scandinavian) helpful

Birkett
(English) living in birches;
calming
*Birk, Birket, Birkie, Birkitt,
Burkett, Burkette, Burkitt*

Birkey
(English) from the birch
tree isle
Birkee, Birkie, Birky

Birley
(English) outdoorsy;
meadow
Berl, Birl, Birlee, Birly

Birney
(English) single-minded;
island
Birne, Birni, Birny, Burney

Birtle
(English) from the hill of
birds; natural

Bish
(Hindi) universal

Bishamon
(Mythology) Japanese god
of war and luck

Bishop
(Greek) supervisor;
serving the bishop
Bish, Bishie, Bishoppe

Bix
(American) hip
Bicks, Bixe

Bjorn
(Swedish) athletic
*Bjarn, Bjarne, Bjonie,
Bjorne, Bjorny*

Black
(Scottish) dark
Blacke, Blackee, Blackie

Blackburn
(Scottish) lives by a brook;
dark

Blade
(Spanish) prepared; knife
Bladie, Blayd

Blagden
(English) likes the dark
valley

Blaine
(Irish) svelte
Blain, Blane, Blayne

Blair
(Irish) open
Blaire, Blare, Blayree

Blaise
(French) audacious
Blasé, Blayse, Blaze

Blake
(English) dark and
handsome
Blaike, Blakey, Blakie

Blakeley
(English) outdoorsy;
meadow
*Blake, Blakelee, Blakely,
Blakie*

Blame
(American) sad
Blaim, Blaime

Blanchard
(Last name as first name)
white
Blan

Blanco
(Spanish) light
Blancoh, Blonco, Blonko

Blanford
(English) from the gray
ford
Blandford

Blank
(American) word as name;
blank slate; open
Blanc

Blanket
(Invented) security
*Blank, Blankee, Blankett,
Blankey, Blankie, Blanky*

Blanton
(English) mild-mannered
Blanten, Blantun

Blasio
(Spanish) stutterer
Blaseo, Blasios, Blaze

Blaze
(English and American)
daring
*Blaase, Blaise, Blazey,
Blazie*

Blazej
(Czech) stutters; insecure

Bleddyn
(Welsh) heroic

Bliss
(English) happy
Blice, Blyss

Blithe
(English) merry
Bly, Blye, Blythe

Blitzer
(German) adventurous
Blitz, Blitze

Blocker
(Last name as first name)
block
Bloc, Block, Blok

Bloo
(American) zany

Blue
(Color name) hip
Bleu, Blu

Blye
(American) joyful
Blie

Bo
(Scandinavian) lively
Beau

Boat
(American) word as name;
sea-loving
Bo

Boaz
(Hebrew) strong; swift
Bo, Boase, Boaze, Boz

Bob
(English) short for Robert;
bright; outstanding
Bobbi, Bobbie, Bobby

Bobby
(English) short for Robert;
bright; outstanding
Bob, Bobbie, Bobi

Bobbydee
(American) combo of
Bobby and Dee; country
boy
*Bobbidee, Bobby D,
Bobby Dee, Bobby-Dee*

Bobbymack
(American) combo of
Bobby and Mack; jovial
*Bobbimac, Bobbymac,
Bobby-Mack*

Bobby-Wayne
(American) combo of
Bobby and Wayne; small-
town boy
*Bob, Bobbiwayne, Bobbi-
Wayne, Bobby, Bobby
Wayne, Bobbywayne,
Wain, Wayne*

Bobo
(African) Tuesday-born

Bodaway
(Native American) fire
maker

Boden
(French) communicator
Bodin, Bodun, Bowden

Bodhi
(Chiense) founder of Ch'an Buddhism in China
Bodhee

Bodil
(Scandinavian) living

Bodua
(African) last one

Bogart
(German) bold, strong man
Bo, Bobo, Bogardte, Boge, Bogert, Bogey, Bogie

Bogdan
(Polish) God's gift

Bogdari
(Polish) gift from God
Bogdi

Boggle
(American) confusing
Bogg

Bogumil
(Polish) loves God

Bojan
(Czech) fighter

Bojesse
(American) comical
Boje, Bojee, Bojeesie, Bojess

Bola
(American) careful; bold
Bolah, Boli

Bolden
(American) bold man
Boldun

Boleslaw
(Polish) in glory
Boleslav

Bolin
(Last name as first name) bold
Bolen

Bolivar
(Spanish) aggressive
Bolley, Bollivar, Bolly

Bolley
(American) strong
Bolly

Bolton
(English) town of the bold

Bomani
(African) fighter
Boman

Bon
(French) good
Bonne

Bonar
(French) gentle
Bonarr, Bonnar, Bonner

Bonaventura
(Spanish) good fortune
Bona, Bonavento, Buenaventura, Buenaventure, Ventura

Bonaventure
(Latin) humble
Bonaventura, Bonnaventura, Buenaventure

Bond
(English) farmer; renegade
Bondee, Bondie, Bondy

Bongo
(American) type of drum; musical
Bong, Bongy

Boni
(Latin) fortunate
Bonne

Bonifacio
(Spanish) benefactor
Bona, Boni, Boniface

Bono
(Spanish) good
Bonno

Booker
(English) lover of books
Book, Booki, Bookie, Booky

Boone
(French) blessed; good
Boon, Boonie, Boony
Booth
(German) protective
*Boot, Boothe, Boothie,
Bootsie*
Boots
(American) cowboy
Bootsey, Bootsie, Bootz
Booveeay
(Invented) form of
Bouvier; elegant
Boo
Bordan
(English) secretive; of the
boar
*Borde, Bordee, Borden,
Bordi, Bordie, Bordy*
Border
(American) word as name;
fair-minded; aggressive
Bord
Borg
(Scandinavian) fortified;
castle
Borge, Borgh
Borges
(Last name as first name)
labyrinthine
Boris
(Russian) combative
Boras, Bore, Bores
Bornami
(Asian) conflicted
Borr
(Russian) contentious
Bos
(English) woodsman
Boz
Boscoe
(English) woodsman
Boseda
(African) Sunday-born

Bosley
(English) thriving; grove
Bos, Boslee, Boslie, Bosly
Bost
(Place name) from Boston,
Massachusetts; audacious
Bostt
Boston
(Place name) distinctive
Boss, Bost
Boswell
(English) well near woods;
dignified
*Bos, Bosswell, Boz,
Bozwell*
Botan
(Japanese) long-living
Botolf
(English) wolf; standoffish
Botof
Bour
(English) loves the stream
Bourbon
(Place name) jazzy
*Borbon, Bourbonn,
Bourbonne*
Bourey
(Vietnamese) countryman
Bourne
(French) planner;
boundary
*Bourn, Bourney, Bournie,
Byrn, Byrne, Byrnie*
Bouvier
(French) elegant; sturdy;
ox
*Bouveah, Bouveay,
Bouviay*
Bowen
(Welsh) shy
Bowie, Bowin
Bowie
(Irish) brash; western
Booie, Bowen

Boyce
(French) defender
Boice, Boy, Boyce

Boyd
(Scottish) fair-haired
Boide, Boydie

Boyne
(Irish) cow; grows

Bovo
(Last name as first name)
macho
Bovoh

Bowing
(Last name as first name)
blond and young
Beau, Bo, Bow, Bowen

Bowman
(Last name as first name)
young; archer
Bow

Bowry
(Irish) form of Bowie; able;
young
Bowy

Boy
(American) boy child of
the family

Boydine
(French) from the woods
Boyse

Boyer
(French) woodsman

Bozidar
(Polish) God's precious
Bovza, Bovzek

Brack
(English) from the plant
bracken; fine
Bracke

Bracken
(English) plant name;
debonair
*Brack, Brackan, Brackin,
Brackun*

Brad
(English) short for
Bradley; expansive
Braddie, Braddy

Bradan
(English) open-minded
*Braden, Bradin, Brady,
Bradyn, Braedyn, Braid*

Bradford
(English) mediator
Brad, Brady

Bradley
(English) prosperous;
expansive
*Brad, Bradie, Bradlee,
Bradlie, Bradly*

Bradshaw
(English) broad-minded
Brad, Brad-Shaw, Bradshie

Brady
(Irish) high-spirited
Brade, Bradee, Bradey

Brahma
(Hindi) worshipful

Brain
(Word as name) brilliant
Brane

Brainard
(English) princely
Brainerd

Bram
(Hebrew) short for
Abraham; great father
Brahm, Bramm

Bran
(Irish) raven; blessed
Brann

Branch
(Latin) growing
Bran, Branche

Branco
(Last name as first name)
authentic
Brank, Branko

Brand
(English) fiery
*Brandd, Brande, Brandy,
Brann*

Brandeis
(Czech) has a charitable
nature

Brando
(American) talented
Brand

Brandon
(English) hill; high-spirited
*Bradonn, Bran, Brandan,
Brandin, Branny*

Brandt
(English) dignified
Bran, Brandtt, Brant

Brandy
(English) firebrand; bold;
brandy drink
*Brand, Brandee, Brandey,
Brandi, Brandie*

Brannon
(Irish) bright-minded
*Bran, Brann, Brannen,
Branon*

Branson
(English) persistent
*Bran, Brans, Bransan,
Bransen*

Brant
(English) hothead
Brandt

Brasil
(Irish) disagrees
Brazil, Breasal, Bresal

Brashier
(French) brash
Brashear, Brasheer

Bratcher
(Last name as first name)
aggressive
Bratch

Bratumil
(Polish) brother's love

Bravillo
(Spanish) brave
Braville

Bravo
(Italian) top-notch
Bravoh, Bravvo

Brawley
(English) meadow man

Braxton
(English) worldly
*Brack, Brackston, Brax,
Braxsten, Braxt*

Bray
(English) vocal
Brae

Brayan
(Origin unknown) to yell
out
Brayen

Braydon
(English) effective
*Braedan, Braedon,
Brayden, Braydun*

Brecht
(Last name as first)
playwright

Breck
(Irish) fair and freckled
Breckie, Breckle, Brek

Brede
(Scandinavian) glacier;
cold heart

Breeahno
(Invented) form of Briano

Breeon
(American) strong

Breeson
(American) strong
Breece, Breese, Bresen

Breeze
(American) happy
Breese, Breez, Breezy

Brencis
(Russian) sad

Brendan
(Irish) armed
Brend, Brenden, Brendie,
Brendin, Brendon

Brennan
(English) pensive
Bren, Brenn, Brennen,
Brennon, Brenny

Brenson
(Last name as first name)
disturbed; masculine
Brens, Brenz

Brent
(English) prepared; on the
mountain
Bren, Brint

Brenton
(English) forward-thinking
Brent, Brenten, Brintin

Brett
(Scottish) man from
Britain; innovative
Bret, Breton, Brette,
Bretton, Britt

Brettson
(American) manly man;
Briton
Brett

Brewster
(English) creative; brewer
Brew, Brewer

Breyen
(Irish) strong; aggressive
Brey, Breyan

Brian
(Irish) strong man of honor
Bri, Briann, Brien, Brienn,
Bry, Bryan

Briander
(American) inquisitive;
rider of waves

Briareus
(Mythology) giant with
one hundred arms; strong

Brice
(Welsh) go-getter
Bryce

Brick
(English) alert; bridge
Bricke, Brik

Brickle
(American) surprising
Brick, Brickel, Brickell,
Bricken, Brickton, Brickun,
Brik

Bridgely
(English) coming from the
bridge
Bridgeley

Bridger
(English) makes bridges
Bridge

Bridon
(English) bright-eyed

Brigdo
(American) leader
Brigg, Briggy

Brigham
(English) mediator
Brigg, Briggie, Briggs,
Brighum

Brighton
(English) from the shining
town

Briley
(English) calm
Bri, Brilee, Brilie, Brily

Brinley
(English) of the joyful
meadow; sweet
Brindley, Brinly, Brynley,
Brynly

Briscoe
(Last name as first name)
forceful
Brisco, Brisko, Briskoe

Brishen
(English) craftsman

Britt
(English) humorous; from
Britain
Brit, Britts

Britton
(English) loyal; from Britain

Brock
(English) forceful
*Broc, Brocke, Brockie,
Brocky, Brok*

Brockly
(English) aggressive
*Brocklee, Brockli, Broklee,
Broklie, Brokly*

Brockton
(English) badger; stuffy
Brock

Brod
(English) short for
Broderick
Broddie, Broddy

Broder
(Scandinavian) true
brother
Brolle, Bror

Broderick
(English) broad-minded;
brother
*Brod, Broddee, Broddie,
Broddy, Broderic,
Broderik, Brodric, Brodrick*

Brodie
(Irish) builder
Brode, Brodee, Brody

Brodny
(Irish) falling aside; brash

Brogan
(Irish) sturdy shoe;
dependable
Brogann

Bromley
(English) meadow of
shrubs; unpredictable
*Brom, Bromlee, Bromlie,
Bromly*

Bron
(Irish) sadness

Bronc
(Spanish) wild; horse
Bronco, Bronk, Bronko

Bronco
(Spanish) wild; spirited
Broncoh, Bronko, Bronnco

Brondo
(Last name as first name)
macho
Bron, Brond

Brone
(Irish) sorrow

Bronson
(English) Brown's son
*Bron, Brondson, Bronni,
Bronnie, Bronny, Bronsan,
Bronsen*

Bronto
(American) short for
brontosaurus; thunderous
*Bront, Brontee, Brontey,
Bronti, Bronty*

Bronze
(Metal) alloy of tin and
copper; brown
Bronz

Brook
(English) easygoing
Brooke, Brookee, Brookie

Brooks
(English) easygoing
Brookes, Brooky

Broughton
(English) from a protected
place

Brow
(American) snob
Browy

Brown
(English) tan
Browne, Brownie, Browny

Brownie
(American) brown-haired
Brown

Bruce
(French) complicated; from a thicket of brushwood
Bru, Brucie, Brucy, Brue

Brumley
(French) smart; scattered
Brum

Bruno
(German) brown-skinned
Brune, Brunne, Brunoh

Brunon
(Polish) brown-haired

Bruiser
(American) tough guy
Bruezer, Bruser, Bruzer

Brush
(American) confident

Brutus
(Latin) aggressive; a bully

Bryan
(Irish) ethical; strong
Brye, Bryen

Bryant
(Irish) honest; strong
Bryan, Bryent

Bryce
(Welsh) spunky
Brice, Bry, Brye

Brychan
(Welsh) speckled

Brydon
(American) magnanimous
Bridon, Brydan, Bryden, Brydun

Bryn
(Welsh) hill-dweller

Brynmor
(Welsh) big hill

Bryson
(Welsh) Bryce's son; smart
Briceson, Bry, Bryse

Bryton
(Welsh) hill town

Bu
(Irish) winner; short for Buagh

Bubba
(German) a regular guy
Bub, Buba, Bubb, Bubbah

Buck
(English) studly; buck deer
Buckey, Buckie, Bucko, Bucky

Buckley
(English) outdoorsy; a meadow for deer
Buckey, Buckie, Bucklee, Bucklie, Bucks, Bucky

Bucko
(American) macho
Bukko

Bucky
(American) warm-hearted
Buck, Buckey, Buckie

Bud
(English) courier
Budd, Buddie, Buddy, Budi, Budster

Buddy
(American) courier
Bud, Buddi, Buddie, Budi

Budington
(English) awakened

Buell
(German) upward; hill
Bue

Buffalo
(American) tough-minded
Buff, Buffer, Buffy

Buford
(English) diligent
Bueford, Bufe, Buforde

Bulgara
(Slavic) hardworking
Bulgar, Bulgarah, Bulgaruh

Bulldog
(American) rough-and-tough
Bull, Dawg, Dog

Bullock
(Last name as first name) practical

Bumpus
(Last name as first name) humorous
Bump, Bumpey, Bumpy

Bunard
(English) good
Bunerd, Bunn

Bunyan
(English) good and burly
Bunyan, Bunyen

Buran
(American) complex
Burann, Burun

Burchard
(English) tree trunks; sturdy
Burckhardt, Burgard, Burgaud, Burkhart

Burditt
(Last name as first name) shy
Burdett, Burdette, Burdey

Burford
(Last name as first name) from the water

Burge
(English) form of Burgess; middle-class
Burges, Burgis, Burr

Burgess
(English) businessman
Berge, Burge, Burges, Burgiss

Burhan
(Last name as first name) complex

Burke
(German) fortified
Berk, Berke, Burk, Burkie

Burl
(German) homespun

Burley
(English) nature-lover; wooded meadow
Burl, Burlea, Burlee, Burli, Burly, Burr

Burnaby
(English) brook man

Burne
(English) lives by the brook
Bourn, Bourne, Burn, Byrn, Byrne, Byrnes

Burnell
(English) of the brook
Burnel

Burnett
(English) by the small brook
Burnet, Burnitt

Burnis
(English) by the brook
Burn, Burnes, Burney, Burr

Burr
(English) prickly; brusque
Burry

Burrick
(English) townsman
Bur, Burr, Burry

Burney
(English) loner; island
Burn, Burne, Burnie, Burny

Burris
(English) sophisticated; living in the town
Berris, Buris, Burr, Burres

Burt
(English) shining man
Bert, Bertee, Burtie, Burty

Burton
(English) protective; town that is well fortified
Burt, Burty, Brutie

Busby
(Scottish) artist; village
Busbee, Busbi, Buzbie,
Buzz, Buzzie

Busher
(Last name as first name)
bold
Bush

Buster
(American) fun
Bustah

Butcher
(English) worker
Butch, Butchy

Butler
(English) directing the
house; handsome
Butler, Butlir, Butlyr,
Buttler

Buxton
(Last name as first name)
kind

Buzz
(Scottish) popular
Buzy, Buzzi, Buzzie, Buzzy

Byford
(English) leaving the
cottage; forever young

Byorn
(American) form of Bjorn

Byram
(English) stealthy; yard
that houses cattle
Bye, Byrem, Byrie, Byrim

Byrd
(English) birdlike
Bird

Byrne
(English) loner
Birn, Birne, Byrn, Byrni,
Byrnie, Byrny

Byrnett
(Last name as first name)
stable
Burn, Burnett, Burney,
Burns, Byrne, Byrney

Byron
(English) reclusive; small
cottage
Biron, Biryn, Bye, Byren,
Byrom, Byrone, Byryn

C

Cab
(American) word as name
Cabby, Kab

Cabell
(Last name as first name)
spontaneous

Cable
(French) rope-making boy;
crafty
Cabel

Cabot
(French) loves the water
Cabbott

Cabrera
(Spanish) able
Cabrere

Cack
(American) laughing
Cackey, Cackie, Cacky,
Cassy, Caz, Kass, Kassy,
Khaki

Cactus
(Botanical) prickly
Cack, Kactus

Cadby
(Norse) spirited heritage

Caddock
(Last name as first name)
high spirits

Cade
(English) stylish; bold;
round
Cadye, Kade

Cadel
(Welsh) fierce

Caden
(English) spirited
*Cadan, Cade, Cadun,
Caiden, Kaden, Kayden*

Cadman
(Irish) fighter
Cadmann

Cadmar
(Greek) fiery
Cadmarr

Cadmus
(Greek) one who excels;
prince
Cad, Cadmuss, Kadmus

Cady
(American) forthright
Cadee, Cadey, Cadie

Caesar
(Latin) focused leader
*Caeser, Caez, Caezer,
Cesaro, Cezar, Seezer*

Cage
(American) dramatic
Cadge

Cailen
(American) gentle
Kail, Kailen, Kale

Cain
(Hebrew) aggressive
*Caine, Cainen, Cane, Kain,
Kane*

Cairn
(Welsh) stone; sturdy
Cairne

Cal
(Latin) short for Calvin;
kind
Callie, Kal

Calbert
(American) cowboy
*Cal, Calbart, Calberte,
Calburt, Callie, Colbert*

Calder
(English) stream; flowing
Cald, Kalder

Calderon
(Spanish) stream; flowing
*Cald, Kald, Kalder,
Kalderon*

Caldwell
(English) refreshing; cold
well

Cale
(Hebrew) slim; good heart
Kale

Caleb
(Hebrew) faithful; brave
*Cal, Calab, Cale, Caley,
Calie, Calub, Kaleb*

Calek
(American) fighter; loyal
Calec, Kalec, Kalek

Calen
(Irish) slim
Cailun

Caley
(Irish) slender

Calf
(American) cowboy
Kalf

Calhoun
(Irish) limited; from the
narrow woods
*Cal, Calhoon, Calhoune,
Callie*

Calixto
(Spanish) handsome
*Calex, Calexto, Cali,
Calisto, Calix, Callie, Cally,
Kalixto*

Callahan
(Irish) spiritual
*Cal, Calahan, Calihan,
Callie*

Callie
(American) short for Calvin; kind
Cal, Calley, Calli, Cally

Callo
(American) attractive
Cal, Cally, Kallo

Cally
(Scottish) peacemaker

Calman
(Last name as first name) caring
Cal

Calum
(Irish, Scottish) peaceful; (American) calm
Cal, Callum, Calym, Calyme

Calvary
(American) word as name; herding all
Cal, Kal, Kalvary

Calvert
(English) respected; herding
Cal, Calber, Calbert, Calver, Kal, Kalvert

Calvin
(Latin) bold
Cal, Calvie, Kal

Cam
(Scottish) short for Cameron; loving
Camm, Cammey, Cammie, Cammy, Kam

Cambell
(American) form of Campbell; reliable; irregular mouth
Cam, Cambel, Cammy, Kambell

Camberg
(Last name as first name) valley man
Cam

Cambridge
(Place name) city in England; twisting; mover
Cambrydge

Camden
(Scottish) conflicted
Cam, Camdan, Camdon

Camerero
(Last name as first name) charismatic

Cameron
(Scottish) mischievous; crooked nose
Cam, Camaron, Camerohn, Cami, Cammy, Camren, Camron

Camilo
(Latin) helpful; (Italian) free
Cam, Camillo

Campbell
(Scottish) bountiful; crooked mouth
Cambell, Cammie, Camp, Campie, Campy

Camrin
(American) form of Cameron; kind

Camron
(Scottish) short for Cameron
Camren

Canaan
(Biblical) spiritual leanings
Cane, Kanaan, Kanan

Canal
(Word as name) waterway
Kanal

Candelario
(Spanish) bright and glowing
Cadelario

Cander
(American) candid
Can, Candor, Candy, Kan, Kander, Kandy

Candido
(Spanish) pure; candid
*Can, Candi, Candide,
Candy*

Candle
(American) bright; hip
Candell

Cannon
(French) courageous
*Canney, Canni, Cannie,
Canny, Canon, Canyn,
Kannon, Kanon*

Canute
(Scandinavian) great
Knut, Knute

Canyon
(Nature) hip

Capote
(Italian) bright

Cappy
(French) breezy; lucky
Cappey, Cappi

Caractacus
(Latin) bold

Carad
(American) wily
Karad

Caravaggio
(Italian) painter

Card
(English) short for Carden;
crafty
Kard

Cardan
(English) crafty; carder
Card, Carden, Cardon

Cardew
(Welsh) dark, sturdy

Cardwell
(English) craftsman
Kardwell

Carel
(Dutch) free

Carew
(Latin) runner
Carrew

Carey
(Welsh) masculine; by the
castle
Care, Cari, Cary, Karey

Cari
(English) masculine
Care, Carie, Cary

Carino
(Last name as first name)
strong

Carl
(Swedish) kingly
Karl

Carlfred
(American) combo of Carl
and Fred; dignified
Carl-Fred, Carlfree

Carlin
(Irish) winning
*Carlan, Carle, Carlen,
Carlie, Carly*

Carlisle
(English) strengthens
Carl, Carly, Carlyle

Carlo
(Italian) sensual; manly
Carl, Carloh

Carlon
(Irish) form of Carl;
winning
Karlon, Carlonn

Carlos
(Spanish) manly; sensual
Carl, Carlo

Carlson
(English) son of a manly
man
Carls, Carlsan, Carlsen

Carlton
(English) leader; town of
Carl
*Carleton, Carltan, Carlten,
Carltown, Carltynne*

Carmel
(Hebrew) growing; garden
Carmell, Karmel

Carmello
(Italian) flourishing
Carm, Carmel, Carmelo,
Karmello

Carmichael
(Scottish) bold; Michael's
follower
Car, Kar, Karmichael

Carmine
(Italian, Latin) dear song
Carmane, Carmin,
Carmyne, Karmen,
Karmine

Carmody
(French) manly; adult
Carmodee

Carnell
(Irish) victor
Car, Carny, Kar, Karnell,
Karney

Carney
(Irish) winner
Carn, Carnay Carnee,
Carnie, Carny

Carol
(Irish) champion
Carroll, Carrol, Carroll

Carr
(Scandinavian) outdoorsy
Car, Kar

Carrew
(Latin) runner

Carrick
(Irish) lives on rocky place

Carroll
(German) masculine;
winner
Carall, Care, Carell, Caroll,
Carrol, Carrolle, Carry,
Caryl

Carson
(English) confident
Carr, Cars, Carsan, Carsen

Carsten
(German) a Christian

Carswell
(English) diligent

Cart
(American) word as name;
practical
Cartee, Cartey, Kart

Carter
(English) insightful
Cart, Cartah, Cartie

Carland
(Last name as first name)
land of free men

Cartrell
(English) practical
Car, Cartrelle, Cartrey,
Cartrie, Cartrill, Kar,
Kartrel, Kartrell

Cartwright
(English) creative
Cart, Cartright, Kart,
Kartwright

Caruso
(Italian) musically inclined
Karuso

Carvell
(English) innovative
Carvel, Carvelle, Carver,
Karvel

Carver
(English) carver
Carve, Carvey, Karver,
Karvey

Cary
(English) pretty brook;
charming
Carey

Casdeen
(American) assertive;
ingenious
Kassdeen

Case
(Irish) highly esteemed
Casey

Casey
(Irish) courageous
*Case, Casey, Casi, Casie,
Kacie, Kacy, Kase, Kaysie*

Cash
(Latin) conceited
Casha, Cashe, Cazh

Cashmere
(American) smooth; soft-
spoken
*Cash, Cashmeer,
Cashmyre, Kashmere*

Cashone
(American) cash-loving
Casho

Casiano
(Latin) empty

Casimir
(Polish) peace-loving
Casmer, Casmir

Casimiro
(Spanish) famous;
aggressor
Casmiro, Kasimiro

Casper
(German) secretive
*Caspar, Casper, Caspey,
Caspi, Caspie, Cass*

Caspian
(Place name) sea near
Iran; daring

Cass
(Irish) short for Cassidy;
funny
Cash, Caz, Kass

Cassidy
(Irish) humorous
*Casidy, Cass, Cassadie,
Cassidee, Cassidie, Kasidy,
Kass, Kassidy*

Cassie
(Irish) short for Cassidy;
clever
Casi, Cass, Cassy

Cassius
(Latin) protective
Cass, Casseus, Casshus

Cast
(Greek) form of Castor;
fiery star
Casta, Caste, Kast

Castellan
(Spanish) adventurer

Casto
(Mythology) from Castor, a
Gemini twin
Cass, Kasto

Castor
(Greek) eager protector
Cass, Caster, Castie

Castulo
(Spanish) aggressor
Castu, Kastulo

Cata
(American) form of
Catarino

Cathal
(Irish) leader

Cathmor
(Irish) brave warrior

Cato
(Latin) zany and bright
Catoe, Kato

Catarino
(Spanish) unflawed; perfect
Catrino

Cavan
(Irish) attractive man
Cavahn, Caven, Cavin

Cavance
(Irish) handsome
*Caeven, Cavanse, Kaeven,
Kavance*

Cavell
(Last name as first name)
opinionated
Cavil, Cavill

Cawley
(Last name as first name)
brash

Cayce
(American) form of Casey;
brave
Cace, Case, Kayce

Cayetano
(Spanish) feisty

Caynce
(Invented) form of Cayce;
daring
Caincy, Cainse, Kaynse

Cazare
(Last name as first name)
daring
Cazares

Cecil
(Latin) unseeing; hard-
headed; blind
*Cece, Cecel, Cecile, Cecilio,
Cicile*

Cedar
(Botanical) tree name;
sturdy
Ced, Sed, Sedar

Cedric
(English) leader
Ced, Ceda, Cedrick

Ceferino
(Spanish) careful

Celedonio
(Spanish) heavenly

Celso
(Italian) heavenly
*Celesteno, Celestino,
Celesto, Celestyno, Celsus,
Selso*

Celumiel
(Spanish) of the heavens
Celu

Centola
(Spanish) tenth child
Cento

Century
(Invented) remarkable
Cen, Cent

Cerf
(French) buck

Cerone
(French) serene; creative
Serone

Cervantes
(Literature) for the
Spanish author; original
Cervantez

Cesar
(Spanish) leader
Cesare, Cezar, Zarr

Chad
(English) firebrand
Chadd, Chaddy

Chadburn
(English) spirited

Chadwick
(English) warrior
Chad, Chadwyck

Chaffee
(Last name as first name)
bold adventurer

Chaggy
(American) cocky
Chagg, Shagg, Shaggy

Chaika
(Hebrew) life
*Chaikeh, Chaikel, Chaiki,
Chai*

Chaim
(Hebrew) life
*Chai, Chayim, Haim, Hy,
Hyman, Hymie, Khaim,
Manny*

Chaise
(French) chases
Chayse

Challen
(American) variant of
Allen; well-liked

Chalmer
(Scottish) the lord's son
Chall, Chally, Chalmers

Chalmers
(French) chambers;
surrounded
Chalm

Chamblin
(American) easygoing
Cham

Chan
(Chinese) bright;
(Vietnamese) truthful

Chanan
(Hebrew) filled with God's
compassion

Chanina
(Hebrew) compassionate
by virtue of God

Chance
(English) good fortune;
happy
*Chancey, Chanci, Chancy,
Chanse, Chanz, Chauncey*

Chancellor
(English) book keeper
Chance, Chancey

Chandell
(African American)
innovator
*Chandelle, Chandey,
Chandie, Shandel,
Shandell*

Chandler
(English) ingenious;
(French) maker of candles
Chand, Chandey, Chandlor

Chaney
(French) strong
*Chane, Chanie, Chayne,
Chaynee*

Chang
(Chinese) free; flowing

Channing
(English) brilliant
Chann, Channy

Chanoch
(Hebrew) dedicated; loyal

Chason
(French) hunts
Chansen

Chante
(French) singer
*Chant, Chanta, Chantay,
Chantie*

Chapa
(Last name as first name)
merchant; spirited
Chap, Chappy

Chaparro
(Spanish) from chaparral
(southern landscape);
cowboy
Chap, Chaps

Chapell
(Hindi) spiritual

Chapen
(French) clergyman
Chapin, Chapland, Chaplin

Chapman
(English) businessman
Chap, Chappy

Charilaos
(Greek) giving

Charles
(German) manly; well-
loved
*Charl, Charley, Charli,
Charlie, Charly, Chas,
Chaz, Chazz, Chuck*

Charleston
(English) Charles's town;
confident
Charlesten

Charles-Wesley
(German) combo of
Charles and Wesley;
strong and sensitive
*Charles Wes, Charles
Wesley*

Charlie
(German) manly
*Charl, Charley, Charli,
Charly*

Charlton
(English) leader
*Charles, Charley, Charlie,
Charlt*

Charome
(American) masculine
*Char, Charoam, Charom,
Charrone, Charry*

Charon
(Greek) mythological
ferryman of the
underworld

Charro
(Spanish) wild-spirited
cowboy
Charo, Charroh

Chas
(American) short for
Charles; happy boy

Chase
(French) hunter
Chace, Chass

Chaskel
(Hebrew) strong

Chat
(American) happy
Chatt

Chatham
(Last name as first name)
serious

Chatwin
(Last name as first name)
thoughtful

Chaucer
(Literature) for Geoffrey
Chaucer; distinguished
Chauce, Chauser

Chauncey
(English) fair-minded
*Chance, Chancey, Chanse,
Chaunce*

Chavakuk
(Hindi) from Charvaka;
jaded

Chavivi
(Hebrew) beloved

Chayne
(Scottish) swagger
Chane, Channe, Chay

Chaz
(German) short for
Charles; manly
*Chas, Chazz, Chazzie,
Chazzy*

Ché
(Spanish) short for José;
aggressive
Chay, Shae, Shay

Chee
(American) high-energy
Che

Chekhov
(Russian) playwright;
genius

Chen
(Chinese) great

Cheney
(French) outdoorsman
Chenay, Cheney

Cheramy
(American) form of
Jeremy; excitable
*Cheramee, Charamie,
Chermy*

Chermon
(French) my dear

Chesley
(American) patient
*Ches, Cheslee, Chez,
Chezlee*

Chester
(English) comfy-cozy
Ches, Chessie, Chessy

Chet
(English) creative
Chett

Chetwin
(English) winding road

Chevalier
(French) gallant
Chev, Chevy

Chevalle
(French) dignified
Chev, Chevi, Chevy

Cheven
(Invented) playful
Chevy

Chevery
(French) from Chevy;
elegant
Chev, Shevery

Cheves
(American) from name
Chivas; jaded
Chevez, Shevas

Chevy
(French) clever
Chev, Chevi, Chevie, Chevv

Chew
(Chinese) mountain

Chiamaka
(African) God is good

Chibale
(Hebrew) loving

Chick
(English) short for
Charles; friendly
Chic, Chickie, Chicky

Chico
(Spanish) boy
Chicoh, Chiko

Chiel
(Hebrew) God lives

Chijoke
(African) talented

Chikosi
(African) the ruins

Chili
(American) appetite for
hot food

Chilton
(English) serene; farm
Chill, Chillton, Chilly, Chilt

Chimanga
(African) grain

Chin
(Korean) precious boy

Chip
(English) chip off the old
block; like father, like son
Chipp, Chipper

Chiram
(Hebrew) held in high
esteem

Chisholm
(Place name) Chisholm
Trail; pioneer spirit
Chis, Chishom, Chiz

Chiura
(Italian) light; textured

Chiztam
(Hebrew) imbued with
God's strength

Chovev
(Hebrew) companion,
admirer

Chow
(Chinese) everywhere

Chris
(Greek) short for
Christopher; close to
Christ
Cris, Chrissy, Chrys

Christer
(Norwegian) religious
Krister

Christian
(Latin) follower of Christ
*Chris, Christen, Christiane,
Christyan, Cristian, Kris,
Krist, Kristian*

Christodoulous
(Greek) filled with sweet
love for Christ

Christophe
(French) beloved of Christ
Cristoph, Kristophe

Christopher
(Greek) the bearer of
Christ
*Chris, Christofer, Crista,
Cristopher, Cristos, Kit,
Kristopher*

Christopherson
(English) son of
Christopher; religious
Christophersen,
Cristophersen,
Cristopherson

Christos
(Greek) form of
Christopher
Chris, Kristos

Chito
(American) fast-food
eater; hungry
Cheetoh, Chitoh

Choicey
(American) word name;
picky
Choicie, Choisie

Chonito
(Spanish) friend
Chonit, Chono

Chopo
(American) cowhand
Chop, Choppy

Choto
(Spanish) kid
Shoto

Chotto
(Last name as first name)
child

Chubby
(American) oversized
Chubbee, Chubbey,
Chubbi, Chubbie

Chuck
(German) rash
Chuckee, Chuckey,
Chuckie, Chucky

Chucky
(German) impulsive
Chuckey, Chucki, Chuckie

Chuhei
(Japanese) shy

Chuna
(Hebrew) warm

Chuneh
(Hebrew) with the Lord's
grace

Chunky
(American) word name;
large
Chunk, Chunkey, Chunki

Churchill
(English) bright
Church

Chutar
(Spanish) aiming for goals
Chuter

Cian
(Irish) old soul

Cicero
(Latin) strong speaker
Cice

Cicil
(English) shy
Cecil, Cice

Cid
(Spanish) leader; lord
Ciddie, Ciddy, Cyd, Sid

Cimarron
(Place name) city in New
Mexico; cowboy
Cimaronn

Cinco
(Spanish) fifth child
Cinko, Sinko

Ciprian
(Latin) from the island of
Cyprus
Cipriano

Ciriaco
(Italian) lordly

Cirill
(English) form of Cyril; lord

Cirillo
(Spanish) lordly
Cirilo

Ciro
(Italian) lordly
Ciroh, Cirro, Cyro

Cirrus
(Latin) thoughtful; cloud formation
Cerrus, Cirrey, Cirri, Cirrie, Cirry, Cirus, Serrus, Serus

Cisco
(American) clever
Sisco, Sysco

Citronella
(American) oil from fragrant grass; pungent
Cit, Citro, Cytronella, Sitronella

Civille
(American) form of place name Seville

Claiborn
(English) born of earth
Claiborne

Clance
(Irish) form of Clancy; redhead; aggressive
Clancy, Clanse, Klance, Klancy

Clair
(English) renowned
Claire, Clare

Clancy
(Irish) lively; feisty redhead
Clance, Clancey, Clancie

Claran
(Latin) bright
Clarance, Claransi, Claranse, Clare, Claren, Clarence, Clary, Klarense

Clarence
(Latin) intelligent
Clarance, Clare, Clarens, Clarense, Clarons, Claronz, Clarrence, Klarence, Klarens

Clarinett
(Invented) plays the clarinet
Clare, Clarinet, Clary, Klare, Klari

Clark
(French) personable; scholar
Clarke

Claude
(Latin) slow-moving; lame
Claud, Claudey, Claudie, Claudy, Klaud, Klaude

Claus
(Greek) victorious
Klaas, Klaus

Claven
(English) endorsed
Klaven

Clavero
(Spanish) lame

Clawdell
(American) form of Claudell
Clawd

Claxton
(English) townie
Clax, Klax

Clay
(English) firm; short for Claybrook and Clayton; reliable
Claye, Klae, Klay

Claybey
(American) southern; earthly
Claybie, Klaybee

Clayborne
(English) earthly
Clabi, Claybie, Claybourne, Clayborn, Klay

Claybrook
(English) sparkling smile
Claibrook, Clay, Claybrooke, Clayie

Clayton
(English) stodgy
Clay, Claytan, Clayten

Cleary
(Irish) smart
Clear, Clearey, Clearie

Cleavon
(English) daring
Cheavaughn, Cleavaughn, Cleave, Cleevaughan, Cleevon

Clem
(Latin) casual
Cleme, Clemmey, Clemmie, Clemmy, Clim

Clement
(Scottish) gentle
Clem, Clemmyl

Clemente
(Spanish) pleasant
Clemen, Clementay

Clements
(Latin) forgiving man
Clem, Clement, Clemmants, Clemment

Clemer
(Latin) mild
Clemmie, Clemmy, Klemer, Klemmie, Klemmye

Clemmie
(Latin) mild
Clem, Klem, Klemmee, Klemmy

Clenzy
(Spanish) forgiving; cleansed
Clense, Clensy, Klenzy

Cleofas
(African American) brave lion

Cleopatrick
(African American) combo of Cleopatra and Patrick
Cleo, Cleopat, Kleo, Kleopatrick, Pat, Patrick

Cleophas
(Greek) seeing glory; known
Cle, Cleofus, Cleoph, Klee, Kleofus, Kleophus

Cleon
(Greek) famed man
Clee, Cleone, Kleon

Clete
(Greek) from Cletus; wanted
Cleet, Cleete

Cletus
(Greek) creative; selected
Clede, Cledus, Cletis

Cleve
(English) precarious
Clive

Cleveland
(English) daring
Cleavelan, Cleve, Clevon, Clevy, Cliveland

Clevis
(Greek) prolific
Cleviss, Clevys, Clevyss

Cliff
(English) short for Clifford; dashing
Clif, Cliffey, Cliffie, Cliffy

Clifford
(English) dashing
Cleford, Cliff, Cliffy, Clyford

Clift
(American) cliff-dweller
Clifte

Clifton
(English) risk-taker
Cliff, Clifftan, Clifften, Cliffy

Cline
(Last name as first name) musical

Clint
(English) short for Clinton; bright
Clent, Clynt, Klint

Clinton
(English) curious; bright; cliff in town
Clenton, Clint, Clinten, Clynton, Klinten, Klinton

Clive
(English) daring; living near a cliff
Cleve, Clyve

Clooney
(American) dramatic
Cloone, Cloonie, Cloony, Clune, Cluney, Clunie, Cluny

Clotaire
(French) famous
Clotie, Klotair, Klotie

Clovis
(German) famed warrior
Clove, Cloves, Clovus, Klove, Kloves, Klovis

Cloyd
(American) form of Floyd; cloying
Cloy, Cloye, Kloy, Kloyd

Clske
(Dutch) dark

Cluny
(American) dramatic

Clwe
(Dutch) face of a mountain

Clyde
(Welsh) adventurer
Clide, Clydey, Clydie, Clydy, Clye, Klyde, Klye

Clydell
(American) countrified
Clidell, Clydel

Clydenestra
(Spanish) form of Clyde
Clyde

Coal
(American) word as a name
Coale, Koal

Cobb
(English) cozy
Cob, Cobbe

Coben
(Last name as first name) creative
Cob, Cobb, Cobe, Cobee, Cobey, Cobi, Coby, Kob, Kobee, Koben, Kobi, Koby

Coby
(American) friendly
Cob, Cobe, Cobey, Cobie

Coca
(American) excitable
Coka, Cokey, Cokie, Koca, Koka

Cochise
(Native American) warrior
Cocheece, Cochize

Cocinero
(Italian) slippery

Coco
(French) brash
Coko, Koko

Cody
(English) comforting
Coday, Code, Codee, Codey, Codi, Codie

Cog
(American) short for Cogdell; necessary
Kog

Cogdell
(Last name as first name) needed
Cogdale

Cohn
(American) winner
Kohn

Cokie
(American) bright
Cokey, Coki, Cokie, Cokki, Kokie

Colbert
(English) cool and calm
Colbey, Colbi, Colbie, Colburt, Colby, Cole

Colborn
(English) intimidating;
cold brook
Colbey, Colborne, Colburn,
Colby, Cole

Colby
(English) bright; secretive;
dark farm
Colbey, Colbi, Colbie, Cole,
Colie

Colden
(English) haunting
Coldan, Coldun, Cole

Cole
(Greek) lively; winner
Coal, Coley, Colie, Kohl,
Kole

Coleman
(English) lively;
peacemaker
Cole, Colemann, Colman,
Kohlman

Colgate
(English) passway
Colgait, Colgaite, Kolgate

Colier
(Last name as first name)
sophisticated

Colin
(Irish) young and quiet;
peaceful; the people's
victor
Colan, Cole, Colen, Collin,
Collyn

Colis
(English) he who delights
others

Colley
(English) dark-haired
Col, Colli, Collie

Collier
(English) hard-working;
miner
Colier, Collie, Colly, Colyer

Collin
(Scottish) shy
Collen, Collie, Collon, Colly

Collins
(Irish) shy; holly
Collens, Collie, Collons,
Colly, Kolly

Colm
(Irish) dove; peaceful

Colorado
(Place name) U.S. state;
multicolored

Colson
(English) precocious; son
of Nicholas
Cole, Colsan, Colsen

Colt
(English) frisky; horse
trainer
Colty, Kolt, Koltt

Colten
(English) dark town;
mysterious
Cole, Collton, Colt, Coltan,
Coltawn, Colton, Kol

Colter
(English) keeping the colts
Colt, Coltor, Colty

Colum
(Latin) peaceful; dove
Colm, Kolm, Kolum

Columbus
(Latin) peaceful
(discovered America)
Colom, Colombo, Columbe

Colwen
(Irish) peaceful
Colwin, Colvin

Comanche
(Native American) tribe;
wild-spirited; industrious
Comanch, Komanche

Commodore
(French) commander

Como
(Spanish) similar
Comoh

Comus
(Greek) humorous
Comes, Comas, Commus, Komus

Conall
(Scottish) highly regarded
Conal

Conan
(Irish) worthy of praise
Conen, Connie, Conny, Conon

Conant
(Irish) top-notch
Conent, Connant

Concord
(English) agreeable
Con, Concor, Conny, Koncord, Konny

Conde
(Last name as first name)
driven

Cong
(Chinese) bright

Coniah
(Irish) pure
Conias, Conah

Conlan
(Irish) winner
Con, Conland, Conlen, Conleth, Conlin, Connie, Conny

Conk
(Invented) from conch (mollusk of the ocean); jazzy
Conch, Conkee, Conkee, Conkey, Conky, Konk, Kanch, Konkey, Konkey

Connaughton
(American) sapient

Connell
(Irish) strong
Con, Conal, Connall, Connel, Connelle, Connie, Conny

Connery
(Scottish) daring
Con, Conery, Connarie, Connary, Connie, Conny

Connie
(Irish) short for Connor
Connery, Conrad, Con, Conn, Connee, Conney, Conni, Conny

Connor
(Scottish) brilliant
Con, Conn, Conner, Conor, Kon, Konnor

Conrad
(German) optimist
Con, Connie, Conny, Conrade, Konrad

Conrado
(Spanish) bright advisor
Conrad, Conrod, Conrodo

Conridge
(Last name as first name)
advisor
Con, Conni, Connie, Conny, Ridge

Conroy
(Irish) wise writer
Conrie, Conroye, Conry, Roy, Roye

Constant
(French) devotee; loyal

Constantine
(Latin) consistent
Con, Conn, Consta, Constance, Constant, Constantin Constantyne, Konstantin

Conway
(Irish) vigilant
Con, Connie, Kon, Konway

Cooke
(Latin) cook
Cook, Cookie, Cooky

Coolidge
(Last name as first name)
wary
Cooledge

Cooney
(Last name as first name)
giving

Cooper
(English) handsome;
maker of barrels
*Coup, Couper, Koop,
Kooper, Kouper*

Cope
(English) able
Cape

Corbell
(Latin) raven; dark
Corbel

Corbet
(Latin) dark
*Corb, Corbett, Corbit,
Corbitt, Korb, Korbet*

Corbin
(Latin) dark and brooding
Corban, Corben, Corby

Corbitt
(Last name as first name)
brooding
*Corbet, Corbett, Corbie,
Corbit, Corby*

Corby
(Latin) dark
*Corbey, Korbee, Korby,
Korry*

Corcoran
(Irish) ruddy-skinned
Corkie, Corky

Cord
(Origin unknown) soap
opera hunk
Corde, Kord

Cordaro
(Italian) roped

Cordel
(French) practical
*Cordel, Cordell, Cordelle,
Cordie, Cordill, Cordy*

Cordell
(Latin) bound; rope

Cordero
(Spanish) gentle
*Cordara, Cordaro,
Cordarro, Kordarro,
Kordero*

Corey
(Irish) laughing
*Core, Corie, Corry, Cory,
Korey, Korrie, Kory*

Corin
(Latin) combative
*Coren, Dorrin, Koren,
Korrin*

Cork
(Place name) county in
Ireland
*Corkee, Corkey, Corki,
Corky, Kork*

Corky
(American) casual
Corkee, Corkey, Korky

Corlon
(American) tasteful

Cormac
(Irish) the raven's
offspring; watchful
Cormack, Cormak

Cormick
(Last name as first name)
old-fashioned
Cormac, Cormack

Corn
(Latin) form of Cornelius;
horn; yellow-haired
Korn

Cornall
(Irish) from Cornelius;
horn; loquacious

Cornelio
(Spanish) hornblower

Cornelius
(Greek) a temptation
Coarn, Conny, Corn, Corni,
Cornie, Corny, Kornelius,
Neel, Neely, Neil, Neiley

Cornell
(French) fair
Corne, Cornelle, Corny,
Kornell

Corodon
(Greek) lark

Corrado
(Italian) worthy advisor

Corrigan
(Irish) aggressive
Coregan, Corie,
Correghan, Corrie, Corry,
Koregan, Korrigan

Cort
(German) eloquent
Corte, Court, Kort

Cortazar
(Last name as first)
creative

Cortez
(Spanish) victorious;
explorer
Cortes

Corvin
(English) friend
Corwin, Corwynn, Korry,
Korvin

Corwin
(English) heart's delight
Corrie, Corry, Corwan,
Corwann, Corwyn,
Corwynne

Cory
(Latin) humorous
Coarie, Core, Corey, Corrie,
Kohry, Kori

Coryell
(Greek) lark; devious

Cosell
(French) outgoing

Cosgrove
(Irish) winner
Cosgrave, Cossy,
Kosgrove, Kossy

Cosma
(Greek) universal
Cos, Kosma

Cosmas
(Greek) universal
Cos, Kosmas, Koz

Cosmo
(Greek) in harmony with
life
Cos, Cosimo, Cosimon,
Cosme, Cosmos, Kosmo

Cosner
(English) organized;
handsome
Cosnar, Kosner

Costas
(Greek) constant
Costa, Costah

Cotton
(Botanical name) casual
Cottan

Coty
(French) comforter
Cotey, Coti, Cotie, Koty

Coug
(American) short for
cougar; fierce
Cougar, Koug, Kougar

Coulter
(English) dealing in colts;
horseman
Colter, Coult, Kolter,
Koulter

Counsel
(Latin) advisor
Consel, Council, Kounse,
Kounsell

Country
(Word as name) cowboy

Court
(English) royal

Courtland
(English) born in the land of the court; dignitary

Courtnay
(English) sophisticated
Cort, Corteney, Court, Courtney, Courtny

Covell
(English) warm
Covele, Covelle

Covet
(American) word as name; desires
Covett, Covette, Kovet

Covington
(English) distinctive
Covey, Coving, Kovey, Kovington

Cowan
(Irish) cozy
Cowen, Cowie, Cowy

Cowboy
(American) western

Cowell
(English) brash; frank
Kowell

Cowey
(Irish) reclusive
Cowee, Cowie, Kowey

Coye
(English) outdoorsman
Coy, Coyey, Coyie

Coyle
(English) in the woods

Coylie
(American) coy
Coyl, Koyl, Koylie

Coystal
(American) bashful
Coy, Koy, Koystal

Crad
(American) practical
Cradd, Krad, Kradd

Craddock
(Last name as first name) practical

Crago
(Last name as first name) macho
Crag, Craggy, Krago

Craig
(Irish) brave climber
Crai, Craigie, Cray, Craye, Crayg, Creg, Cregge, Kraig

Crandal
(English) open
Cran, Crandall, Crandell, Crane

Crandale
(English) from the land of cranes
Crandall, Crandell

Cranley
(English) lives in a field of cranes

Cranston
(English) from the town of cranes

Crawford
(English) flowing
Crafe, Craford, Craw, Fordy

Crayton
(English) substantial
Craeton, Cray, Creighton

Creed
(American) believer
Crede, Creede, Creyd, Kreed

Creighton
(English) sophisticated
Criton

Crenshaw
(Last name as first name) good intentions

Crescin
(Latin) expansive

Crey
(English) short for Creighton; slight
Craedie, Cray, Creydie, Creigh

Creshaun
(African American)
inspired
Creshawn, Kreshaun

Cresp
(Latin) man with curls
*Crisp, Crispen, Crispun,
Crispy, Cryspin, Kresp,
Krisp, Krispin, Krispyn*

Crew
(American) word as name;
sailor
Krew

Cris
(Welsh) short for Crisiant;
crystal-like

Crisanto
(Spanish) anoint

Crisoforo
(Spanish) bearing Christ;
form of Christopher

Crispin
(Latin) man with curls
*Chrispy, Crespen, Crispo,
Crispy, Krispin, Krispo*

Crispo
(Latin) curly-haired
Crisp, Krispo

Crist
(Spanish) Christian

Cristo
(Spanish) mountain of
Christ
Kristo

Cristian
(Greek) form of Christian
Kristian

Cristobal
(Spanish) bearing Christ

Criten
(American) shortened
version of Critendon;
faultfinding
Critan, Kriten

Critendon
(Last name as first name)
critical
Crit, Criten, Krit, Kritendon

Crofton
(Irish) comforter
Croft, Croften

Crompton
(Last name as first name)
giving

Cromwell
(Irish) giving
*Chromwell, Crom,
Crommie*

Cronus
(Greek) reigning

Crosby
(Irish) easygoing
*Crosbee, Crosbie, Cross,
Krosbie, Krosby*

Croston
(English) by the cross
Cro, Croton, Kroston

Cruze
(Spanish) cross
*Cruise, Cruse, Kruise,
Kruze*

Csaba
(Hungarian) shepherd

Ctirad
(Czech) long-suffering

Cuba
(Place name) distinctive;
spicy
*Cubah, Cueba, Kueba,
Kuba*

Cubbenah
(African) Wednesday

Cucuta
(Place name) city in North
Colombia; sharp
Cucu

Cudjo
(Jamaican) Monday

Cuernavaca
(Place name) city in
Mexico; cowhorn
Vaca

Cuffy
(Jamaican) Friday
Cuffee, Cuffey

Cuke
(American) zany
Kook, Kooky, Kuke

Culbert
(Last name as first name)
practical

Culkin
(American) child actor
Culki, Kulkin

Cull
(American) selective
Cullee, Cullie, Cully, Kulley

Cullen
(Irish) attractive
*Culen, Cull, Cullan, Cullen,
Cullie, Cully, Kullen, Kully*

Culley
(Irish) secretive
*Cull, Cullie, Cully, Kull,
Kully*

Culver
(English) peaceful
*Colver, Cull, Culley, Culli,
Cully*

Culverado
(American) peaceful
*Cull, Cullan, Culver, Culvey,
Kull*

Cummings
(Literature) for the poet
E.E. Cummings; innovative
Cumming, Kummings

Cuney
(Last name as first name)
serious
Cune, Kune, Kuney

Cunning
(Irish) from surname
Cunningham; wholesome
Cuning

Cunningham
(Irish) milk-pail town;
practical
Cuningham

Curb
(American) dynamic
Kurb

Curbey
(American) form of Kirby;
high-energy
Curby

Curley
(American) cowboy
Curly, Kurly

Curran
(Irish) smiling hero
*Curan, Curr, Curren, Currey,
Currie, Curt*

Currey
(English) messenger; calm

Currie
(English) messenger;
courteous
Kurrie

Curt
(French) short for Curtis;
kind
Kurt

Curtis
(French) gracious; kind-
hearted
*Curdi, Curdis, Curt, Curtey,
Curtice, Curtie, Curtiss,
Curty, Kurt*

Custer
(Last name as first name)
watchful; stubborn
Cust, Kust, Kuster

Cuthbert
(English) intelligent

Cutler
(English) wily
Cutlar, Cutlur, Cuttie, Cutty

Cutsy
(English) from Cutler;
knife-man
*Cutlar, Cutler, Cuttie, Cutty,
Kutsee, Kutsi, Kutsy*

Cutter
(English) man who cuts
gemstones

Cuttino
(African American) athletic
Kuttino

Cuyler
(American) form of
Schuyler; protective
Kuyler

Cy
(Greek) shining example
Cye, Si

Cyler
(Irish) protective chapel
Cuyler, Cyle

Cyll
(American) bright
Syll, Cyl

Cynric
(Greek) thorn

Cyprien
(French) religious
Cyp, Cyprian

Cyprus
(Place name) island south
of Turkey; outgoing

Cyrano
(Greek) shy heart
*Cyranoh, Cyre, Cyrie,
Cyrno, Cyry*

Cyril
(Greek) regal
Ciril, Cyral, Cyrell, Cyrille

Cyrus
(Persian) sunny
Cye, Syrus

Cyrx
(American) conniving
Cyrxie

Czeslaw
(Polish) honorable
Slav, Slavek

D

Dabney
(English) careful; funny
*Dab, Dabnee, Dabnie,
Dabny*

Dacey
(Irish) southerner
*Dace, Dacian, Dacius,
Dacy, Daicey, Daicy*

Dacias
(Latin) brash
*Dace, Daceas, Dacey,
Dacy, Dayce, Daycie*

Dada
(African) curly-haired

Dade
(Place name) county in
Florida; renegade
Daide, Dayde

Daedalus
(Greek) father of Icarus;
inventor
Daidalos, Dedalus

Dag
(Scandinavian) sunny
*Dagg, Dagget, Daggett,
Dagny*

Dagan
(Hebrew) earthy
Dagon

Daggan
(Scandinavian) day

Dagny
(Scandinavian) day
Dag

Dagoberto
(Spanish) day
Dagbert, Dagobert

Dagwood
(English) comic
Dag, Dawood, Woody

Dahy
(Irish) lithe
Dahey

Dai
(Japanese) great man

Dailey
(English) from Dale; valley
Daley, Daly, Daily

Dainard
(Irish) loved
*Danehard, Danehardt,
Daneard, Daneardt,
Dainehard, Dainhard,
Daynard*

Dairus
(Invented) daring
Daras, Dares, Darus

Daithi
(Irish) speedy

Daivat
(Hindi) powerful man

Dakarai
(African) happy
Dakarrai, Dakk

Dakota
(Native American) friendly
*Daccota, Dack, Dak,
Dakoda, Dakodah,
Dakoetah, Dakotah,
Dekota, Dekohta,
Dekowta, Kota*

Dakote
(Place name) from Dakota
(states North and South
Dakota)
Dako

Dalai
(Indian) peaceful
Dalee

Dalanee
(Invented) form of Delaney
Dalaney, Dalani

Dalbert
(English) man who lives in
the valley
Del, Delbert

Dale
(English) natural
*Dail, Daile, Daley, Dallan,
Dalle, Dallin, Day, Dayl,
Dayle*

Dalen
(English) up-and-coming
*Dalan, Dalin, Dallen,
Dallin, Dalyn*

Daley
(Irish) organized
Dailey, Daily, Dale

Dalgus
(American) loving the
outdoors

Dalhart
(Place name) city in Texas
Dal

Dallas
(Place name) good old
boy; city in Texas
*Dal, Dall, Dalles, Dallice,
Dallis, Dallus, Delles*

Dallin
(English) valley-born; fine
Dal, Dallan, Dallen, Dallon

Dalsten
(English) smart
Dal, Dalston

Dalt
(English) abundant
Dall, Daltt, Daltey

Dalton
(English) farmer
Daleton, Dall, Dallton, Daltan, Dalten

Dalvis
(Invented) form of Elvis; sassy
Dal, Dalves, Dalvus, Dalvy

Daly
(Irish) together
Daley, Dawley

Dalziel
(Scottish) from the field

Damacio
(Spanish) calm; tamed
Damas, Damasio, Damaso, Damazio

Damarcus
(African American) confident
D'Marcus, Damarkes, Damarkus, Demarcus

Damario
(Spanish) tamer of wild things
Damarios, Damarius, Damaro, Damero

Damary
(Greek) tame
Damaree, Damarie

Damascus
(Place name) capital of Syria; dramatic
Damas, Damask

Damaskenos
(Greek) of Damascus; life-changing
Damascus, Damaskinos

Damaso
(Spanish) taming
Damas

Damean
(American) form of Damian; tamed
Dama, Daman, Damas, Damea

Dameetre
(Invented) form of Dmitri; audacious
Dimitri

Damek
(Czech) earth
Adamec, Adamek, Adamik, Adamok, Adha, Damick, Damicke

Damian
(Greek) fate;
(Latin) demon
Daemon, Daimen, Daimon, Daman, Dame, Damean, Damen, Dameon, Damey, Damiano, Damianos, Damianus, Damien, Damion, Damon, Damyan, Damyean, Damyen, Damyon, Damyun, Dayman, Daymian, Daymon, Demyan

Damon
(Greek) dramatic; spirited
Damonn, Damyn

Dan
(Hebrew) short for Daniel; spiritual
Dahn, Dannie, Danny

Dana
(Scandinavian) light-haired
Danah, Dane, Danie, Dayna

Danar
(English) from Denmark; dry

Danaus
(Mythology) king of Argos
Denaus, Dinaus

Dandre
(American) light
*Dan, Dandrae, Dandray,
AeAndrae, DeAndray,
Aiondrae*

Dandy
(Hindi) from Dandin;
spiritual

Dane
(English) man from
Denmark; light
*Dain, Daine, Daney, Danie,
Danyn, Dayne, Dhane*

Daneck
(American) well-liked
*Danek, Danick, Danik,
Danike, Dannick*

Danely
(Scandinavian) Danish
Dainely, Daynelee

Dang
(Vietnamese) worthy

Dangelo
(Italian) angelic
Danjelo

Danger
(American) dangerous
Dang, Dange, Dangery

Daniel
(Hebrew) judged by God;
spiritual
*Da, Danal, Dane, Daneal,
Danek, Dani, Danial,
Daniele, Danil, Danilo,
Danko, Dann, Dannel,
Danney, Danni, Dannie,
Danniel, Danny, Danyal,
Danyel, Danyell, Danyyell,
Deiniol*

Danne
(Biblical) form of Daniel;
faithful
Dann

Danner
(Last name as first name)
rescued by God
Dan, Dann, Danny

Danno
(Hebrew) kind
Dannoh, Dano

Danny
(Hebrew) short for Daniel;
spiritual
*Dan, Dann, Dannee,
Danney, Danni, Dannie*

Danon
(French) remembered
*Danen, Danhann, Dannon,
Danton*

Dante
(Latin) enduring
*Dan, Danne, Dantae,
Dantay, Dantey, Dauntay,
Dayntay, Dontae, Dontay,
Donté*

Danton
(Last name as first name)
Dan's town

Dantre
(African American) faithful
*Dantray, Dantrae, Dontre,
Dantrey, Dantri, Dantry,
Don, Dont, Dontrey, Dontri*

Dantrell
(African American) spunky
Dantrele, Dantrill, Dantrille

Danube
(Place name) flowing; river
*Dannube, Danuube,
Donau*

Daphnis
(Greek) attractive; from
Daphne

Daquan
(African American)
rambunctious
Dakwan, Daquanne,
Dequan, Dequanne,
Dekwan, Dekwohn,
Dekwohnne
Dar
(English) deerlike
Darbrie
(Irish) free man; light-
hearted
Dar, Darb, Darbree, Darbry
Darby
(Irish) free spirit
Dar, Darb, Darbee, Darbey,
Darbie, Darre, Derby
Darce
(Irish) dark
Darcy, Dars, Darsy, D'Arcy
Darcel
(French) dark
Dar, Darce, Darcelle,
Darcey, Darcy, Darsy
Darcy
(French) slow-moving
Darce, Darse, Darsey,
Darsy
Dardanos
(Greek) adored
Dar, Dardanio, Dardanios,
Dardanus
Dare
(Irish) short for Darroh;
dark
Dair, Daire, Darey
Darian
(American) inventive
Dari, Darien, Darion,
Darrian, Darrien, Darrion,
Derreynn
Darin
(Irish) great
Daren, Darren, Darrie,
Daryn

Dario
(Spanish) rich
Darioh, Darrey
Darion
(Irish) great potential
Dare, Darien, Darrion,
Daryun
Darius
(Greek) affluent
Dare, Dareas, Dareus,
Darias, Ariess, Dario,
Darious, Darrius, Derrius,
Derry
Dark
(Slavic) short for Darko;
macho
Dar, Darc
Darko
(Slavic) macho
Dark
Darlen
(American) darling
Darlan, Darlun
Darnell
(English) secretive
Dar, Darn, Darnall, Darnel,
Darnie, Darny
Darnley
(English) sly
Darold
(American) clever
Dare, Darrold, Darroll,
Derold
Daron
(Irish) great
Darren, Dayron
Darrah
(Irish) dark, strong
Darach, Darragh
Darrel
(Aboriginal) blue sky
Darral, Darrell, Darrill,
Darrol, Darroll, Darry,
Darryl, Darryll, Daryl,
Derrel, Derrell, Derril,
Derrill, Deryl, Deryll

Darrell
(French) loved man
Darel, Darol, Darrel, Darrey, Daryl, Derrel, Derrell

Darren
(Irish) great man
Daren, Darin, Daron, Darran, Darrin, Darring, Darron, Darryn, Derrin, Derron, Derry

Darrett
(American) form of Garrett; efficient
Dare, Darry

Darrien
(Greek) with riches
Darian, Darion, Darrian, Darrion, Darryan, Darryen

Darroh
(English) armed; bright
Dare, Daro, Darrie, Darro, Darrohye, Darrow

Darrti
(American) fast; deer
Dart, Darrt

Darryl
(French) darling man
Darrie, Daryl, Derrie, Deryl, Deryll

Darshan
(African American) pious

Dart
(English) decisive
Darte, Dartt

D'Artagnan
(French) leader; ostentatious

Darton
(English) swift; deer

Darwin
(English) dearest friend
Dar, Darwen, Darwinne, Darwon, Darwyn, Derwin, Derwynn

Daryn
(American) form of Darren
Darynn, Deryn

Dash
(American) speedy; dashing
Dashy

Dashawn
(African American) unusual
D'Sean, D'Shawn, Dashaun, Deshaun, Deshawn

Dashell
(African American) dashing
Dashiell

Dasher
(American) dashing; fast
Dash

Dathan
(Biblical) fountain of hope

Davao
(Place name) city in the Philippines; exotic
Davo

Dave
(Hebrew) short for David; loved
Davey, Davi, Davie, Davy

Daven
(American) form of Dave; dashing
Davan

Davenport
(Last name as first name) of the old school; sea-loving

Davey
(Hebrew) short for David; loved
Dave, Davee, Davi, Davie, Davy

Davian
   (Hebrew) dear one
   Daivian, Daivyan, Daveon,
   Davien, Davion, Davyan,
   Davyen, Davyon

David
   (Hebrew) beloved
   Daffy, Daffyd, Dafydd, Dai,
   Davad, Dave, Daved,
   Davee, Daven, Davey,
   Davi, Davide, Davie,
   Davies, Davin, Davis,
   Davon, Davy, Davyd,
   Davydd

David-Drue
   (American) combo of
   David and Drue; sweet
   and loved
   David-Drew, David-Dru,
   David Drue

Davidpaul
   (American) beloved
   David-Paul

Davidson
   (English) son of David
   Davidsen, Davison

Davin
   (Scandinavian) smart
   Dave, Daven, Dayven

Davins
   (American) from David;
   smart
   Davens

Davis
   (Welsh) David's son;
   heart's child
   Dave, Daves, Davidson,
   Davies, Davison, Daviss,
   Davy

Davon
   (American) sweet
   Davaughan, Davaughn,
   Dave, Davone, Devon

Davonnae
   (African American) from
   David; loved
   Davawnae, Davonae

Davonte
   (African American)
   energetic
   D'Vontay, Davontay,
   Devonta

Daw
   (English) quiet
   Dawe, Dawes

Dawber
   (Last name as first name)
   funny
   Daw, Dawb, Dawbee,
   Dawbey, Dawby, Daws

Dawk
   (American) spirited
   Dawkins

Daws
   (English) dedicated
   Daw, Dawsen, Dawz

Dawson
   (English) David's son;
   loved
   Daw, Dawe, Dawes,
   Dawsan, Dawse, Dawsen,
   Dawsey, Dawsin

Dax
   (French) unique; water-
   loving
   Dacks, Daxie

Day
   (English) calm
   Daye

Dayanand
   (Hindi) a loving man

Daymond
   (Invented) compassionate

Dayton
   (English) the town of
   David; planner
   Daeton, Day, Daye,
   Daytan, Daytawn, Dayten,
   Deytawn, Deyton

Deacon
(Greek) giving
Deakin, Decon, Deecon, Deekon, Dekawn, Deke, Dekie, Dekon, Diakonos

Deagan
(Last name as first name) capable
Degan

Deal
(Last name as first name) wheeler-dealer
Deale

Dean
(English) calming
Deane, Deanie, Deany, Deen, Dene, Deyn, Dino

DeAndré
(African American) very masculine
D'André, DeAndrae, DeAndray, Diandray, Diondrae, Diondray

Deangelo
(Italian) sweet; personable
D'Angelo, Dang, Dange, DeAngelo, Deanjelo, Deeanjelo, DiAngelo, Di-Angelo

Deans
(English) sylvan; valley
Dean, Deaney, Deanie

Deanthony
(African American) rambunctious
Deanthe, Deanthoney, Deanthonie, Deeanthie, Dianth

Deanza
(Spanish) smooth
Denza

Dearborn
(Last name as first name) endearing; kind from birth
Dearbourn, Dearburne, Deerborn

Dearing
(Last name as first name) endearing
Dear

Dearon
(American) dear one
Dear

Deason
(Invented) cocky
Deace, Deas, Dease, Deasen, Deasun

Debonair
(French) with a beautiful air; elegant and cultured
Debonaire, Debonnair, Debonnaire

Debythis
(African American) strange
Debiathes

Decatur
(Place name) city in Illinois; special
Dec, Decatar, Decater, Deck

Deccan
(Place name) region in India; scholar
Dec, Dek

Decimus
(Latin) tenth child
Decio

Deck
(Irish) short for Declan; strong; devout
Decky

Declan
(Irish) strong; prayerful
Dec, Deck, Dek, Deklan, Deklon

Deddrick
(American) form of Deidrich; substantial
Dead, Dedric, Dedrick, Dedrik, Dietrich

Dedeaux
(French) sweet
Dede, Dee
Dedric
(German) leader
Dedrick, Deidrich
Dee
(American) short for
names that start with D
D, De
Deek
(American) short for
Deacon; leader
Deke
Deems
(English) merits
Deepak
(Sanskrit) light of
knowledge
Depak, Depakk, Dipak
Deeter
(American) friendly
Deter
DeForest
(French) of the forest
Defforest
DeFoy
(French) child of Foy
Defoy, Defoye
Degraf
(French) child of Graf
DeGraf
Deidrich
(German) leader
*Dedric, Dedrick, Deed,
Deide, Deidrick, Diedrich*
Deinol
(Greek) form of Daniel;
judged by God
Deinorus
(African American)
vigorous
Denorius, Denorus

Deion
(Greek) form of
Dion/Deone (god of wine);
fun-loving; charismatic
Dee
Dejuan
(African American)
talkative
*Dajuan, Dajuwan,
Dejuane, Dejuwan,
Dewaan, Dewan,
Dewaughan, Dewon,
Dewonn, Dewuan Dwon,
Dwonn, Dwonne*
Deke
(Hebrew) from Dekel;
brilliant; sturdy tree
Deek, Dekel
Del
(English) valley; laid-back
and helpful
Dail, Dell, Delle
Delaney
(Irish) challenging
*Del, Delaine, Delainey,
Delainie, Delane, Delanie,
Delany, Dell*
Delano
(Irish) dark
Del, Delaynoh, Dell
Delbert
(English) sunny
*Bert, Bertie, Berty,
Dalbert, Del, Delburt, Dell,
Dilbert*
Delete
(Origin unknown) ordinary
Delette
Delfino
(Spanish) dolphin;
sealoving
Define, Fino
Delgado
(Spanish) slim

Delius
(Greek) from Delos
Deli, Delia, Delios, Delos

Dell
(English) from the country;
sparkles

Delling
(Norse) shines

Delmar
(Last name as first name)
friendly
Delm

Delmer
(American) country
Del, Delmar, Delmir

Delmis
(Spanish) friend
Del, Delms

Delmore
(French) seagoing
*Del, Delmar, Delmer,
Delmor, Delmoor,
Delmoore*

Delmy
(American) from French
Delmore; seagoing
Delmi

Delphin
(French) dolphin
*Delfin, Delfino, Delfinos,
Delfinus, Delphino,
Delphinos, Delphinus,
Delvin*

Delroy
(French) royal; special
*Del, Dell, Dellroy, Delroi,
Roi, Roy*

Delsi
(American) easygoing
*Delci, Delcie, Dels, Delsee,
Delsey, Delsy*

Delt
(American) fraternity boy
Delta

Delton
(English) friend
Delt, Deltan, Delten

Delvan
(English) form of Delwin;
friend
*Del, Dell, Delly, Delven,
Delvin, Delvun, Delvyn*

Delwin
(English) companion
*Dalwin, Dalwyn, Delavan,
Delevan, Dellwin, Delwins,
Delwince, Delwen,
Delwinse, Delwy, Delwyn*

Demarco
(Italian) daring
*D'Marco, Deemarko,
Demarkoe, Demie,
Demmy, Dimarco*

Demarcus
(American) zany; royal
*Damarcus, DaMarkiss,
DeMarco, DeMarcus,
Demarkes, Demarkess,
DeMarko, DeMarkus,
Demarkus, DeMarquess,
DeMarquez, Demarquiss,
DeMarquiss*

Demario
(Italian) bold
*D'Mareo, D'Mario,
Demarioh, Demarrio,
Demie, Demmy, Dimario*

Demarques
(African American) son of
Marques; noble
*Demark, Demarkes,
Demarquis, Demmy*

Demas
(Greek) well-liked
Dimas

Demete
(American) from Greek
Demetrius; a saint
Deme, Demetay

Demetrice
(Greek) form of
Demetrius; fertile

Demetrick
(African American) earthy
Demetrik, Demi, Demitrick

Demetrios
(Greek) earth-loving
*Demeetrius, Demetreus,
Demetri, Demetrious,
Demetris, Demi, Demie*

Demetrius
(Greek) form of Demeter,
goddess of fertility
*Dametrius, Dem, Demetri,
Demetrice, Demetris,
Demitrios, Demmy,
Demos, Dhimitrios,
Dimetre, Dimitri, Dimitrios,
Dimitrious, Dimitry, Dmitri,
Dmitrios, Dmitry*

Demitri
(Greek) fertile; earthy
*Demetrie, Demetry, Demi,
Demie, Demitry, Dmitri*

Demond
(African American) worldly
Demonde

Demos
(Greek) of the people
Demas, Demmos

Demosthenes
(Greek) orator; eloquent
Demos

Demps
(Irish) form of Dempsey;
sturdy
Dempse, Dempse, Dempz

Dempsey
(Irish) respected; judge
*Dem, Demi, Demps,
Dempsie, Dempsy*

Den
(Greek) short for Dennis;
reveler

Denali
(Hindi) great

Denard
(Last name as first name)
envied
*Den, Denar, Denarde,
Denny*

Denby
(Scandinavian)
adventurous
*Danby, Denbee, Denbey,
Denbie, Denney, Dennie,
Denny*

Dene
(Hungarian) reveler

Denham
(Scandinavian) hamlet of
Danes

Denholm
(Scandinavian) house of
Danes

Deni
(English) form of
Dionysius, god of revelry
and wine; festive
Denni

Denis
(Greek) reveler
Den, Denese, Dennis

Denk
(American) sporty
Denky, Dink

Denley
(English) dark
Denlie, Denly

Denman
(English) dark; valley-
dweller
*Den, Deni, Denmin,
Denney, Denni, Dennie,
Dennman, Denny, Dinman*

Denmark
(Scandinavian) place as
name; from Denmark

Dennis
(Greek) reveler
*Den, Denes, Deni, Denies,
Denis, Deniss, Dennes,
Dennet, Denney, Denni,
Dennie, Dennies,
Dennison, Denniz, Denny,
Dennys, Deno, Denys,
Deon, Dino, Dion,
Dionisio, Dionysius,
Dionysus, Diot*

Dennisen
(English) Dennis's son;
partier
*Den, Denison, Dennison,
Dennizon, Dennyson,
Tennyson*

Denny
(Greek) short for Dennis;
fun-loving
*Den, Denee, Deni, Denney,
Denni*

Denton
(English) valley
settlement; happy
*Denny, Dent, Dentan,
Denten, Dentie, Dentin*

Denver
(Place name) capital of
Colorado; climber
Den, Denny

Denzel
(English) sensual
*Den, Denny, Densie, Denz,
Denze, Denzell, Denzelle,
Denziel, Denzil, Denzill,
Denzille, Denzyl, Denzylle,
Dinzie*

Deodar
(Sanskrit) cedar

Deondray
(African American)
romantic
*Deandre, Deeon,
Deondrae, Deondrey,
Deone*

Deone
(Greek) short for
Dionysius, god of wine;
fun-loving; charismatic
*Deion, Deonah, Deonne,
Dion*

Deonté
(French) outgoing
*De'On, Deontae, Deontay,
Deontie, Diontay,
Diontayye*

Deordre
(African American)
outgoing
Deordray

Deotis
(African American) combo
of De and Otis; scholar
Deo, Deoh, Deotus

Depp
(American) dashing
Dep

Derald
(American) combo of
Harold and Derrell; content
Deral, Dere, Derry, Deruld

Derby
(Irish) guileless
Derbey, Derbie

Derek
(German) ruler; bold heart
*Darrick, Darriq, Derak,
Dere, Dereck, Deric,
Derick, Derik, Deriq,
Deriqk, Derk, Derreck,
Derrek, Derrick, Derrik,
Derryck, Derryk, Deryk,
Deryke, Dirk, Dirke, Dyrk*

Derland
(English) from the land of
deer
Durland

Derlin
(English) from Derland,
deer land; sly
*Derl, Derlan, Derland,
Derlen, Derlyn, Durland,
Durlin*

Dermod
(Irish) from Dermot;
guileless; thoughtful
Dermud

Dermond
(Irish) unassuming
*Dermon, Dermun,
Dermund, Derr*

Dermot
(Irish) unabashed; giving
*Der, Dermod, Dermott,
Derree, Derrey, Derri,
Diarmid, Diarmuid*

Deron
(African American)
variation on Darren; smart
*Dare, Daron, DaRon,
Darone, Darron, Dayron,
Dere, DeRronn*

Derrell
(French) another form of
Darrell; loved
Dere, Derrel, Derrill

Derri
(American) breezy
Derree, Derry

Derrick
(German) bold heart
Derak, Derick

Derry
(Irish) red-haired
*Dare, Darry, Derrey, Derri,
Derrie*

Derward
(Last name as first name)
clunky
*Der, Derr, Derwy, Dur, Durr,
Ward*

Derwent
(Last name as first name)
of deer

Derwin
(English) bookish
*Darwin, Darwyn, Derwyn,
Derwynn, Durwen, Durwin*

Des
(Irish) short for Desmond;
delightful

Deseo
(Spanish) desire
Des, Desi, Dezi

Deshan
(Hindi) patriot
Deshad, Deshal

Deshawn
(African American) brassy
*D'Sean, D'Shawn,
Dashaun, Dashawn,
Desean, Deshaun,
Deshaune, Deshawnn,
Deshon*

Deshea
(American) confident
*Desh, DeShay, Deshay,
Deshie*

Deshon
(African American) bold;
open
Desh, Deshan, Deshann

Desiderio
(Italian, Spanish)
desirable
*Deri, Derito, Des, Desi,
Desideratus, Desiderios,
Desiderius, Desie, Diderot,
Didier, Dizier*

Desire
(American) desirable
Des, Desi, Desidero

Desmee
(Irish) form of Desmond;
from Munster, Ireland
*Desi, Dessy, Dezme,
Dezmee, Desmey, Dezmie,
Dezmo, Dezzy*

Desmond
(Irish) from Munster,
Ireland; profound
*Des, Desi, Desmon,
Desmund, Dezmond,
Dizmond*

Desmun
(Irish) form of Desmond;
wise
Dez, Dezmund

Desperado
(Spanish) renegade
*Des, Desesperado, Dessy,
Dezzy*

Destin
(Place name) city in
Florida; destiny; fate
*Desten, Destie, Deston,
Destrie*

Detleff
(Germanic) decisive
Detlef, Detlev

Detroy
(African American)
outgoing
Detroe

Detton
(Last name as first name)
determined
Deet, Dett

Deuce
(American) two in cards;
second child
Doos, Duz

DeUndre
(African American) child of
Undre
*Deundrae, DeUndray,
Deundry*

Dev
(Irish) short for Devlin;
from Dublin; poetic
Deb, Deo

Deval
(Hindi) Godlike
Deven

Devann
(American) divine child
DeVanne, Deven

Devaughan
(American) bravado
*Devan, Devaughn,
Devonne*

Devdan
(Hindi) God's gift
Debdan, Deodan

Devender
(American) poetic
Devander, Deven, Devendar

Deverell
(American) special
*Dev, Devee, Deverel,
Deverelle, Devie, Devy*

Devereux
(French surname) divine
Deveraux

Devin
(Irish) poetic; writer
*Dev, Devan, Deven,
Devinn, Devon, Devvy,
Devyn, Devynn*

Devine
(Latin) divine
Dev, Devinne

Devinson
(Irish) poetic
*Dev, Devan, Devee, Deven,
Davin, Devy*

Devland
(Irish) courageous
*Dev, Devlend, Devlind,
Devvy*

Devlin
(Irish) fearless
*Devlan, Devlen, Devlon,
Devlyn, Devy*

Devo
(American) quirky; fun
Divo

Devon
(Irish) writer
*Deavon, Dev, Deven,
Devin, Devohne, Devond,
Devonn, Devy, Devyn*

Devonte
(African American)
variation on Devon;
outgoing
Devontae, Devontay

Dewayne
(American) spirited
*Dewain, Dewaine, Duwain,
Dwain*

Dewey
(Welsh) valued
*Dew, Dewi, Dewie, Dewy,
Duey*

Dewitt
(English) fair-haired
*Dewie, DeWitt, Dwight,
Witt, Wittie, Witty*

DeWittay
(African American) witty
Dewitt, De Witt, Witt, Witty

Dewon
(African American) clever
Dejuan, Dewan

Dex
(Latin) from Dexter; right-
handed; hearty
Dexe

Dexee
(American) short for
Dexter; lucky
Dex, Dexey, Dexi, Dexie

Dexter
(Latin) skillful; right-
handed
*Decster, Dex, Dext,
Dextah, Dextar, Dextor*

Dezi
(Irish) form of Desi; from
S. Munster, Ireland

Diablo
(Spanish) devil

Diamon
(American) luminous
Dimon, Dimun, Diamund

Diamond
(English) bright; gem
*Dimah, Dime, Dimond,
Dimont*

Diarmid
(Irish) happy for others'
successes
Diarmaid, Diarmait, Diarmi

Diaz
(Spanish) rowdy
Dias, Diazz

Dice
(English) risk-taking
*Dicey, Dies, Dize, Dyce,
Dyse*

Dick
(German) short for
Richard; ruler who
dominates
*Dickey, Dicki, Dickie,
Dicky, Dik*

Dickens
(Literature) for Charles
Dickens; articulate

Dickinson
(Last name as first name)
poetic

Dickon
(Last name as first name)
strong king

Didier
(French) desirable

Diedrich
(German) form of Dedrick;
ruler
*Dedric, Dedrick, Deed,
Died, Dietrich*

Diego
(Spanish) untamed; wild
*Dago, Deago, Deagoh,
Dee, Diago*

Diesel
(American) rugged
*Dees, Deez, Desel, Dezsel,
Diezel*

Dieter
(German) prepared
*Dedrick, Deke, Derek,
Detah, Deter, Diederick,
Dirk*

Dietmar
(German) famous

Digby
(Irish) man of simplicity

Diggory
(French) lost
Diggery, Diggorey, Digory

Dijon
(Place name) city in
France; refined
Dejawn

Dilip
(Hindi) protests; royal
Duleep

Dill
(Irish) faithful
Dillard, Dilly

Dillion
(Irish) from Dillon; loyal

Dillon
(Irish) devoted
*Dill, Dillan, Dillen, Dilly,
Dilon, Dylan, Dylanne,
Dyllon, Dylon*

Dimas
(Spanish) frank

Dimitri
(Russian) fertile;
flourishing
*Demetry, Demi, Demitri,
Demitry, Dmitri*

Dinesh
(Hindi) day lord

Dingo
(Animal) wild spirit

Dino
(Italian) short for Dean;
little sword
*Dean, Deanie, Deano,
Deinoh, Dinoh*

Dinos
(Greek) short for
Constantine; proud
Dean, Dino, Dinohs, Dynos

Dinose
(American) form of Dino;
joyful
*Denoze, Dino, Dinoce,
Dinoz, Dinoze*

Dins
(American) climber
Dinse, Dinz

Dinsdale
(English) hill protector;
innovator

Dinsmore
(Irish) guarded
*Dinnie, Dinnsmore, Dinny,
Dins*

Diogenes
(Greek) honest man
Dee, Dioge, Dioh

Dion
(Greek) short for
Dionysius, god of wine;
reveler
*Deion, Deon, Deonn,
Deonys, Deyon, Dio,
Dionn*

Dionisio
(Spanish) from Dionysius, god of wine and revelry; reveler
Dionis, Dioniso, Dionysio

Dionysus
(Greek) joyous celebrant; god of wine
Dee, Deonysios, Dion, Dionio, Dioniso, Dionysios, Dionysius, Dionysos, Dionysus

Dirk
(Scandinavian) leader
Derk, Dierck, Dieric, Dierick, Dirck, Dirke, Dirky, Durk,

Diron
(American) form of Darren; great
Diran, Dirun, Dyronn

Dit
(Hungarian) short for Ditrik

Dix
(American) energetic
Dex

Dixie
(American) southerner
Dix, Dixee, Dixey, Dixi

Dixon
(English) Dick's son; happy
Dickson, Dix, Dixie, Dixo

Doan
(English) hills; quiet
Doane, Doe

Dobbs
(English) fire

Dobes
(American) unassuming
Dobe, Doe

Dobie
(American) reliable; southern
Dobe, Dobee, Dobey, Dobi

Dobromir
(Polish) good
Dobe, Dobry, Doby

Dobry
(Polish) good
Dobe, Dobree, Dobrey

Doc, Dock
(American) short for doctor; physician
Dok

Dodd
(English) swaggering; has a small-town sheriff feel
Dod

Dodge
(English) swaggering
Dod, Dodds, Dodgson

Dody
(Greek) God's gift
Doe

Dog
(American) good buddy
Daug, Dawg, Dogg, Doggie, Doggy

Doherty
(Irish) rash
Docherty, Doh, Doughertey, Douherty

Dolan
(Irish) dark
Dolen

Dolf
(German) short for Rudolph; wolf
Dolfe, Dolfie, Dolfy, Dolph, Dophe

Dolgen
(American) tenacious
Dole, Dolg, Dolgan, Dolgin

Dolon
(Irish) brunette
Dole, Dolen, Dolton

Dolph
(German) noble wolf
Dolf, Dollfus, Dollfuss, Dollphus, Dolphus

Dom
(Latin) short for Dominic, saint; of the Lord
Dome, Dommie, Dommy

Domenico
(Italian) confident
Dom, Domeniko

Domingo
(Spanish) Sunday-born boy
Demingo, Dom, Domin, Dominko

Dominic
(Latin) child of the Lord; saint
Demenico, Demingo, Dom, Domenic, Domenico, Domenique, Domingo, Domini, Dominick, Dominie, Dominik, Dominique, Domino, Dominy, Nick

Dominique
(French) spiritual
Dom, Dominick, Dominike, Domminique

Domino
(Latin) winner
Domeno, Dominoh, Domuno

Don
(Scottish) short for Donald; powerful
Dahn, Doni, Donn, Donney, Donni, Donnie, Donny

Donaciano
(Spanish) dark
Dona, Donace, Donae, Donase

Donahue
(Irish) fighter
Don, Donahoe, Donohue, Donohue

Donald
(Scottish) world leader; powerful
Don, Donal, Donaldo, Donall, Donalt, Donaugh, Donel, Doneld, Donelson, Donild, Donn, Donnel, Donnell, Donney, Donni, Donnie, Donny

Donatello
(Italian) giving
Don, Donatelo, Donetello, Donny, Tello

Donatien
(French) generous
Don, Donatyen, Donn, Donnatyen

Donato
(Italian) donates

Donder
(Dutch) thunder

Dong
(Chinese) from the east

Donnan
(Irish) brown-haired; popular

Donnell
(Irish) courageous
Dahn, Don, Donel, Donell, Donhelle, Donnie, Donny

Donnelly
(Irish) righteous
Donalee, Donally, Donelli, Donely, Donn, Donnell Donnellie, Donnie

Donnis
(American) from Donald; dark; regal
Don, Donnes, Donnus

Donny
(Irish) fond leader
Donney, Donni, Donnie

Donovan
(Irish) combative
Don, Donavan, Donavon, Donavaughn, Donavyn, Donevin, Donevon, Donivin, Donny, Donoven, Donovon

Don Quixote
(Literature) an original

Dont
(American) dark; giving
Don, Dontay

Dontae
(African American) capricious
Dontay, Donté

Dontave
(African American) wild spirit
Dontav, Donteve

Dontavious
(African American) giving
Dantavius, Dawntavius, Dewontavius, Dontavious

Donté
(Italian) lasting forever
Dantae, Dantay, Dohntae, Dontae, Dontay, Dontey

Donton
(American) confident
Don, Donnee, Dont, Dontie

Dontrell
(African American) jaded
Dontray, Dontree, Dontrel, Dontrelle, Dontrey, Dontrie, Dontrill

Donyale
(African American) regal; dark
Donyel, Donyelle

Donyell
(African American) loyal
Donny, Danyel, Donyal

Donzell
(African American) form of Denzel
Dons, Donsell, Donz, Donzelle

Doocey
(American) clever
Dooce, Doocee, Doocie, Doos

Dooley
(Irish) shy hero
Doolee, Dooli, Dooly

Dor
(Aboriginal) energetic
Doram, Doriel, Dorli

Doran
(Irish) adventurer
Dore, Dorian, Doron, Dorran, Dorren

Dorian
(Greek) the sea's child; mysterious; youthful forever
Dora, Dore, Dorean, Dorey, Dorie, Dorien, Dorrian, Dorrien, Dorryen, Dory

Dorman
(Last name as first name) practical
Dor, Dorm

Doron
(Greek) unlimited passion
Doran, Doroni

Dorral
(Last name as first name) vain
Dorale, Dorry

Dorset
(Place name) county in England
Dorsett, Dorzet

Dorsey
(French) sturdy as a fortress
Dorsee, Dorsie

Dotan
(African) hardworking
Dotann

Dotson
(Last name as first name)
loquacious; son of Dot
Dotsen, Dottson

Dov
(Hebrew) bear

Doug
(Scottish) short for
Douglas; strong
Dougie, Dougy, Dug, Dugy

Dougal
(Irish) dark, mysterious
*Doyle, Dougall, Dugal,
Dugald, Dugall*

Douglas
(Scottish) powerful; dark
river
*Doug, Douggie, Dougie,
Douglace, Douglass,
Douglis, Dugaid*

Dovie
(American) peaceable
*Dove, Dovee, Dovey, Dovi,
Dovy*

Dow
(Irish) brunette
Dowan, Dowe, Dowson

Dowd
(American) serious
Doud, Dowdy, Dowed

Doyal
(American) form of Doyle;
dark and unusual
Doile, Doyl, Doyle

Doyle
(Irish) deep; dark
Doil, Doy, Doyal, Doye, Doyl

Doylton
(Last name as first name)
pretentious
Doyl, Doyle

Dracy
(American) form of Stacy;
secretive
*Dra, Drace, Dracee,
Dracey, Draci, Drase,
Drasee, Drasi*

Dradell
(American) serious
Drade, Dray

Drake
(English) dragonlike; fire-
breathing
Drago, Drakie, Drako

Draper
(English) precise; maker of
drapes
Draiper, Drape

Dravey
(American) groovy
Dravee, Dravie, Dravy

Drew
(Welsh) wise; well-liked
Dru, Druw

Drexel
(American) thoughtful
Drex

Dries
(Dutch) brave
Dre

Driscoll
(Irish) pensive
Driscol, Drisk, Driskell

Dru
(English) wise; popular
Drew, Drue

Drummond
(Scottish) practical
Drum, Drumon, Drumond

Drury
(French) loving man
*Drew, Drewry, Dru, Drure,
Drurey, Drurie*

Dryden
(English) writer; calm
Driden, Drydan, Drydin

Drystan
(Welsh) form of Tristan; mourning
Drestan, Dristan, Drystyn

Duane
(Irish) dark man
Dewain, Dewayne, Duain, Duwain, Duwaine, Duwayne, Dwain, Dwaine, Dwayne

Dub
(Irish) short for Dublin; friendly
Dubby

Dublin
(Place name) city in Ireland; trendy

Duc
(Vietnamese) honest

Dude
(American) cool guy

Dudley
(English) compromiser; rich; stuffy
Dud, Dudd, Dudlee, Dudlie, Dudly

Dueart
(American) kind
Art, Duart, Due, Duey

Duff
(Scottish) dark
Duf, Duffey, Duffie, Duffy

Dugan
(Irish) dark man
Doogan, Dougan, Douggan, Duggan, Duggie, Duggy, Dugin

Duke
(Latin) leader of the pack
Dook, Dukey, Dukie

Dumisani
(African) leader

Dumont
(French) monumental
Dummont, Dumon, Dumonde, Dumonte, Dumontt

Dunbar
(Irish) castle-dweller
Dunbarr

Dunbaron
(American) dark
Baron, Dunbar

Duncan
(Scottish) spirited fighter
Dunc, Dunk, Dunkan, Dunn, Dunne

Dundee
(Australian) spunky

Dunham
(Last name as first name) dark

Dunia
(American) dark
Dunya

Dunk
(Scottish) form of Duncan; dark; combative
Dunc, Dunk

Dunlavy
(English) sylvan
Dunlave

Dunley
(English) meadow-loving
Dunlea, Dunlee, Dunleigh, Dunli, Dunlie, Dunly, Dunnlea, Dunnleigh, Dunnley

Dunlop
(English) sylvan

Dunmore
(Scottish) guarded
Dun, Dunmohr, Dunmoore

Dunn
(Irish) neutral
Dun, Dunne

Dunphy
(American) dark; serious
*Dun, Dunphe, Dunphee,
Dunphey*

Dunstan
(English) well-girded
*Dun, Duns, Dunse,
Dunsten, Dunstin, Dunston*

Dunstand
(English) form of Dunstan;
protected
*Dunsce, Dunse, Dunst,
Dunsten, Dunstun*

Duran
(Last name as first name)
lasting; musical
Durann, Durante, Durran

Durand
(Latin) from Durant;
dependable
Duran, Durayn

Durant
(Latin) lasting; alluring
*Dante, Duran, Durand,
Durante, Durr, Durrie,
Durry*

Durban
(Place name) city in South
Africa
Durb, Durben

Durham
(Last name as first name)
supportive
Duram

Duro
(Place name) Palo Duro
Canyon; enduring
Dure

Durrell
(English) protective
*Durel, Durell, Durr, Durrel,
Durry*

Durward
(English) gatekeeper

Durwin
(English) dear friend
*Derwin, Derwyn, Durwen,
Durwinn, Durwyn*

Durwood
(English) vigilant; home-
loving
*Derrwood, Derwood, Durr,
Durrwood, Durwould,
Durward*

Duryea
(Hindi) invincible

Duster
(American) form of Dusty;
deliberate
*Dust, Dustee, Dustey,
Dusti, Dusty*

Dustin
(German) bold and brave
*Dust, Dustan, Dusten,
Duston, Dustie, Dusty,
Dustyn*

Dusty
(German) short for Dustin;
brave
*Dust, Dustee, Dustey,
Dusti, Dustie*

Dusty-Joe
(American) cowboy
*Dustee, Dusti, Dusty,
Dustyjoe, Joe*

Dutch
(Dutch) from Holland;
optimistic
Dutchie, Dutchy

Duval
(French) valley; peaceful
*Dovahl, Duv, Duvall,
Duvalle*

Dwain
(American) form of
Dwayne; country; dark
Dwaine

Dwan
(African American) fresh
D'wan, D'Wan, Dewan, Dwawn, Dwon

Dwanae
(African American) dark; small
Dwannay

Dwayne
(American) country
Duane, Duwain, Duwane, Duwayne, Dwain, Dwaine

Dweezel
(American) creative
Dweez, Dweezil

Dwight
(English) intelligent; white
Dwi, Dwite

Dwyer
(Irish) wise
Dwire, Dwyyer

Dyer
(English) creative
Di, Dier, Dyar, Dye

Dylan
(Welsh) sea god; creative
Dill, Dillan, Dillon, Dilloyn, Dilon, Dyl, Dylahn, Dylen, Dylin, Dyllan, Dylon, Dylonn

Dynell
(African American) seaman; gambler
Dinell, Dyne

Dyron
(African American) mercurial; sea-loving
Diron, Dyronn, Dyronne

Dyson
(English) sea-loving
Dieson, Dison, Dysan, Dysen, Dysun, Dyzon

Dyvet
(English) worker; dyes
Dye

Eagan
(Irish) form of Egan; intense
Egan, Egon

Eagle
(Native American) sharp-eyed
Eagal, Egle

Eamon
(Irish) form of Edmund; thriving; protective
Amon, Eamen, Emon

Earl
(English) promising; noble
Earle, Earley, Earlie, Early, Eril, Erl

Early
(English) punctual
Earl, Earlee, Earley

Earnest
(English) genuine
Earn, Earnie, Ern, Ernie

Earon
(American) form of Aaron
Earonn

Earvin
(English) sea-loving
Dervin, Ervin

Easey
(American) easygoing
Easy, Ezey

East
(English) from the east
Easte

Easton
(English) outdoorsy; east town
Easten

Eaton
(English) wealthy
Eaten, Etawn, Eton

Eaves
(English) edges by

Eb
(Hebrew) short for
Ebenezer; helpful man

Ebby
(Hebrew) short for
Ebenezer; rock; reliable
Ebbey, Ebbi

Eben
(Hebrew) helpful; loud
Eban

Ebenezer
(Hebrew) base of life; rock
*Eb, Ebbie, Ebby, Eben,
Ebeneezer, Ebeneser*

Eberhardt
(German) brave
Eb, Eber, Eberhard

Ebo
(African) Tuesday-born

Eckhardt
(German) iron-willed
*Eck, Eckhard, Eckhart,
Ekhard*

Ed
(English) short for Edward
Edd, Eddie, Eddy, Edy

Edan
(Scottish) fiery
Edon

Edbert
(German) courageous
Ediberto

Edcell
(English) focused; wealthy
Ed, Edcelle, Eds, Edsel

Eddie
(English) short for Edward
Eddee, Eddey, Eddy

Edel
(German) of noble birth
Adel, Edelmar, Edelweiss

Eden
(Hebrew) delight
*Eadon, Edin, Edon, Edye,
Edyn*

Edenson
(Hebrew) son of Eden;
delight
Edence, Edens, Edensen

Edgar
(English) success
Ed, Eddie, Edghur, Edgur

Edgard
(English) spear thrower
Ed, Eddie, Edgarde

Edgardo
(English) successful
Edgar, Edgard, Edgardoh

Edge
(American) cutting edge;
trendsetter
Eddge, Edgy

Edilberto
(Spanish) noble
Edilbert

Edison
(English) Edward's son;
smart
Ed, Eddie, Edisen, Edyson

Edmond
(English) protective
Ed, Edmon, Edmund

Edmund
(English) protective
Ed, Eddie, Edmond

Edrick
(English) rich leader;
(American) laughing
Ed, Edri, Edrik, Edry

Edsel
(English) rich
Ed, Eddie, Edsil, Edsyl

Eduardo
(Spanish) flirtatious
Ed, Eddie, Edwardo

Edward
(English) prospering;
defender
*Ed, Eddey, Eddi, Eddie,
Eddy, Edwar, Edwerd*

Edwin
(English) prosperous
friend
Ed, Edwinn, Edwynn

Efrain
(Hebrew) fertile
Efren

Efrim
(Hebrew) short for
Ephraim
Ef, Efrem, Efrum

Efton
(American) form of
Ephraim; (Hebrew) fruitful
Ef, Eft, Eften, Eftun

Egan
(Irish) spirited
Eggie, Egin, Egon

Egbert
(English) bright sword
Egber, Egburt, Eggie, Eggy

Egborn
(English) ready; born of
Edgar
*Eg, Egbornem, Egburn,
Eggie*

Egerton
(English) town of a
spearman
*Edgarton, Edgartown,
Edgerton, Egeton*

Eghert
(German) smart
Eghertt, Eghurt

Egil
(Scandinavian) the
sword's edge
Eigil

Egmon
(German) protective
*Egmond, Egmont, Egmun,
Egmund, Egmunt*

Egeus
(American) protective
Aegis, Egis

Egon
(Irish) passionate

Egypt
(Place name)mysterious;
majestic

Ehren
(Hebrew) form of Aaron;
aware

Eikki
(African) strong

Einar
(Scandinavian) lone
fighter

Ekon
(African) muscular

El
(English) old friend

Elam
(Hebrew) from Eliam; God-
centered; distinctive

Elan
(French) finesse
Elann, Elen, Elon, Elyn

Elbis
(American) exalted
Elb, Elbace, Elbase, Elbus

Elbridge
(American) presidential
Elb, Elby

Elder
(English) older sibling
El, Eldor

Eldon
(English) charitable
Edwin, El, Elden, Eldin

Eldorado
(Place name) city in
Arkansas (El Dorado)
El, Eld, Eldor

Eldread
(English) wise advisor
El, Eldred, Eldrid

Eldridge
(English) supportive
Eldredge

Eleazar
(Hebrew) helped by God
*Elazar, Eleasar, Eliasar,
Eliazar, Elieser, Elizar*

Elger
(German) of noble birth
Elger, Ellgar, Ellger

Elgin
(English) elegant
Elgen

Elegy
(Spanish) memorable
Elegee, Elegie, Elgy

Elendor
(Invented) special
Elen, Elend

Eli
(Hebrew) faithful man;
high priest
El, Elie, Eloy, Ely

Elian
(Spanish) spirited
Eliann, Elyan

Elias
(Greek) spiritual
El, Eli, Eliace, Elyas

Eliezer
(Origin unknown) of God
Elieser, Elyeser

Elighie
(American) form of Elijah;
sophisticated, classy

Elihu
(Hebrew) true believer
Elih, Eliu, Ellihu

Elijah
(Hebrew) religious; Old
Testament prophet
El, Elie, Elija

Elijah-Blue
(American) combo of
Elijah and Blue; devout
Elijah-Bleu, Elijah-Blu

Eliseo
(Spanish) daring
Elizeo

Elisha
(Hebrew) of God's
salvation
Elishah, Elysha, Elyshah

Ellard
(German) brave man
Ell, Ellarde, Ellee, Ellerd

Ellery
(English) dominant
El, Ell, Ellary, Ellerie, Ellie

Elliott
(English) God-loving
Elie, Elio, Ell, Elliot

Ellis
(English) form of Elias;
devout
Ellice, Ells

Ellis-Marcelle
(American) combo of Ellis
and Marcelle; achiever
*Ellis, Ellismarcelle,
Marcelle*

Ellison
(English) circumspect
*Ell, Ellason, Ellisen, Ells,
Ellyson*

Ellkan
(Hawaiian) saved by God
Elkan, Elkin

Ellory
(Cornish) graceful swan
Elory, Elorey, Ellorey

Ellsha
(Hebrew) saved by the Lord
*Elljsha, Elisee, Elish,
Elishia, Elishua*

Elman
(American) protective
El, Elle, Elmen, Elmon

Elmer
(English) famed
Ell, Elm, Elmar, Elmir, Elmo, Elmoh

Elmo
(Greek) gregarious
Ellmo, Elmoh

Elmore
(Last name as first name) sassy; royal

Elmot
(American) lovable
Elm

Elmore
(English) radiant
Elm, Elmie, Elmoor, Elmor

Elsworth
(Last name as first name) pretentious
Ells, Ellsworth

Elof
(Swedish) the one heir
Loff

Eloi
(French) chosen one
Eloie, Eloy

Elonzo
(Spanish) sturdy; happy
El, Elon, Elonso

Elrad
(Hebrew) God rules his life

Elroy
(French) giving
Elroi, Elroye

Elsden
(English) spiritual
Els, Elsdon

Elson
(English) from Elston; affluent
Elsen

Elston
(English) sophisticated
Els, Elstan, Elsten

Elton
(English) settlement; famous
Ell, Ellton, Elt, Eltan, Elten

Elvin
(English) friend of elves
El, Elv, Elven

Elvind
(American) form of Elvin/Alvin; friend of elves
Elv

Elvis
(Scandinavian) wise; musical
El, Elvyse, The King

Elvy
(English) elfin; small

Elwell
(English) born in the old-well area

Elwen
(English) friend of elves
Elwee, Elwin Elwy, Elwyn, Elwynn, Elwynt

Elwond
(Last name as first name) steady
Ellwand, Elwon, Eldwund

Elwood
(English) old wood; everlasting
Ell, Elwoode, Elwould, Woodie, Woody, Woodye

Ely
(Hebrew) lifted up
Eli

Emanuel
(Hebrew) with God
Em, Eman, Emanuele

Emberto
(Italian) pushy
Berty, Embert, Emberte

Emerson
(German) Emery's son; able
Emers, Emersen

Emery
(German) hardworking
leader
*Em, Emeri, Emerie,
Emmerie, Emory, Emrie*

Emil
(Latin) ingratiating
Em, Emel, Emele

Emilio
(Italian) competitive;
(Spanish) excelling
Emil, Emile, Emilioh, Emlo

Emjay
(American) reliable
Em-J, Em-Jay, M.J., MJ

Emmanuel
(Hebrew) with God
*Em, Eman, Emmannuel,
Emmanuele, Manny*

Emmett
(Hebrew) truthful; sincere
*Emit, Emmet, Emmit,
Emmitt, Emmyt, Emmytt*

Emory
(German) industrious
leader
*Emery, Emmory, Emorey,
Emori, Emorie*

Emre
(Turkish) bond of brothers
Emra, Emrah, Emreson

Emrick
(German) form of Emergy;
ruler
Emryk

Emuel
(Hebrew) form of
Emmanuel (God with us);
believer
Emanuel, Imuel

Eneas
(Hebrew) much-praised
Ennes, Ennis

Engelbert
(German) angel-bright
*Bert, Bertie, Berty,
Engelber, Inglebert*

Enlai
(Chinese) thankful

Ennis
(Irish) reliable

Enoch
(Hebrew) dedicated
instructor
En, Enoc, Enok

Enos
(Hebrew) mortal
Enoes

Enrick
(Spanish) cunning
Enric, Enrik

Enrico
(Italian) ruler
Enrike, Enriko, Enryco

Enrique
(Spanish) charismatic
ruler
*Enrika, Enrikae, Enriqué,
Enryque, Quiqui*

Enver
(Turkish) brightest child

Enzi
(African) strong boy

Enzo
(Italian) fun-loving

Ephraim
(Hebrew) fertile
*Eff, Efraim, Efram, Efrem,
Ephraime, Ephrame,
Ephrayme*

Erasmus
(Greek) beloved
Eras, Erasmas, Erasmis

Erastus
(Greek) loved baby

Erazmo
(Spanish) loved
Erasmo, Eraz, Ras, Raz

Erbert
(German) from Herbert;
famed fighter
Ebert, Erberto

Ercole
(Italian) glorious God's
child

Erebus
(Greek) nether darkness

Erhardt
(German) strong-willed
*Erhar, Erhard, Erhart,
Erheart*

Eric
(Scandinavian) powerful
leader
*Ehrick, Erek, Erick, Erik,
Eryke*

Erie
(Place name) one of the
Great Lakes; vast

Erikson
(Scandinavian) Erik's son;
bold man
*Ericksen, Eriksen,
Erycksen, Eryksen,
Erykson*

Erin
(Irish) peace-loving
Aaron, Arin, Aron, Eryn

Erlan
(English) aristocratic
*Earlan, Earland, Erland,
Erlen, Erlin*

Ernest
(English) sincere
*Earnest, Ern, Ernie, Erno,
Ernst, Erny, Ernye*

Ernesto
(Spanish) sincere
Ernie, Nesto, Nestoh

Ernie
(English) short for Ernest
Ernee, Erney, Erny

Erol
(American) noble
Eral, Eril, Errol

Eros
(Greek) sensual
Ero

Erose
(Greek) from the word
eros; sensual; resolute
Eroce

Errol
(German) noble
Erol, Erold, Erroll, Erryl

Erskine
(Scottish) high-minded
Ers, Ersk, Erskin

Erv
(English) good-looking

Ervin
(English) sea-loving
*Earvin, Erv, Ervan, Erven,
Ervind, Ervyn*

Ervine
(English) sea-lover
Ervene, Ervin

Erving
(Scottish) good-looking

Erwin
(English) friendly
Erwyn

Esau
(Hebrew) rough-hewn
Es, Esa, Esauw, Esaw

Esaul
(American) combo of Esau
and Saul; hairy
Esau, Esaw, Esawle, Saul

Eskil
(Scandinavian) divine

Esmé
(French) beloved
Es, Esmae, Esmay

Esmond
(French) handsome
Esmand, Esmon, Esmund

Esmun
(American) kind
Es, Esman, Esmon

Espen
(German) bear of God

Espn
(American) form of Espen;
sports enthusiast
ESPN

Esperanza
(Spanish) hopeful
*Esper, Esperance,
Esperence*

Essex
(English) dignified
Ess, Ez

Este
(Spanish) short for
Esteban; crowned

Esteban
(Spanish) royal; friendly
*Estabon, Estebann,
Estevan, Estiban, Estyban*

Estes
(English) eastern; open
Estas, Este, Estis

Estevan
(Spanish) crowned
Estivan, Estyvan

Estridge
(Last name as first name)
fortified
Es, Estri, Estry

Etereo
(Spanish) heavenly;
spiritual
Etero

Ethan
(Hebrew) firm will
Eth, Ethen, Ethin, Ethon

Etheal
(English) of good birth
Ethal

Ethelbert
(German) principled
Ethelburt, Ethylbert

Ettore
(Italian) loyal
Etor, Etore

Euclid
(Greek) brilliant
Euclide, Uclid

Eugene
(Greek) blue-blood
Eugean, Eugenie, Ugene

Eural
(American) from Ural
Mountains; upward
Eure, Ural, Ury

Eurby
(Last name as first name)
sea
Erby, Eurb

Eurskie
(Invented) dorky
Ersky

Eusebio
(Spanish) devoted to God
*Eucebio, Eusabio, Eusevio,
Sebio, Usibo*

Eustace
(Latin) calming
*Eustice, Eustis, Stace,
Stacey, Ustace*

Eustacio
(Spanish) calm; visionary
*Eustacio, Eustase, Eustasio,
Eustazio, Eustes, Eustis*

Evagelos
(Greek) form of Andrew;
strong character
*Evaggelos, Evangelo,
Evangelos*

Evan
(Irish) warrior
*Ev, Evann, Evanne, Even,
Evin*

Evander
(Greek) manly; champion
Evand, Evandar, Evandir

Evans
(Welsh) believer in a
gracious God
Evens, Evyns

Evanus
(American) form of Evan;
heroic
Evan, Evin, Evinas, Evinus

Evaristo
(Spanish) form of Evan;
heroic
Evariso, Evaro

Eve
(Invented) form of Yves
Eeve

Evelyn
(American) writer
Ev, Evlinn, Evlyn

Everard
(German) tough
Ev, Evrard

Everest
(Place name) highest
mountain peak in the
world

Everett
(English) strong
*Ev, Everet, Everitt, Evret,
Evrit*

Everhart
(Scandinavian) vibrant
Evhart, Evert

Everly
(American) singing
*Everlee, Everley, Everlie,
Evers*

Everton
(English) from the town of
boars; fearless

Evetier
(French) good

Evett
(American) bright
Ev, Evatt, Eve, Evidt, Evitt

Evon
(Welsh) form of Evan;
warrior
*Even, Evin, Evonne,
Evonn, Evyn*

Ewald
(Polish) fair ruler

Ewan
(Scottish) youthful spirit
Ewahn, Ewon

Ewand
(Welsh) form of Evan;
warrior
Ewen, Ewon

Ewanell
(American) form of Ewan;
hip
Ewanel, Ewenall

Ewart
(English) shepherd; caring
Ewar, Eward, Ewert

Ewing
(English) law-abiding
Ewin, Ewyng

Excell
(American) competitive
Excel, Exsel, Exsell

Exia
(Spanish) demanding
Ex, Exy

Eza
(Hebrew) from Ezra;
helpful
Esri

Ezekiel
(Hebrew) God's strength
*Eze, Ezek, Ezekhal,
Ezekial, Ezikiel, Ezkeil,
Ezekyel, Ezikiel, Ezikyel,
Ezykiel, Zeke*

Ezequiel
(Spanish) devout

Ezer
(Hebrew) helpful boy

Ezira
(Hebrew) helpful
Ezirah, Ezyra, Ezyrah

Ezra
(Hebrew) helpful; strong
Esra, Ezrah

Ezri
(Hebrew) my help
Ezrey, Ezry

Ezzie
(Hebrew) from the name
Ezra; helpful
Ez

Faakhir
(Arabic) proud

Faber
(German) grower
Fabar, Fabir, Fabyre

Faberto
(Latin) form of Fabian;
grower; deals in beans
*Fabe, Fabey, Fabian,
Fabien, Fabre*

Fabian
(Latin) grower; singer
*Fab, Fabe, Fabean,
Fabeone, Fabie, Fabien,
Fabiano*

Fabio
(Italian) seductive;
handsome
Fab, Fabioh

Fable
(American) storyteller
Fabal, Fabe, Fabel, Fabil

Fabrice
(French) skilled worker
*Fabriano, Fabricius,
Fabritius, Fabrizio,
Fabrizius*

Fabrizio
(Italian) fabulous

Fabron
(French) blacksmith

Fabryce
(Latin) crafty
*Fab, Fabby, Fabreese,
Fabrese, Fabrice*

Fabulous
(American) vain
Fab, Fabby, Fabu

Fachan
(Last name as first name)
precocious

Factor
(English) entrepreneur

Facundo
(Last name as first name)
profound

Faddis
(American) loner; deals in
beans
Faddes, Fadice, Fadis

Faddy
(American) faddish
Fad, Faddey, Faddi

Fadi
(Arabic) saved by grace

Fadil
(Arabic) giving

Fagan
(Irish) fiery
*Fagane, Fagen, Fagin,
Fegan*

Fahd
(Arabic) fierce; panther;
brave
Fahad

Fahim
(Arabic) intelligent

Faheem
(Arabic) brilliant

Fahren
(American) variant of Faron; direct

Fairbanks
(Place name); city in Alaska; forceful
Fairbanx, Farebanks

Fairbairn
(Scottish) fair-haired child

Fairchild
(English) fair-haired child

Fairfax
(English) full of warmth
Fairfacks, Farefax, Fax, Faxy

Faisal
(Arabic) authoritative
Faisel, Faizal, Fasel, Fayzelle

Faizon
(Arabic) understanding

Fakhr
(Arabic) proud

Faladrick
(Origin unknown) variation of Frederick
Faldrick, Faldrik

Falcon
(American) bird as name; dark; watchful
Falk, Falkon

Faldo
(Last name as first) brassy

Faline
(Hindi) fertile

Falk
(Hebrew) falcon
Falke

Falkner
(French) handles falcons
Fowler, Faulkner

Fallows
(English) inactive
Fallow

Fam
(American) family-oriented
Fammy

Famous
(American) ambitious
Fame

Fane
(English) exuberant
Fain, Faine

Fannin
(English) happy
Fane

Faolan
(Irish) wolf; sly
Felan, Phelan

Far
(English) traveler
Farr

Faraji
(African) he who comforts others

Faramond
(English) protected
Faramund, Farrimond, Farrimund, Pharamond, Pharamund

Faran
(American) sincere
Fahran, Faren, Faron, Feren, Ferren

Fareed
(Arabic) special

Fargo
(American) jaunty
Fargouh

Farkas
(Last name as first name) strong man

Farley
(English) open
Farl, Farlee, Farleigh, Farlie, Farly, Farlye

Farmer
(English) he farms

Farnall
(Last name as first name)
strong man
Farnell, Fernald

Farnham
(English) windblown; field
*Farnhum, Farnie, Farnum,
Farny*

Farnley
(English) from a place of
ferns

Farold
(Invented) lively

Farouk
(Arabic) knowing what's
true
Faruq, Faruqh

Farquar
(French) masculine

Farr
(English) adventurer
Far

Farrar
(French) distinguished
Farr

Farrell
(Irish) brave
Farel, Farell, Faryl

Farren
(English) mover
Faran, Faron, Farrin, Farron

Farris
(Arabic) rider; (Irish) rock;
reliable
Fare, Farice, Faris

Farro
(Italian) grain
Farron, Faro

Fasta
(Spanish) offering

Fattah
(Arabic) conquerer

Faulkner
(English) disciplinarian
*Falcon, Falconner, Falkner,
Falkoner*

Faunus
(Latin) god of nature
Fawnus

Faust
(Latin) lucky
Fauston

Favian
(Latin) knowing
Fav, Favion

Fawad
(Arabic) victorious

Fawcett
(American) audacious
*Fawce, Fawcet, Fawcette,
Fawcie, Fawsie, Fowcett*

Faxan
(Anglo-Saxon) outgoing
Faxen, Faxon

Fay
(Irish) raven-haired
Faye, Fayette

Faysal
(Arabic) judgmental

Febronio
(Spanish) bright

Fedde
(Italian) true

Federico
(Spanish) peaceful and
affluent
Federik

Fedor
(German) form of
Theodore; romantic
Faydor, Feodor, Fyodor

Fedrick
(American) form of
Cedrick; wandering
Fed, Fedric, Fedrik

Feibush
(Last name as first name)
particular

Feivel
(Hebrew) bright

Felimy
(Irish) good
Felipe
(Spanish) horse-lover
Felepe, Filipe, Flippo
Felix
(Latin) joyful
Felixce, Filix, Phelix, Philix
Fellini
(Last name as first)
carnivalesque
Felman
(Last name as first name)
smart
Fel, Fell
Felton
(English) farming the field
Fenimore
(Last name as first name)
creative
Fenner
(English) capable
Fen, Fenn, Fynner
Fenris
(Scandinavian) fierce
Fenton
(English) nature-loving
Fen, Fenn, Fennie, Fenny
Fentress
(English) natural
Fentres, Fyntres
Fenwick
(English) from the marsh
village; able
Feo
(Native American) confident
Feeo, Feoh
Ferdinand
(German) adventurer
*Ferdie, Ferdnand, Ferdy,
Fernand*
Ferenc
(Hungarian) free
Fergall
(Irish) bravest man
Fearghall, Forgael

Fergus
(Irish, Scottish) topnotch
*Feargus, Ferges, Fergie,
Fergis, Fergy*
Ferguson
(Irish) bold; excellent
*Fergie, Fergs, Fergus,
Fergusahn, Fergusen,
Fergy, Furgs, Furgus*
Ferlin
(American) countrified
Ferlan
Fermin
(Spanish) strong-willed
Fer, Fermen, Fermun
Fernando
(Spanish) bold leader
*Ferd, Ferdie, Ferdinando,
Ferdy, Fernand*
Fernley
(English) from the fern
meadow; natural
*Farnlea, Farnlee,
Farnleigh, Farnley, Fernlea,
Fernlee, Fernleigh*
Ferrand
(French) gray-haired
Ferrant, Farrand, Farrant
Ferrell
(Irish) hero
Fere, Ferrel, Feryl
Ferris
(Irish) rock
Farris, Farrish, Ferriss
Festatus
(Irish) raven; dark
Festive
(American) word as name;
joyful
Fest, Festas, Festes
Festus
(Latin) happy
Festes
Fhoki
(Japanese) discriminating

Fiachra
(Irish) raven; watchful

Fico
(Italian) form of Frederick;
dedicated

Fidel
(Latin) faithful
Fidele, Fidell, Fydel

Fidencio
(Spanish)
Fidence, Fidens, Fido

Field
(English) outdoorsman
Fields

Fielding
(English) outdoorsman;
working the fields

Fien
(American) elegant
Fiene, Fine

Fiero
(Spanish) fiery

Fife
(Scottish) bright-eyed
Fyfe, Phyfe

Fiji
(Place name) Fiji Islands;
islander
Fege, Fegee, Fijie

Fikry
(American) industrious
Fike, Fikree, Fikrey

Filbert
(English) genius
Fil, Filb, Bert, Phil

Filip
(Greek) horse-lover;
(Belgium) form of Philip
Fil, Fill

Filmer
(English) from Filmore;
famed
Fill, Filmar

Filmore
(English) famed
*Fill, Fillie, Fillmore, Filly,
Fylmore*

Filomelo
(Spanish) friend

Finbar
(Irish) blond

Finch
(Last name as first name)
birdlike

Fineas
(Egyptian) dark

Finian
(Irish) fair
Fin, Finean, Finn, Fynian

Finlay
(Irish) blond soldier
Finley, Findlay, Findley

Finley
(Irish) magical
Fin, Finny, Fynn, Fynnie

Finn
(Scandinavian) fair-haired;
from Finland
Fin, Finnie, Finny

Finnegan
(Irish) fair
*Finegan, Finigan, Finn,
Finny*

Fintan
(Irish) small blond man

Finton
(Irish) magical, fair
Finn, Finny, Fynton

Fiorello
(Italian) flowering

Firman
(French) loyal
*Firmin, Farman, Farmann,
Fermin*

Fishel
(Hebrew) fish
Fish, Fysh

Fisher
(English) he fishes
*Fish, Fischer, Fisscher,
Visscher*

Fisk
(Scandinavian) fisherman
Fiske

Fitch
(French) throws spears

Fitz
(French) bright young
man; son
Fitzy

Fitzgerald
(English) bright young
man; Gerald's son

Fitzhugh
(French) Hugh's son; big-
hearted

Fitzmorris
(Last name as first name)
son of Morris
Fitz, Morrey, Morris

Fitzpatrick
(French) Patrick's son;
noble

Fitzroy
(French) son of Roy; lively

Fitzsimmons
(English) bright young
man; Simmons's son

Flabia
(Spanish) light-haired
Flavia

Flag
(American) patriotic
Flagg

Flaminio
(Spanish) priest;
thoughtful
Flamino

Flann
(Irish) red-haired
Flainn, Flannan, Flannery

Flannan
(Irish) red-haired

Flavean
(Flavian) variant of Flavian

Flavian
(Greek) blond
Flovian

Flavio
(Italian) shining
Flav, Flavioh

Fleada
(American) introvert
Flayda

Fleetwood
(English) from the woods

Flemming
(English) from Flanders;
confident
Fleming, Flyming

Fletcher
(English) kind-hearted;
maker of arrows
*Fletch, Fletchi, Fletchie,
Fletchy*

Flint
(English) stream; nature-
lover
Flinn, Flintt, Flynt, Flynnt

Flip
(English) loves horses;
wild movements

Florentin
(Italian) blooming
Florencio

Florian
(Latin) flourishing
Florean, Florie

Floyd
(English) practical; hair of
gray
Floid

Flux
(Middle English) flowing

Flynn
(Irish) brash
Flin, Flinn, Flinnie, Flinny, Flyne

Flynt
(English) flowing; stream
Flint, Flinte, Flinty, Flynte

Foley
(Last name as first name) creative
Folee, Folie

Folke
(German) of the people

Folker
(German) watchful
Folke, Folko

Fontayne
(French) giving; fountain
Font, Fontaine, Fontane, Fountaine

Fonzie
(German) short for Alphonse
Fons, Fonsi, Fonz, Fonzi

For
(American) representative
Fore

Foran
(American) derivative of foreign; exotic
Foren, Forun

Forbes
(Irish) wealthy
Forb

Ford
(English) strong
Feord, Forde, Fyord

Fordan
(English) river crossing; inventive
Ford, Forday, Forden

Foreign
(American) word as name; foreigner
Foran

Forend
(American) forward
Fore, Foryn, Forynd

Forest
(French) nature-loving
Forrest, Fory, Fourast

Forester
(English) protective; of the forest
Forrester, Forry

Fortney
(Latin) strength of character
Fortenay, Forteney, Forteny, Fortny, Fourtney

Fortune
(French) fortunate man
Fortounay, Fortunae

Fortuno
(Spanish) lucky man
Fortunio

Fost
(Latin) form of Foster; worthwhile
Foste, Fostee, Fosty

Foster
(Latin) worthy
Fauster, Fostay

Fouad
(Arabic) good heart
Fuad

Fowler
(English) hunter; traps fowl
Fowller

Fraime
(Anglo-Saxon) newcomer

Fraine
(English) ash tree; tall
Frayne, Freyne

Francesco
(Italian) flirtatious
Fran, Francey, Frankie, Franky

Franchot
(French) free

Francis
(Latin) free spirit; from
France
*Fran, Frances, Franciss,
Frank, Franky, Frannkie,
Franny, Frans*

Francisco
(Spanish) free spirit; from
Latin *Franciscus*;
Frenchman
*Chuco, Cisco, Francisk,
Franco, Frisco, Paco,
Pancho*

Francista
(Spanish) Frenchman; free
*Cisco, Cisto, Francisco,
Franciscus, Fransico*

Franco
(Spanish) defender; spear
Francoh, Franko

Francois
(French) smooth; patriot;
Frenchman
*Frans, Franswaw, French,
Frenchie, Frenchy*

Frank
(English) short for
Franklin; outspoken;
landowner
*Franc, Franco, Frankee,
Frankie, Frankey, Frankie,
Franko, Franky*

Franklin
(English) outspoken;
landowner
*Francklin, Franclin, Frank,
Frankie, Franklinn,
Franklyn, Franklynn,
Franky*

Frantisek
(Czech) free man

Franz
(German) man from
France; free
Frans

Frasier
(English) attractive; man
with curls
Frase, Fraser, Fraze, Frazer

Frayne
(English) foreigner
*Fraine, Frayn, Frean, Freen,
Freyne*

Fred
(German) short for
Frederick; plainspoken
leader
*Fredde, Freddo, Freddy,
Fredo*

Freddie
(German) short for
Frederick; plainspoken
leader
*Freddee, Freddey, Freddi,
Freddy*

Freddis
(German) from the name
Frederick; friendly
Freddus, Fredes, Fredis

Frederic
(French) peaceful king
Fred, Freddy

Frederick
(German) plainspoken
leader; peaceful
*Fred, Freddy, Frederic,
Fredrich, Fredrik, Fryderyk*

Freeborn
(English) born free

Freed
(English) free boy
Fried

Freedom
(American) loves freedom

Freeman
(English) free man
Free, Freedman, Freman

Fremont
(German) protective;
noble

French
(English) boy from France

Frewen
(Anglo-Saxon) free
Frewin

Frey
(Scandinavian) fertility god

Frick
(English) brave man

Fridmann
(Last name as first name)
free man

Fridolf
(Scandinavian) relishes
peace
*Freydolf, Freydulf, Friedolf,
Fridulf*

Fridolin
(German) free

Frieder
(German) peaceful leader
Frie, Fried, Friedrick

Friederich
(German) form of
Frederick; leader of peace
Fridrich, Friedrich

Friedhelm
(German) peaceful helmet
Friedelm

Frisco
(American) short for
Francisco; free
Cisco, Frisko

Friso
(Anglo-Saxon) best self

Fritz
(German) short for
Frederick and Friedrich
*Firzie, Firzy, Frits, Fritts,
Fritzi, Fritzie, Fritzy*

Frode
(Scandinavian) intellectual

Fromel
(Hebrew) outgoing

Frost
(English) cold; freeze

Froyim
(Hebrew) kind

Fructuoso
(Spanish) fruitful
Fru, Fructo

Fry
(English) new sprout;
growing
Frye, Fryer

Fu
(Japanese) from Fudo, god
of wisdom and fire

Fuddy
(Origin unknown) bright-
eyed
Fuddie, Fudee, Fudi

Fukuda
(Japanese) field

Fulbright
(German) brilliant; full of
brightness
Fulbrite

Fulgentius
(Latin) full of kindness;
shines
Fulgencio

Fulke
(English) folksy
Fulk, Fawke, Fowke

Fuller
(English) tough-willed
Fuler

Fullerton
(English) strong
Fuller, Fullerten

Fulton
(English) fresh mind; field
by the town

Funge
(Last name as first name)
stodgy
Funje, Funny

Furlo
(American) macho
Furl

Fursey
(Irish) spiritual

Fyfe
(Scottish) craftsman
Fife, Fyffe, Phyfe

Furman
(German) form of Firman;
runs a ferry
*Fuhrman, Fuhrmann,
Furmann*

Fyodor
(Russian) divine
Feodor, Fyodr

Gabbana
(Italian) creative
Gabi

Gabe
(Hebrew) short for
Gabriel; devout
*Gabbee, Gabbi, Gabbie,
Gabby, Gabi, Gabie, Gaby*

Gabino
(Spanish) strong believer
Gabby, Gabi

Gable
(French) dashing

Gabor
(Last name as first name)
believer; colorful

Gabriel
(Hebrew) God's hero;
devout
*Gabby, Gabe, Gabi,
Gabreal, Gabrel, Gabriele,
Gabrielle, Gabryel*

Gad
(Hebrew) lucky; audacious
Gadd

Gaddiel
(Hebrew) fortunate
Gadiel

Gaddis
(American) hard to please;
picky
Gad, Gaddes, Gadis

Gadi
(Hebrew) short for
Gaddiel; lucky
Gadish

Gael
(English) speaks Gaelic;
independent

Gaetano
(Italian) from the city of
Gaeta; Italian man
Gaetan, Geitano, Guytano

Gagan
(French) form of Gage;
dedicated
Gage

Gage
(French) dedicated

Gahuj
(African) hunts

Gailen
(French) healer; physician
Galan, Galen, Galun

Gaines
(Last name as first name)
rich
Ganes, Gaynes

Gair
(Irish) little boy
Gaer, Geir

Gaius
(Latin) joyful
Gal

Galbraith
(Irish) sensible
Gal

Galbreath
(Irish) practical man
Galbraith, Gall

Gale
(English) cheerful
Gael, Gail, Gaile, Gaille, Gayle

Galegina
(Native American) lithe; deer

Galen
(Greek) calming; intelligent
Gaelin, Gailen, Gale, Galean, Galey, Gaylen

Galfrid
(Last name as first name) uplifted
Galfryd

Galileo
(Italian) from Galilee; inventor
Galilayo

Gallagher
(Irish) helpful
Galagher, Gallager, Gallie, Gally

Gallant
(American) savoir-faire
Gael, Gail, Gaila, Gaile, Gayle

Gallman
(Last name as first name) lively
Galman, Gallway, Galway

Galo
(Spanish) enthusiastic
Gallo

Galloway
(Irish) outgoing
Gallie, Gally, Galoway, Galway

Galt
(German) empowered

Galton
(English) landowner; reclusive

Galvin
(Irish) sparrow; flighty
Gallven, Gallvin, Galvan, Galven, Galway

Gamal
(Arabic) camel; travels long distances

Gamaliel
(Hebrew) rewarded by God
Gamaleel, Gamalyel

Gamba
(African) warring

Gamberro
(Spanish) hooligan
Gami

Gamble
(Scandinavian) mature wisdom
Gam, Gamb, Gambel, Gambie, Gamby

Gamel
(Hebrew) God rewards him

Gamliel
(Arabic) camel; wanders
Gamaliel

Gammon
(Last name as first name) game
Gamen, Gamon, Gamun

Gan
(Chinese) wanders wide

Gandy
(American) adventurer

Ganesh
(Hindi) Lord of all

Ganon
(Irish) fair-skinned
Gannon, Ganny

Ganso
(Spanish) goose; goofy
Gans, Ganz

Ganya
(Russian) strong

Garai
(African) settled

Garbhan
(Irish) rough boy

Garvan
(English) throws spears;
athletic

Garcia
(Spanish) strong
Garce, Garcey, Garsey

Gard
(English) guard
*Garde, Gardey, Gardi,
Gardie, Gardy, Guard*

Gardner
(English) keeper of the
garden
*Gar, Gard, Gardener, Gardie,
Gardiner, Gardnyr, Gardy*

Garek
(Polish) brave boy
Garreck, Garrik, Gerek

Gareth
(Irish) kind, gentle
Gare

Garfield
(English) armed
Gar, Garfeld

Gariana
(American) form of Gary;
wild heart

Garin
(American) form of Darin;
kind
Gare, Gary

Garland
(French) adorned
*Gar, Garlan, Garlend,
Garlind, Garlynd*

Garmon
(German) man who throws
spears
Garmen

Garn
(American) prepared
Gar, Garnie, Garny, Garr

Garner
(French) guard
Gar, Garn, Garnar, Garnir

Garnett
(English) armed; spear
Gar, Garn, Garnet, Garny

Garnock
(Welsh) from alder-tree
place; outdoor spirit

Garon
(American) gentle
Garonn, Garonne

Garonzick
(Last name as first name)
secure
*Gare, Garon, Garons,
Garonz*

Garp
(German) form of Garbo

Garr
(English) short for Garnett
and Garth; giving
Gar

Garreth
(German) brave
Gareth, Garryth, Garyth

Garrett
(Irish) brave; watchful
*Gare, Garet, Garitt, Garret,
Garritt, Gary, Gerrot*

Garrick
(English) ruler with a
spear; brave
*Garey, Garic, Garick, Garik,
Garreck, Gary, Gerrick,
Gerrieck*

Garridan
(English) form of Gary;
quiet

Garrison
(French) prepared
Garris, Garrish, Garry, Gary

Garroway
(English) throws spears;
physical presence
Garraway

Garson
(English) son of Gar; fort home; industrious

Garth
(Scandinavian) sunny; gardener
Gar, Gare, Garry, Gart, Garthe, Gary

Garthay
(Irish) from Gareth; gentle
Garthae

Garton
(English) place of spear man; rowdy

Garv
(English) peaceful
Garvey, Garvy

Garvy
(Irish) peacemaker
Garvey

Garwood
(English) natural
Garr, Garwode, Garwoode, Woody

Gary
(English) strong man
Gare, Garrey, Garri

Gaspard
(French) holds treasure
Gaspar, Gasper

Gaspare
(Italian) treasure-holder
Casper, Gasp, Gasparo

Gaston
(French) native of Gascony; stranger
Gastawn, Gastowyn

Gate
(English) open
Gait, Gates

Gatsby
(Literature) from Fitzgerald's *The Great Gatsby*; ambitious; tragic

Gaudy
(American) word as name; colorful
Gaudin, Gaudy

Gaurav
(Hindi) proud

Gautier
(French) form of Walter; distinctive
Gauther, Gauthier

Gavard
(Last name as first name) creative
Gav, Gaverd

Gavin
(English) alert; hawk
Gav, Gaven, Gavinn, Gavon, Gavvin, Gavyn

Gavriel
(Herbew) filled by God's strength
Gavryel

Gavril
(Hebrew) strong
Gavrill, Gavryl, Gavryll

Gawain
(Hebrew) archangel
Gawaine, Gawayne, Gwayne

Gawath
(Welsh) white falcon; from Gawain, knight

Gawin
(Scottish) watchful; wise
Gawyn

Gaylin
(Greek) calm
Gaelin, Gayle, Gaylen, Gaylon

Gaylord
(French) high-energy
Gallerd, Galurd, Gaylar, Gayllaird, Gaylor

Gaynor
(Irish) spunky
Gainer, Gaye, Gayner

Gayton
(Irish) fair
Gayten, Gaytun

Geary
(English) flexible
Gearey

Gedaliah
(Hebrew) great in
Jehovah's love
*Gedalia, Gedaliahu,
Gedalya, Gedalyahu*

Geer
(German) spearman
Geere

Gefaniah
(Hebrew) vineyard of the
Lord; grows
*Gefania, Gefanya,
Gephania, Gephaniah*

Gemini
(Astrology) zodiac twins;
intelligent

Genaro
(Latin) dedicated
Genaroe, Genaroh

Gene
(Greek) noble
Geno, Jene, Jeno

General
(American) military rank
as name; leader

Geno
(Italian) spontaneous

Genoah
(Place name) city in Italy
Genoa, Jenoa, Jenoah

Genovese
(Italian) spontaneous;
from Genoa, Italy
*Genno, Geno, Genovise,
Genovize*

Gent
(American) short for
gentleman; mannerly
Gynt, Jent, Jynt

Gentil
(Spanish) charming
Gentilo

Gentry
(American) high breeding
*Genntrie, Gent, Gentree,
Gentree, Gentrie*

Genty
(Irish) man of snow;
changes

Geo
(Greek) form of George;
good
Gee

Geoff
(English) short for
Geoffrey; peaceful
Jeff

Geoffrey
(English) peaceful
*Geffry, Geoff, Geoffie,
Geoffry, Geoffy, Geofry, Jeff*

Georg
(German) works with the
earth

George
(Greek) land-loving; farmer
*Georg, Georgi, Georgie,
Georgy, Jorg, Jorge*

Georgio
(Italian) earth-worker
*Giorgio, Jorgio, Jorjeo,
Jorjio*

Georgios
(Greek) land-loving

Georgy
(Greek) short for George
Georgee, Georgi, Georgie

Geraint
(English) old

Gerald
(German) strong; ruling
with a spear
*Geralde, Gerrald, Gerre,
Gerry*

Gerard
(French) brave
Gerord, Gerr, Gerrard

Gerber
(Last name as first name)
particular
Gerb

Gerbold
(German) bold with a spear
Gerbolde

Gere
(English) spear-wielding;
dramatic
Gear

Gerhard
(German) forceful
Ger, Gerd

Gerlach
(German); athlete with
spears; musical

Germain
(French) growing; from
Germany
*Germa, Germaine,
Germane, Germay,
Germayne, Jermaine*

German
(German) from the country
of Germany

Gerod
(English) form of Gerard;
brave
*Garard, Geraldo, Gerard,
Gerarde, Gere, Gererde,
Gerry, Gerus, Giraud,
Jerade, Jerard, Jere, Jerod,
Jerott, Jerry*

Gerold
(Danish) rules with spears
Gerrold, Gerry

Geronimo
(Italian, Native American)
wild heart
Geronimoh

Gerry
(English) short for Gerald
*Gerr, Gerre, Gerree, Gerrey,
Gerri, Gerrie*

Gersh
(Biblical) short for
Gershon; unwanted
Gershe, Gursh, Gurshe

Gershom
(Biblical) exile

Gervaise
(French) man of honor
Gerv, Gervase, Gervay

Gervasio
(Spanish) aggressive
Gervase, Gervaso, Jervasio

Gervis
(German) honored
*Jervis, Gerv, Gervace,
Gervaise, Gervey, Jervaise*

Gerwyn
(Welsh) fair and lovely

Geshem
(Hebrew) raining

Geter
(Origin unknown) hopeful
Getterr, Getur

Gethin
(Welsh) dark skin

Gevariah
(Hebrew) strength
*Gevaria, Gevarya,
Gevaryah, Gevaryahu*

Ghalby
(Origin unknown) winning
Galby

Ghalib
(Arabic) wins

Ghassan
(Arabic) in the prime of life

Ghayth
(Arabic) victor
Ghaith

Ghoshal
(Hindi) the speaker
Ghoshil

Gi
(Italian) form of John;
short for Gian; live wire

Giacomo
(Italian) replacement;
musical
Como, Gia

Giancarlo
(Italian) combo of Gian
and Carlo; magnetic
*Carlo, Carlos, Gia, Gian,
Giannie, Gianny*

Giann
(Italian) believer in a
gracious God
*Ghiann, Giahanni, Gian,
Gianni, Giannie, Gianny*

Gianni
(Italian) calm; believer in
God's grace
Giannie, Gianny

Gibbs
(English) form of Gibson;
spunky
Gib, Gibb, Gibbes

Gibbon
(Scottish) strong
Gibben, Gibbons

Gibor
(Hebrew) short for
Giborah; strong boy

Gibson
(English) smiling
*Gib, Gibb, Gibbie,
Gibbson, Gibby, Gibsan,
Gibsen, Gibsyn*

Gid
(Hebrew) form of Gideon;
warrior; Bible distributor
Gidd, Giddee, Giddi, Giddy

Gideon
(Hebrew) power-wielding
*Giddy, Gideone, Gidion,
Gidyun*

Gidney
(English) strong
Gidnee, Gidni

Gif
(English) giver
Giff

Giffin
(English) giving
Giffyn

Gifford
(English) generous-
hearted
Giford

Gig
(English) man in the
carriage

Giglio
(Italian) form of the word
gigolo
Gig

Gifford
(English) generous-hearted
Giff, Gifferd, Giffie, Giffy

Gil
(Hebrew) for Gilam; joyful
Gill

Gilad
(Hebrew) testimonial hill;
outspoken
Giladi, Gilead

Gilam
(Hebrew) joyful people

Gilbert
(English) intelligent
*Gil, Gilber, Gilburt, Gill,
Gilly*

Gilberto
(Spanish) bright
*Bertie, Berty, Gil, Gilb,
Gilburto, Gillberto, Gilly*

Gilby
(Irish) blond
Gilbie, Gill, Gillbi

Gilchrist
(Irish) open
Gill

Gildea
(Irish) God's servant
Gildo
(Italian) macho
Gil, Gill, Gilly
Giles
(French) protective
Gile, Gyles
Gilford
(English) kind-hearted
Gill, Gillford, Guilford
Gill
(Hebrew) happy man
Gil, Gilli, Gillie, Gilly
Gillanders
(Scottish) serves
Gillean
(Scottish) able server
Gillan, Gillen, Gillian
Gilles
(French) miraculous
Geal, Zheal, Zheel
Gillespie
(Irish) humble
*Gilespie, Gill, Gilley, Gilli,
Gilly*
Gillett
(French) hospitable
Gelett, Gelette, Gillette
Gilley
(American) countrified
Gill, Gilleye, Gilli, Gilly
Gillian
(Irish) devout
Gill, Gilley, Gilly, Gillyun
Gilman
(Irish) serving well
*Gilley, Gilli, Gillman,
Gillmand, Gilly, Gilmand,
Gilmon*
Gilmer
(English) riveting
Gelmer, Gill, Gillmer, Gilly
Gilmore
(Irish) riveting
Gill, Gillmore, Gilmohr

Gilo
(Hebrew) joyful
Gilon
(Hebrew) joyful
Gill
Gilroy
(Irish) king's devotee
*Gilderoy, Gildray, Gildrey,
Gildroy, Gillroy*
Gilson
(Irish) devoted son
Gilus
(Scottish) Jesus's servant
Ginder
(American) form of
gender; vivacious
*Gin, Gind, Gindyr, Jind,
Jinder*
Gino
(Italian) of good breeding;
outgoing
Geeno, Geino, Ginoh
Ginton
(Hebrew) garden
Giona
(Italian) for John; form of
Giovanni; believer
Giordano
(Italian) delivered
Giorgie, Jiordano
Giorgio
(Italian) earthy; creative
*George, Georgeeo,
Georgo, Jorge, Jorgio*
Giovanni
(Italian) jovial; happy
believer
*Geovanni, Gio, Giovani,
Giovannie, Giovanny,
Vannie, Vanny, Vonny*
Gipsy
(English) travels widely
Girioel
(Welsh) lord

Girvin
(Irish) tough-minded
Girvan, Girven, Girvon

Gitel
(Hebrew) good

Giulio
(Italian) youth

Giuseppe
(Italian) capable
Beppo, Giusepe, Gusepe

Given
(Last name as first name)
gift
Givens, Gyvan, Gyven, Gyvin

Givon
(Hebrew) boy of heights

Gizmo
(American) playful
Gis, Gismo, Giz

Glad
(American) happy
Gladd, Gladde, Gladdi, Gladdie, Gladdy

Gladstone
(English) cheering

Gladus
(Welsh) lame; rueful

Gladwyn
(English) friend who has a
light heart
Glad, Gladdy, Gladwin, Gladwynn

Glaisne
(Irish) serene
Glasny

Glancy
(American) form of Clancy;
ebullient
Glance, Glancee, Glancey, Glanci

Glanville
(French) serene

Glasgow
(Place name) city in
Scotland

Glenard
(Irish) from a glen; nature-
loving
Glen, Glenerd, Glenn, Glennard, Glenni, Glennie

Glen
(Irish) natural wonder
Glenn

Glendon
(Scottish) fortified in
nature
Glen, Glend, Glenden, Glenn, Glynden

Glendower
(Welsh) water valley boy

Glenn
(Irish) natural wonder
Glen, Glenni, Glennie, Glenny, Glynn, Glynny

Glennon
(Last name as first name)
living in a valley
Glenen, Glennen, Glenon

Gloster
(Place name) form of
Gloucester, city area in
England

Glyndwr
(Welsh) water valley life
Glyn, Glynn, Glynne

Glynn
(Welsh) lives in a restful
glen
Glyn, Glin, Glinn

Gobi
(Place name) desert in
Central Asia; audacious
Gobee, Gobie

Gobind
(Sanskrit) the name of a
Hindi deity
Govind

Gockley
(Last name as first name)
peaceful
Gocklee

Goddard
(German) staunch in
spirituality
Godard, Godderd, Goddird

Godfrey
(Irish) peaceful
Godfree, Godfrie, Godfry

Godfried
(German) imbued with
God's peace
Godfreed

Godric
(English) man of God
*Godrick, Godrik, Godryc,
Godryck, Godryk*

Godridge
(Last name as first name)
place of God

Godwin
(English) close to God
*Godwinn, Godwyn,
Godwynn*

Goel
(Hebrew) redeemed

Goethe
(Last name as first name)
poet, playwright; genius

Gofraidh
(Irish) God's peace child
Gothfraidh, Gothraidh

Gohn
(African American) spirited
Gon

Golding
(English) golden boy

Goldo
(English) golden
Golo

Goliath
(Hebrew) large
Goliathe

Gomda
(Native American) wind's
moods

Gomer
(English) famed fighter
Gomar, Gomher, Gomor

Gong
(American) forceful

Gonz
(Spanish) form of
Gonzalo; wild wolf
*Gons, Gonz, Gonza,
Gonzales, Gonzalez*

Gonzales
(Spanish) feisty
Gonzalez

Gonzalo
(Spanish) feisty wolf
Gonz, Gonzoloh

Goodman
(Last name as first name)
a good man
Goodeman

Goodrich
(Last name as first name)
giving; good
Goodriche

Goode
(English) good
Good, Goodey, Goody

Goran
(Croatian) good

Gordo
(American) jovial guy

Gordon
(English) nature-lover; hill
*Gord, Gordan, Gorden,
Gordi, Gordie, Gordy*

Gordy
(English) short for Gordon
Gordee, Gordi, Gordie

Gore
(English) practical; pie-
shaped land

Gorgon
(Place name) form of
Gorgonzola, Italy
Gorgan, Gorgun

Gorham
(English) sophisticated;
name of a silver company
Goram

Gorky
(Place name) Russian
amusement park in the
novel *Gorky Park*;
mysterious
Gork, Gorkee, Gorkey, Gorki

Gorman
(Irish) small man
Gormann, Gormen

Goro
(Japanese) fifth son

Gosheven
(Native American) leaps
well; athletic

Gotam
(Hindi) best cow;
cherished
Gautam, Gautoma

Gottfried
(German) form of
Godfried; peaceful god

Gotzon
(German) angel

Gower
(Welsh) unblemished

Gowon
(African) rainmaking

Gozal
(Hebrew) baby bird; trying
his wings

Grady
(Irish) hardworking
Grade, Gradee, Gradey

Graem
(Scottish) homebody
Graeme

Graham
(English) wealthy; grand
house
Graeham, Graeme, Grame

Grail
(Word as name) desired;
sought after
Grale, Grayle

Gram
(American) form of
Graham; homeloving

Granbel
(Last name as first name)
grand and attractive
Granbell

Granderson
(Last name as first name)
grand
Grand, Grander

Grange
(French) lonely; on the
farm
*Grainge, Granger,
Grangher*

Granison
(Last name as first name)
son of Gran; grandiose
Gran, Grann

Granite
(American) rock; hard
Granet

Grant
(English) expansive
Grandt, Grann, Grannt

Grantly
(French) tall; lithe
*Grantlea, Grantleigh,
Grantley*

Granville
(French) grandiose
*Grann, Granvel, Granvelle,
Gravil*

Gravette
(Origin unknown) grave
Gravet

Gray
(English) hair of gray
Graye, Grey

Graylon
(English) gray-haired
Gray, Grayan, Graylan, Graylin

Grayson
(English) son of man with gray hair
Gray, Grey, Greyson

Graz
(Place name) city in Austria

Graziano
(Italian) dearest
Graciano, Graz

Greenlee
(English) outdoorsy
Green, Greenlea, Greenly

Greeley
(English) careful
Grealey, Greel, Greely

Greenwood
(English) untamed; forest
Greene, Greenwoode, Greenwude, Grenwood

Greer
(Last name as first name) sly
Greere, Grier

Greg
(Latin) short for Gregory; vigilant
Gregg, Greggie, Greggy

Gregoire
(French) watchful
Gregorie

Gregor
(Greek) cautious
Greger, Gregors, Greig

Gregorio
(Greek) careful

Gregory
(Greek) cautious
Greg, Greggory, Greggy, Gregori, Gregorie, Gregry

Gregson
(Last name as first name) son of Greg; careful
Greggsen, Greggson, Gregsen

Grenville
(New Zealand) outdoorsy
Granville, Gren

Gresham
(English) of pasture village; sylvan
Grisham

Greville
(English) thoughtful

Grey
(Last name as first name) quiet; grey-haired
Greyson

Griffin
(Latin) unconventional
Greffen, Griff, Griffee, Griffen, Griffey, Griffie, Griffon, Griffy

Griffith
(Welsh) able leader
Griff, Griffee, Griffey, Griffie, Griffy

Grigg
(Welsh) vigilant

Grigori
(Russian) watchful
Grig, Grigor

Grimbald
(Last name as first name) dark
Grimbold

Grimm
(English) grim; dark
Grim, Grym

Grimshaw
(English) from a dark forest; quiet

Gris
(German) gray
Griz

Griswald
(German) bland
Greswold, Gris, Griswold

Grosvenor
(French) hunts well

Grover
(English) thriving
Grove

Gruver
(Origin unknown)
ambitious
Gruever

Guard
(American) protects

Guerdon
(English) combative

Guido
(Italian) guiding
Guidoh, Gwedo, Gweedo

Guilford
(English) from a ford with
yellow flowers; nature-
lover
Gilford, Guildford

Guillermo
(Spanish) attentive
Guilermo, Gulermo

Gullet
(Latin) throat

Gulshan
(Hindi) gardener;
flourishes

Gulzar
(Arabic) thrives

Gundy
(American) friendly
Gundee

Gunn
(Scandinavian) macho;
gunman
Gun, Gunner

Gunnar
(Scandinavian) bold
Gunn, Gunner, Gunnir

Guntersen
(Scandinavian) macho;
gunman
Gun, Gunth

Gunther
(Scandinavian) able
fighter
*Funn, Gunnar, Gunner,
Guntar, Gunthar, Gunthur*

Gunyon
(American) tough; gunman
Gunn, Gunyun

Gur
(Hindi) from guru; teacher

Gurpreet
(Hindi) devoted follower

Guryon
(Hebrew) lionlike
Garon, Gorion, Gurion

Gus
(Scandinavian) short for
Gustav
*Guss, Gussi, Gussy,
Gussye*

Gustachian
(American) pretentious
Gus, Gussy, Gust

Gustaf
(German) armed; vital
*Gus, Gusstof, Gustav,
Gustovo*

Gustav, Gustave
(Scandinavian) vital
*Gus, Gussie, Gussy, Gusta,
Gustaf, Gustaff, Gusti,
Gustof, Gustoff*

Gustavo
(Spanish) vital; gusto
Gus, Gustaffo, Gustav

Gusto
(Spanish) pleasure
Gusty

Gustus
(Scandinavian) royal
*Gus, Gustaf, Gustave,
Gustavo*

Guth
(Irish) short for Guthrie; in the wind
Guthe, Guthry

Guthrie
(Irish) windy; heroic
Guthree, Guthry

Gutierre
(Spanish) from Walter; distinguished

Guy
(French) assertive; (German) leader
Guye

Guwayne
(American) combo of Guy and Wayne
Guwain, Guwane, Guy, Gwaine, Gwayne

Guzet
(American) bravado
Guzz, Guzzett, Guzzie

Gwandoya
(African) miserable fate

Gwynedd
(Welsh) fair-haired
Gwyn, Gwynfor, Gwynn, Gwynne

Gweedo
(Invented) form of Guido

Gwent
(Place name) city in Wales

Gwill
(American) dark-eyed
Gewill, Guwill

Gwynn
(Welsh) fair
Gwen, Gwyn

Gyan
(Hindi) knowledgeable
Gyani

Gyasi
(African) terrific man

Gylfi
(Scandinavian) king; stealthy

Gyth
(American) capable
Gith, Gythe

Haadee
(Arabic) leader

Haafiz
(Arabic) protector

Haakon
(Scandinavian) chosen son

Haaris
(Arabic) good man

Haas
(Last name as first name) good

Habakkuk
(Hebrew) embrace

Habib
(Arabic) well loved
Habeeb

Habie
(Origin unknown) jovial
Hab

Habimama
(African) believer in God

Hachiro
(Japanese) eighth son

Hachman
(Last name as first name) chops
Hachmann, Hachmin

Hackett
(Last name as first name)
chops

Hackman
(German) fervent; hacks wood
Hackmann

Hadar
(Hebrew) respected
Hadaram, Hadur, Heder

Hadden
(American) bright; natural
Haddan, Haddon, Haddin, Haden, Hadon

Haddy
(English) short for Hadley; sylvan
Had, Haddee, Haddey, Haddi

Hadad
(Arabic) calm

Hades
(Mythology) Greek god of the dead

Hadi
(Arabic) guide

Hadley
(English) lover of nature; meadow with heather
Haddleye, Hadlee, Hadlie, Hadly

Hadrian
(Roman) from Hadria

Hadriel
(Hebrew) blessed

Hadwin
(Last name as first name)
natural man
Hadwyn

Hafiz
(Arabic) guards others
Hafeez, Hapheez, Haphiz

Hagan
(German) defender
Hagen, Haggan, Haggin

Hagar
(Hebrew) wanders

Hagen
(German) chosen one
Hagan, Haggen

Hagley
(Last name as first name)
defensive

Haidar
(Hindi) lionlike
Haider, Haydar, Hyder

Haig
(Last name as first name)
authoritative

Haike
(Asian) of the water

Haim
(Hebrew) alive
Hayim, Hayyim

Haines
(Last name as first name)
confident
Hanus, Haynes

Hakan
(Arabic) fair

Hakim
(Arabic) brilliant
Hakeam, Hakeem, Hakym

Hako
(Japanese) honorable

Hakon
(Scandinavian) chosen son
Haaken, Haakin, Haakon, Hacon, Hagan, Hagen, Hakan, Hako

Hal
(English) home ruler

Haland
(Last name as first name)
island
Halland

Halbert
(Last name as first name)
island
Hal, Bert

Haldane
(German) fierce; person who is half Danish
Haldayn, Haldayne

Haldas
(Last name as first name) dependable

Halden
(German) man who is half Dane
Haldin, Haldane, Haldan, Halfdan

Haldor
(Scandinavian) thunderous rock

Hale
(English) heroic
Hal, Halee, Haley, Hali

Halen
(Swedish) portal to life
Hailen, Hale, Haley, Hallen, Haylen, Haylin

Haley
(Irish) innovative
Hail, Hailee, Hailey, Hale, Halee, Hayley

Halford
(Last name as first name) kind

Hali
(Greek) loves the sea

Hall
(English) solemn

Hallam
(African) gentle

Hallberg
(English) comes from a town of valleys
Halberg, Halburg, Hallburg

Halle
(Scandinavian) rocklike dependability

Halley
(English) holy man

Halliwell
(Last name as first name) sea-loving

Hallward
(English) guards the hall; wily
Halward, Halwerd, Hawarden

Halmer
(English) robust

Halse
(English) on the island
Halce, Halsi, Halsy, Halzee, Halzie

Halsey
(English) isolated; island

Halstead
(Last name as first name) home on the rock
Halsted

Halston
(Origin unknown) fashionable

Halton
(Engilsh) town on a hill; country boy
Halten, Hallton, Halton

Halvard
(Scandinavian) staunch
Halvor, Hallvard

Halwell
(English) special
Hallwell, Halwel, Halwelle

Ham
(Last name as first name) praising

Hamaker
(Last name as first name) industrious
Ham

Hamal
(Arabic) lamb

Hamar
(Scandinavian) hammer

Hamid
(Arabic) grateful
Hameed
Hamidi
(Arabic, African)
praiseworthy
*Ham, Hamedi, Hameedi,
Hamm, Hammad*
Hamil
(English) rough-hewn
*Hamel, Hamell, Hamill,
Hamm*
Hamilton
(English) benefiting
*Hamelton, Hamil,
Hammilton*
Hamish
(Irish) form of James;
supplanting
Hamlet
(German, French)
conflicted; small village;
Shakespearean hero
*Ham, Hamlette, Hamlit,
Hamm*
Hamlin
(German) homebody
*Hamaline, Hamelin,
Hamlen, Hamlyn*
Hammer
(German) works with a
hammer; able
Hammar, Hammur
Hammond
(English) ingenious
*Ham, Hamm, Hammon,
Hamond*
Hamon
(Scandinavian) leader
Hamo
Hamor
(Hebrew) organized
Hamp
(American) fun-loving
Ham, Hampton

Hampden
(English) distinctive; valley
home
Hampton
(English) distinctive
Ham, Hamm, Hamp, Hampt
Han
(Arabic) from Hani;
happiness
Hanani
(Arabic) merciful
Hancock
(English) has a farm;
practical
Haneef
(Arabic) believer
Hanford
(Last name as first name)
forgiving
Hamford
Hani
(Arabic) happy
Hanif
(Arabic) Islam believer
Hanisi
(African) Thursday-born
Hank
(English) short for Henry;
ruler; cavalier
Hankey, Hanks, Hanky
Hanley
(English) natural; meadow
high
*Han, Hanlee, Hanleigh,
Hanly*
Hannes
(Scandinavian) short form
of Johannes; giving
Hahnes
Hannibal
(Slavic) leader
Hanibal, Hanibel, Hann
Hanoch
(Hebrew) loyal

Hans
(Scandinavian) believer; warm
Hahns, Hanz, Hons

Hansa
(Scandinavian) traditional; believer in a gracious Lord
Hans

Hansel
(Scandinavian) gullible; open
Hans, Hansie, Hanzel

Hansen
(Scandinavian) warm; Hans's son
Han, Handsen, Hans, Hansan, Hanson, Hanssen, Hansson, Hanz

Hansraj
(Hindi) king of swans; smooth

Haqq
(Arabic) truth

Harbin
(English) optimist

Harcourt
(English) loves nature

Hardin
(English) lively; valley of hares
Hardee, Harden

Harding
(English) fiery
Harden, Hardeng

Hardwick
(English) castle boy
Harwyck

Hardwin
(English) keeps hares

Hardy
(American) fun-loving; substantial
Hardie, Hardey, Harday, Harding

Harean
(African) aware

Harel
(Scandinavian) ruler

Harence
(English) swift

Harford
(English) jolly
Harferd

Hargrove
(English) fruitful

Harim
(Arabic) above all

Hark
(American) word as name; behold
Harko

Harkin
(Irish) red-faced
Harkan, Harken

Harlan
(English) army land; athletic
Hal, Harl, Harlen, Harlon, Harlynn

Harlemm
(African American) from Harlem; dancer
Harl, Harlam, Harlem, Harlems, Harlum, Harly

Harley
(English) wild-spirited
Harl, Harlee, Harly

Harlow
(English) bold
Harlo, Harloh

Harmon
(German) dependable
Harm, Harman, Harmen

Harmony
(Mythology) from Harmonia; in harmony with life
Harmonio

Harod
(Biblical) king
Harrod

Harold
(Scandinavian) leader of an army
Hal, Harald, Hareld, Harry

Harper
(English) artistic and musical; harpist
Harp

Harpo
(American) jovial
Harpoh, Harrpo

Harrell
(Hebrew) likes the mountain of God; religious

Harrington
(English) comes from the town of Harry; old-fashioned

Harris
(English) dignified
Haris, Harriss

Harrison
(English) Harry's son; adventurer
Harrey, Harri, Harrie, Harris, Harrisan, Harrisen, Harry

Harrod
(Hebrew) victor
Harod, Harry

Harry
(English) home ruler
Harree, Harrey, Harri, Harrie, Harye

Harshad
(Hindi) evokes joy

Harsho
(Hindi) joy

Hart
(English) giving
Harte

Hartley
(English) wilderness wanderer
Hartlee, Hartleigh, Hartly

Hartman
(German) strong-willed
Hart, Hartmann, Harttman

Hartsey
(English) lazing on the meadow; sylvan
Harts, Hartz

Hartwell
(English) good-hearted
Harwell, Harwill

Hartwig
(German) strong

Haruki
(Japanese) child of the spring

Harun
(Arabic) highly regarded

Harv
(German) able combatant
Har

Harvey
(German) fighter
Harv, Harvi, Harvie, Harvy

Harwin
(American) safe
Harwen, Harwon

Harwood
(English) from the deer wood; artistic
Harewood

Hasan
(Arabic) attractive

Hasani
(African) good

Hashim
(Arabic) force for good
Hasheem

Hashum
(African) crushes
Heshum

Hasin
(Arabic) handsome
Hassin, Hasen

Hask
(Hebrew) from Haskell, form of Ekekial; smart
Haske

Haskell
(Hebrew) ingratiating
Hask, Haskel, Haskie, Hasky

Haslett
(English) land of hazel trees; worthy
Haslit, Haslitt, Hazel, Hazlett, Hazlitt

Hassan
(Arabic) good-looking
Hasan

Hasso
(German) sun
Hasson

Hastings
(English) leader
Haste

Haswell
(English) dignified
Has, Haz

Hattan
(Place name) from Manhattan; sophisticate
Hatt

Havard
(American) form of Harvard; guardian
Hav

Havelock
(Czech) form of Paul; prudent

Haven
(English) sanctuary
Haiv, Hav

Haward
(English) guards the hedge; border man
Hawarden

Hawes
(English) stays by the hedges
Haws

Hawke
(English) watchful; falcon
Hauk, Hawk

Hawthorne
(English) observer

Hayden
(English) respectful
Haden, Hadon, Hay, Haydon, Haydyn, Hayton

Haye
(English) open

Hayes
(English) open
Haies, Hay, Haye

Hayman
(English) hedging
Hay

Haymo
(Last name as first name) good-natured

Hayne
(English) working outdoors
Haine, Haines, Haynes

Hayward
(English) creative; good work ethic
Hay, Heyward

Hayword
(English) open-minded
Haword, Hayward, Haywerd

Hazael
(Old English) hazel tree

Hazaiah
(Hebrew) believes God's decisions

Hazard
(Origin Unknown)
Hazzard

Hazen
(English) form of Hayes;
hedges; indecisive
Hazin

Hazleton
(English) from woods of
hazel trees

Hazlewood
(English) from woods of
hazel trees

Hearn
(English) optimistic
Hearne, Hern

Heath
(English) open space;
natural
Heathe, Heith, Heth

Heathcliff
(English) mysterious

Heaton
(English) high-principled
Heat, Heatan, Heaten

Heber
(Greek) from Hebe;
youthful goddess
Hebor

Hector
(Greek) loyal
*Hec, Heck, Heco, Hect,
Hectar, Hecter, Hekter, Tito*

Heddwyn
(Welsh) peaceful; fair-haired
*Hedwin, Hedwyn,
Hedwynn*

Hedley
(English) natural

Hedeon
(Russian) woodsman

Heimdall
(Scandinavian) white; god
Heiman, Heimann

Hein
(German) advising
*Heiiri, Heiner, Heini,
Heinlich*

Heinrich
(German) form of Henry;
leader
*Hein, Heine, Heinrick,
Heinrik*

Heinz
(German) advisor
Heinze

Heladio
(Spanish) boy born in
Greece; ingenious
Eladio, Elado, Helado

Helgi
(Scandinavian) happy
Helge

Helio
(Hispanic) bright

Heller
(German) brilliant

Hellerson
(German) brilliant one's
son; smart
Helley

Helmand
(German) helmet;
protected

Helmar
(German) protected; smart
*Helm, Helmer, Helmet,
Helmut*

Helmut
(German, Polish) brave

Heman
(Last name as first name)
direct

Hender
(German) ruler; illustrious
Hend

Henderson
(English) reliable
*Hender, Hendersen,
Hendersyn*

Hendrik
(German) home ruler
*Heinrich, Hendrick,
Henrick, Hindrick*

Henech
(Last name as first name)
leading the pack
Henach

Henley
(English) surprising
*Henlee, Henly, Henlye,
Hinley*

Henning
(Scandinavian) ruler

Henrik
(Norwegian) leader
Henric, Henrick

Henry
(German) leader
*Hal, Hank, Harry, Henny,
Henree, Henri*

Henson
(Last name as first name)
son of Hen; quiet

Heraldo
(Spanish) divine

Herb
(German) energetic
Herbi, Herbie, Herby, Hurb

Herbert
(German) famed warrior
*Bert, Herb, Herbart,
Herberto, Herbie, Herbirt,
Herby, Hurb, Hurbert*

Hercule
(French) strong
Hercuel, Harekuel, Herkuel

Hercules
(Greek) grand gift
Herc, Herk, Herkules

Heriberto
(Spanish)
Herbert, Heribert

Herman
(Latin) fair fighter
*Heremon, Herm, Hermahn,
Hermann, Hermie,
Hermon, Hermy*

Hermes
(Greek) courier of
messages
Hermez

Hermod
(Scandinavian) greets and
welcomes

Hernando
(Spanish) bold
Hernan

Herndon
(English) nature-loving
Hern, Hernd

Herne
(English) from bird heron;
inventive
Hearne, Hern

Hernley
(English) from the heron
meadow; easygoing
*Hernlea, Hernlee, Hernlie,
Hernly*

Herodotus
(Greek) the father of
history

Herrick
(Last name as first name)
never alone

Herrod
(Biblical) king
Herod

Hershall
(Hebrew) from Hershel;
deer; swift
*Hersch, Herschel, Hersh,
Herzl, Heshel, Hirschel,
Hirsh, Hirshel*

Herschel
(Hebrew) fast; deer
*Hersch, Hersh,
Hershel,Hershell,
Hershelle, Herzl, Hirchel,
Hirsch, Hirshel*

Hershey
(Hebrew) deer; swift; sweet
Hersh, Hershel, Hirsh

Hertzel
(Hebrew) form of
Herschel; deer; swift
Hert, Hertsel, Hyrt

Herve
(French) ready for battle

Hervey
(American) form of Harvey;
ardent and studious
Herv, Herve, Hervy

Herzon
(American) from Hershel;
fast
Herz, Herzan, Herzun

Hesed
(Hebrew) sweet

Hesperos
(Greek) evening star
Hesperios, Hespers

Hess
(Last name as first name)
bold
Hes, Hys

Hessel
(Dutch) bold man

Heston
(Last name as first name)
star quality

Hewitt
(German) smart
*Hew, Hewet, Hewett,
Hewie, Hewit, Hewy, Hugh*

Hewney
(Irish) smart
Owney

Hewson
(Irish) son of Hugh; smart;
giving

Hevel
(Hebrew) alive, breathing

Heywood
(Last name as first name)
thoughtful
Haywood

Hezekiah
(Biblical) strong man
Hezeklah, Zeke

Hiawatha
(Native American) Iroquois
chief
Hia

Hickok
(American) Wild Bill
Hickok, U.S. marshal

Hidalgo
(American) westerner

Hidde
(Japanese) excellent

Hideaki
(Japanese) cautious

Hideo
(Japanese) excellent
Hideyo

Hieremias
(Greek) God lifts him up

Hieronymos
(Greek) alternate of
Jerome
Heronymous

Hifz
(Arabic) memorable

Higinio
(Hispanic) forceful

Hilarion
(Greek) cheery; hilarious
Hilary, Hill

Hilary
(Latin) joyful
*Hilaire, Hill, Hillarie,
Hillary, Hillery, Hilly, Hilorie*

Hildebrand
(German) combative;
sword
Hill, Hilly

Hill
(English) lives on a hill;
dreamy

Hillard
(German) wars; diligent
Hilliard, Hillier, Hillyer

Hillel
(Hebrew) praised; devout
Hilel, Hill

Hillery
(Latin) form of Hilary;
pleasant
Hill

Hilliard
(German) brave;
settlement on the hill
*Hill, Hillard, Millierd, Hilly,
Hillyerd, Hylliard*

Hilton
(English) sophisticated
*Hillten, Hillton, Hiltan,
Hiltawn, Hiltyn, Hylton*

Himesh
(Hindi) snow king

Hines
(Last name as first name)
strong
Hine, Hynes

Hippocrates
(Greek) philosopher
Hipp

Hippolyte
(Greek) frees horses
*Hippolit, Hippolitos,
Hippolytus, Ippolito*

Hiram
(Hebrew) most admired
Hi, Hirom, Hirym

Hiramatsu
(Japanese) exalted

Hiro
(Japanese) giving

Hirsh
(Hebrew) deer; swift
*Hersh, Hershel, Hirschel,
Hirshel*

Hirza
(Hebrew) lithe; deer

Hitchcock
(English) creative; spooky
Hitch

Hjalmar
(Scandinavian) protective
warrior
*Hjalamar, Hjallmar,
Hjalmer*

Ho
(Chinese) good

Hoashis
(Japanese) God

Hobart
(German) haughty
Hobb, Hobert, Hoebard

Hobbes
(English) from Robert;
famed, intelligent
Hob, Hobbs

Hobert
(German) studious

Hobson
(English) helpful backer
*Hobb, Hobbie, Hobbson,
Hobby, Hobsen*

Hockley
(English) high meadow
boy
*Hocklea, Hocklee, Hocklie,
Hockly*

Hockney
(English) from a high
island, a spirited boy
Hockny

Hodge
(English) form of Roger;
vibrant
Hodges

Hodgie
(English) nickname for
Hodge
Hodgy

Hodgson
(English) boy born to
Roger; up-and-coming
Hodge, Hodges

Hoffman
(Last name as first name)
sophisticated

Hogan
(Irish) high-energy; vibrant
Hogahn, Hoge, Hoghan

Hogue
(Last name as first name)
youth
Hoge

Hojar
(American) wild spirit
Hobar, Hogar

Hoke
(Origin unknown) popular

Holbert
(German) capable
Hilbert

Holbrook
(English) educated
*Brooke, Brookie, Brooky,
Holb, Holbrooke*

Holcomb
(Last name as first name)
bright

Holden
(English) quiet; gracious
Holdan, Holdin, Holldun

Holder
(English) musical
Hold, Holdher, Holdyer

Holegario
(Spanish) superfluous
Holegard

Holger
(Last name as first name)
devoted

Holiday
(English) born on a holy
day
Holliday

Hollis
(English) flourishing
*Holl, Hollace, Hollice,
Hollie, Holly*

Holloway
(Last name as first name)
jovial
Hollo, Hollway, Holoway

Hollywood
(Place name) city in
California; showoff
Holly, Wood

Holm
(English) natural; woodsy
Holms

Homain
(Last name as first name)
homebody
Holman, Holmen

Holmes
(English) safe haven
Holmm, Holmmes

Holmfrid
(Last name as first name)
prefers home-and-hearth

Holt
(English) shaded view
Holte, Holyte

Homer
(Greek) secure
*Hohmer, Home, Homere,
Homero*

Honchy
(American) form of
honcho; leader
*Honch, Honchee, Honchey,
Honchi*

Honda
(African) from Hondo;
warrior

Hondo
(African) warring

Honesto
(Spanish) truthful
Honesta, Honestoh

Hong
(Vietnamese) pink;
tasteful

Honorato
(Spanish) full of honor
Honor, Honoratoh

Honoré
(Latin) man who is honored
Honor, Honoray

Hood
(Last name as first name)
easygoing; player
Hoode, Hoodey

Hooker
(English) shepherd

Hoolihan
(American) hooligan
Hool, Hoole, Hooli

Hoop
(American) ball player
Hooper, Hoopy

Hopkins
(Welsh) Robert's son;
famous
*Hopkin, Hopkinson,
Hopkyns, Hopper,
Hoppner*

Hopper
(Last name as first name)
creative

Horace
(Latin) poetic
Horaace, Horase, Horice

Horatio
(Latin) poetic; dashing
Horate, Horaysho

Horsley
(English) calm field of
horses; keeper
*Horslea, Horsleigh,
Horslie, Horsly*

Horst
(German) deep; thicket
Hurst

Horstman
(German) profound
*Horst, Horstmen,
Horstmun*

Horston
(German) thicket; sturdy
Horst

Horton
(English) brash
Horten, Hortun

Hosaam
(Arabic) handsome

Hosea
(Hebrew) prophet

Hosie
(Hebrew) from Hosea;
prophet
Hosaya, Hose

Hosni
(Arabic) excellent

Houghton
(Last name as first name)
bravado

Houston
(English) Texas city;
rogue; hill town
Houst, Hust, Huston

Hovannes
(Hebrew) believer in a
gracious God; form of
Johannes

How
(American) word as a
name
Howe, Howey, Howie

Howard
(English) well-liked
*How, Howerd, Howie,
Howurd, Howy*

Howart
(Origin unknown) admired
Howar

Howe
(German) high-minded
How, Howey, Howie

Howell
(Welsh) outstanding
*Howel, Howey, Howie,
Howill*

Howlan
(English) living on a hill;
high

Howland
(American) well-known
Howlend, Howlond, Howlyn

Hoyt
(Irish) spirited
Hoit, Hoye

Hrothgar
(Literature) king

Huang
(Chinese) rich

Hubbard
(German) fine
Hubberd, Hubert, Hubie

Hubert
(German) intellectual
*Bert, Bertie, Burt, Hubart,
Huberd, Hue, Huebert,
Hugh*

Hubie
(English) short for Hubert
Hube, Hubee, Hubey, Hubi

Huckleberry
(American) glossy black
berry; (Literature) from
Twain's *Huckleberry Finn*;
mischevious

Hud
(English) charismatic
cowboy
Hudd

Hudson
(English) Hugh's son;
charismatic adventurer
Hud, Hudsan, Hudsen

Hudya
(Arabic) going the right
way

Huelett
(American) bright;
southern
*Hu, Hue, Huel, Hugh,
Hulette*

Huey
(French) hearty

Hugh
(English) intelligent
*Hue, Huey, Hughey, Hughi,
Hughie, Hughy*

Hughdonald
(American) combo of Hugh
and Donald; southern
*Huedonald, Hughdon,
Hughdonal, Hughdonn*

Hughie
(English) intelligent; lucky
in parentage
Hughee, Hughi, Hughy

Hugo
(Latin) spirited heart

Huland
(English) bright
Hue, Huel, Huey, Hugh

Hulbard
(Last name as first name)
singing; bright
Hulbert, Hulburt

Hull
(English) spirited;
confident

Humberto
(Spanish) brilliant
*Hum, Humb, Humbert,
Humbie*

Hume
(Last name as first name)
daunting

Humphrey
(German) strong
peacemaker
*Hum, Humfry, Hump,
Humphry, Humprey*

Hunn
(German) combative
Hun

Hunt
(English) active

Hunter
(English) hunter;
adventurer
Hunt

Hunting
(English) hunter
Huntyng

Huntington
(Last name as first name) town of hunters

Huntler
(English) hunter
Huntt

Huntley
(English) hunter
Hunt, Hunter, Huntlea, Huntlee, Huntlie, Huntly

Huon
(Hebrew) form of John; believer

Hurd
(Last name as first name) tends the herd

Hurlbert
(English) shining army man
Hulbert, Hurlburt, Hurlbutt

Hurley
(Irish) the tide; flowing
Hurlea, Hurlee, Hurli, Hurly

Hurst
(Last name as first name) entrepreneurial

Husky
(American) big
Husk, Huskee, Huskey, Huski

Hussein
(Arabic) attractive man
Husain, Husane, Husein, Hussain

Hutch
(American) safe haven; unique
Hut, Hutchey, Hutchie, Hutchy

Hutter
(Last name as first name) tough
Hut, Hutt, Huttey, Huttie, Hutty

Hutton
(English) sophisticated
Hutt, Huttan, Hutten, Hutts

Huxford
(Last name as first name) outdoorsman

Huxley
(English) outdoorsman
Hux, Huxel, Huxle, Huxlee, Huxlie

Hwang
(Japanese) yellow

Hyacinthe
(French) flowering
Hyacinthos, Hyacinthus, Hyakinthos

Hyatt
(English) secure
Hy, Hye, Hyett, Hyut

Hyde
(English) special; a hyde is 120 acres
Hide, Hy

Hyghner
(Last name as first name) lofty goals
High, Highner, Hygh

Hyll
(Origin unknown) open-minded
Hy, Hye, Hyell

Hyman
(Hebrew) life
Hy, Hymen, Hymie

I

Iagan
(Scottish) fire

Iago
(Spanish) feisty villain
Iagoh, Jago

Iain
(Scottish) believer

Ian
(Scottish) believer;
handsome
Iain, Ean, Eon, Eyon

Ib
(Arabic) joy

Ibrahim
(Arabic) fathering many
Ibraham, Ibrahem

Ibu
(Japanese) creative

Icarus
(Mythology) ill-fated
Ikarus

Ich
(Hebrew) short for
Ichabod; has-been
Ick, Ickee, Ickie, Icky

Ichabod
(Hebrew) glory in the past;
slim
*Ich, Icha, Ickabod, Ika,
Ikabod, Ikie*

Idi
(African, Arabic) born
during Idd Festival

Idris
(Welsh) impulse-driven
Idriss, Idriys

Idwal
(Welsh) known

Iefan
(Welsh) form of John;
believer in God's grace

Ieuan
(Welsh) form of Ivan;
grace

Ifan
(Welsh) form of John;
believer

Ifor
(Welsh) archer

Iggy
(Latin) short for Ignatius;
spunky
Iggee, Iggey, Iggi, Iggie

Ignace
(French) fiery
Iggy, Ignase

Ignatius
(Latin) firebrand
*Ig, Iggie, Iggy, Ignacius,
Ignashus, Ignatious,
Ignnatius*

Igor
(Russian) warrior

Ihsan
(Arabic) charitable

Ike
(Hebrew) short for Isaac
and Eisenhower; friendly
Ika, Ikee, Ikey, Ikie

Ilan
(Hebrew) tree
Illan

Illtyd
(Welsh) from well-
populated homeland
Illtud

Ilom
(Welsh) happy

Immanuel
(Hebrew) honored
Emmanuel, Imanuel

Imran
(Arabic) host

Inder
(Hindi) the lord of sky gods is Indra; ethereal
Inderjeet, Inderjit, Inderpal, Indervir, Indra, Indrajit

Indiana
(Place name) U.S. state; rowdy; dashing
Indio, Indy

Indore
(Place name) city in India
Indor

Indra
(Hindi) lord of sky gods

Ing
(Scandinavian) he who is foremost
Inge

Ingelbert
(German) combative
Ing, Inge, Ingelbart, Ingelburt, Inglebert

Inger
(Scandinavian) fertile
Ingemar, Ingmar

Ingmar
(Scandinavian) fertile
Ing, Ingamar, Ingamur, Inge, Ingemar, Ingmer

Ingmer
(Scandinavian) short for Ingemar; famed
Ing, Ingamar, Ingemar, Ingmar

Ingra
(English) short for Ingram; kind-hearted
Ingie, Ingrah, Ingrie

Ingram
(English) angelic; kind
Ing, Ingraham, Ingre, Ingrie, Ingry

Ingvar
(Scandinavian) fertility god
Ingevar

Inigo
(Spanish) from Ignatius; eager

Iniko
(Japanese) serves

Innis
(Irish) isolated
Ines, Inis, Innes, Inness, Inniss

Innocencio
(Spanish) innocent

Inteus
(Native American) proud, unashamed

Ior
(Welsh) short for Iorworth; attractive

Iorgos
(Greek) outgoing

Ira
(Hebrew) cautious
Irae, Irah

Iram
(English) smart
Irem, Irham, Irum

Iranga
(Sri Lanken) special

Irv
(English) short for Irving

Irvin
(English) attractive
Irv, Irvine

Irving
(English) attractive
Irv, Irve, Irveng, Irvy

Irwin
(English) practical
Irwen, Irwhen, Irwie, Irwinn, Irwy, Irwynn

Isa
(African) saved

Isaac
(Hebrew) laughter
*Isaak, Isack, Izak, Ize,
Izek, Izzy*

Isadore
(Greek) special gift
*Isador, Isedore, Isidore,
Issy, Izzie, Izzy*

Isai
(Hebrew) believer

Isaiah
(Hebrew) saved by God
*Isa, Isay, Isayah, Isey,
Izaiah, Izey*

Isak
(Scandinavian) laughter
Isac

Isam
(Arabic) protector

Isas
(Japanese) worthwhile

Isham
(Last name as first name)
athletic

Ishan
(Hindi) sun

Ishmael
(Hebrew) outcast son of
Abraham in the Bible
Hish, Ish, Ishmel, Ismael

Isidore
(Greek, French) gift
Isi, Izzie

Isidoro
(Spanish) gift
*Cedro, Cidro, Doro, Izidro,
Sidro, Ysidor*

Isidro
(Greek) gift
Isydro

Israel
(Hebrew) God's prince;
conflicted
Israyel, Issy, Izzy

Israj
(Hindi) king of gods

Issa
(Hebrew) laughing

Isser
(Slavic) creative

Itzak
(Hebrew) form of Isaac
Itzik

Ivan
(Russian) believer in a
gracious God; reliable one
Ivahn, Ive, Ivey, Ivie

Ivar
(Scandinavian) Norse god

Ive
(English) able
Ivee, Ives, Ivey, Ivie

Ives
(American) musical
Ive

Ivo
(Polish) yew tree; sturdy
*Ivar, Ives, Ivon, Ivonnie,
Yvo*

Ivor
(Scandinavian) outgoing;
ready
Ifot, Ivar, Ive, Iver, Ivy

Izaak
(Polish) full of mirth

Izacz
(Slavic) spicy; happy
Isaac, Izak, Izie, Izze, Izzee

Izador
(Spanish) gift
*Dorrie, Dory, Isa, Isador,
Isadoro, Isidoros, Isodore,
Iza, Izadoro*

Izzy
(Hebrew) friendly
Issie, Issy, Izi, Izzee, Izzie

Ja
(Korean) gorgeous

Jaan
(Scandinavian) from John; believes in the Lord

Jabal
(Place name) short for Japalpur (city in India); attractive

Jabari
(African American) brave

Jabbar
(Arabic) comforting

JaBee
(American) combo of Jay and B
J.B., Jabee, Jaybe, Jaybee

Jaber
(American) form of Arabic Jabir; comforting
Jabar, Jabe, Jabir

Jabez
(Hebrew) sorrow
Jabezz

Jabin
(Hebrew) God's own

Jabir
(Arabic) supportive
Jabbar

Jabon
(American) wild
Jabonne

Jabot
(French) shirt ruffle

Jace
(American) audacious
Jase, Jhace

Jacee
(American) combo of Jay and C
J.C., Jacey, JayC, Jaycee, Jaycie, Jaycy

Jacek
(Polish) hyacinth; growing
Jack, Yahcik

Jacett
(Invented) jaunty
Jaycett

Jachym
(Hebrew) from Jacob; supplants; helpful
Jach

Jacinto
(Spanish) hyacinth; fragrant
Jacint

Jack
(Hebrew) believer in a gracious God; personality-plus
Jackee, Jackie, Jacko, Jacky, Jax

Jackal
(Sanskrit) wild dog; betrays
Jackel, Jackell, Jackyl, Jackyll

Jackie
(English) personable
Jackee, Jackey, Jacki, Jacky, Jaki

Jackson
(English) Jack's son; full of personality
Jackee, Jackie, Jacks, Jacsen, Jakson, Jax, Jaxon

Jacksonville
(Last name as first name) town of Jack's son; sturdy
Jacsonville, Jaksonville

Jacob
(Hebrew) replacement;
best boy
*Jaccob, Jacobe, Jacobee,
Jake, Jakes, Jakey, Jakob*

Jacobo
(Spanish) warm
Jake, Jakey

Jacobs
(Biblical) replacing
Jakobs, Jakey

Jacobus
(Latin) from Jacob
Jakobus

Jacoby
(Hebrew) from Jacob
Jacobey, Jakobey, Jakoby

Jacquard
(French) class act
*Jackard, Jackarde,
Jacquarde, Jaqard,
Jaquard, Jaquarde*

Jacques
(French) romantic;
ingenious
*Jacquie, Jacue, Jaques,
Jock, Jok*

Jacy
(American) from Jacob;
replacement

Jadaan
(Last name as first name)
content
Jada, Jadan, Jade, Jay

Jadall
(Invented) punctual
Jada, Jade

Jade
(Spanish) valued (jade
stone)
Jadee, Jadie, Jayde

Jadee
(American) combo of Jay
and D
J.D., Jadee, JayD, Jaydy

Jadney
(Last name as first name)
pleased
Jad

Jadon
(American) devout; ball-
of-fire
*Jade, Jadin, Jadun, Jadun,
Jadyn, Jaiden, Jaydie,
Jaydon*

Jadrien
(Invented) combo of Jaden
and Adrien; audacious

Jaegel
(English) salesman
Jaeg, Jaeger, Jael

Jaeger
(German) outdoorsman
Jaegir, Jagher, Jagur

Jael
(Hebrew) climber

Jaequon
(African American) combo
of Jae and Quon; outgoing
Jaequan, Jayquon, Jayquan

Jaewon
(African American) form of
Juwon
Jaewan, Jaywan, Jaywon

Jafar
(Arabic) from the stream
Gafar, Jafari

Jaffey
(English) form of Jaffe
Jaff

Jagan
(English) confident
Jagen, Jagun, Jago

Jagger
(English) brash
Jagar, Jager, Jaggar, Jagir

Jaggerton
(English) brash
Jag, Jagg

Jagit
(Invented) brisk
Jaggett, Jaggit, Jagitt

Jago
(English) self-assured

Jaguar
(Spanish) fast
Jag, Jagg, Jaggy, Jagwar, Jagwhar

Jahan
(Sanskrit) worldly

Jahi
(African) runs well; dignity

Jahmal
(Arabic) beautiful
Jahmaal, Jahmall

Jahmil
(Arabic) beautiful
Jahmeel, Jahmyl

Jai
(American) adventurer
Jay

Jaidev
(Hindi) God's victory

Jaime
(Spanish) follower
Jaimey, Jaimie, Jamee, Jaymie

Jaimini
(Hindi) winner

Jair
(Hebrew) teacher
Jairo

Jairaj
(Hindi) Lord's victor

Jairo
(Spanish) God enlightens
Jaero, Jairoh

Jairus
(Biblical) faithful

Jaison
(American) form of Jason
Jaizon

Jaja
(African) praise-worthy

Jajuan
(African American) combo
of Ja and Juan; loves God

Jakar
(Place name) from Jakarta,
Indonesia
Jakart, Jakarta, Jakarte

Jake
(Hebrew) short for Jacob
Jaik, Jakee, Jakey, Jakie, Jayke

Jakeem
(Arabic) has been lifted

Jakey
(American) nickname for
Jake; friendly
Jaky

Jakob
(Hebrew) form of Jacob
Jakab, Jake, Jakeb, Jakey, Jakie, Jakobe, Jakub

Jal
(Arabic) from Jalal; great;
travels

Jaleel
(Arabic) handsome
Jalil

Jalen
(American) vivacious
Jalon, Jaylen, Jaylin, Jaylon

Jamail
(Arabic) good-looking
Jahmil, Jam, Jamaal, Jamahal, Jamal, Jamil, Jamile, Jamy

Jamaine
(Arabic) good-looking

Jamar
(American) from Jamal;
attractive
Jamarr, Jemar, Jimar

JaMarcus
(African American) combo
of Jay and Marcus;
attractive
Jamarcus, Jamark, Jamarkus

Jamari
(African American) attractive

Jamarr
(African American) attractive; formidable
Jam, Jamaar, Jamar, Jammy

Jamel
(Arabic) form of Jamal
Jameel, Jamele, Jimelle

James
(English) dependable; steadfast
Jaimes, Jamsey, Jamze, Jaymes, Jim, Jimmy

Jameson
(English) able; James's son
Jamesan, Jamesen, Jamesey, Jamison, Jamsie

Jamie
(English) short for James
Jaimey, Jaimie, Jamee, Jamey, Jay, Jaymey, Jaymsey

Jamil
(Arabic) beautiful
Jameel, Jamyl

Jamin
(Hebrew) favored son
Jamen, James, Jamie, Jamon, Jaymon

Jamisen
(American) form of James/Jamie; lively
Jami, Jamie, Jamis, Jamison

Jan
(Dutch) form of John; believer
Jaan, Jann, Janne

Jan-Erik
(Slavic) combo of Jan and Erik; reliable
Jan-Eric

Janesh
(Hindi) thankful

Janson
(Scandinavian) Jan's son; hardworking
Jan, Janne, Janny, Jansahn, Jansen, Jansey

Jantz
(Scandinavian) short for Jantzen
Janson, Janssen, Jantzon, Janz, Janzon

Janus
(Latin) Roman god of beginnings and endings; optimistic; born in January
Jan, Janis

Japheth
(Hebrew) grows
Japhet

Jaquawn
(African American) rock
Jacquon, Jakka, Jaquan, Jaquan, Jaquie, Jaqwen, Jequon, Jock

Jarah
(Hebrew) sweet

Jard
(American) form of Jared; longlasting
Jarra, Jarrd, Jarri, Jerd, Jord

Jareb
(Hebrew) contender
Jarib, Yarev, Yariv

Jared
(Hebrew) descendant; giving
Jarad, Jarod, Jarode, Jarret, Jarrett, Jerod, Jerrad, Jerrod

Jarek
(Slavic) fresh
Jarec

Jarell
(Scandinavian) giving
Jare, Jarelle, Jarey, Jarrell, Jerrell

Jaren
(Hebrew) vocal
Jaron, Jayrone, J'ron

Jarenal
(American) form of Jaren;
long-lasting
*Jaranall, Jaret, Jarn,
Jaronal, Jarry, Jerry*

Jareth
(American) open to
adventure
Jarey, Jarith, Jarth, Jary

Jarman
(German) stoic
Jerman

Jaromil
(Czech) spring love
Jarmil

Jarred
(Hebrew) form of Jared
*Jared, Jere, Jerod, Jerred,
Jerud*

Jarrell
(English) jaunty
*Jare, Jarell, Jarrel, Jarry,
Jerele, Jerrell*

Jarrett
(English) confident
*Jare, Jaret, Jaritt, Jarret,
Jarrit, Jarritt, Jarry, Jarryt,
Jarrytt, Jerot, Jerret, Jerrett,
Jurett, Jurette*

Jarrod
(Hebrew) form of Jared
Jare, Jarod, Jarry, Jerod

Jarvey
(German) celebrated
*Garvey, Garvy, Jarvee,
Jarvi, Jarvy*

Jarvis
(German) athletic
*Jarv, Jarvee, Jarves, Jarvey,
Jarvhus, Jarvie, Jarvus,
Jarvy*

Jary
(Spanish) form of Jerry;
leader
Jaree

Jase
(American) hip

Jashon
(African American) combo
of Jason and the letter
h**Jason**
(Greek) healer; man on a
quest
*Jace, Jacey, Jaisen, Jase,
Jasen, Jasey, Jasyn, Jayson,
Jaysun*

Jason-Joel
(American) combo of
Jason and Joel; popular
Jasonjoel, Jason Joel

Jaspal
(Pakistani) pure

Jasper
(English) guard; country
boy
Jasp, Jaspur, Jaspy, Jaspyr

Jaster
(English) form of Jasper;
vigilant
Jast

Jathan
(Invented) combo of Jake
and Nathan; attractive
*Jae, Jath, Jathe, Jathen,
Jathun, Jay*

Javan
(Biblical) righteous
Javin, Javon

Javaris
(African American) ready
Javares, Javarez

Javas
(Sanskrit) bright eyes

Javier
(Spanish) affluent;
homeowner
Havyaire, Javey, Javiar

Javon
(Hebrew) hopeful
Javan, Javaughn, Javen, Javonn, Javonte

Javonte
(African American) jaunty
Javaughantay, Javawnte, Ja-Vonnetay, Ja-Vontae

Javy
(American) short for Javaris; prepared
Javey, Javie

Jawdat
(Arabic) excellent
Gawdat

Jawhar
(Arabic) gem

Jawon
(African American) shy
Jawan, Jawaughn, Jawaun, Jawuane, Jewan, Jewon, Jowon

Jax
(American) form of Jackson; fun
Jacks, Jaxx

Jay
(English) short for a name starting with J; colorful
Jai, Jaye

Jaya
(American) jazzy
Jay, Jayah

Jayant
(Hindi) winner

Jaydon
(American) bright-eyed
Jayde, Jayden, Jaydey, Jaydi, Jaydie, Jaydun, Jaydy

Jaylin
(American) combo of Jay and Lin

Jaymes
(American) form of James
Jaimes, James

JayR
(American) actor
J.R.

Jayson
(Greek) form of Jason

Jazeps
(Latvian) God will increase

Jazon
(Polish) heals

Jazz
(American) jazzy
Jazze, Jazzee, Jazzy

Jean
(French) form of John; kind
Jeanne, Jeannie, Jene

Jean-Baptiste
(French) combo of Jean and Baptiste; John the Baptist; religious
John-Baptiste

Jean-Claude
(French) combo of Jean and Claude; gracious

Jean-Francois
(French) combo of Jean and Francois; smooth

Jean-Michel
(French) combo of Jean and Michel; godly

Jean-Paul
(French) combo of Jean and Paul; small and giving

Jean-Philippe
(French) combo of Jean and Philippe; handsome

Jean-Pierre
(French) combo of Jean and Pierre; giving and dependable

Jeb
(Hebrew) jolly
Jebb, Jebby

Jebediah
(Hebrew) close to God
Jeb, Jebadiah, Jebby, Jebedyah

Jecori
(American) exuberant
Jekori

Jed
(Hebrew) helpful
Jedd, Jeddy, Jede

Jediah
(Hebrew) God's help
Jedi, Jedyah

Jedidiah
(Hebrew) close to God
Jed, Jeddy, Jeddyah, Jedidyah

Jedrek
(Polish) virile
Jedrick, Jedrus

Jeevan
(African American) form of Jevon; lively
Jevaughn, Jevaun

Jeff
(English) short for Jeffrey or Jefferson
Geoff, Jeffie, Jeffy

Jefferson
(English) dignified
Jeff, Jeffarson, Jeffersen, Jeffursen, Jeffy

Jeffery
(English) alternate for Jeffrey; peaceful
Jeffrey, Jeffrie, Jeffry, Jefry

Jeffrey
(English) peaceful
Geoffrey, Jeff, Jeffree, Jeffrie, Jeffry, Jeffy, Jefree

Jehan
(French) for John; spiritual

Jehu
(Hebrew) true believer

Jela
(African) honors

Jelani
(African American) trendy
Jelanee, Jelaney, Jelanne

Jem
(English) short for James
Jemmi, Jemmy, Jemmye, Jemy

Jemarr
(African American) worldly
Jemahr

Jemonde
(French) man of the world
Jemond

Jenda
(Czech) form of John; humble

Jenkins
(Last name as first name) God is gracious
Jenkin, Jenks, Jenky, Jenkyns, Jenx, Jinx

Jennett
(Hindi) heavenly
Jennet, Jennit, Jennitt, Jennyt, Jennytt, Jinnat

Jennings
(Last name as first name) attractive
Jennyngs

Jensi
(Hungarian) noble
Jenci, Jens

Jenson
(English) son of Jen; blessed
Jensen, Jenssen, Jensson

Jep
(American) easygoing
Jepp

Jephtha
(Biblical) judges others; outgoing

Jerald
(English) form of Gerald;
merry
*Jere, Jereld, Jerold, Jerrie,
Jerry*

Jeramy
(Hebrew) exciting
*Jeramah, Jeramie, Jere,
Jeremy*

Jerard
(French) confident
Jerrard

Jere
(Hebrew) short for Jeremy
Jeree, Jerey

Jeremiah
(Hebrew) prophet uplifted
by God; far-sighted
*Jeramiah, Jere, Jeremyah,
Jerome, Jerry*

Jeremie
(Hebrew) loquacious
Jeremee, Jeremy

Jeremy
(English) talkative
*Jaramie, Jere, Jeremah,
Jereme, Jeremey, Jerrey,
Jerry*

Jeriah
(Hebrew) uplifted; from
Jeremiah

Jericho
(Arabic) nocturnal
*Jerako, Jere, Jerico, Jeriko,
Jerycho, Jerycko, Jeryco,
Jeryko*

Jerick
(American) form of
Jericho; tenacious
*Gericho, Jereck, Jerik, Jero,
Jerok, Jerrico*

Jeril
(American) form of Jarrell;
leader
Jerill, Jerl, Jerry

Jerma
(American) form of
Germain; man of Germany
*Jermah, Jermane,
Jermayne*

Jermain
(French) from Germany
*German, Germane,
Germanes, Germano,
Germanus, Jermaine,
Jerman, Jermane, Jermayn,
Jermayne*

Jermaine
(German) form of
Germaine
*Germain, Germaine, Jere,
Jermain, Jermane,
Jermene, Jerry*

Jermey
(American) short for
Jermaine; friendly
Jermy

Jermon
(African American)
dependable
Jermonn

Jerney
(Slavic) from Greek,
Jerome; funny

Jernigan
(Last name as first name)
spontaneous
Jerni, Jerny

Jero
(American) jaunty
*Jeroh, Jerree, Jerri, Jerro,
Jerry*

Jerod
(Hebrew) form of Jerrod
and Jarrod

Jerold
(English) merry
Jerrold, Jerry

Jerome
(Latin) holy name; blessed
Jarome, Jere, Jerohm, Jeromy, Jerree, Jerrome, Jerry, Jirome

Jerone
(English) hopeful
Jere, Jerohn, Jeron, Jerrone

Jeronimo
(Italian) form of Gerome; Geronimo, Apache Indian chief; excited
Gerry, Jero, Jerry

Jerral
(American) form of Gerald/Jerald; exciting
Jeral, Jere, Jerry

Jerram
(Hebrew) God has uplifted
Jeram, Jerem, Jerrem, Jerrym, Jerym

Jerrell
(American) exciting
Jarell, Jerre, Jerrel, Jerrie, Jerry

Jerrett
(Hebrew) form of Jarrett
Jeret, Jerete, Jerod, Jerot, Jerret

Jerrick
(American) combo of Jerry and Derek (Derrick); lively
Jerick, Jerrie

Jerry
(German) strong
Gerry, Gery, Jerre, Jerri, Jerrie, Jerrye

Jerse
(Place name) calm; rural
Jerce, Jercey, Jersey, Jersy, Jerzy

Jervis
(Greek) honorable
Gervase

Jesmar
(American) from Jesse; Biblical
Jess, Jessie, Jezz, Jezzie

Jesper
(American) easygoing
Jesp, Jess

Jess
(Hebrew) wealthy
Jes

Jesse
(Hebrew) wealthy
Jess, Jessee, Jessey, Jessi, Jessye

Jessup
(Last name as first name) rich
Jesop, Jesopp, Jess, Jessa, Jessie, Jessopp, Jessy, Jesup, Jesupp, Jessupp

Jesuan
(Spanish) devout

Jesus
(Hebrew) saved by God
Hesus, Jesu, Jesuso, Jezus

Jesus-Amador
(Spanish) combo of Jesus and Amador; loving the Lord
Jesusamador, Jesus Amador

Jesus-Angel
(Spanish) combo of Jesus and Angel; angel of God
Jesusangel, Jesusangelo

Jet
(English) black gem

Jetal
(American) zany
Jetahl, Jetil, Jett, Jettale, Jetty

Jethro
(Hebrew) fertile
Jeto, Jett, Jetty

Jeton
(French) a chip for
gamblers; wild spirit
Jet, Jetawn, Jets, Jett, Jetty

Jett
(American) wild spirit
Jet, Jets, Jetty, The Jet

Jettie
(American) from name
Jett; free
Jette, Jettee, Jetti

Jetty
(American) from the name
Jett; free
Jettey

Jevan
(African American) spirited
*Jevaughn, Jevaun, Jevin,
Jevon*

Jevon
(African American) spirited
Jevaun

Jex
(American) form of Jack;
personable

Jhonatan
(African) spiritual
Jhon, Jon

Ji
(Chinese) organized;
orderly

Jibben
(American) form of Jivan;
(Hindi) alive

Jibri
(Arabic) angel

Jie
(Chinese) wonderful

Jim
(Hebrew) short for James
*Jem, Jihm, Jimi, Jimmee,
Jimmy*

Jimbo
(American) cowhand;
endearment for Jim
*Jim, Jimb, Jimbee, Jimbey,
Jimby*

Jimbob
(American) countrified
*Gembob, Jim Bob, Jim-
Bob, Jymbob*

Jimmy
(English) short for James
*Jim, Jimi, Jimmey, Jimmi,
Jimmye, Jimy*

Jimmydee
(American) combo of
Jimmy and Dee; southern
boy
*Jimmy D, Jimmy Dee,
Jimmy-Dee*

Jimmy-John
(American) country boy
*Jimmiejon, Jimmyjohn,
Jimmy-Jon, Jymmejon*

Jimoh
(African) Friday's child

Jin
(Chinese) golden

Jinan
(Place name) city in China
Jin

Jindrich
(Czech) ruling
*Jindra, Jindrik, Jindrisek,
Jindrousek*

Jing
(Chinese) unblemished;
capital

Jiri
(Czech) working the earth
Jira, Jiricek

Jiro
(Japanese) second boy
born

Jivon
(Hindi) living; vibrant

Joab
(Hebrew) praising God;
hovering
Joabb

Joachim
(Hebrew) a king of Judah;
powerful; believer
*Akim, Jakim, Yachim,
Yakim*

Joah
(Greek) form of Jonah;
unfortunate

Joaquin
(Spanish) bold; hip
*Joakeen, Joaquim,
Joaquin, Juakeen,
Jwaqueen*

Job
(Hebrew) patient
Jobb, Jobe, Jobi, Joby

Jobson
(English) son of Job;
patient

Joby
(Hebrew) patient; tested
Job, Jobee, Jobi

Jock
(Hebrew) grace in God;
athlete
Jockie, Jocky

Jody
(Hebrew) believer in
Jehovah; (American)
combo of Joe and Dee
*Jodee, Jodey, Jodie, Jodye,
Joe*

Joe
(Hebrew) short for Joel
and Joseph
Jo, Joey, Joeye, Joie

Joebob
(American) combo of Joe
and Bob
J.B., Jobob, Joe-Bob

Joedan
(American) combo of Joe
and Dan
*Jodan, Jodin, Jodon, Joe-
Dan, Joedanne*

Joel
(Hebrew) prophet in the
Bible
Joelie, Joell, Jole, Joly

Joemac
(American) combo of Joe
and Mac
*J.M., Joe-Mac, Joe-Mack,
Jomack*

Joergen
(Scandinavian) earth
worker

Joey
(Hebrew) short for Joel
and Joseph
Joee, Joie

Joffre
(German) form of Jeffrey;
bright star

Johann
(German) spiritual
musician
*Johan, Johane, Yohann,
Yohanne, Yohon*

Johannes
(Hebrew) form of John, the
Biblical name
Johan, Jon

Johar
(Hindi) gem

John
(Hebrew) honorable;
Biblical name
*Jahn, Jhan, Johne, Johnne,
Johnni, Johnnie, Johnny,
Johnnye, Jon*

Johnnie
(Hebrew) endearment for
John; honorable man
*Gianni, Johnie, Johnny,
Jonni, Jonny*

Johnny-Dodd
    (American) country sheriff
    *Johnniedodd, Johnny
    Dodd*
Johnpaul
    (American) combo of John
    and Paul
    *John Paul, John-Paul,
    Jonpaul*
Johnny-Ramon
    (Spanish) renegade
    *Johnnyramon, Johnny
    Ramon*
Johnson
    (English) John's son;
    credible
    *Johnsen, Johnsonne,
    Jonsen, Jonson*
Joji
    (Japanese) form of John;
    believes
Jojo
    (American) friendly;
    popular
    Jo-Jo
Jolon
    (Native American) oak
    valley dweller
Jomar
    (African American) helpful
    Joemar, Jomarr
Jomei
    (Japanese) lightens
Jon
    (Hebrew) alternative for
    John
    Jonni, Jonnie, Jonny, Jony
Jonah
    (Hebrew) peacemaker
    Joneh
Jonas
    (Hebrew) capable; active
    Jon

Jonathan
    (Hebrew) gracious
    *Johnathan, Johnathon,
    Jonathon*
Jon-Eric
    (American) combo of Jon
    and Eric
    Joneric, Jon Eric, John-Eric
Jones
    (American) saucy
Jon-Jason
    (American) combo of Jon
    and Jason
    *Johnjace, John-Jaison,
    John-Jazon, Jon Jason,
    Jonjason, Jon-Jayson*
Jonjay
    (American) combo of Jon
    and Jay; jaunty; believer
    Jonjae, Jon Jay, Jon-Jay
Jonmarc
    (American) combo of Jon
    and Marc
    *Jon Marc, Jon-Marc, John
    Mark*
Jonnley
    (American) form of Jon;
    believer
    Jonn, Jonnie
Jonte
    (American) from John;
    loves God
    Johatay, Johate, Jontae
Joplin
    (Place name) city in
    Montana; sings
    Joplyn
Jordahno
    (Invented) form of Giordano
Jordan
    (Hebrew) descending
    *Jorden, Jordon, Jordun,
    Jordy, Jordyn*
Jordane
    (Hebrew) form of Jordan;
    down-flowing river

Jordison
(American) son of Jordi;
glowing
*Jordisen, Jordysen,
Jordyson*

Jordy
(Hebrew) from Jordan
Jordie, Jordey

Jorge
(Spanish) form of George;
farmer
Jorje, Quiqui

Jorgen
(Scandinavian) farmer
Jorgan

Jory
(Hebrew) descendant
Jorey

Jos
(Place name) city in Nigeria

José
(Spanish) asset; favored
Joesay, Jose, Pepe, Pepito

Josef
(Hebrew) asset;
supported by Jehovah
*Jodie, Joe, Joey, Josep,
Joseph, Josephe, Jozef,
Yusif*

Josh
(Hebrew) saved by the
Lord; devout
*Joshua, Joshuam,
Joshyam, Josue, Jozua*

Josha
(Hebrew) variant of Joshua

Joshuah
(Hebrew) devout

Josia
(Hebrew) form of Josiah;
supported by the Lord
Josea

Josiah
(Hebrew) Jehovah bolsters
Josyah

Joss
(English) form of Joseph;
cool
Josslin, Jossly

Josue
(Spanish) devout

Jotham
(Biblical) a king of Judah;
believer in perfect Jehovah
Jothem, Jothym

Jourdain
(French) flowing
Jordane, Jorden

Jovan
(Slavic) gifted
Jovahn, Jovohn

Jovani
(Italian) Roman god Jove;
jovial
*Jovani, Jovanni, Jovanny,
Jovany*

Jove
(Mythology) Roman sky
god

Juanantonio
(Spanish) combo of Juan
and Antonio; believer in a
gracious God
*Juan Antonio, Juan-
Antonio*

Joza
(Czech) from Joseph; he
adds to life

Jozef
(Polish) supported by
Jehovah; asset
Joe, Joze

Juan
(Spanish) devout; lively
Juann, Juwon

Juancarlos
(Spanish) combo of Juan
and Carlos; debonair

Juan-Fernando
(Spanish) combo of Juan and Fernando; believer in a gracious God
Juanfernand, Juanfernando, Juan Fernando

Juanjose
(Spanish) combo of Juan and Jose; active
Juan-Jose

Juanmiguel
(Spanish) combo of Juan and Miguel; hopeful
Juan-Miguel

Juanpablo
(Spanish) combo of Juan and Pablo; believer
Juan Pablo, Juan-Pablo

Jubal
(Hebrew) celebrant

Jubilo
(Spanish) rejoicing; jubilant
Jube

Judah
(Biblical) praised
Juda

Judas
(Latin) Biblical traitor

Judd
(Latin) secretive
Jud

Jude
(Latin) form of Judas; disloyal
Judah

Judge
(English) judgmental
Judg

Judson
(Last name as first name) mercurial
Juddsen, Juddson, Judsen, Judssen

Judule
(American) form of Judah; judicious
Jud, Judsen, Judsun

Jules
(Greek) young Adonis
Jewels, Jule

Julian
(Greek) gorgeous
Juliane, Julien, Julyon, Julyun

Julio
(Spanish) handsome; youthful
Huleeo, Hulie, Julie

Julius
(Greek) attractive
Juleus, Jul-yus, Jul-yuz

Ju-Long
(Chinese) powerful

Jumaane
(African) Tuesday-born

Jumah
(African) from Jumapili; Sunday-born
Juma

Jumbe
(African) strong
Jumbey, Jumby

Jumoke
(African) beloved

Jun
(Japanese) follows the rules

Juneau
(Place name) capital of Alaska
Juno, Junoe

Junior
(Latin) young son of the father, senior
Junnie, Junny, Junyer

Junius
(Latin) youngster
Junie, Junnie, Junny

Jupiter
(Roman) god of thunder
and lightning; guardian
Jupe

Jura
(Place name) mountain
range between France and
Switzerland
Jurah

Jurass
(American) from Jurassic
period of dinosaurs;
daunting
Jurases, Jurassic

Jurgen
(Scandinavian) working
the earth

Juri
(Slavic) farms

Jus
(French) just
Just, Justice, Justis

Juste
(French) law-abiding
Just, Zhuste

Justice
(Latin) just
*Jusees, Just, Justice, Justiz,
Justus, Juztice*

Justie
(Latin) honest; fair
Jus, Justee, Justey, Justi

Justin
(Latin) fair
*Just, Justan, Justen,
Justun, Justyn, Justyne*

Justinian
(Latin) ruler; Roman
emperor
Justinyan

Justino
(Spanish) fair
Justyno

Justiz
(American) judging; fair
Justice, Justis

Justus
(German) fair

Jute
(Botanical) practical

Juvenal
(Latin) young
Juve

Juventino
(Spanish) young
Juve, Juven, Juvey, Tino, Tito

Juwon
(African American) form of
Juan; devout; lively
Jujuane, Juwan, Juwonne

K

Kabir
(Hindi) spiritual leader
Kabar

Kabonero
(African) symbol

Kabonesa
(African) born in hard
times

Kacancu
(Rukonjo) firstborn

Kacy
(American) happy
*K.C., Kace, Kacee, Kase,
Kasee, Kasy, Kaycee*

Kadar
(Arabic) empowered
Kader

Kade
(American) exciting
*Cade, Caden, K.D. Kadey,
Kaid, Kayde, Kydee*

Kadeem
(Arabic) servant
Kadim

Kaden
(American) exciting
*Cade, Caden, Caiden,
Caidin, Caidon, Caydan,
Cayden, Caydin, Caydon,
Kadan, Kadon, Kadyn,
Kaiden*

Kadir
(Hindi) talented
Kadeer, Qadeer, Qadir

Kadmiel
(Hebrew) God-loving

Kado
(Japanese) through life's
gate

Kaelan
(Irish) strong
*Kael, Kaelen, Kaelin,
Kaelyn*

Kaemon
(Japanese) happy

Kaeto
(American)
Cato, Cayto, Caytoe, Kato

Kahale
(Hawaiian) homebody

Kahil
(Turkish) ingénue; (Arabic)
friend; (Greek) handsome
*Cahill, Kaleel, Kalil, Kayhil,
Khalil*

Kaholo
(Hawaiian) boy who runs

Kai
(Hawaiian, African)
attractive
Kay, Keh

Kaid
(English) round; happy
*Caiden, Cayde, Caydin,
Kaden, Kadin, Kayd*

Kaihe
(Hawaiian) spear

Kailin
(Irish) sporty
*Kailyn, Kale, Kalen, Kaley,
Kalin, Kallen, Kaylen*

Kaipo
(Hawaiian) embraces

Kairo
(Arabic) from Cairo; exotic

Kaiser
(German) title that means
emperor

Kaj
(Scandinavian) earthy

Kala
(Hawaiian) sun boy

Kalama
(Hawaiian) source of light
Kalam

Kalani
(Hawaiian) of one sky
Kalan

Kale
(American) healthy;
vegetable
*Kail, Kayle, Kaylee, Kayley,
Kaylie*

Kaleb
(American) form of Caleb
Caleb

Kalgan
(Place name) city in China
Kal

Kali
(Polynesian) comforts

Kalil
(Arabic) best friend
*Kahil, Kahleel, Kahlil,
Kaleel, Khaleel, Khalil*

Kalkin
(Hindi) tenth child

Kallen
(Greek) handsome
Kallan, Kallin, Kallon,
Kallun, Kalon, Kalun,
Kalyn

Kalogeros
(Greek) beautiful in aging

Kalunga
(African) watchful; the
personal god of the
Mbunda of Angola

Kalvin
(Latin) form of Calvin;
blessing
Kal

Kamaka
(Hawaiian) pretty face

Kamal
(Arabic) perfect
Kameel, Kamil

Kamau
(African) quiet soldier
Kamall

Kameron
(Scottish) form of
Cameron
Kameren, Kammeron,
Kammi, Kammie, Kammy,
Kamran, Kamrin, Kamron

Kamon
(American) alligator,
(Place name) Cayman
Islands
Cayman, Caymun, Kame,
Kammy, Kayman, Kaymon

Kana
(Japanese) strength of
character

Kance
(American) combo of Kane
and Chance; attractive
Cance, Cance, Cans,
Kaince, Kans, Kanse,
Kaynce

Kane
(American, English)
sterling spirit
Cahan, Cahane, Cain, Kain,
Kaine, Kaney, Kanie, Kayne

Kang
(Korean) healthy

Kaniel
(Hebrew) confident;
supported by the Lord;
hopeful
Kane, Kan-El, Kanel,
Kanelle, Kaney

Kano
(Place name) city in
Nigeria
Kan, Kanoh

Kant
(German) philosopher
Cant

Kantu
(Hindi) joyous

Kanye
(American) unbreakable

Kaori
(Japanese) scented

Kaper
(American) capricious
Cape, Caper, Kahper, Kape

Kapila
(Hindi) foresees
Kapil

Kapono
(Hawaiian) anointed one

Kapp
(Greek) short for the
surname Kaparos
Kap, Kappy

Karcher
(German) beautiful blond
boy

Kare
(Scandinavian) large
Karee

Kareem
(Arabic) generous
*Karehm, Karem, Karim,
Karreem, Krehm*

Karey
(Greek) form of Cary or
Carey
Karee, Kari, Karrey, Karry

Kari
(Scandinavian) hair curls

Karif
(Arabic) fall-born
Kareef

Kareem
(Arabic) generous
Karam, Karim

Karl
(German) manly; forceful
*Carl, Kale, Karel, Karll,
Karlie, Karol, Karoly*

Karmel
(Hebrew) red-haired
*Carmel, Carmelo, Karmeli,
Karmelli, Karmelo,
Karmello, Karmi*

Karney
(Irish) wins
Carney

Karolek
(Polish) form of Charles;
grown man
Karol

Karr
(Scandinavian) curly hair
Carr

Karsten
(Greek) chosen one

Karu
(Hindi) cousin
Karun

Kaseem
(Arabic) divides
*Kasceem, Kaseym, Kasim,
Kazeem*

Kaseko
(African) ridiculed

Kasem
(Asian) joyful

Kasen
(Spanish) helmet;
protected

Kasey
(Irish) form of Casey
Kasi, Kasie

Kasi
(African) short for Kasiya;
leaving
Kasee, Kasey, Kasie

Kasim
(Hindi) shining

Kasimir
(Arabic) serene
Kasim Kazimir, Kazmer

Kasper
(German) reliable
*Caspar, Casper, Kasp,
Kaspar, Kaspy*

Kass
(German) standout among
men
Cass, Kasse

Kassidy
(Irish) form of Cassidy
*Kass, Kassidi, Kassidie,
Kassie*

Kato
(African) second of twins

Katzir
(Hebrew) reaping
Katzeer

Kauai
(Place name) Hawaiian
island; breezy spirit
Kawai

Kaufman
(Last name as first name)
serious
Kauffmann, Kaufmann

Kavan
(Irish) good-looking
Cavan, Kaven, Kavin

Kavi
(Hindi) poetic

Kay
(Greek) joyful
Kai, Kaye, Kaysie, Kaysy, Keh

Kayin
(African) desired baby

Kayle
(Hebrew) faithful
Kail, Kayl

Kaylen
(Irish) form of Kellen; laughing
Kaylan, Kaylin, Kaylon, Kaylyn

Kayven
(Irish) handsome
Cavan, Kavan, Kave

Kazan
(Greek) creative
Kazann

Kazimierz
(Polish) practical
Kaz

Kazuo
(Japanese) peaceloving

Kealoha
(Hawaiian) bright path

Keandre
(American) combo of Ke and Andre; grateful
Keondre

Keane
(German) attractive
Kean, Keen, Keene, Kiene

Keanu
(Hawaiian) cool breeze over mountains
Keahnu

Kearn
(Irish) outspoken
Kearny, Kern, Kerne, Kerney

Kearney
(Irish) sparkling
Karney, Karny, Kearns, Kerney, Kirney

Keary
(Irish) form of Kerry; dark

Keaton
(English) nature-lover
Keaten, Keatt, Keatun, Keton

Keats
(Literature) for poet John Keats; melancholy
Keatz

Keawe
(Hawaiian) lovable

Keb
(Egyptian) loves the earth

Kecalf
(American) inventive
Keecalf

Kechel
(African American)
Kach, Kachelle

Kedar
(Hindi) powerful
Kadar, Keder

Kedem
(Hebrew) old soul

Kedrick
(American) form of Kendrick
Ked, Keddy, Kedric, Kedrik

Kee-Bun
(Taiwanese) good news
Keebun

Keefe
(Irish) handsome
Keaf, Keafe, Keef, Keeffe, Kief

Keegan
(Irish) ball-of-fire
Keagan, Keagin, Kegan, Kege, Keghun

Keelan
(Irish) slim
Kealan, Keallan, Keallin, Keilan, Keillan, Kelan

Keeley
(Irish) handsome
Kealey, Kealy, Keelee, Keelie, Keely, Keilie

Keen
(German) smart
Kean, Keane, Keene, Keeney, Kene

Keenan
(Irish) bright-eyed
Kenan

Keeney
(American) incisive
Kean, Keane, Keaney, Keene, Kene

Kefir
(Hebrew) young lion; high spirits

Keir
(Irish) brunette

Keirer
(Irish) dark
Kerer

Keiron
(Irish) dark
Keiren, Keronn

Keitaro
(Japanese) blessed baby
Keita

Keith
(English) witty
Keath, Keeth, Keithe

Keithen
(Scottish) gentle
Keith

Kekoa
(Hawaiian) one warrior

Kel
(Irish) fighter; energetic
Kell

Kelby
(English) snappy; charming
Kel, Kelbey, Kelbi, Kelbie, Kelbye, Kell, Kellby, Kelly

Kelcy
(English) helpful
Kelci, Kelcie, Kelcye, Kelsie

Kele
(Hawaiian) watches like a hawk

Kelle
(Scandinavian) springlike

Kelemen
(Hungarian) softspoken

Kell
(English) fresh-faced
Kel, Kelly

Kellagh
(Irish) hardworking
Kellach

Kellen
(Irish) strong-willed
Kel, Kelen, Kelin, Kell, Kellan, Kellin, Kelly, Kelyn

Keller
(Last name as first name) bountiful
Kel, Keler, Kelher, Kell, Kylher

Kelly
(Irish) able combatant
Keli, Kellee, Kelley, Kelli, Kellie

Kelmen
(Hungarian) form of Kelemen; softspoken

Kelsey
(Scandinavian) unique among men
Kel, Kells, Kelly, Kels, Kelsi, Kelsie, Kelsy, Kelsye, Kelzie, Kelzy

Kelton
(Irish) energetic
Keldon, Kelltin, Kellton, Kelten, Keltin, Keltonn

Kelts
(Origin unknown)
energetic
*Kel, Kelly, Kelse, Kelsey,
Keltz*

Kelvin
(English) goal-oriented
*Kelvan, Kelven, Kellven,
Kelvon, Kelvun, Kelvynn,
Kilvin*

Kelvis
(Invented) combo of K and
Elvis; ambitious
Kellvis, Kelviss, Kelvys

Kemal
(Turkish) honored infant;
generous

Kemp
(English) champion

Kemper
(American) high-minded
Kemp, Kempar

Kempton
(American) takes the high
road

Kemuel
(Hebrew) God's advocate

Ken
(Scottish) short for
Kenneth; cute
Kenn, Kenny, Kinn

Kendall
(English) shy
*Ken, Kend, Kendahl,
Kendal, Kendoll, Kendy,
Kenney, Kennie, Kenny,
Kindal*

Kendan
(English) strong; serious
Ken, Kend, Kenden

Kendrick
(English) heroic
*Kendricks, Kendrik,
Kendryck, Kenric, Kenrick,
Kenricks, Kenrik*

Kenel
(Invented) form of Kendall;
hopeful
Kenele

Kenelm
(English) handsome boy
Kenhelm, Kennelm

Kenlee
(American) combo of Ken
and Lee

Kenley
(English) distinguished
*Kenlea, Kenlee, Kenleigh,
Kenlie, Kenly*

Kenn
(English) river; flowing

Kennard
(English) courageous;
selfless
*Ken, Kenard, Kennaird,
Kennar, Kenny*

Kennedy
(Irish) leader
*Canaday, Canady,
Kennedey, Kennedie,
Kennidy*

Kenner
(English) capable
Kennard

Kennet
(Scandinavian) good-
looking
Kenet, Kennete

Kenneth
(Scottish) handsome;
(Irish) good-looking
*Ken, Keneth, Kenith,
Kennath, Kennie, Kenny*

Kenny
(Scottish) short for Kenneth
*Kennee, Kenney, Kenni,
Kennie*

Kenrick
(English) heroic boy

Kent
(English) fair-skinned
Kennt, Kentt

Kentaro
(Japanese) large baby boy

Kentlee
(Last name as first name)
dignified
*Ken, Kenny, Kent, Kentlea,
Kentleigh, Kently*

Kenton
(English) from Kent
Kentan, Kentin, Kenton

Kentrell
(English) white

Kenward
(Last name as first name)
bold

Kenway
(Last name as first name)
bold

Kenyatta
(African) from Kenya;
patriotic

Kenyon
(Irish) dear blond boy
*Ken, Kenjon, Kenny,
Kenyawn, Kenyun*

Kenzie
(Scottish) form of Kinsey;
leads
Kensie

Keola
(Hawaiian) vibrant

Keon
(American) unbridled
enthusiasm
*Keion, Keonne, Keyon,
Kion, Kionn*

Keontay
(African American)
outrageous
Keon, Keontae, Keontee

Kepler
(German) loves astrology;
starry-eyed
*Kappler, Keppel, Keppeler,
Keppler*

Kerel
(African) forever young

Kerem
(Hebrew) works in
vineyard

Kerey
(Irish) dark

Kerm
(Irish) form of Kermit;
guileless
Kurm

Kermit
(German) droll
*Kerm, Kermee, Kermet,
Kermey, Kermi, Kermie,
Kermy*

Kern
(Irish) dark; musically
inclined
*Curran, Kearn, Kearne,
Kearns*

Kernaghan
(Last name as first name)
dark
Carnahan, Kernohan

Kernis
(Invented) dark; different
Kernes

Kerr
(Scandinavian) serious
Karr, Kerre, Kurr

Kerrick
(English) rules

Kerry
(Irish) dark
*Keary, Kere, Keri, Kerrey,
Kerrie*

Kers
(Todas) an Indian plant

Kersen
(Indonesian) cherry bright

Kerstie
(American) spunky
Kerstee, Kersty

Kerwyn
(Irish) energetic
*Kerwen, Kerwin, Kerwun,
Kir, Kirs, Kirwin*

Keshawn
(African American) friendly
*Kesh, Keshaun, Keyshawn,
Shawn*

Keshet
(Hebrew) rainbow; bright
hopes

Keshon
(African American)
sociable
Kesh

Keshua
(African American) form of
the feminine name Kesha
Keshe

Kesin
(Hindi) needy

Kesley
(American) derivative of
Lesley; active
Keslee, Kesli, Kezley

Kesse
(American) attractive
*Kessee, Kessey, Kessi,
Kessie*

Kester
(Scottish) form of
Christopher; Christ-loving

Kestrel
(English) soars

Ketchum
(Place name) city in Idaho
*Catch, Ketch, Ketcham,
Ketchim*

Kettil
(Scandinavian) self-
sacrificing
Keld, Kjeld, Ketil, Ketti

Keung
(Chinese) universal spirit

Kevin
(Irish) handsome; gentle
*Kev, Kevahngn, Kevan,
Keven, Kevvie, Kevvy*

Key
(English) key
Keye, Keyes

Keyohtee
(Invented) form of Quixote

Keyshawn
(African American) clever;
believer

Khadim
(Hindi) forever
*Kadeem, Kadeen,
Kahdeem, Khadeem*

Khalid
(Arabic) everlasting
Khalead, Khaled, Khaleed

Khalil
(Arabic) good friend

Khaliq
(Arabic) ingenious
Kaliq, Khalique

Khambrel
(American) articulate
*Kambrel, Kham,
Khambrell, Khambrelle,
Khambryll, Khamme,
Khammie, Khammy*

Khan
(Turkish) shares; prince

Khayru
(Arabic) giving
Khiri, Khiry, Kiry

Khevin
(American) form of Kevin;
good-looking
Khev

Khouri
(Arabic) spiritual
*Couri, Khory, Khourae,
Kori*

Khyber
(Place name) pass on
border of Pakistan and
Afghanistan
Kibe, Kiber, Kyber

Kibbe
(Nayas) nocturnal bird

Kibo
(Place name) mountain
peak (highest peak of
Kilimanjaro); spectacular
Kib

Kidd
(Last name as first name)
adventurous

Kiel
(Place name) city in North
Germany

Kieran
(Irish) handsome brunette
*Keiran, Kier, Kieren, Kierin,
Kiers, Kyran*

Kidder
(Last name as first name)
brash; confident

Kiefer
(Irish) loving
*Keefer, Kieffer, Kiefner,
Kieffner, Kiefert, Kuefer,
Kueffner*

Kieran
(Scottish) dark-haired
*Keiran, Keiren, Keiron,
Kern, Kernan, Kiernan,
Kieron, Kyran*

Kier
(Icelandic) large vat or tub

Kiet
(Asian) respected

Kiev
(Place name) capital city
of Ukraine

Kiho
(Hawaiian) moves
carefully

Killi
(Irish) form of Killian;
fighter
*Killean, Killee, Killey,
Killyun*

Killian
(Irish) effervescent
*Kilean, Kilian, Killean,
Killee, Killi, Killie, Killyun,
Kylian*

Kim
(Vietnamese) gold
(English) enthusiastic
Kimmie, Kimmy, Kimy, Kym

Kimball
(Greek) inviting
*Kim, Kimb, Kimbal,
Kimbie, Kimble, Kymball*

Kimberly
(English) bold
*Kim, Kimbo, Kimberleigh,
Kimberley*

Kin
(Japanese) gold

Kincaid
(Scottish) vigorous
Kincaide, Kinkaid

Kinch
(Last name as first) knife
blade

King
(English) royal leader

Kingman
(Last name as first name)
gracious man

Kingsley
(English) royal nature
*King, Kings, Kingslea,
Kingslee, Kingsleigh,
Kingsly, Kins*

Kingston
(English) gracious
King, Kingstan, Kingsten

Kingswell
(English) royal; king

Kinnard
(Last name as first name)
leaning
Kinnaird

Kinnel
(Place name) from
Kinnelon, New Jersey

Kinsey
(English) affectionate;
winning
Kensey, Kinsie

Kinton
(Hindi) adorned

Kioshi
(Japanese) thoughtful
silence

Kip
(English) focused
Kipp, Kippi, Kippie, Kippy

Kipling
(Literature) for writer
Rudyard; adventurous
Kiplen, Kippling

Kipp
(American) hill; upward
bound
Kip, Kyp

Kiral
(Greek) lord

Kiran
(Hindi) light

Kirby
(English) brilliant
*Kerb, Kirb, Kirbee, Kirbey,
Kirbie, Kyrbee, Kyrby*

Kiri
(Vietnamese) like
mountains, everlasting

Kiril
(Russian) lord
*Cyril, Cyrill, Kirill, Kirillos,
Kyril, Kyrill*

Kirk
(Scandinavian) believer
Kerk, Kirke, Kurk

Kirkland
(Last name as first name)
church land

Kirkley
(Last name as first name)
church wood
*Kirklea, Kirklee, Kirklie,
Kirkly*

Kirkwell
(Last name as first name)
wood; giving of faith

Kirkwood
(English) heavenly
Kirkwoode, Kurkwood

Kirton
(English) from town of
churches

Kirvin
(American) form of Kevin;
good-looking
*Kerven, Kervin, Kirv,
Kirvan, Kirven*

Kit
(Greek) mischievous
Kitt

Kito
(African) precious

Kiva
(Hebrew) from Akiva;
replacement

Kizza
(African) child born after
twins' birth

Klaus
(German) wealthy
Klaas, Klaes, Klas, Klass

Klay
(English) form of Clay;
reliable
Klaie, Klaye

Kleber
(Last name as first name)
serious
Klebe

Kleef
(Dutch) boy from the cliff;
daring

Klein
(Last name as first name)
bright
Kleiner, Kleinert, Kline

Klemens
(Latin) gentle
*Klemenis, Klement,
Kliment*

Kleng
(Scandinavian) claw;
struggles

Klev
(Invented) form of Cleve
Kleve

Knight
(English) protector
Knighte, Nighte

Knightley
(English) protects
*Knight, Knightlea,
Knightlee, Knightlie,
Knightly, Knights*

Knoll
(American) flamboyant
Noll

Knowles
(English) outdoorsman
Knowlie, Knowls, Nowles

Knox
(English) bold

Knud
(Scandinavian) ruler

Knut
(Scandinavian) aggressive
Canute, Cnut, Knute

Kobe
(Hebrew) cunning
Kobee, Kobey, Kobi, Koby

Kobi
(Hebrew) cunning; smart
*Cobe, Cobey, Cobi, Cobie,
Coby, Kobe, Kobey, Kobie,
Koby*

Kodiak
(American) bear; daunting

Kody
(English) brash
*Kodee, Kodey, Kodi,
Kodie, Kodye*

Kofi
(African) Friday-born

Kohana
(Hawaiian) best

Kohler
(German) coal

Kojo
(African) Monday-born

Koka
(Hawaiian) man from
Scotland; strategist

Kolby
(American) form of Colby;
congenial
Kelby, Kole, Kollby

Kolton
(English) coal town

Komic
(Invented) funny
Com, Comic, Kom

Konane
(Hawaiian) spot of
moonlight

Kondo
(African) fights

Kong
(Chinese) heavenly

Konnor
(Irish) another spelling of
Connor; brilliant
Konnar, Konner

Kono
(African) industrious

Konrad
(German) bold advisor
*Khonred, Kon, Konn,
Konny, Konraad, Konradd,
Konrade, Kord, Kort*

Konstantin
(Russian) forceful
*Kon, Konny, Kons,
Konstance, Konstantine,
Konstantyne*

Konstantinos
(Greek) steadfast
*Constance, Konstance,
Konstant, Tino, Tinos*

Koren
(Greek) strong-willed

Koresh
(Hebrew) farms
Choresh

Korey
(Irish) lovable
Kori, Korrey, Korrie

Kornel
(Czech) horn;
communicator
*Kornelisz, Kornelius,
Kornell*

Kornelius
(Latin) another spelling of
Cornelius
*Korne, Kornellius,
Kornelyus, Korney,
Kornnelyus*

Korrigan
(Irish) another spelling of
Corrigan
*Koregan, Korigan, Korre,
Korreghan, Korri, Korrigon*

Kort
(German) talkative

Kory
(Irish) hollow
Kori, Korre, Korrey, Korrye

Kosey
(African) temperamental;
lionlike

Koshy
(American) jolly
Koshee, Koshey, Koshi

Kosmo
(Greek) likes order
Kosmy, Cosmos

Kostas
(Russian) from Kostyn and
Konstantin; loyal

Koster
(American) spiritual
Kost, Kostar, Koste, Koster

Kosumi
(Native American) fishes
with a spear; smart

Kovit
(Asian) talented

Kraig
(Irish) another spelling for
Craig
Krag, Kragg, Kraggy

Kramer
(German) shopkeeper;
humorous

Kricker
(Last name as first name)
reliable
Krick

Kris
(Greek) short for Kristian
and Kristopher
Krissy, Krys

Krishna
(Hindu) pleasant
Krishnah

Krispin
(Irish) form of Crispin;
curly hair

Krister
(Scandinavian) religious

Kristian
(Greek) another form of
Christian
Kris, Krist, Kristyan

Kristo
(Greek) short for
Kristopher

Kristopher
(Greek) bearer of Christ
Kris, Krist, Kristo, Kristofer

Kruz
(Spanish) delight

Krystyn
(Polish) Christian
Krys, Krystian

Krzysztof
(Polish) bearing Christ
Kreestof

Kubrick
(Last name as first name)
creative
Kubrik

Kueng
(Chinese) of the universe;
fine

Kugonza
(African) in love

Kumar
(Hindi) boy

Kuper
(Hebrew) copper, red hair

Kurt
(Latin) wise advisor
Curt, Kurty

Kurtis
(Latin) form of Curtis
*Kurt, Kurtes, Kurtey,
Kurtie, Kurts, Kurtus,
Kurty*

Kutty
(English) knife-wielding
Cutty

Kwako
(African) Wednesday-born

Kwame
(African) Saturday's child
Kwamee, Kwami

Kwan
(Korean) bold character

Kwasi
(African) born on Sunday
Kweisi, Kwesi

Kwintyn
(Polish) fifth child
Kwint, Kwintin, Kwynt

Kyan
(Place name) village in
Japan
Kyann

Kyle
(Irish) serene
*Kiel, Kiyle, Kye, Kyl, Kyley,
Kylie, Kyly*

Kyle-Evan
(American) combo of Kyle
and Evan
Kyle Evan

Kyler
(English) peaceful
*Cuyler, Kieler, Kiler, Kye,
Kylor*

Kylerton
(American) form of Kyle
Kylten

Kynan
(Welsh) leads

Kynaston
(English) serene

Kyne
(English) blue-blooded

Kyrone
(African American) combo
of K and Tyrone; brash
*Keirohn, Keiron, Keirone,
Keirown, Kirone, Kyron*

Kyros
(Greek) masterful

Kyzer
(American) wild spirit
Kaizer, Kizer, Kyze

Laban
(Hebrew) white
Lavan

Labarne
(American) form of Laban;
(Hebrew) white
Labarn

Labaron
(French) the baron
LaBaron, LaBaronne

Labhras
(Irish) form of Lawrence;
introspective
Lubhras

LaBryant
(African American) son of
Bryant; brash
*Bryant, La Brian, La Bryan,
Labryan, Labryant*

Lachlan
(Scottish) feisty
*Lachlann, Lacklan,
Lackland, Laughlin, Lock,
Locklan*

Lachtna
(Irish) gray; aging with
grace

Lacy
(Scottish) warlike
Lacey

Ladan
(Hebrew) having seen;
aware

Ladarius
(Origin unknown) combo
of La and Darius

Ladd
(English) helper; smart
*Lad, Laddee, Laddey,
Laddie, Laddy*

Ladden
(American) athletic

Laddie
(English) youthful
*Lad, Ladd, Laddee,
Laddey, Laddy*

Ladisiao
(Spanish) helpful
Laddy

Lado
(Spanish) artistic

Lael
(Hebrew) belonging to
Jehovah
Lale

Laertes
(Literature) from
Shakespeare's *Hamlet*;
action-oriented

Lafaye
(American) cheerful
*Lafay, Lafayye, Laphay,
Laphe*

Lafayetta
(Spanish) from the French
name Lafayette; bold
Lafay

Lafayette
(French) ambitious
Lafayet, Lafayett

Lafe
(American) punctual
Laafe, Laife, Laiffe

Lafi
(Polynesian) shy

Lagos
(Place name) city in
Nigeria
Lago

Lagrand
(African American) the grand
Grand, Grandy, Lagrande

Lahahana
(Hawaiian) warm as sunshine

Laionela
(Hawaiian) lion boldness

Laird
(Scottish) rich
Layrd, Layrde

Lais
(Indian) leonine

Lake
(English) tranquil water

Lakista
(African American) bold man

Lakshman
(Hindi) promising

Lal
(Slavic) from Lala; tulip; colorful

Lalo
(Latin) singer of a lullaby
Laloh

Lamalcom
(African American) son of Malcolm; kingly
LaMalcolm, LaMalcom, Mal, Malcolm, Malcom

Lamar
(Latin) renowned
Lamahr, Lamarr, Lemar, Lemarr

Lamber
(German) form of Lambert; ingratiating
Lambur

Lambert
(German) bright
Lamb, Lamber, Lambie, Lamburt, Lammie, Lammy

Lamond
(French) worldly
Lammond, Lamon, Lamonde, Lemond

Lamont
(Scandinavian) lawman
Lamon

Lamonte
(French) mountain

Lance
(German) confident
Lanse, Lantz, Lanz

Lancelot
(French) romantic
Lance, Lancelott, Launcelot, Launcey

Landan
(English) from the plains; quiet

Lander
(English) landed
Land, Landor

Landers
(English) wealthy
Land, Landar, Lander, Landor

Landis
(English) owning land; earthy
Land, Landes, Landice, Landise, Landly, Landus

Lando
(American) masculine
Land

Landon
(English) plain; old-fashioned
Land, Landan, Landen

Landry
(French) entrepreneur
Landré, Landree

Lane
(English) secure
Laine, Laney, Lanie, Lanni, Layne

Lang
(English) top
Lange

Langdon
(English) long-winded
Lang, Langden, Langdun

Langford
(English) healthy
Lanford, Langferd

Langham
(Last name as first name)
long
Lang

Langilea
(Polynesian) loud as
thunder

Langiloa
(Polynesian) stormy;
moody

Langley
(English) natural
*Lang, Langlee, Langli,
Langly*

Langston
(English) long-suffering
Lang, Langstan, Langsten

Langton
(English) long
Lange

Langundo
(Polynesian) graceful

Langward
(Last name as first name)
long

Langworth
(Last name as first name)
of long worth

Lani
(Hawaiian) lithe

Lanny
(American) popular
*Lann, Lanney, Lanni,
Lannie*

Lansing
(Place name) city in
Michigan
Lance, Lans

Lanty
(Irish) lively
*Laughun, Leachlainn,
Lochlainn, Lochlann*

Lanu
(Native American) circular

Laoghaire
(Irish) caretaker of cows

Laoiseach
(Place name) from the
county Leix in Ireland

Lap
(Vietnamese) independent

Laphonso
(African American)
prepared; centered

Lapidos
(Greek) cologne
Lapidus

Laquintin
(American) combo of La
and Quintin

Laramie
(French) pensive
Laramee

Lare
(American) wealthy
Larre, Layr

Largel
(American) intrepid
Large

Lariat
(American) roper
Lare, Lari

Larkin
(Irish) brash
*Lark, Larkan, Larken,
Larkie, Larky*

Larndell
(American) generous
*Larn, Larndelle, Larndey,
Larne*

Larne
(Place name) district in
Northern Ireland
Larn, Larney, Larny

Larnell
(American) giving
Larne

Laron
(American) outgoing
Larron, Larrone

Larrimore
(Last name as first name)
loud
Larimore, Larmer, Larmor

Larrmyne
(American) boisterous
*Larmie, Larmine, Larmy,
Larmyne*

Larry
(Latin) extrovert
*Lare, Larrey, Larri, Larrie,
Lary*

Lars
(Scandinavian) short for
Lawrence and Laurens
Larrs, Larse, Larsy

Lashaun
(African American)
enthusiastic
*Lashawn, La-Shawn,
Lashon, Lashond*

Laskey
(Last name as first name)
jovial
Lask, Laski

Lassen
(Place name) a peak in
California in the Cascade
Range
*Lase, Lasen, Lassan,
Lassun*

Lassit
(American) broad-minded
Lasset, Lassitte

Lassiter
(American) witty
*Lassater, Lasseter, Lassie,
Lassy*

Laszlo
(Hungarian) famous
leader
Laslo, Lazuli

Lateef
(Arabic) a gentle man

Latham
(Scandinavian) farmer;
knowing
Lathe, Lay

Lathrop
(English) home-loving
*Lathe, Lathrap, Latrope,
Lay, Laye, Laythrep*

Latimer
(English) interprets;
philanthropic
Latymer

Latorris
(African American)
notorious
LaTorris

Latravious
(African American) healthy
Latrave

Latty
(English) giving
Lat, Latti, Lattie

Laughlin
(Irish) servent

Laurence
(Latin) glorified
*Larence, Laurance,
Laurans, Laure, Lorence*

Laurens
(German) brilliant
*Larrie, Larry, Laure,
Laurins, Lorens, Lors*

Laurent
(French) martyred
Laurynt

Lavan
(Latin) pure

Lavaughn
(African American) perky
Lavan, Lavon, Lavonn, Levan, Levaughn

Lavaughor
(African American) laughing
Lavaugher, Lavawnar

Lavesh
(Hindi) little piece; calm

Lavi
(Hebrew) uniter

Lawford
(English) dignified
Laford, Lauford, Lawferd

Lawler
(Last name as first name) honoring; teacher
Lawlor, Lollar, Loller

Lawrence
(Latin) honored
Larrie, Larry, Laurence, Lawrance, Lawrunce

Lawrie
(Latin) form of Lawry; anointed
Lowrie

Lawson
(English) Lawrence's son; special
Law, Laws, Lawsan, Lawsen

Lawton
(Last name as first name) honored town

Layshaun
(African American) merry
Laysh, Layshawn

Laysy
(Last name as first name) sophisticated
Lay, Laycie, Laysee

Layt
(American) fascinating
Lait, Laite, Late, Layte

Layton
(English) musical
Laytan, Laytawn, Layten

Laz
(Spanish) short for Lazaro; God-loved

Lazar
(Hebrew) from Lazarus; helped by God
Lazare, Lazaro, Lazear, Lazer

Lazarus
(Greek) renewed
Eleazer, Lasarus, Lazerus, Lazoros

Leal
(Greek) self-assured

Leamon
(American) powerful
Leamm, Leamond, Leemon

Leand
(Greek) from Leander; leonine
Leander

Leander
(Greek) ferocious; lion-like
Anders, Leann, Leannder

Lear
(Greek) royal
Leare, Leere

Learly
(Last name as first name) terrific
Learley

Leary
(Irish) herds; high goals

Leather
(American) word as name; tough
Leath

Leavery
(American) giving
Leautree, Leautri, Leautry, Levry, Lo, Lotree, Lotrey, Lotri, Lotry

Leben
(Last name as first name)
small; hopeful

Lebna
(African) soulful

Lebron
(French) form of Lebrun

Lechoslaw
(Polish) glorious Pole;
envied
Lech, Leslaw, Leszek

Lectoy
(American) form of Lecter
and Leroy; good-old-boy
Lec, Lecto, Lek

Lee
(English) loving
Lea, Lee, Leigh

Leeander
(Invented) form of Leander

Leenoris
(African American) form of
Lenore; respected
Lenoris

Leeodis
(African American) combo
of Lee and Odis; carefree
Lee-Odis, Leotis

Leeron
(African American) combo
of Lee and Ron
Leerawn

Leggett
(Last name as first name)
able
Legate, Leggitt, Liggett

Lei
(Hawaiian) wreath;
decorative

Leibel
(Hebrew) lion

Leif
(Scandinavian) loved one
Laif, Leaf, Leife

Leigh
(English) smooth

Leighton
(Last name as first name)
hearty
*Laytan, Layton, Leighten,
Leightun*

Leith
(Scottish) broad

Lel
(Gypsy) taker

Leland
(English) protective
*Leeland, Leighlon, Leiland,
Lelan, Lelond*

Leldon
(American) form of Eldon;
bookish
Leldun

Lem
(Hebrew) from Lemuel;
loves God

Lemar
(American) form of Lamar;
famed landowner
Lemarr

Lemetrias
(African American) form of
Lemetrius
Lem

Lemon
(American) fruit; tart
Lemonn, Lemun, Limon

Lemuel
(Hebrew) religious
Lem, Lemmie, Lemmy, Lemy

Len
(German) short for
Leonard
Lennie, Lynn

Lenard
(American) form of
Leonard; heart of a lion
Lenerd

Leni
(Polynesian) lives for
today

Lennan
(Irish) gentle
Lennart
(Scandinavian) brave
Lenn, Lenne
Lenno
(Italian) brave
Lennon
(Irish) renowned; caped
Lenn, Lennan, Lennen
Lennor
(Last name as first name)
brave
Lennox
(Scottish) authoritative
*Lennix, Lenocks, Lenox,
Linnox*
Lenny
(German) short for
Leonard
*Lenn, Lenney, Lenni,
Lennie, Leny, Linn*
Lensar
(English) stays with
parents
Lenton
(American) religious
Lent, Lenten, Lentun
Lenvil
(Invented) typical
Lenval, Level
Leo
(Latin) lionlike; fierce
Leocadio
(Spanish) lion-hearted
Leo
Leolin
(Polynesian) watchful
Leoline, Llewelyn
Leoliver
(American) combo of Leo
and Oliver; audacious
Leo
Leon
(Greek) tenacious
Lee, Leo, Leone, Leonn

Leonard
(German) courageous
*Lee, Leo, Leonar, Leonerd,
Leonord, Lynar, Lynard,
Lynerd*
Leonardo
(Italian) lion-hearted
Leo
Leoncio
(Spanish) lion-hearted
Leon, Leonce, Leonse
Leondras
(African American) lionine
*Leon, Leondre, Leondrus,
Leonid*
Leonidus
(Latin) strong
*Leon, Leone, Leonidas,
Leonydus*
Leopaul
(American) combo of Leo
and Paul; brave; calm
Leo-Paul
Leopold
(German) brave
Lee, Leo
Leor
(Latin) listens
Leoti
(American) outdoorsy
Lee, Leo
Leovardo
(Spanish) form of
Leonardo; brave
Leo, Leovard
Lepoldo
(Spanish) form of Leopold;
brave
Lee, Lepold, Poldo
Lepolo
(Polynesian) handsome
Lerey
(American) form of Larry
Lerrie, Lery

Leron
(American) combo of Lee
and Ron; courageous
*LeRon, Lerone, Liron,
Lirone, Lyron*

Leroy
(French) king; royal
*Leeroy, Leroi, Le-Roy, Roy,
Roye*

Les
(English) short for Leslie
Lez, Lezli

Leshawn
(African American) cheery
*Lashawn, Leshaun, Le-
Shawn*

Leslie
(Scottish) fortified
*Lee, Les, Lesley, Lesli,
Lezlie, Lezly*

Lesner
(Last name as first name)
serious
Les, Lez, Lezner

Lester
(American) large persona
Les, Lestor

Lev
(Russian) lionine

Levar
(American) softspoken
Levarr

Leverett
(Last name as first name)
planner
*Lev, Leveret, Leverit,
Leveritt*

Leverton
(Last name as first name)
town of Lever; organized

Levi
(Hebrew) harmonious
Lev, Levey, Levie, Levy

Levonne
(African American)
forward-thinking
Lavonne, Leevon, Levon

Lew
(Polish) lion-like
Leu

Leward
(French) contentious
Lewar, Lewerd

Lew-Gene
(American) combo of Lew
and Gene; renowned
fighter
Lou-Gene

Lewie
(French) form of Louie
Lew, Lewee, Lewey, Lewy

Lewin
(Last name as first name)
lion-like

Lewis
(German, French) powerful
ruler
*Lew, Lewey, Lewie, Lewus,
Lewy*

Lewy
(Irish) giving

Lex
(English) short for
Alexander; mysterious
*Lexa, Lexe, Lexi, Lexie,
Lexy*

Leyland
(Last name as first name)
protective

Li
(Chinese) strong man

Liam
(Irish) protective;
handsome
Leam, Leeam, Leeum

Liang
(Chinese) good man

Liberio
(Spanish) liberated
Libere, Lyberio

Liberty
(American) freedom-loving
Lib

Libor
(Czech) free

Librada
(Italian, Spanish) free

Lictor
(Invented) form of Lecter;
disturbed
Lec, Lek

Lidio
(Greek) pleasant man

Lidon
(Hebrew) judge

Liem
(Vietnamese) truthful

Lif
(Scandinavian) full of life

Lihau
(Hawaiian) cool; fresh

Like
(Asian) soft-spoken

Liko
(Hawaiian) budding;
flourishing

Lillo
(American) triple-threat
talent
Lilo

Limo
(Invented) from the word
limousine; sporty
Lim

Limu
(Polynesian) seaweed;
natural

Linc
(English) short for Lincoln;
leader
Link, Links

Lincoln
(English, American) quiet
Linc, Link

Lindberg
(German) blond good
looks
*Lin, Lind, Lindburg, Lindie,
Lindy, Lyndberg, Lyndburg*

Lindell
(Last name as first name)
in harmony with nature
*Lindall, Lindel, Lyndall,
Lyndell*

Linden
(Botanical) tree
Lindun

Lindoh
(American) sturdy
Lindo, Lindy

Lindsay
(English) natural
*Lind, Lindsee, Lindsey,
Linz, Linzee, Lyndsey,
Lyndzie, Lynz, Lynzie*

Lindy
(German) form of
Lindberg; daring
Lind

Linford
(Last name as first name)
bold man
Lynford

Linfred
(Last name as first name)
proactive

Linley
(English) open-minded
Lin, Linlee, Linleigh, Lynlie

Linnard
(German) form of Leonard;
bold
Linard, Lynard

Lino
(American) form of Linus
Linus

Linus
(Greek) blond
Linas, Line, Lines

Linton
(English) lives near lime
trees
Lintonn, Lynton, Lyntonn

Linwood
(American) open

Lionel
(French) fierce
*Li, Lion, Lionell, Lye, Lyon,
Lyonel, Lyonell*

Liron
(Hebrew) my song
Lyron

Lisiate
(Polynesian) courageous

Lisimba
(African) attacked by lion;
victim

Lister
(Origin unknown)
intelligent

Litton
(English) centered
Lyten, Lyton, Lytton

Liu
(Asian) quiet

Liuz
(Polish) light

Livingston
(English) comforting
Liv, Livey, Livingstone

Liwanu
(Asian) released

Llano
(Place name) river in
Texas; flowing
Lano

Llewellyn
(English) fiery; fast
Lew, Lewellen, Lewellyn

Lloyd
(English) spiritual; joyful
Loy, Loyd, Loydde, Loye

Lobo
(Spanish) wolf
Loboe, Lobow

Lochan
(Irish) lively; (Hindu) eyes

Lochlain
(Irish) assertive
*Lochlaine, Lochlane,
Locklain*

Lock
(English) natural
Locke

Lodewuk
(Scandinavian) warrior
Ladewijk, Ludovic

Lodge
(English) safe haven

Lodur
(Scandinavian) vivid

Loey
(American) daring
Loie, Lowee, Lowi

Lofton
(Last name as first name)
lofty
Loften

Logan
(Irish) eloquent
Logen, Loggy, Logun

Lohan
(Last name as first name)
capable

Lokela
(Hawaiian) famed
spearthrower

Lokene
(Hawaiian) form of
Rodney; open-minded

Lokni
(Hawaiian) red rose

Loman
(Irish) bare

Lomas
(Spanish) good man

Lombard
(Italian) winning

Lombardi
(Italian) winner
Bardi, Bardy, Lom,
Lombard, Lombardy

Lon
(Irish) intense

Lonato
(Native American)
flintstone; calm

London
(English) ethereal; capital
of Great Britain
Londen

Long
(Last name as first name)
Chinese dragon;
methodical

Lonnie
(Spanish) short for Alonzo
Lonney, Lonni, Lonny

Lono
(Slavic) form of Lonna;
light

Loocho
(Invented) form of Lucho

Lorance
(Latin) form of Lawrence;
long-suffering; patient
Lorans, Lorence

Lorca
(Last name as first) poet,
playwright; tragic

Lorcan
(Irish) fiery

Lord
(English) regal
Lorde

Lordlee
(English) regal
Lordly, Lords

Loredo
(Spanish) smart; cowboy
Lorado, Loredoh, Lorre,
Lorrey

Loren
(Latin) hopeful; winning
Lorin, Lorrin

Lorens
(Scandinavian) form of
Laurence

Lorenzo
(Spanish, Italian) bold and
spirited
Larenzo, Loranzo, Lore,
Lorence, Lorenso, Lorentz,
Lorenz, Lorrie, Lorry

Lorimer
(Last name as first name)
brash
Lorrimer

Loring
(German) brash
Looring, Lorrie, Louring

Lorne
(Latin) grounded
Lorn, Lorny

Lorry
(English) form of Laurie
Lore, Lorri, Lorrie, Lorry,
Lory

Lot
(Hebrew) furtive
Lott

Lothario
(German) lover
Lotario, Lothaire, Lotherio,
Lothurio

Lou
(German) short for Louis
Lew

Loudon
(American) enthusiastic
Louden, Lowden, Lowdon

Louie
(German) short for Louis
Louey

Louis
(German, French) powerful ruler
Lew, Lewis, Lou, Louie, Lue, Luie, Luis

Loundis
(American) visionary
Lound, Loundas, Loundes, Lowndis

Louvain
(English) city in Belgium; wanderer

LouVon
(American) combo of Lou and Von; searching
Lou Von, Louvaughan, Louvawn, Lou-Von

Lovell
(English) brilliant
Lovall, Love, Lovelle, Lovie

Lovett
(Last name as first name) loving
Lovat, Lovet

Low
(American) word as a name; low-key
Lowey

Lowell
(English) loved
Lowall, Lowel

Lowry
(Last name as first name) leader
Lowree, Lowrey

Loyal
(English) true to the word
Loy

Loys
(American) loyal
Loyce, Loyse

Lubomil
(Polish) loves grace

Luboslaw
(Polish) loves glory

Luc
(French) light; laidback
Lucca, Luke

Luca
(Italian) light-hearted
Louca, Louka, Luka

Lucan
(Irish) light

Lucas
(Greek) patron saint of doctors/artists; creative
Lucca, Luces, Luka, Lukas, Luke, Lukes, Lukus

Lucho
(Spanish) lucky; light

Lucian
(Latin) soothing
Lew, Luciyan, Lushun

Luciano
(Italian) light-hearted
Luca, Lucas, Luke

Lucious
(African American) light; delicious
Luceous, Lushus

Lucius
(Latin) sunny
Lucca, Luchious, Lushus

Lucky
(American) lucky
Luckee, Luckey, Luckie

Ludger
(Scandinavian) wielding spears

Ludie
(English) glorious
Ludd

Ludlow
(German) respected
Ludlo, Ludloe

Ludolf
(English) form of Rudolf; glorious

Ludomir
(Polish) of well-known ancestry

Ludoslav
(Polish) of glorified people

Ludovic
(Slavic) smart; spiritual
Luddovik, Lude, Ludovik, Ludvic, Vick

Ludwig
(German) talented
Ludvig, Ludweg, Ludwige

Luigi
(Italian) famed warrior
Lui, Louie

Luis
(Spanish) outspoken
Luez, Luise, Luiz

Luister
(Irish) form of Louis; strong

Lujo
(Spanish) luxurious
Luj

Luka
(Italian, Croatian) easygoing
Luca, Luke

Lukah
(Invented) form of Luca

Lukas
(Greek) light-hearted; creative
Lucus

Luke
(Latin) worshipful
Luc, Lucc, Luk, Lukus

Lukman
(Last name as first name) vivacious

Lulani
(Hawaiian) light sky

Lumer
(American) light
Lumar, Lume, Lumur

Luna
(Spanish) moon

Lundy
(Scandinavian) island-lover

Lunn
(Irish) smart and brave
Lun, Lunne

Lunt
(Scandinavian) grove-dweller

Luong
(Vietnamese) from the land of bamboo

Lusk
(Last name as first name) hearty
Lus, Luske, Luskee, Luskey, Luski, Lusky

Lutalo
(African) bold fighter

Lute
(Polynesian) pigeon; inconspicuous

Luther
(German) reformer
Luthar, Luth, Luthur

Luthus
(American) form of Luther; prepared and armed
Luth, Luthas

Lux
(English) light

Lyal
(English) form of Lyle; islander
Lye

Lyle
(French) unique
Lile, Ly, Lyle

Lyman
(English) meadow-man; sportsman
Leaman, Leyman

Lyndall
(English) nature-lover
Lynd, Lyndal, Lyndell

Lyndon
(English) verbose
Lindon, Lyn, Lynd,
Lyndonn

Lynge
(Scandinavian) sylvan
nature

Lynn
(English) water-loving
Lin, Linn, Lyn, Lynne

Lynshawn
(African American) combo
of Lyn and Shawn; helpful
Linshawn, Lynnshaw,
Lynshaun

Lynton
(English) town of nature
lovers
Linton

Lyon
(Place name) city in France
Lyone

Lyron
(Hebrew) my song

Lysande
(Greek) freewheeling
Lyse

Lysander
(Greek) lover
Lysand

Lyulf
(German) haughty;
combative
Lyulfe, Lyulff

Mablevi
(African) do not deceive

Mac
(Irish, Scottish) short for
"Mc" or "Mac" surname;
friendly
Mack, Mackee, Macki,
Mackie, Macky

MacAdam
(Scottish) son of Adam;
first

Macaffie
(Scottish) charming
Mac, Mack, Mackey,
McAfee, McAffee, McAffie

Macario
(Spanish) blessed
Macareo, Makario

Macarlos
(Spanish) manly
Carlos

Macauley
(Scottish) righteous;
dramatic
Mac, Macaulay, McCauley

Macauliffe
(Last name as first name)
bookish
Macaulif, Macauliff

Macbey
(American) form of Mackey
Mackbey, Makbee, Makbi

Macdowell
(Last name as first name)
giving
Macdowl

Macedonio
(Spanish) from
Macedonia; travels
MacEgan
(Last name as first name)
son of Egan; capable
Macgowan
(Irish) able; gallant
Macgowen, Macgowyn
Mackeane
(Last name as first name)
attractive
Mackeene
Mackenna
(Irish) giving; leader
Mackena
Mackenzie
(Irish) giving
*Mack, Mackenzy,
Mackinsey, Makinzie,
McKenzie*
Mackeon
(Last name as first name)
smiling
Mackie
(Irish) friendly
Mackey
MacKinley
(Irish) son of Kinley;
educated
Mackinney
(Last name as first name)
good-looking
Mackinny
Macklin
(Irish) good-humored
Maclain
(Irish) natural wonder
McLain, McLaine, McLean
Maclean
(Irish) dependable
Macleen
MacMurray
(Irish) loves the sea
Macnair
(Scottish) practical

Macon
(Place name) city in
Georgia; creative
Makon
Macy
(French) lasting; wealthy
*Mace, Macee, Macey,
Macye*
Madan
(Hindi) god of love; loving
Madden
(Pakistani) planner
*Maddin, Maddyn, Maden,
Madin, Madyn*
Maddock
(Welsh) generous
*Maddoc, Madocock,
Maddox, Madox*
Maddox
(English) giving
Maddocks, Maddy, Madox
Madhav
(Hindi) sweet
Madhu
Madison
(English) good
*Maddison, Maddy,
Madisan, Madisen, Son*
Madock
(American) giving
Maddock, Maddy, Madoc
Madras
(Place name) city in India
Madu
(African) manly
Madzimoyo
(African) nourished by
water; simple
Magaidi
(African) last
Magdaleno
(Spanish) from
Magdelene; spiritual
Magee
(Irish) practical; lively
Mackie, Maggy, McGee

Magglio
(Hispanic) athletic
Magic
(American) magical
Majic
Magne
(Latin) great
Magnus
(Latin) outstanding
Maggy, Magnes
Maguire
(Irish) subtle
Macky, Maggy, McGuire
Mahan
(American) cowboy
*Mahahn, Mahand, Mahen,
Mayhan*
Mahatma
(Sanskrit) spiritually
elevated
Mahir
(Arabic) skilled
Mahler
(Last name as first) famous
composer; sweeping, free
Mahluli
(African) conqueror
Mahmud
(Arabic) remarkable
Maimon
(Arabic) of good fortune
Main
(Place name) river in
Gemany; leader
Mainess, Mane, Maness
Maisel
(Persian) warrior
Meisel
Maitland
(English) of the meadow;
fresh ideas
Majeed
(Arabic) majestic
Majid
Majid
(Arabic) glorious

Major
(Latin) leading
*Mage, Magy, Majar, Maje,
Majer*
Makale
(Invented) form of Mikhail
Makio
(Hawaiian) from Makimo;
great
Makoto
(Japanese) true
Maks
(Russian) short for
Maksimilian
Maksimilian
(Russian) competitor
Maksim
Makya
(Native American) hunter
Mal
(Hindi) gardens; flourishes
Malachi
(Hebrew) angelic;
magnanimous
*Malachy, Malakai, Malaki,
Maleki*
Malawa
(African) flowering
Malcolm
(Scottish) peaceful
*Mal, Malkalm, Malkelm,
Malkolm*
Maldon
(French) strong and
combative
Maldan, Malden
Malfred
(German) feisty
Malfrid, Mann
Malik
(Arabic) angelic
Malic
Malise
(French) masterful
Malla-Ki
(Invented) form of Malachi

Mallin
(English) rowdy; warrior
Malen, Malin, Mallan, Mallen, Mallie, Mally

Mallory
(French) wild spirit
Mal, Mallie, Malloree, Mallorie, Mally, Malory

Maloney
(Irish) religious
Mal, Malone, Malonie, Malony

Malvin
(English) open-minded
Mal, Malv, Malven, Malvyne

Mamun
(Arabic) trustworthy

Manasseh
(Hebrew) cannot remember
Manases

Manchester
(English) dignity; (Place name) city in England

Manchu
(Chinese) unflawed

Mandell
(German) tough; almond
Mandee, Mandel, Mandela, Mandie, Mandy

Mandy
(Latin) lovable
Mandey

Manfred
(English) peaceful
Manferd, Manford, Mannfred, Mannie, Manny, Mannye

Manfredo
(Italian) strong peacefulness

Manila
(Place name) capital of Philippines
Manilla

Maninder
(Hindi) masculine; potent

Manley
(English) virile; haven
Man, Manlee, Manlie, Manly

Mann
(German) masculine
Mannes, Manning

Manning
(English) heroic
Man, Maning, Mann

Mannis
(Irish) great
Manish, Manus

Mannix
(Irish) spiritual
Manix, Mann, Mannicks

Manny
(Spanish) short for Manuel
Manney, Manni, Mannie

Manolo
(Spanish) from Spanish shoe designer Manolo Blahnik; cutting-edge

Mansfield
(English) outdoorsman
Manesfeld, Mans, Mansfeld, Mansfielde

Manse
(English) winning

Manshel
(English) or Mansel (of the house); domestic

Mantel
(English) formidable
Mantell, Mantle

Manton
(English) man's town; special

Manu
(Hindi) father of people; masculine

Manuel
(Hebrew, Spanish) gift
from God
*Mann, Mannuel, Manny,
Manual, Manuelle*

Manus
(American) strong-willed
*Manes, Mann, Mannas,
Mannes, Mannis, Mannus*

Manvel
(French) great town;
hardworking
*Mann, Manny, Manvil,
Manville*

Mao
(Chinese) hair

Marc
(French) combative
*Markee, Markey, Markeye,
Markie Mark, Markie,
Marko, Marky*

Marc-Anthony
(French) combo of Marc
and Anthony
*Marcantony, Mark-
Anthony, Markantony*

Marcel
(French) singing God's
praises
Marcell, Mars, Marsel

Marcellus
(Latin) romantic;
persevering
*Marcel, Marcelis, Marcey,
Marsellus, Marsey*

March
(English) fruitful month
Marche

Marcial
(Spanish) martial;
combative
Mars

Marciano
(Italian) manly; macho
Marcyano

Marcin
(Polish) form of Martin;
warlike

Marco
(Italian) tender
*Marc, Mark, Markie,
Marko, Marky*

Marconi
(Italian) inventive; tough

Marcos
(Spanish) outgoing
*Marco, Marko, Markos,
Marky*

Marco-Tulio
(Spanish) fighter;
substantial
Marco Tulio, Marcotulio

Marcoux
(French) aggressive; manly
Marce, Mars

Marcus
(Latin) combative
Marc, Mark, Markus, Marky

Marcus-Anthony
(Spanish) valuable;
aggressive
*Marc Anthony, Marc-
Antonito, Marcus-
Antoneo, Marcusantonio,
Markanthony, Taco, Tonio,
Tono*

Marek
(Polish) masculine

Margarito
(Spanish) from Margarite;
sunny

Marguez
(Spanish) noble
Marguiz

Mariano
(Italian) combative; manly
Mario

Marin
(French) ocean-loving
Maren, Marino, Maryn

Mariner
(Greek) from Marinos;
sea-farer

Mario
(Italian) masculine
*Marioh, Marius, Marrio,
Morio*

Marion
(Latin) suspicious
Mareon, Marionn

Marius
(German) masculine; virile
Marrius

Marjuan
(Spanish) contentious
*Marhwon, Marwon,
Marwond*

Markell
(African American)
personable
Markelle

Markham
(English) homebody
*Marcum, Markhum,
Markum*

Markos
(Greek) warring; masculine
Marc, Mark

Marl
(English) rebel
Marley, Marli

Marley
(English) secretive
Marlee, Marleigh, Marly

Marlin
(English) opportunistic;
fish
Marllin

Marlo
(English) hill by a lake;
optimistic
*Mar, Marl, Marlow,
Marlowe*

Marlon
(French) wizard; strange
*Marlan, Marlen, Marlin,
Marly*

Marmaduke
(English) haughty
*Duke, Marmadook,
Marmahduke*

Marmion
(French) famed
Marmeonne, Marmyon

Marnin
(Hebrew) ebullient

Marq
(French) noble
Mark, Marque, Marquie

Marque
(French) noble; smart
Marcqe, Marcque, Marqe

Marquel
(French) nobleman

Marques
(African American) noble
*Marqes, Marqis, Marquez,
Marquis*

Marquise
(French) noble
*Mark, Markese, Marky,
Marq, Marquese, Marquie,
Marquis*

Mars
(Latin) warlike; god of war
Marrs, Marz

Marsdon
(English) comforting
*Marr, Mars, Marsden,
Marsdyn*

Marsh
(English) handsome
*Marr, Mars, Marsch,
Marsey, Marsy*

Marshall
(French) giving care
*Marsh, Marshal, Marshel,
Marshell, Marsy*

Marshawn
(American) combo of Mark
and Shawn; outgoing
Marston
(English) personable
*Mars, Marst, Marstan,
Marsten*
Martial
(French) form of Mark;
combative
Martin
(Latin) combative; from
Mars
*Mart, Marten, Marti,
Martie, Marton, Marty*
Marty
(Latin) short for Martin
*Mart, Martee, Martey,
Marti, Martie, Martye*
Marv
(English) short for Marvin;
good friend
Marve, Marvy
Marvell
(French) marvelous man
*Marvel, Marvil, Marvill,
Marvyl, Marvyll*
Marvin
(English) steadfast friend
Marv, Marven, Marvy
Marwood
(English) forest man
Masa
(African) centered
Masaaki
(African) from Maskini;
unfortunate
Masajiro
(Japanese) integrity
Masahiro, Masaji
Masamba
(African) departs
Masamitsu
(Japanese) feeling
Masanao
(Japanese) good

Masayuki
(Japanese) problematic
Mashael
(Invented) form of Michael
Mashawn
(African American)
vivacious
*Masean, Mashaun,
Mayshawn*
Maslen
(American) promising
Mas, Masline, Maslyn
Mason
(French) ingenious;
reliable; stone mason
Mace, Mase
Masood
(Iranian) helpful
Massey
(English) doubly excellent
Maccey, Masey, Massi
Massimo
(Italian) great
*Masimo, Massey,
Massimmo*
Masura
(Japanese) fated for good
life
Mateo
(Italian) gift
Mateus
(Italian) God's gift
Mathau
(American) spunky
Mathou, Mathow, Mathoy
Mather
(English) leader; army;
strong
Mathar
Matheson
(English) son of God's gift
*Mathesen, Mathisen,
Mathison, Mathysen,
Mathyson*

Matheu
(French) form of Matthew;
God's gift
Matt, Matty

Mathias
(German) form of
Matthew; dignified
*Mathies, Mathyes, Matt,
Matthias, Matty*

Mathieu
(French) from Matthew

Matias
(Spanish) gift from God
Mathias, Matios, Mattias

Matin
(Hebrew) gift

Matisse
(French) gifted

Matland
(English) Mat's land;
homesteader

Matlock
(American) rancher
Lock, Mat, Matt

Mato
(Native American) bear;
brawler

Matson
(Hebrew) son of Matthew
*Matsan, Matsen, Matt,
Matty*

Matt
(Hebrew) short for
Matthew
Mat, Matte

Matteson
(English) son of Matt;
God's gift

Matthew
(Hebrew) God's gift
*Math, Matheu, Mathieu,
Matt, Mattie, Mattsy, Matty*

Matthewson
(Last name as first name)
son of Matthew; devout
*Mathewsen, Mathewson,
Matthewsen*

Matti
(Scandinavian) form of
Matthias; God's gift
Mat, Mats

Mattison
(Last name as first name)
son of Matti; worldly
*Matisen, Matison,
Matisen, Mattysen,
Mattyson, Matysen,
Matyson*

Matts
(Swedish) gift from God

Matty
(Hebrew) short for
Matthew
Mattey, Matti

Matunde
(African) from Matthew;
God's gift

Mauri
(Latin) short for Maurice;
dark

Maurice
(Latin) dark
*Maur, Maurie, Maurise,
Maury, Moorice, Morice,
Morrie, Morry*

Mauricio
(Italian) dark
Mari, Mauri, Maurizio

Maurizio
(Italian) dark
*Marits, Miritza, Moritz,
Moritza, Moritzio*

Maury
(Latin) short for Maurice;
dark
Mauree, Maurey

Maverick
(American)
unconventional
*Mav, Mavarick, Mavereck,
Mavreck, Mavvy*

Mavis
(French) bird; thrush; free
Mavas, Mavus

Mawali
(African) vibrant

Mawulol
(African) thanks God

Max
(Latin) best
*Mac, Mack, Macks, Maxey,
Maxie, Maxx, Maxy*

Maxfield
(English) of the great field;
lives large

Maxime
(French) greatest
Max, Maxeem, Maxim

Maximilian
(Latin) most wonderful
*Max, Maxemillion, Maxie,
Maxima, Maximillion,
Maxmyllyun, Maxy*

Maximino
(Spanish) maximum; tops
*Max, Maxem, Maxey, Maxi,
Maxim, Maxy*

Maxinen
(Spanish) maximum
Max, Maxanen, Maxi

Maxwell
(English) full of excellence
*Maxe, Maxie, Maxwel,
Maxwill, Maxy*

Mayer
(Hebrew) smart
Mayar, Maye, Mayor, Mayur

Mayfield
(English) grace

Maynard
(English) reliable
Mayne, Maynerd

Mayo
(Irish) nature-loving
*Maio, Maioh, May, Mayes,
Mayoh, Mays*

Mayon
(Place name) volcano in
the Philippines
May, Mayan, Mays, Mayun

Mays
(English) of the field;
athlete

Maz
(Hebrew) aid
*Maise, Maiz, Mazey, Mazi,
Mazie, Mazy*

Mazal
(Arabic) sedate

McCoy
(Irish) jaunty; coy
Coye, MacCoy

McDonald
(Scottish) open-minded
Mac-D, Macdonald

McFarlin
(Last name as first name)
son of Farlin; confident
Far, Farr

McGill
(Irish) tricky

McGowan
(Irish) feisty
Mac-G, Mcgowan

McGregor
(Irish) philanthropic
Macgregor

McKay
(Scottish) connives

McKinley
(Last name as first name)
son of Kinley; holding his
own
Kin, Kinley, McKinlee

McLean
(Scottish) stays lithe

McLin
(Irish) careful
Mac, Mack

Mead
(English) outdoorsman
Meade, Meede

Meallan
(Irish) sweet
Maylan, Meall

Medford
(French) natural; comical
Med, Medfor

Medgar
(German) strong

Medwin
(German) friendly

Mehmet
(Sanskrit) royal

Meindert
(German) hearty boy
Meinhard, Meinrad

Meir
(Hebrew) teacher
Mayer, Myer

Mel
(Irish) short for Melvin
Mell

Melanio
(Spanish) royal

Melar
(English) mill man;
pleases

Melbourne
(Place name) city in
Australia; serene
*Mel, Melborn, Melbourn,
Melburn, Melburne*

Melburn
(English) sylvan; outdoorsy
*Mel, Melbourn, Melburne,
Milbourn, Milburn*

Melchor
(Polish) city's king

Meldon
(English) destined for fame
Melden, Meldin, Meldyn

Meldric
(English) leader
Mel, Meldrik

Melecio
(Spanish) cautious
Melesio, Melezio, Mesio

Meletius
(Greek) ultra-cautious
Meletios, Meletus

Melito
(Spanish) small and calm

Melos
(Greek) favorite
Milos

Melquiades
(Spanish) gypsy

Melroy
(American) form of Elroy
Mel

Melton
(English) nature; natural
Mel, Meltan

Melville
(French) mill town
Mel, Mell, Melvil, Melvill

Melvin
(English) friendly
*Mel, Melvine, Melvon,
Melvyn, Milvin*

Melvis
(American) form of Elvis;
songbird
Mel, Melv

Memphis
(Place name) city in
Tennessee
Memphus

Menas
(Hebrew) forgets

Mendel
(English) methodical
*Mendl, Menka, Menke,
Mela, Menlin*

Mensa
(African) third son; genius
Mensah

Mercer
(English) affluent
Merce, Mercur, Murcer

Mercutio
(Literature) from
Shakespeare's *Romeo and
Juliet*; mercurial

Meredith
(Welsh) protector
*Merdith, Mere, Meredyth,
Meridith, Merrey*

Merlin
(English) clever
*Merl, Merlan, Merle,
Merlinn, Merlun, Murlin*

Merrick
(English) bountiful
seaman
*Mere, Meric, Merik,
Merrack, Merrik*

Merrie
(English) giving
Merey, Meri, Merri

Merrill
(French) renowned
*Mere, Merell, Merill,
Merrell, Merril, Meryll*

Merritt
(Latin) worthy
Merid, Merit, Merret, Merrid

Merv
(Irish) short for Mervin;
bold
Murv

Mervin
(Irish) bold
*Merv, Merven, Mervun,
Mervy, Mervyn, Murv,
Murvin*

Meshach
(Hebrew) fortunate
*Meeshak, Meshack,
Meshak*

Mesquite
(American) rancher; spiny
shrub
Meskeet

Meyer
(Hebrew) brilliant
Maye, Meier, Mye, Myer

Meyshaun
(African American)
searching
*Maysh, Mayshaun,
Mayshawn, Meyshawn*

Micha
(Hebrew) prophet; sees all
Mica, Micah, Michah

Michael
(Hebrew) spiritual patron
of soldiers
*Mical, Michaelle, Mickey,
Mikael, Mike, Mikey,
Mikiee, Miko*

Michel
(French) fond
Mich, Michelle, Mike, Mikey

Michelangelo
(Italian) God's
angel/messenger; artistic
*Michel, Michelanjelo,
Mikalangelo, Mike, Mikel,
Mikelangelo*

Michon
(French) form of Michel;
godlike
*Mich, Michonn, Mish,
Mishon*

Mick
(Hebrew) closest to God
Mic, Mik

Mickel
(American) form of
Michael; friend
Mick, Mikel

Mickey
(American) enthusiastic
*Mick, Micki, Mickie, Micky,
Miki, Myck*

Mickey-Lee
(American) friendly
Mickey Lee, Mickeylee,
Mickie-Lee

Miga
(Spanish) persona;
essence

Miguel
(Spanish) form of Michael
Megel, Migel, Migelle

Miguelangel
(Spanish) angelic
Miguelanjel

Mihir
(Hindi) sunny

Mika
(Hebrew) form of Micah
Mikah, Mikie, Myka,
Mykie, Myky

Mikael
(Scandinavian) warrior
Michael, Mikel, Mikkel

Mike
(Hebrew) short for
Michael
Meik, Miik, Myke

Mikhail
(Russian) god-like;
graceful
Mika, Mikey, Mikkail,
Mykhey

Mikolas
(Greek) form of Nicholas;
bright
Mick, Mickey, Mickolas,
Mik, Miko, Mikolus, Miky

Milagros
(Spanish) miracle
Milagro

Milam
(Last name as first name)
uncomplicated
Mylam

Milan
(Place name) city in Italy;
smooth
Milano

Milburn
(Scottish) volatile
Milbyrn, Milbyrne,
Millburn

Miles
(German) forgiving
Mile, Miley, Myles, Myyles

Miley
(American) reliable;
forgiving
Mile, Miles, Mili, Mily,
Myles, Myley

Milford
(English) from a calm
(mill) setting; country
Milferd, Milfor

Millard
(Latin) old-fashioned
Milard, Mill, Millerd,
Millurd, Milly

Miller
(English) practical
Mille, Myller

Mills
(English) safe
Mill, Milly, Mylls

Milo
(German) soft-hearted
Miles, Milos, Mye, Mylo

Milos
(Slavic) kind
Mile, Miles, Myle, Mylos

Milton
(English) innovative
Melton, Milt, Miltey, Milti,
Miltie, Milty, Mylt, Mylton

Mimi
(Greek) outspoken
Mims

Miner
(Last name as first name)
hard-working; miner
Mine, Miney

Mingo
(American) flirtatious
Ming-O, Myngo

Minnow
(American) beachcomber

Minter
(Last name as first name)
dull

Mirlam
(American) great
Mir, Mirsam, Mirtam

Mirsab
(Arabic) judicious

Misael
(Hebrew) godlike

Misha
(Russian) short for Mikhail

Mitch
(English) short for
Mitchell; optimist

Mitchell
(English) optimistic
*Mitch, Mitchel, Mitchelle,
Mitchie, Mitchill, Mitchy,
Mitshell, Mytchil*

Mitchum
(Last name as first name)
dramatic; known
Mitchem

Modesto
(Spanish) modest
Modysto

Modred
(Greek) unafraid
Modrede, Modrid

Moe
(American) short for
names beginning with Mo
or Moe; easygoing
Mo

Moey
(Hebrew) easygoing
Moe, Moeye

Mohammad
(Arabic) praiseworthy
*Mohamad, Mohamid,
Mohamud, Muhammad*

Mohan
(Hindi) compelling

Mohana
(Sanskrit) handsome
Mohann

Mohawk
(Place name) river in New
York

Mohsen
(Persian) one who does
good deeds
Mosen

Moises
(Hebrew) drawn from the
water
Moe

Mojave
(Place name) desert in
California; towering man
Mohave, Mohavey

Moline
(American) narrow
Moleen, Molene

Momo
(American) rascal

Monahan
(Irish) believer
*Mon, Monaghan,
Monehan, Monnahan*

Money
(American) word as name;
popular
Muney

Monico
(Spanish) form of Monaco;
player
Mon

Monroe
(Irish) delightful;
presidential
Mon, Monro, Munro,
Munroe

Montague
(French) forward-thinking
Mont, Montagew,
Montagu, Montegue,
Monty

Montana
(Spanish) mountain;
(Place name) U.S. state;
(American) sports icon
Mont, Montane,
Montayna, Monty

Monte
(Spanish) short for
Montgomery and
Montague; handsome
Mont, Montee, Monti,
Monts, Monty

Monteague
(African American) combo
of Monty and Teague;
creative
Mont, Montegue, Monti,
Monty

Montgomery
(English) wealthy
Mongomerey, Monte,
Montgomry, Monty

Montraie
(African American) fussy
Mont, Montray, Montraye,
Monty

Montrel
(African American)
popular
Montrell, Montrelle,
Monty

Montrose
(French) high and mighty
Mont, Montroce, Montros,
Monty

Monty
(English) short for
Montgomery and
Montague
Monte, Montee, Montey,
Monti

Moody
(American) expansive
Moodee, Moodey, Moodie

Moon
(African) dreamer

Mooney
(American) dreamer
Moon, Moonee, Moonie

Moore
(French) dark-haired
Mohr, Moores, More

Mooring
(Last name as first name)
centered
Moring

Moose
(American) large guy
Moos, Mooz, Mooze

Mordecai
(Hebrew) combative
Mord, Morde, Mordekai,
Morducai, Mordy

Moreland
(Last name as first name)
of wealth
Mooreland, Moorland,
Moorlande, Morland,
Morlande

Morell
(French) secretive
More, Morelle, Morey,
Morrell, Mourell, Murell

Morey
(Latin) dark
Morrie, Morry

Morgan
(Celtic) confident; seaman
Morg, Morgen, Morghan

Morlen
(English) outdoorsy
Morlan, Morlie, Morly

Moroni
(Place name) city in
Comoros; joyful
*Maroney, Maroni, Marony,
Moroney, Morony*

Morpheus
(Greek) god of dreams;
shapes

Morris
(Latin) dark
*Maurice, Moris, Morse,
Mouris*

Morrison
(Last name as first name)
son of Morris; dark
*Morrisen, Morrysen,
Morryson*

Morrley
(English) outdoors-loving
*More, Morlee, Morley,
Morly, Morrs*

Morrow
(Last name as first name)
follower
Morrowe

Morry
(Hebrew) taught by God;
old friend
Morey, Morrey, Mory

Morse
(English) bright; code-
maker
*Morce, Morcey, Morry,
Morsey*

Mortimer
(French) deep
*Mort, Mortemer, Mortie,
Morty, Mortymer*

Morton
(English) sophisticated
*Mort, Mortan, Mortun,
Morty*

Moses
(Hebrew) appointed for
special things
*Mosa, Mose, Mosesh,
Mosie, Mozes, Mozie*

Moshe
(Hebrew) special
Mosh, Moshie

Moss
(Irish) giving
Mossy

Mostyn
(Welsh) mossy

Motor
(American) word as name;
speedy; active
Mote

Mottel
(Hebrew) from Max; fighter

Mozam
(Place name) from
Mozambique
Moze

Mudge
(Last name as first name)
friendly
Mud, Mudj

Muhammad
(Arabic) form of
Mohammed; praised
Muhamed, Muhammed

Mukul
(Hindi) bird; beginnings

Mulder
(American) of the dark

Muldoon
(Last name as first name)
different
Muldoone, Muldune

Mundo
(Spanish) short for
Edmundo; prosperous
Mun, Mund

Mungo
(Scottish) loved; congenial
*Mongo, Mongoh, Munge,
Mungoh*

Murcia
(Place name) region in
Spain
Mursea

Murdoch
(Scottish) rich
*Merdock, Merdok, Murd,
Murdock, Murdok, Murdy*

Murfain
(American) bold spirit
*Merfaine, Murf, Murfee,
Murfy, Murphy*

Murff
(Irish) short for Murphy;
feisty
Merf, Murf

Murl
(English) nature-lover; sea

Murphy
(Irish) fighter
*Merph, Merphy, Murfie,
Murph*

Murray
(Scottish) sea-loving;
sailor
Mur, Muray, Murrey, Murry

Murrell
(English) nature-lover; sea

Murtough
(Irish) of the sea
Murtagh, Murrough

Muslim
(Arabic) religious

Mustafa
(Arabic) chosen one;
(Turkish) ingenious

Mutka
(African) New Year's baby

Myreon
(Greek) blessed; smell of
oil
Myron

Mycheal
(African American)
devoted
Mysheal

Myles
(German) form of Miles

Mylos
(Slavic) kind
Milos

Myrle
(American) able
Merl, Merle, Myrie, Myryee

Myron
(Greek) notable
Mi, Miron, My, Myrayn

Myrzon
(American) humorous
Merzon, Myrs, Myrz

Mystikal
(American) musician;
mystical

Nabil
(Arabic) of noble birth;
honored
Nabeel, Nobila

Nachman
(Last name as first name)
unique
*Menachem, Menahem,
Nacham, Nachmann,
Nahum*

Nachson
(Last name as first name)
son of Nach; up-and-
coming

Nachum
(Hebrew) comforts others
Nada
(Arabic) morning dew;
giver
Nadah
Nadim
(Arabic) fellow celebrant
Nadeem
Nadir
(Arabic) rare man
Nadeer, Nadeir
Naeem
(Arabic) happy
Nafis
(Hebrew) struggles
Naftali
(African) runs in woods
*Naphtali, Naphtali, Neftali,
Nefthali, Nephtali,
Nephthali*
Nagel
(English) smooth
*Naegel, Nageler, Nagelle,
Nagle, Nagler*
Nagid
(Arabic) regal
Nahir
(Hebrew) light
Naheer, Nahor
Nahum
(Arabic) content
Nemo
Naim
(Arabic) content
Naeem
Nairn
(Last name as first name)
born again
Nairne
Nairobi
(Place name) city in
Kenya; starting out
Najib
(Arabic) noble
Nageeb, Nagib, Najeeb

Naldo
(Italian) from Reynaldo;
smart tutor
Nalin
(Hindi) lotus; pretty boy
Naleen
Namir
(Hebrew) leopard; fast
Nameer
Nando
(Spanish) short for
Fernando
Nandor
(Hungarian) short for
Ferdinand
Nandy
(Hindi) from the god
Nandin; destructs
Nanson
(American) spunky
*Nance, Nanse, Nansen,
Nansson*
Napier
(French) mover
Neper
Napoleon
(German) lion of Naples;
domineering
*Nap, Napo, Napoleone,
Napolion, Napolleon,
Nappy*
Narciso
(Spanish) form of Greek
Narcissus, who fell in love
with his reflection; vain
Narcis
Narcissus
(Greek) self-loving; vain
*Narciss, Narcissah,
Narcisse, Nars*
Naren
(Hindi) best

Nasario
(Spanish) dedicated to God
Nasar, Nasareo, Nassario, Nazareo, Nazarlo, Nazaro, Nazor

Nash
(Last name as first name) exciting
Nashe, Nashey

Nashua
(Native American) thunderous

Nasser
(Arabic) winning
Naser, Nasir, Nasr, Nassar, Nasse, Nassee, Nassor

Nat
(Hebrew) short for Nathaniel
Natt, Natte, Nattie, Natty

Natal
(Hebrew) gift of God
Natale, Natalino, Natalio, Nataly

Nate
(Hebrew) short for Nathan and Nathaniel
Natey

Natividad
(Spanish) a child born at Christmastime

Nathan
(Hebrew) short for Nathaniel; magnanimous
Nat, Nate, Nathen, Nathin, Natthaen, Natthan, Natthen, Natty

Nathaniel
(Hebrew) God's gift to mankind
Nat, Nate, Nathan, Nathaneal, Nathanial, Nathe, Nathenial

Nation
(American) patriotic

Nato
(American) gentle
Nate, Natoe, Natoh

Navarro
(Spanish) wild spirit
Navaro, Navarroh, Naverro

Nayan
(Hebrew) form of Nathan; God-given

Naylor
(English) likes order
Nailer, Nailor

Naveed
(Hindi) wishing you well
Navid

Nazaire
(Biblical) from Nazareth; religious boy
Nasareo, Nasarrio, Nazario, Nazarius, Nazaro, Nazor

Neal
(Irish) winner
Neale, Nealey, Neall, Nealy, Neel, Neelee, Neely, Nele

Neander
(Greek) from Neanderthal
Ander, Nean, Neand

Nebo
(Mythology) Babylonian god of wisdom

Nebraska
(Place name) U.S. state
Neb

Nectarios
(Greek) sweet nectar; immortal man
Nectaire, Nectarius, Nektario, Nektarios, Nektarius

Ned
(English) short for Edward; comforting
Neddee, Neddie, Neddy

Nedrun
(American) difficult
*Ned, Nedd, Neddy,
Nedran, Nedro*

Neely
(Scottish) winning
Neel, Neels

Negasi
(African) destined for
royalty

Nehemiah
(Hebrew) compassionate
*Nechemia, Nechemiah,
Nechemya, Nehemyah,
Nemo*

Neil
(Scottish) victor
*Neal, Neale, Neall, Nealle,
Nealon, Neel, Neile, Neill,
Neille, Neils, Nels, Nial,
Niall, Niel, Niles*

Neirin
(Irish) light

Nellie
(English) short for Nelson;
singing
*Nell, Nellee, Nelli, Nells,
Nelly*

Nels
(Scandinavian) victor

Nelson
(English) broad-minded
*Nell, Nels, Nelsen, Nelsun,
Nilsson*

Nemesio
(Spanish) from Nemesis, a
god who avenges wrongs
Nemo

Nemo
(Literature) from Herman
Melville's Moby Dick;
courageous

Neptune
(Latin) god of the sea
*Neptoon, Neptoone,
Neptunne*

Ner
(Hebrew) light, fire

Nereus
(Greek) of the sea
Nereo

Nero
(Latin) unyielding
Neroh

Nery
(Spanish) daring
Neree, Nerey, Nerrie, Nerry

Nesbit
(Last name as first name)
man who wanders
*Naisbit, Naisbitt, Nesbitt,
Nisbet, Nisbett*

Nesto
(Greek) adventurer
Nestoh, Nestoro

Nestor
(Greek) wanderer
*Nest, Nester, Nestir, Nesto,
Nesty*

Netar
(African American) bright
Netardas

Netzer
(American) form of Nestor
Net

Nevada
(Place name) U.S. state
Nev, Nevadah

Neville
(French) innovator
*Nev, Nevil, Nevile, Nevvy,
Nevyle, Niville*

Nevin
(Irish) small holy man
*Nev, Nevan, Neven,
Nevins, Nevon, Niven*

Newbie
(American) novice
New, Newb

Newbury
(Last name as first name)
renewal
Newbery, Newberry

Newcomb
(Last name as first name)
renewal
Newcombe

Newell
(English) fresh face in the
hall
*New, Newall, Newel, Newy,
Nywell*

Newland
(Last name as first name)
of a new land

Newlin
(Welsh) able; new pond
Newl, Newlynn, Nule

Newman
(English) attractive young
man
*Neuman, Neumann, New,
Newmann*

Newport
(Last name as first name)
from a new seaport

Newt
(English) new

Newton
(English) bright; new mind
New, Newt

Neyman
(American) son of Ney;
bookish
Ney, Neymann, Neysa

Nezer
(Arabic) winning boy

Niall
(Irish) winner
Nial

Niaz
(Hindi) gift

Nicah
(Greek) victorious
Nik, Nike

Nicandro
(Spanish) a man who
excels
*Nicandreo, Nicandrios,
Nicandros, Nikander,
Nikandreo, Nikandrios*

Nicholas
(Greek) winner; the
people's victory
*Nichelas, Nicholus, Nick,
Nickee, Nickie, Nicklus,
Nickolas, Nicky, Nikolas,
Nyck, Nykolas*

Nichols
(English) kind-hearted
*Nicholes, Nick, Nicky,
Nikols*

Nick
(English) short for Nicholas
Nic, Nik

Nicklaus
(Greek) form of Nicholas
Nicklaws, Niklus

Nickleby
(Last name as first name)
betting on the odds

Nickler
(American) fleet-footed;
perspicacious

Nicky
(Greek) short for Nicholas
*Nick, Nickee, Nickey, Nicki,
Nik, Nikee, Nikki*

Nico
(Italian) victor
Nicos, Niko, Nikos

Nicodemus
(Greek) people's victory
Nicodemo, Nikodema

Nicol
(Italian) from Nicola; victor

Nicolas
(Italian) form of Nicholas;
victorious
Nic, Nico, Nicolus

Nicomedes
(Greek) thinking of victory
Nicomedo, Nikomedes

Niels
(Scandinavian) victorious
Neels

Nigel
(English) champion
Nigie, Nigil, Nygelle

Night
(American) nocturnal

Nike
(Greek) winning
Nykee, Nykie, Nyke

Nikhil
(Russian) from Nicola;
victor

Nikita
(Russian) not yet won
Nika

Niklas
(Scandinavian) winner
Niklaas, Nils, Klaas

Nikolai
(Russian) winning
Nika

Nikolas
(Greek) form of Nicholas
*Nik, Nike, Niko, Nikos,
Nyloas*

Nikos
(Greek) victor
Nicos, Niko, Nikolos

Nikostratos
(Greek) the army's victory
*Nicostrato, Nicostratos,
Nicostratus*

Niles
(English) smooth
Ni, Nile, Niley, Nyles, Nyley

Nimrod
(Hebrew) renegade
Nimrodd, Nymrod

Ninian
(Armenium) studious

Nino
(Spanish) child; young boy

Ninyun
(American) spirited
*Ninian, Ninion, Ninyan,
Nynyun*

Nissan
(Hebrew) omen
Nisan, Nissyn

Nissim
(Hebrew) Nisan is seventh
Jewish month; believer

Niven
(Last name as first name)
smooth

Nix
(American) negative
Nicks, Nixy

Nixon
(English) audacious
Nickson, Nixen, Nixun

Njord
(Scandinavian) man of the
north
Njorth

Noah
(Hebrew) peacemaker
Noa, Noe, Nouh

Noam
(Hebrew) sweet man
Noahm, Noe

Noble
(Latin) regal
*Nobe, Nobee, Nobel,
Nobie, Noby*

Noe
(Spanish) quiet;
(Polish) comforter
Noeh, Noey

Noel
(French) born on
Christmas
Noelle, Noelly, Nole, Nollie

Noey
(Spanish) form of Noah;
he who wanders
Noe, Noie

Nolan
(Irish) outstanding; noble
*Nole, Nolen, Nolline,
Nolun, Nolyn*

Nolden
(American) noble
Nold

Noll
(Scandinavian) from Nolly
(Oliver); smiling

Nolly
(Scandinavian) hopeful
*Nole, Noli, Noll, Nolley,
Nolleye, Nolli, Nollie*

Noor
(Hindi) light
Nour, Nur

Norb
(Scandinavian) innovative
*Noberto, Norbie, Norbs,
Norby*

Norbert
(German) bright north
Norb, Norbie, Norby

Nordin
(Nordic) handsome
*Nord, Nordan, Norde,
Nordee, Nordeen, Nordi,
Nordun, Nordy*

Norman
(English) sincere; man of
the North
*Norm, Normen, Normey,
Normi, Normie, Normon,
Normun, Normy*

Norris
(English) from the north

Norshawn
(African American) combo
of Nor and Shawn
*Norrs, Norrshawn,
Norshaun*

North
(American) directional
Norf, Northe

Northcliff
(English) from the north
cliff
*Northcliffe, Northclyff,
Northclyffe*

Northrop
(English) northerner
Northrup

Norton
(English) dignified man of
the North
Nort, Nortan, Norten

Norval
(English) from the North
Norvan

Norville
(French) resident of a
northern village; warm-
hearted
*Norval, Norvel, Norvil,
Norvill, Norvyl*

Norshell
(African American) brash
Norshel, Norshelle

Norward
(English) going north
Norwerd

Norwell
(English) northward
bound

Norwin
(English) friendly
*Norvin, Norwen, Norwind,
Norwinn*

Norwood
(English) of the north
woods

Nowell
(Last name as first name)
dependable
Nowe

Nowey
(American) knowing
Nowee, Nowie

Nueces
(Place name) river in Texas

Nuell
(American) form of Newell
(last name); in charge
Nuel

Nuey
(Spanish) short for Nueva
Nui, Nuie

Nuncio
(Spanish) messenger;
informant
Nunzio

Nunry
(Last name as first name)
giving
Nunri

Nuri
(Arabic) light
Noori, Nur, Nuriel, Nuris

Nuriel
(Hebrew) light of God
*Nooriel, Nuriya, Nuriyah,
Nurya*

Nuys
(Place name) from Van
Nuys, California
Nies, Nyes, Nys

Nye
(Welsh) focused
Ni, Nie, Nyee

Nyle
(American) form of
Niles/Nile; smooth
Nyl, Nyles

O

Oak
(English) sturdy
Oake, Oakes, Oakie

Oakley
(English) sturdy; strong
*Oak, Oakie, Oaklee,
Oakleigh, Oakly, Oklie*

Oba
(Hebrew) from Obadiah;
God's servant

Obadiah
(Hebrew) serving God
*Obadyah, Obediah, Obee,
Obie, Oby*

Obasi
(African) God-loving

Obataiye
(African) world leader

Obayana
(African) king by the fire

Obbie
(Biblical) from Biblical
prophet Obadiah; serving
God
Obey, Obi, Obie

Obedience
(American) strict
Obie

Oberon
(German) strong-bearing
*Auberon, Auberron,
Obaron, Oberahn,
Oberone, Oburon*

Obert
(German) rich man

Obey
(American) short for
Obadiah
Obe, Obee, Obie, Oby

Obi
(African) big heart

Obie
(Hebrew) from Obadiah;
serves the Lord
Obbie, Obe, Oby

Obike
(African) loved by his
family

Ocean
(Greek) ocean; child born
under a water sign
Oceane, Oceanus

Ocie
(Greek) short for Ocean
Osie

Octavio
(Latin) eight; able
*Octave, Octavian,
Octavien, Octavioh,
Octavo, Ottavio*

Odakota
(Native American) has
many friends

Ode
(Greek) poetry as a name;
poetic
Odee, Odie

Oded
(Hebrew) supportive

Odell
(American) musical
*Dell, Odall, Ode, Odey,
Odyll*

Oder
(Place name) river in
Europe
Ode

Odhran
(Irish) green; creative
Odran, Oran

Odin
(Scandinavian) Norse god
of magic; soulful
Odan, Oden

Odinan
(Hungarian) rich; powerful

Odion
(African) the first twin

Odisoose
(Invented) form of
Odysseus
Ode

Odissan
(African) wanderer

Odolf
(Japanese) from the field
of deer; lithe

Odom
(African) the oak; strong

Odysseus
(Greek) wanderer
Ode, Odey, Odie

Ofer
(Hebrew) deer, fleetfooted

Og
(Aramaic) king

Ogano
(Japanese) wise

Ogdon
(English) literate
Og, Ogdan, Ogden

Oghe
(Irish) horserider
Oghie, Oho

Ogle
(American) word as name;
leer; stare
Ogal, Ogel, Ogll, Ogul

Ogun
(Japanese) undaunted

Ohanko
(Japanese) invincible

Ohanzee
(Native American)
shadowy figure

Ohin
(Japanese) wanted child

Oisin
(Irish) fawn; gentle

Oistin
(Latin) much revered

Ojay
(American) brash
O.J., Oojai

Ojo
(African) he came of a
hard birth

Okan
(Turkish) horse
Oke

Okapi
(African) graceful

Okechuku
(African) God's blessing

Okello
(African) child after twins
were born

Okemos
(African) advises

Okie
(American) man from
Oklahoma
Okey, Okeydokey

Oko
(Japanese) evoker;
charming

Okon
(Japanese) from the
darkness

Okoth
(African) sad child; born
during rainfall

Okpara
(African) first son

Oktawian
(African) eighth child

Ola
(African) child much
honored

Oladele
(African) honored at home

Olaf
(Scandinavian) watchful
Olay, Ole, Olef, Olev, Oluf

Olafemi
(African) lucky child

Olajuwon
(Arabic) honorable
Olajuwan, Olujuwon

Olakeakua
(Hawaiian) living for God

Olamina
(African) rich of spirit

Olan
(Scandinavian) royal
ancestor
Olin, Ollee

Olaniyan
(African) honored all
around

Olav
(Scandinavian) traditional
Ola, Olov, Oluf

Oldrich
(Czech) leader; strong
*Olda, Oldra, Oldrisek,
Olecek, Olik, Olin,
Olouvsek*

Ole
(Scandinavian) watchful
Olay

Oleg
(Russian) holy; religious
Olag, Ole, Olig

Olvery
(English) draws others
near

Olin
(English) holly; jubilant
Olen, Olney, Olyn

Olindo
(Latin) sweet fragrance

Oliver
(Latin) loving nature
*Olaver, Olive, Ollie, Olliver,
Olly, Oluvor*

Olivier
(French) eloquent
Oliveay

Oliwa
(Hawaiian) from an army of elves

Ollie
(English) short for Oliver
Olie, Ollee, Olley, Olly

Olney
(English) lonely field

Olo
(Spanish) short for Orlando; showy

Olorun
(African) blessed; counsels others

Olubayo
(African) full of happiness

Olufemi
(African) God's loved child
Olviemi

Olugbala
(African) the people's God

Olujimi
(African) hand in hand with God

Olumide
(African) God has come

Olumoi
(African) blessed by God

Olushegun
(African) marches with God

Olushola
(African) blessed

Oluwa
(African) believer

Oluyemi
(African) man full of God

Omaha
(Place name) city in Nebraska

Omanand
(Hindi) joyful thinker

Omar
(Arabic) spiritual
Omahr, Omarr

Omie
(Italian) homebody
Omey, Omi, Omye

Omri
(Hebrew) Jehovah's servant; giving

On
(African) desirable

Onacona
(Native American) white owl; watchful

Oukounaka
(Asian) from the surf

Onan
(Turkish) rich

Onani
(Asian) sweet

Onaona
(Hawaiian) fragrant

Ondrej
(Czech) masculine
Ondra, Ondravsek, Ondrejek, Ondrousek

Onesimo
(Spanish) number one
Onie

Onkar
(Hindi) purest one

Onofrio
(German) smart
Ono, Onofreeo, Onofrioh

Onslow
(Arabic) climbing passion's hill
Ounslow

Onur
(Turkish) promising boy

Onwoachi
(African) God's world

Oqwapi
(Native American) red cloud

Oral
(Latin) eloquent

Oran
(Irish) pale
Orin, Orran, Orren, Orrin

Orban
(Hungarian) city man;
sophisticated

Ordell
(Latin) the start

Oren
(Hebrew) from Owen;
sturdy tree

Orenthiel
(American) sturdy as a
pine
Ore, Oren

Orenthiem
(American) sturdy as a
pine
Orenth, Orenthe

Orestes
(Greek) leader
*Oresta, Oreste, Restie,
Resty*

Orev
(Hebrew) raven; observing

Orford
(Last name as first name)
noble

Ori
(Hebrew) flame of truth

Oriol
(Spanish) best
Orioll

Orion
(Greek) fiery hunter
Oreon, Ori, Orie, Ory

Orji
(African) sturdy tree

Orlando
(Spanish) famed;
distinctive
*Orl, Orland, Orlie,
Orlondo, Orly*

Orleans
(Latin) the golden boy
Orlins

Orman
(Latin) noble
*Ormand, Ormond,
Ormonde*

Orme
(English) kind
Orm

Ormond
(English) kind-hearted
*Ormand, Ormande, Orme,
Ormon, Ormonde,
Ormund, Ormunde*

Oro
(Spanish) golden child

Oron
(Hebrew) light spirit

Orpheus
(Greek) darkness of night;
mythological musician

Orran
(Irish) green-eyed
Ore, Oren, Orin

Orrick
(English) sturdy as an oak
Oric, Orick, Orreck, Orrik

Orrie
(American) short for
Orson; solid
Orry

Orrin
(English) river boy

Orris
(Latin) from Horatio;
inventive
Oris, Orriss

Orry
(Latin) Oriental; exotic
Oarrie, Orrey, Orrie

Orson
(Latin) strong as a bear
*Orsan, Orsen, Orsey,
Orsun*

Orth
(English) honest
Orthe

Orton
(Last name as first name)
reaching

Orval
(American) form of Orville;
bold
Orvale

Orunjan
(African) god of the noon-
time sun

Orville
(French) brave
Orv, Orvelle, Orvie, Orvil

Orvin
(Last name as first name)
fated for success
Orwin, Orwynn

Orway
(American) kind
Orwaye

Osakwe
(Japanese) good destiny

Osanmwesr
(Japanese) leaving

Osayaba
(Japanese) wonders

Osbert
(English) smart

Osborne
(English) strong-spirited
*Osborn, Osbourne,
Osburn, Osburne, Ossie,
Oz, Ozzie, Ozzy*

Osburt
(English) smart
*Osbart, Osbert, Ozbert,
Ozburt*

Oscar
(Scandinavian) divine
Ozkar

Oscard
(Greek) fighter
Oscar, Oskard

Osceola
(Native American) black
drink

Osei
(African) gracious

Osgood
(English) good man
Osgude, Ozgood

Oshea
(Hebrew) kind spirit

Osiel
(Spanish)

Osileani
(Polynesian) talking
forever

Oslo
(Place name) capital of
Norway
Os, Oz

Osman
(Spanish) verbose
*Os, Osmen, Osmin, Ossie,
Oz, Ozzie*

Osmar
(English) amazing; divine

Osmond
(English) singing to the
world
*Os, Osmonde, Osmund,
Ossie, Oz, Ozzy*

Osrec
(Scandinavian) leader
Os, Ossie

Osred
(Scandinavian) leads
mankind

Osric
(Scandinavian) leader
Osrick

Ossie
(Hebrew) powerful
Os, Oz, Ozzy

Osten
(Last name as first name)
religious leader
Ostin, Ostyn

Osvaldo
(German) divine power
Osvald, Oswaldo

Oswald
(English) divine power
*Oswalde, Oswold, Oswuld,
Oszie, Oz*

Oswin
(English) God's ally
*Osvin, Oswinn, Oswyn,
Oswynn*

Ota
(Czech) affluent

Otik
(German) lucky

Otadan
(Native Amercian)
abundance

Othell
(African American) thriving
Oth, Othey, Otho

Othello
(Spanish) bold
Otello, Othell

Othman
(Last name as first name)
man of bravery

Othniel
(Hebrew) rendered brave
by God's love

Otis
(Greek) intuitive
*Oates, Odis, Otes, Ottes,
Ottis*

Otokar
(Czech) prudent in wealth

Otoniel
(Spanish) fashionable
Otonel

Otskai
(Native American) leaving

Ottah
(African) thin boy

Ottar
(Scandinavian) warring
Otomars, Ottomar

Otto
(German) wealthy
Oto, Ott, Ottoh

Ottokar
(German) can-do spirit;
fighter
Otokars, Ottocar

Ottway
(German) fortunate
Otwae, Otway

Otu
(Native American)
industrious

Ouray
(Native American) arrow
man

Oved
(Hebrew) serving
Obed

Overton
(Last name as first name)
leader
Ove, Overten

Ovidio
(Spanish) from Ovid
(Roman poet); creative
Ovido

Owen
(Welsh) well-born; high-
principled
Owan, Owin, Owwen

Owney
(Irish) old one
Oney

Ox
(American) animal; strong
Oxy

Oxford
(English) scholar; ox
crossing
Fordy, Oxferd, Oxfor

Oz
(Hebrew) courageous;
unusual

Ozell
(English) strong
Ozel

Oziel
(Spanish) strong

Ozni
(Hebrew) knows God

Ozuru
(Japanese) stork; lively hope

Ozzie
(English) short for Oswald
Oz, Ozzee, Ozzey, Ozzy

Pablo
(Spanish) strong; creative
Pabel, Pabo, Paublo

Pacian
(Spanish) peaceful
Pacien, Pace

Pack
(German) from Packard
(Richard); outdoorsman
Pac, Pak

Packer
(Last name as first name)
orderly
Pack

Packy
(German) from Packard, a
form of Richard;
outdoorsman
Packey

Paco
(Spanish) energetic
*Pak, Pakkoh, Pako,
Paquito*

Padden
(English) form of Patton;
confident
Paddin, Paddyn

Paddy
(Irish) short for Patrick;
noble; comfortable
*Paddey, Paddi, Paddie,
Padee*

Padget
(French) learning; growing
Padgett, Pagas

Padraic
(Irish) form of Patrick;
cocky
*Padraick, Padraik, Padrayc,
Padrayck, Padrayk*

Padre
(Spanish) father; cajoles
Padrae, Padray

Page
(French) helpful
Pagey, Paige, Payg

Pageman
(Last name as first name)
sharp

Pago
(Place name) for Pago
Pago, American Samoa;
hospitable
Pay

Paine
(Latin) countryman
Payne

Paki
(African) has seen the
truth

Pall
(Scandinavian) form of
Paul; wise friend

Palladin
(Greek) confrontational;
wise
*Palidin, Palladyn,
Palleden, Pallie, Pally*

Pallaton
(Native American) tough;
fighter
Palladin

Palma
(Latin) successful
Palmer
(English) open
*Pallmar, Pallmer, Palmar,
Palmur*
Palti
(Hebrew) getaway
Pampa
(Place name) city in Texas
Pan
(Greek mythology) god of
forest and shepherds
Pann
Panama
(Place name) canal
connecting North and
South America; rounder
Pan
Pancho
(Spanish) short for
Francisco; jaunty
Panchoh, Ponchito
Pancrazio
(Italian) all-powerful
Pankraz
Panfilo
(Spanish) loving all nature
Panos
(Greek) rock; sturdy
Pantaleon
(Spanish) pants; trousers;
manly
Pant, Pantalon
Pantias
(Greek) philosophical
Paolo
(Italian) form of Paul;
small and high-energy
Paoloh, Paulo
Paquito
(Spanish) dear Paco
Paris
(English) lover; France's
capital
Pare, Paree, Parris

Parish
(French) priest's place;
lovely boy
Parrish, Parrysh, Parysh
Park
(English) calming
Parke, Parkey, Parks
Parker
(English) manager
Park, Parks
Parley
(Scottish) reluctant
Parly
Parnell
(French) ribald
*Parne, Parnel, Parnelle,
Perne, Parle*
Parnelli
(Italian) frisky
Parnell
Paros
(Place name) Greek
island; charming
Par, Paro
Parr
(English) protective
Par, Parre
Parris
(French) priest's place;
lovely boy
*Paris, Pariss, Parriss,
Parrys, Parryss*
Parrish
(French) separate and
unique; district
Parry
(Welsh) young son
Parrie, Pary
Parryth
(American) up-and-coming
*Pareth, Parre, Parry,
Parythe*
Parson
(English) clergyman
Parsen

Parthik
(Greek) virginal
Partholon
(Irish) form of
Bartholomew; earthy
Parlan
Paryon
(Greek) form of Parion,
ancient Greek city
Pascal
(French) boy born on
Easter or Passover;
spiritual
*Pascalle, Paschal, Pasco,
Pascual, Paskalle, Pasky*
Pasquale
(Italian) spiritual
*Pask, Paskwoll, Pasq,
Pasquell, Posquel*
Pass
(Russian) from Pasha
(form of Paul); small; kind
Pastor
(English) clergyman
Pastar, Paster
Pat
(English) short for Patrick;
noble
*Pattey, Patti, Patty, Pattye,
Pattee*
Pate
(Latin) from Patrick; noble
Pait, Payte
Patek
(Latin) from Patrick; noble
Patec, Pateck
Pater
(French) fathers
Paterson
(Last name as first name)
intelligent father
Patricio
(Spanish) form of Patrick;
noble
Patricyo

Patrick
(Irish) aristocrat
*Paddy, Partric, Patric,
Patrik, Patriquek, Patryk,
Pats, Patsy*
Patriot
(American) patriotic
Patterson
(English) intellectual
*Paterson, Pattersen,
Pattersun, Pattersund*
Pattison
(English) son of Pat; noble
*Pattisen, Pattysen,
Pattyson, Patysen,
Patyson*
Patton
(English) brash warrior
*Patten, Pattun, Patun,
Peyton*
Paul
(Latin) small; wise
Pauley, Paulie, Pauly
Pauli
(Italian) dear Paul
*Paulee, Pauley, Paulie,
Pauly*
Paulin
(German) form of Paul;
small boy
Paulyn
Paulis
(Latin) form of Paul; small
boy
Pauliss, Paulys, Paulyss
Paulo
(Spanish) form of Paul
Paulos
(Greek) small
Paulus
(Latin) small
Paul, Paulie, Paulis, Pauly
Pavel
(Russian) inspired
Pasha

Pavlof
(Last name as first name)
reactive; small
Pavel

Pavun
(Indian) belonging to the
middle

Pawel
(Polish) believer
Pawl

Pax
(Latin) peace-loving
Paks, Paxy

Paxon
(German) peaceful
Packston, Packton

Paxton
(English) from a town of
peace; gentle boy
Paxten

Payne
(Latin) countryman
Paine, Payn

Payton
(English) soldier's town
*Pate, Paton, Payten,
Paytun, Peyton*

Peabo
(Irish) rock

Peale
(English) bellringer in a
church; religious
Peal, Peel, Peele

Peat
(English) form of Pete;
knowing

Pecos
(Place name) Texas river;
cowboy
Peck, Pekos

Pedaias
(Biblical) God loves
Pedaiah

Peader
(Scottish) rock or stone;
reliable
Peder, Peter

Pearson
(English) dark-eyed
*Pearse, Pearsen, Pearsun,
Peerson*

Pederson
(Scandinavian) form of
Peterson; son of Peter;
smart boy
Pedersen

Pedro
(Spanish) audacious
Pedra, Pedrin, Pedroh

Peer
(Scandinavian) rock

Peerson
(English) son of Peter;
smart
Peersen

Pegasus
(Mythology) horse; rider

Pelle
(Swedish) for Peter; rock
Pele, Pelee

Pelly
(English) happy
Peli, Pelley, Pelli

Pelon
(Spanish) joyful

Pelton
(Last name as first name)
town of Pel; respectful

Pembroke
(French) sophisticated
*Brookie, Pemb,
Pembrooke, Pimbroke*

Pender
(Last name as first name)
loves music

Penley
(Last name as first name)
strong

Penn
(German) strong-willed
Pen, Pennee, Penney,
Pennie, Penny

Penrod
(German) respected leader

Penrose
(Last name as first name)
liked

Pentecost
(Religion) pious person
Penticost, Pentycost

Pentige
(Last name as first name)
worthy

Pentz
(Last name as first name)
visionary

Penuel
(Hebrew) face of God

Pepin
(German) ardent
Pepen, Pepi, Pepp, Peppi,
Peppy, Pepun

Pepper
(Botanical) live wire
Pep, Pepp, Peppy

Peppino
(Spanish) energetic

Per
(Scandinavian) secretive

Percival
(French) mysterious
Parsival, Perc, Perce,
Perceval, Percey, Percy,
Perseval, Purcival, Purcy

Percy
(French) short for Percival
Percee, Percey, Perci, Percie

Peregrino
(Italian) bird; ordinary

Perfecto
(Spanish) perfect
Perfek

Pericles
(Greek) fair leader
Periklees, Perikles, Perry

Perine
(Latin) adventurer
Perrin, Perrine, Perry,
Peryne

Perk
(American) perky
Perkey, Perki, Perky

Perkin
(English) opinionated
Parkin

Perkins
(English) political
Perk, Perkens, Perkey

Pernell
(French) from Parnell;
small Peter; smart
Pernel

Peron
(Last name as first name)
leader

Perrin
(Latin) traveler
Perrine, Pero, Per

Perris
(Greek) legendary
kidnapper of Helen of
Troy; daring
Paris, Peris, Periss, Perrys,
Perys

Perry
(English) tough-minded
Parry, Perr, Perrey, Perri,
Perrie

Perryman
(Last name as first name)
nature-lover
Perry

Perseus
(Greek) destroyer;
mythological hero

Perth
(Place name) capital of
Western Australia
Purth

Perun
(Hindi) from the name
Perunkulam

Pete
(English) easygoing
Petey, Petie

Peter
(Greek) dependable; rock
*Per, Petar, Pete, Petee,
Petey, Petie, Petur, Pyotr*

Pethuel
(Aramaic) God's vision

Petra
(Place name) city in
Arabia; dashing

Petter
(Scandinavian) form of
Peter; dependable
Petya

Peverel
(Latin, French) of the piper
Peverell, Peveril

Peyton
(English) form of Payton
Pey, Peyt

Pharis
(Irish) heroic
Farres, Farrus, Pharris

Phelan
(Irish) the small wolf;
fierce

Phelgen
(Last name as first name)
stylish
Phelgon

Phelim
(Irish) wolfish; fierce
Phelym

Phelps
(English) droll
Felps, Filps

Phex
(American) kind
Fex

Phil
(Greek) short for Philip
Fill, Phill

Philander
(Greek) lover of many;
infidel
*Filander, Phil, Philandyr,
Philender*

Philemon
(Greek) showing affection
Filemon, Philamon, Philo

Philetus
(Greek) collector

Philip
(Greek) outdoorsman;
horse-lover
*Felipe, Filipp, Flippo, Phil,
Phillie, Phillip, Phillippe,
Philly*

Philippe
(French) form of Philip
Felipe, Filippe, Philipe

Philo
(Greek) lover
Filo

Phineas
(English) far-sighted
*Fineas, Finny, Pheneas,
Phineus, Phinny*

Phoenix
(Greek) bird of
immortality; everlasting
Fee, Feenix, Fenix, Nix

Photius
(Greek) scholarly

Picardus
(Hispanic) adventurous

Pickford
(Last name as first name)
old-fashioned

Pico
(Spanish) the epitome;
peak

Pierce
(English) insightful;
piercing
*Pearce, Peerce, Peers,
Peersey, Percy, Piercy,
Piers*

Piero
(Italian) form of Peter;
dependable
Pierro

Pierre
(French) socially adroit
Piere

Pierrepont
(French) social
Pierpont

Piers
(English) from Philip;
horse lover

Pierson
(English) son of Pier; rock
Peirsen, Pearson

Pietro
(Italian) reliable
Pete

Pilar
(Spanish) basic
Pilarr

Pilgrim
(English) a traveler
Pilgrym

Pillion
(French) excellence
Pilion, Pillyon, Pilyon

Pilot
(French) excellence

Pim
(Dutch) precise

Pin
(Vietnamese) joyful

Pincus
(American) dark
*Pincas, Pinchas, Pinchus,
Pinkus*

Pinechas
(Hebrew) form of Paul;
dark

Piney
(American) living among
pines; comfortable
Pine, Pyney

Pinkston
(Last name as first name)
different
Pink, Pinky

Pinky
(American) familiar form
of Pinchas

Pinya
(Hebrew) loyal

Pio
(Italian) pious

Pip
(German) ingenious
Pipp, Pippin, Pippo, Pippy

Pippin
(English) shy

Pirney
(Scottish) from the island

Pitch
(American) musical

Piton
(Spanish) form of Felix;
prideful

Pitt
(English) swerving
dramatically

Pittman
(English) blue-collar
worker

Pius
(Polish) pious

Placid
(Latin) calm
Plasid

Placido
(Italian) serene songster
*Placeedo, Placidoh,
Placydo*

Plan
(American) word as name;
organized
Plash
(American) splashy; zany
Plat
(French) from the
flatlands; landowner
Platt
Platinum
(English) worthwhile
Plato
(Greek) broad-minded
Plata, Platoh
Playtoh
(Invented) form of Plato
Pluck
(American) audacious;
plucky
Plutarco
(Greek) nefarious
Poe
(Last name as first name)
dark spirit
Poet
(American) writer
Poe
Policarpo
(Greek) with much fruit
Polk
(Last name as first name)
political
Pollard
(German) closed-minded
*Polard, Pollar, Pollerd,
Polley*
Pollock
(Last name as first name)
creative
Pollux
(Last name as first name)
underdog
Polo
(Greek) adventurer
Poloe, Poloh

Polonice
(Polish) respects
Polygnotos
(Greek) lover of many
Pomeroy
(Last name as first name)
polite
Pomposo
(Spanish) pompous
Ponce
(Spanish) fifth; wanderer
Poncey, Ponciano, Ponse
Ponipake
(Hawaiian) good luck
Pons
(Spanish) fifth; explores
Ponse
Pontius
(Latin) the fifth
Pontias, Pontus
Pony
(Scottish) dashing
Poney, Ponie
Poogie
(American) snuggly
*Poog, Poogee, Poogi,
Poogs, Pookie*
Poole
(Place name) area in
England
Pool
Pope
(Greek) father
Po
Porfirio
(Spanish) audacious
Port
(Latin) gatekeeper
Porte
Porter
(Latin) decisive
Poart, Port, Portur, Porty
Powder
(American) cowboy
Powd, Powe

Powell
(English) ready
Powers
(English) wields power
Prairie
(American) rural man or
rancher
Prair, Prairey, Prairi, Prairy
Prakash
(Indian) light
Pratt
(Last name as first name)
talkative
Praxedes
(Last name as first name)
prayerful
Preemoh
(Invented) form of Primo
Prentice
(English) learning
*Prenticce, Prentis,
Prentiss, Printiss*
Prescott
(Last name as first name)
sophisticated
Preston
(Last name as first name)
village of a priest;
religious home
Presley
(English) songbird;
meadow of the priest
Preslee, Preslie, Presly
Preston
(English) spiritual
Prestyn
Preto
(Latin) important
Price
(Welsh) vigorous
Pricey, Pryce
Priestley
(English) cottage of the
priest
Priestlea, Priestlee, Priestly

Primerica
(American) form of
America; patriotic
Prime
Primitivo
(Spanish) primitive
Primi, Tito, Tivo
Primo
(Italian) top-notch
Preemo, Primoh, Prymo
Prince
(Latin) regal leader
Preenz, Prins, Prinz, Prinze
Prine
(English) prime
Prisciliano
(Spanish) wise old man
Procopio
(Greek, Spanish) making
progress; prominent nose
Procter
(Last name as first name)
leads
Proctor
Prometheus
(Mythology) friend of man;
bringer of fire
Prop
(American) word as name;
fun-loving
Propp
Prosper
(Italian) having good
fortune
Pros
Proteus
(Greek) first
Pryor
(Latin) spiritual director
Pry, Prye
Publias
(Greek) thinker
Publius

Pullman
(English) train man;
motivator
*Pulman, Pulmann,
Pullmann*

Purvin
(English) helpful
Pervin

Purvis
(French) provider
Pervis, Purviss

Pushkin
(Last name as first) poet;
playful

Putnam
(English) fond of water
*Puddy, Putnum, Puttie,
Putty*

Pynchon
(Last name as first)
brilliant; inventive

Pyre
(Latin) fire; excitable

Q

Qabil
(Arabic) capable

Qadim
(Arabic) able

Qadir
(Arabic) talented
*Qadar, Qadeer, Quadeer,
Quadir*

Qamar
(Arabic) moon; dreamy

Qasim
(Arabic) generous

Qimat
(Hindi) valued

Quaashie
(African American)
ambitious

Quaddus
(African American) bright

Quadrees
(Latin) fourth
Kwadrees, Quadrhys

Quan
(Vietnamese) dignified

Quanah
(Native American) good-
smelling
Quan

Quannell
(African American) strong-
willed
*Kwan, Kwanell, Kwanelle,
Quan, Quanelle, Quannel*

Quant
(Latin) knowing his worth
*Quanta, Quantae,
Quantal, Quantay,
Quantea, Quantey,
Quantez*

Quaronne
(African American)
haughty
*Kwarohn, Kwaronne,
Quaronn*

Quashawn
(African American)
tenacious
*Kwashan, Kwashaun,
Kwashawn, Quasha,
Quashie, Quashy*

Qudamah
(Arabic) courage

Qued
(Native American)
decorated robe

Quelatikan
(Native Amercan) blue horn

Quenby
(English) giving
Quenbee, Quenbie,
Quenbey

Quennell
(French) strength of an
oak
Quenell, Quennel

Quentin
(Latin) fifth
Kwent, Qeuntin, Quantin,
Quent, Quenten, Quenton,
Quientin, Quienton, Quint,
Quintin, Quinton, Qwent,
Qwentin, Qwenton

Quick
(American) fast;
remarkable

Quico
(Spanish) stands by his
friends
Paco

Quiessencia
(Spanish) essential;
essence
Quiess, Quiessence

Quigley
(Irish) loving nature
Quiglee, Quigly, Quiggly,
Quiggy

Quillan
(Irish) club; joined
Quill, Quillen, Quillon

Quimby
(Norse) woman's house

Quincy
(French) fifth; patient
Quensie, Quincee,
Quincey, Quinci, Quincie,
Quinnsy, Quinsey

Quinlan
(Irish) fit physique
Quindlen, Quinlen,
Quinlin, Quinn, Quinnlan

Quinn
(Irish) short for Quinton;
bright
Kwen, Kwene, Quenn,
Quin

Quintavius
(African American) fifth
child
Quint

Quintin
(Latin) planner
Quenten, Quint, Quinton

Quinto
(Spanish) fifth
Quiqui

Quintus
(Spanish) fifth child
Quin, Quinn, Quint

Quiqui
(Spanish) friend; short for
Enrique
Kaka, Keke, Quinto,
Quiquin

Quirin
(English) a magic spell

Quirinus
(Latin) spear; Roman god
of war

Quito
(Spanish) lively
Kito

Qunnoune
(Native Amercian) tall

Quoitrel
(African American)
equalizer
Kwotrel, Quoitrelle

Quon
(Chinese) bright; light

Qusay
(Arabic) rough hewn
Qussay

Raashid
(Arabic) form of Rashad;
wise man

Rab
(Scottish) short for
Raibeart; bright
Rabbie

Rabbaanee
(African) easygoing

Rabbi
(Hebrew) master

Rabbit
(Literature) for John
Updike's novels; fast
Rab

Rabul
(Hispanic) rich

Rachins
(Hebrew) merciful

Racqueab
(Arabic) homebody

Rad
(Scandinavian) helpful;
confident
Radd

Radbert
(English) intelligent
Rad

Radborne
(English) born happy
Radbourne, Radburn

Radcliff
(English) from the bright
cliff; able

Raddy
(Slavic) cheerful
*Rad, Radde, Raddie,
Radey*

Radford
(English) helpful
*Rad, Raddey, Raddie,
Raddy, Radferd*

Radimir
(Polish) joyful

Radley
(English) sways with the
wind
Radlea, Radlee, Radleigh

Radnor
(English) boy of the bright
shore; natural

Radolf
(Anglo-Saxon) warrior

Radomir
(Slavic) delightful

Rady
(Filipino) happy

Raeshon
(American) form of
Raeshawn; brainy
*Rayshawn, Rashone,
Reshawn*

Raekwon
(African American) proud
Raykwonn

Rael
(African) from Roe; lamb

Rafael
(Hebrew, Spanish)
renewed
*Rafaelle, Rafayel,
Rafayelle, Rafe, Raphael,
Raphaele*

Rafe
(Irish) tough
Raff, Raffe, Raif

Rafeeq
(Arabic) gregarious

Rafferty
(Irish) wealthy
*Rafarty, Rafe, Raff, Raferty,
Raffarty, Raffertie, Raffety*

Raffin
(Hebrew) from Raphael; healed by God

Rafi
(Arabic) musical; friend
Rafee, Raffy

Rage
(American) trendsetter

Raghib
(Arabic) rapturous

Ragnar
(Scandinavian) power fighter

Raheem
(Arabic) having empathy
Rahim

Rahman
(Arabic) full of compassion
Raman, Rahmahn

Rahn
(American) form of Ron; kind
Rahnney, Rahnnie, Rahnny

Rai
(Japanese) next child

Rain
(English) helpful; smart
Raine, Rainey, Rainey, Raini, Rains, Raney, Rayne

Rainer
(German) advisor
Rainor, Rayner, Raynor

Rainey
(German) generous
Rain, Raine, Raney, Raynie

Rainier
(Place name) distinguished

Raj
(Sanskrit) with stripes
Rajiv

Raja
(Sanskrit) king
Raj

Rajab
(Arabic) glorified

Rajan
(Pakistani) kingly

Rajendra
(Hindi) strong king

Rajesh
(Hindi) king rules

Rajoseph
(American) combo of Ra and Joseph
Raejoseph

Rakesh
(Hindi) king

Raleigh
(English) jovial
Ralea, Ralee, Raleighe, Rawlee, Rawley, Rawlie

Ralf
(American) form of Ralph
Raulf

Ralik
(Hindi) purified

Ralis
(Latin) thin
Rallus

Ralph
(English) advisor to all
Ralf, Ralphie, Ralphy, Raulf, Rolf

Ralphie
(English) form of Ralph
Ralphee, Ralphi

Ralston
(English) Ralph's town; quirky boy
Ralfston, Rolfston

Ram
(Sanskrit) compelling; pleasant
Rama, Ramm

Rambert
(German) pleasant kid
Ramburt

Rambo
(American) daring; action-oriented
Ram

Ramel
(Hindi) godlike
Raymel

Rami
(Spanish) from Ramiro;
flirtatious
Ramiah

Ramiro
(Spanish) all-knowing
judge
*Rameero, Ramero, Ramey,
Rami*

Ramone
(Spanish) wise advocate;
romantic
*Ramond, Raymond,
Romon*

Ramp
(American) word as name;
hyper
Ram, Rams

Rams
(English) form of Ramsey;
boisterous; strong
Ramm, Ramz

Ramsden
(English) born in ram
valley; loves the outdoors

Ramsey
(English) savvy
*Rams, Ramsay, Ramsy,
Ramz, Ramzee, Ramzy*

Ran
(Scottish) short for
Ronald; powerful
Ranald

Rance
(American) renegade
Rans, Ranse

Ranceford
(English) from the ford of
Laurence; rooted in reality

Rancye
(American) form of Rance
Rancel, Rancy

Rand
(Place name) ridge of
gold-bearing rock in South
Africa

Randal
(English) secretive
*Randahl, Randel, Randey,
Randull, Randy, Randall*

Randolph
(English) protective
*Rand, Randolf, Randolphe,
Randy*

Randy
(English) short for Randall
or Randolph
*Randee, Randey, Randi,
Randie*

Ranen
(Hebrew) joyful

Rangarajan
(Hindi) charming

Ranger
(French) vigilant
Rainge, Range, Rangur

Rani
(Hebrew) joyful
Ran, Ranie, Rannie

Rank
(American) top
Ran

Rankin
(English) shielded

Ransell
(English) short form of
Laurence or Ransom
Rancell

Ransford
(English) the raven's ford;
watchful

Ransley
(English) the raven's field;
watchful

Ransom
(Latin) wealthy
*Rance, Ranse, Ransome,
Ransum, Ransym*

Rante
(American) from Randy;
amorous

Ranulf
(English) a lord chancellor
from 1107–1123; regal

Raoul
(Spanish) confidant
Raul, Raulio

Raphael
(Hebrew) archangel in the
Bible; painter
Rafael, Rafe, Rapfaele

Raqib
(Arabic) glorified

Rascheed
(Arabic) giving

Rashad
(Arabic) wise
*Rachad, Rashaud, Rashid,
Rashod, Roshad*

Rashard
(American) good

Rasheed
(Arabic) intelligent

Rashid
(Arabic) focused

Rasmus
(Greek) from Erasmus;
beloved

Rasool
(Arabic) herald

Rasputin
(Russian) a Russian mystic
Rasp

Rastus
(Greek) form of Erastus
Rastas

Raudel
(African American) rowdy
Raudell, Rowdel

Rauf
(Arabic) compassionate

Raul
(French) sensual
Rauly, Rawl

Raven
(American) bird; dark and
mysterious
Rave, Ravey, Ravy, Rayven

Ravi
(Hindi) sun god
Ravee

Ravid
(Hebrew) searching

Ravindra
(Hindi) a strong sun

Rawdan
(English) hilly;
adventurous
Rawden, Rawdin, Rawdon

Rawle
(French) form of Raul;
sensitive

Rawleigh
(American) form of Raleigh
Rawlee, Rawli

Rawlins
(French) from Roland;
famed

Ray
(French) royal; king
Rae, Raye, Rayray

Raybourne
(English) from the deer
brook; sylvan
Rayburn, Raybin

Rayce
(American) form of
Raymond; advisor
Rays, Rayse

Rayfield
(English) woodsy; capable
Rafe, Ray, Rayfe

Raymond
(English) strong
*Rai, Ramand, Ramond,
Ray, Raymie, Raymonde,
Raymun, Raymund, Raymy*

Raymont
(American) combo of Ray and Mont; distinguished
Raemon, Raymon, Raymonte

Raynaldo
(Spanish) form of Renaldo; innovative
Ray, Rayni, Raynie, Raynoldo

Raynard
(French) judge; sly
Ray, Raynaud, Renard, Renaud, Rey, Reynard, Reynaud

Rayner
(French) form of Raymond; counselor
Ray, Rayne

Rayshan
(African American) inventive
Ray, Raysh, Raysha, Rayshun

Rayshawn
(African American) combo of Ray and Shawn
Raeshaun, Rayshaun, Rayshie, Rayshy

Razi
(Aramaic) secretive

Reace
(Welsh) passionate
Reece, Rees, Rees, Reese

Read
(English) red-haired
Reade, Reed, Reid

Reagan
(Irish) kingly
Ragan, Raghan, Reagen, Reegan, Regan

Reaner
(Last name as first name) even-tempered
Rean, Rener

Rebel
(American) outlaw
Reb, Rebbe, Rebele

Red
(English) man with red hair
Redd, Reddy

Redford
(English) handsome man with ruddy skin
Readford, Red, Reddy, Redferd, Redfor

Redmon
(German) protective
Redd, Reddy, Redmond, Redmun, Redmund

Reece
(Welsh) vivacious
Rees, Reese, Reez

Reed
(English) red-haired
Read, Reede, Reid

Reem
(Hebrew) horned animal or unicorn

Rees
(Welsh) form of the name Rhys; ardor
Reece, Reese, Reez, Rez

Reese
(Welsh) vivacious
Reis, Rhys

Reeves
(English) giving
Reave, Reaves, Reeve

Reg
(Scandinavian) short for Regner; judgmental

Regal
(American) debonair
Regall

Regent
(Latin) royal; grand

Reggie
(English) short for
Reginald; wise advisor
*Reg, Reggey, Reggi,
Reggye*

Reginald
(English) wise advisor
*Reg, Reggie, Reginal,
Regineld*

Regine
(French) artistic
Regeen

Regis
(Latin) king; gilded talker
Reggis

Regulo
(Italian) from Reginald;
counsels

Rehoboam
(Biblical) son of Solomon

Reid
(English) red-haired
Reide

Reidar
(Scandinavian) soldier

Reilly
(Irish) daring
Rilee, Riley, Rilie

Reinald
(French) judges

Reinhart
(German) brave-hearted
*Reinhar, Reinhardt,
Rhinehard, Rhinehart*

Reith
(American) shy

Remi
(French) fun-loving
*Remee, Remey, Remmy,
Remy*

Remigio
(Italian) from Rheims,
France; sharp mind

Remington
(Last name as first name)
intellectual
Rem, Remmy

Remuda
(Spanish) herd of horses,
or changing horses (a
relay); rancher
Rem, Remmie, Remmy

Remus
(Latin) fast
Reemus, Remes, Remous

Renard
(French) smart
Renardt

Renato
(Italian) born again
Renata, Renate

Renaud
(English) powerful
Renny

René
(French) born again
*Renee, Rennie, Renny, Re-
Re*

Renferd
(English) peaceloving
Renfred

Renfro
(Welsh) calm
*Renfroe, Renfrow,
Renphro, Rinfro*

Renny
(French) able
Renney, Renni, Rennye

Reno
(Place name) city in Nevada
Reen, Reenie, Renoh

Renshaw
(English) born in the raven
wood

Renton
(English) born in the town
of deer

Renwick
(English) born in the village of deer

Renzo
(Italian) adorned; from Lorenzo

ReShard
(African American) rough
Reshar, Reshard

Resugio
(Spanish) form of Refugio
Resuge

Rett
(Literature) form of Rhett, from *Gone with the Wind*

Reuben
(Hebrew) religious; (Spanish) creative
Rube, Rubey, Rubie, Rubin, Ruby, Rubyn

Rev
(Invented) ramped up
Revv

Revin
(American) distinctive
Revan, Revinn, Revun

Rex
(Latin) kingly
Rexe

Rexford
(American) form of Rex; noble
Rex, Rexferd, Rexfor, Rexy

Rey
(Spanish) short for Reynaldo
Ray, Reye, Reyes

Reynard
(French) brilliant
Raynard, Rayne, Renardo

Reynaud
(French) advisor/judge

Reynold
(English) knowledgeable tutor
Ranald, Ranold, Reinold, Renald, Renalde, Rey, Reye, Reynolds

Reza
(Iranian) content

Rhene
(American) smiley
Reen, Rheen

Rhett
(American) romantic
Rhet, Rhette

Rhodes
(Greek) lovely
Rhoades, Rodes

Rhodree
(Welsh) ruler
Rodree, Rodrey, Rodry

Rhyon
(American) form of Ryan
Rhyan, Rhyen

Rhys
(Welsh) loving
Reece, Reese

Rian
(Irish) little king

Riao
(Spanish) form of Rio; river; flowing

Ribal
(American) form of ribald; revels

Ricardo
(Spanish) snappy
Recardo, Ric, Riccardo, Ricky

Rice
(English) rich
Ryes

Rich
(English) affluent
Richie, Ritchie

Richard
(English) wealthy leader
*Rich, Richerd, Richey,
Richi, Richie, Rickie, Ricky,
Ritchie*

Richardean
(American) combo of
Richard and Dean;
unusual
*Richard Dean, Richard-
Dean, Richardene*

Richey
(German) ruler
*Rich, Richee, Richie, Ritch,
Ritchee, Ritchee, Ritchey*

Richie
(English) short for Richard
*Richey, Richi, Ritchey,
Ritchie*

Richman
(German) has power

Richmond
(German) rich and
protective
*Rich, Richie, Richmon,
Richmun, Ricky, Ritchmun*

Richshae
(English) from Richard;
reliable

Richter
(Last name as first name)
hopeful
Rick, Ricky, Rik, Rikter

Rick
(German) short for
Richard; friendly
*Ric, Rickey, Ricki, Rickie,
Ricky, Rik*

Rickard
(Scandinavian) from
Richard; reliable
*Rick, Rickert, Rickward,
Rikkert*

Rico
(Italian) spirited; ruler
*Reco, Reko, Ricko, Rikko,
Riko*

Ricotoro
(Spanish) combo of Rico
and Toro; brave bull
*Ricky, Rico-Toro, Rikotoro,
Toro*

Riddock
(Irish) man of the field

Rider
(American) horse rider
Ryder

Ridge
(English) on the ridge;
risk-taker

Ridglee
(English) man of the ridge
Ridgley, Ridglea

Ridhaa
(Arabic) delight

Ridley
(English) ingenious
*Redley, Rid, Ridley, Ridlie,
Ridly, Rydley*

Riemer
(English) from Rheims,
France; loving

Rigby
(English) high-energy
Rigbie, Rigbye, Rygby

Rigel
(Arabic) foot; star in
constellation Orion

Rigoberto
(Spanish) strong
Bert, Berto, Rigo

Rike
(American) form of Nike;
high-spirited
Rikee, Rykee, Rykie, Ryky

Rilee
(American) form of Riley
Rilea, Rileigh

Rileigh
(American) form of Riley
Ryleigh

Riley
(Irish) brave
Reilly, Rylee, Ryley, Rylie, Ryly

Rimon
(Hebrew) pomegranate

Ringo
(English) funny
Ring, Ringgoh, Ryngo

Rio
(Spanish) water-loving
Reeo

Rione
(Spanish) flowing
Reo, Reone, Rio

Rio Grande
(Spanish) a river in Texas
Rio, Riogrande

Riordan
(Irish) lordly
Rearden

Rip
(English) serene
Ripp, Rippe

Ripley
(English) serene
Riplee

Ris
(English) outdoorsman;
smart
Rislea, Rislee, Risleigh, Riz, Rizlee

Rishab
(American) from Rashad;
showy

Rishi
(Arabic) first

Rishon
(Hebrew) first

Risley
(English) smart and quiet
Rislee, Risleye, Rizlee, Rizley

Ritch
(American) leader
Rich, Richee, Richey, Ritch, Ritchal, Ritchee, Ritchi

Ritchie
(English) form of Richie
Ritchee, Ritchey, Ritchy

Rito
(American) spunky
Reit

Ritt
(German) debonair
Rit, Rittie, Rittly

Ritter
(German) debonair
Riter, Rittyr

Rivan
(Literature) from Eddings'
The Rivan Codex; esoteric

River
(English) flowing water; hip
Riv, Ryver

Roald
(Scandinavian) famous
ruler

Roam
(American) wanderer
Roamey, Roamy, Roma, Rome

Roan
(English) form of Rowan
(berry tree); red hair

Roar
(Irish) from Roark; mighty

Roarke
(Irish) ruler
Roark, Rork, Rourke

Rob
(English) short for Robert;
smart
Robb

Robbie
(English) short for Robert;
smart
Robbee, Robbey, Robbi, Robby

Robert
(English) brilliant;
renowned
*Bob, Bobbie, Bobby, Rob,
Robart, Robbie, Robby,
Roberto, Robs, Roburt*

Roberto
(Spanish) form of Robert;
bright and famous
Berto, Rob, Robert, Tito

Roberts
(Last name as first name)
luminous
*Rob, Robards, Robarts,
Roburts*

Robert-Lee
(American) patriotic
*Bobbylee, Robby Lee,
Robert Lee, Robert-E-Lee,
Robertlee*

Robeson
(English) Rob's son; bright
Roberson, Robison

Robin
(English) gregarious
*Robb, Robbin, Robby,
Robyn*

Roble
(Last name as first name)
divine
Robel, Robl, Robley

Robson
(English) sterling
character
Robb, Robbson, Robsen

Rocco
(Italian) tough
*Roc, Rock, Rockie, Rocko,
Rocky, Rok, Rokee, Rokko,
Roko*

Rochester
(English) guarded
Roche

Rock
(American) hardy
Roc, Rocky, Rok

Rocket
(American) word as a
name; snappy
Rokket

Rockleigh
(English) dependable;
outdoorsy
*Rocco, Rock, Rocklee,
Rockley, Rocky, Roklee*

Rockney
(American) brash

Rockwell
(American) spring of
strength
Rock, Rockwelle, Rocky

Rocky
(English) hardy; tough
*Rocco, Rock, Rockee,
Rockey, Rocki, Rockie*

Rod
(English) brash
Rodd, Roddy

Rodas
(Spanish) Spanish name for
the Rhone River in France
Rod, Roda

Roddick
(Last name as first name)
goes far

Roddy
(German) short for
Roderick; effective
Roddee, Roddi, Roddie

Rodel
(American) generous
Rodell, Rodey, Rodie

Rodeo
(Spanish) roundup;
cowboy
Rodayo, Roddy, Rodyo

Roderick
(German) effective leader
*Roddy, Roddyrke, Roderic,
Roderik, Rodreck, Rodrick,
Rodrik*

Rodger
(German) form of Roger
Rodge, Roge

Rodman
(German) hero
Rodmin, Rodmun

Rodney
(English) open-minded
*Rod, Roddy, Rodnee,
Rodni, Rodnie*

Rodolfo
(Spanish) spark
Rod, Rudolfo, Rudolpho

Rodree
(American) leader
Rodrey, Rodri, Rodry

Rodrigo
(Spanish) feisty leader
*Rod, Roddy, Rodrego,
Rodriko*

Rodriguez
(Spanish) hot-blooded
*Rod, Roddy, Rodreguez,
Rodrigues*

Rodwell
(German) renowned

Roe
(English) deer

Roemello
(Italian) form of Romulus;
Roman man; ingenious

Rogan
(Irish) spirited redhead

Rogelio
(Spanish) aggressive
Rojel, Rojelio

Roger
(German) famed warrior
*Rodge, Rodger, Roge,
Rogie, Rogyer, Rogers*

Rohan
(Hindi) going higher

Roi
(French) form of Roy

Roland
(German) renowned
*Rolend, Rollan, Rolland,
Rollie, Rollo, Rolund*

Rolando
(Spanish) famous
Rolan

Role
(American) brash
Roel, Roll

Rolf
(German) kind advisor
Rolfee, Rolfie, Rolfy, Rolph

Rollie
(English) short for Roland
Rollee, Rolley, Rolli, Rolly

Rollins
(German) form of Roland;
dignified
Rolin, Rolins, Rollin, Rolyn

Rollo
(German) famous

Rolshawn
(American) combo of
Roland and Shawn;
notorious

Rolt
(Latin) wolfish

Roly
(English) short for Roland;
famed

Roman
(Latin) fun-loving
*Romen, Romey, Romi,
Romun, Romy, Romain*

Rombert
(Latin) from Rome;
admired

Rome
(Place name) city in Italy
Romeo

Romeo
(Italian) romantic lover
*Romah, Rome, Romeoh,
Romero, Romey, Romi,
Romy*

Romer
(American) form of Rome
Roamar, Roamer

Romney
(Welsh) roamer
Rom, Romnie

Romulo
(Spanish) man from Rome
Romo

Romulus
(Latin) presumptuous
Rom, Romules, Romulo

Ron
(English) short for Ronald;
kind
Ronn

Ronak
(Scandinavian) powerful

Ronald
(English) helpful
*Ron, Ronal, Ronel,
Ronney, Ronni, Ronnie,
Ronuld*

Ronan
(Irish) seal; playful

Rondel
(French) poetic
*Ron, Rondal, Rondell,
Rondie, Rondy*

Ronford
(English) distinguished
Ronferd, Ronnforde

Roni
(Hebrew) joyful
Rone, Ronee

Ronnie
(English) short for Ronald
*Ronnee, Ronney, Ronni,
Ronny*

Ronson
(Scottish) Ron's son;
likable

Roone
(Irish) distinctive; bright
face
Rooney, Roune

Rooney
(Irish) man with red hair
Rooni, Roony

Roose
(Last name as first name)
high-energy
Rooce, Roos, Rooz, Ruz

Roosevelt
(Dutch) strong leader
*Rooseveldt, Rosevelt,
Rosy, Velte*

Rooster
(American) loud
Roos, Rooz

Roper
(American) roper
Rope

Roque
(Spanish, Portugese) form
of Rocco

Rory
(German) strong
*Roree, Rorey, Roreye,
Rorie*

Rosalio
(Spanish) rose; charmer

Rosano
(Italian) rosy prospects;
romantic

Roscoe
(English) woods; nature-
loving
*Rosco, Roskie, Rosko,
Rosky*

Roser
(American) redhead;
outgoing
Rozer

Roshaun
(African American) loyal
Roshawn

Rosk
(American) swift
Roske

Rosling
(Scottish) redhead;
explosive
Roslin, Rosy, Rozling

Ross
(Latin) attractive
Rossey, Rossie, Rossy

Rossa
(American) exuberant
Ross, Rosz

Rossain
(American) hopeful
Rossane

Rossano
(Italian) handsome

Roswell
(English) fascinating
*Roswel, Roswelle, Rosy,
Rozwell, Well*

Roth
(German) man with red
hair
Rothe, Rauth

Roupen
(American) quiet
Ropan, Ropen, Ropun

Rover
(English) wanderer
Rovar, Rovey, Rovur, Rovy

Rovonte
(French) roving

Rowan
(English) red-haired;
adorned
Rowe, Rowen

Rowand
(Last name as first)
reliable

Rowdy
(English) athletic; loud
*Roudy, Rowdee, Rowdi,
Rowdie*

Rowe
(English) outgoing
Roe, Row, Rowie

Rowell
(English) rocker
Roll, Rowl

Rowland
(Scandinavian) famous;
form of Roland

Rowley
(English) from the rough
meadow; spirited

Roy
(French) king
Roi

Royal
(French) king
Roy, Royall, Royalle, Roye

Royalton
(French) king
Royal, Royallton

Royce
(English) affluent
Roy, Royse

Roycie
(American) form of Royce;
kind
*Rory, Roy, Royce, Royse,
Roysie*

Royd
(English) good humor

Royden
(English) outdoors; regal
Roy, Roydin

Royle
(English) kingly

Ruadhan
(Hindi) brash

Ruari
(Irish) red-haired
Ruairi, Ruaridh

Rube
(Spanish) short for Ruben
Rubino

Ruben
(Spanish) form of Reuben
Rube, Ruby

Rudeger
(German) friendly
Rudger, Rudgyr, Rudigar,
Rudiger, Rudy

Rudo
(African) loving

Rudolf
(German) wolf
Rodolf, Rudy

Rudolph
(German) wolf
Rodolf, Rodolph, Rud,
Rudee, Rudey, Rudi,
Rudolpho, Rudy

Rudow
(German) lovable

Rudy
(German) short for
Rudolph
Rude, Rudee, Rudey, Rudi

Rudyard
(English) closed off
Rud, Rudd, Ruddy

Rueban
(American) form of Ruben;
talented
Ruban

Rufino
(Spanish) redhead

Rufus
(Latin) redhead
Fue, Rufas, Rufes, Ruffie,
Ruffis, Ruffy, Rufous

Rugby
(English) braced for
contact
Rug, Rugbee, Rugbie,
Ruggy

Ruiz
(Spanish) chummy

Rulon
(Native American) spirited
Rulonn

Rumford
(English) lives at river
crossing; grounded

Runako
(African) attractive

Rune
(German) secretive
Roone, Runes

Rupad
(Hindi) secretive
Rupesh

Rupchand
(Sanskrit) as beautiful as
the moon

Rupert
(English) prince
Rupe

Rurik
(Russian) famous

Rush
(English) loquacious
Rusch

Rushford
(English) from the ford of
rushes; found

Rusk
(Spanish) innovator
Rusck, Ruske, Ruskk

Ruskin
(French) red-haired

Ruslan
(English) rusty hair

Russ
(French) short for Russell;
dear

Russell
(French) man with red
hair; charmer
Russ, Russel, Russy, Rusty

Rustice
(French) rusty hair

Rustin
(English) redhead
Rustan, Ruston, Rusty

Rusty
(French) short for Russell
Rustee, Rustey, Rusti

Rutherford
(English) dignified
*Ruthe, Rutherfurd,
Rutherfyrd*

Rutland
(Norse) red land

Rutledge
(English) substantial
Rutlidge

Rutley
(English) from red country;
fertile

Ruvim
(Hebrew) meaningful

Ryan
(Irish) royal; good-looking
*Rhine, Rhyan, Rhyne, Ry,
Ryane, Ryann, Ryanne,
Ryen, Ryun*

Ryander
(American) competitive;
obstinate

Ryder
(English) outdoorsy; man
who rides horses
Rider, Rye

Rye
(Botanical) grain; basic

Ryerson
(English) fit outdoorsman
Rye

Ryker
(English) of the rye land;
farms

Ryland
(English) excellent
Rilan, Riland, Rye, Rylan

Rylandar
(English) farmer
Rye, Rylan, Ryland

Ryle
(American) form of Kyle

Ryman
(English) man of rye;
fundamental

Ryne
(Irish) form of Ryan; royal
Rine, Ryn, Rynn

Ryszard
(Polish) courageous leader
Reshard

Ryton
(English) from town of rye;
fundamental

S

Saad
(Aramaic) helping others

Saahdia
(Aramaic) helped by the
Lord
Saadya, Seadya

Saarik
(Hindi) sings like a bird
*Saariq, Sareek, Sareeq,
Sariq*

Sabene
(Latin) optimist
*Sabe, Sabeen, Sabin,
Sabyn, Sabyne*

Saber
(French) armed; sword
Sabar, Sabe, Sabre

Sabin
(Latin) Sabine, tribe of
Italy; daring
*Sabeeno, Sabino, Savin,
Savino*

Sable
(French) animal; brown-
haired child

Sacha
(Russian) defends; charms
Sascha, Sasha

Sachar
(Hebrew) well-rewarded
Sacar

Saddam
(Arabic) powerful ruler
Saddum

Sadiki
(African) loyal
Sadeeki

Sadler
(English) practical
*Sadd, Saddle, Sadlar,
Sadlur*

Sae
(American) talkative
Saye

Saeed
(African) lucky

Safar
(Arabic) from Saphar,
second month of Islamic
calendar; devout
Safer, Safyr

Safford
(English) boy from river of
willows

Saffron
(Botanical) spice/plant;
orange-haired
Saffran, Saffren, Saphron

Sagaz
(Spanish) clever
Saga, Sago

Sage
(Botanical) wise
Saje

Sager
(American) rewarded;
short
Sayger

Saginaw
(Place name) city in
Michigan; (Native
American) bold
Sag, Saggy

Sagiv
(Hebrew) the best
Segev

Saguaro
(Botanical) cactus; prickly
Seguaro

Sahil
(Hindi) leader
Sahel

Saied
(Arabic) fortunate

Saith
(English) to speak
Saithe, Saythe

Sail
(American) water; natural

Sainsbury
(English) from the home of
saints; religious
Sainsberry

Saint
(Latin) holy man

Sajan
(Hindi) beloved

Sal
(Italian) short for Salvador
and Salvatore
Sall, Sallie, Sally

Saladin
(Arabic) devout
Saladdin

Salado
(Spanish) funny
Sal

Salehe
(African) good

Salem
(Hebrew) peaceful

Salford
(Place name) city in
England

Salim
(Arabic) safe; peaceful
Saleem

Salisbury
(English) born in the willows
Salisbery, Salisberry, Saulsberry, Saulsbery, Saulsbury, Saulisbury

Salman
(Arabic) protected

Salt
(American) salt-of-the-earth
Salty

Salute
(American) patriotic

Salvador
(Spanish) savior; spirited
Sal, Sally, Salvadore

Salvatore
(Italian) rescuer; spirited
Sal, Sallie, Sally, Salvatori, Salvatorre

Salvio
(Latin) saved
Salvian, Salviano, Salviatus

Sam
(Hebrew) short for Samuel; wise
Samm, Sammey, Sammi, Sammy

Sami
(Lebanese) high

Samir
(Arabic) special
Sameer, Samere, Samyr

Sammon
(Arabic) grocer
Sammen

Sammy
(Hebrew) wise
Samie, Sammee, Sammey, Sammi, Sammie, Samy

Samos
(Place name) casual

Samson
(Hebrew) strong man
Sam, Sampson

Samuel
(Hebrew) man who heard God; prophet
Sam, Samael, Sammeul, Sammie, Sammo, Sammuel, Sammy, Samual

Samvel
(Hebrew) know the name of God
Samvell, Samvelle

Sanborn
(English) one with nature
Sanborne, Sanbourn, Sandy

Sancho
(Latin) genuine
Sanch, Sanchoh

Sandberg
(Last name as first name) writer
Sandburg

Sander
(Greek) savior of mankind; nice
Sandor

Sanders
(English) kind
Sandars, Sandors, Saunders

Sanderson
(Last name as first name) defender
Sandersen

Sandhurst
(English) from the sandy thicket; undaunted
Sandhirst

Sanditon
(English) from the sandy town; perseveres

Sandy
(English) personable
Sandee, Sandey, Sandi

Sanford
(English) negotiator
*Sandford, Sandy, Sanferd,
Sanfor*

Sanjay
(Sanskrit) wins every time

Sanorelle
(African American) honest
*Sanny, Sano, Sanorel,
Sanorell*

Sansone
(Italian) strong

Santana
(Spanish) saintly
*Santa, Santanah,
Santanna, Santee*

Santiago
(Spanish) sainted; valuable
*Sandiago, Santego,
Santiagoh, Santy, Tago*

Santino
(Italian) sacred
Santeeno, Santyno

Santos
(Italian) holy; blessed
Sant, Santo

Sapir
(Hebrew) sapphire; jewel
Safir, Saphir, Saphiros

Sarday
(American) extrovert
Sardae, Sardaye

Sargent
(French) officer/leader
Sarge, Sergeant

Sasha
(Russian) helpful
Sacha, Sash, Sasha

Sassacus
(Native American) wild
soul

Sasson
(Hebrew) happy

Satchel
(American) unique
Satch, Satchell

Saturnin
(Spanish) from planet
Saturn; melancholy
Saturnino

Saunder
(English) defensive;
focused
Saunders

Saul
(Hebrew) gift
Sawl, Saulie, Sol, Solly

Savage
(Last name as first name)
wild
Sav

Saviero
(Spanish) from Xavier;
renewal

Saville
(French) stylish
Savelle, Savile, Savill

Savion
(American) from Savion
Glover, actor/dancer
Xavion, Savionn

Savoy
(Place name) region in
France
Savoe

Savyon
(Spanish) great attitude

Sawyer
(English) hardworking
Saw, Sawyrr

Saxe
(English) short for Saxon
Sax, Saxee, Saxey, Saxie

Saxon
(English) sword-fighter;
feisty
*Sackson, Sax, Saxan,
Saxe, Saxen*

Saxton
(Place name) stern
Saxten

Sayre
(Welsh) skilled
Saye, Sayer, Sayers

Scafell
(Place name) mountain in England

Scanlon
(Irish) devious
Scan, Scanlin, Scanlun, Scanne

Scant
(American) word as name; too little
Scanty

Schae
(American) safe; careful
Schay

Schaffer
(German) watchful
Schaffur, Shaffer

Schelde
(Place name) river in Europe; calm
Shelde

Schmidt
(German) hardworking; blacksmith
Schmit

Schneider
(German) stylish; tailor
Sneider, Snider

Schubert
(German) cobbler
Shubert

Schumann
(Last name as first) famous composer; romantic

Schuyler
(Dutch) protective
Skylar, Skyler

Scipio
(Greek) leader

Scirocco
(Italian) warmth of the wind
Cirocco, Sirocco

Scorpio
(Latin) lethal
Scorp, Scorpioh

Scott
(English) from Scotland; happy
Scot, Scotty

Scotty
(English) happy
Scottee, Scottey, Scotti

Scout
(French) hears all; scouts for information

Scribner
(English) the one who writes

Scully
(Irish) vocal
Scullee, Sculley, Scullie

Seabert
(English) shines like the sea
Seabright, Sebert, Seibert

Seabrook
(English) outdoorsy
Seabrooke

Seabury
(English) lives by the sea
Seaberry, Seabry

Seal
(American) singer; water; natural

Seaman
(English) seafarer

Seamus
(Gaelic) replacement; bonus
Seemus, Semus

Sean
(Hebrew, Irish) grace in God
Seann, Shaun, Shaune, Shawn

Searcy
(English) fortified
Searcee, Searcey

Searles
(English) fortified
Searl, Searle, Serles, Serls

Seaton
(Place name) Seaton, Illinois; calm
Seaten, Seeten, Seeton

Seaver
(Last name as first name) safe
Seever

Sebastian
(Latin) dramatic; honorable
Bastian, Seb, Sebashun, Sebastien, Sebastion, Sebastuan, Sebo

Sebe
(Latin) short for Sebastian
Seb, Sebo, Seborn, Sebron, Sebrun

Secondo
(Italian) second-born boy
Segundo

Sedgley
(American) classy
Sedg, Sedge, Sedgeley, Sedgely

Sedgwick
(English) from place of swords; defensive
Sedgewick, Sedgewyck, Sedgwyck

Seely
(Last name as first name) fun-loving
Sealy, Sealey, Seeley

Seerath
(Indian) great

Seferino
(Spanish) flying in the wind
Cefirino, Sebarino, Sephirio, Zefarin, Zefirino, Zephir, Zephyr

Sefton
(English) from the town in the rushes; safe

Seger
(Last name as first name) singer
Seager, Seeger, Sega, Segur

Segundo
(Spanish) second child

Sekani
(African) laughing

Sela
(Hebrew) from the cliff; dares
Selah

Selby
(English) from a village of mansions; rich
Selbey, Shelbey, Shelbie, Shelby

Seldon
(English) from the willow valley; swaying
Selden, Sellden, Shelden

Selestino
(Spanish) heavenly
Celeste, Celestino, Celey, Sele, Selestyno

Selig
(German) blessed boy
Seligman, Seligmann, Zelig

Selkirk
(Scottish) church home boy; conflicted

Sellers
(English) dweller of marshland; sturdy
Sellars

Selvon
(American) gregarious
*Sel, Selman, Selv,
Selvaughn, Selvawn*

Selwyn
(English) friend from the
mansion; wealthy
*Selwin, Selwinn, Selwynn,
Selwynne*

Seminole
(Native American) tribe
name; unyielding

Sender
(Hebrew) form of
Alexander; protective

Seneca
(Native American) tribe
name; revered

Senior
(French) older
Sennyur, Senyur, Sinior

Sennen
(English) aged

Sennett
(French) old spirit
Sennet

Septimus
(Latin) seventh child;
neglected

Sequoia
(Native American) tree;
sturdy

Serafín
(Spanish) from the
Hebrew Seraphim, full of
fire

Seraphim
(Hebrew) full of fire
*Sarafim, Saraphim,
Serafim, Serephim*

Sereno
(Latin) serene
Cereno

Serge
(French) gentle man
Serg

Sergeant
(French) officer; leader
Sarge, Sargent

Sergei
(Russian) good looking
*Serg, Serge, Sergie, Sergy,
Surge*

Sergio
(Italian) handsome
*Serge, Sergeeo, Sergeoh,
Sergyo*

Servacio
(Spanish) saved

Servas
(Latin) saved
Servaas, Servacio, Servatus

Sesame
(Botanical) seed; flavors
*Sesamey, Sessame,
Sessamee*

Seth
(Hebrew) chosen
Sethe

Seton
(English) from sea town;
loves the water

Seven
(American) dramatic;
seventh child
Sevene, Sevin

Several
(American) multiplies
Sevral, Sevrull

Severin
(Latin) severe
*Saverino, Sverinus,
Seweryn*

Severence
(French) strict
Severince, Severynce

Severn
(English) having
boundaries

Severo
(Italian) unbending; harsh

Sevester
(American) form of Sylvester
Seveste, Sevy

Seward
(English) guarding the sea
Sew, Sewerd, Sward

Sewell
(Last name as first name) seaward
Seawell, Seawel, Sewel

Sexton
(English) church-loving
Sextan, Sextin, Sextown

Sextus
(Latin) sixth child; mischievous
Sesto, Sixto, Sixtus

Seymour
(French) prayerful
Seamore, See, Seye, Seymore

Shabat
(Hebrew) the end
Shabbat

Shachar
(Hebrew) the dawn

Shade
(English) secretive
Shadee, Shadey, Shady

Shadow
(English) mystique
Shade, Shadoe

Shad
(African) joyful

Shadman
(Hebrew) farm

Shadrach
(Biblical) godlike; brave
Shad, Shadd, Shadrack, Shadreck, Shadryack

Shafiq
(Arabic) forgiving
Shafeek, Shafik

Shafir
(Hebrew) handsome
Shafeer, Shafer, Shefer

Shahzad
(Persian) royalty; king

Shai
(Hebrew) the gift

Shakil
(Arabic) attractive
Shakeel, Shakill, Shakille, Shaqueel, Shaquil, Shaquille

Shakir
(Arabic) appreciative
Shakee, Shakeer

Shakur
(Arabic) thankful
Shakurr

Shale
(Hebrew) short for Shalev; calm
Shaile, Shayle

Shalom
(Hebrew) peaceful
Sholem, Sholom

Shaman
(Russian) mystical
Shamain, Shamon, Shayman

Shamir
(Hebrew) thorn
Shameer

Shamus
(Irish) seizing
Schaemus, Schamus, Shamuss

Shanahan
(Irish) giving
Shanihan, Shanyhan

Shance
(American) form of Chance; open
Shan, Shanse

Shand
(English) loud
Shandy

Shandee
(English) noisy
Shandi, Shandy

Shane
(Irish) easygoing
Shain, Shay, Shayne

Shani
(African) a wonder;
(Hebrew) red

Shanley
(Irish) old soul
Shannley

Shannon
(Irish) wise
*Shana, Shanan, Shane,
Shanen, Shann, Shannen,
Shanon*

Shante
(American) poised
Shantae, Shantay

Shaq
(Arabic) short for
Shaquille
Shack, Shak

Shaquille
(Arabic) handsome
*Shak, Shakeel, Shaq,
Shaquil, Shaquill*

Sharif
(Arabic) truthful
Shareef, Sheref

Shashhi
(Hindi) moon

Shasta
(Place name) Oregon
mountain; high hopes

Shaun
(Irish) form of Sean
Seanne, Shaune, Shaunn

Shavon
(American) combo of Sha
and Von; open mind
*Shavonne, Shivaun,
Shovon*

Shaw
(English) safe; in a tree
grove
Shawe

Shawn
(Irish) form of Sean
*Shawnay, Shawne,
Shawnee, Shawney*

Shawnell
(African American)
talkative
Shaunell

Shawner
(American) form of Shawn

Shawon
(African American)
optimistic
*Shawan, Shawaughn,
Shawaun*

Shay
(Irish) short for Shamus;
bolstering
Shai

Shayan
(Native American) from
Cheyenne; tribe; erratic

Shayde
(Irish) confident
Shaedy, Sheade

Shaykeen
(African American)
successful
Shay, Shaykine

Shayshawn
(American) combo of Shay
and Shawn; able
*Shaeshaun, Shaeshawn,
Shayshaun*

Shea
(Irish) vital
Shay

Sheehan
(Irish) clever
Shehan, Shihan

Sheen
(English) bright and shining; talented
Shean, Sheene

Shel
(Hebrew) mine

Shelby
(English) established
Shel, Shelbee, Shelbey, Shelbie, Shell, Shelly

Sheldon
(English) quiet
Shel, Sheld, Shelden, Sheldin, Shell, Shelly

Shelley
(English) form of Shelby; meadow ledge boy
Shelly

Shelton
(English) from the village of ledges

Shem
(Hebrew) famous

Shen
(Chinese) introspective

Shenandoah
(Place name) valley; nostalgic

Sheng
(Chinese) winning

Shep
(English) watchful
Shepp, Sheppy

Shepherd
(Last name as first name) vigilant
Shepard, Sheperd, Shephard

Shepley
(English) from the sheep meadow; tender
Sheplea, Shepleigh, Shepply, Shipley

Sherborn
(English) from the bright shiny stream; careful
Sherborne, Sherbourn, Sherburn, Sherburne

Sheridan
(Irish) wild-spirited
Sharidan, Sheridon, Sherr, Sherrey, Shuridun

Sherill
(English) from the shining hill; special
Sherrill

Sherlock
(English) fair-haired; smart
Sherlocke, Shurlock

Sherm
(English) worker; shears
Shermy

Sherman
(English) tough-willed
Cherman, Shermann, Shermy, Shurman

Sherrerd
(English) from open land; rancher
Sherard, Sherrard, Sherrod

Sherrick
(Last name as first name) already gone
Sherric, Sherrik, Sherryc, Sherryck, Sherryk

Sherwin
(English) fleet of foot
Sherwind, Sherwinn, Sherwyn, Sherwynne

Sherwood
(English) bright options
Sherwoode, Shurwood, Woodie, Woody

Shevon
(African American) zany
Shavonne, Shevaughan, Shevaughn

Shiloh
    (Hebrew) gift from God;
    charmer
    Shile, Shilo, Shy, Shye

Shingo
    (Japanese) clutch

Shipley
    (English) meadow of
    sheep
    Ship

Shipton
    (English) from the ship
    village; sailor

Shire
    (Place name) English
    county; humorous
    Shyre

Shiva
    (Hindi) of great depth and
    range; life/death
    Shiv

Shlomo
    (Hebrew) form of
    Solomon; peace-loving
    Shelomi, Shelomo, Shlomi

Shomer
    (Hebrew) watches

Shon
    (American) form of Shawn
    Sean, Shaun, Shonn

Shontae
    (African American) hopeful
    *Shauntae, Shauntay,
    Shawntae, Shontay,
    Shontee, Shonti, Shontie,
    Shonty*

Shorty
    (American) small in stature
    Shortey, Shorti

Shoshone
    (Native American) tribe;
    wanderer
    Shoshoni

Shoval
    (Hebrew) on the right path

Shura
    (Russian) protective
    Schura, Shoura

Shuu
    (Japanese) responsible

Si
    (Hebrew) short for Simon
    Sy

Sicily
    (Place name) traveler
    Sicilly

Sid
    (French) short for Sidney
    *Cyd, Sidd, Siddie, Siddy,
    Syd, Sydd*

Sidney
    (French) attractive
    *Ciddie, Cidnie, Cyd,
    Cydnee, Sidnee, Sidnie,
    Syd, Sydney*

Sidonio
    (Spanish) from Sidney; sly

Sidor
    (Russian) gifted
    Isidor, Sydor

Sidus
    (Latin) star
    Sydus

Siegfried
    (German) victor
    *Siegfred, Sig, Sigfred,
    Sigfrid, Siggee, Siggie,
    Siggy*

Sierra
    (Spanish) dangerous
    *See-see, Serra, Siera,
    Sierrah*

Sig
    (German) short for
    Sigmund and Siegfried
    Siggey, Siggi, Sigi, Syg

Sigga
    (Scandinavian) from
    Siegfried; peaceful;
    winning
    Sig

Sigmund
(German) winner
*Siegmund, Sig, Siggi,
Siggy, Sigi, Sigmon,
Sigmond*

Signe
(Scandinavian) victor
Signy

Sigwald
(German) leader
Siegwald

Sigurd
(Scandinavian) winning
personality

Silas
(Latin) saver
Si, Siles, Silus

Sill
(English) beam of light
Sills

Silous
(American) form of Silas;
brooding
Si, Silouz

Silvano
(Latin) of the woods;
unique
*Silvan, Silvani, Silvio,
Sylvan*

Silver
(Spanish) form of Silva;
outgoing
Sylver

Silverman
(German) works with
silver; craftsman

Silverton
(English) from town of
silversmiths
Silvertown

Silvester
(Latin) from the woods
*Silvestre, Silvestro,
Sylvester*

Simba
(African) lionlike

Simcha
(Hebrew) joyful

Simeon
(French) listener
*Si, Simion, Simone,
Simyon, Sy*

Simms
(Hebrew) good listener
Sims

Simon
(Hebrew) good listener;
thoughtful
*Si, Siman, Simen, Simeon,
Simmy, Sye, Symon, Syms*

Simpson
(Hebrew) simplistic
*Simpsen, Simpsun,
Simson*

Sinclair
(French) prayerful
*Clair, Sinc, Sinclare,
Synclaire*

Sindbad
(Literature) from *The
Arabian Nights*; daring
Sinbad

Singer
(Last name as first name)
vocalist
Synger

Sinjin
(English) form of St. John;
religious

Sion
(Hebrew) heavenly peak
Zion

Siraj
(Arabic) shines

Sirius
(Star) shining

Sisto
(American) cowboy

Sisyphus
(Greek) in mythology, a
cruel king

Six
(American) number as name
Syx

Sixtus
(Latin) sixth child

Sivney
(Irish) satisfied
Sivneigh, Sivnie

Skeeter
(English) fast
Skeater, Skeet, Skeets

Skeetz
(American) zany
Skeet, Skeeter, Skeets

Skelly
(Irish) bard
Scully

Skerry
(Scandinavian) from the island of stone; pragmatist

Skilling
(English) masterful
Skillings

Skinner
(English) skins for a living

Skip
(American) short for Skipper
Skipp, Skyp, Skyppe

Skippy
(American) fast
Skippee, Skippie, Skyppey

Skye
(Dutch) goal-oriented
Sky

Skylar
(Dutch) protective
Skilar, Skye, Skyeler, Skylir

Slade
(English) quiet child
Slaid, Slaide, Slayd, Slayde

Sladkey
(Slavic) glorious
Sladkie

Slam
(American) friendly
Slams, Slamz

Slater
(Last name as first name) precocious
Slaiter, Slayter

Slavek
(Polish) smart; glorious
Slavec, Slavik

Slavin
(Irish) mountain man; hermit
Slawin, Slaven

Slawomir
(Slavic) great glory; famed
Slavek, Slavomir

Slim
(English) nickname for slim guy

Sloan
(Irish) sleek
Sloane, Slonne

Slocum
(Last name as first name) happy
Slo, Slocom, Slocumb

Slover
(Last name as first name)
Slove

Sly
(Latin) from Sylvester; of the forest

Smedley
(English) of the flat meadow
Smedleigh, Smedly

Smerdyakov
(Russian) sinister

Smith
(English) crafty; blacksmith
Smid, Smidt, Smit, Smitt, Smitti, Smitty

Smithson
(Last name as first name) son of Smith; craftsman

Smitty
(English) craftsman
Smittey

Smokey
(American) smokin'
Smoke, Smokee, Smoky

Snake
(Place name) U.S. river

Snowden
(English) from a snowy hill; fresh
Snowdon

Snyder
(German) tailor's clothing; stylish
Schneiger, Snider

So
(Vietnamese) smart

Socorro
(Spanish) helpful
Sokorro

Socrates
(Greek) philosophical; brilliant
Socratez, Socratis, Sokrates

Sofian
(Arabic) devoted

Sofus
(Greek) wise
Sophus

Sohan
(Hindi) charmer

Sohil
(Hindi) beautiful

Sol
(Hebrew) short for Solomon
Solly

Solly
(Hebrew) short for Solomon
Sollee, Solley, Solli, Sollie

Solomon
(Hebrew) peaceful and wise
Salamon, Sol, Sollie, Solly, Soloman

Somerby
(English) from the summer village; lighthearted
Somerbie, Somersby, Sommersby

Somerley
(Irish) summer sailor
Somerled, Sorley

Somers
(English) loving summer
Sommers

Somerset
(English) talented
Somer, Somers, Sommerset, Summerset

Somerton
(English) from summer town
Somervile, Somerville

Sommar
(English) summer
Somer, Somers, Somm, Sommars, Sommer

Son
(English) boy
Sonni, Sonnie, Sonny

Sonny
(English) boy
Son, Sonney, Sonni, Sonnie

Sonteeahgo
(Invented) form of Santiago

Sophocles
(Greek) playwright

Soren
(Scandinavian) good communicator
Soryn

Sorrel
(French) reddish-brown horse; horse lover
Sorre, Sorrell, Sorrey

Sothern
(English) from the south; warm-hearted
Southern

Sound
(American) word as a name; dynamic

Southwell
(English) living by the southern well

Spanky
(American) outspoken; stubborn
Spank, Spankee, Spankie

Sparky
(Latin) ball of fire; joyful
Spark, Sparkee, Sparkey, Sparki, Sparkie

Spaulding
(Last name as first name) comic
Spalding, Spaldying, Spauldyng

Speed
(English) plucky

Speers
(English) good with spears; swift-moving
Speares, Spears, Spiers

Spence
(English) short for Spencer
Spens, Spense

Spencer
(English) giver; provides well
Spence, Spencey, Spenser, Spensor, Spensy

Sperry
(Last name as first name) inventive
Sperrey

Spider
(American) scary
Spyder

Spidey
(American) zany

Spike
(American) word as name
Spiker

Spiker
(English) go-getter
Spike, Spikey, Spyk

Spiridon
(Greek) like a breath of fresh air
Speero, Spero, Spiridon, Spiro, Spiros, Spyridon, Spyros

Spiro
(Greek) coil; spiral
Spi, Spiroh, Spiros, Spy, Spyro

Springer
(English) fresh
Spring

Sprague
(French) high-energy

Spud
(English) energetic

Spurgeon
(Botanical) from the shrub spurge; natural
Spurge

Spunk
(American) spunky; lively
Spunki, Spunky

Spurs
(American) boot devices used to spur horses; cowboy
Spur

Squire
(English) land-loving
Squirre, Skwyre

Stace
(English) optimist
Stayce

Stacey
(English) hopeful
Stace, Stacee, Stacy, Stase, Stasi

Stadler
(Last name as first name) staid
Stadtler

Stafford
(English) dignified
Staff, Staffard, Stafferd, Staffi, Staffie, Staffor, Staffy

Stamos
(Greek) reasonable
Stammos, Stamohs

Stan
(Latin) short for Stanley

Stanbury
(English) fortified
Stanberry, Stanbery, Stanburghe, Stansberry, Stansburghe, Stansbury

Stancliff
(English) from the stone cliff; prepared
Stancliffe, Stanclyffe, Stanscliff, Stanscliffe

Standish
(English) farsighted
Standysh

Stanfield
(English) from the stone field; able
Stansfield

Stanford
(English) dignified
Stan, Stanferd, Stann

Stanislaus
(Latin) glorious
Staneslaus, Stanis, Stanislus, Stann, Stanus

Stanislav
(Russian) glory in leading
Slava, Stasi

Stanley
(English) traveler
Stan, Stanlea, Stanlee, Stanli, Stanly

Stanmore
(English) lake of stones; ill-fated

Stanton
(English) stone-hard
Stan

Stanway
(English) came from the stone road
Stanaway, Stannaway, Stannway

Stanwick
(English) born in village of stone; hard
Stanwicke, Stanwyck

Stanwood
(English) stone woods man; tough

Stark
(German) high-energy
Starke, Starkey

Starling
(English) singer; bird
Starlling

Starr
(English) bright star
Star, Starri, Starrie, Starry

Stavros
(Greek) winner
Stavrohs, Stavrows

Steadman
(English) landowner;
wealthy
*Steadmann, Sted,
Stedmann*

Steed
(English) horse of high
spirits

Steele
(English) hardworking
Steel, Stille

Stefan
(Scandinavian) crowned;
(German) chosen one
*Stefawn, Steff, Steffan,
Steffie, Steffon, Steffy,
Stefin, Stephan*

Stefano
(Italian) supreme ruler
*Stef, Steffie, Steffy,
Stephano, Stephanos*

Stehlin
(Last name as first name)
genius
Staylin, Stealan, Stehlan

Stein
(German) stonelike
Steen, Sten, Steno

Steinar
(Scandinavian) muse; rock
*Steinard, Steinart,
Steinhardt*

Steinbeck
(Last name as first) writer
John

Stellan
(Swedish) star

Sten
(Scandinavian) star stone
Stene, Stine

Stennis
(Scottish) prehistoric
standing stones; eternal

Stepan
(English) from Stephen;
crowned
Stepen, Stepyn

Steph
(English) short for
Stephen; triumphant
Stef, Steff, Steffy

Stephan
(Greek) form of Stephen;
successful

Stephanos
(Greek) crowned; martyr
*Stef, Stefanos, Steph,
Stephanas*

Stephen
(Greek) victorious
*Stephan, Stephon, Stevee,
Steven, Stevey, Stevi,
Stevie, Stevy*

Stephene
(French) form of Stephen;
wearing a crown
Stef, Steff, Steph

Sterling
(English) worthwhile

Stern
(German) bright; serious
Stearn, Sterns

Stetson
(American) cowboy
Stetsen, Stetsun, Stettson

Steubing
(Last name as first name)
stepping
*Steuben, Stu, Stuben,
Stubing*

Steve
(Greek) short for Steven
and Stephen; prosperous
Stevie

Steven
(Greek) victorious
*Stevan, Steve, Stevey,
Stevie*

Steveo
(American) form of Steve
Stevie
(English) short for Steven,
Stephen
Stevee, Stevey, Stevi,
Stevy
Stewart
(English) form of Stuart;
steward or keeper
Stewert, Stu, Stuie
Stian
(Scandinavian) traveler
Stieran
(Scandinavian) wandering
Steeran, Steeren, Steeryn,
Stieren, Stieryn
Stig
(Scandinavian) upwardly
mobile
Stigg, Styg, Stygg
Stiles
(English) practical
Stile, Stiley, Styles
Stillman
(English) quiet boy
Sting
(English) spike of grain
Stoat
(English) small mammal
also called ermine; white
Stoate, Stote
Stobart
(German) harsh
Stobe, Stobey, Stoby
Stock
(American) macho
Stok
Stockard
(English) dramatic
Stock, Stockerd, Stockord
Stocker
(English) foundation
Stock

Stockley
(English) in a field of tree
stumps (stock); rooted in
reality
Stockton
(English) strong foundation
Stockten
Stockwell
(English) from the well by
tree stumps; grounded
Stoddard
(English) caretaker of
horses
Stoddart
Stoli
(Russian) celebrant
Stone
(English) athletic
Stonee, Stoney, Stonie,
Stony
Stonewall
(English) fortified
Stone, Stoney, Wall
Stoney
(American) form of Stone;
friendly
Stonee, Stoni, Stonie
Storey
(English) one story of a
house; storyteller
Story
Storm
(English) impetuous;
volatile
Storme, Stormy
Stowe
(English) secretive
Stow, Stowey
Strahan
(Irish) sings stories
Strachan
Stratford
(English) river-crossing
boy; happy
Strafford

Strato
(Invented) strategic
Strat, Stratt

Stratton
(Scottish) home-loving
Straton, Strattawn

Straus
(German) ostrich; in
disbelief
Strauss

Stretch
(American) easygoing
Stretcher

Strickland
(English) field of flax;
outdoorsy

Strider
(Literature) from Tolkien's
Lord of the Rings; great
warrior

Strike
(American) word as name;
aggressive
Striker

Stroheim
(Last name as first) great
director

Strom
(German) water-lover
Strome, Stromm

Strong
(English) strength of
character

Strother
(Irish) strict
*Strothers, Struther,
Struthers*

Struther
(Last name as first name)
flowing
*Strother, Strothers,
Struthers*

Stu
(English) short for Stuart
Stew, Stue, Stuey

Stuart
(English) careful; watchful
Stewart, Stu, Stuey

Studs
(American) cocky
Studd, Studds

Sture
(Scandinavian) difficult
Sturah

Styles
(English) practical
Stile, Stiles, Style

Stylianos
(Greek) stylish
Styli

Sudbury
(English) southern town
boy; lackadaisical
*Sudbery, Sudberry,
Sudborough*

Suffield
(English) man from south
field; farms

Suffolk
(English) from southern
folks

Sugar-Ray
(American) strong; singer
Sugar Ray

Sujay
(Hindi) good
Sujit

Sulaiman
(Arabic) loves peace
Suleiman, Suleyman

Sullivan
(Irish) dark-eyed; quiet
*Sullavan, Sullie, Sullivahn,
Sully*

Sully
(Irish) melancholy; hushed
Sull, Sullee, Sulley, Sullie

Sultan
(American) bold
Sultane, Sulten, Sultin

Suman
(Hindi) ingenious

Sumner
(Last name as first name) honorable; fortified

Sumney
(American) ethereal
Summ, Summy, Sumnee, Sumnie

Sunil
(Hindi) blue; sad

Sunny
(American) happy baby boy
Sunney, Sunnie

Sutcliff
(English) from the south cliff; edgy
Sutcliffe

Sutherland
(Scandinavian) sunny; southerner
Southerland

Sutter
(English) southern
Sutt, Suttee, Sutty

Sutton
(English) sunny; southerner

Svatomir
(Slavic) known for being spiritual

Svatoslav
(Slavic) having the glory of being devout

Sven
(Scandinavian) young boy
Svein, Svend, Swen

Swahili
(Arabic) language of East Africa; verbal

Swain
(English) rigid; leading the herd
Swaine, Swayne

Swanton
(English) where swans live; sylvan boy

Sweeney
(Irish) hero
Schwennie, Sweeny

Swift
(English) fast
Swifty

Swinburne
(English) seeing pigs in the stream
Swinborn, Swinbourne, Swinburn, Swinbyrn, Swynborne

Swindell
(English) polished
Schwindell, Swin, Swindel

Swinford
(English) seeing pigs in the ford
Swynford

Swinton
(English) from the town of swine

Swithin
(English) swift
Swithinn, Swithun

Sy
(Latin) short for Silas,
Sylas, Si

Sydney
(French) form of Sidney
Cyd, Syd, Sydie

Sylvain
(Latin) reclusive
Syl

Sylvan
(Spanish) nature-loving
Silvan, Syl, Sylvany, Sylvin

Sylvester
(Latin) forest dweller; heavy-duty
Sil, Silvester, Sly, Syl

Symms
(Last name as first name)
landowner
Symotris
(African American)
fortunate
Sym, Symetris, Symotrice, Syms
Syon
(Sanskrit) lucky boy

Tab
(German) intelligent
Tabby, Tabbey, Tabby
Tabbai
(Hebrew) good boy
Tabbebo
(Native American) boy of
the sun
Tabib
(Turkish) physician
Tabeeb
Tabor
(Aramaic) unfortunate
Taber, Taibor, Tayber, Taybor
Tad
(Greek) short for
Thaddeus
Tadd, Taddee, Taddey, Taddie, Taddy
Tadeusz
(Polish) praise-worthy
Tad, Taduce

Tadhg
(Irish) poetic
Taidghin, Teague, Teige
Tadi
(Native American) wind
child
Tadzi
(Polish) praised
Taff
(American) sweet
Taf, Taffee, Taffey, Taffi, Taffy
Taft
(English) flowing
Tafte, Taftie, Taffy
Taggart
(Last name as first name)
keeps track; singer
Taghee
(Native American) chief
Taighe, Taihee, Tyee, Tyhee
Taha
(Polynesian) first
Tahatan
Taheton
(Native American) like a
hawk
Tahi
(Polynesian) by the sea
Tahir
(African) pure
Tahoe
(Place name) Lake Tahoe,
Nevada
Taho
Tahoma
(Native American)
mountain peak; high hopes
Tohoma
Tai
(Vietnamese) talented
Taimah
(Native American) thunder

Taiwo
(African) first of twins
Taizo
(Japanese) third son
Taj
(Sanskrit) royal; crowned
Takeshi
(Japanese) unbending
Taklishim
(Native American) gray-haired
Takoda
(Native American) friend
Tal
(Hebrew) worrier
Tallee, Talley, Talli, Tally
Talbot
(French) skillful
Tal, Talbert, Talbott, Tallbot, Tallbott, Tally
Talcot
(English) lake-cottage dweller; laidback
Tale
(African) green; open
Talfryn
(Welsh) on the high hill
Talib
(African) looking for enlightenment
Taliesin
(Welsh) head that shines
Taltesin
Talli
(Hebrew) dew; fresh
Talmai
(Aramaic) born on a hill
Talmadge
(English) natural; living by lakes
Tal, Tally, Tamidge
Talman
(Hebrew) from my hill
Tallie, Tally, Talmon

Talon
(French) wily
Tallie, Tallon, Tally, Tawlon
Talor
(French) cutter; tailor
Tam
(Hebrew) truthful
Tammy
Taman
(Hindi) needed
Tamarius
(African American) stubborn
Tam, Tamerius, Tammy, T'Marius
Tamir
(Arabic) owner
Tammany
(Native American) friendly boy
Tamanend
Tammy
(English) short for Thomas and Tamarius
Tammee, Tammie, Tammey
Tan
(Japanese) high achiever
Tanafa
(Polynesian) drumbeat
Tanaki
(Polynesian) boy who counts
Tanay
(Hindi) son
Tandie
(African American) virile
Tane
(Polynesian) sky god; fertile
Tain
Tangaloa
(Polynesian) gutsy
Tanh
(Vietnamese) having his way

Tani
(African American) short for Tanier; hide tanner

Tank
(American) big; bullish

Tankie
(American) large
Tank, Tankee, Tanky

Tanner
(English) tanner of skins
Tan, Tanier, Tann, Tannar, Tanne, Tanney, Tannie, Tannor, Tanny

Tano
(Mythology) from Tane, fertility god

Tanton
(English) town of tanners

Taos
(Place name) town in New Mexico
Tao, Tayo

Tap
(American) light touch
Tapp, Tappi, Tappy

Tarhe
(Native American) strength of a tree

Tarik
(Arabic) knocks
Taril, Tarin, Tariq

Tariq
(African American) conquerer
Tarik

Tarlach
(Hebrew) wild

Tarleton
(English) stormy
Tally, Tarlton

Taro
(Japanese) first-born son

Tarquin
(Roman clan) impulsive

Tarrance
(Latin) smooth
Terance, Terrance, Terry

Tarrant
(Place name) county in Texas; lawful

Tarri
(American) form of Terry
Tari, Tarree, Tarrey, Tarry

Tarso
(Italian) dashing

Tarun
(Arabic) knocks

Taryll
(American) form of Terrell
Tarell

Tas
(Place name) from Tasmania
Taz

Tashunka
(Native American) horse lover
Tasunke

Tassilo
(Scandinavian) fearless protector

Tassos
(Italian) dark

Tatankamimi
(Native American) the buffalo walks

Tate
(English) happy
Tait, Taitt, Tatey, Tayt, Tayte

Tatonga
(Native American) deer; swift

Tatry
(Place name) mountains in Poland
Tate, Tatree, Tatri

Tau
(African) lionine

Taurean
(African American)
reclusive; quiet
Taureen

Taurus
(Astrological sign) macho
Tar, Taur, Tauras, Taures

Tava
(Polynesian) fruit; fertile

Tavares
(African American) hopeful
Tavarus

Tavarius
(African American) fun-
loving
*Tav, Taverius, Tavurius,
Tavvy*

Tavas
(Hebrew) peacock;
handsome

Tavi
(Aramaic) good

Tavish
(Scottish) upbeat
Tav, Taven, Tavis, Tevis

Tavor
(Aramaic) unfortunate
Tabor

Tawa
(Native American) sun boy

Tawagahe
(Native American) builder

Tawanima
(Native American)
measures the sun
Tewanima

Tawfiq
(Arabic) fortunate
Tawfi

Tawl
(Arabic) tall
Taweel

Tawno
(American) small

Tay
(Scottish) river in
Scotland; jaunty
Tae, Taye

Tayib
(Arabic) city in Israel;
spiritual

Taylor
(English) tailor
Tailor, Talor, Tayler, Tayley

Tayton
(American) form of Payton
*Tate, Taye, Tayte, Tayten,
Taytin*

Taz
(Arabic) cup; vibrant

Teague
(Irish) bard; poet
Teaguey, Tege

Tearlach
(Scottish) adult man; bold

Techomir
(Czech) famed comfort

Techoslav
(Native American) glorious
comfort

Tecumseh
(Native American)
shooting star; bright

Ted
(English) short for
Theodore
*Teddee, Teddey, Teddi,
Teddy*

Teddy-Blue
(American) smiley
*Blu, Blue, Teddie-Blue,
Teddy, Teddyblu, Teddy-
Blu, Teddyblue*

Tedmund
(American) shy
Tedmond

Tedrick
(African American) form of
Cedrick
Ted, Tedrik

Tedshawn
(American) combo of Ted and Shawn
Teddshawn, Tedshaun

Tedwayne
(American) combo of Ted and Wayne; friendly
Ted Wayne, Ted-Wayne

Tegan
(Irish) form of Teague; literary figure
Tege, Tegen, Tegun, Teige

Tejomay
(Hindi) glorious
Tej

Tekonsha
(Native American) caribou

Telamon
(Greek) mythological hero

Telek
(Polish) ironworker

Telem
(English) from Teleson; amulet

Telemachus
(Mythological) son of Ulysses

Telesphoros
(Greek) leading to an end; centered

Telford
(English) cutting iron; targeted
Telfer, Telfor, Telfour

Teller
(English) relates stories; storytelling
Tellie, Telly

Telvis
(American) form of Elvis
Telly

Tem
(African) short form of Teman; spiritual

Teman
(Hebrew) Temani are Jews from Yeman; spiritual

Tempest
(French) stormy; volatile
Tempie, Tempy, Tempyst

Temple
(Latin) spiritual
Tempie, Templle, Tempy

Templeton
(English) from religious place
Temp, Tempie, Temple, Temps

Ten
(American) tenth

Tendoy
(Native American) he who climbs higher
Tendoi

Teneangopte
(Native American) bird; flies high

Tennant
(American) capable
Tenn

Tennessee
(Native American) able fighter; U.S. state
Tenns, Tenny

Tennyson
(English) storyteller
Tenie, Tenn, Tenney, Tenneyson, Tennie, Tenny, Tennysen

Teo
(Greek) gift of God

Teodoro
(Spanish) God's gift
Tedoro, Teo, Teodore, Theo

TeQuarius
(African American) secretive
Teq, Tequarius, Tequie

Terach
(Hebrew) wild goat; contentious
Tera, Terah

Terard
(Invented) form of Gerard
Terar, Tererd, Terry

Terence
(Irish) tender
Tarrance, Terencio, Terrance, Terrence, Terrey, Terri, Terry

TeRez
(African American) creative

Termell
(Invented) form of Terrell; militant
Termel

Terrance
(Latin) calm
Terance, Terence, Terre, Terree, Terrence, Terrie, Terry

Terrelle
(German) thunderous; outspoken
Terel, Terele, Terell, Teril, Terille, Terral, Terrale, Terre, Terrel, Terril, Terrill, Terrille, Terry, Tirill, Tirrill, Tyrel, Tyril

Terrill
(African American) combo of Terry and Derrell
Terrall, Terrel, Terrell, Terryl, Terryll, Tirrell, Tyrrell

Terry
(English) short for Terrence
Terree, Terrey, Terri, Terrie

Tesher
(Hebrew) gift

Teshombe
(African American) able

Tet
(Vietnamese) Vietnamese New Year

Teva
(Hebrew) natural
Tevah

Tevaughn
(African American) tiger
Tev, Tevan, Tevaughan, Tivan, Tivaughan

Tevey
(Hebrew) good
Tev, Tevi, Tevie

Tevin
(African American) outgoing
Tev, Tevan, Tivan

Tevis
(American) flamboyant
Tev, Tevas, Teves, Teviss, Tevy

Tevita
(Spanish) variant of Evita; strong

Tex
(American) from Texas; cowboy
Texas, Texx

Texas
(Place name) U.S. state; cowboy
Tex

Thabiti
(African) real man

Thad
(Greek) short for Thaddeus; brave
Thadd, Thaddy

Thaddeus
(Greek) courageous
Taddeo, Tadeo, Tadio, Thad, Thaddaus, Thaddius, Thaddy, Thadeus, Thadius

Thady
(Irish) thankful
Thad, Thaddee, Thaddie, Thaddy, Thads

Thai
(Vietnamese) winner

Thandiwe
(African) loved

Thane
(English) protective
Thain, Thaine, Thayn, Thayne

Thang
(Vietnamese) victorious

Thanh
(Vietnamese) tops

Thanos
(Greek) praiseworthy
Thanasis

Thanus
(American) landowner; wealthy
Thainas, Thaines

Thatcher
(English) practical
Thacher, Thatch, Thatchar, Thaxter

Thaw
(Word as name) cool

Thayer
(English) protected; sheltered
Thay, Thayar

Themba
(African) hopeful

Theo
(Greek) godlike

Theobald
(German) brave man
Thebaud, Thebault, Thibault, Thibaut, Tibold, Tiebold

Theodore
(Greek) God's gift; a blessing
Teador, Ted, Tedd, Teddey, Teddie, Teddy, Tedor, Teodor, Teodoro, Theeo, Theo, Theodor, Theos

Theodoric
(African American) God's gift
Thierry

Theodoros
(Greek) God's gift
Theo, Theodor

Theophilos
(Greek) loved by God
Teofil, Theo, Theophile

Therman
(Scandinavian) thunderous
Thur, Thurman, Thurmen

Theron
(Greek) industrious
Therron, Theryon

Theseus
(Mythology) brave

Thiassi
(Scandinavian) wily
Thiazi, Thjazi

Thierno
(American) humble
Therno, Their

Tho
(Vietnamese) long-living

Thomas
(Greek) twin; lookalike
Thom, Thomes, Thommy, Thomus, Tom, Tomas, Tommi, Tomus

Thompson
(English) prepared
Thom, Thompsen, Thompsun, Thomson, Tom, Tommy

Thor
(Scandinavian) protective; god of thunder
Thorr, Tor, Torr

Thorald
(Scandinavian) thundering
Thorold, Torald

Thorbert
(Last name as first name) warring

Thorburn
(Last name as first name) warlike

Thorer
(Scandinavian) warrior
Thorvald

Thorin
(Scandinavian) form of Thor; god of thunder
Thorrin, Thors

Thorley
(Last name as first name) warrior
Thorlea, Thorlee, Thorleigh, Thorly, Torley

Thormond
(Last name as first name) world of thunder
Thurmond, Thurmund

Thorn
(English) thorny; bothersome

Thorndike
(Last name as first name) powerful
Thorndyck, Thorndyke

Thorne
(English) complex
Thorn, Thornee, Thorney, Thornie, Thorny

Thornley
(Last name as first name) empowered
Thornlea, Thornleigh, Thornly

Thornston
(Scandinavian) protected
Thornse, Thors

Thornton
(English) difficult
Thorn, Thornten

Thorpe
(English) homebody
Thor, Thorp

Thrace
(Place name) region in southeast Europe
Thrase

Thu
(Vietnamese) born in the fall

Thuc
(Vietnamese) alert

Thuong
(Vietnamese) in pursuit

Thurlow
(Last name as first name) helping

Thurman
(Last name as first name) popular
Thurmahn, Thurmen, Thurmie, Thurmy

Thurmond
(Norse) sheltered
Thurman, Thurmon

Thurston
(Scandinavian) thundering
Thor, Thors, Thorst, Thorstan, Thorstein, Thorsteinn, Thorsten, Thur, Thurs, Thurstain, Thurstan, Thursten, Torstein, Torsten, Torston

Thurstron
(Scandinavian) volatile
Thorst, Thorsten, Thorstin, Thurs, Thurstran

Thuy
(Vietnamese) kind

Tiago
(Hispanic) brave
Ti, Tia

Tiarnach
(Irish) lordlike
Tighearnach

Tibor
(Czech) artist
Tybald, Tybalt, Tybault

Tien
(Vietnamese) first and
foremost

Tiernan
(Irish) regal
Tierney

Tige
(American) easygoing
Tig, Tigg

Tiger
(American) ambitious;
strong
*Tig, Tige, Tigur, Tyg, Tyge,
Tyger, Tygur*

Tiki
(Mythology) first man

Tilak
(Hindi) leader; troubled

Tilden
(Place name) Tilden,
Nebraska; conservative

Tilford
(Last name as first name)
tilling the soil

Till
(German) short for
Tillman; tiller of soil

Tillery
(German) ruler
Till, Tiller

Tillman
(German) leader
Tilman

Tilon
(Hebrew) mound; giver

Tilton
(English) prospering
Till, Tillie, Tylton

Tim
(Greek) short for Timothy
Timmy, Tym

Timber
(American) word as name
*Timb, Timby, Timmey,
Timmi, Timmy*

Timin
(Irish) honors God

Timmy
(Greek) truthful
*Timi, Timmee, Timmey,
Timmie*

Timo
(Finnish) form of Timothy
or Timon

Timon
(Literature) from
Shakespeare's *Timon of
Athens*; wealthy man
Tim

Timothy
(Greek) reveres God
*Tim, Timathy, Timmie,
Timmothy, Timmy, Timo,
Timon, Timoteo, Timothe,
Timothey, Timothie,
Timuthy, Tymmothy,
Tymothy*

Timur
(African) timid

Tin
(Vietnamese) proud;
pondering

Tinks
(American) coy
*Tink, Tinkee, Tinki, Tinky,
Tynks, Tynky*

Tino
(Spanish) respected
Tyno

Tinsley
(English) personable
Tensley, Tins, Tinslee,
Tinslie, Tinsly

Tip
(American) small boy
Tipp, Tippee, Tippey, Tippi,
Tippy, Typp

Tipu
(Hindi) tiger

Tiru
(Hindi) pious

Tisa
(African) ninth child

Titan
(Greek) powerful giant
Titun, Tityn

Tito
(Latin) honored
Teto, Titoh

Titus
(Latin) heroic
Titas, Tite, Tites

Tivon
(African American) popular

Toa
(Polynesian) brave-
hearted

Toafo
(Polynesian) in the wild;
spontaneous

Toal
(Irish) from strong roots

Tobes
(Hebrew) form of Tobias;
believing the Lord is good
Tobee, Tobi, Tobs

Tobias
(Hebrew) believing the
Lord is good
Tobe, Tobey, Tobi, Tobiah,
Tobie, Tobin, Toby, Tobyas,
Tovi

Tobbar
(African American)
physical

Tobikuma
(Japanese) cloud; misty

Tobin
(Hebrew) form of Tobias;
believing the Lord is good
Toban, Toben, Tobun,
Tobyn

Toby
(Hebrew) short for Tobias;
having faith in the Lord
Tobe, Tobee, Tobey, Tobie,
Toto

Todd
(English) sly; fox
Tod, Toddy

Todros
(Hebrew) gifted; treasure
Todos

Togo
(Place name) country in
West Africa; jaunty

Tohon
(Native American) loves
the water

Tokala
(Native American) fox; sly

Toks
(American) carefree

Tokutaro
(Japanese) virtuous son

Tolan
(American) studious
Tolen, Toll

Tolbert
(English) bright prospects
Talbart, Talbert, Tolbart,
Tolburt, Tollee, Tolley,
Tollie, Tolly

Toledo
(Place name) city in Ohio;
casual
Tol, Tolly

Tolfe
(American) outgoing

Tolomey
(French) planner

Tom
(English) short for
Thomas; twin
Thom, Tommy

Tomas
(Spanish) form of Thomas

Tomasso
(Italian) doubter
Maso, Tom

Tomer
(Hebrew) tall

Tomi
(Spanish) short for Tomas;
twin

Tomlin
(Last name as first name)
ambitious

Tommie
(Hebrew, English) short
for Thomas
*Tomee, Tommee, Tommey,
Tommi, Tomy*

Tomochichi
(Hawaiian) seeking truth
and beauty
Tomocheechee

Tong
(Chinese) name of a secret
society; keeps a secret

Toni
(Greek, Italian, American,
English) soaring
Tonee, Toney, Tonie, Tony

Tonion
(American) from
Tony/Anthony; priceless

Toopweets
(Native American) strong
man

Topwe
(American) jovial

Tor
(Scandinavian) thunder;
brash
*Thor, Torr, Torri, Torrie,
Torry*

Torao
(Japanese) tiger male; wild

Torcall
(Scandinavian) summoned
by thunder

Tord
(Dutch) peaceful

Torger
(Scandinavian) Thor's
spear
Terje, Torgeir

Toribio
(Spanish) strong; bullish

Toril
(Hindi) having attitude

Torin
(African American) like
thunder

Torio
(Spanish) fierce

Torkel
(Scandinavian) protective
*Thorkel, Torkil, Torkild,
Torkjell, Torquil*

Torless
(Literature) from *The
Confusions
of Young Torless* by Musil

Tormod
(Scottish) man of the
north

Torn
(Last name as first name)
whirlwind
Torne, Tornn

Toro
(Spanish) bull

Torolf
(Scandinavian) wolf of Thor
Thorolf, Tolv, Torolv, Torulf

Toronto
(Place name) jaded
Torontoe

Torq
(Scandinavian) form of Thor, god of thunder
Tork

Torquil
(Scandinavian) a kettle of thunder; trouble

Torr
(English) tower; tall
Torre

Torrence
(Latin) smooth
Torrance, Torence, Torey, Tori, Torr, Torrance, Torrie, Tory

Torri
(English) calming
Toree, Tori, Torre, Torree, Torrey, Torry

Toru
(Scandinavian) thundering

Toshiro
(Japanese) smart

Tov
(Hebrew) good
Tovi, Toviel, Tovya, Tuvia, Tuviah, Tuviya

Tova
(Hebrew) good
Tov

Tove
(Scandinavian) ruling; leads
Tuve

Townie
(American) jovial
Townee, Towney, Towny

Townley
(Last name as first name) citified
Townlea, Townlee, Townleigh, Townlie, Townly

Townsend
(Last name as first name) went to town

Toyah
(Place name) town in Texas; saucy
Toy, Toya, Toye

Trace
(French) careful
Trayse

Tracy
(French) spunky
Trace, Tracee, Tracey, Traci

Trae
(American) form of Trey; third

Trahan
(English) handsome
Trace, Trahahn, Trahain, Trahane, Trahen

Trahaearn
(Welsh) strong man
Trahern, Traherne

Trai
(Vietnamese) pearl in the oyster

Trampus
(American) talkative
Amp, Tramp, Trampy

Trap
(American) word as name; masculine
Trapp, Trappy

Traves
(American) traversing different roads
Trav, Travus, Travys

Travers
(English) helpful

Travis
(English) conflicted
Tavers, Traver, Travers, Traves, Travess, Travey, Travus, Travuss, Travys

Travon
(African American) brash
Travaughn

Trayton
(English) third
Tray, Trey

Treebeard
(Literature) from Tolkein's
The Lord of the Rings;
noble; strong

Trefor
(Welsh) form of Trevor;
large home

Tremayne
(French) protector
*Tramaine, Treemayne,
Trem, Tremain, Tremaine,
Tremane, Tremen*

Trent
(Latin) quick-minded
*Trente, Trenten, Trentin,
Trenton, Trenty, Trint, Trynt*

Trenton
(Latin) fast-moving
*Trent, Trentan, Trenten,
Trentin*

Treva
(Irish) wise
Trevan

Trevan
(African American)
outgoing
Trevahn, Trevann

Trevelyan
(English) from Elyan's
home; comforted

Trevon
(African American)
studious
Trevaughan

Trevor
(Irish) wise
*Trefor, Trev, Trevar, Trever,
Trevis, Trevur, Treve*

Trey
(English) third-born;
creatively brilliant
Trae, Tray, Tre, Treye

Trigg
(American) short for
Trigger; quick-witted
Trig, Trygg

Trinee
(Spanish) musical
Triney, Trini

Trinity
(Latin) triad
Trinitie

Trip
(English) wanderer
Tripe, Tripp

Tripsy
(English) dancing
Trippsie, Tryppsi

Tristan
(English) impulsive
*Trestan, Trestyn, Trist,
Tristen, Tristie, Triston,
Tristy, Tristyn*

Triste
(French) sad; wistful
Tristan

Tristram
(Welsh) sorrowful

Trivett
(Last name as first name)
trinity
Trevett, Triv

Trivin
(American) form of Devin;
clever
Trevin

Trocky
(American) manly
Trockey, Trockie

Trond
(Scandinavian) from
Trondheim, Norway; blond

Trowbridge
(Place name) Trowbridge
Park, Michigan; staunch

Troy
(French) good-looking
Troi, Troye, Troyie

Troylane
(American) combo of Troy and Lane
Troy Lane, Troy-Lane

Trudell
(English) remarkable for honesty
Trude, True

True
(English) truthful
Tru

Truitt
(English) honest
Tru, True, Truett, Truitte

Truk
(Place name) islands in the West Pacific; tough
Truck

Truman
(English) honest man
Tru, True, Trueman, Trumaine, Trumann

Trumble
(Last name as first name) sincere
Trumball, Trumbell, Trumbull

Trusdale
(English) truthful
Dale, Tru, True

Tsalani
(African) says good-bye; leaving

Tsatoke
(Native American) hunter on a horse

Tsela
(Native American) star

Tsin
(Native American) riding a horse

Tsoai
(Native American) tree; big

Tu
(Vietnamese) fourth

Tuan
(Vietnamese) simple

Tucker
(English) stylish
Tuck, Tucky, Tuckyr

Tucks
(English) short for Tucker; fanciful
Tuk

Tudor
(Welsh) leader; special

Tukuli
(African) moon child

Tullis
(Latin) important
Tull, Tullice, Tullise, Tully

Tully
(Irish) short for Tullis; interesting
Tull, Tulley, Tulli, Tullie

Tulsa
(Place name) city in Oklahoma; rancher

Tulsi
(Hindi) holy

Tumaini
(African) optimist

Tune
(American) dancer; musical
Toone, Tuney

Tung
(Chinese, Vietnamese) dignified; wise

Tunu
(Place name) from Tununak, Alaska; natural

Tuong
(Vietnamese) everything

Tupi
(Spanish) a language family with Brazilian roots

Turk
(English) tough
Terk, Turke

Turlough
(Hebrew) form of Tuvyeh; good

Turner
(Latin) skilled

Turone
(African American) form of Tyrone
Ture, Turrey, Turry

Turner
(Latin) skilled
Turn

Tut
(Arabic) brave
Tuttie, Tutty

Tuvia
(Hebrew) good
Tuvyah

Tuwa
(Native American) earth-loving

Tuyen
(Vietnamese) angelic

Twain
(English) dual-faceted
Twaine, Tway, Twayn

Twyford
(English) debonair

Ty
(English) short for Tyler
Ti, Tie, Tye

Tybalt
(Greek) always right

Tyce
(American) lively
Tice

Tycho
(Scandinavian) focused
Tyge, Tyko

Tydeus
(Mythology) determined

Tyee
(African American) goal-oriented

Tygie
(American) energetic
Tygee, Tygey, Tygi

Tyke
(Scandinavian) determined

Tyler
(English) industrious
Tile, Tiler, Ty, Tye, Tylar, Tyle, Tylir, Tylor

Tymon
(Polish) honored by God

Tynan
(Place name) a town in, Texas; rancher

Tyonne
(African American) feisty
Tye, Tyon

Typhoon
(English) volatile
Tifoon, Ty, Tyfoon, Tyfoonn

Tyr
(Scandinavian) Norse god; daring warrior

Tyre
(English) thunders
Tyr

Tyree
(African American) courteous
Ty, Tyrae, Tyrie, Tyry

Tyreece
(African American) combative
Tyreese

Tyrell
(African American) personable
Trelle, Tyrel, Tyrelle, Tyril, Tyrrel

Tyron
(African American) self-reliant
Tiron, Tyronn

Tyrone
(Greek) self-starter;
autonomous
*Terone, Tiron, Tirone,
Tirus, Ty, Tyronne, Tyron,
Tyroon, Tyroun*

Tyroneece
(African American) ball of
fire
Tironeese, Tyronnee

Tys
(American) fighter
*Thysen, Tyes, Tys, Tyse,
Tysen*

Tyson
(French) son of Ty
*Tieson, Tison, Tyse, Tysen,
Tysson, Tysy*

Tzach
(Hebrew) unblemished
Tzachai, Tzachar

Tzadik
(Hebrew) fair
*Tzadok, Zadik, Zadoc,
Zadok, Zaydak*

Tzadkiel
(Hebrew) righteous
Zadkiel

Tzalmon
(Hebrew) dark
Zalmon

Tzephaniah
(Hebrew) man protected
by God
*Tzefanya, Zefania,
Zefaniah, Zephania,
Zephaniah*

Tzevi
(Hebrew) graceful; deer
Tzeviel, Zevi, Zeviel

Tzuriel
(Hebrew) depends on God
Zuriel

Ualtar
(Irish) strong
Ualtarr

Uba
(African) rich

Ubald
(French) brave one
Ubaldo, Ube

Ubanwa
(African) wealth in
children

Uben
(German) practice
Ubin, Ubyn

Ubrig
(German) big
Ubrigg, Ubryg, Ubrygg

Ubrigens
(German) bothered
Ubrigins, Ubrigyns

Uchtred
(English) cries
*Uchtrid, Uchtryd, Uctred,
Uctrid, Uctryd, Uktred,
Uktrid*

Udall
(English) certain; valley of
trees
*Eudall, Udahl, Udawl,
Yudall*

Udeh
(Hindi) praised

Udel
(English) growing

Udell
(English) from a tree grove
Del, Dell, Udale, Udall

Udenwa
(African) thriving
Udo
(German) shows promise
Udolf
(German) stodgy
Ufer
(German) dark mind
Ugo
(Italian) bright mind
Uhr
(German) disturbed
Uilleac
(Irish) ready
Uilleack, Uilleak, Uilliac, Uilliack, Uilliak, Uillyac, Uillyack, Uillyak
Uilleog
(Irish) prepared
Uilliog, Uillyog
Ukel
(American) player
Ukal, Uke, Ukil
Ukraine
(Place name) republic
Ulan
(Place name) city in Russia, Ulan Ude
Ulane
Uland
(African) first-born twin
Ulande
Ulas
(German) noble
Ulbrich
(German) aristocratic
Ulfat
(Norse) wolf
Ulff
(Scandinavian) wolf; wild
Ulf, Ulv
Ulfred
(Norse) noble
Ulgar
(German) high-born

Ulices
(Latin) form of Ulysses; wanderer
Uly
Ulick
(Irish) for William; up-and-coming
Ulissus
(Invented) form of Ulysses
Ulland
(English) noble lord
Uland, Ullund
Ullock
(Irish) nobleman
Ulman
(German) the wolf's infamy
Ulmann, Ullman, Ullmann
Ulmer
(German) wolf; cagy
Ulriah
(German) from Ulric; powerful wolf
Ulria, Ulrya, Ulryah
Ulrich
(German) ruling; powerful
Ric, Rick, Rickie, Ricky, Ulrek, Ulric, Ulriche, Ulrick, Ulrico
Ulster
(Scandinavian) wolf
Ultan
(Irish) noble
Ultann
Ultar
(Scandinavian) wolf
Ultarr
Ultman
(Hindi) godlike
Ulysses
(Latin) forceful
Ule, Ulesses, Ulises, Ulisses
Umar
(Hindi) doing well

Umbard
(German) from Humbert; renowned
Umbarde

Umber
(French) brown; plain

Umberto
(Italian) earthy

Umed
(Hindi) has an aim

Umher
(Arabic) controlling

Umi
(African) life

Unique
(American) word as name
Uneek, Unik

Unitas
(American) united

Unser
(Last name as first name) drives hard and fast

Unten
(English) not a friend
Untenn

Unus
(Latin) one
Unuss

Unwin
(Last name as first name) modest

Updike
(Last name as first name) from up above

Upjohn
(English) creative
Upjon

Upton
(English) highbrow writer
Uppton, Uptawn, Upten, Uptown

Upwood
(Last name as first name) upper woods is home

Uranus
(Greek) the heavens

Urban
(Latin) city dweller
Urb, Urbain, Urbaine, Urbane, Urben, Urbin, Urbun, Urby

Uri
(Hebrew) short for Uriel; light

Ury
(Hebrew) shining, lit by God

Uriah
(Hebrew) bright; led by God
Uri, Urie, Uryah

Urian
(Irish) from heaven
Urion

Urias
(Hebrew) Lord as my light; old-fashioned
Uraeus, Uri, Uria, Urius

Uriel
(Hebrew) light; God-inspired

Urien
(Mythology) lights life

Urs
(Scandinavian) bear; growly
Urso

Ursan
(French) from Orson; softspoken
Ursen, Ursyn

Urteil
(German) judgment
Urteel, Urtiel

Urvano
(Spanish) city boy
Urbano

Urvine
(Place name) form of Irvine, California
Urveen, Urvene, Urvi

Ury
(Hispanic) God-loving

Usaid
(Arabic) laughs

Usaku
(Japanese) moonlit

Usher
(Latin) decisive

Utah
(Place name) U.S. state

Uthman
(Arabic) bird
Uthmann

Utz
(American) befriends all

Uwe
(Welsh) gentle

Uziah
(Hebrew) believes

Uziel
(Hebrew) soothed by
God's strength

Uzondu
(African) attracts others

Vachel
(French) keeps cows
Vachell

Vadim
(French) creative
Vadeem

Vadin
(Hindi) speaks well

Vaduz
(Place name) city in
Germany

Vail
(English) serene
*Bail, Bale, Vaile, Vaill,
Vale, Valle*

Vaino
(Welsh) from Vanora;
white

Val
(Latin) short for Valery and
Valentine; strong
Vall

Vala
(Latin) from Valentine;
powerful

Valdemar
(Scandinavian) famous
leader
Waldemar

Valenti
(Italian) mighty; romantic
*Val, Valence, Valentin,
Valentyn*

Valentin
(Russian) healthy; robust
Val, Valeri

Valentine
(Latin) robust
*Val, Valentijn, Valentin,
Valentinian, Valentino,
Valentinus, Valentyn,
Valentyne, Valyntine*

Valentino
(Italian) strong; healthy
Val

Valeri
(Russian) athletic; mighty
Val, Valerian, Valerio, Valry

Valerian
(Russian) strong leader
*Valerien, Valerio, Valerius,
Valery, Valeryan*

Vali
(Scandinavian) brave man

Valin
(Latin) from Valentin;
tenacious
Valen, Valyn

Valu
(Polynesian) eight

Van
(Dutch) descendant
Vann, Von, Vonn

Vance
(English) brash
Vans, Vanse

Vanda
(Russian) form of Walter;
wars

Vandan
(Hindi) saved

Vander
(Greek) short for Evander
Vand

Vandiver
(American) quiet
*Van, Vand, Vandaver,
Vandever*

Vandwon
(African American) covert
Vandawon, Vandjuan

Vandyke
(Last name as first name)
educated

Vane
(Last name as first name)
gifted

Vannevar
(Scandinavian) from
Evander; good

Vanslow
(Scandinavian)
sophisticated
*Vansalo, Vanselow,
Vanslaw*

Vanya
(Russian) right
Van, Yard, Yardy

Vardon
(French) green hill is home
Varden, Verdon, Verdun

Varen
(Hindi) rain god Varun

Varesh
(Hindu) God is superior

Varick
(German) defender
Varrick, Warick, Warrick

Varil
(French) faithful

Varkey
(American) boisterous

Varlan
(American) tough
Varland, Varlen, Varlin

Varma
(Hindi) fruitful

Varner
(Last name as first name)
formidable
Varn

Vartan
(Russian) gives roses

Varun
(Hindi) water lord;
excellent
Varoun

Vas
(Slavic) protective
Vaston, Vastun, Vasya

Vasant
(Sanskrit) brings spring

Vashon
(American) delightful
Vashaun, Vashonne

Vasil
(Slavic) form of William;
quiet
*Vasile, Vasilek, Vasili,
Vasilis, Vasilos, Vasily,
Vassily*

Vasilis
(Russian) king
Vasileios, Vasilij, Vasily, Vaso, Vasos, Vassilij, Vassily, Vasya, Wassily

Vasin
(Hindi) rules all

Vassil
(Bulgarian) king
Vass

Vasu
(Sanskrit) rich boy

Vaughn
(Welsh) compact
Vaughan, Vaunie, Von

Vea
(Vietnamese) short for Veasna; lucky

Veasna
(Vietnamese) fortunate

Veejay
(American) talkative
V.J., Vee-Jay, Vejay

Vegas
(Place name) from Las Vegas, Nevada
Vega

Vejis
(Invented) form of Regis; outgoing
Veejas, Veejaz, Vejas, Vejes

Velle
(American) tough
Vell, Velley, Velly, Veltree

Veltry
(African American) hopeful

Velvet
(American) smooth
Vel, Velvat, Velvit

Venancio
(Spanish) glorious

Vencel
(Hungarian) king

Venedict
(Greek) from Benedict; blessed
Venedikt, Venka, Venya

Venezio
(Italian) glorious
Venetziano, Veneziano

Ventura
(Spanish) good fortune

Venturo
(Italian) lucky
Venturio

Verdun
(French) from verdant; growing

Vere
(Latin) springlike

Vered
(Hebrew) rose-loving

Vergel
(Spanish) writer
Vergele, Virgil

Verile
(German) macho
Verill, Verille, Verol, Verrill

Verlie
(American) from Verle; countrified
Verley

Verlyn
(African American) growing
Verle, Verlin, Verllin, Verlon, Verlyn, Virle, Vyrle

Vermont
(Place name) U.S. state

Vern
(Latin) short for Vernon
Verne, Vernie, Verny

Vernados
(Greek) hearty

Verner
(German) resourceful
Vern, Verne, Vernir, Virner

Verniamin
(Greek) form of Benjamin; son of the right hand

Vernon
(Latin) fresh and bright
*Lavern, Vern, Vernal,
Verne, Vernen, Vernin,
Verney*

Verona
(Italian) man of Venice or
Verona, both Italian cities
Verone

Verrier
(French) faithful

Verrill
(German) manly
*Verill, Verrall, Verrell,
Verroll, Veryl*

Vester
(Latin) from Vesta; he who
guards the fire

Vesuvio
(Place name) Mount
Vesuvius; spontaneous

Vic
(Latin) short for Victor
Vick, Vickey, Vik

Vicente
(Spanish) winner
Vic, Vicentay, Visente

Victor
(Latin) victorious
*Vic, Vick, Vickter, Victer,
Victorien, Victorin, Vidor,
Vikki, Viktor, Vitorio,
Vittorio*

Vittorios
(Italian) victor

Vida
(Hebrew) beloved; vibrant

Vidal
(Spanish) full of vitality
Bidal, Videl, Videlio

Vidalo
(Spanish) energetic
Vidal

Vidar
(Scandinavian) soldier

Vidkun
(Scandinavian) gives

Vidor
(Hungarian) delightful

Viggo
(Scandinavian) exuberant
Viggoa, Vigo

Vigile
(American) vigilant
Vegil, Vigil

Vihs
(Hindu) increase

Vijay
(Hindi) winning
Bijay, Vijun

Vila
(Czech) from William
Vili, Ville

Viliami
(Slavic) from William; high
goals

Villard
(French) village man

Villiers
(French) kind-hearted

Vilmos
(Italian) happy
Villmos

Vilok
(Hindu) to see

Vimal
(Hindi) unblemished

Vin
(Italian) short for Vincent
Vinn, Vinney, Vinni, Vinnie

Vinay
(Hindi) good manners

Vince
(English) short for Vincent
Vee, Vence, Vins, Vinse

Vincent
(Latin) victorious
*Vencent, Vicenzio, Vin,
Vince, Vincens, Vincente,
Vincentius, Vincents,
Vincenty, Vincenz,
Vincenzio, Vincenzo,
Vincien, Vinicent, Vinnie,
Vinny, Vinzenze, Wincenty,
Vinciente, Vinn, Vinny*

Vincenzo
(Italian) conquerer
Vincenze, Vinnie, Vinny

Vine
(Latin) from Vin; wins

Vinod
(Hindi) effervescent

Vinson
(English) winning attitude
Venson, Vince, Vinny, Vins

Vinton
(English) town of wine;
reveler

Vireo
(Latin) brave

Virgil
(Latin) holding his own;
writer
*Verge, Vergil, Vergilio,
Virge, Virgie, Virgilio, Virgy*

Virginius
(Latin) virginal
Virginio

Vischer
(Last name as first name)
longing
Visscher

Vitale
(Italian) important

Vitalis
(Latin) bubbly; vital

Vitas
(Latin) animated
Vidas, Vite

Vito
(Italian) short for Vittorio;
lively; victor
*Veto, Vital, Vitale, Vitalis,
Vitaly, Vitas, Vite, Vitus,
Witold*

Vittorio
(Italian) victorious
*Vite, Vito, Vitor, Vitorio,
Vittore*

Vitus
(Latin) winning

Vivar
(Greek) alive
Viv

Vivek
(Hindi) wise

Vivian
(Latin) lively
*Viviani, Vivien, Vivyan,
Vyvian, Vyvyan*

Vlad
(Russian) short for
Vladimir

Vladimir
(Russian) glorious leader
*Vlada, Vladameer,
Vladamir, Vlademar,
Vladimeer, Vlakimar,
Wladimir, Wladimyr*

Vladislav
(Czech) glorious leader

Vladja
(Russian) short for
Vladislav

Volf
(Hebrew) form of Will;
bold

Volker
(German) prepared to
defend
Volk

Volney
(Greek) hidden

Volya
(Slavic) hopes

Von
(German) bright
Vaughn, Vonn, Vonne

Vonzie
(American) form of Fonzie;
personable
*Vons, Vonze, Vonzee,
Vonzey, Vonzi*

Voshon
(Slavic) generous

Vui
(African) saves

Waclaw
(Polish) glorified

Wade
(English) mover; crossing
a river
Wadie, Waide, Wayde

Wadell
(English) southerner
Waddell, Wade

Waden
(American) form of Jaden;
fun
Wade, Wedan

Wadley
(Last name as first name)
by the water
Wadleigh, Wadly

Wadsworth
(English) homebody
Waddsworth, Wadswurth

Wagner
(German) musical; practical
*Wagg, Waggner, Waggoner,
Wagnar, Wagnur*

Wagon
(American) conveyance
Wag, Wagg, Waggoner

Wain
(English) industrious

Wainwright
(Last name as first name)
works hard
*Wain, Wainright, Wayne,
Wayneright, Waynewright,
Waynright, Wright*

Wait
(American) word as name;
patient
Waite

Wake
(Place name) island in the
Marshall Islands

Wakefield
(English) the field worker
Field, Wake

Wakely
(Last name as first name)
wet

Wakeman
(Last name as first name)
wet
Wake

Wal
(Arabic) short for Waleed;
baby

Walbert
(German) protective;
stodgy

Walcott
(Last name as first name)
steadfast
Wallcot, Wallcott, Wolcott

Waldemar
(German) famous leader
*Valdemar, Waldermar,
Waldo*

Walden
(English) calming
*Wald, Waldan, Waldi,
Waldin, Waldo, Waldon,
Waldy, Welti*

Waldo
(German) short for
Oswald; zany
Wald, Waldoh, Waldy

Waleed
(Arabic) newborn
Waled, Walid

Walenty
(Polish) strong

Walerian
(Polish) powerful

Wales
(English) from Wales in
the United Kingdom
*Wael, Wail, Wails, Wale,
Waley, Wali, Waly*

Walford
(English) wealthy; from
Wales

Walfred
(English) from Wales; loyal

Wali
(Arabic) newborn

Walker
(English) distinctive
Walk, Wally

Wallace
(English) from Wales;
charming
*Wallas, Walley, Walli,
Wallice, Wallie, Wallis,
Wally, Walsh, Welsh*

Waller
(English) man from Wales;
confident

Wallis
(English) man from Wales;
smooth

Walls
(American) walled
Walen, Wally, Waltz, Walz

Wally
(English) short for Walter
Wall, Walley, Walli, Wallie

Walmond
(Last name as first name)
laidback

Walsh
(English) inquisitive
*Walls, Welce, Welch, Wells,
Welsh*

Walt
(German) army leader
Waltey, Waltli, Walty

Walter
(German) army leader
*Walder, Wallie, Wally, Walt,
Walther, Waltur, Walty, Wat*

Walther
(German) army leader;
powerful

Walton
(English) shut off;
protected
Walt, Walten, Waltin

Walworth
(English) introvert

Walwyn
(English) reticent
*Walwin, Walwinn,
Walwynn, Walwynne,
Welwyn*

Wang
(Chinese) hope; wish

Waqar
(Arabic) talkative

Warburton
(Last name as first name)
still

Ward
(English) vigilant; alert
Warde, Warden, Worden

Wardell
(English) guarded

Warden
(English) watchful
*Warde, Wardie, Wardin,
Wardon*

Wardley
(English) careful
Wardlea, Wardleigh

Ware
(English) aware; cautious
Warey, Wary

Warfield
(Last name as first name)
cautious

Warford
(Last name as first name)
defensive

Waring
(English) dashing
Wareng, Warin, Warring

Wark
(American) watchful

Warley
(Last name as first name)
worthy people

Warner
(German) protective
Warne

Warren
(German) safe haven
*Ware, Waren, Waring,
Warrenson, Warrin,
Warriner, Warron, Warry,
Worrin*

Warton
(English) defended town

Warwen
(American) defensive
Warn, Warwun, Warwun

Warwick
(English) lavish
*War, Warick, Warrick,
Warweck, Warwyc,
Warwyck, Wick*

Washburn
(English) bountiful
*Washbern, Washbie,
Washby*

Washington
(English) leader
Wash, Washe, Washing

Wasim
(Arabic) pretty baby

Wat
(English) short for
Watkins; jolly

Watford
(Last name as first name)
softspoken

Watkins
(English) able
*Watkens, Wattie, Wattkins,
Watty*

Watson
(English) helpful
*Watsen, Watsie, Watsun,
Watsy, Wattsson*

Wave
(American) word as a
name
Waive, Wave, Wayve

Waverley
(Place name) city in New
South Wales
Waverlee, Waverli, Waverly

Way
(English) landed; smart
Waye

Wayland
(English) form of Waylon;
country boy

Wayling
(English) the right way
*Waylan, Wayland, Waylen,
Waylin*

Waylon
(English) country boy
*Wallen, Walon, Way,
Waylan, Wayland, Waylen,
Waylie, Waylin, Waylond,
Waylun, Wayly, Weylin*

Wayman
(English) traveling man
*Way, Waym, Waymon,
Waymun*

Waymon
(American) knowing the
way
Waymond

Wayne
(English) wheeler and
dealer
*Wain, Wanye, Way, Wayn,
Waynell, Waynne*

Wazir
(Arabic) minister, advisor

Webb
(English) intricate mind
Web, Webbe, Weeb

Weber
(German) intuitive
Webb, Webber, Webner

Webley
(English) weaves; intuitive
Webbley, Webbly, Webly

Webster
(English) creative
Web, Webstar, Webstur

Weddel
(Last name as first name)
has an angle

Weebie
(American) wily
Weebbi

Weido
(Italian) bright;
personable
Wedo

Wel-Quo
(Asian) bothered
Wel

Welborne
(Last name as first name)
where the well is
*Welborn, Welbourne,
Welburn, Wellborn,
Wellborne, Wellbourn,
Wellburn*

Welby
(German) astute
*Welbey, Welbi, Welbie,
Wellby*

Weldon
(Last name as first name)
where the well is

Welford
(English) unusual
Walferd, Wallie, Wally

Wellington
(English) nobility
Welling

Wells
(English) unique
Well, Wellie, Welly

Welsh
(English) form of Walsh
Welch, Wellsh

Welton
(English) spring town

Wenceslaus
(Polish) glorified king
*Wenceslas, Wenzel,
Wiencyslaw, Wenczeslaw*

Wendell
(German) full of
wanderlust
*Wandale, Wend, Wendall,
Wendel, Wendey, Wendie,
Wendill, Wendle, Wendull,
Wendy*

Wenford
(English) confessing
Wynford

Went
(American) ambitious
Wente, Wentt

Wenworth
(English) adventures
Werner
(German) warrior
Wes
(English) short for Wesley
Wess, Wessie, Wessy
Wesh
(German) from the west
Wesley
(English) bland
Wes, Weslee, Wesleyan,
Weslie, Wesly, Wessley,
West, Westleigh, Westley,
Westly, Wezlee, Wezley
Wesson
(American) from the west
Wess, Wessie
West
(English) westerner
Weste, Westt
Westbrook
(Last name as first name)
from the west brook;
nature-loving
Brook, West, Westbrooke
Westby
(English) near the west
Westcott
(English) from a western
cottage
Wescot, Wescott, Westcot
Westie
(American) capricious
West, Westee, Westey,
Westt, Westy
Westleigh
(English) western
Westlea, Westlie, Wezlee
Westley
(English) from the west
fields
Westoll
(American) open
West, Westall

Weston
(English) good neighbor
West, Westen, Westey,
Westie, Westy, Westin
Wether
(English) light-hearted
Weather, Weth, Wethar,
Wethur
Wetherby
(English) light-hearted
Weatherbey, Weatherbie,
Weatherby, Wetherbey,
Wetherbie
Wetherell
(English) light-hearted
Wetherly
(English) light-hearted
Whalley
(Last name as first name)
predicts
Wharton
(Last name as first name)
provincial
Warton
Wheat
(Invented) fair-haired
Wheatie, Wheats, Wheaty,
Whete
Wheatley
(Last name as first name)
fair-haired; fields of wheat
Whatley, Wheatlea,
Wheatleigh, Wheatly
Wheaton
(Last name as first name)
blond; wheat town
Wheel
(American) important
player
Wheele
Wheeler
(English) likes cars; wheel
maker
Weeler, Wheel, Wheelie,
Wheely

Wheeless
(English) off track
Whelus

Wheelie
(American) big-wig
Wheeley, Wheels, Wheely

Whip
(American) friendly

Whistler
(English) melodic
*Whis, Whistlar, Whistle,
Whistlerr*

Whit
(English) short for
Whitman
*Whitt, Whyt, Whyte, Wit,
Witt*

Whitby
(English) white-haired;
white-walled town

Whitcomb
(English) light in the
valley; shining
Whitcombe, Whitcumb

Whitelaw
(English) white
Whitlaw

Whitey
(English) fair-skinned
White

Whitfield
(English) from a white
field

Whitford
(English) the light source

Whitley
(English) white area is
home
*Whitlea, Whitlee,
Whitleigh*

Whitman
(English) man with white
hair
Whit, Whitty, Witman

Whitmore
(English) white
*Whitmoor, Whittemore,
Witmore, Wittemore*

Whitney
(English) likes white
spaces
*Whit, Whitnee, Whitnie,
Whitt, Whittney, Widney,
Widny, Witt*

Whitson
(English) son of Whit
Whitt, Witt

Whittaker
(English) outdoorsy
*Whitaker, Whitt, Witaker,
Wittaker*

Wick
(American) burning
Wic, Wik, Wyck

Wickham
(Last name as first name)
living in a hamlet
Wick

Wickley
(Last name as first name)
coming from a small home
Wicley

Wilberforce
(German) wild and strong

Wilbert
(German) smart
Wilberto, Wilburt

Wilbur
(English) fortified
*Wilbar, Wilber, Willbur,
Wilburt, Willbur, Wilver*

Wilburn
(German) brilliant
Bernie, Wil, Wilbern, Will

Wilder
(English) wild man
Wildar, Wilde, Wildey

Wildon
(Last name as first name)
willing support
Wilden, Willdon

Wiles
(American) tricky
Wyles

Wiley
(English) cowboy
Wile, Willey, Wylie

Wilford
(English) willowy; peaceful
wishes

Wilfred
(German) peacemaker
*Wilferd, Wilfrid, Wilfride,
Wilford, Wilfried, Wilfryd,
Will, Willfred, Willfried,
Willie, Willy*

Wilfredo
(Italian) peaceful
Fredo, Wifredo, Willfredo

Wilhelm
(German) resolute;
determined
Wilhelmus, Wilhem, Willem

Wilkie
(English) willful

Wilkins
(English) affectionate
*Welkie, Welkins, Wilk,
Wilkens, Wilkes, Wilkie,
Wilkin, Willkes, Willkins*

Wilkinson
(English) son of Wilkin;
capable
Willkinson

Will
(English) short for William;
likable
Wil, Wilm, Wim, Wyll

Willard
(German) courageous
Wilard, Willerd

William
(English) staunch
protector
*Bill, Will, Willeam, Willie,
Wills, Willy, Willyum,
Wilyam*

Williams
(German) brave
Williamson

Willie
(German) short for
William; protective
*Will, Wille, Willey, Willeye,
Willi, Willy, Wily*

Willis
(German) youthful
*Willace, Willece, Willice,
Wills, Willus*

Willoughby
(Last name as first name)
lives with grace
Willoughbey, Willoughbie

Wills
(English) willful

Wilmer
(German) resolute;
ambitious
*Willmar, Willmer, Wilm,
Wilmar, Wilmyr, Wylmar,
Wylmer*

Wilmot
(German) tough-minded

Wilson
(English) extraordinary
*Willson, Wilsen, Wilsun,
Willson*

Wilt
(English) talented
Wiltie

Wilton
(English) practical and
open
*Will, Wilt, Wiltie, Wylten,
Wylton*

Win
(German) flirtatious
Winn, Winnie, Winny

Winchell
(English) meandering
Winchie, Winshell

Wind
(American) word as name;
breezy
Windy

Windell
(German) wanderer
Windelle, Windyll

Windsor
(English) royal
*Win, Wincer, Winnie,
Winny, Winsor, Wyndsor,
Wynser*

Winfield
(English) peace in the
country
*Field, Winifield, Winnfield,
Wynfield, Wynnfield*

Winfried
(English) peaceful

Wing
(Chinese) in glory
Wing-Chiu, Wing-Kit

Wingate
(Last name as first name)
glorified

Wingi
(American) spunky

Wings
(American) soaring; free
Wing

Winkel
(American) bright;
conniving
Wink, Winky

Winlove
(Filipino) winning favor

Winslow
(English) friendly
Winslo, Wynslo, Wynslow

Winsome
(English) gorgeous;
charming
Wins, Winsom, Winz

Winston
(English) dignified
*Win, Winn, Winnie, Winny,
Winstan, Winsten,
Winstonn, Winton,
Wynstan, Wynsten,
Wynston*

Winter
(English) born in winter
*Win, Winnie, Winny,
Wintar, Winterford, Wintur,
Wynter, Wyntur*

Winthrop
(English) winning; stuffy
*Win, Winn, Winnie, Winny,
Wintrop*

Winton
(English) winning
Wynten, Wynton

Winward
(English) friendly

Wiss
(American) carefree
Wissie, Wissy

Wit
(Polish) life
Witt, Wittie, Witty

Witek
(Polish) from Victor;
conqueror

Witha
(Arabic) vibrant, handsome

Witold
(Polish) lively

Witt
(Slavic) lively
Witte

Witter
(Last name as first name)
alive

Witton
(Last name as first name)
lively

Witty
(American) humorous
Wit, Witt, Witte, Wittey, Wittie

Wize
(American) smart
Wise, Wizey, Wizi, Wizie

Wladymir
(Polish) famous ruler
Vladimir

Wladyslaw
(Polish) good leader
Slaw

Wohn
(African American) form of
John

Wojtek
(Polish) comforter; warrior

Wolcott
(English) home of wool

Wolf
(German) short for
Wolfgang
Wolff, Wolfie, Wolfy

Wolfe
(German) wolf; ominous
Wolf, Wolff, Wulf, Wulfe

Wolfgang
(German) talented; a wolf
walks
Wolf, Wolff, Wolfgans, Wolfy, Wulfgang

Wolley
(American) form of Wally
Wolly

Wood
(English) short for
Woodrow
Woode, Woody

Woodery
(English) woodsman
Wood, Wooderree, Woodree, Woodri, Woodry, Woods, Woodsry, Woody

Woodfield
(Last name as first name)
enjoys the woods

Woodfin
(English) attractive
Wood, Woodfen, Woodfien, Woodfyn, Woodie, Woody

Woodford
(Last name as first name)
forester

Woodrow
(English) special
Wood, Woodrowe, Woody

Woodruff
(Last name as first name)
smooth; natural

Woodson
(Last name as first name)
son of Wood; suave

Woodward
(English) watchful
Wood, Woodie, Woodard, Woodwerd, Woody

Woodville
(Last name as first name)
from town of trees

Woody
(American) jaunty
Wooddy, Woodey, Woodi, Woodie

Woolsey
(English) leader
Wools, Woolsi, Woolsie, Woolsy

Worcester
(English) secure

Word
(American) talkative
Words, Wordy, Wurd

Worden
(American) careful
Word, Wordan, Wordun

Wordsworth
(English) poetic
Words, Worth

Worie
(English) cautious

Worsh
(American) from the word
worship; religious
Wor

Worth
(English) deserving;
special
*Werth, Worthey, Worthie,
Worthington, Worthy,
Wurth*

Worthington
(English) fun; worthwhile
*Worth, Worthey, Worthing,
Worthingtun, Wurthington*

Wrangle
(American) cowboy
Wrang, Wrangler, Wrangy

Wray
(American) cornered

Wren
(American) leader of men
Ren, Rin, Rinn, Wrenn

Wright
(English) clear-minded;
correct
Right, Rite, Wrighte, Write

Wrisley
(American) smart
Wrisee, Wrislie, Wrisly

Wriston
(American) good
proportions
Wryston

Wulf
(Hebrew) wolf
Wolf

Wyatt
(French) ready for combat
*Wiatt, Wy, Wyat, Wyatte,
Wye, Wyeth*

Wybert
(Last name as first name)
good profile

Wyborn
(Last name as first name)
well-born

Wyck
(English) light

Wyclef
(American) trendy
Wycleff

Wycliff
(English) edgy
*Cliffie, Cliffy, Wicliff, Wyclif,
Wycliffe*

Wydee
(American) form of Wyatt;
fighter
Wy, Wydey, Wydie

Wylie
(English) charmer
Wiley, Wye, Wylee

Wymann
(English) contentious
Wimann, Wye, Wyman

Wymer
(English) rambunctious;
fighter

Wyn
(Welsh) gregarious

Wyndham
(English) from a hamlet
Windham, Wynndham

Wynne
(English) dear friend
Winn, Wyn, Wynn

Wyshawn
(African American) friendly
*Shawn, Shawny, Why,
Whysean, Wieshawn, Wye,
Wyshawne, Wyshie, Wyshy*

Wystan
(English) struggles

Wythe
(English) fair

Wyton
(English) fair-haired;
crowd-pleaser
Wye, Wytan, Wyten, Wytin

Wyze
(American) sizzle; capable
Wise, Wye, Wyse

Xan
(Greek) short for
Alexander; defends
mankind

Xander
(Greek) short for
Alexander
*Xan, Xande, Xandere,
Xandre*

Xanthin
(Greek) from Xanthe; gold
hair

Xanthus
(Greek) golden-haired
child

Xanthos
(Greek) attractive

Xat
(American) saved
Xatt

Xaver
(Spanish) from Xavier;
home

Xaverius
(Spanish) from Xavier;
home
Xaverious, Xaveryus

Xavier
(Arabic) shining
*Saverio, Xaver, Zavey,
Zavier*

Xavion
(Spanish) from Xavier;
home

Xaxon
(American) happy
Zaxon

Xayvion
(African American) dwells
in new house
*Savion, Sayveon, Sayvion,
Xavion, Xayveon, Zayvion*

Xebec
(French) from Quebec;
cold
Xebeck, Xebek

Xen
(African American) original
Zen

Xenik
(Russian) sly
*Xenic, Xenick, Xenyc,
Xenyck, Xenyk*

Xeno
(Greek) gracious
*Xenoes, Zene, Zenno,
Zenny, Zeno, Zenos*

Xenon
(Greek) gracious

Xenophon
(Greek) gracious

Xenos
(Greek) with grace
Xeno, Zenos

Xerarch
(Greek) dancing
Xerarche

Xeres
    (Persian) from Xerxes;
    leads
    Xeries

Xerxes
    (Persian) leader
    Xerk, Xerky, Zerk, Zerkes,
    Zerkez

Xhosas
    (African) South African
    tribe
    Xhoses, Xhosys

Xiaoping
    (Chinese) brightest star

Ximen
    (Spanish) obeys
    Ximenes, Ximon, Ximun

Ximena
    (Spanish) good listener

Xing-Fu
    (Chinese) happy

Xi-Wang
    (Chinese) optimistic

Xuthus
    (Last name as first name)
    long-suffering

Xyle
    (American) helpful
    Zye, Zyle

Xylo
    (Greek) from Xylon; noisy

Xylon
    (Greek) forester

Xyshaun
    (African American) zany
    Xye, Zye, Zyshaun,
    Zyshawn

Xyst
    (English) a portico;
    systematic
    Xist

Xystum
    (Greek) promenade
    Xistoum, Xistum, Xysoum

Xystus
    (Greek) promenade
    Xistus

Yaameen
    (Hebrew) right hand

Yachna
    (Hebrew) gracious

Yadon
    (Last name as first name)
    different
    Yado, Yadun

Yadua
    (Hindi) judged

Yael
    (Hebrew) teacher
    Yail, Yaley, Yalie

Yagil
    (Hebrew) celebrant

Yahya
    (Arabic) vital
    Yahiya

Yakar
    (Hebrew) adored

Yakez
    (Scandinavian) celestial

Yale
    (German) producer

Yamato
    (Japanese) mountain;
    scaling heights

Yana
    (Native American) bearlike

Yancy
(American) vivacious
Yanci, Yancie, Yancy, Yanzie

Yanis
(Hebrew) God's gift
Yannis, Yantsha

Yank
(American) Yankee
Yanke

Yankel
(Hebrew) supportive
Yaki, Yakov, Yekel

Yannis
(Greek) believer in God
Yannie

Yanton
(Hebrew) from Jonathon;
overwhelming

Yao
(Chinese) athletic;
Thursday's child

Yaphet
(Hebrew) from Japheth;
gorgeous
Yapheth, Yefat, Yephat

Yarb
(Gypsy) spicy

Yarden
(Hebrew) flowing
*Yard, Yardan, Yarde,
Yardene, Yardun*

Yardley
(English) adorned;
separate
*Yard, Yarde, Yardie,
Yardlea, Yardlee, Yardly,
Yardy*

Yarkon
(Hebrew) green

Yarom
(Hebrew) sings
Yaron

Yash
(Hindi) famous

Yasin
(Arabic) seer

Yasir
(Arabic) rich

Yasmuji
(Asian) flowering

Yasuo
(Japanese) calm

Yasutaro
(Japanese) peaceful

Yates
(English) smart; closed
Yate, Yattes, Yeats

Yave
(Hindi) from Yavar; giving

Yavin
(Hebrew) believes

Yawo
(African) Thursday's child

Yazeed
(Arabic) growing in spirit

Yeats
(English) gates
Yates

Yediel
(Hebrew) loved by Jehovah

Yehoshua
(Hebrew) alive by God's
salvation

Yehuda
(Hebrew) praised
Yehudi

Yemin
(Hebrew) guarded

Yemyo
(Asian) serene

Yen
(Chinese) calming;
capable

Yens
(Vietnamese) Yen; calm

Yeoman
(English) helping
*Yeomann, Yo, Yoeman,
Yoman, Yoyo*

Yero
(African) studious

Yesel
(Hebrew) won by God

Yeshaya
(Hebrew) treasured

Yesher
(Hebrew) God's salvation

Yeshurun
(Hebrew) focuses on God

Yevgeny
(Russian) life-giving

Yianni
(Greek) creative

Yigal
(Turkish) lively

Yimer
(Scandinavian) giant

Yishai
(Hebrew) from Jessie; proud

Yisrael
(Hebrew) struggles with God

Yitro
(Hebrew) from Jethro; jolly

Yitzhak
(Hebrew) laughing
Yitz, Yitzchak

Yngvar
(Scandinavian) god of fertility
Ingvar;

Yo
(Vietnamese) truthful

Yoav
(Hebrew) form of Joab

Yobachi
(African) prayerful

Yochanan
(Hebrew) from John; believes in a gracious Lord
Yohanan

Yoel
(Hebrew) form of Joel

Yogi
(Japanese) yoga practicer

Yohann
(German) form of Johann
Yohan, Yohn

Yojiro
(Japanese) hopes

Yonah
(Hebrew) form of Jonah

Yonatan
(Hebrew) from Jonathon; straightforward
Yonathan, Yonathon

Yong
(Chinese) brave

Yoosef
(Hebrew) favorite
Yosef

Yoran
(Hebrew) to sing

Yorick
(Literature) Hamlet's jester

York
(English) affluent
Yorke, Yorkee, Yorkey, Yorki, Yorky

Yorker
(English) rich
York, Yorke, Yorkur

Yosef
(Hebrew) form of Joseph
Yose, Yoseff, Yosif

Yosemite
(Place name) natural wonder

Yoshe
(Hebrew) wise

Yoshiaki
(Japanese) attractive

Yoshikatsu
(Japanese) good

Yoshinobu
(Japanese) goodness

Yoshio
(Japanese) giving

Yossel
(Hebrew) favored
Yoska, Yossi

Yosuke
(Japanese) helps

Young
(English) fledgling
Jung, Younge

Yov
(Russian) reliable

Yovan
(Slavic) form of Jovan

Yu
(Chinese) shiny; smart

Yuan
(Chinese) circle

Yudel
(Hebrew) jubilant
Yudi

Yui
(Chinese) moon;
universal

Yuji
(Japanese) snow

Yuke
(American) short for Yukon

Yuki
(Japanese) loves snow

Yukichi
(Japanese) lucky snow

Yukio
(Japanese) man of snow

Yukon
(Place name) individualist

Yul
(Chinese) infinity

Yule
(English) Christmas-born
Yuel, Yul, Yuley, Yulie

Yuli
(Basque) childlike

Yuma
(Place name) city in
Arizona; cowboy
Yumah

Yurcel
(Turkish) the best

Yuri
(Russian) dashing
*Yurah, Yure, Yurey, Yurie,
Yurri, Yury*

Yurik
(Japanese) Yuri's child

Yuris
(Latin) farmer
Yures, Yurus

Yursa
(Japanese) lily; delicate

Yutu
(African) hunter

Yuval
(Hebrew) celebrant

Yves
(French) honest;
handsome
Eve, Ives

Yvonn
(French) attractive
Von, Vonn, Yvon

Z

Zab
(American) slick
*Zabbey, Zabbi, Zabbie,
Zabby*

Zac
(Hebrew) short for
Zachariah; Lord
remembers
*Zacary, Zach, Zachary,
Zachry*

Zacary
(Hebrew) form of Zachary
Zac, Zacc, Zaccary, Zaccry,
Zaccury

Zaccheus
(Hebrew) unblemished
Zac, Zacceus, Zack

Zace
(American) pleasure-
seeking
Zacey, Zacie, Zase

Zach
(Hebrew) short for Zachary
Zac, Zachy

Zachariah
(Hebrew) Lord remembers
Zac, Zacaria, Zacarias,
Zacary, Zacaryah, Zaccaria,
Zaccariah, Zaccheus, Zach,
Zachaios, Zacharia,
Zacharias, Zacharie,
Zachary, Zacheriah,
Zachery, Zacheus, Zachey,
Zachi, Zachie, Zachy, Zack,
Zackariah, Zackerias,
Zackery, Zak, Zakarias,
Zakarie, Zakariyyah, Zakery,
Zechariah, Zekariah,
Zekeriah, Zeke, Zhack

Zacharias
(Hebrew) devout
Zacharyas

Zachary
(Hebrew) spiritual
Zacary, Zacchary, Zach,
Zackar, Zackarie, Zak,
Zakari, Zakri, Zakrie, Zakry

Zack
(Hebrew) short for
Zachary
Zacky, Zak

Zade
(Arabic) flourishing;
trendy
Zaid

Zadok
(Hebrew) unyielding
Zadek, Zaydie, Zadik,
Zayd, Zaydok

Zafar
(Hindi) victor
Zaphar

Zafir
(Arabic) wins
Zafeer, Zafyr

Zahavi
(Hebrew) golden child

Zahir
(Hebrew) bright
Zaheer, Zahur

Zahur
(Arabic) flourishes

Zain
(American) zany
Zane, Zayne

Zaire
(Place name) country in
Africa; brash

Zakary
(Hebrew) form of Zachary

Zaki
(Arabic) virtuous
Zak

Zale
(Greek) strong
Zail, Zaley, Zalie, Zayle

Zalman
(Hebrew) peaceful
Salman, Zaloman

Zamil
(German) from Samuel;
jovial
Zameel, Zamyl

Zamir
(Hebrew) lyrical
Zameer, Zamyr

Zan
(Hebrew) well-nourished
Xan, Zander, Zandro,
Zandros, Zann

Zander
(Greek) short for
Alexander
*Zande, Zandee, Zandey,
Zandie, Zandy*

Zandy
(American) high-energy
Zandee, Zandi

Zane
(English) debonair
Zain, Zay, Zayne, Zaynne

Zano
(American) unique
Zan

Zappa
(American) zany
Zapah, Zapp

Zaquan
(American) combo of Za
and Quan; duplicitous
Zaquon, Zequan, Zequon

Zared
(Arabic) gold

Zarek
(Aramaic) light

Zartavious
(African American)
unusual
Zar, Zarta

Zashawn
(African American) fiery
*Zasean, Zash, Zashaun,
Zashe, Zashon, Zashone*

Zavier
(Arabic) form of Xavier

Zavion
(American) smiling
Zavien

Zawon
(American) combo of Za
and Won; doubter
Zawan, Zewan, Zewon

Zbigniew
(Polish) free of malice;
calming

Zeandre
(American) combo of Zee
and Andre; confident
Zeandrae, Zeandray

Zeb
(Hebrew) short for
Zebediah
Zebe

Zebby
(Hebrew) believer;
rambunctious
Zabbie, Zeb, Zebb, Zebbie

Zebediah
(Hebrew) gift from God
*Zeb, Zebadia, Zebb,
Zebbie, Zebby, Zebedee,
Zebediah, Zebi, Zebidiah*

Zebulon
(Hebrew) uplifted
*Zebulen, Zebulun,
Zevulon, Zevulun*

Zechariah
(Hebrew) form of
Zachariah
Zeke

Zed
(Hebrew) energetic
Zedd, Zede

Zedediah
(Hebrew) gift from God
Zededia, Zedidia, Zedidiah

Zedekiah
(Hebrew) believing in a
just God
*Zed, Zeddy, Zedechia,
Zedechiah, Zedekias*

Zeeman
(Dutch) seafaring
Zeaman

Zeevy
(American) sly
Zeeve, Zeevi, Zeevie

Zeffy
(American) explosive
Zeff, Zeffe, Zeffi, Zeffie

Zeke
(Hebrew) friendly;
outgoing
Zeek, Zekey, Zeki

Zel
(American) hearty

Zelig
(Hebrew) holy; happy
Selig, Zel, Zeligman, Zelik

Zen
(Japanese) spiritual

Zenas
(Greek) from Zeus;
powerful
Zenios, Zenon

Zeno
(Greek) philosophical;
stoic
Zeney, Zenie, Zenno, Zeny

Zenobios
(Greek) living Zeus; lively
Zenobius, Zinov, Zinovi

Zenon
(Greek, Polish) godlike

Zent
(American) zany
Zynt

Zephaniah
(Hebrew) protected by
God
Zeph, Zephan

Zephariah
(Hebrew) Jehovah's light

Zephyr
(Greek) breezy
*Zayfeer, Zayfir, Zayphir,
Zefar, Zefer, Zefir, Zeffer,
Zefur, Zephir, Zephiros,
Zephirus, Zephyrus*

Zero
(Arabic) nothing
Zeroh

Zerond
(American) helpful
Zerre, Zerrie, Zerry, Zerund

Zeshon
(African American) zany
Zeshaune, Zeshawn

Zeth
(American) form of Seth;
unpredictable
Zethe

Zeus
(Greek) vibrant
Zues

Zev
(Hebrew) form of Zebulon;
respected
Zevv

Zevediah
(Hebrew) form of
Zebediah; broken dreams
Zevedia, Zevidia, Zevidiah

Zevi
(Hebrew) brisk
Zevie

Zevulon
(Hebrew) form of Zebulon;
honorable
Zevulonn

Zhivago
(Russian) dashing;
romantic
Vago

Zhong
(Chinese) middle brother;
loyal

Zia
(Hebrew) in motion
Zeah, Ziah

Zie
(American) compelling
Zye, Zyey

Ziggy
(American) zany

Zigmand
(American) form of
Sigmund
Zig, Ziggy

Zikomo
(African) grateful

Zimran
(Hebrew) sacred
Zindel
(Yiddish) form of
Alexander
Zindil
Zino
(Greek) philosopher
Zeno
Zion
(Hebrew) sign
Sion, Zeione, Zi, Zione, Zye
Zipkiyah
(Native American) archer
Ziv
(Hebrew) energetic
Zeven, Zevy, Ziven, Zivon
Ziven
(Polish) lively
Ziv, Zivan, Zyvan
Ziya
(Turkish) light
Zoilo
(Greek) life
Zol
(American) jaunty
Zoll
Zoltan
(Hungarian) lively
Zoma
(American) loquacious
Zome
Zorba
(Greek) pleasure seeker
Zorbah, Zorbe
Zorby
(Greek) tireless
Sorby, Zorb, Zorbie
Zorshawn
(African American) jaded
*Zahrshy, Zorsh, Zorshie,
Zorshon, Zorshy*
Zowie
(Greek) life
Zowey, Zowy

Zuberi
(African) powerful
Zooberi, Zubery
Zuhayr
(Arabic) flowers
Zuhair
Zuni
(Native American) creative
Zuriel
(Hebrew) believer
Zvon
(Croatian) short for
Zvonimir
Zevon, Zevonn
Zyke
(American) high-energy
Zykee, Zyki, Zykie, Zyky

Bibliography

"America's 40 Richest Under 40." Fortune Online. 16 Sept. 2002 <http://www.fortune.com>.

"The American States." Collin, P.H., ed. Webster's Concise Desk Dictionary. New York: Barnes & Noble Books, 2001.

"The Animal Kingdom." Collin, P.H., ed. Webster's Concise Desk Dictionary. New York: Barnes & Noble Books, 2001.

Baby Center Baby Name Finder Page. 1 Dec. 2002 <http://www.babycenter.com/babyname>.

Baby Chatter Page. 1 Dec. 2002 <http://www.baby chatter.com>.

Baby Names/Birth Announcements Page. 1 Oct. 2002 <http://www.princessprints.com>.

Baby Names Page. 1 Dec. 2002 <http://www.yourbabysname.com>.

Baby Names Page. 1 Nov. 2002 <http://www.baby names.com>.

Baby Names Page. 1 Oct. 2002 <http://www.babyshere.com>.

Baby Names World Page. 15 Jan. 2003 <http://www.babynameworld.com>.

Baby Zone Page. "Around-the-World Names." 15 Jan. 2003 <http://www.babyzone.com/babynames>.

"Biographical Names." Collin, P.H. ed. Webster's Concise Desk Dictionary. New York: Barnes & Noble Books, 2001.

"Biographical Names." The Merriam-Webster Dictionary. Springfield, Mass: Merriam Webster, Inc., 1998.

"Books of the Bible." Collin, P.H., ed. Webster's Concise Desk Dictionary. New York: Barnes & Noble Books, 2001.

Celebrity Names Page. 1 Nov. 2002 <http://www.celebnames.8m.com>.

"Common English Given Names." The Merriam-Webster Dictionary. Springfield, Mass: Merriam Webster, Inc., 1998.

Death Penalty Info Page. 1 Feb. 2003 "Current Female Death Row Inmates." <http://www.death penaltyinfo.org/womencases.html>.

Dunkling, Leslie. The Guinness Book of Names. Enfield, UK: Guinness Publishing, 1993.

eBusinessRevolution Page. 1 Nov. 2002 <http:// www.ebusinessrevolution.com/babynames/a.html>.

ePregnancy Page. 1 Dec. 2002 <http://www.Epreg nancy.com/directory/Baby_Names>.

"Fifty Important Stars." Gove, Philip Babcock, ed. Webster's Third New International Dictionary of the English Language Unabridged. Springfield, Mass: Merriam-Webster, Inc., 1981.

"Gambino Capos Held in 1989 Mob Hit." Jerry Capeci. This Week in Gangland, The Online Column Page. 1 Aug. 2002 <http://www.gang landnews.com/column289.htm>.

Hanks, Patrick, and Flavia Hodges. *A Dictionary of First Names.* Oxford: Oxford University Press, 1992.

Hanley, Kate and the Parents of Parent Soup. *The Parent Soup Baby Name Finder: Real Advice from Real Parents Who Have Named Their Babies and Lived To Tell About It—with More Than 15,000 Names.* Lincolnwood, Illinois: Contemporary Books, 1998.

Harrison, G.B. ed. *Major British Writers.* New York: Harcourt, Brace &World, Inc., 1959.

HypoBirthing Page. "Baby Names." 1 Oct. 2002 <http://www.hypobirthing.com>.

Indian Baby Names Page. 1 Nov. 2002 <http:// www.indiaexpress.com/specials/baby names>.

Irish Names Page. 15 Jan. 2003 <http://www.hylit.com/info>.

Jewish Baby Names Page. 15 Jan. 2003 <http://www.jewishbabynames.net>.

Lansky, Bruce. *The Mother of All Baby Name Books: Over 94,000 Baby Names Complete with Origins and Meanings.* New York: Meadowlark Press (Simon and Schuster), 2003.

Kaplan, Justin, and Anne Bernays. *The Language of Names: What We Call Ourselves and Why It Matters.* New York: Simon & Schuster, 1997.

"Months of the Principal Calendars." Gove, Philip Babcock, ed. Webster's Third New International Dictionary of the English Language Unabridged. Springfield, Mass: Merriam-Webster Inc., 1981.

"Most Popular Names of the 1990s." Social Security Administration Online. 1 Nov. 2002 <http://www.ssa.gov/OACT/babynames>.

"Most Popular Names of the 1980s." Social Security Administration Online. 1 Nov. 2002 <http://www.ssa.gov/OACT/babynames>.

"Most Popular Names of the 1970s." Social Security Administration Online. 1 Nov. 2002 <http://www.ssa.gov/OACT/babynames>.

"Most Popular Names of the 1960s." Social Security Administration Online. 1 Nov. 2002 <http://www.ssa.gov/OACT/babynames>.

"Most Popular Names of the 1950s." Social Security Administration Online. 1 Nov. 2002 <http://www.ssa.gov/OACT/babynames>.

"Most Popular Names of 2001." Social Security Administration Online. 1 Nov. 2002 <http://www.ssa.gov/OACT/babynames>.

"Most Powerful Women in Business." Fortune Online. 14 Oct. 2002 <http://www.fortune.com>.

"Movie-Star Names." Internet Movie Database online. 1 Nov. 2002 <http://www.imdb.com>.

Norman, Teresa. *A World of Baby Names: A Rich and Diverse Collection of Names from Around the World.* New York: Perigee (Penguin Putnam), 1996.

Origins/Meanings of Baby Names from Around the World Page. 1 Nov. 2002 <http:// www.Baby NamesOrigins.com>.

Oxygen Page. "Baby Names." 1 Nov. 2002 <http://www.oxygen.com/babynamer>.

Parenthood Page. 1 Nov. 2002 <http:// www.parenthood.com/parent_cfmfiles/babynames.cfm>.

"The Plant Kingdom." Collin, P.H., ed. Webster's Concise Desk Dictionary. New York: Barnes & Noble Books, 2001.

Popular Baby Names Page. 1 Nov. 2002 <http://www.popularbabynames.com>.

"Presidents of the United States." Collin, P.H. ed. Webster's Concise Desk Dictionary. New York: Barnes & Noble Books, 2001.

"Prime Ministers of the U.K." Collin, P.H. ed. Webster's Concise Desk Dictionary. New York: Barnes & Noble Books, 2001.

Racketeering and Fraud Investigations Page. 4 Feb. 2003 <http://www.oig.dol.gov/public/media/oi/mainz01.htm>.

Rick Porelli's AmericanMafia.com Page. 21 June 2002 <http://www.americanmafia.com/news/6-21-02_Feds_Bust.html>.

Rosenkrantz, Linda, and Pamela Redmond Satran. *Baby Names Now*. New York: St. Martin's Press, 2002.

Rosenkrantz, Linda, and Pamela Redmond Satran. *Beyond Charles and Diana: An Anglophile's Guide to Baby Naming*. New York: St. Martin's Press, 1992.
Rosenkrantz, Linda, and Pamela Redmond Satran. *Beyond Jennifer and Jason*. New York: St. Martin's Press, 1994.

Ryan, Joal. *Puffy, Xena, Quentin, Uma: And 10,000 Other Names for Your New Millenium Baby*. New York: Plume (Penguin Putnam), 1999.

Schwegel, Janet. *The Baby Name Countdown*. New York: Marlowe & Company (Avalon), 2001.
Shaw, Jessica. *The Everything Baby Names Book*. Massachusetts: Adams Media Corporation, 1996.

"Signs of the Zodiac." Gove, Philip Babcock, ed. *Webster's Third New International Dictionary of the English Language Unabridged*. Springfield, Mass: Merriam-Webster Inc. Publishers, 1981.

Television-show credits. 1 Oct. 2002–25 Feb. 2003.

Texas Department of Criminal Justice Page.
"Offenders on Death Row." 1 Feb. 2003
<http://www.tdcj.state.tx.us/stat/offender-
sondrow.htm>.

Trantino, Charlee. *Beautiful Baby Names from Your
Favorite Soap Operas.* New York: Pinnacle Books,
1996.

20,000+ Names Page. "20,000+ Names from
Around the World." 1 Nov. 2002
<http:// www.20000-names.com>.

United Kingdom Baby Name Page. 15 Jan. 2003
<http://www.baby-names.co.uk>.

Wallace, Carol McD. *The Greatest Baby Name Book
Ever.* New York: Avon, 1998.

Notes

Mom's Picks

_____

_____

_____

_____

_____

_____

_____

_____

_____

_____

_____

_____

_____

Dad's Picks

_____

_____

_____

_____

_____

_____

_____

_____

_____

_____

_____

_____

_____

Our Picks

_____

_____

_____

_____

_____

_____

_____

_____

_____

_____

_____

_____

_____

Our Picks

_____

_____

_____

_____

_____

_____

_____

_____

_____

_____

_____

_____

_____

_____

Notes

_____

_____

_____

_____

_____

_____

_____

_____

_____

_____

_____

_____

_____

_____

Notes

_____

_____

_____

_____

_____

_____

_____

_____

_____

_____

_____

_____

_____

Notes

Notes

Notes

Notes